Cork In

A complete illustrated textbook on cork insulation–the origin of cork and history of its use for insulation–the study of heat and determination of the heat conductivity of various materials–complete specifications and directions for the proper application of cork insulation in ice and cold storage plants and other refrigeration installations–the insulation of household refrigerators, ice cream cabinets and soda fountains

Pearl Edwin Thomas

Alpha Editions

This edition published in 2020

ISBN : 9789354010088

Design and Setting By
Alpha Editions
email - alphaedis@gmail.com

Cork Insulation

A COMPLETE ILLUSTRATED TEXTBOOK ON CORK INSULATION—THE ORIGIN OF CORK AND HISTORY OF ITS USE FOR INSULATION—THE STUDY OF HEAT AND DETERMINATION OF THE HEAT CONDUCTIVITY OF VARIOUS MATERIALS—COMPLETE SPECIFICATIONS AND DIRECTIONS FOR THE PROPER APPLICATION OF CORK INSULATION IN ICE AND COLD STORAGE PLANTS AND OTHER REFRIGERATION INSTALLATIONS—THE INSULATION OF HOUSEHOLD REFRIGERATORS, ICE CREAM CABINETS AND SODA FOUNTAINS.

BY

PEARL EDWIN THOMAS

Engineering Graduate, [illegible], The Pennsylvania State College
Identified with the Cork and Insulation Industries since 1912

PUBLISHERS
NICKERSON & COLLINS CO.
CHICAGO

To
the Memory of
JAMES EDWARD QUIGLEY

PREFACE

In submitting this first complete treatise on the sources, harvesting, manufacture, distribution and uses of cork and cork insulation products, the author believes that he has succeeded in adding to scientific literature a work for which there is at this period a real necessity and a genuine demand.

The collection of data on which the matter herein published is based has necessitated many years of careful research in a field widely scattered and requiring thought and discriminating care in the separation of the grain from the chaff in published matter sometimes of a more or less dissolute nature and frequently of an unreliable character. Such matter as is here presented can be considered authentic and authoritative and relied upon unreservedly.

When consideration is given to the fact that in the half century just passed the cork industry has developed and progressed from a mere matter of production of bottle stoppers to a diversified line of products covering hundreds of separate items and involving cork imports valued at millions of dollars per annum, some conception of the magnitude and importance of the cork industry of the world can be formed.

For the architect, engineer, consulting expert, equipment designer, car and steamship builder, plant owner, industrial manager, and for every one interested in any way in refrigeration, ice making, cold storage, the operation of markets, dairies, creameries, ice cream plants, the manufacture of household and commercial refrigerators, insulating against both heat and cold, sound-proofing, moisture-proofing, humidity and temperature control, this book will be found indispensable.

The rapid strides of the development of the cork industry in this country have astonished even those who have been and are now directly associated with the cork business, and it is appreciated that as yet the possibilities of future application of cork to other and more remote industrial purposes have scarcely been touched.

While the main idea sought to be brought out emphatically in this work is that of insulation, it is thought possible that the subjects covered herein may lead to further important developments and progress in the industry.

In addition to the direct credit given in the body of the text, and in foot-notes, grateful acknowledgement is also made to the following individuals and concerns whose courtesy and cooperation made possible many of the very valuable illustrations contained in this work, as follows: Armstrong Cork & Insulation Co., United Cork Companies, Cork Import Corporation, Spanish Cork Insulation Co., John R. Livezey, Edward J. Ward, Rhinelander Refrigerator Co., Leonard Refrigerator Co., Gifford-Wood Co., and the American Society of Refrigerating Engineers.

P. EDWIN THOMAS.

Chicago, July, 1928.

TABLE OF CONTENTS.

Part I.—The Cork Industry.

CHAPTER VI.

Part II.—The Study of Heat.

CHAPTER VII.

CHAPTER VIII.

CHAPTER IX.

CHAPTER XVIII.

CORK INSULATION

Part I—The Cork Industry.

CHAPTER I.

THE ORIGIN OF CORK.

1.—Early Uses of Cork.—The story of cork is so little known and shrouded with so much mystery that the world has never had a complete and comprehensive account of it. The utility and general uses of the "cork of commerce," as well as its native land, are no longer a part of the mysticism; but its character, composition and chemical construction are still the subject of research and experimentation.

The uses of the outer bark of the cork oak tree have been traced far back into a dim past, but for our purpose it will be enough to go back no further than the first century of the Christian era. The elder Pliny wrote about the cork oak tree then, in his work on natural history, and recognized twenty centuries ago at least four of the principal functions that cork fills in the world today, which involved a recognition of the two principal properties of cork bark that make its use of so much value as a commercial insulating material—its marked ability to retard the flow of heat and its freedom from capillarity. These two properties, in combination, were provided by Nature to make this interesting and remarkable material the foundation, when put through proper manufacturing processes, for the best cold storage and refrigerator insulation yet known to mankind.

As is often the case with many important discoveries, the first use of cork probably came through accident; for its employment "attached as a buoy to the ropes of ships' anchors and the drag nets of fishermen" suggests that a piece of cork bark found its way to the sea where its unusual buoyancy was first noted and utilized by fishermen and sea-faring men as floats for nets, buoys for anchors, cork jackets for life preservers, and later as plugs for vintage casks sealed in with pitch and as winter sandals for women.

Since Pliny was writing history, some two thousand years ago, it is safe to assume that the very first use ever made of cork must date well before his time, perhaps 500 B. C., or 1000 B. C.—there is now no means of knowing.

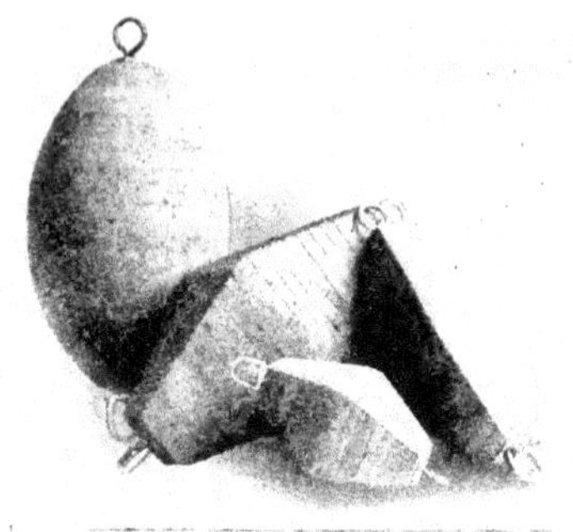

FIG. 1.—CORK MOORING AND ANCHORAGE BUOYS.

2.—**Beginning of the Cork Industry.**—During many centuries of the Christian era the great cork forests, bordering the Mediterranean sea, were ravaged by wars and fires and the demand for timber and charcoal. But at least some of these sturdy cork oak trees managed to escape and later, under kindlier treatment, spread out over the mountain slopes and gave to Spain, Portugal and Algeria one of their chief present sources of revenue—the growing of "corkwood."

It was not until the sixteenth or seventeenth century, however, that the real beginnings of the great cork industry, as it is known today, may be said to have begun, with the general introduction of the glass bottle. Then cork bottle stoppers quickly came into general use, being elastic, compressible, tasteless, odorless, and impervious to water, and gave the cork industry such impetus as to establish it upon a sound footing for all time.

3.—Source of Supply.—While southern France and Italy, including the isles of Corsica, Sardinia and Sicily, are factors in the harvesting and supplying of the crude material, yet Spain, Portugal, Algeria and Tunis continue to supply the world with the bulk of the raw cork that is consumed. Morocco, in north and northwest Africa, provides an enormous and for the greater part an undeveloped area of cork forests, but this field is now being opened up under careful supervision, and should grow rapidly in importance as a source of supply.

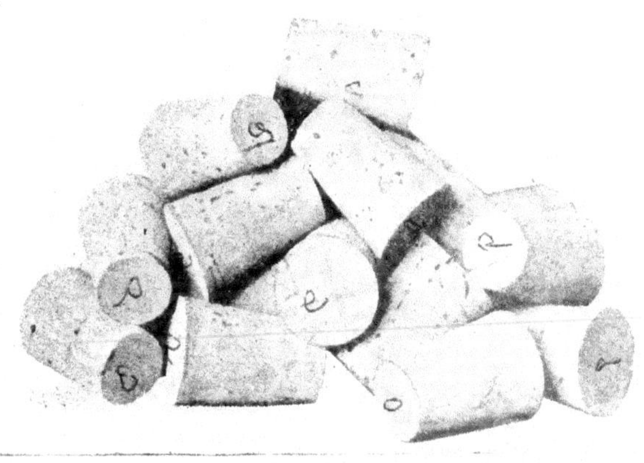

FIG. 2.—CORK BOTTLE STOPPERS.

The total area covered by cork forests in all countries is estimated at from four to five million acres,* and the annual yield of corkwood in 1913 at about two hundred thousand tons.† The shaded areas on the accompanying map represent the principal places in the world where the cork oak grows. It flourishes best in an altitude of 1,600 to 3,000 feet, in an average mean temperature of 55° F., and the Mediterranean basin is therefore particularly suitable for the growing of the cork oak and the harvesting of its outer bark of quality.

*Armstrong Cork Company, 1909.
†U. S. Tariff Commission's 1924 Dictionary of Tariff Information.

Many attempts have been made to transplant this interesting tree, but the result of every such effort has been futile. Just before the Civil war, in 1859, the United States Government provided funds to bring Portugese cork acorns to several of the Southern States for planting; but after a dozen years or so it was concluded, in spite of the neglect of the seedlings occasioned by the War of the Rebellion, that the experiment was not a commercial success. Some of these cork oak trees are still standing in Mississippi and Georgia, but the outer bark never matured satisfactorily.

FIG. 3.—SOURCE OF THE WORLD'S SUPPLY OF CORK.

In 1872 another effort was made to grow the cork oak in southern California, but the outcome proved no better there than it did at an earlier date in the East. Four of these trees are now standing in the Methodist churchyard at Fourth and Arizona Streets, Santa Monica, California, and a half dozen more have recently been located by H. H. Wetzel in Santa Monica canyon; but while the trees themselves have flourished, the quality of their salient product is inferior and of no commercial value.

FIG. 4.—CORK OAK TREE GROWING IN SANTA MONICA, CALIF.

4.—Home of the Industry.—The ancient Spanish province of Catalonia, in the northeast or Barcelona area, has long been recognized as the greatest cork manufacturing district in the world, the towns of Palamos, Palafrugell, San Feliu de Guixols, Bisbal, Figueras and others being devoted almost exclusively to cork and cork products. Domestic cork factories are scattered throughout the cork areas of Spain and Portugal, to the extent of perhaps a thousand different estab-

FIG. 5.—LOADING CORKWOOD FOR EXPORT AT PORT OF PALAMOS, SPAIN.

lishments, while the remainder of the yield, in the form of baled corkwood, cork waste, shavings and cork refuse of all kinds, is exported to Sweden, Denmark, Russia, Austria, Germany, France, Great Britain and the United States, the last four named ordinarily absorbing perhaps eighty-five per cent of the total product of the producing countries, to be worked into hundreds of different cork articles of trade.

Because most people think of Spain as an easy-going country of medieval ways, with no great wealth or material development, it can not be amiss to say a word about Barcelona, the capital, so to speak, of the cork industry, and which must be ranked today among the great cities of the world. The Barcelona district of Spain would be an amazing surprise to any one coming to it with no better idea of what to expect. Barcelona is today an enormous city of nearly a million population, extending from the sea to the foothills of the Pyrennes, filling the plain in between and stretching out into the valleys and well along the coast.

From a point on Tibidabo some 1,500 feet above the Mediterranean sea, can be seen an immense metropolis spread out with the exact regularity of any of our modern cities of the Middle West. Off to one side a splotch by the harbor faintly marks the old Barcelona of crooked, narrow streets, but even this is fast giving way to make room for new, wide thoroughfares that link modern highway and transportation lines.

Modern office and public buildings, hotels and shops, flats and apartments, broad avenues and boulevards lined with trees and completely equipped with excellent electric tram and omnibus service, athletic stadiums and open air theatres, palatial villas and residences, electric trains every few minutes from the heart of the city out into the country, a subway under construction, at night the central squares lit up with flashing Broadway sky signs—there is little indeed to suggest the Spain of our fancy.

Barcelona began to grow after the International Exposition of 1888, when new capital gave an immense impetus to its many industries; and while it is the chief seaport of Spain, it is as a manufacturing center that it has risen to the position of one of the great cities of the world.

5.—Characteristics of the Cork Oak.—The botanical name for the cork oak is *Quercus suber*. "It grows and develops in ground of little depth, and often quite stony, being seldom found in calcareous soil, preferring a sandy soil of felspar."* It ordinarily attains a height of from twenty-five to fifty feet, but occasionally grows to a height of more than one hundred

*Consul Schenck's Report, 1890.

and fifty feet and to a diameter of as much as four feet.† Its branches usually are full-spread and are covered with small evergreen leaves having a velvety feel and a glossy appearance. Its roots spread considerably and attain much strength, often being visible above ground.

During April and May the yellowish blossoms appear, which are followed by the acorns that ripen and at once fall to the ground during the last four months of the year. These acorns are bitter to the taste, but give a peculiarly piquant flavor to Spanish mountain hams when fed to swine. The

FIG. 6.—TYPICAL CORK FOREST IN SPAIN.

cork oak offers but little shade, which permits the soil to become very dry and of inferior producing value unless the young trees are grown close together until they are about twenty-five years old. If the soil is poor, the outer bark is thin but of fine texture; if the soil is rich, the bark is thick, spongy and inclined to be coarse. These characteristics are carefully studied from an agricultural standpoint, in the various cork growing districts, and are dealt with as reason dictates.

The outer bark of the cork oak consists of thin-walled cells filled with air, is destitute of intercellular spaces, and is impermeable to air and water. These cells are so small that

†Henry Vincke, 1925.

they can be visualized only with a high powered microscope, there being about four hundred million per cubic inch, but each cell contains a microscopic bit of air and is sealed against all other cells so that the entrapped air can not move about within the material. It is this peculiar structure of cork bark that makes it an excellent nonconductor of heat and, at the same time, impervious to air and water, which latter property is absolutely essential in an insulating material that is to be employed in cold storage and refrigerator construction where moisture is always present.

CHAPTER II.

CORK STRIPPING.

6.—**Removing the Outer Bark.**—The cork of commerce, or corkwood, is the outer bark of the cork tree, which belongs to the oak family and which has been described. This outer bark can readily be removed during the summer months, generally during July and August, without harm to the tree, although considerable skill is required if injury to the inner or sap-carrying bark is to be avoided. French strippers sometimes use crescent-shaped saws, but Spanish strippers invariably use a long-handled hatchet, the handle tapered at the butt in the shape of a wedge.

When cork oak trees attain a diameter of about five inches, or measure forty centimeters in circumference according to the Spanish practice, which fixes the age of the tree at about twenty years, the virgin outer bark is removed. It is customary to cut the bark clear through around the base of the tree and again around the trunk just below the main branches, the two incisions then being connected by probably two vertical cuts. By using the long handle of the hatchet as a wedge and lever, the tree's outer bark is easily pried off. The lower portions of the limbs are stripped in like manner, frequently yielding a finer grade of corkwood than that of the trunk. The thickness of this virgin outer bark varies from about one-half to two and one-half inches, while the yield per tree also varies from a half hundred to several hundred pounds, depending on both its size and age when the virgin stripping is accomplished.

7.—**Virgin Cork.**—This virgin cork bark, called "borniza" in Spain, is rough, coarse and dense in texture. It is therefore of limited commercial value, except as used by florists and others for decorative purposes, and, when ground, as packing for grapes, although it has of recent years come into

FIG. 7.—REMOVING THE OUTER BARK FROM THE CORK OAK TREE.

use also in the manufacture of linoleum and, when treated, in the manufacture of cork insulation.

So long as the inner bark or skin is not injured, the removal of the outer bark is beneficial rather than harmful to the cork oak tree; for this unscarred inner bark, with its life-giving sap, immediately undertakes the formation of a new covering of better quality. Each year this inner bark, the tree's real skin, forms a layer of cells within, increasing the

FIG. 8.—VIRGIN CORK AND SECOND STRIPPING BARK.

diameter of the trunk, and a layer of cells without, adding thickness to the covering of outer bark. If the inner bark is injured, the growth of the outer bark is permanently stopped at that point, the injured area appearing as scarred

FIG. 9.—CORK BARK—"BACK" AND "BELLY".

and uncovered for the remainder of the life of the tree. Also, stripping is never done during a "sirocco,"—a hot southernly wind blowing from the African coast to Italy, Sicily and Spain,—which would dry the inner bark too rapidly and exclude all further formation of outer bark.

8.—Secondary Bark.—After eight or ten years the outer bark is again removed, known as "pelas" or secondary bark and, while of much better quality than the virgin bark, it is not as fine in texture as future strippings, which follow every eight or ten years from the time the tree is about forty years of age until it is a hundred or more years old. When the cork oak has been stripped about five times, or when about ninety years old, subsequent strippings yield a bark that is more grainy and of less value for taper corks and cork paper. The second and all subsequent strippings of the outer bark of

FIG. 10.—HANDLING CORKWOOD IN THE FOREST.

the cork oak tree is known as the cork of commerce, while the term "cork waste" is employed to describe the residue from the cutting of natural cork articles, and also the forest waste or refuse remaining after the selection of the commercial bark.

9.—Boiling and Baling.—As the outer bark of the cork oak is removed, under the regulations and precautions that are prescribed by the different cork growing countries, it is piled for a few days to dry out, after which it is weighed, removed to the boiling station and there stacked for a few weeks of seasoning preliminary to being boiled. The outer surface of cork bark is rough and woody and contains considerable grit, due to its long exposure to the elements. After boiling, this "hard-back," as it is called, is readily scraped off; but since the weight is thereby reduced about twenty per cent, and corkwood is sold by weight, it is the tendency to want to slight this operation. The same boiling process removes the tannic acid, increases the volume and the elasticity of the bark, renders it soft and pliable and flattens it out for baling after

FIG. 11.—CORKWOOD SORTING AND STORAGE YARD IN SPAIN.

first being sorted as to quality and thickness. Sometimes the boiling is not done until the raw cork bark comes into the possession of those in Spain or Portugal who intend to utilize it in their own domestic manufacturing plants, because then the complete boiling operation can be carefully supervised and controlled. However, it is customary, if the forest is distant, water is plentiful and the quantity of bark is ample to justify the equipment, to set up the copper vats at a convenient point and carry out the boiling operation right in the forest.

The mountaneous nature of the country, where most of the cork trees abound, makes its desirable that the Spaniard's much abused friend, the faithful burro, be employed to transport corkwood to domestic factories, or to the railway for freighting to the seaport warehouses in Spain and Portugal, the city of Seville, Spain, being probably the largest depository of corkwood in the world.

Before exporting, the bales are opened, the edges of each piece of bark are trimmed and the corkwood is again sorted into many grades of thickness and quality. This final sorting, before re-baling for shipment, is done by experts who "know cork," because the successful and economical manufacture of cork products hinges on it. The large, flat pieces, known as planks or tables, are first laid in the baling box to form the bottom and sides of the bale, smaller pieces being filled in the center and larger pieces used again to cover the top. Pressure is then applied to make a compact mass, which steel hoops bind securely.

CHAPTER III.

USES OF CORKWOOD AND UTILIZATION OF CORK WASTE.

10.—Hand Cut Corks.—Soon after the general introduction of the glass bottle, in the seventeenth century, the manufacture of cork stoppers consumed the bulk of the corkwood

FIG. 12. SPANIARDS CUTTING CORK BY HAND.

that was harvested, and continued to do so for several centuries. The manufacture of these "corks" was orginally done by hand in the producing countries. The slabs or pieces of cork bark were sliced to a width equal to the length of the stopper desired, and these strips were then cut into squares, or "quarters," from which the corks were rounded by hand. The greatest skill was acquired by the Catalons, who today rank as the most adept cork workmen in the world.

The manufacture of bottle corks by hand was never carried

on to any great extent in the United States, although prior to the Civil War there were a few such establishments in Boston, New York and Philadelphia. In Spain and Portugal, however, there are to this day many small hand cork manufactories, although machinery is used by the large and more modern plants. While Portugal attained rank with Spain as a cork manufacturing country, it has since come to export a much larger proportion of its corkwood in unmanufactured form than does Spain. Probably three-fourths of the corkwood grown in Spain is consumed in Spain; that is, is manufactured into some cork product, and in addition, Spain imports large quantities from Portugal and Algeria. Spain, in a word, is the cork clearing house of the world, and cork is one of the principal industries, if not *the* principal industry, of the Spanish people.

11.—**Other Uses.**—In addition to "straight" and "taper" corks, about which more will be said presently, a great variety

FIG. 13. CORK WASHERS AND GASKETS—ONE OF MANY USES FOR CORK.

of disks, washers, floats, buoys, life rings, balls, mats, handle grips, gaskets, bobbers, life preservers, as well as shoe insoles, polishing disks, cork paper, tropical helmets, rafts, bungs, French heels for shoes, bedding, sound isolation, heat and cold insulation, floor tiles, roof tiles, sweat bands, lining for hats, the basis for ladies' hat and dress trimmings, pulley and clutch inserts, Spanish black for paint, cigarette tips, wadding for gun cartridges, packing for glass and fruits, bulletin boards, the basis of linoleum manufacture, an important ingredient in good stucco plaster, and probably a hundred or so additional items of importance are manufactured from corkwood and cork waste.

12.—Importance of Sorting.—"In taking up the processes of manipulation we naturally start from the beginning, but the beginning in this case has a peculiar significance as relating to the whole, for it is apparent to utilize corkwood to the fullest extent its qualities must be studied and the best used first, so that the beginning of the corkwood industry is peculiar in this fact, that it takes the best part and leaves but scrap, which must be studied carefully to realize the value lost in the first process; therefore, in the manufacture of one

FIG. 14.—CORKWOOD STORAGE YARD AT ALGECIRAS, SPAIN.

article of corkwood it is necessary to make provision for the scrap (waste) created, and this is a characteristic of all such (cork) establishments."*

The bulkiness of corkwood is probably its outstanding characteristic when considered in relation to its value, and since the harvest occurs but once each year and the corkwood comes to market soon after the crop is taken, a large stock must necessarily be kept on hand by cork factories. The raw material is frequently purchased, or contracted for, a year in advance of its fabrication. Thus great piles appear in the

*Gilbert E. Stecher, 1914, "Cork—Its Origin and Industrial Uses," D. Van Nostrand Co., New York, N. Y.

yards and sheds of cork plants, covering much area and involving considerable capital, for a shortage in raw material would not only throw men out of work and put the plant into disuse but would cause the loss of much business through inability to supply the trade with first-grade cork materials, the other grades always being compelled to await a favorable market.

For whatever purpose it is to be used, all corkwood upon reaching the factory is again sorted by highly skilled men; and the original twenty or twenty-five grades are re-classed into perhaps one hundred and twenty-five or one hundred and fifty grades, according to quality and thickness. Success in the "cork business" hinges on the care and skill displayed in the various sorting operations that are meticulously followed at every step from the stripping of the bark to the packing of the finished product for delivery to consumers. So slight is the difference between many of the grades that the inexperienced eye would detect none whatever, yet the speed with which this sorting work is skillfully done is often astounding.

The importance of the initial sorting operations is increasing as the uses of cork increase; because various grades can now be used for so many different things, without longer being thought of as a by-product. In order that the full value be obtained from all corkwood, the sorter must have a thorough understanding of the uses to which the many grades of the material may be put, and for that reason he is now thought of as an expert and a valuable member of the manufacturing organization.

13.—Cork Stoppers.—No account of the uses of corkwood and the utilization of cork waste can be given without at least a short description of the modern processes followed in manufacturing cork stoppers, for the waste from the production of these stoppers has long been an appreciable percentage of the total cork waste annually made available for utilization, although this percentage is now decreasing.

The sorted slabs of corkwood are first placed in a steam box, which process increases its flexibility greatly, its bulk slightly, and otherwise prepares it for the mechanical operations that rapidly follow. First, the steamed corkwood is usually scraped, often by hand and sometimes by knives mounted on a vertical shaft revolving at about 1,500 r.p.m., to remove the hard-back, or "raspa," provided this operation was not satisfactorily performed at the time of boiling. The cork slabs are next cut into strips of width equal to the length of the stopper to be cut, because the cutting is done across and not with the grain of the bark. A circular knife does this slicing, following which the strips go to the "blocking" machine. There a tubular punch, with sharpened edges and of given diameter, is rotated at about 2,000 r.p.m. to punch or cut out thousands of cork stoppers per day, although the operator must use caution in avoiding defective spots and at

FIG. 15.—CORK PUNCHINGS—STOPPERS REMOVED.

the same time must keep the punchings as close as possible to minimize the waste. Next, smaller stoppers are punched from the waste from the first punchings, if quality and remaining area permit, for every economy of raw stock must be followed.

These stoppers have straight sides, but if tapered corks are desired, larger in diameter at the top than at the bottom, the cylindrical pieces must be handled on another machine where a circular, razor-edged knife, revolving at top speed and set at the proper taper angle to the cork to be shaped, takes off the necessary cutting in the form of a very thin cork shaving.

14.—Cork Disks.—The wide use of the patented "Crown" bottle cap, with which the reader is undoubtedly familiar, requiring a thin cork disk, created an outlet for very thin bark for which there was virtually no previous demand. A revolving blade slices the cork bark, on a plane parallel to its "back" and "belly", to the required thickness, ranging from one-eighth to one-quarter inch, and from these sheets the natural cork disks are punched. A great deal of cork waste results from this manufacturing process, and its utilization is important enought to form virtually a separate branch of the corkwood industry.

The manufactured stoppers and disks must, in their turn, be sorted as to grade and quality. They are then washed and bleached by soaking in water and a chemical, and are

FIG. 16.—CORK PUNCHINGS—DISKS REMOVED.

then dried by spinning in a perforated centrifugal cylinder mounted within a metal jacket connected to a drain. Some stoppers, usually "straights", and all disks, are given a bath of hot paraffin, or glycerine and paraffin, which improves their resistance and retards discoloration, the operation usually being done in a steam jacketed kettle and then "tumbled" to remove the excess water and paraffin.

15.—Artificial Cork.—The working up of the waste from corkwood, and virgin cork, which is classed as waste, into many products of utility and value is probably the most important phase of the cork business today, just as the successful utilization of by-products in any modern industry is usually necessary for successful operation.

It was noted that in the handling of corkwood the best was utilized first; and similarly, in the working up of cork waste, the best is granulated in an iron rotary cutter mill, of size that will pass a ⅛-inch mesh, screened and mixed with an unusually tenacious glue, dried by steam, hydraulically pressed into sheets, dried again, and then punched out into "composition" disks for Crown caps, gaskets, insoles and a variety of products, frequently termed "artificial" cork products.

FIG. 17.—CORK INSOLES FOR SHOES.

Granulated cork for many purposes is made by grinding the waste in a metal roller, cage or bur mill, and screening into various degrees of fineness. If cork-flour is required, a tube mill is used.

The manufacture of "Spanish black" for use as a base for oil paints of the same color, is produced from cork waste by burning inferior grades in a retort, and grinding the carbonized material in a ball mill until the required fineness is obtained.

16.—Cork Insulation.—Probably the most important use to which cork waste is now being put, and which rivals the cork stopper industry, is in the manufacture of cork insulation for the retarding of heat and sound.

Steam pipes are insulated to prevent heat from escaping; cold rooms and cold pipes are insulated to prevent heat from entering. Cork is employed as a thermal insulation to prevent the entrance of heat, or to preserve cold temperatures; and its success, either in board or slab form for application to floors, walls and ceilings of cold rooms, or in special molded forms for ready application to cold pipes and fittings, is due

FIG. 18.—PURE CORKBOARD INSULATION 1, $1\frac{1}{2}$, 2, 3, AND 4 INCH THICKNESSES, IN STANDARD 12X36 INCH SHEETS.

not alone to its remarkable heat retarding properties and its ready adaptability but more particularly to its entire freedom

FIG. 19.—CORK PIPE COVERING FOR REFRIGERATED LINES AND TANKS.

from capillarity. This property, the force that causes a blotter to suck up ink, is entirely lacking in cork, as evidenced by its long and successful use as stoppers in vessels containing liquids.

Machines are insulated—perhaps more properly spoken of today as isolated—to permanently reduce the transmission of vibration and sound to an irreducable minimum. Cork iso-

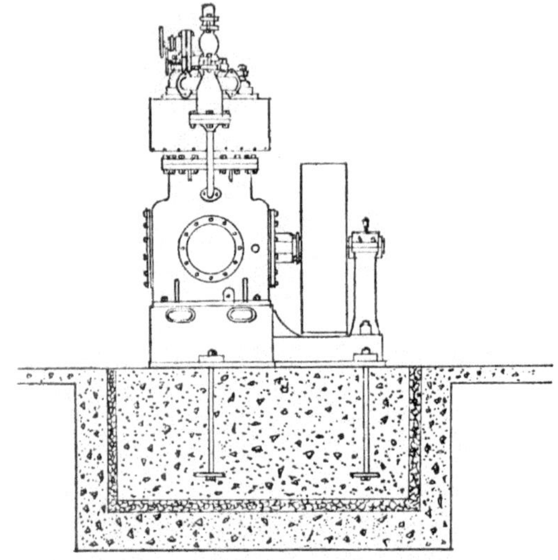

FIG. 20.—MACHINE BASE COMPLETELY ISOLATED WITH CORKBOARD INSULATION TO REDUCE VIBRATION AND NOISE.

lation is already widely used in the industries; but, since it takes so little to accomplish so much, the total quantity of cork consumed in its manufacture is a small factor in the cork industry.

Cork insulation takes on several forms of corkboard, or sheet cork, and molded cork pipe covering; and it is the detailed treatment of the uses of these remarkable cork products that shall comprise the greater part of this text.

CHAPTER IV.

EARLY FORMS OF CORK INSULATION.

17.—Natural Cork and Composition Cork.—The first mention of the use of cork as insulation appears to be by the elder Pliny in the first century of the Christian era when he called attention to its use by women as winter foot gear. Undoubtedly it was utilized as sandals because of its insulating qualities and its freedom from capillarity. Pliny spoke of cork bark being used as a covering for roofs. John Evelyn, the English writer and diarist (1620-1706), mentions that cork was much used by old people for linings to the soles of their shoes. The poor of Spain laid planks of cork on the floor like tiles, to obviate the need for a floor covering that would be warm to the touch. They also lined the inside of their stone houses with cork bark, to make their homes easier to heat and to correct the precipitation of moisture on the walls. Ground cork and India rubber formed the basic ingredients of the quiet, resilient floors of the reading rooms of the British Museum. Bee hives have long been constructed of pieces of cork bark, because of its warmth to the touch. Shelves of cork have been used for centuries to preserve objects from dampness. The primitive races of northern Africa used cork mixed with clay for the walls of their crude dwellings, and cork slabs as roof tiles. Cork was, and still is, the basis in Europe for certain cements and plastics for preventing the escape of heat, which are formed to steam pipes, and hot surfaces in general. Powdered cork and starch were molded into cylinders to fit pipes of different sizes, and were then split and made ready for application to pipes requiring insulation, after which the cork composition was spirally wrapped with cloth and coated with tar or pitch. Narrow cork pieces were laid around steam pipes, as lagging, wired in place and spirally wrapped and coated. Cork was early used by the medical profession because of its sound isolation qualities, as lining for doors of consulting rooms and as floors in hospitals. In tropical countries, cork lined hats and cork helmets have long served to prevent sunstroke. Brick paste, as it was called, was made by mixing the coarsest cork powder with milk of lime, compressed into bricks and slabs, dried and used for the covering of damp walls and pitched

FGI. 21.—CORK TILE FLOOR IN MODERN OFFICE.

roofs. In gunpowder plants and powder storage magazines, such composition slabs prevented the caking of the powder through dampness; and used under wood flooring, they destroyed the sound vibrations.

Thus, it will be noted that the thermal insulating, as well as the sound isolating, qualities of cork bark were known and utilized, although probably not very clearly understood, as early as the year One. Many of these uses have persisted through the ages*; for cork insoles are today an important

*See appendix for "Pulverized Cork—Subirine" and "Cork as a Building Material."

item in the construction of high grade shoes, cork tile floors are essential to edifices and libraries, cork linoleum is so common in public buildings and in certain types of homes as to be classed as essential, and corkboard effectively and efficiently prevents condensation on and the flow of heat through the walls and roofs of buildings. All that was needed to establish cork as the standard insulation of the world was the discovery of a practical method of utilizing cork waste

FIG. 22.—CORKBOARD INSULATION BEING APPLIED TO SAW-TOOTH ROOF CONSTRUCTION.

in the form of molded slabs or boards of convenient size, ample strength and high permanent insulating value under actual service conditions.

18.—Impregnated Corkboard.—About the year 1890 the German firm of Grünzweig & Hartmann acquired patents in Germany and in the United States for a type of insulation known as "Impregnated Corkboard", and soon became the leaders in their own country in the manufacture of these "impregnated" cork slabs for insulating purposes, particularly for cold storage work. The United States patent rights for this new type of insulation were subsequently acquired by the Armstrong Cork Company of Pittsburgh, about the year 1900, following which a plant for its manufacture was established at Beaver Falls, Pa., such location being selected principally because the necessary clay for the preparation of the foreign binder to stick the granules of cork together was available there in generous quantity and at a point not far distant from Pittsburgh.

The business grew rapidly, especially among the brewers, for the insulation of their cellars; but it was soon discovered that this impregnated corkboard was inferior in insulating quality, and in structural strength in service, to a brand of "pure" corkboard being made under the patents of one John T. Smith, an American, and subsequently the manufacture and use of the impregnated, or "composition," corkboard gave way entirely to the pure corkboard insulation.

CHAPTER V.

DISCOVERY OF SMITH'S CONSOLIDATED CORK, AND THE FIRST PURE CORK INSULATION.

19.—Smith's Discovery.—The manufacture of pure cork insulation was begun in 1893, in the United States, under the original John T. Smith patents, by Messrs. Stone and Duryée. Cork covering was produced first, and then the manufacture of pure corkboard followed within a very few years.

It is interesting to know that the discovery of the process of baking cork particles under pressure to bind them together, which later made pure cork insulation possible, was purely an accident; and that the process was not thought of in connection with cork covering and corkboard until Messrs. Stone and Duryée later applied it to that purpose.

In the "Boat Works" of John T. Smith on lower South Street, on the East River, in New York, was a large cast-iron kettle with a fire box under it, the kettle being used to steam oak framing for row boats that Smith manufactured there for many years. He also produced boat fenders, life preservers and ring buoys, in the manner common in those days, by packing granulated cork in canvas jackets. Girls packed the cork in these jackets, using tin forms or cylinders to keep the canvas distended until filled. One of these cylinders became clogged in the hands of one of Smith's employees and was laid aside for the moment, but it inadvertently rolled into the dying embers of the fire box during clean-up late that evening.

Early the next morning, Smith, owner and fireman, cleaned out the fire box and found his misplaced utensil. But the hot ashes had not consumed the cork particles that had clogged it. The heat had been sufficient merely to bind the mass together in the form of a very substantial chocolate-brown cork cylinder.

Smith noted this peculiar fact with much interest, if not with actual astonishment, and put the tin form and cork cylinder aside for future secret study and investigation. He repeated the original and wholly unintentional experiment enough times to satisfy himself that for some good reason a certain degree of heat applied for a given time served to glue cork particles together without the addition of a foreign

FIG. 23.—ARTIST'S CONCEPTION OF THE DISCOVERY OF PURE CORK-BOARD INSULATION BY JOHN T. SMITH.

substance or binder of any kind or character, to produce what he later termed "Smith's Consolidated Cork". He thereupon applied for and was granted basic patents in the United States, Germany, France and England covering the broad principles involved.

20.—Cork Covering for Steam Pipes.—In 1893 Messrs. Stone and Duryée purchased the Smith patent rights for the United States, France and England and began the manufacture, at No. 184-6 North Eighth street, Brooklyn, New York, of asbestos-lined cork covering for steam pipes, the suggestion probably having come to Junius H. Stone, who had previously been engaged in the steam pipe covering business, from the original Smith cork cylinder, which, incidentally, Smith had failed to utilize to any good purpose whatever.

But not long thereafter the patent rights on "85 per cent Magnesia" steam pipe covering expired, and the resultant competition so reduced prices as to seriously interfere with the further sale of the cork product.

21.—Cork Covering for Cold Pipes.—Then the Engineering department of the United States Navy became interested in molded cork covering for cold pipes, to replace hair felt and such other fibrous materials as possessed a marked affinity for moisture, and it was subsequently tried out as insulation for brine lines on one of the large battleships then building.

The adaptability and suitability of this very early form of pure cork covering for cold lines was quickly apparent to the Navy's engineers, and the material rapidly found favor in other Governmental departments. Thus the real field of usefulness for Smith's Consolidated Cork—as an insulating material for cold surfaces—was discovered; and soon thereafter, with the encouragement of the Navy department again, the firm of Stone & Durýee began the manufacture of the very first pure corkboard that was ever produced, sold or used.

It cannot be out of place to remark here that the various U. S. Governmental departments are constantly on the lookout for new and better materials for use in the construction of governmental equipment of every conceivable sort. To our Government's engineers may be credited the discovery, early development or initial successful use of many materials and products that have influenced the course of human progress. Merely as an instance, this is taken from the August 23d, 1926, issue of the Chicago *Daily Tribune*, under the caption of "Science Marches On":

> Army experts in aerial photography, improving a process invented by the Eastman Kodak Company, are able to take photographs not only at great distances but through mist and smoke screens.

22.—Pure Corkboard.—Mr. Harvey H. Durýee, of the firm of Stone & Durýee, was of French Hugenot descent, and it pleased him to designate the products of his firm "Nonpareil", from the French words "non pareil", meaning no parallel, or no equal. The firm of Stone & Durýee subsequently became The Nonpareil Cork Works, and with the construction of a factory at Camden, N. J., it became the Nonpareil Cork Manufacturing Company.

In June, 1904, the Armstrong Cork Company purchased the patents, plant and business of the Nonpareil Cork Manufacturing Company; and, by the time the patents expired,

FIG. 24.—AN EXAMPLE OF THE VERSATILITY OF MODERN CORK PIPE COVERING, LAGS AND DISKS, ON TANK HEADER, RECEIVER, PIPING AND FITTINGS.

both pure corkboard insulation* and cork pipe covering† were the standard of the world wherever the use of refrigeration had been scientifically introduced.

*See Appendix for "Some Uses of Corkboard Insulation".
†See Appendix for "Cork Pipe Covering Specifications" and "Instructions for the Proper Application of Cork Pipe Covering."

CHAPTER VI.

EXTENT OF THE CORK INDUSTRY.

23.—Is Source of Supply Adequate?—The question that is most frequently asked today is this: "Can the production of corkwood be increased sufficiently by the cork producing countries to keep pace with the world's constantly increasing demand for cork products of every kind?"

In attempting an answer to such a question, if indeed an answer should be attempted, it must be remembered that corkwood is an agricultural product, and that in agriculture price controls production, with certain important limitations, rather than production establishing price as it does in many of the industries not associated with agriculture. In other words, if an agricultural product grown in volume will bring a price that will make such growing of the product profitable, it will continue to be produced in volume; otherwise, not. If that volume demand should grow beyond the ultimate capacity of the producing soil and climate, then other soil will be prepared and utilized in a suitable climate, if that is possible and not too costly. Now a look back into the history of the cork industry should furnish much information and possibly serve as a guide in reaching conclusions about the ultimate extent of the cork industry, with particular emphasis upon cork insulation.

24.—Cork Stopper Industry.—The cork stopper industry, which was for many years the most important branch of the cork industry, had its permanent origin in the town of Llacostera, Province of Gerona, Spain, late in the year 1750,* and was incident to the real beginnings of the use of the

*Gilbert E. Stecher, 1914, "Cork—Its Origin and Industrial Uses," D. Van Ostrand Co., New York, N. Y.

glass bottle, although corkwood was used centuries before as stoppers for casks and other kinds of liquid-containing vessels. The cork trade was later disrupted by the many wars that followed one another in rapid succession, which drove the industry to the mountains to struggle for years until some semblance of peace was restored. The principal dangers having passed, the cork stopper industry slowly but surely grew until it virtually became a necessity in the life of Spain.

FIG. 25.—LOADING CRATED CORKBOARD AT PALAMOS, SPAIN.

It was customary in those days to hold all manufacturing processes as valuable secrets, but the cork stopper industry of Spain soon attracted so much attention that other and neighboring countries sought to learn the secrets of its processes. French agents in the Province of Catalonia obtained sufficient information, it is said, to return to France and establish their own plants, which greatly disturbed the Spanish manufacturers because they had never had any competition up to that time. But by about 1850 the trade in cork and cork products had grown so that there was plenty of business for all, and the industry expanded until it surpassed the expectations of the most optimistic. In fact, a shortage of corkwood came about in Spain; and, in an effort to fill the demands, the cork bark was stripped from the trees more frequently than was usual or desirable, and as a consequence the grade deteriorated until the situation became alarming.

25.—Cork a National Necessity.—The Spanish Government then passed the necessary laws to protect its cork forests as

FIG. 26.—CORK REFUSE—USED IN THE MANUFACTURE OF MANY "ARTIFICIAL" CORK PRODUCTS.

a national necessity, these laws governing the stripping of the corkwood from the trees. But the demand for corkwood kept right on growing in other countries, and the raw stock came to be so heavily exported from Spain and Portugal that it finally interfered so seriously with the local production of finished cork products as to bring about a convention of the principal representatives of the cork industry in Madrid, in December, 1911. Resolutions were passed calling upon the Spanish Government to impose an export duty on corkwood, ranging from about 90 cents to $90.00 per ton.

New export duties were then decided upon by the Government and an effort was made to put the new laws in force in 1912, but all these efforts were without much success. In Portugal, one of the restrictive laws that were passed made it impossible to export from the country pieces of corkwood larger than about 4x8 inches. That law, while almost never enforced, still remains to harry the inexperienced buyer who has failed to provide in advance for its temporary nonexistence, so to speak.

26.—Effect of U. S. Tariff Act of 1913.—For one reason or another, the governments of Portugal and Spain both failed in their efforts to restrict the exportations of raw cork, although the cork manufacturing industry remains very strong in both of these countries, particularly in Spain. Considerable impetus was given the manufacture of cork insulation in Spain when the United States Tariff Act of 1913, which reduced the United States import on finished cork insulation to a *specific* duty of ¼c per pound, became effective. The Act of 1922 restored the former rate of duty of the Act of 1909, or 30 per centum ad valorem*, but meanwhile several large insulation factories were constructed in Spain and one in Portugal and the size of these investments coupled with the constantly mounting labor rate in the United States keeps these foreign plants of domestic concerns operating at capacity.

The United States Tariff Commission's Comparison of Tariff Acts—1922, 1913 and 1909—subdivides "Cork" into eighteen groups, as follows:

TARIFF SUBDIVISIONS OF CORK INTO GROUPS.

Description Cork:	Paragraph under act of 1922 No.	 1913 No.	 1909 No.
Artificial and manufactures of	1412	340	429
Bark, squares, etc.	1412	340	429
Bark, unmanufactured	1559	464	547
Carpet	1020	276	347
Composition or compressed	1412	340	429
Disks	1412	340	429
Granulated or ground	1412	340	429
Insulation	1412	340	429
Manufacturers of, n. s. p. f.	1412	340	429
Paper	1412	340	429

*Duties imposed by a government on commodities imported into its territory from foreign countries are designated as *specific* and *ad valorem*—the former when fixed at a specified amount, the latter when requiring payment of a sum to be ascertained by a determined percentage on the value of the goods imported.

TARIFF SUBDIVISIONS OF CORK INTO GROUPS.—*Continued*

Description Cork:	Paragraph under act of 1922 No.	 1913 No.	 1909 No.
Refuse and shavings	1559	464	547
Stoppers	1412	340	429
Substitutes	1412	340	429
Tile	1412	340	429
Wafers	1412	340	429
Washers	1412	340	429
Waste	1559	464	547
Wood or cork bark, unmanufactured	1559	464	547

Act of 1922

Paragraph 1020.—Linoleum, including corticine and cork carpet, 35 per centum ad valorem; floor oilcloth, 20 per centum ad valorem; mats or rugs made of linoleum or floor oilcloth shall be subject to the same rates of duty as herein provided for linoleum or floor oilcloth.

Paragraph 1412.—Cork bark, cut into squares, cubes, or quarters, 8 cents per pound; stoppers over three-fourths of an inch in diameter, measured at the larger end, and discs, wafers, and washers over three-sixteenths of one inch in thickness, made from natural cork bark, 20 cents per pound; made from artificial or composition cork, 10 cents per pound; stoppers, three-fourths of one inch or less in diameter, measured at the larger end, and discs, wafers, and washers, three-sixteenths of one inch or less in thickness, made from natural cork bark, 25 cents per pound; made from artificial or composition cork, 12½ cents per pound; cork, artificial, commonly known as composition or compressed cork, manufactured from cork waste or granulated cork, in the rough and not further advanced than in the form of slabs, blocks, or planks, suitable for cutting into stoppers, discs, liners, floats, or similar articles, 6 cents per pound; in rods or sticks suitable for the manufacture of discs, wafers, or washers, 10 cents per pound; granulated or ground cork, 25 per centum ad valorem; cork insulation, wholly or in chief value of cork waste, granulated or ground cork, in slabs, boards, planks, or molded forms; cork tile; cork paper, and manufactures, wholly or in chief value of cork bark or artificial cork and not specially provided for, 30 per centum ad valorem.

Paragraph 1559.—Cork wood, or cork bark, unmanufactured, and cork waste, shavings, and cork refuse of all kinds (Free).

Act of 1913

Paragraph 276.—Linoleum, plain, stamped, painted, or printed, including corticine and cork carpet, figured or plain, also linoleum known as granite and oak plank, 30 per centum ad valorem; inlaid linoleum, 35 per centum ad valorem; oilcloth for floors, plain, stamped, painted, or printed, 20 per centum ad valorem; mats or rugs made of oilcloth, linoleum, corticine, or cork carpet shall be subject to the same rate of duty as herein provided for oilcloth, linoleum, corticine, or cork carpet.

Paragraph 340.—Cork bark, cut into squares, cubes, or quarters, 4 cents per pound; manufactured cork stoppers, over three-fourths of an inch in diameter, measured at the larger end, and manufactured cork discs, wafers, or washers, over three-sixteenths of an inch in thickness, 12 cents per pound; manufactured cork stoppers, three-fourths of an inch or less in diameter, measured at the larger end, and manufactured cork discs, wafers, or washers, three-sixteenths of an inch or less in thickness, 15 cents per pound; cork, artificial, or cork substitutes manufactured form cork waste, or granulated cork, and not otherwise provided for in this section, 3 cents per pound; cork insulation, wholly or in chief value of granulated cork, in slabs, boards, planks, or molded forms, 1/4 cent per pound; cork paper, 35 per centum ad valorem; manufactures wholly or in chief value of cork or of cork bark, or of artificial cork or cork substitutes, granulated or ground cork, not specially provided for in this section, 30 per centum ad valorem.

Paragraph 464.—Cork wood, or cork bark, unmanufactured, and cork waste, shavings, and cork refuse of all kinds (Free).

Act of 1909

Paragraph 347.—Linoleum, corticene, and all other fabrics or coverings for floors, made in part of oil or similar product, plain, stamped, painted or printed only, not specially provided for herein, if nine feet or under in width, 8 cents per square yard and 15 per centum ad valorem; over nine feet in width, 12 cents per square yard and 15 per centum ad valorem; and any of the foregoing of whatever width, the composition of which forms designs or patterns, whether inlaid or otherwise, by whatever name known, and cork carpets, 20 cents per square yard and 20 per centum ad valorem; mats for floors made of oilcloth, linoleum, or corticene, shall be subject to the same rate of duty herein provided for oilcloth, linoleum, or corticene; oilcloth for floors, if nine feet or less in width, 6 cents per square yard and 15 per centum ad valorem; over nine feet in width, 10 cents per square yard and 15 per centum ad valorem; . . . .

Paragraph 429.—Cork bark cut into squares, cubes, or quarters, 8 cents per pound; manufactured corks over three-fourths of an inch in diameter, measured at larger end, 15 cents per pound; three-fourths of an inch and less in diameter, measured at larger end, 25 cents per pound; cork, artificial, or cork substitutes, manufactured from cork waste or granulated cork, and not otherwise provided for in this section, 6 cents per pound; manufactures, wholly or in chief value of cork, or of cork bark, or of artificial cork or cork substitutes, granulated or ground cork, not specially provided for in this section, 30 per centum ad valorem.

Paragraph 547.—Cork wood, or cork bark, unmanufactured. (Free).

27.—Effect of the World War.—While there was an apparent shortage of corkwood for a brief time just prior to the beginning of the World War, yet the demand for corkwood by France, Germany, Austria and other belligerent countries quickly dropped off to almost nothing, which left the United States as virtually the only country requiring any appreciable exports of corkwood or cork waste. The situation in the cork producing countries became rapidly worse as the war continued until the time soon came when it did not pay, in many cases, to bring in the cork harvest.

FIG. 27.—CORKWOOD STOCKS ON HAND IN STORAGE YARD IN SPAIN.

In Catalonia, for example, the situation become so acute at one time that valuable cork oak trees were cut down and burned as fuel and the cork workers threatened to burn all cork manufacturing plants if enough employment was not given them to keep body and soul together. The situation was quickly recognized as acute, and large owners moved rapidly to provide enough relief to tide over the difficulties occasioned by the World War. Sufficient capital was invested in stocks to provide the cork workers with just enough wages to buy necessary food and drink, although it was not known then by those owners and operators how long they would have to continue the very unusual procedure before the war would end and thus give them an opportunity of turning those stocks back into capital, regardless of whether a profit could be realized or a heavy loss would be suffered.

Conservation of valuable cork forests and cork manufactories and the prevention of civil war and incident loss of life was the first and only consideration of those large operators; but they met the situation with such remarkable foresight attended by such complete success that the King of Spain is said to have personally thanked the men who so ably and generously gave of their time and money.

28.—Recovery of the Industry.—If a crop of wheat is wanted next year, the planting usually is done in the fall of this year. With cork, however, it is from eight to nine years after the stripping of the virgin bark before the secondary bark can be stripped and another equal period before the first real crop of corkwood is available. When there is not a favorable price offered for corkwood, the trees are not stripped, that is, the older ones that have previously been brought into bearing and are ready for stripping are allowed to go over another year, or two, or three, as desired and those ready for their initial stripping, of the virgin bark, are not touched. Thus it can be seen what happened to much of the cork forests during the World War; and when the demand for corkwood suddenly returned to normal again, with the recovery of Europe, and with an unusually brisk demand in the United States due to an active cold storage building program, to the adoption of corkboard as standard for household refrigerators, and to the demand for corkboard as insulation for roofs and residences, a temporary shortage of raw cork waste was felt early in 1926, its price trebled, and the price of many finished cork products rose by July first to double what they were early in 1925, all because the raw product supply could not, by the nature of the industry, expand suddenly to take care of wide and sudden fluctuations in demand.

The resultant (August, 1926) price of cork waste aided in bringing in a full harvest in the cork producing countries for the first time since 1914, many young trees were put in line for productivity by receiving their initial stripping, and with the complete cessation of the Riffian wars in Northern

Africa much is being done by France and Spain to open up that enormous area of virgin cork forests as a very appreciable future source of supply.

29.—Changing Demands.—The growth of "prohibition" throughout the world and the increasing substitution of "Crown" caps and screw closures for cork stoppers has effected a material decrease in the total quantity of corkwood required for use in connection with bottles containing liquids. The use of granulated cork for the packing of glass and fruit is decreasing in favor of certain very soft woods. The world's demand for corkwood for miscellaneous purposes, such as life preservers, floats, buoys, etc., probably has not changed a great deal in many years and probably will not change much in the years to come. The demand for cork waste, however, for cork insulation has increased irregularly but slowly and certainly ever since pure corkboard insulation was first made some thirty-four years ago, the industry getting its first important impetus when the basic pure cork insulation patents expired, and its second important impetus in 1925 when corkboard began to be used in large quantities as a recognized essential insulation for electric household refrigerators and standard insulation for industrial roof slabs.

At one time the breweries utilized about two-thirds of all cork insulation that was produced. Then ice, ice cream and cold storage plants replaced the breweries as the large consumers of cork insulation. The mechanically-cooled cork-insulated ice cream cabinet is replacing the ice plant as an adjunct to the ice cream factory, the cork-insulated mechanically-cooled commercial and household refrigerators are making inroads on the use of ice, and thus it will be observed that as new applications are made others are slightly reduced, so that the world's urgent need for cork insulation, that is, for use with cold storage temperatures where cork insulation is now essential, has a habit of slowly increasing with the growth of population and with the increasing per capita use of refrigeration in the preservation of food. A great proportion of all foodstuffs is today preserved by cooling, one place or another, by ice or mechanical refrigeration, and cork insulation is an essential item of all cold storage equipment.

FIG. 28.—CORKBOARD INSULATION BEING APPLIED OVER ROOF DECK OF INDUSTRIAL BUILDING.

Thus the basic essential requirements for cork insulation by the industries of the world must be somewhat comparable to shfting sands—constantly moving about but added to but slowly. On the other hand, there is a growing demand for cork insulation for use wherever moisture is encountered, such as for the insulation of industrial roofs, which field is enormous in scope, and if the demand for corkboard for roofs continues at the pace it has already set for itself, then no one dare predict the ultimate requirements for cork insulation, and, in turn, for cork waste and corkwood.

Of course, if the ultimate cost were low enough, cork, because it combines within itself so many unusual and useful qualities, would be utilized in many more ways and to a much greater extent than it is at present employed. Cost, however, is usually the final determining factor in the industries of the world; and, should the demand exceed the supply, additional cork will be made available or the price of cork will advance to a point sufficient to discourage further increase in its use and consumption. In such event, possibly substitutes will be found for enough of the miscellaneous uses to which cork is put to release sufficient material for all the essential cork products, such as cork insulation, that would be required.

30.—Tables of U. S. Imports (1892-1924).—In order that the reader may form a comprehensive idea of the cork industry, past and present, a number of tables of cork imports into the United States from various countries are given here.

IMPORTS OF MERCHANDISE

Fiscal Year	Corkwood or Cork Bark Unmanufactured (Free)	Cork, Manufactures of (Dutiable)	Total Value of Imports
1892	$1,368,244.00	$ 321,480.00	$1,689,724.00
1893	1,641,294.00	351,731.40	1,993,025.40
1894	985,913.00	295,069.00	1,280,982.00
1895	1,049,073.00	351,757.00	1,400,830.00
1896	1,209,450.00	409,887.00	1,619,337.00
1897	1,323,409.00	428,243.00	1,751,652.00
1898	1,152,325.00	294,863.00	1,447,188.00
1899	1,147,802.00	394,565.00	1,542,367.00
1900	1,444,825.00	464,658.00	1,909,483.00
1901	1,729,912.00	541,083.00	2,270,995.00
1902	1,816,107.00	648,827.00	2,464,934.00
1903	1,737,366.00	830,214.00	2,567,580.00
1904	1,484,405.00	810,738.00	2,295,138.00
1905	1,729,143.00	1,009,176.00	2,738,319.00

IMPORTS OF MERCHANDISE—*Continued*

FISCAL YEAR OF 1906—JUNE 30, 1905, TO JUNE 30, 1906

IMPORTS INTO UNITED STATES FROM	Cork Bark, or Wood Unmanufactured[1]	Cork Waste, Shavings, etc.		Cork Discs, Wafers and Washers		All Other Manufactures
	Dollars	Pounds	Dollars	Pounds	Dollars	Dollars
EUROPE:						
Austria and Hungary	7,194					5
Belgium	224					18
Bulgaria						
Czechoslovakia						
Denmark	67					
Finland						
France	120,953					11,405
Germany	25,147					139,082
Italy	50,842					30
Netherlands						1
Norway	1,774					
Poland and Danzig						
Portugal	988,757					8,441
Rumania						
Russia in Europe						91
Spain	481,675					1,300,747
Sweden						
United Kingdom	5,553					15,093
All others						1
AMERICA:						
Canada						1,248
Central American States						
Cuba						
Mexico	62					10
South American Continent						
West Indies						
ASIA:						
China						
Japan						
All others	2,734					
AFRICA:						
Algeria	151,220					
Morocco						
All others	932					
Totals	1,837,134					1,476,172

FISCAL YEAR OF 1907—JUNE 30, 1906, TO JUNE 30, 1907

IMPORTS INTO UNITED STATES FROM	Cork Bark, or Wood Unmanufactured[1]	Cork Waste, Shavings, etc.		Cork Discs, Wafers and Washers		All Other Manufactures
	Dollars	Pounds	Dollars	Pounds	Dollars	Dollars
EUROPE:						
Austria and Hungary						
Belgium	22,116					561
Bulgaria						
Czechoslovakia						
Denmark	23					
Finland						
France	82,802					6,093
Germany	49,261					171,853
Italy	92,758					77
Netherlands						150
Norway						35
Poland and Danzig						
Portugal	1,333,815					57,608
Rumania						
Russia in Europe	20,396					
Spain	588,077					1,452,010
Sweden						
United Kingdom	16,206					19,223
All others						
AMERICA:						
Canada	482					313
Central American States						
Cuba						2
Mexico	341					4
South American Continent						
West Indies						
ASIA:						
China						
Japan						
All others						1
AFRICA:						
Algeria	146,708					
Morocco						
All others	3,067					
Totals	2,356,052					1,707,930

[1]Includes cork waste, shavings, etc., prior to July 1, 1918.

IMPORTS OF MERCHANDISE—*Continued*

FISCAL YEAR OF 1908—JUNE 30, 1907, TO JUNE 30, 1908

IMPORTS INTO UNITED STATES FROM	Cork Bark, or Wood Unmanufactured[1]	Cork Waste, Shavings, etc.		Cork Discs, Wafers and Washers		All Other Manufactures
	Dollars	Pounds	Dollars	Pounds	Dollars	Dollars
EUROPE:						
Austria and Hungary						116
Belgium						
Bulgaria						
Czechoslovakia						
Denmark						
Finland						
France	104,913					5,735
Germany	61,686					322,675
Italy	38,084					45
Netherlands						
Norway						
Poland and Danzig						
Portugal	1,268,611					76,940
Rumania						
Russia in Europe	7,164					532
Spain	467,046					1,726,965
Sweden						
United Kingdom	12,694					22,125
All others						
AMERICA:						
Canada	93					831
Central American States						
Cuba						310
Mexico	362					
South American Continent						
West Indies						
ASIA:						
China						
Japan						
All others						
AFRICA:						
Algeria	132,060					
Morocco						
All others	19					
Totals	2,092,732					2,156,274

FISCAL YEAR OF 1909—JUNE 30, 1908, TO JUNE 30, 1909

IMPORTS INTO UNITED STATES FROM	Cork Bark, or Wood Unmanufactured[1]	Cork Waste, Shavings, etc.		Cork Discs, Wafers and Washers		All Other Manufactures
	Dollars	Pounds	Dollars	Pounds	Dollars	Dollars
EUROPE:						
Austria and Hungary						
Belgium	40					
Bulgaria						
Czechoslovakia						
Denmark						
Finland						
France	109,263					2,253
Germany	53,097					115,470
Italy	66,258					48
Netherlands	17					203
Norway						
Poland and Danzig						
Portugal	1,197,430					42,907
Rumania						
Russia in Europe	736					
Spain	453,084					849,788
Sweden						
United Kingdom	3,347					14,298
All others						
AMERICA:						
Canada						235
Central American States	88					
Cuba						434
Mexico						
South American Continent						
West Indies	219					
ASIA:						
China						
Japan						3
All others						
AFRICA:						
Algeria	132,972					
Morocco						
All others						
Totals	2,016,551					1,025,639

[1]Includes cork waste, shavings, etc., prior to July 1, 1918.

IMPORTS OF MERCHANDISE—*Continued*

FISCAL YEAR OF 1910—JUNE 30, 1909, TO JUNE 30, 1910

IMPORTS INTO UNITED STATES FROM	Cork Bark, or Wood Unmanufactured[1]	Cork Waste, Shavings, etc.		Cork Discs, Wafers and Washers		All Other Manufactures
	Dollars	Pounds	Dollars	Pounds	Dollars	Dollars
EUROPE:						
Austria and Hungary						9
Belgium	58					4,173
Bulgaria						
Czechoslovakia						
Denmark	22					11
Finland						
France	108,860					8,098
Germany	20,091					200,256
Italy	36,801					453
Netherlands						4,014
Norway						
Poland and Danzig						
Portugal	1,888,738					51,854
Rumania						
Russia in Europe	4,200					
Spain	913,528					1,332,392
Sweden						
United Kingdom	17,133					16,539
All others						25
AMERICA:						
Canada						1,002
Central American States						
Cuba	184					232
Mexico						
South American Continent	10					
West Indies						41
ASIA:						
China						
Japan						12
All others						
AFRICA:						
Algeria	162,655					
Morocco						
All others						
Totals	3,152,280					1,619,111

FISCAL YEAR OF 1911 JUNE 30, 1910, TO JUNE 30, 1911

IMPORTS INTO UNITED STATES FROM	Cork Bark, or Wood Unmanufactured[1]	Cork Waste, Shavings, etc.		Cork Discs, Wafers and Washers		All Other Manufactures
	Dollars	Pounds	Dollars	Pounds	Dollars	Dollars
EUROPE:						
Austria and Hungary						374
Belgium						
Bulgaria						
Czechoslovakia	24					
Denmark						3
Finland						
France	145,323					20,698
Germany	85,911					137,429
Italy	56,757					973
Netherlands	4,384					696
Norway						
Poland and Danzig						
Portugal	1,785,848					67,055
Rumania						
Russia in Europe	4,094					308
Spain	2,010,216					2,096,706
Sweden						
United Kingdom	4,151					10,152
All others						
AMERICA:						
Canada	1,046					15
Central American States						10
Cuba						
Mexico						
South American Continent						
West Indies						
ASIA:						
China						
Japan						1
All others						
AFRICA:						
Algeria	176,976					
Morocco						
All others	50					582[2]
Totals	4,274,810					2,335,003

[1]Includes cork waste, shavings, etc., prior to July 1, 1918. [2]Australia.

IMPORTS OF MERCHANDISE—*Continued*

FISCAL YEAR OF 1912—JUNE 30, 1911, TO JUNE 30, 1912

IMPORTS INTO UNITED STATES FROM	Cork Bark, or Wood Unmanufactured[1]	Cork Waste, Shavings, etc.		Cork Discs, Wafers and Washers		All Other Manufactures
	Dollars	Pounds	Dollars	Pounds	Dollars	Dollars
EUROPE:						
Austria and Hungary						
Belgium						
Bulgaria						
Czechoslovakia						
Denmark	4,345					
Finland						
France	122,414					26,758
Germany	72,240					283,325
Italy	56,938					358
Netherlands						2,509
Norway						
Poland and Danzig						
Portugal	1,440,491					52,534
Rumania						
Russia in Europe	4,525					
Spain	1,282,871					1,972,758
Sweden						
United Kingdom	2,108					8,137
All others						
AMERICA:						
Canada	2					11
Central American States						
Cuba						
Mexico						2
South American Continent						
West Indies						
ASIA:						
China						
Japan						23
All others						
AFRICA:						
Algeria	256,385					
Morocco						
All others						
Totals	3,242,319					2,346,415

FISCAL YEAR OF 1913—JUNE 30, 1912, TO JUNE 30, 1913

IMPORTS INTO UNITED STATES FROM	Cork Bark, or Wood Unmanufactured[1]	Cork Waste, Shavings, etc.		Cork Discs, Wafers and Washers		All Other Manufactures
	Dollars	Pounds	Dollars	Pounds	Dollars	Dollars
EUROPE:						
Austria and Hungary						44
Belgium	230					1
Bulgaria						
Czechoslovakia						
Denmark	5,737					
Finland						
France	106,077					12,413
Germany	10,661					54,954
Italy	115,330					267
Netherlands						
Norway						
Poland and Danzig						
Portugal	1,480,329					47,483
Rumania						
Russia in Europe	938					11
Spain	1,250,722					2,229,266
Sweden						
United Kingdom	1,474					6,097
All others						2
AMERICA:						
Canada						137
Central American States						
Cuba						
Mexico	721					3
South American Continent						
West Indies						
ASIA:						
China						2
Japan						4
All others						
AFRICA:						
Algeria	153,798					
Morocco						
All others	26,053[2]					
Totals	3,152,070					2,350,684

[1]Includes cork waste, shavings, etc., prior to July 1, 1918. [2]Australia.

IMPORTS OF MERCHANDISE—*Continued*

FISCAL YEAR OF 1914—JUNE 30, 1913, TO JUNE 30, 1914

IMPORTS INTO UNITED STATES FROM	Cork Bark, or Wood Unmanufactured[1]	Cork Waste, Shavings, etc.		Cork Discs, Wafers and Washers		All Other Manufactures
	Dollars	Pounds	Dollars	Pounds	Dollars	Dollars
EUROPE:						
Austria and Hungary						
Belgium						175
Bulgaria						
Czechoslovakia						
Denmark						
Finland						
France	138,944					13,087
Germany	7,479					34,338
Italy	75,227					862
Netherlands						14
Norway						
Poland and Danzig						
Portugal	1,941,618					86,984
Rumania						
Russia in Europe						
Spain	1,421,894					2,478,364
Sweden						
United Kingdom	197					33,399
All others						4
AMERICA:						
Canada						443
Central American States						
Cuba						81
Mexico						1
South American Continent						
West Indies						
ASIA:						
China						6
Japan						26
All others						
AFRICA:						
Algeria	266,435					
Morocco						
All others						
Totals	3,851,794					2,647,838

FISCAL YEAR OF 1915—JUNE 30, 1914, TO JUNE 30, 1915

IMPORTS INTO UNITED STATES FROM	Cork Bark, or Wood Unmanufactured[1]	Cork Waste, Shavings, etc.		Cork Discs, Wafers and Washers		All Other Manufactures
	Dollars	Pounds	Dollars	Pounds	Dollars	Dollars
EUROPE:						
Austria and Hungary						39
Belgium						
Bulgaria						
Czechoslovakia						
Denmark						
Finland						
France	17,000					12,977
Germany	10,389					20,870
Italy	47,884					361
Netherlands						240
Norway						
Poland and Danzig						
Portugal	1,595,945					61,961
Rumania						
Russia in Europe						
Spain	898,415					1,923,371
Sweden						
United Kingdom	3,698					2,335
All others						1,850
AMERICA:						
Canada						6
Central American States						
Cuba						
Mexico	18,647					8
South American Continent						
West Indies						2
ASIA:						
China						
Japan						39
All others						
AFRICA:						
Algeria	170,917					
Morocco						
All others						
Totals	2,762,895					2,024,059

[1]Includes cork waste, shavings, etc., prior to July 1, 1918.

IMPORTS OF MERCHANDISE—*Continued*

FISCAL YEAR OF 1916—JUNE 30, 1915, TO JUNE 30, 1916

IMPORTS INTO UNITED STATES FROM	Cork Bark, or Wood Unmanufactured[1]	Cork Waste, Shavings, etc.		Cork Discs, Wafers and Washers		All Other Manufactures
	Dollars	Pounds	Dollars	Pounds	Dollars	Dollars
EUROPE:						
Austria and Hungary						
Belgium						
Bulgaria						
Czechoslovakia						
Denmark						
Finland						
France	86,822					5,679
Germany						10
Italy	2,671					1,985
Netherlands						14
Norway						
Poland and Danzig						
Portugal	1,906,694					83,680
Rumania						
Russia in Europe						
Spain	928,477					847,224
Sweden						
United Kingdom	2,545					2,231
All others	8,207					
AMERICA:						
Canada	102					92
Central American States						
Cuba						25
Mexico						3
South American Continent						
West Indies						
ASIA:						
China						
Japan						300
All others						
AFRICA:						
Algeria	199,366					
Morocco						
All others						
Totals	3,134,884					941,243

FISCAL YEAR OF 1917—JUNE 30, 1916, TO JUNE 30, 1917

IMPORTS INTO UNITED STATES FROM	Cork Bark, or Wood Unmanufactured[1] (Dollars)	Cork Waste, Shavings, etc. (Pounds)	Cork Waste, Shavings, etc. (Dollars)	Cork Discs, Wafers and Washers (Pounds)	Cork Discs, Wafers and Washers (Dollars)	All Other Manufactures (Dollars)
EUROPE:						
Austria and Hungary						
Belgium						
Bulgaria						
Czechoslovakia						
Denmark	56,396					
Finland						
France	101,810					3,633
Germany						
Italy	6,326					
Netherlands						
Norway						
Poland and Danzig						
Portugal	2,404,678					105,647
Rumania						
Russia in Europe						
Spain	1,058,574					2,026,785
Sweden						
United Kingdom	7,304					3,094
All others						
AMERICA:						
Canada	621					16,799
Central American States						
Cuba	1,572					1,111
Mexico	10					4
South American Continent	6					
West Indies						
ASIA:						
China						84
Japan						1,290
All others						
AFRICA:						
Algeria	233,062					
Morocco						
All others						
Totals	3,870,389					2,158,447

[1]Includes cork waste, shavings, etc., prior to July 1, 1918.

IMPORTS OF MERCHANDISE—*Continued*

FISCAL YEAR OF 1918—JUNE 30, 1917, TO JUNE 30, 1918

IMPORTS INTO UNITED STATES FROM	Cork Bark, or Wood Unmanufactured[1]	Cork Waste, Shavings, etc.		Cork Discs, Wafers and Washers		All Other Manufactures
	Dollars	Pounds	Dollars	Pounds	Dollars	Dollars
EUROPE:						
Austria and Hungary						
Belgium						
Bulgaria						
Czechoslovakia						
Denmark						
Finland						
France	88,518					7,486
Germany						
Italy	44,727					72,548
Netherlands						
Norway						
Poland and Danzig						
Portugal	1,754,750					152,099
Rumania						
Russia in Europe						
Spain	946,373					1,778,279
Sweden						
United Kingdom	30,107					1,474
All others						3,307
AMERICA:						
Canada						163
Central American States						
Cuba						
Mexico						
South American Continent						90
West Indies						
ASIA:						
China						
Japan						1,700
All others						
AFRICA:						
Algeria	197,352					
Morocco						
All others						
Totals	3,061,827					2,017,146
CALENDAR YEAR 1918						
EUROPE:						
Austria and Hungary						
Belgium						
Bulgaria						
Czechoslovakia						
Denmark						
Finland						
France	6,586	1,415,529	19,890	9,491	11,304	8,007
Germany						
Italy	43,928					72,548
Netherlands						
Norway						
Poland and Danzig						
Portugal	1,275,137	9,558,460	187,417	118,282	32,328	90,463
Rumania						
Russia in Europe						
Spain	459,087	21,952,679	373,112	434,850	395,211	1,133,193
Sweden						
United Kingdom						934
All others						
AMERICA:						
Canada						307
Central American States						
Cuba						
Mexico						
South American Continent						
West Indies						
ASIA:						
China						
Japan	26					881
All others						
AFRICA:						
Algeria	112,832	4,237,282	52,033			
Morocco						
All others				4,675	3,110	
Totals	1,898,193	37,163,950	632,452	567,298	441,953	1,306,333

[1]Includes cork waste, shavings, etc., prior to July 1, 1918.

IMPORTS OF MERCHANDISE—CALENDAR YEAR OF 1919

IMPORTS INTO UNITED STATES FROM	Cork Bark, or Wood Unmanufactured		Cork Waste, Shavings, etc.		Cork Discs, Wafers and Washers		Cork Insulation		All Other Manufactures	
	Pounds	Dollars	Pounds	Dollars	Pounds	Dollars	Pounds	Dollars	Pounds	Dollars
EUROPE:										
Austria and Hungary										
Belgium										
Bulgaria										
Czechoslovakia										
Denmark			509,755	9,897						
Finland										
France			6,745,875	96,872	44	29				2,330
Germany										
Italy	294,054	34,021	11,220,152	168,298	2,198	1,685				219
Netherlands										
Norway										
Poland and Danzig										
Portugal	21,180,579	1,490,049	57,477,704	1,187,487	530,014	313,932				17,905
Rumania										
Russia in Europe										
Spain	4,981,255	224,123	43,925,182	863,496	593,701	393,065				443,910
Sweden			954,592	25,600						
United Kingdom										4,492
All others										
AMERICA:										
Canada			210,106	4,502	1,179	866				172,851
Central American States	59,918	3,329								5
Cuba					31,006	26,917				
Mexico										
South American Continent										
West Indies										
All others										
ASIA:										
China										60
India										
Japan										1,582
All others										
AFRICA:										
Algeria and Tunis	1,771,136	50,984	10,598,333	202,404						
Morocco										
All others										
TOTALS	28,286,942	1,802,506	131,641,699	2,558,556	1,158,142	736,494				643,354

IMPORTS OF MERCHANDISE—CALENDAR YEAR OF 1920

IMPORTS INTO UNITED STATES FROM	Cork Bark, or Wood Unmanufactured		Cork Waste, Shavings, etc.		Cork Discs, Wafers and Washers		Cork Insulation		All Other Manufactures	
	Pounds	Dollars	Pounds	Dollars	Pounds	Dollars	Pounds	Dollars	Pounds	Dollars
EUROPE:										
Austria and Hungary										
Belgium										
Bulgaria										
Czechoslovakia										
Denmark										
Finland										
France	1,624,400	18,795	3,681,032	59,419						1,324
Germany										
Italy	2,256,128	93,459	4,654,965	78,839	2	2				3,049
Netherlands										18
Norway			760,572	23,291						
Poland and Danzig										
Portugal	33,609,583	1,746,828	56,915,839	1,565,558	353,609	161,554				
Rumania										20,500
Russia in Europe										
Spain	13,784,431	517,854	62,387,764	1,495,938	1,201,544	798,551				
Sweden	26,675	1,510	3,077,913	86,158						676,457
United Kingdom	1,877,034	137,148			1,700	1,711				25,864
All others										10,180
AMERICA:										
Canada			460,065	7,461						302,502
Central American States										
Cuba					1,193	1,620				74
Mexico										
South American Continent	114,680	2,681	183,533	5,167						
West Indies										
All others										
ASIA:										
China					100	127				13
India										
Japan					7	11				2,111
All others										
AFRICA:										
Algeria and Tunis	7,113,050	196,733	13,704,660	291,491						
Morocco										
All others	3,566,057	10,000								
TOTALS	63,972,038	2,725,008	145,826,343	3,613,322	1,558,155	963,576				1,042,092

IMPORTS OF MERCHANDISE—CALENDAR YEAR OF 1921

IMPORTS INTO UNITED STATES FROM	Cork Bark, or Wood Unmanufactured		Cork Waste, Shavings, etc.		Cork Discs, Wafers and Washers		Cork Insulation		All Other Manufactures	
	Pounds	Dollars	Pounds	Dollars	Pounds	Dollars	Pounds	Dollars	Pounds	Dollars
EUROPE:										
Austria and Hungary										
Belgium										207
Bulgaria										
Czechoslovakia										
Denmark			6,905	218						56
Finland			120,733	2,689						
France	4,252	172	3,045,134	53,853	538	144				1,066
Germany	50,735	3,507	10,912	231	138	141				6,867
Italy	1,960,152	23,000	4,899,437	64,325						60
Netherlands			168,169	7,030						774
Norway										
Poland and Danzig										
Portugal	10,935,201	592,324	44,780,656	636,376	171,789	89,360				18,841
Rumania										
Russia in Europe										
Spain	7,238,590	254,568	21,435,765	415,091	322,820	273,743				539,138
Sweden			1,316,405	30,379						2,242
United Kingdom										9,456
All others			*98,560	*1,540						2
AMERICA:										
Canada			571,700	6,748	259	320				114,529
Central American States										
Cuba										
Mexico										
South American Continent	3,576	179	12,000	77						
West Indies										
All others										
ASIA:										
China										
India										
Japan										4,151
All others										
Algeria and Tunis	1,955,362	86,197	11,788,465	178,655						
Morocco										
All others										
TOTALS	22,147,868	959,947	88,255,141	1,397,212	495,544	363,708				697,389

*July 1 to December 31

IMPORTS OF MERCHANDISE—CALENDAR YEAR OF 1922

IMPORTS INTO UNITED STATES FROM	Cork Bark, or Wood Unmanufactured		Cork Waste, Shavings, etc.		Cork Discs, Wafers and Washers		Cork Insulation		All Other Manufactures	
	Pounds	Dollars	Pounds	Dollars	Pounds	Dollars	Pounds	Dollars	Pounds	Dollars
EUROPE:										
Austria and Hungary										3
Belgium			23,143	75						2
Bulgaria										
Czechoslovakia	227,433	12,320	2,014,879	93,940						
Denmark			650,756	10,461						3,969
Finland			219,200	2,197						
France	19,419	654	12,046,993	146,897	5	2				1,758
Germany			222,664	1,140						29,443
Italy	3,216,535	46,647	8,364,649	101,327						116
Netherlands										457
Norway										
Poland and Danzig										
Portugal	35,866,940	927,975	98,705,242	1,138,757	101,271	25,555	61,839	1,687		22,835
Rumania										
Russia in Europe										
Spain	16,304,990	491,401	39,678,712	653,502	35,018	32,470	1,506,606	89,199		722,743
Sweden	1,323	53	948,740	11,738						2,899
United Kingdom	11,834	450	1,192	81						3,641
All others										248
AMERICA:										
Canada			823,196	13,690	8	2	9,263	116		219,125
Central American States										
Cuba										
Mexico										
South American Continent					352	176				
West Indies										
All others										
ASIA:										
China										404
India										
Japan										1,307
All others										
AFRICA:										
Algeria and Tunis	4,468,012	80,559	20,842,098	310,516						
Morocco										
All others										
TOTALS	60,116,486	1,560,059	184,541,464	2,484,321	136,654	58,205	1,577,708	91,002		1,008,950

IMPORTS OF MERCHANDISE—CALENDAR YEAR OF 1923

IMPORTS INTO UNITED STATES FROM	Cork Bark, or Wood Unmanufactured		Cork Waste, Shavings, etc.		Cork Discs, Wafers and Washers		Cork Insulation		All Other Manufactures	
	Pounds	Dollars	Pounds	Dollars	Pounds	Dollars	Pounds	Dollars	Pounds	Dollars
EUROPE:										
Austria and Hungary										
Belgium										
Bulgaria			237,440	4,545						
Czechoslovakia										
Denmark	12,664	1,080	17,560	339					200	97
Finland										
France	3,092,831	39,146	16,744,377	166,392	51	215			1,153	2,785
Germany	5,985	543	55,789	964	225	100	49,118	7,115	569,537	84,545
Italy	239,659	15,936	522,336	6,765	2,244	1,013	9,260	332	3,103	88
Netherlands			2,619,139	15,600					951	664
Norway			54,560	699						
Poland and Danzig										
Portugal	34,133,657	1,077,213	60,205,134	713,496	51,887	29,608	216,995	5,633	14,368	3,541
Rumania										
Russia in Europe										
Spain	20,863,917	492,722	49,263,374	653,135	229,700	200,681	16,633,218	556,464	886,948	408,949
Sweden	1,400	42	866,820	8,818	3,730	503	26,005	1,575		
United Kingdom	15,068	1,017	510,960	11,754	8,285	8,749			3,771	2,073
All others									100	17
AMERICA:										
Canada	20	2	107,725	937			4,080	250	1,429	995
Central American States										
Cuba										
Mexico									40	3
South American Continent										
West Indies							452,829	22,994		
All others										
ASIA:										
China	990	46							40	15
India										
Japan										
All others										
AFRICA:										
Algeria and Tunis	2,546,197	129,098	33,365,914	367,699	2,860	1,329				
Morocco	2,063,161	19,572								
All others										
TOTALS	62,975,549	1,775,417	164,571,128	1,951,143	298,982	242,207	17,391,505	594,363	1,481,643	503,772

IMPORTS OF MERCHANDISE—CALENDAR YEAR OF 1924

IMPORTS INTO UNITED STATES FROM	Cork Bark, or Wood Unmanufactured		Cork Waste, Shavings, etc.		Cork Discs, Wafers and Washers		Cork Insulation		All Other Manufactures	
	Pounds	Dollars	Pounds	Dollars	Pounds	Dollars	Pounds	Dollars	Pounds	Dollars
EUROPE:										
Austria and Hungary			71,680	1,630					50	45
Belgium										
Bulgaria										
Czechoslovakia										
Denmark	30,564	640	215,417	4,005						
Finland										
France	6,435,202	40,978	4,256,710	41,922					770	555
Germany	201,049	2,604					14,621	1,862	601,641	72,508
Italy	189,946	3,274	63,798	828	1,263	467	12	6	1,025	406
Netherlands										
Norway										
Poland and Danzig										
Portugal	30,139,141	582,500	62,505,298	555,797	73,081	36,048	82,795	1,470	80,781	17,452
Rumania										
Russia in Europe										
Spain	11,099,475	388,182	36,192,050	513,012	354,678	345,777	18,830,938	714,586	4,185,466	567,406
Sweden										
United Kingdom	330,673	1,254					18	89	3,321	3,971
All others									710	297
AMERICA:										
Canada			1,900	38	612	70	60,000	1,781	1,331	1,443
Central American States									4	3
Cuba					122	75				
Mexico			120,000	150						
South American Continent										
West Indies	2,670	210								
All others										
ASIA:										
China									54	31
India										
Japan	16	12							81	10
All others										
AFRICA:										
Algeria and Tunis	14,020,601	219,351	26,725,384	255,751						
Morocco										
All others										
TOTALS	62,449,337	1,239,005	130,152,237	1,373,133	429,756	382,437	18,988,384	719,794	4,875,234	664,127

VALUE OF IMPORTS OF CORK TO THE UNITED STATES (FISCAL YEAR)

Corkwood, or cork bark, and manufactures of cork

YEAR	VALUE
1892	$ 1,689,724.00
1893	1,993,025.40
1894	1,280,982.00
1895	1,400,830.00
1896	1,619,337.00
1897	1,751,652.00
1898	1,447,188.00
1899	1,542,367.00
1900	1,909,483.00
1901	2,270,995.00
1902	2,464,934.00
1903	2,567,580.00
1904	2,295,138.00
1905	2,738,319.00
14 Years	$26,971,554.40
Yearly Average	$ 1,926,539.60

YEAR	VALUE
1906	$ 3,313,306.00
1907	4,063,982.00
1908	4,249,006.00
1909	3,042,190.00
1910	4,771,391.00
1911	6,609,813.00
1912	5,588,734.00
1913	5,502,754.00
1914	6,499,632.00
1915	4,786,954.00
1916	4,076,127.00
1917	5,028,836.00
1918	5,028,973.00
1918**	1,840,409.00
1919*	5,740,910.00
1920*	8,313,998.00
1921*	3,418,256.00
1922*	5,202,537.00
1923*	5,067,902.00
1924*	4,328,496.00
19½ Years	$96,604,206.00
Yearly Average	$ 4,954,061.88

*Calendar Year.
**July 1 to Dec. 31, 1918.

IMPORTS ENTERED UNITED STATES FOR CONSUMPTION

FOR FISCAL YEAR, 1903

CORK, and MANUFACTURES OF:	Rate of Duty	Quantities Lbs.	Values $	Duties $	Value per Unit of Quantity $	Actual and Computed Ad Valorem Rate %
Unmanufactured						
Cork wood, or cork bark	Free		1,737,366.00			
Manufactures of						
Artificial cork, or cork substitutes, mfd. from cork waste or granulated cork and n. o. p. f.						
Bark, cut in squares, cubes or quarters	8c lb.	4.00	2.00	0.32	.50	16.00
Corks (or cork stoppers):						
$\frac{3}{4}$" or less in diam. at large end	25c lb.	79,214.40	36,073.00	19,803.60	.455	54.90
For mfg. in bonded whse. and export						
Reciprocity treaty with Cuba						
Over $\frac{3}{4}$" in diam. at large end	15c lb.	1,409,507.16	704,429.00	211,426.08	.50	30.01
For mfg. in bonded whse. and export						
Reciprocity treaty with Cuba						
Cork disks, wafers or washers						
$\frac{3}{16}$" or less in thickness						
For mfg. in bonded whse. and export						
Reciprocity treaty with Cuba						
Over $\frac{3}{16}$" in thickness						
For mfg. in bonded whse. and export						
Reciprocity treaty with Cuba						
Cork insulation; wholly or in chief value of granulated cork in slabs, boards, planks, or molded forms						
Cork Tile						
Granulated or ground cork						
Waste, shavings, or refuse of all kinds						
Cork Paper						
All other manufactures wholly or in chief value of cork or cork bark, or of artificial cork or cork substitutes, granulated or ground cork not specifically provided for	25%		54,290.49	13,572.62		25.00
	Remitted	959.00	795.00		.829	
Reciprocity treaty with Cuba						
TOTALS	Free		1,737,366.00			
	Dutiable		795,589.49	244,802.62		30.77

FOR FISCAL YEAR, 1904

CORK, and MANUFACTURES OF:	Rate of Duty	Quantities Lbs.	Values $	Duties $	Value per Unit of Quantity $	Actual and Computed Ad Valorem Rate %
Unmanufactured						
Cork wood, or cork bark	Free		1,484,405.00			
Manufactures of						
Artificial cork or cork substitutes mfd. from cork waste or granulated cork and n. o. p. f.						
Bark, cut in squares, cubes or quarters	8c lb.	1,580.00	212.00	126.40	.134	59.62
Corks (or cork stoppers):						
$\frac{3}{4}$" or less in diam. at large end	25c lb.	351,447.76	69,537.00	87,861.94	.198	126.35
For mfg. in bonded whse. and export						
Reciprocity treaty with Cuba						
Over $\frac{3}{4}$" in diam. at large end	15c lb.	1,309,663.33	640,569.51	196,449.50	.489	30.67
For mfg. in bonded whse. and export						
Reciprocity treaty with Cuba						
Cork disks, wafers or washers						
$\frac{3}{16}$" or less in thickness						
For mfg. in bonded whse. and export						
Reciprocity treaty with Cuba						
Over $\frac{3}{16}$" in thickness						
For mfg. in bonded whse. and export						
Reciprocity treaty with Cuba						
Cork insulation; wholly or in chief value of granulated cork in slabs, boards, planks or molded forms						
Cork Tile						
Granulated or ground cork						
Waste shavings or refuse of all kinds						
Cork Paper						
All other manufactures wholly or in chief value of cork or cork bark, or of artificial cork or cork substitutes, granulated or ground cork, not specifically provided for	25%		67,289.00	16,822.25		25.00
	Remitted	293.00	232.00		.792	
Reciprocity treaty with Cuba						
TOTALS	Free		1,484,405.00			
	Dutiable		777,839.51	301,260.09		38.73

IMPORTS ENTERED UNITED STATES FOR CONSUMPTION—*Continued*

FOR FISCAL YEAR, 1905

CORK, and MANUFACTURES OF:	Rate of Duty	Quantities Lbs.	Values $	Duties $	Value per Unit of Quantity $	Actual and Computed Ad Valorem Rate %
Unmanufactured						
Cork wood, or cork bark	Free		1,728,743.00			
Manufactures of						
Artificial cork, or cork substitutes, mfd. from cork waste or granulated cork and n. o. p. f.						
Bark, cut in squares, cubes or quarters	8c lb.	340.00	167.00	27.20	.491	16.29
Corks (or cork stoppers):						
¾" or less in diam. at large end	25c lb.	110,670.08	51,152.56	27,667.52	.489	51.09
For mfg. in bonded whse. and export						
Reciprocity treaty with Cuba						
Over ¾" in diam. at large end	15c lb.	1,633,226.97	859,780.00	244,984.06	.526	28.49
For mfg. in bonded whse. and export						
Reciprocity treaty with Cuba						
Cork disks, wafers or washers						
3/16" or less in thickness						
For mfg. in bonded whse. and export						
Reciprocity treaty with Cuba						
Over 3/16" in thickness						
For mfg. in bonded whse. and export						
Reciprocity treaty with Cuba						
Cork insulation, wholly or in chief value of granulated cork in slabs, boards, planks, or molded forms						
Cork Tile						
Granulated or ground cork						
Waste, shavings, or refuse of all kinds						
Cork Paper						
All other manufactures wholly or in chief value of cork or cork bark, or of artificial cork or cork substitutes, granulated or ground cork, not specifically provided for	25%		38,298.55	9,574.63		25.00
Reciprocity treaty with Cuba						
TOTALS	Free		1,728,743.00			
	Dutiable		952,398.11	282,253.41		29.64

FOR FISCAL YEAR, 1906

CORK, and MANUFACTURES OF:	Rate of Duty	Quantities Lbs.	Values $	Duties $	Value per Unit of Quantity $	Actual and Computed Ad Valorem Rate %
Unmanufactured						
Cork wood, or cork bark	Free		1,837,354.00			
Manufactures of						
Artificial cork, or cork substitutes, mfd. from cork waste or granulated cork and n. o. p. f.						
Bark, cut in squares, cubes or quarters	8c lb.	5,993.00	1,289.00	479.44	.215	37.19
Corks (or cork stoppers):						
¾" or less in diam. at large end	25c lb.	213,468.47	95,629.36	53,367.11	.448	55.81
For mfg. in bonded whse. and export						
Reciprocity treaty with Cuba						
Over ¾" in diam. at large end	15c lb. Remitted	1,939,781.00 3,004.00	1,279,974.50 1,025.00	290,967.17	.660	22.73
For mfg. in bonded whse. and export						
Reciprocity treaty with Cuba						
Cork disks, wafers or washers						
3/16" or less in thickness						
Reciprocity treaty with Cuba						
Over 3/16" in thickness						
For mfg. in bonded whse. and export						
Reciprocity treaty with Cuba						
Cork insulation, wholly or in chief value of granulated cork in slabs, boards, planks, or molded forms						
Cork Tile						
Granulated or ground cork						
Waste, shavings, or refuse of all kinds						
Cork Paper						
All other manufactures wholly or in chief value of cork or cork bark, or of artificial cork or cork substitutes, granulated or ground cork, not specifically provided for	25%		83,421.48	20,855.37		25.00
Reciprocity treaty with Cuba						
TOTALS	Free		1,837,354.00			
	Dutiable		1,461,339.34	365,669.00		25.02

IMPORTS ENTERED UNITED STATES FOR CONSUMPTION—*Continued*

FOR FISCAL YEAR, 1907

CORK, and MANUFACTURES OF:	Rate of Duty	Quantities Lbs.	Values $	Duties $	Value per Unit of Quantity $	Actual and Computed Ad Valorem Rate %
Unmanufactured						
Cork wood, or cork bark	Free		2,358,873.00			
Manufactures of						
Artificial cork, or cork substitutes, mfd. from cork waste or granulated cork and n. o. p. f						
Bark, cut in squares, cubes or quarters	8c lb.	217.00	133.00	17.36	.613	13.05
Corks (or cork stoppers):						
3/4" or less in diam. at large end	25c lb.	91,591.00	54,413.00	22,897.75	.594	42.08
For mfg. in bonded whse. and export						
Reciprocity treaty with Cuba						
Over 3/4" in diam. at large end	15c lb.	2,186,088.00	1,489,448.00	327,913.51	.681	22.02
	Remitted	1,191.50	494.50		.415	
Reciprocity treaty with Cuba						
Cork disks, wafers or washers						
3/16" or less in thickness						
For mfg. in bonded whse. and export						
Reciprocity treaty with Cuba						
Over 3/16" in thickness						
For mfg. in bonded whse. and export						
Reciprocity treaty with Cuba						
Cork insulation: wholly or in chief value of granulated cork in slabs, boards, planks, or molded forms						
Cork Tile						
Granulated or ground cork						
Waste, shavings, or refuse of all kinds						
Cork Paper						
All other manufactures wholly or in chief value of cork or cork bark, or of artificial cork or cork substitutes, granulated or ground cork, not specifically provided for	25%		159,541.50	39,885.38		25.00
Reciprocity treaty with Cuba						
TOTALS	Free		2,358,873.00			
	Dutiable		1,704,030.00	390,714.00		22.93

FOR FISCAL YEAR, 1908

CORK, and MANUFACTURES OF:	Rate of Duty	Quantities Lbs.	Values $	Duties $	Value per Unit of Quantity $	Actual and Computed Ad Valorem Rate %
Unmanufactured						
Cork wood, or cork bark	Free	60,664,316.00	2,092,732.00		.033	
Manufactures of						
Artificial cork, or cork substitutes, mfd. from cork waste or granulated cork and n. o. p. f	8c lb.	3,395.00	1,638.00	271.60	.482	16.58
Bark, cut in squares, cubes or quarters	8c lb.	208.00	194.00	16.64	.932	8.57
Corks (or cork stoppers):						
3/4" or less in diam. at large end	25c lb.	49,483.25	29,863.00	12,370.81	.603	41.42
For mfg. in bonded whse. and export						
Reciprocity treaty with Cuba						
Over 3/4" in diam. at large end	15c lb.	2,435,154.91	1,814,519.00	365,273.24	.745	20.13
	Remitted	2,028.00	938.00		.462	
Reciprocity treaty with Cuba	15c lb. less 20%	450.00	185.00	54.00	.411	29.18
Cork disks, wafers or washers						
3/16" or less in thickness						
Reciprocity treaty with Cuba						
Over 3/16" in thickness						
For mfg. in bonded whse. and export						
Cork insulation; wholly or in chief value of granulated cork in slabs, boards, planks, or molded forms						
Cork Tile						
Granulated or ground cork						
Waste, shavings, or refuse of all kinds						
Cork Paper						
All other manufactures wholly or in chief value of cork or cork bark, or of artificial cork or cork substitutes, granulated or ground cork, not specifically provided for	25%		159,229.50	39,807.38		25.00
Reciprocity treaty with Cuba	25% less 20%		123.00	24.60		20.00
TOTALS	Free	60,664,316.00	2,092,732.00			
	Dutiable		2,006,689.50	417,818.27		20.82

IMPORTS ENTERED UNITED STATES FOR CONSUMPTION—*Continued*

FOR FISCAL YEAR, 1909

CORK, and MANUFACTURES OF:	Rate of Duty	Quantities	Values	Duties	Value per Unit of Quantity	Actual and Computed Ad Valorem Rate
		Lbs.	$	$	$	%
Unmanufactured						
Cork wood, or cork bark	Free	78,330,391.00	2,016,534.00		.026	
Manufactures of						
Artificial cork, or cork substitutes, mfd. from cork waste or granulated cork and n. o. p. f.						
Bark, cut in squares, cubes or quarters	8c lb.	8.00	5.00	.64	.625	12.80
Corks (or cork stoppers):						
¾" or less in diam. at large end	25c lb.	52,762.00	31,362.00	13,190.50	.594	42.06
For mfg. in bonded whse. or export						
Reciprocity treaty with Cuba						
Over ¾" in diam. at large end	15c lb.	1,163,580.50	885,536.00	174,537.08	.761	19.71
	Remitted	595.00	324.00		.545	
Reciprocity treaty with Cuba	15c lb. less 20%	1,051.00	434.00	126.12	.413	29.06
Cork disks, wafers or washers						
$\frac{3}{16}$" or less in thickness						
Reciprocity treaty with Cuba						
Over $\frac{3}{16}$" in thickness						
For mfg. in bonded whse. or export						
Reciprocity treaty with Cuba						
Cork insulation: wholly or in chief value of granulated cork in slabs, boards, planks, or molded forms						
Cork Tile						
Granulated or ground cork						
Waste, shavings, or refuse of all kinds						
Cork Paper						
All other manufactures wholly or in chief value of cork or cork bark, or of artificial cork or cork substitutes, granulated or ground cork, not specifically provided for	25%		184,765.15	46,191.29		25.00
Reciprocity treaty with Cuba						
TOTALS	Free	78,330,391.00	2,016,534.00		.026	
	Dutiable		1,102,426.15	234,045.63		21.23

FOR FISCAL YEAR, 1910

CORK, and MANUFACTURES OF:	Rate of Duty	Quantities	Values	Duties	Value per Unit of Quantity	Actual and Computed Ad Valorem Rate
Unmanufactured						
Cork wood, or cork bark	Free	109,271,575.00	3,152,280.00		.029	
Manufactures of						
Artificial cork, or cork substitutes, mfd. from cork waste or granulated cork and n. o. p. f.	6c lb.[1]	183.00	103.00	10.98	.563	16.66
Bark, cut in squares, cubes or quarters	8c lb.	1,649.00	310.00	131.92	.188	42.55
Corks (or cork stoppers):						
¾" or less in diam. at large end	25c lb.	41,699.00	29,820.00	10,424.75	.715	34.96
For mfg. in bonded whse. or export						
Reciprocity treaty with Cuba						
Over ¾" in diam. at large end	15c lb.	1,709,941.55	1,344,688.10	256,491.24	.786	19.07
	Remitted	557.00	236.00		.424	
Reciprocity treaty with Cuba	15c lb. less 20%	710.00	232.00	85.20	.327	36.72
Cork disks, wafers or washers						
$\frac{3}{16}$" or less in thickness						
Reciprocity treaty with Cuba						
Over $\frac{3}{16}$" in thickness						
For mfg. in bonded whse. or export						
Reciprocity treaty with Cuba						
Cork insulation: wholly or in chief value of granulated cork in slabs, boards, planks, or molded forms						
Cork Tile						
Granulated or ground cork						
Waste, shavings, or refuse of all kinds						
Cork Paper						
All other manufactures wholly or in chief value of cork or cork bark, or of artificial cork or cork substitutes, granulated or ground cork, not specifically provided for	25% [2]		49,619.00	12,404.75		25.00
	30% [1]		126,611.00	37,983.30		30.00
Reciprocity treaty with Cuba						
TOTALS	Free	109,271,575.00	3,152,280.00		.029	
	Dutiable		1,551,619.10	317,532.14		20.47

[1] Aug 6, 1909 to June 30, 1910, under Act of 1909. [2] July 1 to Aug. 5, 1909, under Act of 1897.

IMPORTS ENTERED UNITED STATES FOR CONSUMPTION—*Continued*

FOR FISCAL YEAR, 1911

CORK, and MANUFACTURES OF:	Rate of Duty	Quantities Lbs.	Values $	Duties $	Value per Unit of Quantity $	Actual and Computed Ad Valorem Rate %
Unmanufactured						
Cork wood, or cork bark	Free	139,602,251.00	4,286,760.00		.031	
Manufactures of						
Artificial cork, or cork substitutes, mfd. from cork waste or granulated cork and n. o. p. f.	6c lb.	1.00	1.00	.06	1.00	6.00
Bark, cut in squares, cubes or quarters	8c lb.	542.00	136.00	43.36	.258	31.88
Corks (or cork stoppers):						
3/4" or less in diam. at large end	25c lb.	30,771.00	23,296.00	7,692.76	.757	33.02
For mfg. in bonded whse. and export						
Reciprocity treaty with Cuba						
Over 3/4" in diam. at large end	15c lb.	2,553,357.42	2,155,098.00	383,003.62	.844	17.77
	Remitted	614.00	389.00		.633	
Reciprocity treaty with Cuba						
Cork disks, wafers or washers						
3/16" or less in thickness						
For mfg. in bonded whse. and export						
Reciprocity treaty with Cuba						
Over 3/16" in thickness						
For mfg. in bonded whse. and export						
Reciprocity treaty with Cuba						
Cork insulation; wholly or in chief value of granulated cork in slabs, boards, planks, or molded forms						
Cork Tile						
Granulated or ground cork						
Waste, shavings, or refuse of all kinds						
Cork Paper						
All other manufactures wholly or in chief value of cork or cork bark, or of artificial cork or cork substitutes, granulated or ground cork, not specifically provided for	30%		210,825.21	63,247.56		30.00
Reciprocity treaty with Cuba						
TOTALS	Free	139,602,251.00	4,286,760.00		.031	
	Dutiable		2,389,715.21	453,987.36		19.00

FOR FISCAL YEAR, 1912

CORK, and MANUFACTURES OF:	Rate of Duty	Quantities Lbs.	Values $	Duties $	Value per Unit of Quantity $	Actual and Computed Ad Valorem Rate %
Unmanufactured						
Cork wood, or cork bark	Free	118,432,309.00	3,247,086.00		.027	
Manufactures of						
Artificial cork, or cork substitutes, mfd. from cork waste or granulated cork and n. o. p. f.	6c lb.	77.00	8.00	4.62	.104	57.75
Bark, cut in squares, cubes or quarters						
Corks (or cork stoppers):						
3/4" or less in diam. at large end	25c lb.	21,998.58	17,900.00	5,499.63	.814	30.73
For mfg. in bonded whse. and export						
Reciprocity treaty with Cuba						
Over 3/4" in diam. at large end	15c lb.	2,346,323.41	1,891,372.00	351,948.53	.806	18.61
	Remitted	693.00	341.00		.492	
Reciprocity treaty with Cuba						
Cork disks, wafers or washers						
3/16" or less in thickness						
For mfg. in bonded whse. and export						
Reciprocity treaty with Cuba						
Over 3/16" in thickness						
For mfg. in bonded whse. and export						
Reciprocity treaty with Cuba						
Cork insulation; wholly or in chief value of granulated cork in slabs, boards, planks, or molded forms						
Cork Tile						
Granulated or ground cork						
Waste, shavings, or refuse of all kinds						
Cork Paper						
All other manufactures wholly or in chief value of cork or cork bark, or of artificial cork or cork substitutes, granulated or ground cork, not specifically provided for	30%		268,464.00	80,539.20		30.00
Reciprocity treaty with Cuba						
TOTALS	Free	118,432,309.00	3,247,086.00		.027	
	Dutiable		2,178,085.00	437,991.98		20.11

IMPORTS ENTERED UNITED STATES FOR CONSUMPTION—*Continued*

FOR FISCAL YEAR, 1913

CORK and MANUFACTURES OF:	Rate of Duty	Quantities Lbs.	Values $	Duties $	Value per Unit of Quantity $	Actual and Computed Ad Valorem Rate %
Unmanufactured						
Cork wood, or cork bark	Free	133,227,878.00	3,152,070.00	....	.024	.....
Manufactures of						
Artificial cork, or cork substitutes, mfd from cork waste or granulated cork and n. o. p. f.	....	....	....	....	.....	.....
Bark, cut in squares, cubes or quarters	8c lb.	99.00	32.00	7.92	.323	24.75
Corks (or cork stoppers):						
¾" or less in diam. at large end	25c lb.	20,635.50	15,637.00	5,158.88	.758	32.99
For mfg. in bonded whse. and export	....	....	....	....	.....	.....
Reciprocity treaty with Cuba	....	....	....	....	.....	.....
Over ¾" in diam. at large end	15c lb.	2,490,194.73	2,171,955.00	373,529.21	.872	17.20
	Remitted	455.00	275.25	....	.605	.....
Reciprocity treaty with Cuba	....	....	....	....	.....	.....
Cork disks, wafers or washers	....	....	....	....	.....	.....
3/16" or less in thickness	....	....	....	....	.....	.....
For mfg. in bonded whse. and export	....	....	....	....	.....	.....
Reciprocity treaty with Cuba	....	....	....	....	.....	.....
Over 3/16" in thickness	....	....	....	....	.....	.....
For mfg. in bonded whse. and export	....	....	....	....	.....	.....
Reciprocity treaty with Cuba	....	....	....	....	.....	.....
Cork insulation: wholly or in chief value of granulated cork in slabs, boards, planks, or molded forms	....	....	....	....	.....	.....
Cork Tile	....	....	....	....	.....	.....
Granulated or ground cork	....	....	....	....	.....	.....
Waste, shavings, or refuse of all kinds	....	....	....	....	.....	.....
Cork Paper	....	....	....	....	.....	.....
All other manufactures wholly or in chief value of cork or cork bark, or of artificial cork or cork substitutes, granulated or ground cork, not specifically provided for	30%	....	157,250.00	47,175.00	.....	30.00
Reciprocity treaty with Cuba	....	....	....	....	.....	.....
TOTALS	Free	133,227,878.00	3,152,070.00	....	.....	.....
	Dutiable	....	2,345,149.25	425,871.01	.....	18.16

FOR FISCAL YEAR, 1914

CORK and MANUFACTURES OF:	Rate of Duty	Quantities Lbs.	Values $	Duties $	Value per Unit of Quantity $	Actual and Computed Ad Valorem Rate %
Unmanufactured						
Cork wood, or cork bark	Free	88,282,529.00	2,646,018.00	....	.03	.....
Manufactures of						
Artificial cork, or cork substitutes, mfd from cork waste or granulated cork and n. o. p. f.	6c lb.[1]	695.00	151.00	41.70	.217	27.62
	3c lb.[2]	1,511.00	470.00	45.33	.311	9.64
Bark, cut in squares, cubes or quarters	8c lb.[1]	1,120.00	343.00	89.60	.306	26.12
	4c lb.[2]	1,696.00	298.00	67.84	.177	22.76
Corks (or cork stoppers): ¾" or less in diam. at large end	25c lb.[1]	4,717.50	3,831.00	1,179.38	.812	30.78
	15c lb.[2]	82,865.00	53,947.00	12,429.75	.651	23.04
For mfg. in bonded whse. and export	Free[2]	71.00	53.00	....	.747	.....
Over ¾" in diam. at large end	15c lb.[1]	548,452.25	477,615.00	82,267.84	.871	17.21
	12c lb.[2]	251,744.00	192,517.00	30,209.28	.765	15.69
For mfg. in bonded whse. and export	Free[1]	378.00	193.00	....	.511	.....
	Free[2]	127.00	80.00	....	.63	.....
Reciprocity treaty with Cuba	12c less 20%[2]	146.00	81.00	14.02	.555	17.30
Cork disks, wafers or washers	....	....	....	....	.....	.....
3/16" or less in thickness	15c lb.[2]	2,065,567.00	1,675,683.00	309,835.05	.811	18.49
Over 3/16" in thickness	12c lb.[2]	19,469.00	9,443.00	2,336.28	.485	24.74
For mfg. in bonded whse. and export	Free[2]	126.00	70.00	....	.555	.....
Cork insulation: wholly or in chief value of granulated cork in slabs, boards, planks, or molded forms	¼c lb.[2]	2,692.00	201.00	6.73	.075	3.34
Cork Tile	....	....	....	....	.....	.....
Granulated or ground cork	....	....	....	....	.....	.....
Waste, shavings, or refuse of all kinds	Free[2]	90,487,964.00	1,205,776.00	....	.013	.....
Cork Paper	35%[2]	....	95,154.00	33,303.90	.....	35.00
All other manufactures wholly or in chief value of cork or cork bark, or of artificial cork or cork substitutes, granulated or ground cork, not specifically provided for	30%	....	118,653.00	35,595.90	.....	30.00
Reciprocity treaty with Cuba	....	....	....	....	.....	.....
TOTALS	Free	178,771,195.00	3,852,190.00	....	.....	.....
	Dutiable	....	2,628,387.00	507,422.60	.....	19.31

[1]Old law, July 1 to Oct. 3, 1913 [2]New law, Oct. 4, 1913 to June 30, 1914.

IMPORTS ENTERED UNITED STATES FOR CONSUMPTION—*Continued*

FOR FISCAL YEAR, 1915

CORK and MANUFACTURES OF:	Rate of Duty	Quantities Lbs.	Values $	Duties $	Value per Unit of Quantity $	Actual and Computed Ad Valorem Rate %
Unmanufactured						
Cork wood, or cork bark	Free	24,897,803.00	1 420 581.00		.057	
Manufactures of						
Artificial cork, or cork substitutes, mfd. from cork waste or granulated cork and n. o. p. f.	3c lb.	1,155.00	320.00	34.65	.277	10.83
Bark, cut in squares, cubes or quarters	4c lb.	6,125.00	1,112.00	245.00	.182	22.03
Corks (or cork stoppers):						
3/4" or less in diam. at large end	15c lb.	131,269.00	82,576.00	19,690.35	.629	23.85
For mfg. in bonded whse. and export	Free	734.00	930.00		1.257	
Reciprocity treaty with Cuba						
Over 3/4" in diam. at large end	12c lb.	194,721.00	166,705.00	23,366.52	.856	14.02
For mfg. in bonded whse. and export	Free	163.00	131.00		.805	
Reciprocity treaty with Cuba						
Cork disks, wafers or washers						
3/16" or less in thickness	15c lb.	1,918,643.00	1,160,316.00	287,796.45	.605	24.80
For mfg. in bonded whse. and export	Free	126.00	68.00		.54	
Reciprocity treaty with Cuba						
Over 3/16" in thickness	12c lb.	7,841.00	4,996.00	940.92	.638	18.83
For mfg. in bonded whse. and export	Free	254.00	160.00		.63	
Reciprocity treaty with Cuba						
Cork insulation; wholly or in chief value of granulated cork in slabs, boards, planks, or molded forms						
Cork Tile						
Granulated or ground cork						
Waste, shavings, or refuse of all kinds	Free	96,575,427.00	1,334,262.00		.014	
Cork Paper	35%		111,069.00	38,874.15	.35	35.00
All other manufactures wholly or in chief value of cork or cork bark, or of artificial cork or cork substitutes, granulated or ground cork, not specifically provided for	30%		41,466.00	12,439.80	.301	30.00
Reciprocity treaty with Cuba						
TOTALS	Free	121,474,507.00	2,756,132.00		.023	
	Dutiable		1,568,560.00	383,387.84		24.44

FOR FISCAL YEAR, 1916

CORK and MANUFACTURES OF:	Rate of Duty	Quantities Lbs.	Values $	Duties $	Value per Unit of Quantity $	Actual and Computed Ad Valorem Rate %
Unmanufactured						
Cork wood, or cork bark	Free	32,866,700.00	1,517,366.00		.046	
Manufactures of						
Artificial cork, or cork substitutes, mfd. from cork waste or granulated cork and n. o. p. f.						
Bark, cut in squares, cubes or quarters						
Corks (or cork stoppers):						
3/4" or less in diam. at large end	15c lb.	143,889.00	86,681.00	21,583.35	.602	24.90
For mfg. in bonded whse. and export						
Reciprocity treaty with Cuba						
Over 3/4" in diam. at large end	12c lb.	125,917.00	84,065.00	15,110.04	.672	17.97
For mfg. in bonded whse. and export						
Reciprocity treaty with Cuba						
Cork disks, wafers or washers						
3/16" or less in thickness	15c lb.	674,066.00	464,931.00	101,109.90	.689	21.75
For mfg. in bonded whse. and export						
Reciprocity treaty with Cuba						
Over 3/16" in thickness	12c lb.	21,710.00	22,657.00	2,605.20	1.044	11.50
For mfg. in bonded whse. and export						
Reciprocity treaty with Cuba						
Cork insulation; wholly or in chief value of granulated cork in slabs, boards, planks, or molded forms	1/4c lb.	956,979.00	39,651.00	2,392.46	.041	6.03
Cork Tile						
Granulated or ground cork						
Waste, shavings, or refuse of all kinds	Free	122,577,224.00	1,617,518.00		.013	
Cork Paper	35%		136,615.00	47,815.25		35.00
All other manufactures wholly or in chief value of cork or cork bark, or of artificial cork or cork substitutes, granulated or ground cork, not specifically provided for	30%		43,668.00	13,100.40		30.00
Reciprocity treaty with Cuba						
TOTALS	Free	155,443,924.00	3,134,884.00		.021	
	Dutiable		878,268.00	203,716.60		23.20

IMPORTS ENTERED UNITED STATES FOR CONSUMPTION—*Continued*

FOR FISCAL YEAR, 1917

CORK and MANUFACTURES OF:	Rate of Duty	Quantities Lbs.	Values $	Duties $	Value per Unit of Quantity $	Actual and Computed Ad Valorem Rate %
Unmanufactured						
Cork wood, or cork bark	Free	40,273,005.00	2,125,633.00	......	.055	.....
Manufactures of						
Artificial cork, or cork substitutes, mfd. from cork waste or granulated cork and n. o. p. f.	......	......	......	......	......	......
Bark, cut in squares, cubes or quarters	4c lb.	573.00	116.00	22.92	.202	19.76
Corks (or cork stoppers):						
3/4" or less in diam. at large end	15c lb.	147,394.00	96,289.00	22,109.10	.652	22.96
For mfg. in bonded whse. and export	......	......	......	......	......	......
Reciprocity treaty with Cuba	......	......	......	......	......	......
Over 3/4" in diam. at large end	12c lb.	290,156.00	178,872.00	34,818.72	.458	19.47
For mfg. in bonded whse. and export	......	......	......	......	......	......
Reciprocity treaty with Cuba	......	......	......	......	......	......
Cork disks, wafers or washers	......	......	......	......	......	......
3/16" or less in thickness	15c lb.	2,759,446.00	1,933,621.00	413,916.90	.616	21.41
For mfg. in bonded whse. and export	......	......	......	......	......	......
Reciprocity treaty with Cuba	15c lb. less 20%	1,006.00	1,111.60	120.72	1.104	10.87
Over 3/16" in thickness	12c lb.	53,186.00	37,721.00	6,382.32	.711	16.92
Reciprocity treaty with Cuba	12c lb. less 20%	877.00	889.00	84.19	1.014	9.47
Cork insulation; wholly or in chief value of granulated cork in slabs, boards, planks, or molded forms	1/4c lb.	4,038,372.00	181,698.00	10,095.93	.045	5.56
Cork Tile	......	......	......	......	......	......
Granulated or ground cork	......	......	......	......	......	......
Waste, shavings, or refuse of all kinds	Free	120,677,624.00	1,743,184.00	......	.015	
Cork Paper	35%	......	138,214.00	48,374.90		35.00
All other manufactures wholly or in chief value of cork or cork bark, or of artificial cork or cork substitutes, granulated or ground cork, not specifically provided for.	30%	......	58,273.00	17,481.90		30.00
Reciprocity treaty with Cuba	......	......	......	......	......	......
TOTALS	Free	160,950,629.00	3,868,817.00	......	.024	......
	Dutiable	......	2,626,804.00	553,407.60		21.07

FOR FISCAL YEAR, 1918

CORK and MANUFACTURES OF:	Rate of Duty	Quantities Lbs.	Values $	Duties $	Value per Unit of Quantity $	Actual and Computed Ad Valorem Rate %
Unmanufactured						
Cork wood, or cork bark	Free	30,750,497.00	1,479,072.00	......	.048	.....
Manufactures of						
Artificial cork, or cork substitutes, mfd. from cork waste or granulated cork and n. o. p. f.	3c lb.	100.00	25.00	3.00	.25	12.00
Bark, cut in squares, cubes or quarters	4c lb.	5.00	1.00	.20	.20	20.00
Corks (or cork stoppers):						
3/4" or less in diam. at large end	15c lb.	177,292.00	70,233.00	26,593.80	.399	37.86
For mfg. in bonded whse. and export	......	......	......	......	......	......
Reciprocity treaty with Cuba	......	......	......	......	......	......
Over 3/4" in diam. at large end	12c lb.	189,585.00	128,145.00	22,750.20	.675	17.75
For mfg. in bonded whse. and export	......	......	......	......	......	......
Reciprocity treaty with Cuba	......	......	......	......	......	......
Cork disks, wafers or washers	......	......	......	......	......	......
3/16" or less in thickness	15c lb.	2,258,233.00	1,401,694.00	338,734.95	.62	24.17
For mfg. in bonded whse. and export	......	......	......	......	......	......
Reciprocity treaty with Cuba	......	......	......	......	......	......
Over 3/16" in thickness	12c lb.	57,785.00	44,157.00	6,934.20	.762	15.70
For mfg. in bonded whse. and export	......	......	......	......	......	......
Reciprocity treaty with Cuba	......	......	......	......	......	......
Cork insulation: wholly or in chief value of granulated cork in slabs, boards, planks, or molded forms	1/4c lb.	3,771,294.00	181,402.00	9,428.23	.048	5.20
Cork Tile	......	......	......	......	......	......
Granulated or ground cork	......	......	......	......	......	......
Waste shavings or refuse of all kinds	Free	95,051,164.00	1,582,755.00	......	.017	
Cork Paper	35%	......	107,462.00	37,611.70	......	35.00
All other manufactures wholly or in chief value of cork or cork bark, or of artificial cork or cork substitutes, granulated or ground cork, not specifically provided for.	30%	......	44,403.00	13,320.90	......	30.00
Reciprocity treaty with Cuba	......	......	......	......	......	......
TOTALS	Free	125,801,661.00	3,061,827.00	......	.024	......
	Dutiable	.	1,977,522.00	455,377.18	......	23.03

IMPORTS ENTERED UNITED STATES FOR CONSUMPTION—*Continued*

FOR CALENDAR YEAR, 1918

CORK and MANUFACTURES OF:	Rate of Duty	Quantities Lbs.	Values $	Duties $	Value per Unit of Quantity $	Actual and Computed Ad Valorem Rate %
Unmanufactured						
Cork wood, or cork bark	Free	22,560,059.00	1,297,636.00		.058	
Manufactures of						
Artificial cork, or cork substitutes, mfd. from cork waste or granulated cork and n. o. p. f.						
Bark, cut in squares, cubes or quarters	4c lb.	5.00	1.00		.20	20.00
Corks (or cork stoppers):						
3/4" or less in diam. at large end	15c lb.	64,556.00	20,605.00	9,683.40	.319	47.00
For mfg. in bonded whse. and export						
Reciprocity treaty with Cuba						
Over 3/4" in diam. at large end	12c lb.	101,021.00	72,426.00	12,122.52	.716	16.74
For mfg. in bonded whse. and export						
Reciprocity treaty with Cuba						
Cork disks, wafers or washers						
3/8" or less in thickness	15c lb.	2,010,408.00	1,316,590.00	301,561.20	.655	22.90
For mfg. in bonded whse. and export						
Reciprocity treaty with Cuba						
Over 3/8" in thickness	12c lb.	71,112.00	46,495.00	8,533.44	.654	18.35
For mfg. in bonded whse. and export						
Reciprocity treaty with Cuba						
Cork insulation, wholly or in chief value of granulated cork in slabs, boards, planks, or molded forms	1/4c lb.	1,349,570.00	63,704.00	3,373.92	.047	5.30
Cork Tile						
Granulated or ground cork						
Waste, shavings, or refuse of all kinds	Free	72,421,740.00	1,233,009.00		.017	
Cork Paper	35%		116,665.00	40,832.75		35.00
All other manufactures wholly or in chief value of cork or cork bark, or of artificial cork or cork substitutes, granulated or ground cork, not specifically provided for	30%		32,546.00	9,763.80		30.00
Reciprocity treaty with Cuba						
TOTALS	Free	94,981,799.00	2,530,645.00		.027	
	Dutiable		1,669,032.00	385,871.23		23.12

FOR CALENDAR YEAR, 1919

CORK and MANUFACTURES OF:	Rate of Duty	Quantities Lbs.	Values $	Duties $	Value per Unit of Quantity $	Actual and Computed Ad Valorem Rate %
Unmanufactured						
Cork wood, or cork bark	Free	28,286,942.00	1,802,506.00		.064	
Manufactures of						
Artificial cork, or cork substitutes, mfd from cork waste or granulated cork and n. o. p. f.	3c lb.	175,331.00	116,505.00	5,259.93	.666	4.51
Bark, cut in squares, cubes or quarters	4c lb.	6,135.00	3,129.00	245.40	.51	7.84
Corks (or cork stoppers):						
3/4" or less in diam. at large end	15c lb.	76,397.00	65,150.00	11,459.55	.853	17.59
For mfg. in bonded whse. and export						
Reciprocity treaty with Cuba						
Over 3/4" in diam. at large end	12c lb.	73,728.00	59,966.00	8,847.36	.815	14.74
For mfg. in bonded whse. and export						
Reciprocity treaty with Cuba						
Cork disks, wafers or washers						
3/8" or less in thickness	15c lb.	766,947.00	452,331.00	115,042.05	.589	25.43
Reciprocity treaty with Cuba	15c lb. less 20%	24,106.00	18,617.00	2,892.72	.773	15.54
Over 3/8" in thickness	12c lb.	12,651.00	8,991.00	1,518.12	.714	16.88
For mfg. in bonded whse. and export						
Reciprocity treaty with Cuba						
Cork insulation: wholly or in chief value of granulated cork in slabs, boards, planks, or molded forms	1/4c lb.	5,719,668.00	411,472.00	14,299.17	.072	3.47
Cork Tile						
Granulated or ground cork						
Waste, shavings, or refuse of all kinds	Free	131,641,699.00	2,558,556.00		.019	
Cork Paper	35%		101,569.00	35,549.15		35.00
All other manufactures wholly or in chief value of cork or cork bark, or of artificial cork or cork substitutes, granulated or ground cork, not specifically provided for	30%		51,286.00	15,385.80		30.00
Reciprocity treaty with Cuba						
TOTALS	Free	159,928,641.00	4,361,062.00		.027	
	Dutiable		1,289,016.00	210,499.25		

IMPORTS ENTERED UNITED STATES FOR CONSUMPTION—*Continued*

FOR CALENDAR YEAR, 1920

CORK and MANUFACTURES OF:	Rate of Duty	Quantities Lbs.	Values $	Duties $	Value per Unit of Quantity $	Actual and Computed Ad Valorem Rate %
Unmanufactured						
Cork wood, or cork bark	Free	53,927,976.00	2,596,600.00		.048	
Manufactures of						
Artificial cork, or cork substitutes, mfd. from cork waste or granulated cork and n. o. p. f.	3c lb.	6.00	1.00	.18	.167	18.00
Bark, cut in squares, cubes or quarters	4c lb.	1,387.00	403.00	55.48	.291	13.77
Corks (or cork stoppers):						
¾" or less in diam. at large end	15c lb.	103,961.00	88,509.00	15,594.15	.85	17.62
For mfg. in bonded whse. and export						
Reciprocity treaty with Cuba						
Over ¾" in diam. at large end	12c lb.	67,790.00	39,430.00	8,134.80	.58	20.63
Reciprocity treaty with Cuba	12c lb. less 20%	176.00	74.00	16.90	.421	22.84
Cork disks, wafers or washers						
⅜" or less in thickness	15c lb.	1,382,697.00	905,429.00	207,404.55	.065	22.91
For mfg. in bonded whse. and export						
Reciprocity treaty with Cuba						
Over ⅜" in thickness	12c lb.	11,764.00	6,736.00	1,411.68	.572	20.96
For mfg. in bonded whse. and export						
Reciprocity treaty with Cuba						
Cork insulation: wholly or in chief value of granulated cork in slabs, boards, planks, or molded forms	¼c lb.	9,000,101.00	771,123.00	22,500.25	.086	2.92
Cork Tile						
Granulated or ground cork						
Waste, shavings, or refuse of all kinds	Free	169,549,364.00	3,741,730.00		.022	
Cork Paper	35%		62,560.00	21,896.00		35.00
All other manufactures wholly or in chief value of cork or cork bark, or of artificial cork or cork substitutes, granulated or ground cork, not specifically provided for	30%		94,938.00	28,481.40		30.00
Reciprocity treaty with Cuba						
TOTALS	Free	223,477,340.00	6,338,330.00		.028	
	Dutiable		1,969,203.00	305,495.39		

FOR CALENDAR YEAR, 1921

CORK and MANUFACTURES OF:	Rate of Duty	Quantities Lbs.	Values $	Duties $	Value per Unit of Quantity $	Actual and Computed Ad Valorem Rate %
Unmanufactured						
Cork wood, or cork bark	Free	22,147,868.00	959,947.00		.044	
Manufactures of						
Artificial cork, or cork substitutes, mfd. from cork waste or granulated cork and n. o. p. f.	3c lb.	220.00	41.00	6.60	.187	16.10
Bark, cut in squares, cubes or quarters	4c lb.	8.00	2.00	.32	.25	16.00
Corks (or cork stoppers):						
¾" or less in diam. at large end	15c lb.	72,718.00	59,451.00	10,907.70	.818	18.35
For mfg. in bonded whse. and export						
Reciprocity treaty with Cuba						
Over ¾" in diam. at large end	12c lb.	84,519.00	42,846.00	10,142.28	.506	23.66
For mfg. in bonded whse. and export						
Reciprocity treaty with Cuba						
Cork disks, wafers or washers						
⅜" or less in thickness	15c lb.	509,765.00	380,069.00	76,464.75	.748	20.12
For mfg. in bonded whse. andexport						
Reciprocity treaty with Cuba						
Over ⅜" in thickness	12c lb.	29,205.00	22,918.00	3,504.60	.792	15.29
For mfg. in bonded whse. and export						
Reciprocity treaty with Cuba						
Cork insulation: wholly or in chief value of granulated cork in slabs, boards planks or molded forms	¼c lb.	8,971,847.00	517,772.00	22,429.62	.058	4.33
Cork Tile						
Granulated or ground cork						
Waste, shavings, or refuse of all kinds	Free	88,255,141.00	1,397,212.00		.016	
Cork Paper	35%		25,462.00	8,911.70		35.00
All other manufactures wholly or in chief value of cork or cork bark, or of artificial cork or cork substitutes, granulated or ground cork, not specifically provided for	30%		51,893.00	15,567.90		30.00
Reciprocity treaty with Cuba						
TOTALS	Free	110,403,009.00	2,357,159.00		.021	
	Dutiable		1,100,454.00	147,935.47		

IMPORTS ENTERED UNITED STATES FOR CONSUMPTION—*Continued*

FOR CALENDAR YEAR, 1922

CORK and MANUFACTURES OF:	Rate of Duty	Quantities Lbs.	Values $	Duties $	Value per Unit of Quantity $	Actual and Computed Ad Valorem Rate %
Unmanufactured						
Cork wood or cork bark	Free	60,116,486.00	1,560,059.00	....	.026	.....
Manufactures of						
Artificial cork, or cork substitutes, mfd. from cork waste or granulated cork and n. o. p. f.	.....	....	....	....	.....	.....
Bark, cut in squares, cubes or quarters	4c lb.[1]	1,174.00	105.00	46.96	.089	44.72
Corks (or cork stoppers):						
3/4" or less in diam. at large end	15c lb.[1]	93,528.00	59,804.00	14,029.20	.64	23.46
	25c lb.[2]	24,051.00	20,551.00	6,012.75	.838	29.25
Reciprocity treaty with Cuba	.....	....	....	....	.....	.....
Over 3/4" in diam. at large end	12c lb.[1]	61,048.00	28,464.00	7,325.76	.465	25.74
	20c lb.[2]	24,042.00	22,601.00	4,808.40	.94	21.27
Reciprocity treaty with Cuba	.....	....	....	....	.....	.....
Cork disks, wafers or washers	.....	....	....	....	.....	.....
3/16" or less in thickness	15c lb.[1]	260,109.00	144,750.00	39,016.35	.556	26.95
	25c lb.[2]	33,496.00	15,234.00	8,374.00	.455	54.97
Reciprocity treaty with Cuba	.....	....	....	....	.....	.....
Over 3/16" in thickness	12c lb.[1]	18,014.00	13,338.00	2,161.68	.743	16.21
	20c lb.[2]	3,835.00	2,497.00	767.00	.65	30.71
Cork insulation; wholly or in chief value of granulated cork in slabs, boards planks, or molded forms	1/4c lb.[1]	13,040,492.00	776,655.00	32,601.23	.06	4.20
	30%[2]	1,577,708.00	91,002.00	27,300.60	.058	30.00
Granulated or ground cork	25%[2]	25.00	9.00	2.25	.36	25.00
Waste, shavings, or refuse of all kinds	Free	184,541,464.00	2,484,321.00	....	.014	.....
Cork Paper	35%[1]	....	15,185.00	5,314.75	.....	35.00
	30%[2]	1,070.00	1,411.00	423.30	1.32	30.00
All other manufactures wholly or in chief value of cork or cork bark, or of artificial cork or cork substitutes, granulated or ground cork, not specifically provided for	30%[1]	....	67,397.00	20,219.10	.....	30.00
	30%[2]	123,780.00	24,278.00	7,283.40	.196	30.00
Reciprocity treaty with Cuba	.....	....	....	....	.....	.....
TOTALS	Free	244,657,950.00	4,044,380.00	....	.017	.....
	Dutiable		1,283,281.00	175,686.73	.....	.....

FOR CALENDAR YEAR, 1923

CORK and MANUFACTURES OF:	Rate of Duty	Quantities Lbs.	Values $	Duties $	Value per Unit of Quantity $	Actual and Computed Ad Valorem Rate %
Unmanufactured						
Cork wood, or cork bark	Free	62,975,549.00	1,776,417.00	....	.028	.....
Manufactures of						
Artificial cork, or cork substitutes, mfd. from cork waste or granulated cork and n. o. p. f.	6c lb.[6]	590.00	308.00	35.40	.521	11.49
	10c lb.[6]	201.00	171.00	20.10	.851	11.75
Bark, cut in squares, cubes or quarters	8c lb.	799.00	218.00	63.92	.273	29.32
Corks (or cork stoppers):						
3/4" or less in diam. at large end	25c lb.	123,153.00	163,001.00	30,788.25	1.324	18.89
For mfg. in bonded whse. and export	.....	....	....	....	.....	.....
Reciprocity treaty with Cuba	.....	....	....	....	.....	.....
Over 3/4" in diam. at large end	20c lb.	113,301.00	112,563.00	22,660.20	.994	20.13
For mfg. in bonded whse. and export	.....	....	....	....	.....	.....
Reciprocity treaty with Cuba	.....	....	....	....	.....	.....
Cork disks, wafers or washers	.....	....	....	....	.....	.....
3/16" or less in thickness	25c lb.	315,333.00	209,084.00	78,833.25	.664	37.70
For mfg. in bonded whse. and export	.....	....	....	....	.....	.....
Reciprocity treaty with Cuba	.....	....	....	....	.....	.....
Over 3/16" in thickness	20c lb.[3]	55,540.00	53,523.00	11,108.00	.964	20.75
	10c lb.[4]	123.00	48.00	12.30	.391	25.63
Reciprocity treaty with Cuba	.....	....	....	....	.....	.....
Cork insulation; wholly or in chief value of granulated cork in slabs, boards, planks or molded forms	30%	13,976,878.00	496,133.00	148,839.90	.034	30.00
Cork Tile	30%	16,800.00	1,875.00	562.50	.112	30.00
Granulated or ground cork	25%	11,273.00	242.00	60.50	.022	25.00
Waste shavings, or refuse of all kinds	Free	164,571,128.00	1,951,143.00	....	.012	.....
Cork Paper	30%	6,977.00	6,211.00	1,863.30	.891	30.00
All other manufactures wholly or in chief value of cork or cork bark, or of artificial cork or cork substitutes, granulated or ground cork not specifically provided for	30%	1,176,886.00	181,223.00	54,366.90	.154	30.00
Reciprocity treaty with Cuba	.....	....	....	....	.....	.....
TOTALS	Free	227,546,677.00	3,727,560.00	....	.016	.....
	Dutiable	15,797,854.00	1,224,600.00	349,214.52	.078	.....

[1]Old law, Jan. 1 to Sept. 21, Act of Oct. 3, 1913, and Emergency Tariff Act of May 27, 1921. New law, Sept. 22 to Dec. 31. [3]Made from natural cork bark. [4]Made from Artificial or Composition Cork. [5]In the rough, not further advanced than slabs, blocks or planks. [6]In rods or sticks suitable for the manufacture of disks, wafers, or washers.

IMPORTS ENTERED UNITED STATES FOR CONSUMPTION—*Continued*
FOR CALENDAR YEAR, 1924

CORK and MANUFACTURES OF:	Rate of Duty	Quantities Lbs.	Values $	Duties $	Value per Unit of Quantity $	Actual and Computed Ad Valorem Rate %
Unmanufactured						
Cork wood or cork bark	Free	61,556,348.00	1,234,424.00	......	.02	.....
Manufactures of						
Artificial cork or cork substitutes, mfd. from cork waste or granulated cork and n. o. p. f.	6c lb.[3]	1,025.00	201.00	61.50	.196	30.60
Bark, cut in squares, cubes or quarters	8c lb.	804.00	267.00	64.32	.332	24.09
Corks (or cork stoppers):						
¾″ or less in diam. at large end	25c lb.[1]	159,781.00	233,280.00	39,945.25	1.46	17.12
	12½c lb.[2]	138.00	70.00	17.25	.508	24.64
Reciprocity treaty with Cuba	.....	.....	.....	.....		.....
Over ¾″ in diam. at large end	20c lb.[1]	113,886.00	156,051.00	22,777.20	1.37	14.60
	10c lb.[2]	25.00	16.00	2.50	.64	15.63
Reciprocity treaty with Cuba	.....	.....	.....	.....	.....	.....
Cork disks, wafers or washers	.....	.....		.....	.....	.....
⅛″ or less in thickness	25c lb.[1]	317,761.00	275,100.00	79,440.25	.855	28.88
For mfg. in bonded whse. and export	.....	.....	.....	.....		.....
Reciprocity treaty with Cuba	.....	.....		.....		.....
Over ⅛″ in thickness	20c lb.[1]	80,613.00	110,451.00	16,122.60	1.37	14.60
For mfg. in bonded whse. and export	.....	.....	.....	.....		.....
Reciprocity treaty with Cuba	20c lb. less 20%	122.00	75.00	19.52	.615	26.03
Cork insulation: wholly or in chief value of granulated cork in slabs, boards, planks, or molded forms	30%	21,363,488.00	781,568.00	234,470.40	.037	30.00
Cork Tile	.....					.....
Granulated or ground cork	25%	608,221.00	8,697.00	2,174.25	.014	25.00
Waste, shavings, or refuse of all kinds	Free	131,048,779.00	1,377,714.00	.....	.011	
Cork Paper	30%	38.00	24.00	7.20	.632	30.00
All other manufactures wholly or in chief value of cork or cork bark, or of artificial cork or cork substitutes, granulated or ground cork, not specifically provided for	30%	4,099,843.00	273,867.00	82,160.10	.067	30.00
Reciprocity treaty with Cuba	.....	.....	.....	.....	.....	.....
TOTALS	Free	192,605,127.00	2,612,138.00	......	.014	.....
	Dutiable	26,745,745.00	1,839,667.00	477,262.34	.07	.....

[1] Made from natural cork bark. [2] Made from artificial or composition cork. [3] In the rough, not further advanced than slabs, blocks or planks.

CORK IMPORTS ENTERED UNITED STATES FOR CONSUMPTION BY YEARS 1903 TO 1924 INCLUSIVE

YEAR		FREE		DUTIABLE		TOTAL	
		Quantity	Value	Quantity	Value	Quantity	Value
Fiscal	1903	...	$1,737,366.00	...	$ 795,589.49	...	$2,532,955.49
"	1904	...	1,484,405.00	...	777,839.51	...	2,262,244.51
"	1905	...	1,728,743.00	...	952,398.11	...	2,681,141.11
"	1906	...	1,837,354.00	...	1,461,339.34	...	3,298,693.34
"	1907	...	2,358,873.00	...	1,704,030.00	...	4,062,903.00
"	1908	60,664,316	2,092,732.00	...	2,006,689.50	...	4,099,421.50
"	1909	78,330,391	2,016,534.00	...	1,102,426.15	...	3,118,960.15
"	1910	109,271,575	3,152,280.00	...	1,551,619.10	...	4,703,899.10
"	1911	139,602,251	4,286,760.00	...	2,389,745.21	...	6,676,505.21
"	1912	118,432,309	3,247,086.00	...	2,178,085.00	...	5,425,171.00
"	1913	133,227,878	3,152,070.00	...	2,345,149.25	...	5,497,219.25
"	1914	178,771,195	3,852,190.00	...	2,628,387.00	...	6,480,577.00
"	1915	121,474,507	2,756,132.00	...	1,568,560.00	...	4,324,692.00
"	1916	155,443,924	3,134,884.00	...	878,268.00	...	4,013,152.00
"	1917	160,950,629	3,868,817.00	...	2,626,804.00	...	6,495,621.00
"	1918	125,801,661	3,061,827.00	...	1,977,522.00	...	5,039,349.00
Calender	1918	94,981,799	2,530,645.00	...	1,669,032.00	...	4,199,677.00
"	1919	159,928,641	4,361,062.00	...	1,289,016.00	...	5,650,078.00
"	1920	223,477,340	6,338,330.00	...	1,969,203.00	...	8,307,533.00
"	1921	110,403,009	2,357,159.00	...	1,100,454.00	...	3,457,613.00
"	1922	244,657,950	4,044,380.00	...	1,283,281.00	...	5,327,661.00
"	1923	227,546,677	3,727,560.00	15,797,854	1,224,600.00	243,344,531	4,952,160.00
"	1924	192,605,127	2,612,138.00	26,745,745	1,839,667.00	219,350,872	4,451,805.00
			$69,739,327.00		$37,319,704.66		$107,059,031.66

CORK INSULATION

Part II—The Study of Heat

CHAPTER VII.

HEAT, TEMPERATURE AND THERMAL EXPANSION.

31.—Molecular Theory of Heat.—The sensation of *heat* is normally recorded by the sense of touch if heat is transferred from a gas, liquid or solid to the human body; and the sensation of *cold* results from a transfer of heat from the human body to a gas, liquid or solid. For the purpose of our study of heat, it will be best to think principally in terms of *heat*, rather than in terms of *cold*.

For many centuries it was generally believed that *heat* was an invisible, elastic and weightless fluid, termed *caloric*, which was responsible for all thermal phenomena by entering gases, liquids and solids in some mysterious or hypothetical manner, possibly even combining temporarily with them. It was not until about the beginning of the nineteenth century that the materialistic conception of heat was rather definitely disproven by certain experiments conducted by Count Rumford (Benjamin Thompson) (1753-1814), an American philosopher who made important contributions to physics and agriculture and later become adviser to the King of Bavaria, and by Sir Humphry Davy (1778-1829), an English chemist. But it remained for James Prescott Joûle (1818-1889), an English physicist, to prove, about the middle of the nineteenth century, that a definite amount of mechanical work is equivalent to a definite amount of heat, when it soon became evident that *heat is a form of energy*.

The *kinetic* theory of heat holds, briefly, that the molecules of a body have a certain amount of independent, though irregular, motion, and any increase in the energy of that motion manifests itself in the body becoming warmer, and any decrease by its becoming cooler, heat, in a word, being considered as kinetic energy of molecular motion.

The *molecular* theory of heat goes one step farther and holds that heat is in part the kinetic energy of molecular motion, as just elaborated, and in remaining part the potential energy of molecular arrangement. The molecular theory of heat permits a readier grasp of the facts concerning heat than seems otherwise possible, and for that reason is today generally accepted.

32.—Temperature.—It is a mere matter of observation that if several spoonfuls of ice water are added to a cup of hot coffee, the entire contents of the cup quickly become cooler, the heat flowing from the hot coffee to the cold water until a quiescent state, in which there is no tendency to further change of any kind, known as *thermal equilibrium,* is established between them. If the same cup is then allowed to stand in a closed room, without outside interference or disturbance of any kind, the heat will flow from the coffee to the cup to the table to the air of the room until all substances in the room settle to a state of thermal equilibrium; and when a number of bodies have settled to such a common state of thermal equilibrium they are said to have the same temperature.

The transfer of heat is always from the body of higher temperature to the one of lower temperature until those temperatures are exactly the same, or until thermal equilibrium is established between them. *Temperature* may be thought of as the thermal condition of a body, or the measure of the degree of hotness; but it must not be confused with *quantity of heat.* A cup of coffee may be at exactly the same temperature as the water in a 1,000-gallon hot water tank, yet the tank contains a vastly greater *quantity* of heat than the cup, owing to the vastly greater quantity of liquid held by the tank.

When a substance is hot its temperature is said to be high, and when cold its temperature is said to be low.

33.—Dissipation of Energy.—Every actual case of motion is attended by friction and/or collision on the part of the moving body, and that part of its energy not employed in doing work is thus dissipated. This dissipation of energy is always accompanied by the generation of heat, or, stated another way, such dissipation of energy is the conversion of mechanical energy into heat. A familiar example of the generation of heat by the dissipation of energy is the stamping of one's feet in cold weather to make them warm. Another example of the dissipation of energy is furnished by the change in potential energy resulting from the drop in temperature of superheated steam caused by the radiation or loss of heat from uninsulated boiler surfaces or steam pipe lines.

34.—Effects of Heat.—The heating of a substance, by the dissipation of energy, by contact with a hot body, or by any other means, may produce these effects:

(a) Rise in temperature.
(b) Meltage or vaporization.
(c) Contraction or expansion.
(d) Dissociation, if a chemical compound.
(e) Exhibition of electrical phenomena.

35.—Thermometers.—The most convenient instrument to measure temperature, rise and fall, is a mercury thermometer,

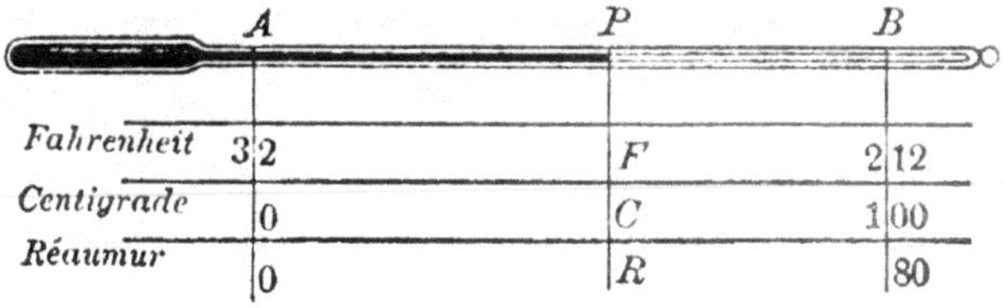

	A	*P*	*B*
Fahrenheit	32	*F*	212
Centigrade	0	*C*	100
Réaumur	0	*R*	80

FIG. 29.—COMPARISON OF THREE TYPES OF THERMOMETERS—(A) FREEZING POINT; (B) BOILING POINT; (P) THERMOMETER READING.

which employs a glass tube of uniform bore having a blown bulb on one end. A part of the air contained in the bulb and tube is expelled by expansion resulting from heating, and the open end of the tube is then immersed in pure mercury. As the tube cools the air within it cools and contracts, and atmospheric pressure relieves the condition by forcing mercury into the open end of the tube. This method is used to fill the bulb completely and the tube only to a point where the lowest temperature the thermometer is to measure is to be indicated on the tube or glass stem. Then, after heat applied to the the bulb has raised the mercury to the very top, the open end of the tube is sealed in a blowpipe flame. As the tube and mercury cool, the contracting mercury moves down the glass stem, leaving a vacuum at the top of the tube.

Since the temperature of melting ice and that of steam, under a constant pressure, have been found by very careful experiment to be invariable, their respective temperatures at a pressure of 76 centimeters (29.922 inches) of mercury have been selected as the fixed points on a thermometer. The instrument is placed in an ice bath and the *freezing point* is marked on the tube; it is then enveloped in steam and the *boiling point* is similarly recorded, proper corrections being made to compensate for any pressure different from 76 c.m.

The number of spaces, or *degrees*, into which the distance between the *fixed points* is divided has been subject to much discretion, but the three scales most used are the *Fahrenheit*, the *Centigrade* and the *Réaumur*. Gabriel Daniel Fahrenheit (1686-1736), a German physicist, introduced the Fahrenheit scale about 1714, and it is today in common use in all English-speaking countries in spite of the unreasonableness of designating the freezing point as 32°, the boiling point as 212° and dividing the scale between into 180 equal parts. René Antoine Ferchault de Réaumur (1638-1757), a French physicist, devised the Réaumur scale in 1731, which is today in common use in the households of Europe, the zero point corresponding to the temperature of melting ice and 80° to the temperature of boiling water. Some erroneously credit Anders Celsius (1701-1744), a Swedish astronomer, with the Centigrade scale, which fixes zero as the temperature of melting ice and 100 as the temperature of boiling water, but the Celsius scale (now in disuse entirely) reversed these fixed points and designated 100 as the temperature of melting ice and zero as the temperature of boiling water. The Centigrade scale was evidently designed as part and parcel of the metric system, which originated in France and was there definitely adopted in 1799. The Centigrade scale is in general use among scientific men throughout the world.

36.—Air Thermometer.—Galileo Galilei, commonly called Galileo (1564-1642), an Italian astronomer and physicist, invented the air thermometer about 1593 for the use of physicians. It consisted of a sizable blown glass bulb on the end of a tube of small bore, a scale being attached to the tube. The

TEMPERATURE CONVERSION TABLE

Centigrade to Fahrenheit to Reaumur.

C.	F.	R.	C.	F.	R.	C.	F.	R.
+100°	+212.0°	+80.0°	+53°	+127.4°	+42.4°	+ 6°	+42.8°	+4.8°
99	210.2	79.2	52	125.6	41.6	5	41.0	4.0
98	208.4	78.4	51	123.8	40.8	4	39.2	3.2
97	206.6	77.6	50	122.0	40.0	3	37.4	2.4
96	204.8	76.8	49	120.2	39.2	2	35.6	1.6
95	203.0	76.0	48	118.4	38.4	1	33.8	0.8
94	201.2	75.2	47	116.6	37.6	Zero	32.0	Zero
93	199.4	74.4	46	114.8	36.8	− 1	30.2	− 0.8
92	197.6	73.6	45	113.0	36.0	2	28.4	1.6
91	195.8	72.8	44	111.2	35.2	3	26.6	2.4
90	194.0	72.0	43	109.4	34.4	4	24.8	3.2
89	192.2	71.2	42	107.6	33.6	5	23.0	4.0
88	190.4	70.4	41	105.8	32.8	6	21.2	4.8
87	188.6	69.6	40	104.0	32.0	7	19.4	5.6
86	186.8	68.8	39	102.2	31.2	8	17.6	6.4
85	185.0	68.0	38	100.4	30.4	9	15.8	7.2
84	183.2	67.2	37	98.6	29.6	10	14.0	8.0
83	181.4	66.4	36	96.8	28.8	11	12.2	8.8
82	179.6	65.6	35	95.0	28.0	12	10.4	9.6
81	177.8	64.8	34	93.2	27.2	13	8.6	10.4
80	176.0	64.0	33	91.4	26.4	14	6.8	11.2
79	174.2	63.2	32	89.6	25.6	15	5.0	12.0
78	172.4	62.4	31	87.8	24.8	16	3.2	12.8
77	170.6	61.6	30	86.0	24.0	17	1.4	13.6
76	168.8	60.8	29	84.2	23.2	18	−0.4	14.4
75	167.0	60.0	28	82.4	22.4	19	2.2	15.2
74	165.2	59.2	27	80.6	21.6	20	4.0	16.0
73	163.4	58.4	26	78.8	20.8	21	5.8	16.8
72	161.6	57.6	25	77.0	20.0	22	7.6	17.6
71	159.8	56.8	24	75.2	19.2	23	9.4	18.4
70	158.0	56.0	23	73.4	18.4	24	11.2	19.2
69	156.2	55.2	22	71.6	17.6	25	13.0	20.0
68	154.4	54.4	21	69.8	16.8	26	14.8	20.8
67	152.6	53.6	20	68.0	16.0	27	16.6	21.6
66	150.8	52.8	19	66.2	15.2	28	18.4	22.4
65	149.0	52.0	18	64.4	14.4	29	20.2	23.2
64	147.2	51.2	17	62.6	13.6	30	22.0	24.0
63	145.4	50.4	16	60.8	12.8	31	23.8	24.8
62	143.6	49.6	15	59.0	12.0	32	25.6	25.6
61	141.8	48.8	14	57.2	11.2	33	27.4	26.4
60	140.0	48.0	13	55.4	10.4	34	29.2	27.2
59	138.2	47.2	12	53.6	9.6	35	31.0	28.0
58	136.4	46.4	11	51.8	8.8	36	32.8	28.8
57	134.3	45.6	10	50.0	8.0	37	34.6	29.6
56	132.8	44.8	9	48.2	7.2	38	36.4	30.4
55	131.0	44.0	8	46.4	6.4	39	38.2	31.2
54	129.2	43.2	7	44.6	5.8	40	40.0	32.0

Fahrenheit degrees = 1.8 × Centigrade degrees + 32°.
Centigrade degrees = (Fahrenheit degrees) − 32°+1.8.

bulb was heated in order to expand and expel some of its air content, and then the stem was inserted in a colored liquid, as pigmented water or alcohol. As the air in the bulb and stem cooled, the air contracted, and atmospheric pressure caused the liquid to rise in the tube. Fixed points were then established on the scale, and any rise in temperature caused the colored liquid to drop and any drop in temperature caused the liquid to rise. The instrument was remarkable for its

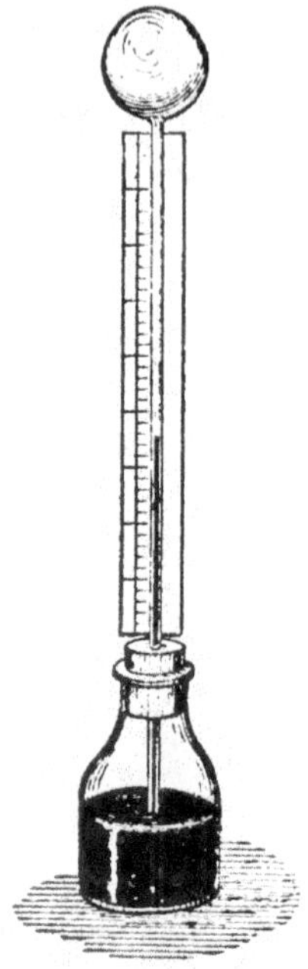

FIG. 30.—EARLY FORM OF AIR THERMOMETER.

sensitiveness, but its readings changed for every change in barometric pressure.

The modern "air thermometer" is an apparatus for measuring the *ratio* of two temperatures by observation of the pressures of a confined portion of hydrogen gas at the respective temperatures, based on the necessary modification of the Law of Charles, laid down in 1787, which claimed to establish that "the volume of a given mass of any gas under constant pressure increases by a constant fraction of its volume at zero for each rise of temperature of 1°C." The ratio of standard steam temperature (the minimum temperature of pure steam at 76 c.m. pressure) to ice temperature (the temperature of pure melting ice at 76 c.m. pressure) has been found by the air thermometer to be 1.367, or

$$\frac{\text{Steam temp.}}{\text{Ice temp.}} = \frac{S}{I} = 1.367$$

On the Centigrade scale S — I = 100, and from these two simple equations we find that S = 373° and I = 273°, approximately, Centigrade. Any other temperature may be determined by measuring its ratio to I or to S by means of the air thermometer. Temperatures measured in this way are called ***absolute temperatures***, and thus it will be noted that the absolute zero on the *Absolute scale* is 273 degrees below the freezing point on the Centigrade scale. It has been established, since Jacques Alexandre César Charles (1746-1822), a French physicist and aeronaut, gave us his Law of Charles, that the volumes of the same mass of gas under constant pressure are proportional to the temperature on this Absolute scale, or

$$\frac{v}{v_1} = \frac{t+273}{t_1+273} = \frac{T}{T_1}$$

if $t + 273$ is expressed by T, and $t_1 + 273$ by T_1.

37.—Expansion and Contraction.—If equal volumes of various gases are heated, under constant pressure, they were thought by Joseph Louis Gay-Lussac (1778-1850), a French chemist and physicist, to expand equivalent amounts for the same rise in temperature, but very careful measurements have since demonstrated quite perceptible differences of expansion of various gases, ammonia, for example, being distinctly different in its expansion from hydrogen. Gases that are near their points of liquefaction depart widely from Gay-Lussac's law; ammonia, sulphur dioxide and methyl chloride gases are easily liquefied and are commonly referred to as vapors. Hydrogen, on the other hand, is not easily liquefied under ordinary pressures, and hence follows Gay-Lussac's law quite closely. The point of importance here is that all gases expand when heated and contract when cooled.

Liquids, with notable exceptions, expand when heated and contract when cooled, the amount in any case depending entirely upon the volume of the substance. An exception is water, which contracts when heated from 0° C. (32° F.) to 4° C. (39.2° F.).

Solids, with a few exceptions, expand in all directions when heated and contract when cooled. An exception is iodide of silver, which, within a certain temperature range, contracts when heated and expands when cooled.

38.—**Force of Expansion and Contraction.**—The force of

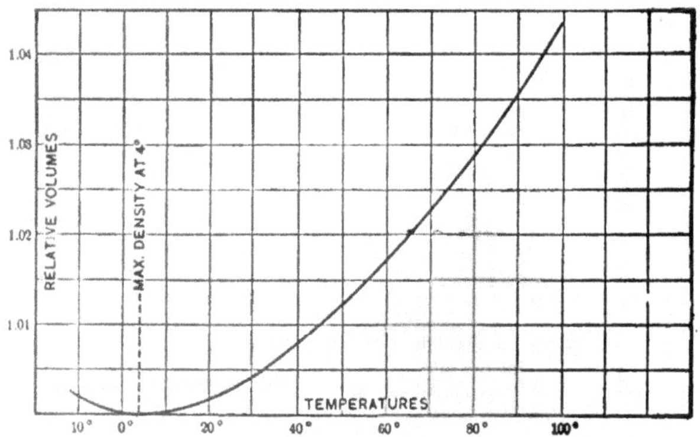

FIG. 31.—GRAPHIC REPRESENTATION OF THE EXPANSION AND CONTRACTION OF WATER WITH CHANGE OF TEMPERATURE.

expansion or of contraction of a substance is equal to the force required to compress or expand it to the same extent by mechanical means. This force must be computed by some method suited to the conditions, such as illustrated in this example*: A bar of iron, one square inch in cross-sectional area, if placed under the tension of a ton, increases in length 0.0001 of itself. The coefficient of linear expansion of this

*Henry S. Carhart and Horatio N. Chute, 1901, "Physics," Allyn and Bacon, Boston and Chicago.

iron is 0.0000122. Since 0.0001 ÷ 0.0000122 = 8+, then a change of temperature of approximately 8° C. will produce the same change in the length of the bar as a force of one ton.

39.—Application of Expansion and Contraction.—Many of the phenomena that are commonly encountered are traceable directly to the expansion and contraction that results from the rise and fall of temperature. One of the commonest of these is the explanation for a pendulum clock losing time in hot weather and gaining time in cold weather, due to the expansion and contraction, respectively, of its pendulum with the seasons. The wagon-maker heats his iron tires, thus expanding them, and after being put in place they contract and bind the wooden wheel solidly and securely. Very hot water if poured into a cold glass will often crack the glass due to unequal expansion of the inner and outer surfaces. The steel framework of modern buildings is put together with red-hot rivets hammered down as tight as possible with pneumatic hammers. When the rivets cool they contract and draw the steel members together with an enormous force. Virtually all pipe lines must be so arranged or equipped as to allow for expansion and contraction, to avoid serious damage and trouble from leaks. Paved streets, cement sidewalks, viaducts, bridges and all such items of general utility must be provided with a certain freedom of motion of their standardized parts to prevent buckling and cracking from expansion and contraction. The terrific force exerted by the expansion of freezing water splits off the solid rock from the side of the granite hills with the ease of a mythological giant. Pavements come up, trees are lifted out of the ground, building foundations are damaged, water pipes burst, mountain ranges slowly crumble away, all because the terrific force exerted by the expansion of freezing water is irresistible.

Other phenomena are traceable to expansion and contraction due to humidity rather than to temperature.

40.—Coefficient of Expansion.—It has been noted that, with very few exceptions, substances expand in every direction when heated. Expansion in length is quite naturally termed *linear expansion,* expansion in area is known as *superficial expansion* and expansion in volume is called *cubical expan-*

sion. If a substance is heated from 0° C. to 1° C., the fraction of its length that the body expands is its *cofficient of linear expansion,* the fraction of its area that the body expands is its *coefficient of superficial expansion* and the fraction of its volume that the body expands is its *coefficient of cubical expansion.*

The expansion of most substances has been found to be nearly constant for each degree of temperature, and it is therefore the practice to determine the *mean* coefficient for a change of several degrees. If l_1 is the length of an iron bar at temperature t_1 and l_2 the length at temperature t_2, then the expansion in length for 1° C. is expressed by

$$\frac{l_2 - l_1}{t_2 - t_1} = \frac{l_2 - l_1}{t}$$

if $t_2 - t_1$ is expressed by t. Now the fraction of its length that a body expands when heated from 0° C. to 1° C. is taken as its coefficient of linear expansion, which shall be designated as a. Therefore, the original length, l_1, times the coefficient of linear expansion of the material, a, or l_1 a, must equal the expansion in length for 1° C., or

$$l_1 a = \frac{l_2 - l_1}{t}, \text{ or } a = \frac{l_2 - l_1}{l_1 t}, \text{ or } l_2 = l_1(1+at);$$

and, similarly, if k is the coefficient of cubical expansion, v_1 and v_2 the volumes at temperatures t_1 and t_2, respectively, then

$$k = \frac{v_2 - v_1}{v_1 (t_2 - t_1)} = \frac{v_2 - v_1}{v_1 t}, \text{ or } v_2 = v_1 (1+kt).$$

Superficial and cubical expansion for solids are computed from the linear expansion, the coefficient of superficial expansion being twice and the coefficient of cubical expansion being three times the coefficient of linear expansion.

41.—Determination of the Expansion of Substances.—The linear or cubic expansion of a solid may be determined by the actual measurement of its dimensions at different temperatures, or its cubic expansion may be determined indirectly by measuring the volume of the solid at various temperatures by the *gravimetric method,* in common use by chemists.

The determination of the expansion of water and all other

volatile liquids is attended by difficulties due to the formation of vapor when heated. The most accurate results are obtained by first determining the volume of a glass vessel at each of various temperatures by weighing the vessel full of mercury at those temperatures and then using the vessel to determine the density of the given liquid at the various temperatures. The accompanying table gives the results obtained in this way for water by Edward L. Nichols and William S. Franklin (The Elements of Physics; The MacMillan Co., New York City).

DENSITIES AND SPECIFIC VOLUMES OF WATER.

Temperature	Density	Volume
—10°C.	0.99815	1.00186
— 8°	0.99869	1.00131
— 6°	0.99912	1.00088
— 4°	0.99945	1.00055
— 2°	0.99970	1.00031
0°	0.999874	1.000127
+ 1°	0.999930	1.000070
2°	0.999970	1.000030
3°	0.999993	1.000007
4°	1.000000	1.000000
5°	0.999992	1.000008
6°	0.999970	1.000030
7°	0.999932	1.000068
8°	0.999881	1.000119
9°	0.999815	1.000185
10°	0.999736	1.000265
15°	0.999143	1.000858
20°	0.998252	1.001751
25°	0.997098	1.002911
30°	0.995705	1.004314
35°	0.994098	1.005936
40°	0.99233	1.00773
45°	0.99035	1.00974
50°	0.98813	1.01201
55°	0.98579	1.01442
60°	0.98331	1.01697
65°	0.98067	1.01971
70°	0.97790	1.02260
75°	0.97495	1.02569
80°	0.97191	1.02890
85°	0.96876	1.03224
90°	0.96550	1.03574
95°	0.96212	1.03938
100°	0.95863	1.04315

The cubic expansion of various gases may be obtained by means of careful measurements employing especially constructed laboratory apparatus. There are perceptible differences of expansion of various gases at equal pressures for a given rise in temperature; carbon dioxide, ammonia and water vapor, for example, being distinctly different from hydrogen, nitrogen and oxygen, disproving the accuracy of Gay-Lussac's law.

CHAPTER VIII.

MEASUREMENT OF HEAT, CHANGE OF STATE, HUMIDITY.

42.—First Law of Thermodynamics.—When a given substance is heated by the dissipation of energy there is a definite relation between the amount of work done and the thermal effect produced, and consequently heat may be measured in units of mechanical work.

43.—Methods of Heat Measurement.—An amount of heat required to produce a given thermal effect can be measured by the direct determination of the amount of work required to produce a like effect, but this direct method of heat measurement is not easy of accomplishment due in part to the difficulty of applying mechanical work wholly to the heating of a given substance. The work spent in a given portion of an electric circuit, however, can be measured with great accuracy and such work can be readily employed to produce any given thermal effect.

Another method of measuring heat employs the relation between the amount of work dissipated in heating water and the rise of temperature thus produced. This method is practical, even though the energy-values are given indirectly, because the procedure may be carried out with accuracy. The melting of ice, and the vaporization of water, are also frequently employed in the measurement of heat, since the heat (work) necessary to melt a given quantity of ice or to convert a given quantity of water into steam are known quantities by determination.

44.—Units of Heat.—The work required to heat a given quantity of water has been shown to be approximately proportional to the rise of temperature, and for most purposes this proportion is sufficiently exact. Consequently, *the amount* *of heat required to raise the temperature of one gram of water one degree Centigrade* has been adopted by physicists as a practical unit of heat and is known as the *calorie.* (The *standard calorie* is the amount of heat required to raise one gram of water from 14.5° C. to 15.5° C. hydrogen thermometer, and is equivalent to 4.189 joules*. Engineers have fixed upon *the amount of heat required to raise the temperature of one pound of water one degree Fahrenheit* as a practical unit of heat, called the *British thermal unit* (B.t.u.), and which is equivalent to approximately 778 foot-pounds.)

45.—Thermal Capacity of a Substance.—The number of thermal units (units of work) or the quantity of heat required to raise the temperature of a body through one degree is the *thermal capacity* of that body at that temperature; thermal capacity varies slightly with temperature, but for many purposes is assumed to be constant. The thermal capacities of equal masses of different substances differ widely, being the product of specific heat and mass.

46.—Specific Heat.—Substances in general have each a definite *specific heat,* which may be defined as the increase in heat content of a unit mass of the substance per degree increase in temperature; or, the number of thermal units (units of work) necessary to raise the temperature of a unit mass of a substance through one degree, at any temperature, is its *specific heat* at that temperature. Since the *Standard thermal unit* (calorie) is the amount of heat required to raise the temperature of one gram of water from 14.5° C. to 15.5° C., then *specific heat* may be expressed as the ratio of the amount of heat required to raise a given weight of the substance from 14.5° C. to 15.5° C., to that required to raise an equal weight of water through the same temperature range. By ignoring the variation in the specific heat of a substance at different temperatures and by taking one gram as the unit of weight and 1° C. as the rise of temperature, the definition becomes:

$$\text{Specific Heat} = \frac{\text{Heat units required to raise one gram of substance } 1^\circ \text{ C.}}{\text{Heat units required to raise one gram of water } 1^\circ \text{ C.}}$$

Taking the calorie as the heat unit, the denominator becomes

*Edward L. Nichols and Wm. S. Franklin, 1904, "The Elements of Physics," The MacMillan Co., New York, N. Y.

equal to unity, by definition. Hence the specific heat of a substance is equal to the number of calories required to raise the temperature of one gram 1° C., and it will be observed that the same figure is given by the number of B.t.u. required to raise one pound of the substance 1° F., since by definition one B.t.u. will raise one pound of water 1° F.

The *mean specific heat* of a substance, between any two temperatures, is determined by dividing the heat given off per unit mass in cooling from the one temperature to the other, by the difference in the temperatures. The accompanying table gives the *specific heats* of various substances for the mean temperatures shown, and in terms of water at 15° C. (5° F.).

SPECIFIC HEATS OF VARIOUS MATERIALS.*

Substance	Mean Temperature	Specific Heat
Water	5°	1.0041
Water	15°	1.0000
Water	20°	0.9987
Ice	—10°	0.502
Paraffin	10°	0.694
Copper	50°	0.092
Zinc	50°	0.093
Iron	15°	0.109
Platinum	50°	0.032
Mercury	20°	0.033

47.—**Heat of Combustion.**—Most chemical actions are accompanied by the generation or the absorption of heat; those involving the generation of heat are known as *exothermic* reactions, and those during the progress of which heat is absorbed are called *endothermic* reactions. The most important case of exothermic reaction is combustion, the heat generated per unit mass of a substance burned being the *heat of combustion* of that substance. The accompanying table gives the heat of combustion of a few substances in B.t.u. per pound of substance.

HEAT OF COMBUSTION OF VARIOUS MATERIALS.†

Substance	Product of Combustion	Heat of Combustion B.t.u. per pound
Carbon	CO_2	14,600
Carbon	CO	4,450
Carbon Monoxide	CO_2	10,150
Hydrogen	H_2O	62,000
Methane	(CO_2) (H_2O)	23,550
Sulphur	SO_2	4,050

48.—**Changes of State with Rise of Temperature.**—When a body changes from the solid to the liquid state by the appli-

*Carhart & Chute, 1904, "Physics," Allyn and Bacon, Boston and Chicago.
†Thos. A. Marsh, M.E., 1924.

cation of heat, it is said to melt, or fuse, or liquefy, and the temperature at which fusion or liquefaction occurs is the *melting point.* The temperature of the substance then remains constant until the complete change to the liquid state has been accomplished, when, under continued application of heat, the temperature rises again until the liquid begins to boil or vaporize, and the temperature at which vaporization occurs is the *boiling point.* The temperature again remains constant until the liquid is entirely changed to vapor, when the temperature once more begins to rise.

49.—The Melting Point.—The temperature at which the solid and liquid forms of a substance are capable of existing together in equilibrium, is the melting point of that substance, and such temperature is invariable for every crystalline substance if the pressure is constant. Some substances, like wax, resin, glass and wrought iron, have no sharply defined melting points. They first soften and then pass more or less slowly into the condition of a viscous liquid, which property permits of the bending and forming of glass and the welding and forging of iron.

Most substances expand on melting, or occupy a larger volume in the liquid state than in the solid. A notable and important exception is water, which upon freezing, or solidifying, increases its volume nine per cent. If this expansion is resisted, water in freezing is capable of exerting an enormous force.

The accompanying table gives the melting points of some solids at atmospheric pressure.

MELTING POINTS OF VARIOUS SOLIDS.

Substance	Temperature, F.
Nickel	2732°
Gold	1947°
Aluminum	1214°
Zinc	786°
Lead	620°
Tin	449°
Mercury	—38°

50.—Heat of Fusion.—When a solid begins to melt, or fuse, by the application of heat, the heat-energy imparted to the substance is fully employed in producing change of state, its temperature remaining constant until fusion is completed.

The heat of fusion of a substance is the number of thermal units required to change a unit mass of a solid at its melting point into liquid at the same temperature. The accompanying table gives the heat of fusion of various substances.

HEAT OF FUSION OF VARIOUS SUBSTANCES.*

Substance	B.t.u. per Pound
Bismuth	22.7
Lead	9.7
Mercury	5.04
Nickel	8.3
Platinum	49.0
Silver	38.0
Tin	25.7
Zinc	50.6
Ice	144.0
Hydrogen	28.8

51.—The Boiling Point.—The temperature at which the liquid and its pure vapor can exist together in equilibrium, is the boiling point of that liquid, and such temperature is invariable if the pressure is constant.

The vapor of a substance under given pressure will condense to a liquid if it is cooled below the temperature that is its boiling point at that pressure; and the vapor of a substance at given temperature will condense to a liquid if its pressure is increased beyond a certain maximum value for that substance, although all vapors have a *critical* temperature above which they can not be liquified regardless of the amount of pressure to which they are subjected.

The accompanying table gives the boiling points of various liquids at atmospheric pressure.

BOILING POINTS OF VARIOUS LIQUIDS.*

Substance	Boiling Point, F.
Ether	95°
Chloroform	142°
Alcohol	172.2°
Benzine	176.7°
Water	212°
Glycerine	554°
Mercury	675°
Sulphur dioxide	14°
Ammonia	— 29°
Carbon dioxide	—108.5°
Oxygen	—296°
Hydrogen	—422°

52.—Vaporization.—The conversion of a substance into the gaseous form is called *vaporization*. If the change to a gas takes place slowly and from the surface of a liquid, at a tem-

*Chas. R. Darling, 1908.

perature below the normal boiling point, it is called evaporation; but if rapid internal evaporation visibly agitates a liquid, and the bubbles that rise through the liquid are pure vapor, the process is called *boiling*. If a small quantity of liquid is placed on hot metal, it assumes a globular form and vaporizes at a rate somewhere between ordinary evaporation and boiling. The vapor acts as a cushion and prevents actual contact between the liquid and the metal, while the globular form is due to surface tension. This variety of vaporization is called the *spheroidal state,* and the phenomenon is sometimes also referred to as the *caloric paradox*.

When a substance passes directly from the solid to the gaseous state, without passing through the intermediate state of a liquid, it is said to *sublime*. Some substances, such as iodine and camphor, sublime at atmospheric pressure but melt if the pressure be sufficiently increased. If ice is held at a temperature below freezing, it sublimes (evaporates) slowly, which fact is of some importance in the storing of ice.

53.—Heat of Vaporization.—When a liquid begins to boil, or vaporize, by the application of heat, the heat-energy imparted to the substance is fully employed in producing change of state, its temperature remaining constant until vaporization is complete. *The heat of vaporization* of a liquid is the number of thermal units required to change a unit mass of the liquid at its boiling point into vapor at the same temperature. The accompanying table gives the heat of vaporization of various substances at atmospheric pressure.

HEAT OF VAPORIZATION OF VARIOUS SUBSTANCES.*

Substance	B.t.u. per Pound
Water	967
Ether	164
Mercury	112
Turpentine	133
Air	99
Carbon dioxide	88
Ammonia	531
Oxygen	101
Hydrogen	360

54.—Superheating and Undercooling of Liquids.—When pure water that is free from air is heated in a clean vessel, its temperature usually rises as much as from eight to twelve degrees above its normal boiling point before it begins to

*Chas. R. Darling, 1908.

vaporize, and when vaporization begins it occurs violently and is attended by an immediate fall of temperature to the normal boiling point. If pure water is cooled, its temperature usually falls a number of degrees below its normal freezing point before freezing actually begins, but a large amount of ice is then suddenly formed and the temperature quickly rises to the normal freezing point. These phenomena are common to most liquids, but the converse is not true; that is, water vapor will not condense until it reaches its normal condensing point, and ice begins to melt immediately upon reaching its normal melting point.

55.—Critical Temperatures.—When a liquid and its vapor are confined in a vessel and heated, a portion of the liquid vaporizes, the pressure increases, the density of the vapor increases and possibly the density of the liquid decreases. When that temperature is reached where the density of the liquid and of the vapor become identical, the liquid and the vapor are physically identical and this temperature is called the *critical temperature* of the liquid. Thus the heat of vaporization of a liquid is zero at its critical temperature. In the following table the critical temperatures of various substances are given:

CRITICAL TEMPERATURES OF VARIOUS REFRIGERANTS*.

Substance	Chemical Symbol	Degrees F.
Sulphur dioxide	SO_2	311.0
Ammonia	NH_3	271.4
Methyl chloride	CH_3Cl	289.0
Carbon dioxide	CO_2	88.2
Ethyl chloride	C_2H_5Cl	360.5
Butane	C_4H_{10}	311.0
Nitrous oxide	N_2O	95.7
Propane	C_3H_8	216.0
Ethane	C_2H_6	90.0
Methane	CH_4	—115.6
Ether	$C_4H_{10}O$	......

56.—Saturated Vapor.—A vapor is said to be saturated when it is at its maximum pressure for a given temperature, or when it is at its minimum temperature for a given pressure.

57.—Effect of Pressure on Melting Point.—Change of pressure varies but slightly the melting points of substances, but the lowering of the melting point of ice by increase of pressure

*Compiled from data by H. D. Edwards and U. S. Bureau of Standards.

is responsible for several common phenomena. The melting of ice at a point where it is subjected to pressure and the immediate freezing of the resulting water when it flows out of the region of pressure is known as *regelation*. The exceptional ease with which a skater glides over the ice when the temperature of the atmosphere is not too low is due largely to the formation of a thin layer of water in the region of extra pressure under the skate runners, which water freezes almost instantly when the skate has passed and the pressure is relieved. Similarly, the ready packing of snow into balls is made possible by the melting of the snow crystals at their points of contact under the extra pressure of the hands and the immediate freezing of the resulting water as it flows out of the small regions of pressure, although snow must be near the

FIG. 32.—MELTAGE OF LOWER TIERS OF ICE IN LARGE ICE STORAGES DUE TO PRESSURE IS AN IMPORTANT CONSIDERATION IN THE DESIGN OF SUCH STRUCTURES.

melting point in order that regelation may be caused by the slight pressure produced by the hands. John Tyndall (1820-1893), a British physicist, regarded the apparent plasticity of glacier-ice as due to continued minute fracture and regelation. The phenomenon of regelation is of practical importance to the manufacturer of ice because of the meltage of the lower layers of ice cakes due to the pressure of the layers stored above.

58.—Effect of Pressure on Boiling Point.—Change of pressure varies greatly the boiling point of a liquid. At a pressure of 9.198 c.m. of mercury the boiling point of water is but 50° C., at a pressure of 76 c.m. its boiling point is 100° C., and at a pressure of 358.1 c.m. its boiling point is 150° C. At a pressure of 86.64 c.m. the boiling point of liquid ammonia is −30° C., and at a pressure of 1,945.6 c.m. its boiling point is 60° C. The variation of boiling point with change of pressure is of utmost importance in connection with mechanical refrigeration, as is shown in any text pertaining to the ammonia refrigerating machine.

59.—Boiling and Melting Points of Mixtures.—When pure water has a foreign substance dissolved in it, such as finely divided ammonium nitrate, for example, a thermometer will show a sensible fall of temperature, known as *heat lost in solution,* while its freezing point is lowered and its boiling point is raised. Similarly, ice in a strong solution of common salt (NaCl) has a very low melting point, about 5° F. (−15° C.), and remains at that temperature until all the ice is melted by heat absorbed from surrounding objects; thus a vessel of water, or a can of ice cream mix, surrounded by cracked ice and salt, gives up its heat to the low temperature mixture until the water or cream is frozen.

It is commonly supposed that salt sprinkled on icy sidewalks melts the ice; but the fact is that the salt lowers the melting point of the ice below surrounding temperatures (if they are not below about 5° F.) and these surrounding substances then give up heat to the ice, which melts it.

The use of ice and salt as a freezing mixture is so common as to require no further treatment here. However, it is believed that it offers such possibilities in the industries as to justify serious study and application.

60.—Cold by Evaporation.—If a few drops of ether are placed on the bulb of a thermometer, the mercury column will drop due to the fact that some of the heat of the mercury will be used to do work on the ether in evaporating it. Sprinkling the lawn, shrubbery and trees cools the surrounding air, because of the heat expended in evaporating the water. A liquid is cooled in a porous vessel by the evaporation from the outside surface of that part of the liquid that seeps through the vessel. Liquid carbon dioxide (CO_2) evaporates so rapidly as to readily freeze itself*. The rapid evaporation of liquid ammonia is one of the properties that makes this chemical of so much value as a refrigerating medium.

61.—Condensation and Distillation.—All the heat that disappears during the vaporization of a liquid is generated again when the vapor is condensed back to its original liquid form, which principle is employed to advantage in steam heating. Some gases will assume a liquid form through their affinity for a liquid, as exemplified by the affinity of ammonia gas for water, the gas being rapidly absorbed by the water with a marked rise of temperature.

Pure water, free from foreign substances such as vegetable and mineral matter, is obtained by *distillation,* which involves both vaporization and condensation. Alcohol may be separated from fermented liquors, for example, through distillation, because if two or more liquids are mixed together the more volatile will be vaporized by heat first and can be condensed and collected by itself.

62.—The Dew Point.—The dew point of the atmosphere at given pressure is the temperature at which the water vapor of that atmosphere becomes saturated and begins to condense. For example†, air at 64° F. temperature, 30 inches barometric pressure and containing 6.24 grains of moisture per cubic foot, when cooled to 62° F. will have reached its dew point, while air at the same temperature and pressure but containing 5.19 grains of moisture per cubic foot must be cooled to 57° F. before its dew point is reached.

The amount of moisture that a given volume of air can retain at given pressure depends on the temperature of the air. For example, a cubic foot of air at 64° F. temperature and 30 inches barometric pressure can contain 6.55 grains of moisture before precipitation takes place, while a cubic foot of air at 60° F. temperature and 30 inches barometric pressure requires but 5.75 grains of moisture to saturate it.

63.—Humidity.—The amount of water in the air at any given temperature and pressure is called the *absolute humidity*

*See "Solid Carbon Dioxide—A New Commercial Refrigerant," by the Dry Ice Corporation of America, 50 East 42d St., New York City.

†Carrier Air Conditioning Co., Newark, N. J.

of such air at that temperature and pressure. However, such absolute humidity cannot exceed a certain fixed value, known as absolute humidity at saturation, for any given temperature and pressure and cannot, of course, be less than zero. For example*, air at 64° F. temperature and 30 inches barometric pressure cannot have an absolute humidity of more than 6.56 grains of moisture per cubic foot, nor less than zero, which is perfectly dry air containing no moisture.

The amount of moisture in the air expressed in hundredths of what that air would contain were it saturated at the given temperature and pressure, is called *relative humidity.* For example*, air at 64° F. temperature, 30 inches barometric pressure and having an absolute humidity of 6.24 grains of moisture per cubic foot, has a relative humidity of 95 (95/100th

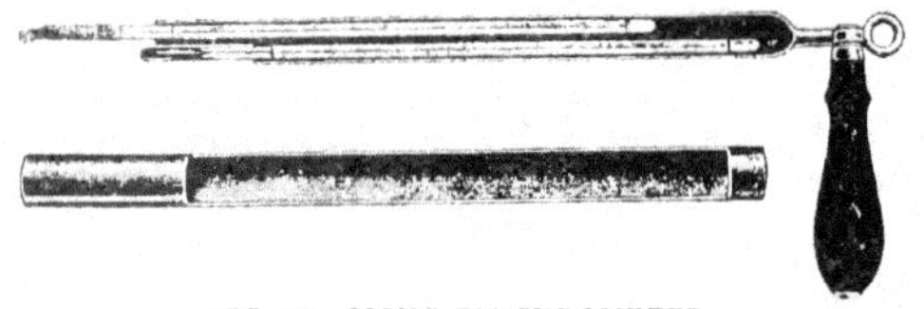

FIG. 33.—SLING PSYCHROMETER.

of 6.56 grains, the maximum amount of moisture such air would contain if completely saturated). When the relative humidity is low, the air is said to be dry; and when the relative humidity is high, the air is said to be moist.

The relative humidity and the dew point of air are usually determined by the use of an instrument called a psychrometer. The *sling psychrometer* consists of a wet bulb and a dry bulb thermometer suitably mounted and attached to a handle so that they may be rotated. A wet bulb thermometer is one having a piece of soft cloth or wick, which is kept moist with water, covering its bulb; while a dry bulb thermometer has its bulb exposed to the air. When the sling psychrometer is rotated or whirled at from 150 to 200 revolutions per minute (r.p.m.), evaporation takes place on the wet bulb thermometer and a *depressed* temperature reading is secured, and by means of the temperature readings on the wet and dry bulb thermometers it is possible to determine the relative humidity;†

*Carrier Air Conditioning Co., Newark, N. J.
†See Appendix for "Relative Humidity Table, Percent."

the dew point and the amount of water vapor in the air (absolute humidity) from psychrometric tables published by the United States Department of Agriculture, Weather Bureau Bulletin No. 235*.

Air that is saturated has a dew point and dry bulb and wet bulb temperatures that are identical; and if such air is cooled, the volume will be contracted and some of the moisture will be condensed. If air is but partly saturated, and the temperature is reduced, by removal of heat from such air, the dry bulb temperature falls and the wet bulb temperature falls until they finally reach the dew point temperature, at which point the air is completely saturated.

RELATIVE HUMIDITIES IN VARIOUS CITIES.

(U. S. Weather Reports.)

Average Annual Humidities for Various Cities of United States.		
City	8 a. m.	8 p. m.
Albany, N. Y.	78	72
Asheville, N. C.	85	71
Atlanta, Ga.	79	65
Atlantic City, N. J.	80	79
Augusta, Ga.	82	66
Baltimore, Md.	72	66
Boston, Mass.	73	70
Hartford. Conn.	74	68
Jacksonville, Fla.	83	77
Key West, Fla.	78	77
Macon, Ga.	83	....
New Haven, Conn.	75	72
New York, N. Y.	75	62
Norfolk, Va.	80	75
Philadelphia, Pa.	74	66
Portland, Me.	75	73
Providence, R. I.	74	71
Savannah, Ga.	81	75
Washington, D. C.	76	68
Wilmington, N. C.	81	77
Birmingham, Ala.	79	65
Galveston, Texas	84	78
Mobile, Ala.	84	74
Montgomery, Ala.	82	64
New Orleans, La.	83	72
Pensacola, Fla.	80	75
San Antonio, Texas	81	53
Tampa, Fla	84	76
Buffalo, N. Y.	77	73
Chattanooga, Tenn.	80	63
Chicago, Ill.	78	71

*Address, "Superintendent of Documents, Government Printing Office, Washington, D. C." Price, 10 cents.

RELATIVE HUMIDITIES IN VARIOUS CITIES.—*Continued.*

(U. S. Weather Reports.)

Average Annual Humidities for Various Cities of United States.

City	8 a. m.	8 p. m.
Cincinnati, Ohio	76	62
Cleveland, Ohio	77	70
Columbus, Ohio	79	66
Detroit, Mich.	80	71
Duluth, Minn.	81	71
Grand Rapids, Mich.	82	70
Indianapolis, Ind.	77	64
Louisville, Ky.	76	61
Dayton, Ohio	80	67
Milwaukee, Wis.	78	72
Nashville, Tenn.	80	62
Pittsburgh, Pa.	77	66
Rochester, N. Y.	75	71
Syracuse, N. Y.	77	....
Toledo, Ohio	79	69
Davenport, Iowa	80	65
Des Moines, Iowa	80	63
Kansas City, Mo.	77	62
Memphis, Tenn.	79	65
St. Louis, Mo.	77	63
St. Paul, Minn.	80	63
Springfield, Ill.	79	65
Fort Worth, Texas	78	....
Lincoln, Neb.	79	59
Oklahoma City, Okla.	80	59
Omaha, Neb.	78	60
Sioux City, Iowa	81	61
Wichita, Kan.	78	57
Denver, Colo.	63	41
El Paso, Texas	54	26
Helena, Mont.	68	50
Phoenix, Ariz.	54	28
Pueblo, Colo.	64	37
Reno, Nev.	72	39
Salt Lake City, Utah	60	45
Santa Fe, N. Mex.	58	40
Spokane, Wash.	77	50
Los Angeles, Cal.	78	62
Portland, Ore.	86	63
Sacramento, Cal.	82	52
San Diego, Cal.	79	70
San Francisco, Cal.	87	72
Seattle, Wash.	87	67

CHAPTER IX.

TRANSFER OF HEAT.

64.—Heat Transference.—Heat is transmitted from a region of higher temperature to a region of lower temperature by its natural and continual tendency toward temperature equilibrium. When such temperature equilibrium does not exist, that is, when there is a temperature difference, the natural direction of the flow of heat is toward the lower temperature level.

There are three quite distinct processes by means of which heat is transferred from one place to another, viz:

1. **Conduction,** in which heat is conveyed by matter without any visible motion of the matter itself. This method of transfer is assumed to be accomplished by invisible molecular motion or communication.

2. **Convection,** in which heat is transferred by the visible motion of heated matter, as by a current of warm air or the flow of hot water through a pipe circuit. This method of transfer is generally accomplished through the fact of the unequal weights of any given matter at different temperatures.

3. **Radiation,** in which heat is disseminated by a wave motion in the ether, as light is propogated, without the aid of matter. It is by this method that heat and light reach the earth from the sun.

The rate of heat transfer from one region to another obviously depends, therefore, upon the area of the transmitting surface, the difference in temperature levels, and a unit heat transfer coefficient that combines the heat that may be transmitted by conduction, convection and radiation. The actual magnitude of this composite heat transfer coefficient is determined in practice by calculation based on theoretical analysis and experimentation. The actual amount of heat transmitted in any case,—being the product of this coefficient, the area, and the temperature difference,—may be expressed in symbols, thus:

$$H=K\ A\ (t_1-t_2)$$

in which H is the total heat transfer in B.t.u. per hour, K is the total heat transfer coefficient in B.t.u. per hour per degree temperature difference F., A is the area of the heat transmitting surface in square feet, and (t_1-t_2) is the temperature difference in degrees Fahrenheit between the regions of highest and lowest levels.

It is evident, therefore, that if the heat transmitting area and the temperature levels are held constant, the heat transfer depends entirely upon conduction, convection and radiation.

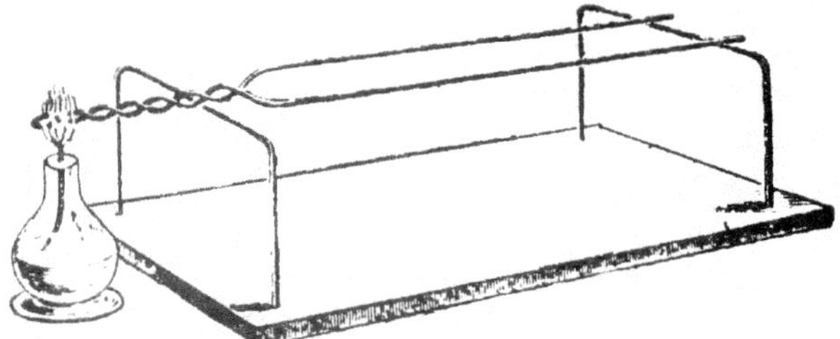

FIG 34.—TRANSFER OF HEAT BY CONDUCTION.

65.—Conduction.—Heat transfer by conduction is accomplished in a body of material by the vibration or impact of the molecules or particles of matter that compose the body itself, such molecular disturbance being produced by an unbalanced thermal condition within the mass. Thus heat may be interchanged between different parts of the same body, or between two separate bodies in actual contact, by conduction; but due to friction and adhesion between the molecules of a body, the vibration or impact of the particles of matter will become slower as the heat energy passes from one molecule to the other, and consequently the amount of heat that will be transmitted through the body will be something less than that applied to it. The amount of heat that will be transmitted through a given material, due to a given temperature difference, depends on the characteristic internal thermal conductivity of the material, each material having its own characteristic rate of conduction. The metals are the best conductors of heat. Wood, paper, cloth and organic substances as a class are poor conductors, as are pulverized or powdered materials, partly because of lack of continuity in the material.

The rate of heat transfer through a homogeneous material having parallel sides, depends on the temperature difference, the kind and condition of the material, the thickness of the material, and its absolute temperature. The heat transmitted by conduction may, in general, be expressed in symbols, thus:

$$H_1 = \frac{C}{X} A\ (t_1 - t_2)$$

in which H_1 is the total heat transmitted by conduction in B.t.u. per hour, C is the coefficient of specific internal conductivity in B.t.u. per hour per degree difference in temperature Fahrenheit per inch of thickness of the material, X is the thickness of the material in inches, A is the area of the transmitting surface in square feet, and $(t_1 - t_2)$ is the difference beween the high and the low surface temperatures.

Only *homogeneous* materials can have a specific internal conductivity; and while such conductivity is known to increase slowly with rise of temperature, it usually may be considered as constant for such temperatures as are encountered in cold storage work. *Resistance* to heat flow is the reciprocal of conduction; and for a given section of a compound wall the resistances, not the conductions, are additive.

Radial conduction in cylindrical layers of materials is not as easily handled as conduction through layers of materials having parallel sides. Using the insulated steam pipe as an example, the flow of heat will be relatively more rapid through the material near the pipe than farther out, since the area for the heat to pass through is increasing toward the outside. Thus resistances are not directly additive when considering radial conduction in cylinders, but the problem is capable of mathematical solution.

The *rate* at which the temperature of a material rises should never be taken as an indication of its internal conductivity; because if equal bars of iron and lead, for example, are placed so that one end of each is heated alike, the temperature of the other end of the lead bar will rise first to the point of igniting a match, even though iron is a better conductor of heat, which is accounted for by the fact that iron has approximately four times the specific heat of lead and thus requires about four times as much heat to produce the same change of temperature. This leads to the consideration of *conduction with changing temperature*. So long as the temperature of parts of the conducting or insulating material is changing, such as when a heating or cooling process is beginning and a *steady state* has not been reached, the amounts of heat entering and leaving the material are not the same. The thermal capacity, or specific heat, of the material determines the time required to reach a steady state.

The *thermometric conductivity* of a material is the change in temperature that is produced in a *unit volume* of the material by the heat conducted through a unit area in a unit of time with a unit temperature gradient. This value, which is entirely different from thermal conductivity, is of importance where protection against the effects of fire is the consideration.

The internal thermal conductivities of various materials, as determined under laboratory test conditions, from experiments by the United States Bureau of Standards and others, are shown in the accompanying table. (Additional tables containing full data will be found in the Article on "Tests by Various Authorities on Many Materials.")

To determine the heat transmitted by conduction through a 4-inch sheet of corkboard, having surface temperatures of 80° and 20° F., where t_1 is 80, t_2 is 20, X is 4 and C (from the accompanying table) is 0.308, apply such values to the formula, thus:

$$H_1 = \frac{0.308}{4}(80-20) = 4.62 \text{ B.t.u. per hour.}$$

All liquids, except molten metals, are relatively poor conductors of heat, while the conductivity of gases is very small. However, on account of convection primarily and radiation secondarily, it is very difficult to determine the conductivity of liquids and gases.

66.—Convection.—Convection is the transfer of heat by displacement of movable media, that is, the carrying of heat

INTERNAL THERMAL CONDUCTIVITY OF VARIOUS MATERIALS. (C)*

Material	Description	B.t.u. per 24 hours	B.t.u. per hour	Lb. per cu. ft.
Air	Ideal air space	4.2	0.175	0.08
Air Cell, ½ inch	Asbestos paper and air spaces	11.0	0.458	8.80
Air Cell, 1 inch	Asbestos paper and air spaces	12.0	0.500	8.80
Aluminum	Cast	24.000	1000.000	162
Ammonia Vapor	32° F.	3.19	0.133	0.21
Aqua Ammonia	64° F.	75.90	3.160	56.50
Asbestos Mill Bd.	Pressed asbestos—not very flexible	20.00	0.830	61.00
Asbestos Paper	Asbestos and organic binder	12.	0.500	31.0
Asbestos Wood	Asbestos and cement	65.0	3.700	123.0
Balsa Wood	Very light and soft—across grain	8.4	0.350	7.5
Boiler Scale		305	12.700	......
Brass		15.000	625.000	250.
Brick	Heavy	120	5.000	131.
Brick	Light, dry	84	3.500	115.
Brine	Salt	27.1	1.130	73.4
Cabot's Quilt	Eel grass enclosed in burlap	7.7	0.321	16.0
Calorax	Fluffy finely divided mineral matter	5.3	0.221	4.0
Celite	Infusorial earth powder	7.4	0.308	10.6
Cement	Neat Portland, dry	150.0	6.250	170.
Charcoal	Powdered	10.0	0.417	11.8
Charcoal	Flakes	14.6	0.613	15.0
Cinders	Anthracite, dry	20.3	0.845	40.0
Concrete		125.0	5.200	136.0
Concrete	Of fine gravel	109.0	4.540	124.0
Concrete	Of slag	50.0	2.080	94.5
Concrete	Of granulated cork	43.	1.790	7.5
Copper		50.000	2083.000	556.0
Cork	Granulated ⅛-3/16 inch	8.1	0.337	5.3
Cork	Regranulate 1/16-⅛ inch	8.0	0.333	10.0
Corkboard	No artificial binder—low density	6.7	0.279	6.9
Corkboard	No artificial binder—high density	7.4	0.308	11.3
Cotton Wool	Loosely packed	7.0	0.292	......
Cypress	Across grain	16.0	0.666	29.0
Fibrofelt	Felted vegetable fibers	7.9	0.329	11.3
Fire Felt Roll	Asbestos sheet coated with cement	15.0	0.625	43.0
Fire Felt Sheet	Soft, flexible asbestos sheet	14.0	0.583	26.0
Flaxlinum	Felted vegetable fibers	7.9	0.329	11.3
Fullers Earth	Argillaceous powder	17.0	0.708	33.0
Glass		124.0	5.160	150.0
Glass		178.0	7.420	185.0
Granite		600	25.000	166.0
Granulated Cork	About 3/16 inch	7.5	0.313	8.1
Gravel	Dry, coarse	62.0	2.582	115.0
Gravel	Dry, fine	39.0	1.630	91.25
Ground Cork		7.1	0.294	9.4
Gypsum Plaster		54.0	2.250	......
Hair Felt		5.9	0.246	17.0
Hard Maple	Across grain	27.0	1.125	44.0
Ice		408	17.000	57.4
Infusorial Earth	Natural blocks	14.0	0.583	43.0
Insulex	Asbestos and plaster blocks—porous	22.0	0.916	29.0
Insulite	Pressed wool pulp—rigid	7.1	0.296	11.9
Iron	Cast	7.740	321.500	450.0
Iron	Wrought	11.600	483.000	485.0
Kapok	Imp. vegetable fiber—loosely packed	5.7	0.238	0.88
Keystone Hair	Hair felt confined with building paper	6.5	0.271	19.0
Limestone	Close grain	368	15.300	185.0
Limestone	Hard	214.0	9.330	159.0

*W. H. Motz, M. E., 1926, "Principles of Refrigeration," Nickerson & Collins Co., Chicago.

INTERNAL THERMAL CONDUCTIVITY OF VARIOUS MATERIALS (C)—*Continued.*

Material	Description	B.t.u. per 24 hours	B.t.u. per hour	Lb. per cu. ft.
Limestone	Soft	100.0	4.167	113.0
Linofelt	Vegetable fiber confined with paper	7.2	0.300	11.3
Lithboard	Mineral wool and vegetable fibers	9.1	0.379	12.5
Mahogany	Across grain	22.0	0.916	34.0
Marble	Hard	445	18.530	175.0
Marble	Soft	104	4.330	156.0
Mineral Wool	Medium Packed	6.6	0.275	12.5
Mineral Wool	Felted in blocks	6.9	0.288	18.0
Oak	Across grain	24.0	1.000	38.0
Paraffin	"Parowax," melting point 52° C.	38.0	1.582	56.0
Petroleum	55° F.	24.7	1.030	50.0
Plaster		132.0	5.500	105.0
Plaster	Ordinary mixed	90	3.750	83.5
Plaster	Board	73	3.040	75.0
Planer Shavings	Various	10.0	0.417	8.8
Pulp Board	Stiff pasteboard	11.0	0.458	......
Pumice	Powdered	11.6	0.483	20.0
Pure Wool		5.9	0.246	6.9
Pure Wool		5.9	0.246	6.3
Pure Wool		6.3	0.263	5.0
Pure Wool		7.0	0.292	2.5
Rice Chaff		16.0	0.667	10.0
Rock Cork	Mineral wool and binder—rigid	8.3	0.346	21.0
Rubber	Soft	45	7.875	94.0
Rubber	Hard, vulc.	16.0	0.667	59.0
Sand	River, fine, normal	188.0	7.830	102.0
Sand	Dried by heating	54.0	2.250	95.0
Sandstone		265	11.100	138.0
Sawdust	Dry	12.0	0.500	13.4
Sawdust	Ordinary	25.0	1.040	16.0
Shavings	Ordinary	17.0	0.707	8.0
Silicate Cotton		14.0	0.583	8.55
Slag Wool		18.0	0.750	15.0
Snow on Ref. Coils		75	3.130	......
Tar Roofing		17.0	0.707	55.0
Vacuum	Silvered vacuum jacket	0.1	0.004	.....
Virginia Pine	Across grain	23.0	0.958	34.0
Water	Still, 32° F.	100	4.166	62.4
White Pine	Across grain	19.0	0.791	32.0
Wool Felt	Flexible paper stock	8.7	0.363	21.0

from one point or object to another by means of an outside agent, such as air or water, or any moving gas or fluid. The phenomenon is due to the fact that, in general, liquids and gases are lighter when warm than when cold. Land and sea breezes, trade winds and ocean currents carry great quantities of heat from one place on the earth to another; while the heating of buildings by hot water circulating through pipes, or by hot air furnaces, is another familiar application of *convection currents.*

It is, at best, a complicated process to attempt to calculate heat transfer by convection, because there are so many factors involved that are incapable of accurate determination. Perhaps the most important of these pertains to the conditions that exist between the conducting solid material and the gas or liquid in contact in which convection occurs. The resistance to heat transfer at the surface of a solid when in contact with a gas or liquid is known to be important, but its nature and extent is not generally understood.

Fluids, in general, *conduct* heat less rapidly than is commonly supposed, the difficulty of considering their heat conduction separate from their heat convection probably accounting for this misconception. The fact is important, however, in the consideration of the surface or contact thermal resistance between solids and fluids; because the finite layer of fluid in actual contact with a solid is *always at rest,* and a finite thickness next adjacent is moving very slowly. The resistance of this stagnant layer of fluid, through relatively low conduction, is responsible for the *surface resistance* to heat transfer; and such surface resistance in any example must be dependent upon the actual conditions of the case.

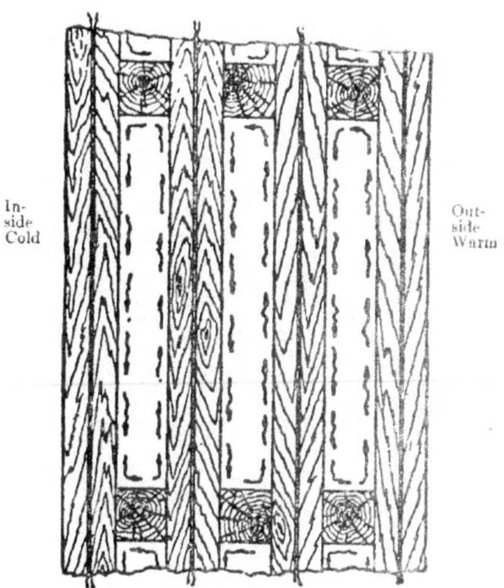

FIG. 35.—TRANSFER OF HEAT BY CONVECTION.

The transfer of heat by *evaporation* and *condensation* is

usually classed as convection, although in several respects it differs widely from convection as just discussed. In ordinary convection, it has been noted that the surface layer of fluid plays an important part; but in the steam boiler the finite layer of water next the hot boiler wall is heated and vaporized, thus absorbing a very large amount of heat. Such steam is instantly replaced by other water and the process is continued, a procedure distinctly different from the usual convective heating process and one in which the rate of heat transfer is much higher. By drainage, on the condenser end of the system, the film of condensed water is quickly removed, which differs from the usual transfer by convection.

The transfer of heat by evaporation and condensation has a definite bearing on the effect of moisture in insulating materials and in air-space construction.

Thus, in general, the rate of heat transfer by convection is dependent on the kind of fluid in contact, the temperature differences, the velocity of the convecting fluid, the character of surfaces (such as shape and roughness), and the area of the surface.

67.—Radiation.—Radiation is the mode of transfer of heat, for example, from the sun to the earth, which is accomplished even though the intervening space is entirely devoid of ordinary matter. The transfer of heat by radiation is effected by wave motion exactly similar in general character to the wave motion that constitutes light, these waves being transmitted by a medium, known as ether, that fills all space, although, contrary to popular belief, considerable obstruction is offered to the passage of these waves.

The molecular disturbance in a hot body produces a commotion in the immediate adjacent ether, which spreads out in all directions as an ether wave disturbance, and when these waves impinge on a cool body they produce a molecular disturbance in it. In a word, the heat energy of a hot body is constantly passing into space as radiant energy in the luminiferous ether, and becomes heat energy again only when and as it is absorbed by bodies upon which it falls; and energy transmitted in this way is referred to as *radiant heat,* although it is transmitted as radiant energy and is transferred again into heat only by absorption. Radiant heat and light are physically identical, but are perceived through different avenues of sensation; radiations that produce sight when received through the eye, give a sensation of warmth through the nerves of touch. The sensation of warmth felt in bright sunlight on a cool day is a good illustration of this phenomenon.

FIG. 36.—TRANSFER OF HEAT BY RADIATION—THE RADIOMETER.

The rate of heat transfer by radiation depends on the characters of both the hot radiating and the cold receiving surfaces (the reflecting power of the hot surface and the absorbing power of the cold surface), the temperature differences, the relative absolute temperatures, and the distance between surfaces.

The blacker an object the more heat it will, in general,

lose by radiation; non-metals radiate heat at a much more rapid rate than metals of similar surface; and rough surfaces radiate heat at a more rapid rate than smooth, polished surfaces. Thus stoves and radiators* intended to give out heat should present a non-metal surface, the color and relative degree of smoothness being of lesser importance. Metal cooking utensils should be tinned or nickeled in order to radiate as little heat as possible. A brightly tinned hot air furnace pipe may lose less heat by radiation than when covered with thin asbestos paper, because the surface of the non-metallic asbestos paper radiates heat more rapidly than the bright tin.

The heat radiated to a body may be partly rejected, absorbed, or transmitted through the body. The capacity of a surface to absorb radiant energy depends both on the lack of polish of the surface and the nature of the material. Lampblack is the best absorber of radiant energy and polished brass is the poorest. In cold climates dark clothes are worn because they absorb and transmit the greatest proportion of radiant energy, while in hot climates white clothes are preferred because they reject radiant energy to the maximum extent.

It has been noted that if no heat is supplied or taken away, all *surfaces* in an enclosure come to the same temperature; the rate, however, at which this equalization takes place depends on the radiating and the reflecting powers of such surfaces. Thus the temperature of a surface may be higher than the air adjacent to it. A wall in direct sunlight is often a good many degrees warmer than the atmosphere, which fact is important in the consideration of insulation for buildings since the temperature of the outside wall surface—not that of the air—helps determine the heat leakage.

The Stefan-Baltzmann radiation law for calculating heat losses is as follows:

$$H_2 = R\ A\ h\ (T_1)^4 - (T_2)^4$$

where H_2 is the total heat radiated in a given time in B.t.u., R is a constant (see accompanying table for values for various radiating materials), A is the area of the radiating surface in square feet, h is the time in hours, T_1 is the higher tem-

*It must be remembered that heat is transferred by conduction, convection and radiation,—not by radiation alone,—and that heat transfer by radiation is spoken of here, which is of secondary importance to the total heat transfer.

perature absolute in degrees F. and T_2 is the lower temperature absolute in degrees F. (Absolute temperature is 460 degrees below zero F., or 273 degrees below zero C.) If large temperature differences are not involved, then use the formula:

$$H_2 = R\ A\ h\ (T)^4$$

where T is the absolute temperature in degrees F.

TABLE OF STEFAN-BALTZMANN CONSTANTS (R).

Material	Constant (R)
Lampblack	0.900
Smooth glass	0.154
Dull brass	0.0362
Dull steel plate	0.338
Slightly polished copper	0.0278
Dull oxidized wrought iron	0.154
Clean, bright wrought iron	0.0562
Highly polished wrought iron	0.0467
Polished aluminum plate	0.053
Water	0.112
Ice	0.106

68.—Flow of Heat.—Generally the transfer of heat takes place by all three processes—conduction, convection and radiation—simultaneously. Thus heat is distributed throughout a room from a hot stove or furnace partly by radiation, principally by convection currents of air and to a slight extent by conduction. Such a body is said to emit* heat, and the rate at which a body emits heat depends upon its excess of temperature above its surroundings, upon the extent and character of the body and its surface, upon the nature of the surrounding gas or liquid, upon the freedom of motion of the surrounding fluid, and upon the nature of surrounding bodies.

Thus it is evident that many variables enter into the determination of heat transfer by radiation and by convection. Reliable experimental information is lacking, because it is very difficult to ascertain the exact effect of each. However, the engineer is concerned primarily with the combined transference of heat by conduction, convection and radiation. The heat transferred by convection and radiation may be determined by experimentation. The combined coefficient, or rate, of this heat transfer by convection and radiation is the heat given off or absorbed per square foot of surface, per hour, per degree of temperature difference F. In the case of cold stor-

*This term is variously used to indicate the emission of heat by a body by radiation only, by radiation and convection, and by all three methods combined.

age wall insulation, this temperature difference would be the difference between the temperature of the surface of the wall and the average temperature of the surrounding air; while the velocity of the air across the surface of such wall must affect the coefficient, or rate, of heat transfer by convection and radiation.

The values for the coefficient of convection and radiation for various materials under *still air* conditions are given in the accompanying table, and are based upon experiments made at the Engineering Experiment Station of the University of Illinois.

This coefficient is generally denoted by the symbol K_1, and is called the coefficient of radiation and convection for inside surfaces. In an actual plant, the outside walls are exposed to the more rapid movement of the air, so that the coefficient of radiation and convection is larger for the outside surfaces. The symbol for this coefficient is K_2, and it is, in general, 2.5 to 3 times the inside wall coefficient K_1, due to the greater velocity of the outside air. Thus, as a general rule, the value of the outside coefficient, K_2, may be considered to be three times the inside coefficient, K_1.

COEFFICIENTS OF RADIATION AND CONVECTION (K1) IN B.t.u. PER HOUR PER DEGREE TEMPERATURE DIFFERENCE F.

Material	Coefficient K_1
Brick wall	1.40
Concrete	1.30
Wood	1.40
Corkboard	1.25
Magnesia board	1.45
Glass	2.00
Tile plastered on both sides	1.10
Asbestos board	1.60
Sheet asbestos	1.40
Roofing	1.25

69.—Total Heat Transfer.—In its simplest form, total heat transfer is the heat passing into, through and out of a single wall of given area. If the surface temperatures and the temperatures in the surrounding air are taken, the total heat transmission may be separated into internal and external conductivity, the external conductivity being sometimes called "surface effects." In the case of a good insulator, as used for cold storage rooms, internal conduction is the essential factor; while in the case of a poor insulator, as the metal in a boiler tube, good conduction is necessary and surface transmission is all-important. Between these extreme conditions, the relative importance of conduction and surface transmission (convection and radiation) varies with each case considered. In determining the total transmission of three-inch corkboard insulation in still air, an error of about ten per cent is introduced if the surface effects on both sides are disregarded; while in the case of a single thickness of brick, the resistance

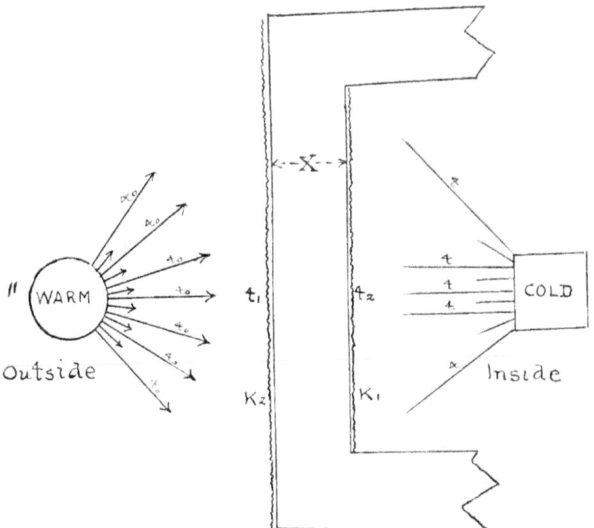

FIG. 37.—HEAT TRANSFER THROUGH A WALL.

to the flow of heat of the two surfaces is about eight times the internal resistance of the brick. In general, the better the substance as an insulator, the less is the error due to disregarding surface effects.

It has been observed that heat may be transmitted from a region of high temperature through a wall into a region of lower temperature by means of conduction, convection and radiation. The accompanying figure shows graphically the transfer of heat from the outside through a wall to the inside.

It will be seen that the heat passes by convection and radiation from the surface of a warm body at t_0 degrees F. to the outside surface of the wall, where it is absorbed by that surface, conducted through the wall and then given off by the inside surface of the wall by means of convection and radiation to the surface of the cold body at t degrees F.

The heat is conducted through the wall, due to the temperature difference between the outside and the inside surfaces of the wall, the temperature at the outside surface being noted as t_1 and the temperature at the inside surface as t_2. The amount of heat conducted through this wall, as previously mentioned, would depend on the internal thermal conductivity (C) and the thickness of the wall (X). Since heat is conducted through the wall because of temperature differences at the surfaces of the wall, it is proper to say that this temperature difference exists within very thin layers of air at such surfaces. On the outside of the wall in the figure, this is represented by the difference between the temperature of the outside air, t_0, and the temperature at the outside surface, t_1, and on the inside this is represented by the difference between the temperature of the inside surface, t_2, and the temperature of the inside air, t.

The total amount of heat passing from the warm body on the outside to the cold body on the inside depends on the combined conduction, convection and radiation effects. The quantity of heat transferred from the outside air to the wall depends on the coefficient of the combined radiation and convection, K_2, sometimes called the surface coefficient, and the temperature of the outside air, t_0, and the temperature at the outside surface, t_1. The heat given off by the inside surface of the wall to the inside air will depend on the coefficient of the combined radiation and convection for such inside surface, K_1, and the temperature of the inside surface, t_2, and the temperature of the inside air, t.

Thus, the total heat transmission from the surface of the outside hot body to the surface of the inside cold body will depend on the combined heat transfer coefficient, K, and the temperature of the outside air, t_0, and the temperature of the inside air, t. From this analysis, the value of the unit total heat transfer coefficient, K, may be expressed as follows:

$$K=\frac{1}{\frac{1}{K_1}+\frac{X}{C}+\frac{1}{K_2}}$$

From this formula, it will be noted that the unit total heat transfer coefficient, K, in B.t.u. per hour, per degree temperature difference F., for a given wall, depends on the combined convection and radiation coefficient for the inside and outside surfaces, K_1 and K_2, respectively, the thickness of the wall, X, and the internal conductivity of the material, C. The values of the conductivity, C, for various materials and the values of the coefficients of the combined inside convection and radiation, K_1, are given in the accompanying tables. The values of K_2, in general, may be taken as three times K_1.

In the case of a solid wall made up of layers of different materials, in intimate contact, having different conductivities, C_1, C_2, C_3, etc., of various thicknesses, X_1, X_2, X_3, etc., respectively, the foregoing formula becomes:

$$K=\frac{1}{\frac{1}{K_1}+\left\{\frac{X_1}{C_1}+\frac{X_2}{C_2}+\frac{X_3}{C_3}+\text{etc.}\right\}+\frac{1}{K_2}}$$

Suppose it is desired to determine how much heat per hour is transmitted through an outside heavy brick wall 18 inches thick, 20 feet high, and 25 feet long, when the outside temperature is 80° F. and the inside temperature is 20° F. From the tables, C equals 5, K_1 equals 1.4, and K_2 equals three times 1.4, or 4.2. Thus the heat transmission coefficient is found as follows:

$$K=\frac{1}{\frac{1}{1.4}+\left\{\frac{18}{5}\right\}+\frac{1}{4.2}}=0.2196$$

The area, A, is equal to 20x25, or 500 square feet, and t_1 equals 80° F, and t_2 equals 20° F. The total heat transfer is therefore:

$$H = K\,A\,(t_1 - t_2)$$
$$= 0.2196 \times 500 \times (80^\circ - 20^\circ)$$
$$= 6588 \text{ B.t.u. per hour.}$$

Suppose it is desired to determine the heat transmission of a similar brick wall of equal thickness insulated with 4 inches of corkboard applied directly to the wall in ½-inch Portland cement mortar and finished with Portland cement plaster ½-inch thick. From the table, K_1 (for plastered surface) equals 1.1, C_1 equals 5, X_1 equals 18, C_2 equals 0.308, X_2 equals 4, C_3 (for 1-inch thick Portland cement) equals 6.25, X_3 equals 1, and K_2 equals 4.2. Thus the heat transmission coefficient for this composite wall is found as follows:

$$K = \frac{1}{\frac{1}{1.10} + \left\{ \frac{18}{5} + \frac{4}{.308} + \frac{1}{6.25} \right\} + \frac{1}{4.2}} = 0.05588$$

The total heat transfer is therefore:

$$H = K\,A\,(t_1 - t_2)$$
$$= 0.05588 \times 500 \times (80^\circ - 20^\circ)$$
$$= 1676.4 \text{ B.t.u. per hour.}$$

Suppose it is desired to determine the heat transmission of a similar brick wall of equal thickness insulated with four 2-inch air spaces formed by four double layers of 1-inch white pine. From the tables, K_1 (for inside brick) equals 1.4, K_1' (for each of 8 inside surfaces of wood) equals 1.4, C_1 (for brick) equals 5, X_1 (for brick) equals 18, C_2 (for white pine) equals 0.791, X_2 (8 layers wood) equals 8, K_2 (for outside brick) equals 4.2. The value of K is then as follows:

$$K = \frac{1}{\frac{1}{1.4} + 8\left\{ \frac{1}{1.4} \right\} + \left\{ \frac{18}{5} + 8\,\frac{1}{0.791} \right\} + \frac{1}{4.2}} = 0.04906$$

The total heat transfer is therefore:

$$H = K\,A\,(t_1 - t_2)$$
$$= 0.04906 \times 500 \times (80^\circ - 20^\circ)$$
$$= 1471.8 \text{ B.t.u. per hour.}$$

It will be noticed at once that an 18-inch brick wall insulated with four 2-inch air spaces formed by four double layers of 1-inch white pine shows, by this method of computation, a lower total heat transfer than a similar brick wall insulated with 4 inches of corkboard. Experience teaches that the figures just shown are not accurate and the same problem is solved by a different method in the next Article.

70.—Air Spaces.—It should be especially noted here that a high vacuum is necessary to appreciably lower the normal rate of heat transfer by convection across air spaces, and that such rate increases very appreciably as the temperature differences increase. Also, that the amount of heat passing across an air space by radiation is very much enlarged when there is a large temperature difference between radiating and receiving surfaces, for it will be remembered that the rate of heat transfer by radiation is proportional to the difference between the fourth powers of the absolute temperatures of the surfaces involved, subject only to correction for losses due to imperfections in radiating and absorbing surfaces.

The United States Bureau of Standards, in the accompanying table, gives some interesting and valuable data on the heat *conduction* of air spaces, in which X is the width of the air spaces in inches and C is the heat conductivity in B.t.u. per square foot, per degree difference F., per inch thickness, per hour, from which table it should be especially noted that the thermal conductivity of air spaces *is not* proportional to the thickness of the spaces.

THERMAL CONDUCTIVITY OF AIR SPACES (C) IN B.t.u. PER HOUR, PER DEGREE DIFFERENCE F., PER INCH THICKNESS.

Thickness (X)	Conductivity (C)
⅛-inch	0.2625
¼-inch	0.3375
⅜-inch	0.4083
½-inch	0.4833
⅝-inch	0.5667
¾-inch	0.6833
⅞-inch	0.8333
1-inch	0.9167
2-inch	1.7917
3-inch	2.5833

The determination of the heat transmission of an 18-inch brick wall insulated with four 2-inch air spaces formed by four double layers of 1-inch white pine, based on the thermal conductivities of air spaces as determined by the Bureau of Standards, becomes a different problem from that presented in the preceding Article. From the tables, K_1 (for inside wood) equals 1.4, C_1 (for brick) equals 5, C_2 (for 2-inch air space) equals 1.7917, C_3 (for white pine) equals 0.791, X_1 equals 18, X_2 equals 4, X_3 equals 8 and K_2 equals 4.2. The value of K is then as follows:

$$K=\frac{1}{\frac{1}{1.4}+\left\{\frac{18}{5}+\frac{4}{1.7917}+\frac{8}{0.791}\right\}+\frac{1}{4.2}}=0.05915$$

The total heat transfer is therefore:

$$\begin{aligned}H&=K\ A\ (t_1-t_2)\\&=0.05915\times500\times(80^\circ-20^\circ)\\&=1774.5\text{ B.t.u. per hour.}\end{aligned}$$

71.—**Heat Transfer by Conduction Only.**—It will be noted that the heat that passes through an insulated wall depends mostly upon the internal thermal conductivity of the materials that compose the wall, and that the resistance to the flow of heat at the surface (convection and radiation) but slightly reduces the total heat transfer. This may be seen by calculation from the example of the 18-inch brick wall insulated with 4 inches of corkboard, as follows:

$$K=\frac{1}{\frac{18}{5}+\frac{4}{.308}+\frac{1}{6.25}}=0.0597$$

The heat transfer (by conduction only) is therefore:

$$\begin{aligned}H&=K\ A\ (t_1-t_2)\\&=0.0597\times500\times(80^\circ-20^\circ)\\&=1791\text{ B.t.u. per hour.}\end{aligned}$$

Thus it is seen that the increase in heat flow in this example due to neglecting the surface effects is but 6.8%, under the normal conditions assumed; and for practical purposes, in connection with the computation of refrigeration losses due to heat leakage, the following formula is followed:

$$H=\frac{A\ (t_1-t_2)}{\frac{X_1}{C_1}+\frac{X_2}{C_2}+\frac{X_3}{C_3}+\text{etc.}}$$

The internal heat conductivities available for the determination of heat losses by calculation were, for the most part, secured under favorable conditions, in testing laboratories; and much practical experience with cold storage insulation and refrigeration teaches that the results obtained by computation are about 25% lower than is safe to expect in actual service under plant working conditions.

72.—Heat Loss Through Insulation.—The internal conductivity of various insulating materials depends, in general, upon the structure and density of the material; and since the conductivity of still air is very low, probably because of the very loose arrangement of the molecules, then a material containing a large percentage of "dead air" will transfer a

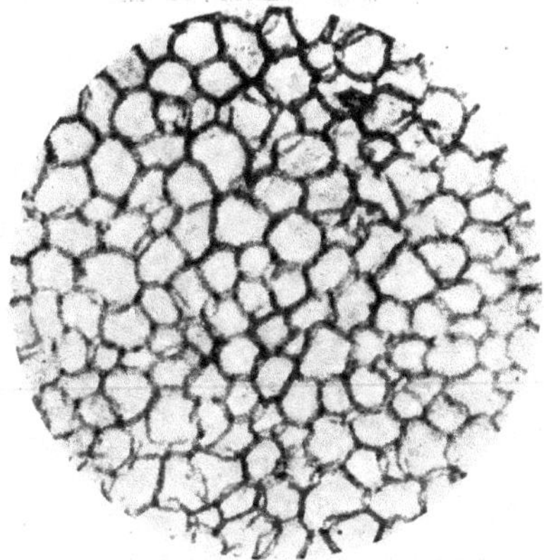

FIG. 38.—CORK UNDER POWERFUL MICROSCOPE, SHOWING SEALED AIR CELL CONSTRUCTION.

minimum amount of heat. But to keep air still, to keep it from circulating, even when it is confined, is difficult, especially when it is recalled that heat applied to the surface of one side of a compartment containing air will warm up that surface, the heat will be transmitted in more or less degree through the wall to the air on the inside, it will be taken up by the particles of air in contact therewith, and warm air being at once lighter than cold air it will rise and be replaced by cold air. Thus the heat is quickly and effectively carried across the air space to the wall on the other side, by convection, and by conduction passes through the opposite wall to the space beyond.

An automobile can attain a greater speed on a two mile track than it can attain on a quarter mile track. Similarly, air can attain a greater velocity in a large space than it can in a small one. Thus this principle is one of the two main guides in the selection of an efficient insulating material. First, the material must contain air in the very smallest possible units, such as atoms, so that convection is reduced to a minimum; and since these atoms of air must each be confined, a material must be selected that is very light and of little density so that conduction is also reduced to a minimum. Secondly, such material must at the same time be impervious to moisture, so that its initial ability to retard heat will prevail in service. Such a material will be as efficient from the standpoint of heat transfer as it is possible to obtain; that is, a very light material containing myriads of microscopic air cells, each cell sealed unto itself. A material of such character is *cork,* the outer bark of the cork oak tree, native of the Mediterranean basin.

CHAPTER X.

DETERMINATION OF THE HEAT CONDUCTIVITY OF VARIOUS MATERIALS.*

73.—Methods Employed.—It is a complicated as well as an expensive procedure to determine with any degree of accuracy the heat conductivity of given materials.† In spite of this fact, a great many experiments and tests have been made over a period of many years; but in the absence of any standard in apparatus or uniformity of procedure, the results have varied so much as often to be of no real value whatever.

Most common of the test methods employed are:

(a) Ice-box Method.
(b) Oil-box Method.
(c) Hot-air-box Method.
(d) Cold-air-box Method.
(e) Flat-plate (or Hot-plate) Method.

74.—The Ice-box Method.—The most common of all methods of comparing the heat insulating value of two materials has been by the use of two identical cubical metal boxes covered with the materials to be tested, each filled with ice, and observing the rate at which the ice melts. Since it is difficult to keep the entire box at 32° F., even though containing ice, this method may lead to inaccurate results even as a *comparative* test of two materials. As a method of testing any one material, it is far too unreliable to be of any practical value whatever.

75.—The Oil-box Method.—The oil-box method of comparative testing consists in covering two identical cubical

*For a comprehensive treatment of heat transmission, consult "Heat Transmission of Insulating Materials," in eleven parts, published by The American Society of Refrigerating Engineers, 37 W. 39th St., New York City. Price, $2.50.

†For a comprehensive treatment of methods to be employed in testing insulating materials, consult "An Investigation of Certain Methods for Testing Heat Insulators," by E. F. Grundhofer, The Pennsylvania State College Engineering Experiment Station Bulletin No. 33. Price, 25 cents. Address: State College, Pa.

metal boxes with the materials to be tested, each filled with mineral oil and the oil surrounding an electrical heater and an agitator. By varying the heat supplied, any desired difference in temperature may be maintained between the contents of the boxes and the surrounding air of the room. By measuring the electrical input by ammeters and voltmeters, the amount of heat lost through the respective materials under test can be determined by calculation. Inaccuracies occur due to uncertainty of the temperature at the top of the box and loss of heat through agitator rod, box supports, evaporation of oil and conduction through overflow pipe. For

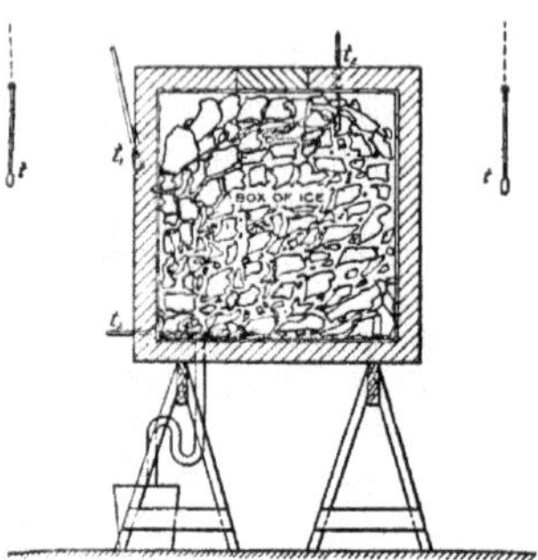

FIG. 39.—THE ICE-BOX METHOD OF TESTING HEAT TRANSMISSION.

the comparative testing of two materials of equal thickness, the results are reasonably accurate; but as a method of testing any one material the results will usually be too high, and unreliable.

76.—The Hot-air-box Method.—The hot-air-box method of testing consists of a cubical box constructed wholly of the material to be tested, with only such light wooden reinforcing as may be required for strength or rigidity. Inside the box is placed an electrical heater and an electrical fan, which permits of a uniform box temperature maintained at any desired temperature difference between the air in the box and the surrounding outside air. By measuring the electrical input, the amount of heat lost through the material under test can be determined by calculation, as in the case of the oil-box method, but the inaccuracies are reduced, by comparison, to the loss of heat through the box supports, and are correspondingly more reliable. This method of testing has con-

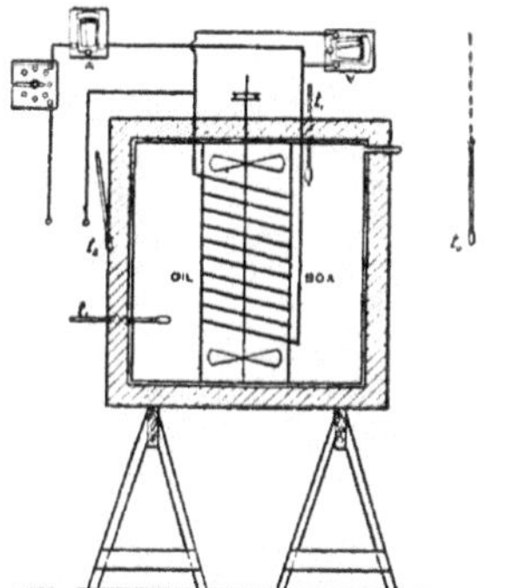

FIG. 40.—THE OIL-BOX METHOD OF TESTING HEAT TRANSMISSION.

siderable merit, and can be used with fairly good results as a method of testing any one material alone.

77.—The Cold-air-box Method.—The cold-air-box method

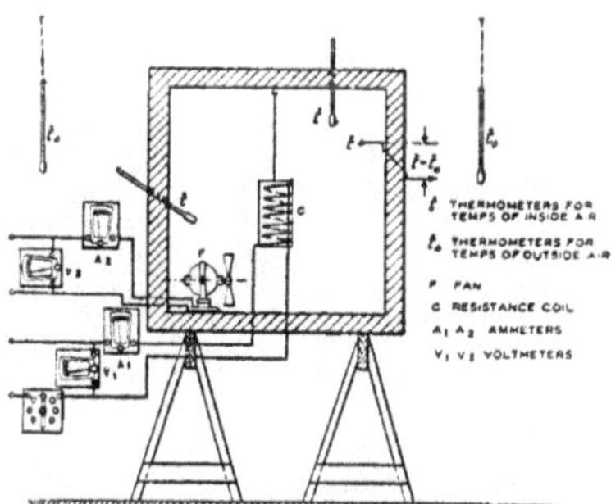

FIG. 41.—THE HOT-AIR-BOX METHOD OF TESTING HEAT TRANSMISSION.

of testing consists in the substituting for the heater and the fan in the hot-air-box method, a container of cracked ice suspended inside the cubical test box near the top. The air in the test box will be maintained at a lower temperature than the outside room, and since the amount of heat required to melt one pound of ice is definitely known, the amount of heat lost through the walls of the test box may be determined by weighing the water resulting from the melting of ice and carried outside of the box through a small rubber tube.

The results are reasonably reliable since the suspended container of cracked ice sets up a natural circulation of air within the test box and keeps it at a very nearly uniform temperature.

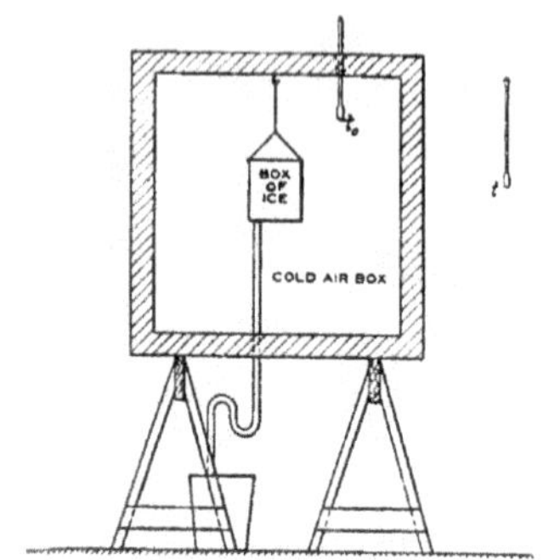

FIG. 42.—THE COLD-AIR-BOX METHOD OF TESTING HEAT TRANSMISSION.

78.—The Hot-plate Method.—The hot-plate method has probably been most widely used by investigators, including the United States Bureau of Standards, to determine the *relative* conductivity of insulating materials. The inaccuracies in this method, for absolute conductivity determination, lie in the determination of the heat loss from the edges, which is ordinarily considerable, and the uncertainty of the contact between the material and the plates.

The method consists of an electrically heated plate placed between two sheets of the material to be tested, and outside of these sheets are placed two hollow plates cooled by circulating water. By measuring the electrical input, the amount of heat lost through the insulating materials can be determined by calculation. The temperature difference between the hot and the water-cooled plates is measured by thermal junctions. Knowing these factors, also the area and the thickness, the *relative* conductivity of the materials under test may be computed with precision.

An instrument of this general character, which shows refinements over previous apparatus, has lately been designed and constructed. The hot plate consists of two ⅛-inch copper plates 12 inches square, between which are the heating

FIG. 43.—THE HOT-PLATE METHOD OF TESTING HEAT TRANSMISSION—GENERAL VIEW OF THERMAL CONDUCTIVITY APPARATUS, 8-IN. SQUARE.

coils consisting of nichrome resistance ribbon wound with even spacing on a slate core and insulated from the copper plates by two sheets of mica bond. *In order to minimize the loss of heat from the edges of the hot plate,* each copper plate is divided into an inner test area 8x8 inches and an outer guard ring. A compensating winding for furnishing auxiliary current is wound around the outer edges of the plate, to prevent the lateral flow of heat from the inner test area to the outer guard ring, a 1/16-inch air space being left between the areas and the areas being held in place by four pieces of Advance wire soldered to the copper plates.

By the use of a galvanometer, the inner area and the outer guard ring are kept at the same temperature, this condition being indicated by a zero reading, and under which condition it is assumed that no heat flows from the 8x8 inch

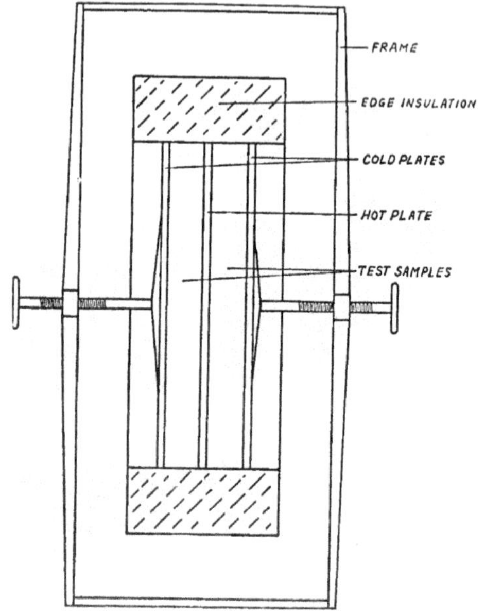

FIG. 44.—DIAGRAMMATIC SKETCH OF APPARATUS FOR THE PLATE METHOD OF MEASURING THE THERMAL CONDUCTIVITY OF MATERIALS.

inner portion of the test area to the outer portion of the test area or guard ring.

Direct current from a generating set is supplied to the main heating grid and also to the auxiliary guard ring circuit; *and to prevent any variation in current due to voltage fluctuation*, a ballast tube, similar to that used with radio sets, is placed in the main line and automatically keeps the current constant to the main heating grid.

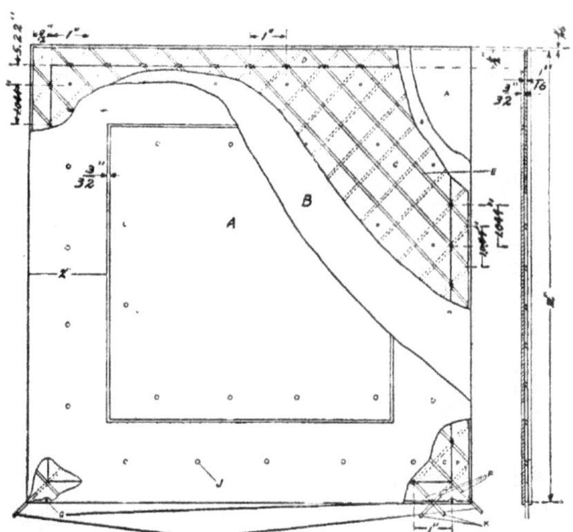

FIG. 45.—DETAILS OF HEATING PLATE FOR THERMAL CONDUCTIVITY APPARATUS.

(A) Copper plates. (B) Micanite insulation. (C) Fibre board—main heater. (D) Fibre board—edge heater. (E) Constantan ribbon 1-16-in. No. 36. (F) Brazed joints. (G) Steel pins for suspension. (H) Copper leads to main heater. (J) Brass screws. (K) Copper leads to edge heater.

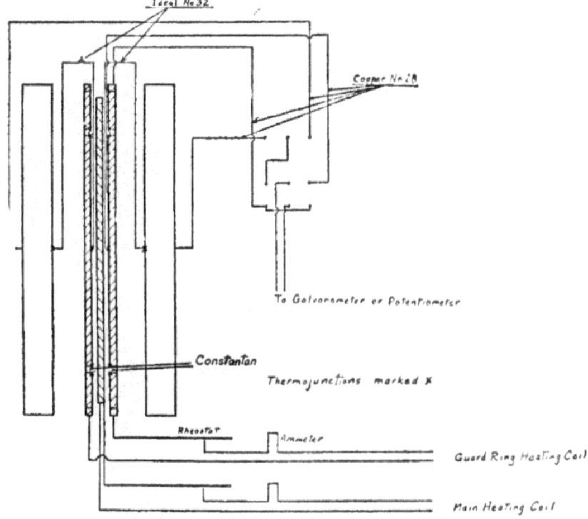

FIG. 46.—ARRANGEMENT OF ELECTRICAL CONNECTIONS TO THERMO-JUNCTIONS.

79.—Tests by Various Authorities on Many Materials.— Probably the most comprehensive and the most widely accepted data* on the rate of heat flow through most of the materials with which an engineer has to deal is given in "Results of Tests to Determine Heat Conductivity of Various Insulating Materials," by Charles H. Herter,† being the ninth section of the "Report of Insulation Committee" of the American Society of Refrigerating Engineers, published in the January, 1924, number of "Refrigerating Engineering." The complete "Report of Insulation Committee," in eleven sections, is now available in data pamphlet form from the American Society of Refrigerating Engineers, New York City (Price, $2.50).

In his report, Mr. Herter says, in part:

The original program merely called for a "Summary of Test Results," with a tabulation giving but one recommended average value for materials such as cork, wood, asbestos, brick, stone, etc. When, however, in the course of compiling it was found that each material occurs in many varieties with correspondingly differing heat resistances, it was thought best to tabulate all values conveniently available and to let the reader select the value applying to his material. As explained in detail further on, a close approximation to the correct value can be obtained from the attached tables if care is exercised to ascertain the important properties of one's material, such as density, moisture content, mean temperature exposed to, and perhaps the relative size of grains. If these characteristics are alike in different articles, their resistance to heat also will be practically alike.

In most of the older textbooks but one value appears for each material, and since no specification is given, and fabricated materials are continually being changed in composition, old and indefinite values are liable to be misleading. All vague results are intended to be excluded from these tables, and the opinion is held that such values properly qualified as to density and temperature are more trustworthy than those identified merely by name. . . . .

Reasons for Method of Classification.

To facilitate the finding of the heat conductivity value for any material it was first suggested to arrange the tables in alphabetical order. Since, however, many materials have several designations, and in many cases a suitable insulator is sought and not a specific product, it was concluded to arrange all values in four groups and

*See Appendix for "Heat Transmission: A National Research Council Project."
†Refrigerating Engineer, New York City.

to enumerate the items approximately in the order of their insulating value, the material with lowest rate of conduction coming first. Thus, a glance at a table discloses at once the relative heat resistance of any material listed, and over how large a range it extends due to natural variations in physical condition such as density and moisture content. The influence of temperature level is also evident from the tables.

Another important advantage gained by the group method is that a comparison can readily be made of similar materials tested in various parts of the world. The fact that the results thus obtained with similar materials by widely separated experimenters are usually in good accord, tends to prove that the values found are correct and have been verified. This knowledge forms a good basis for estimating the heat insulating quality of some new material which may not be listed in these tables. . . . .

Results of Tests.

All the values given are derived from tests. In every instance the authority for the result given is indicated in column 10 of the tables. . . . .

In the past many materials were tested in such a way that the resistance at the surfaces, that is the temperature drop caused by the inability of the surrounding air to take up heat rapidly enough, was included in the insulating power per inch thickness of the material. As explained in another section of this report, the proper basis for comparing the heat insulating value of materials employed in thicknesses exceeding those of glass and paper is their internal conductivity. Accordingly, these are the values included in the attached tables, and this explains why the results of some widely advertised tests could not be included. . . . .

Explanation of Tables.

For simplicity and to prevent error in using these tables, they have been given identical arrangement. Each table has 10 columns, numbered.

Column 1 contains name and particulars of material in question.

Columns 2 and 3 give the density in two ways, by specific gravity or ratio of weight of material to the weight of an equal volume of water. In other words, the specific gravity of water is established at 1, and its weight is figured at 62.35 lb. per cu. ft., while in column 3 the apparent weight of the insulator as derived from its bulk, is given in lb. per cu. ft.

Density.

One of the first things to be done in trying to place insulation engineering on a scientific basis is to emphasize the importance of density. Frequently it is not advantageous for a manufacturer to discuss density; first, because it is difficult for him to keep within a narrow limit, nature's products not always being uniform; second, because moisture absorption from the atmosphere may change it against his will, and third, a rival may claim to make an equivalent material of a lower density, which, as is well illustrated in Table II, (Mineral Matter) would be likely to yield a better insulating effect. Thus, in Table II the heat conductivity of the heaviest American corkboard listed (15.6 per cu. ft.) is 0.3513 B.t.u. per hour against 0.2693 B.t.u. for the 6.9 lb. variety. Incidentally, it should be borne in mind that the structural strength of porous material diminishes as its density is lowered.

A light variety of corkboard may be a good insulator, and less expensive to make because it contains less cork and more air, but the delicate product requires great care in shipping and handling, it is weaker and, unless specially treated, it will offer less resistance to air and moisture penetration. In view of these facts, it is customary to employ for moulded cork pipe covering a quality of pure compressed cork varying in density from 20.5 lb. per cu. ft. ("ice water thickness," 1-in. pipe) to 15.5 lb. per cu. ft. ("special thick brine covering" for 6-in. pipe) while the weight of American commercial pure corkboard now (1923) varies from 10 lb. per cu. ft. in one-inch thick boards to 8 lb. per cu. ft. in 6 in. thick slabs.

Frequently thin boards are obtained by sawing up thick slabs, and so the only way to determine the true density is to weigh the boards used.

These variations in density involve of course variations in conductivity.

A good example of the value of comparison will be found in the case of snow and ice, where the values of c found by nine different experimenters are quite consistent when lined up in the order of density.

Mean Test Temperature.

Columns 4 and 5 of the tables are intended to state the mean temperature of sample while being tested for heat conductivity. The Centigrade thermometer scale is preferred in testing laboratories, but the Fahrenheit scale continues to be used by most English speaking engineers, hence both are given.

In the past many investigators were not aware that the mean absolute temperature has any influence upon the heat conduction of a material. When, in 1908, Nusselt extended his tests over a wide range of temperature, this fact became evident. For example, by increasing the temperature of an infusorial earth block from 32° to 842° F. he found the conductivity to increase from 0.51 to 1.02 B.t.u. or to just double the initial value. The effect of absolute temperature is noticeable in all materials, but the rate of change differs and is only very roughly proportional to the absolute mean temperature of the sample.

It has also been proved that the effectiveness of insulators depends upon their containing the greatest possible number of minute air cells. The solid portions or thin walls of these air cells conduct heat readily, but across the cells heat is conducted chiefly by radiation. As explained in another section of this report, radiation increases with the fourth power of the absolute temperature of the heat exchanging surfaces, and this explains why in careful testing we find that the insulating effect changes as the mean working temperature is changed. The amount of change varies with each material.

Units of Heat Conductivity.

Columns 6, 7 and 8 express the heat conductivity in various units as defined. The physicist who prefers to work with the Centigrade-Gram-Second system expresses his results in gram-calories of heat passing in one second through a plate one centimeter square, one centimeter thick, per one degree C. difference in temperature of the two faces of plate.

Using this extremely small unit the conductivity even of silver is equal to but 1 gram-calorie. For 6.9 lb. corkboard it is 0.00009275 gram-calorie. In order to eliminate from the tables at least three of the decimals, the true numbers in column 6 are given as they appear after multiplication by 1000. (It would be wrong to write kilogram calories instead.)

The results of most European tests are expressed in technical, metric system units, as shown in column 7. In this case the heat flow is measured in kilogram-calories per hour passing through a plate of one square meter area one meter thick, which may be written as equivalent to 1 m^3 (1 meter cube) per degree C. difference in temperature between hot and cold faces.

Finally in column 8 appear the values for heat conductivity in technical English units, the figures as given representing the number of British thermal units (B.t.u.) passing per hour through a plate of the material one square foot in area, one inch thick, and per degree Fahrenheit difference in temperature *of the two faces.* These last four words must be added, otherwise those who carelessly omit them invariably think it is understood that the difference between warm and cold *air* each side of board is meant. This mistake is cleared up in another section of this report.

Since in refrigerating plants heat must usually be removed throughout 24 hours, it has long been the custom to use 24 hours as the time unit for expressing the insulating effect of walls, etc. Outside of the laboratory temperature conditions due to atmospheric changes (sun, wind, rain) are never constant throughout 24 hours, and so the committee has decided to adopt the hourly basis for measuring heat flow. This also conforms with the practice of other than refrigerating engineers.

In addition to the three units appearing in columns 6, 7 and 8, a fourth one is being advocated by physicists. Their viewpoint is that it is illogical when using the foot (12 in.) as the unit of length for determining areas to use some other unit, the inch, for the thickness. Accordingly, in modern textbooks such as "Mechanical Engineers' Handbook" by L. S. Marks, 1916, page 304, and in "Heat Transmission by Radiation, Conduction and Convection," by R. Royds, 1921, heat conduction per hour is based on a piece one square foot in area, and one foot thick.

Anyone preferring to calculate with this new unit need only divide the values per inch thickness (col. 8) by 12.

In the metric system the same unit, either the meter or the centimeter, is used for both area and thickness.

Conversion Factors Used.

For the convenience of those accustomed to the use of the units employed in either columns 6, 7 or 8, the value appearing at the original source was translated into the other units by means of the following conversion factors, using a 20-inch slide rule:

Value in col. 6 $\times$ 0.36 = value in col. 7
Value in col. 6 $\times$ 2.90291 = value in col. 8
Value in col. 7 $\div$ 0.36 = value in col. 6
Value in col. 7 $\times$ 8.06364 = value in col. 8
Value in col. 8 $\times$ 0.344482 = value in col. 6
Value in col. 8 $\times$ 0.124013 = value in col. 7

Column 9 simply gives the reciprocals of the values in column 8, for convenience in calculations as brought out in another section. Thus the values in column 9 represent the heat resistivity of the various materials enumerated, that property really being the reason for their use by refrigerating engineers and others.

Column 10 gives the source of the information found in the preceding columns. This is quite useful, because it affords an opportunity to look up the references given and to satisfy oneself whether or not the testing method used was likely to give trustworthy results. Every investigator publishing his work is convinced that his results are of a high order of accuracy, and it is only the additional experience acquired from subsequent investigations that enables us to critically evaluate past accomplishments.

Results of Conduction Tests.

The present survey of the field of heat conductors (there are "poor conductors of heat" but no "non-conductors of heat") furnishes the desired numerical proof for the existence of a number of peculiarities in insulators.

In these tables an attempt is made to list the various materials approximately in the order of their power to resist heat flow, the best resistor coming first. This plan could not be strictly adhered to, because it was considered desirable for comparison to list together material of the same name but of various densities, and to keep together materials of the same family, for example, the corkboards.

It will be noted with surprise that some of the loose insulating materials show as low a heat conduction as does air alone. This is due to the fact that in a filled space the diminished convection and radiation offset the conduction proceeding through the fibers of the insulator. The packing of an air space with insulating material is, therefore, of particular advantage.

In the absence of a series of tests of each material at various densities, it is hardly possible to state just which density or rate of packing will result in least heat conduction. Randolph, Table III (Animal Matter), obtained lower heat conduction with eiderdown at 6.8 lb. per cu. ft. than he did with 4.92 lb., because in the latter case there was a better chance for convection. His tests on absorbent cotton, Table I (Vegetable Matter), lead to the same conclusion. The heat conduction of dry granulated cork seems to depend more upon the state of division and absence of foreign substances than on the density, some grades at 3 lb. per cu. ft. showing just as favorable as grades three times as dense.

Comparisons of this kind should be made at like temperature levels. In Nusselt's series of tests on 10-lb. granulated cork it will be observed that the heat conductivity increased from 0.25 B.t.u. at 32° F. to 0.44 at 392° F. The temperature coefficient, or the increase in c per degree change from standard mean test temperature, such as 68° F., is appreciable in all materials, but more so in some than in others. All so-called insulators are more effective per degree difference at low than at high temperatures, that property being due to radiation in the minute air cells, and due to included moisture, but in metals there is no uniform behavior in this respect, the conductivity increasing in one metal and decreasing in another. . . . .

Test Reports to Be Specific.

It should be evident from the foreging that the heat conductivity of any material is not a fixed figure. Honest investigators will not fail to carefully describe the sample they tested and to at least give its dimensions, density and range of surface temperatures used, otherwise their results may not fit in with correctly made tests and will be of no service to discriminating engineers.

Temperature Level Important.

Heretofore there was no universally recognized mean temperature of samples under test. To obtain results within a convenient time a fairly large temperature difference is often resorted to. Thus the sample is dried out much beyond its normal commercial state of dryness. Investigators rarely report the state of dryness after tests are concluded. They aim to give us a favorable looking value of a bone-dry sample, kiln-dried for weeks in some cases, when, in commercial applications we are interested in the heat conductivity of samples *as received on the job.* The low mean temperature should be used in the first test, and some higher mean temperature in subsequent tests. These results should *not* be averaged up into a single value.

The successive drying out of a sample is revealed by a (temporary) lowering of the heat conductivity as higher temperatures are reached; for illustration see Randolph's diatomaceous earth and asbestos compositions, 20.6 lb. per cu. ft. At 50° and 752° F. face temperatures a value of c was obtained of 0.462 B.t.u. against 0.718 (55% more) with 50° and 212° face temperatures, when in reality, with constant moisture content, the order of these values should be reversed, in conformity with the results of other investigations.

To avoid drying out the sample unduly, the cold side of the plate is cooled by refrigerated brine, at the British National Physical Laboratory (Table I, Vegetable Matter), and in some European laboratories by liquid air or other cold fluid.

Materials used in refrigeration, and in the construction of buildings, should have their normal rated heat conductivity referred to 68° F. (20° C.) arithmetical mean test temperature.

While in the tables columns 4 and 5 are supposed to give the true mean test temperature, or else the range used, this rule could not be adhered to in cases where the original investigator neglected to specifically state that the temperature given (if any) actually represents the mean test temperature. It is possible that some (as Norton) meant it to be the temperature of the hot face. Others, like Taylor and Griffiths, gave both face temperatures, a method which has much in its favor. In general, the data given contain all that is available. The results of older determinations were not obtained from the original sources stated, but were taken simply from standard reference books, such as the Smithsonian Physical Tables or Landolt-Boernstein's Chemical-Physical Tables, 1912.

Moisture Content.

As already pointed out, the subject of moisture has not received its full share of attention in the past. From a few isolated tests and observations in practice, and knowing that water conducts heat at about 14 times the rate at which heat flows across dry air cells, there remains no doubt as to the harmful influence of moisture. Quantitative measurements, however, are as yet incomplete.

In Table 1 (Vegetable Matter), Biquard gives for French impregnated corkboard weighing dry 17.17 lb. per cu. ft., $c = 0.4195$ B.t.u per hr. After the weight was increased by water absorption to 19.34 lb., c became 0.613 B.t.u. Here 12.7% increase in weight caused the conductivity to increase by 49.7%, equivalent to 4% for each 1% gain in weight.

In Table I, near the end, Nusselt gives for Austrian "cement wood," dry, 44.6 lb. per cu.ft., $c = 0.968$ B.t.u. After moisture had increased the weight to 51.4 lb., c was 1.21 B.t.u. Here 15.2% increase in weight caused the conductivity to increase by 25%, equivalent to only 1.65% loss of heat for each 1% gain in weight.

In Table II (Mineral Matter), Randolph gives for diatomaceous earth and asbestos at 20.6 lb. per cu. ft. a value of $c = 0.57777$ B.t.u for a plain air-dry sample, against $c = 0.499$ when first *dried for three days at 572° F.* The ratio is 1.158 to 1. Actually such a sample will soon go back to air-dry condition, if not worse, and then the wonderfully high insulating effect will not longer obtain.

A similar experiment is Nusselt's who, as shown in Table II, decreased, by roasting, the weight of fine river sand from 102.4 to 94.8 lbs. (excess 8%) thereby lowering c from 7.825 down to 2.26 B.t.u. The ratio of c is as 346% to 100% or 43% heat loss for each 1% moisture.

Under the item masonry, Table II, tests are given of a porous brick, showing the following results:

At 46.1 lb. (100 %) $c = 1.17$ B.t.u. (100 %)
At 49.7 lb. (107.7%) $c = 1.095$ B.t.u. (144.8%)
At 58.8 lb. (127.5%) $c = 2.743$ B.t.u. (234.2%)

It will be noted that for each 1% increase in weight, c increased 5.82% in the second test and 4.88%, on the average, in the third test.

In the case of the machine made brick weighing 101.1 lb. per cu. ft. the addition of moisture increased c from 3.34 up to 6.64 B.t.u. per hour.

Further tests are necessary before the influence of moisture can be expressed by a correct formula, but for the time being it may be assumed that each 1% gain in weight by moisture absorption causes the heat conductivity of previously dry slabs and bricks to increase by about 5%. Thus 20% addition in weight is likely to double the original conductivity. Cork and other pipe coverings long in use afford a good chance for checking this estimate.

If we figure that the British slag wool, Table II (Mineral Matter), originally had a value of $c = 0.29$, as is probable, then its value of $c = 0.35$, after 14 years use, represents a loss of 0.006 B.t.u. or 20.7%. This change in insulating effect is caused by moisture. Losses up to this magnitude must be expected whenever corkboard is incorporated in forms exposed to wet concrete. Hence this practice is to be discouraged.

Observations of this kind from actual practice are of greater value to refrigerating engineers than are tests of kiln dried samples.

Tables I to IV (Vegetable Matter, Mineral Matter, Animal Matter and Metals) contain no test results on air spaces and surface resistance. Reliable data on these items have appeared but recently, but it is intended to compile this information and to include it in a future report.

THERMAL CONDUCTIVITY OF MATERIALS CONSISTING MAINLY OF VEGETABLE MATTER

A. S. R. E. Insulation Committee Report, Revised 1924.

MATERIAL	Density		Temp. of Sample, mean or range		Thermal Conductivity			Resistance per inch thickness (R) 1/Col. 8	Authority
	Grams per cu. cm. (Specific gravity)	Pounds per cu. ft.	°C.	°F.	Gram Calorie, sec., cm.^{3} deg. C. x 1000	Kg. Calorie hour, m^3, deg. C.	B.t.u. hour, sq. ft., 1 in. °F Commercial conductivity		
Column 1	2	3	4	5	6	7	8	9	10
Sea weed, including air	....	....	0–18	From 32–64	0.0615	0.02215	**0.1788**	5.6	Rubner, 1895
Plant fibers, including air	....	....	0–18	32–64	0.0645	0.02322	**0.1874**	5.63	Rubner, 1895
Plant fibers, without air	....	....	0–18	32–64	1.42	0.511	**4.12**	0.2428	Rubner, 1895
Kapok, hollow vegetable fibers loosely packed	0.014	0.874	20–40	Between 68–104	0.082	0.0295	**0.238**	4.2	Bureau of Standards
Kapok, of Java	0.0157	0.98	15	59	0.0945	0.034	**0.2742**	3.647	Biquard
Cotton, compressed	0.101	6.3	10–100	50–212	0.071	0.02557	**0.2061**	4.85	Randolph
Cotton, loose	0.021	1.31	10–100	50–212	0.1114	0.04013	**0.3237**	3.092	Randolph
Cotton, compressed	....	....	....	....	0.0335	0.01205	**0.0972**	10.28	Forbes, 1872
Cotton, loose	....	....	....	....	0.0433	0.0156	**0.1258**	7.95	Forbes, 1872
Cotton (values of *c* increase along a straight line)	0.081	5.055	−200	−328	0.0764	0.0275	**0.222**	4.52	Nusselt & Groeber (Sphere)
			−150	−238	0.09035	0.0325	**0.2622**	3.816	
			−100	−148	0.1042	0.0375	**0.3027**	3.30	
			− 50	− 58	0.1181	0.0425	**0.343**	2.916	
			0	32	0.1334	0.0480	**0.387**	2.584	
			+ 50	122	0.1487	0.0535	**0.432**	2.314	
			100	212	0.164	0.0590	**0.476**	2.10	
			150	302	0.18075	0.0650	**0.524**	1.909	
Cellular rubber (expanded after vulcanizing under very high gas pressure), sample but $^1/_8$ in. thick. A spongy solid; cells unbroken	0.059 to 0.12	3.7 to 7.5	....	....	0.085	0.0306	**0.247**	4.05	Griffiths
Pure wool	0.10 / 0.11	6.24 / 6.87	30	86	0.084	0.0303	**0.244**	4.1	Bureau of Standards
Pure wool	0.08	4.99	30	86	0.090	0.0324	**0.2613**	3.826	Bureau of Standards
Pure wool; very loose packing; air circulation likely	0.04	2.5	30	86	0.101	0.0364	**0.2934**	3.41	Bureau of Standards
Cotton wool, medium packed	0.08	4.99	30	86	0.10	0.036	**0.2903**	3.442	Bureau of Standards
Wool felt, flexible paper stock	0.33	20.6	30	86	0.125	0.045	**0.363**	2.754	Bureau of Standards
Cotton wool, scrap from spinning mill	0.081	5.06	0	32	0.1306	0.047	**0.379**	3.639	Nusselt, 1908
			50	122	0.150	0.054	**0.436**	2.304	
			100	212	0.164	0.059	**0.476**	2.100	

THERMAL CONDUCTIVITY OF MATERIALS CONSISTING MAINLY OF VEGETABLE MATTER—*Continued*

A. S. R. E. Insulation Committee Report, Revised 1924

Cotton wool, absorbent	0.029	1.81	77.4	171.3	0.1883	0.0678	**0.547**	1.829	Desvignes
	0.0153	0.955	10–100	50–212	0.1191	0.0429	**0.346**	2.89	
	0.0250	1.56	...	...			**0.3125**	3.20	
	0.0352	2.198	...	...	0.1025	0.0369	**0.2977**	3.36	
Woolen fibres; pure, clean; dried at 212°F	0.0444	2.773	...	...	...	...	**0.2867**	3.49	
Note effect of density. (Density of sample is	0.0545	3.402	...	...	0.08965	0.03228	**0.2604**	3.84	Randolph
never exactly uniform, therefore proportion-	0.0823	5.14	...	...			**0.2522**	3.96	
ality varies slightly)	0.106	6.62	...	...	0.0718	0.02588	**0.2087**	4.79	
	0.140	8.74	...	...	...	...	**0.1773**	5.64	
	0.163	10.17	...	...		...	**0.1662**	6.02	
CORK	0.192	11.98	...	...	0.0552	0.0199	**0.1604**	6.23	
Cork, granulated, expanded ("Expansitschrot")	0.0476	2.972	20	68	0.0805	0.029	**0.234**	4.28	Groeber
No. 1, grains 1/32 to 1/16 inch			100	212	0.10	0.036	**0.2905**	3.44	(Sphere)
No. 3, grains 1/8 to 3/16 inch	0.0454	2.835	20	68	0.09165	0.033	**0.2662**	3.76	Groeber
			65	149	0.1028	0.037	**0.2987**	3.35	(Sphere)
Cork, ground; grains less than 1/16 inch	0.15	9.36	30	86	0.102	0.0367	**0.2963**	3.374	Bureau of Standards
Cork, granulated, fine. Sample No. 1	...	...	−9–+9	15–49	0.103	0.0371	**0.299**	3.343	Griffiths
			0	32	0.0861	0.031	**0.250**	4.00	
			50	122	0.1139	0.041	**0.331**	3.02	
Cork, regranulated; grains 1/32 to 1/8 inch	0.161	10.05	100	212	0.1334	0.048	**0.387**	2.584	Nusselt, 1908
(Scrap from Cork boards)			150	302	0.1445	0.052	**0.419**	2.387	
			200	392	0.1528	0.055	**0.444**	2.252	
Cork, granulated (or regranulated), grains 1/8	0.085		0	32	0.1055	0.038	**0.3067**	3.26	
to 3/16 inch		5.30	20	68	0.1167	0.042	**0.3387**	2.95	Groeber (Sphere)
			60	140	0.1389	0.050	**0.4033**	2.48	
Regranulated cork (waste product from baked pure cork board), grains about 3/16 inch	0.13	8.12	30	86	0.107	0.0385	**0.3105**	3.22	Bureau of Standards
Cork, granulated	0.078	4.867	15	59	0.1111	0.040	**0.3225**	3.10	Biquard
Granulated cork, coarse—	0.085	5.3	−9–15	16–58	0.112	0.0403	**0.325**	3.078	Griffiths
Sample No. 1, two tests	0.0866	5.4	−11–+1	10–34	0.110	0.0396	**0.319**	3.136	
Granulated cork, coarse— Sample No. 2	0.117	7.3	−15–+8	4–46	0.118	0.0425	**0.343**	2.917	Griffiths
Cork, ground, safe temp. 356°F	0.168	10.48	100	212	0.15	0.054	**0.436**	2.293	Skinner
			200	392	0.19	0.0684	**0.552**	1.8115	
Cork, granulated	0.087	5.43	78.3	172.9	0.1878	0.0679	**0.548**	1.827	Desvignes

A collection of accurate heat conductivity tests of (dry) corkboards of various densities and compositions made at the Laboratory for Physics, Technical High School, Munich, now arranged to show the influence of density upon the amount of heat conducted. Abstracted from paper by Profs. O. Knoblauch, E. Raisch and H. Reiher, *Gesundheits-Ingenieur*, Vol. 43, No. 52, Dec. 25, 1920.

Temperatures indicated represent mean temperature of Sample during test.

Corkboard ("Expansit steine") made from expanded cork granules (subjected to superheated steam), without foreign binder— Sample No. 1	0.061	3.81	0	32	0.0917	0.033	**0.266**	3.76	Nusselt (cube)
			20	68	...	0.035	**0.2823**	3.54	
			100	212		0.042	**0.3387**	2.95	

THERMAL CONDUCTIVITY OF MATERIALS CONSISTING MAINLY OF VEGETABLE MATTER—*Continued*

A. S. R. E. Insulation Committee Report, Revised 1924

MATERIAL	Density		Temp. of Sample, mean or range		Thermal Conductivity			Resistance per inch thickness (R) 1/Col. 8	Authority
	Grams per cu. cm. (Specific gravity)	Pounds per cu. ft.	°C.	°F.	Gram Calorie, sec., cm.², deg. C. x 1000	Kg. Calorie hour, m², deg. C.	B.t.u. hour, sq. ft., 1 in. °F Commercial conductivity		
Column 1	2	3	4	5	6	7	8	9	10
No. 2	0.150	9.36	0	32		0.037	**0.2985**	3.35	Nusselt (cube)
No. 3	0.154	9.62	15	59	0.1194	0.043	**0.347**	2.88	Poensgen
			50	122		0.044	**0.355**	2.82	
No. 4	0.160	9.98	0	32		0.037	**0.2985**	3.35	Poensgen
No. 5	0.163	10.175	0	32	0.1111	0.040	**0.3225**	3.1	Poensgen
			15	59		0.042	**0.3387**	2.95	
No. 6	0.166	10.36	30	86		0.044	**0.355**	2.82	Poensgen
Change in c is 0.000598 B. t. u. per °F.			45	113		0.046	**0.371**	2.7	
No. 7	0.169	10.55	0	32	0.100	0.036	**0.2903**	3.445	Poensgen
No. 8	0.171	10.67	0	32		0.037	**0.2985**	3.35	Poensgen
No. 9	0.175	10.92	0	32		0.039	**0.3145**	3.18	Poensgen
			15	59	0.114	0.041	**0.3305**	3.02	
No. 10, Granules expanded, impregnated	0.180	11.24	50	122		0.042	**0.3387**	2.95	Noell
No. 11	0.184	11.48	0	32		0.039	**0.3145**	3.18	Noell
No. 12	0.186	11.61	0	32		0.042	**0.3387**	2.95	Noell
No. 13	0.189	11.80	0	32	0.114	0.041	**0.3305**	3.02	Noell
No. 14	0.189	11.80	0	32		0.042	**0.3387**	2.95	Noell
			15	59		0.043	**0.347**	2.88	
No. 15, "M. I. K.," impregnated	0.193	12.05	25	77	0.1222	0.044	**0.355**	2.82	Poensgen
No. 16	0.195	12.17	0	32		0.043	**0.347**	2.88	Poensgen
No. 17			10	50		0.043	**0.347**	2.88	
Change in c is 0.000356 B.t.u. per °F.	0.199	12.42	25	77		0.044	**0.355**	2.82	Nusselt (cube)
			35	95		0.045	**0.363**	2.755	
No. 18, Asphalt impreg. Excess pitch removed under vacuum	0.200	12.48	18	64.4	0.1696	0.061	**0.492**	2.075	Nusselt (cube), 1908
No. 19	0.202	12.61	0	32		0.042	**0.3387**	2.95	Nusselt (cube), 1908
No. 20	0.202	12.61	0	32		0.043	**0.347**	2.88	Nusselt (cube), 1908
			10	50		0.044	**0.355**	2.82	
No. 21	0.215	13.42	15	59	0.125	0.045	**0.363**	2.755	Nusselt (cube)
			30	86		0.046	**0.371**	2.7	
No. 22	0.219	13.67	0	32		0.043	**0.347**	2.88	Nusselt (cube)
No. 23	0.220	13.74	0	32		0.061	**0.492**	2.03	Nusselt (cube)

THERMAL CONDUCTIVITY OF MATERIALS CONSISTING MAINLY OF VEGETABLE MATTER—*Continued*

A. S. R. E. Insulation Committee Report, Revised 1924

No. 24	0.226	14.10	0	32	....	0.0395	**0.3185**	3.14	Nusselt (cube)
No. 25	0.227	14.17	0	32	....	0.048	**0.387**	2.584	Nusselt (cube)
No. 26	0.228	14.24	0	32	....	0.044	**0.355**	2.82	Nusselt (cube)
No. 27	0.229	14.30	0	32	....	0.044	**0.355**	2.82	Nusselt (cube)
No. 28	0.242	15.11	0	32	....	0.059	**0.476**	2.10	Nusselt (cube)
No. 29	0.248	15.49	0	32	....	0.043	**0.347**	2.88	Nusselt (cube)
			0	32	0.1334	0.048	**0.387**	2.584	
			15	59	0.1362	0.049	**0.395**	2.53	
No. 30	0.254	15.86	25	77	0.139	0.050	**0.403**	2.48	Poensgen
Change in c is 0.000330 B.t.u. per °F.			45	113	0.1416	0.051	**0.411**	2.43	
			65	149	0.1445	0.052	**0.419**	2.39	
No. 31	0.259	16.17	0	32	....	0.039	**0.3145**	3.18	Poensgen
No. 32	0.265	16.54	0	32	....	0.048	**0.387**	2.584	Poensgen
No. 33	0.266	16.60	0	32	0.139	0.050	**0.403**	2.48	Poensgen
No. 34	0.269	16.80	0	32	0.139	0.050	**0.403**	2.48	Poensgen
No. 35	0.289	18.04	0	32	....	0.051	**0.4355**	2.294	Poensgen
No. 36	0.301	18.80	0	32	....	0.0435	**0.351**	2.85	Poensgen
No. 37	0.324	20.22	0	32	....	0.046	**0.371**	2.7	Poensgen
			0	32	....	0.039	**0.3145**	3.18	
			15	59	....	0.048	**0.387**	2.584	
No. 38	0.335	20.91	25	77	....	0.054	**0.4355**	2.294	Nusselt (cube)
			35	95	....	0.057	**0.460**	2.173	
			45	113	....	0.059	**0.476**	2.10	
			0	32	0.1528	0.055	**0.444**	2.25	
No. 39	0.350	21.85	10	50	0.1556	0.056	**0.452**	2.21	Poensgen
			25	77	0.1584	0.057	**0.460**	2.17	
			60	140	0.1611	0.058	**0.468**	2.137	
No. 40	0.354	22.10	0	32	0.1528	0.055	**0.444**	2.25	Poensgen
No. 41	0.434	27.10	0	32	0.175	0.063	**0.508**	1.97	Poensgen
No. 42	0.483	30.17	0	32	0.2612	0.094	**0.758**	1.328	Poensgen
No. 43			10	50	0.1556	0.056	**0.452**	2.21	Poensgen
Corkboard 2.56 inch thick, coated with 0.197 inch cement each side	0.446	27.85	15	59	0.1611	0.058	**0.468**	2.138	(plate with guard ring)
			50	122	0.1639	0.059	**0.476**	2.10	
Corkboard substitute ("Korkersatzplatten")	0.24 to 0.35	15 to 21.85	0	32	0.133 to 0.175	0.048 to 0.063	**0.387** to **0.508**	2.58 to 1.97	Hencky
			20	68	0.139 to 0.18	0.05 to 0.065	**0.404** to **0.524**	2.45 to 1.91	
Same, heavier	0.48	30.0	0	32	0.2445	0.088	**0.710**	1.408	Hencky
			20	68	0.250	0.090	**0.726**	1.377	

French corkboard tests reported by A. Desvignes, First International Congress of Refrigeration, Paris, 1908, and by R. Biquard, Laboratory of Physics at the Conservatoire des Arts et Métiers, First French Congress, Toulouse, and Second International Congress of Refrigeration, Vienna, 1910. Temperatures given are mean temperatures of samples under test. Approximate range 60° to 100° C.

THERMAL CONDUCTIVITY OF MATERIALS CONSISTING MAINLY OF VEGETABLE MATTER—*Continued*

A. S. R. E. Insulation Committee Report, Revised 1924

MATERIAL	Density: Grams per cu. cm. (Specific gravity)	Density: Pounds per cu. ft.	Temp. of Sample, mean or range: °C.	Temp. of Sample, mean or range: °F.	Thermal Conductivity: Gram Calorie, sec., cm.^{3} deg. C. x 1000	Thermal Conductivity: Kg. Calorie hour, m^3, deg. C.	Thermal Conductivity: B.t.u. hour, sq. ft., 1 in. °F Commercial conductivity	Resistance per inch thickness (R) $\frac{1}{\text{Col. 8}}$	Authority
COLUMN 1	2	3	4	5	6	7	8	9	10
Corkboard (without foreign binder)	0.175	10.92	75.4	167.6	0.1873	0.0674	**0.544**	1.84	Desvignes
Cork, granulated, compounded with silicate of soda	0.195	12.16	76.4	1695.5	0.1873	0.0674	**0.544**	1.84	Desvignes
Cork, granulated, conglomerated with caseine	0.203	12.67	75.2	167.4	....	0.0689	**0.556**	1.8	Desvignes
Cork, granulated, conglomerated with odorless pitch	0.270	16.87	77.7	172	....	0.0874	**0.705**	1.418	Desvignes
Cork, granulated, mixed with diatomite and calcined	0.318	19.85	79.8	175.6	....	0.0888	**0.7165**	1.395	Desvignes
Corkboard, impregnated with pitch	0.275	17.17	15	59	....	0.052	**0.4195**	2.384	Biquard
Same, damp	0.310	19.34	15	59	....	0.076	**0.613**	1.631	Biquard
Cork, granulated (slab), conglomerated with caseine (sample 3.94 in. thick)	0.148	9.24	5 15 30	41 59 86	....	0.042 0.0437 0.0477	**0.3387** **0.3525** **0.385**	2.95 2.837 2.6	Biquard
Same, after 20 days immersion in water (swelling 4%)	0.280	17.48	7.5 20	45.5 68	....	0.082 0.093	**0.6615** **0.750**	1.511 1.333	Biquard
Same, dry, surface coated with rosin. Sample 3.94 in. thick	0.185	11.55	30	86	....	0.049	**0.3953**	2.53	Biquard
Sample 7.08 in. thick	0.275	17.17	5 15 30	41 59 86	....	0.049 0.052 0.057	**0.3953** **0.4195** **0.460**	2.53 2.384 2.173	Biquard
Sample 4.72 in. thick	0.285	17.79	5 15 30	41 59 86	....	0.0495 0.053 0.0585	**0.3995** **0.4275** **0.472**	2.504 2.34 2.12	Biquard
Sample 5.90 in. thick	0.275	17.17	5 15 30	41 59 86	....	0.049 0.053 0.058	**0.3953** **0.4275** **0.468**	2.53 2.34 2.138	Biquard
Same, after 20 days immersion in water, 7.08 in. thick	0.310	19.34	7.5 20	45.5 68	....	0.073 0.078	**0.589** **0.629**	1.70 1.59	Biquard

Tests of some British corkboard conducted at the National Physical Laboratory, London, given in Special Report No. 5 of Food Investigation Board of Great Britain. "*Ice and Cold Storage*," London, Feb., 1922.

THERMAL CONDUCTIVITY OF MATERIALS CONSISTING MAINLY OF VEGETABLE MATTER—*Continued*

A. S. R. E. Insulation Committee Report, Revised 1924

Cork slab, baked—			Face temp.	range					
Sample No. 1, from a warship after 10 years' service. Mean temperature = m			27–58 tm. 40	80–128 tm. 104	0.102	0.0367	**0.296**	3.38	
Sample No. 2			−8–+10 tm. 1	16–50 tm. 33	0.105	0.0378	**0.305**	3.28	Dr. Ezer Griffiths, Senior Assistant, Heat Division, British National Physical Laboratory. (Refrigerating World, April, 1922)
			19–37 tm. 28	66–98 tm. 82	0.1 7	0.0385	**0.3105**	3.22	
Sample No. 3			22–96 tm. 58	70–204 tm. 136	0.117	0.0421	**0.3395**	2.947	
			13–25 tm. 20	55–77 tm. 68	0.113	0.0407	**0.328**	3.05	
			−14.5–−1.7 tm. −8	6–29 tm. 17.6	0.114	0.0410	**0.331**	3.02	
Cork Plaster			−7.5–6 tm. −1	18–42 tm. 30	0.135	0.0486	**0.392**	2.552	
Corkboard made in United States. Tested at United States Bureau of Standards, Washington, D. C. Paper by M. S. Van Dusen, *A. S. R. E. Journal*, Nov., 1920.									
Corkboard. No artificial binder used. Low density. Values for c below 86 and above 150°F. extrapolated from straight line curve	0.1105	6.9	0	32	0.0860	0.03096	**0.2497**	4.005	Bureau of Standards
			10	50	0.08825	0.03177	**0.2562**	3.9	
			20	68	0.0905	0.03258	**0.2628**	3.806	
			30	86	0.09275	0.0334	**0.2693**	3.713	
			40	104	0.0950	0.0342	**0.2759**	3.623	
			60	140	0.0995	0.0358	**0.2888**	3.462	
			80	176	0.1040	0.03743	**0.3020**	3.313	
Same, more dense	0.16	9.98	30	86	0.104	0.03743	**0.302**	3.313	Bureau of Standards
Same, still more dense	0.18	11.24	30	86	0.106	0.03818	**0.308**	3.246	Bureau of Standards
Same, high density. Values for c below 86 and above 150°F. extrapolated from straight line curve	0.224	14	0	32	0.109	0.0392	**0.3165**	3.158	Bureau of Standards
			10	50	0.11112	0.040	**0.3224**	3.10	
			20	68	0.11325	0.0408	**0.3287**	3.042	
			30	86	0.11537	0.0415	**0.3347**	2.988	
			40	104	0.11750	0.0423	**0.341**	2.933	
			60	140	0.12175	0.0438	**0.3535**	2.83	
			80	176	0.1260	0.0453	**0.366**	2.733	
Corkboard, "Nonpareil." (Has no artificial binder). Thickness tested 2.03 in. (in 1917)	0.156	9.74					**0.29** to **0.32**	3.45 to 3.125	Willard & Lichty
Corkboard, "Nonpareil" (average weight, 9 lb./cu. ft.) No kiln drying hotbox method. Note unusually rapid increase in c. (0.001473 B.t.u. per °F. rise in tm.). Face temperatures given.	0.1442	9	13.1	42–69 tm. 55.5	Test: 8–28	1919	**0.300**	3.333	A. J. Wood and E. F. Grundhofer, Pa. State College Exp. Bull. No. 30, May, 1920
			22.8	44–102 tm. 73	7–9	1919	**0.3276**	3.055	
			31.1	46–131 tm. 88.5	7–7	1919	**0.3486**	2.870	

THERMAL CONDUCTIVITY OF MATERIALS CONSISTING MAINLY OF VEGETABLE MATTER—*Continued*

A. S. R. E. Insulation Committee Report, Revised 1924

MATERIAL	Density		Temp. of Sample, mean or range		Thermal Conductivity			Resistance per inch thickness (R) 1/Col. 8	Authority
	Grams per cu. cm. (Specific gravity)	Pounds per cu. ft.	°C.	°F.	Gram Calorie, sec., cm.^{3} deg. C. x 1000	Kg. Calorie hour, m^3, deg. C.	B.t.u. hour, sq. ft., 1 in. °F Commercial conductivity		
Column 1	2	3	4	5	6	7	8	9	10
Corkboard, without foreign binder, 1 in. thick	......	......			0.118	0.0425	0.344	2.908	Bureau of Standards 1919 according to Sam. Cabot, Boston, Mass.
Corkboard, without foreign binder. No kiln drying before test. Hotbox in cold room. (Increase in c is 0.00150 B. t. u. per °F. rise in tm.)	......	......	7.5	39–60 tm. 45.5	Test: 17-4-3	......	0.360	2.78	R. B. Fehr, Pa. State College Exp. Bull. No. 24, Feb., 1918
			13.1	39–72 tm. 55.5	17-4-4a	......	0.369	2.71	
			19.7	38–97 tm. 67.5	17-4-4b	......	0.390	2.565	
			20.8	29–110 tm. 69.5	17-4-5a	......	0.396	2.526	
Corkboard with bituminous binder	0.25	15.6	30	86	0.121	0.0436	0.3513	2.849	Bureau of Standards
"Universal Insulite," pressed wood pulp board, labeled "waterproofed," offered as wall board, ¼ and ½ in. thick	0.19	11.86	30	86	0.102	0.0367	0.2963	3.376	Bureau of Standards
"Lyxnayr" (waste fibre from bark of eucalyptus tree, used in place of animal hair). Normal moisture content 12%. After 24 hrs. immersion in water a further 66% of its own weight is absorbed. Carbonizing starts at 302°F. (150°C.)	......	......	−12 to +12	10 to 54	0.107	0.0385	0.3105	3.22	Griffiths
Celotex insulating lumber, 7/16 in. thick. A wall board; made from bagasse (sugar cane waste). Wood fibres and binder	0.2635	16.45	......	......	0.1137	0.0409	0.33	3.03	Geo. F. Gebhardt, Chicago (plate), Sweet's Cat., 1922
Upson processed wall board, made of ground wood and chemical fibre (cellulose). Mat pebbled surface. Thicknesses, ⅛ to ⅜ in.	Compares with Rigid. Not		Celotex as regards moisture proof.		weight and conductivity (per inch thickness).				

THERMAL CONDUCTIVITY OF MATERIALS CONSISTING MAINLY OF VEGETABLE MATTER—*Continued*

A. S. R. E. Insulation Committee Report, Revised 1923

Cornell-Wood-Board, of ground wood (paper) pulp, oatmeal finish, 3/16 in. thick; rigid. Not moisture proof.	0.458	28.5	......	......	0.1721	0.062	**0.50**	2.00	Herter c estimated
NOTE—Owing to their thinness wall boards are not effective as insulators. It is the film of air on either side that provides a moderate insulating effect.									
"Beaver Board." A 4-ply, all spruce fibre wall Board, 3/16 in. thick	0.5	31	......	......	0.333	0.12	**0.968**	1.033	Herter c estimated
Linofelt. Flax fibre confined with (either Kraft or waterproofed) paper, 3/8 to 3/4 in. thick. Flexible and soft	0.18	11.24	30	86	0.103	0.0371	**0.299**	3.341	Bureau of Standards
Cotton seed hull fibre, loosely packed	0.071	4.43	30	86	0.108	0.0389	**0.314**	3.184	Bureau of Standards
Straw fibres, pressed	0.139	8.675	0	32	0.1084	0.039	**0.3146**	3.18	Knoblauch
			20	68	0.1111	0.040	**0.3225**	3.10	
Cabot's car quilt No. 1. Eel grass enclosed in burlap. Thickness, 0.83 in	0.25	15.6	30	86	0.108	0.0389	**0.314**	3.184	Sam. Cabot
			30	86	0.11	0.0396	**0.3193**	3.133	Bureau of Standards
Car quilt (Asb.) No. 2. Thickness, 0.87 in	......	......	30	86	0.114	0.041	**0.331**	3.02	Bureau of Standards for Cabot, 1919
Car quilt No. 3x. Thickness, 0.87 in	......	......	30	86	0.115	0.0414	**0.334**	2.99	Bureau of Standards for Cabot
Fibrofelt. Felted vegetable fibres, 3/8 to 1 in. thick, flexible	0.18	11.24	30	86	0.113	0.0407	**0.328**	3.05	Bureau of Standards
Flaxlinum. Felted flax fibres, 3/4 to 1 in. thick; semi rigid	0.18	11.24	30	86	0.113	0.0407	**0.328**	3.05	Bureau of Standards
Flax and Paper Lining for insulating steel railway cars—									
Sample No. and Thickness — Actual Thickness									
U2, 3/4" — 0.79					0.119	0.0428	**0.346**	2.89	
U4, 1/2" — 0.512					0.123	0.0443	**0.357**	2.80	Tests by
U4, 3/4" — 0.83	......	......	usually	about	0.124	0.0446	**0.360**	2.773	Bureau of Standards
U4, 1/4" — 0.374			30	86	0.126	0.0454	**0.366**	2.73	in 1919
U1, 1" — 1.14			mean	temp.	0.129	0.0464	**0.374**	2.67	according to
U7, 1" — 0.98					0.131	0.04415	**0.380**	2.63	Sam. Cabot
U5, 1/4" — 0.452					0.146	0.0525	**0.424**	2.358	Boston, Mass.
U6, 1/4" — 0.492					0.157	0.0565	**0.456**	2.19	
Burrash, confined with cloth	0.14	8.74	30	86	0.116	0.0418	**0.3367**	2.97	Bureau of Standards
Peat ("Torfmull")	......	......	0	32	0.111	0.04	**0.3224**	3.10	Nusselt
			20	68	0.1138	0.041	**0.3307**	3.02	

THERMAL CONDUCTIVITY OF MATERIALS CONSISTING MAINLY OF VEGETABLE MATTER—*Continued*

A. S. R. E. Insulation Committee Report, Revised 1924

MATERIAL	Density		Temp. of Sample, mean or range		Thermal Conductivity			Resistance per inch thickness (R) 1/Col. 8	Authority
	Grams per cu. cm. (Specific gravity)	Pounds per cu. ft.	°C.	°F.	Gram Calorie, sec., cm.², deg. C. x 1000	Kg. Calorie hour, m², deg. C.	B.t.u hour, sq. ft., 1 in. °F Commercial conductivity		
COLUMN 1	2	3	4	5	6	7	8	9	10
Peat ("Torfmull"), dry	0.190	11.85	20	68	0.1138	0.041	**0.3307**	3.02	Nusselt
			20	68	0.1668	0.060	**0.484**	2.068	
Peat, moisture content about 50%	0.160	9.98	50 dry	122	0.125	0.045	**0.363**	2.755	
			25 damp	77	0.1528	0.055	**0.444**	2.252	
Peat ("Torfmull"), exceedingly hygroscopic. Absorbs 25 to 30% moisture from air	0.190	11.85	50 dry	122	0.125	0.045	**0.363**	2.755	Nusselt, 1908 (Sphere)
			25 damp	77	0.1445	0.052	**0.419**	2.387	
	0.195	12.17	40 dry	104	0.125	0.045	**0.363**	2.755	
			20 damp	68	0.1945	0.070	**0.564**	1.772	
Peat boards, light	0.230	14.35	0	32	0.1362	0.049	**0.395**	2.53	Henckу
			20	68	0.1389	0.050	**0.403**	2.48	
Peat boards, medium	0.370	23.1	0	32	0.2028	0.073	**0.5886**	1.698	Hencky
			20	68	0.2082	0.075	**0.605**	1.653	
Peat boards, hard, as floor tiles	0.730	45.6	0	32	0.264	0.095	**0.766**	1.305	Hencky
			20	68	0.2788	0.100	**0.8064**	1.239	
Peat dust, Holland, dry	0.201	12.54	78.2	173	0.2087	0.0751	**0.606**	1.65	Desvignes
	......	......	−8 – +1 tm. −2	17–39 tm. 28	0.225	0.081	**0.653**	1.532	
Cellular bricks, made up of cardboard (Sir Alfred Ewing's design)	......	......	13–21 tm. 17	55–70 tm. 63	0.236	0.0819	**0.685**	1.46	Griffiths
	......	......	38–82 tm. 69	100–180 tm. 140	0.282	0.1015	**0.818**	1.222	
Strawboard	......	......	......	......	0.33	0.1187	**0.9575**	1.044	Barratt
Strawboard, paste board	......	......	......	below 32	0.453	0.1631	**1.316**	0.76	Forbes
Charcoal, Sample No. 1	......	......	−11–46 tm. 17	12.2–115 tm. 53.6	0.120	0.0432	**0.348**	2.873	Griffiths
	......	......	−15– +5 tm. −5	7–41 tm. 22	0.120	0.0432	**0.348**	2.873	
Sample No. 2	......	......	−13–9 tm. −2	8–48 tm. 28	0.127	0.0457	**0.369**	2.71	Griffiths
Charcoal, loose	0.184	11.48	15	59	......	0.045	**0.363**	2.755	Biquard
Charcoal, composition slab	0.230	14.36	15	59	......	0.046	**0.3712**	2.695	Biquard

THERMAL CONDUCTIVITY OF MATERIALS CONSISTING MAINLY OF VEGETABLE MATTER—*Continued*

A. S. R. E. Insulation Committee Report, Revised 1924

Charcoal flakes, Cartvale, and binder, in board form ("Iris-Platte," German)	0.204	12.74	20	68	0.1334	0.048	**0.3873**	2.582	Knoblauch & Poensgen
			50	122	....	0.049	**0.3953**	2.53	
Charcoal flakes Cartvale, loose	0.185	11.55	25	77	....	0.052	**0.4195**	2.385	Knoblauch & Poensgen, 1912
Flake charcoal	0.190	11.85	0	32	0.1389	0.050	**0.403**	2.48	Nusselt, 1908
			40	104	0.1556	0.056	**0.452**	2.212	
			80	176	0.175	0.063	**0.508**	1.969	
Charcoal flakes	0.241	15.04	77.9	172.2	0.2098	0.0755	**0.609**	1.642	Desvignes
Charcoal, granulated, 0.04 to 0.39 in., sifted	0.242	15.1	78.7	173.7	0.244	0.0878	**0.708**	1.412	Desvignes
Sponge rubber (used in upholstery). Vulcanizing rubber mixed with ammonium carbonate; cells broken. Sample 1 in. thick	0.224	14	....	...	0.13	0.0468	**0.3775**	2.65	Griffiths
Waterproofed Lith board; mineral wool; vegetable fibres, and waterproofing binder. Rigid	0.20	12.5	30	86	0.131	0.0472	**0.3802**	2.630	Bureau of Standards
Wood felt. Flexible paper stock	0.33	20.6	30	86	0.125	0.0450	**0.363**	2.755	Bureau of Standards
Cardboard, corrugated packing; 35 layers of 0.1969 in. = or total 6.88 in. thick	....	....	7.5	45.5	....	0.048	**0.387**	2.583	Biquard
			15	59	....	0.052	**0.4195**	2.385	
			20	68	....	0.054	**0.436**	2.292	
			30	86	....	0.060	**0.484**	2.068	
Blotting paper	....	....	....	...	0.15	0.054	**0.435**	2.294	Lees & Chorlton
Wall pulp board; stiff paste board	0.69	43.0	30	86	0.17	0.0612	**0.494**	2.066	Bureau of Standards
Corkment linoleum, dry (soft, elastic, insulating lining under regular linoleum), 0.36 in. thick	0.535	33.4	20	68	0.01918	0.069	**0.5565**	1.797	Groeber (plate)
WOODS									
Fir sawdust, compressed	....	....	....	...	0.123	0.04425	**0.357**	2.8	Forbes
Planer Shavings, various	0.14	8.74	30	86	0.14	0.0504	**0.4063**	2.46	Bureau of Standards
Sawdust, various	0.19	11.86	30	86	0.14	0.0504	**0.4063**	2.46	Bureau of Standards
Sawdust, uniform, free from ships; dry	0.215	13.425	0	32	0.1668	0.060	**0.484**	2.067	Nusselt
			20	68	0.1721	0.062	**0.500**	2.000	
Sawdust, pine. fine, dry, loose	0.025	1.56	74.5	166	0.196	0.0706	**0.57**	1.754	Desvignes
Sawdust, pine, fine, dry	0.058	3.62	77.6	171.7	0.2089	0.0752	**0.606**	1.65	Desvignes
Ceiba wood, across grain, untreated	0.113	7.05	30	86	0.113	0.0407	**0.328**	3.05	Bureau of Standards
Balsa wood, across grain, very light; untreated	0.113	7.05	30	86	0.107	0.0385	**0.3105**	3.22	Bureau of Standards
Same sample, but with 13% waterproofing cpd.	0.128	7.98	30	86	0.119	0.0428	**0.3455**	2.895	Bureau of Standards
Balsa wood, across grain, untreated	0.118	7.36	30	86	0.119	0.0428	**0.3455**	2.895	Bureau of Standards
Balsa wood—									
Sample D 0.512 in., treated					0.121	0.0436	**0.3517**	2.84	Bureau of Standards, 1919 for Welin Marine Equipment Co., Long Island City, New York (accord. to Sam. Cabot, Inc., Boston, Mass.)
Sample D 0.472 in., untreated					0.122	0.0439	**0.354**	2.82	
Sample B 0.764 in., treated					0.133	0.0479	**0.386**	2.59	
Sample B 0.759 in., untreated	....		30	86	0.136	0.049	**0.395**	2.53	
Sample B 0.280 in., untreated					0.139	0.050	**0.404**	2.47	
Sample E 0.280 in., treated					0.146	0.0525	**0.424**	2.357	
Sample A 0.76 in., treated					0.146	0.0525	**0.424**	2.357	

THERMAL CONDUCTIVITY OF MATERIALS CONSISTING MAINLY OF VEGETABLE MATTER—*Continued*

A. S. R. E. Insulation Committee Report, Revised 1924

MATERIAL	Density		Temp. of Sample, mean or range		Thermal Conductivity			Resistance per inch thickness (R) $\frac{1}{\text{Col. 8}}$	Authority
	Grams per cu. cm. (Specific gravity)	Pounds per cu. ft.	°C.	°F.	Gram Calorie, sec., cm.[3] deg. C. x 1000	Kg. Calorie hour, m[3], deg. C.	B.t.u. hour, sq. ft., 1 in. °F Commercial conductivity		
COLUMN 1	2	3	4	5	6	7	8	9	10
Balsa wood, medium weight	0.143	8.93	30	86	0.132	0.0475	**0.383**	2.61	Bureau of Standards
Balsa wood, heavy	0.33	20.6	.....	.....	0.200	0.072	**0.581**	1.721	Bureau of Standards
Cypress, across grain	0.46	28.7	30	86	0.23	0.0828	**0.668**	1.497	Bureau of Standards
Fir, pine, across grain	.....	.....	.....	.....	0.088	0.03165	**0.2555**	3.917	Forbes
Fir, pine, along grain	.....	.....	.....	.....	0.30	0.108	**0.8715**	1.148	Forbes
Fir, across grain; thickness tested, 1.06 in.	0.534	33.37	.....		0.306 to 0.348	0.1104 to 0.1252	**0.89 to 1.01**	1.124 to 0.99	Willard & Lichty
Fir, dry, across grain (Kiefernholz)	0.546	34.1	0 15 30	32 59 86	0.333 0.361 0.3888	0.12 0.13 0.14	**0.968** **1.048** **1.130**	1.034 0.954 0.885	Poensgen (plate with guard ring)
Fir, dry, along grain	0.551	34.4	20 25	68 77	0.8335 0.888	0.30 0.32	**2.42** **2.582**	0.413 0.3873	Poensgen (plate with guard ring)
White pine, across grain	0.50	31.2	30	86	0.27	0.0972	**0.784**	1.275	Bureau of Standards
White pine, across grain; thickness of sample, 0.519 in.	0.45	28.1	20–120	68–248	0.255	0.0918	**0.74**	1.352	Taylor
White pine, along grain; thickness of sample, 0.732 in.	0.45	28.1	30–80	86–176	0.613	0.2208	**1.78**	0.562	Taylor
White pine, across grain, "Swedish deal," dry	0.407	25.53	82.6	181	.....	0.1194	**0.964**	1.037	Desvignes
Virginia pine, across grain	0.55	34.3	30	86	0.33	0.1188	**0.958**	1.044	Bureau of Standards
Pitch pine, good quality, across grain	.....	.....	20–32 tm. 26	67–91 tm. 79	0.357	0.1285	**1.036**	0.965	Griffiths
Yellow pine, across grain	.....	.....	.....	.....	0.36	0.1295	**1.045**	0.957	Bacon
Mahogany, across grain	0.55	34.3	30	86	0.31	0.1116	**0.900**	1.111	Bureau of Standards
Mahogany	0.55	34.3	20 100	68 212	0.51 0.60	0.1838 0.216	**1.482** **1.743**	0.675 0.573	Barratt
White wood	0.58	36.2	20 100	68 212	0.41 0.45	0.1475 0.162	**1.190** **1.307**	0.84 0.765	Barratt
Boxwood	0.90	56.2	20 100	68 212	0.36 0.41	0.1295 0.1475	**1.045** **1.190**	0.957 0.84	Barratt

THERMAL CONDUCTIVITY OF MATERIALS CONSISTING MAINLY OF VEGETABLE MATTER—*Continued*

A. S. R. E. Insulation Committee Report, Revised 1924

Teak wood, dry, across grain	0.642	40.5	0	32	0.3888	0.14	**1.130**	0.885	Poensgen
			15	59	0.4167	0.15	**1.21**	0.826	
			50	122	0.472	0.17	**1.372**	0.728	
Teak wood, dry, along grain	0.604	37.7	12	53.6	0.888	0.32	**2.582**	0.3873	Poensgen
			18	64.4	0.917	0.33	**2.663**	0.3755	
			50	122	0.945	0.34	**2.743**	0.3645	
Teak wood, across grain					0.64	0.2306	**1.86**	0.538	Bacon
Oak, across grain	0.61	38	30	86	0.35	0.126	**1.016**	0.985	Bureau of Standards
White oak, across grain; thickness of sample, 0.516 in.	0.60	37.45	20–80	68–176	0.455	0.164	**1.3215**	0.7565	Taylor
White oak, along grain; thickness of sample, 0.754 in.	0.60	37.45	40–70	104–158	0.944	0.3397	**2.74**	0.365	Taylor
Oak, dry, across grain	0.825	51.5	0	32	0.472	0.17	**1.372**	0.728	Poensgen
			15	59	0.500	0.18	**1.452**	0.689	
Oak, dry, along grain	0.819	51.1	12	53.6	0.834	0.30	**2.42**	0.413	Poensgen
			20	68	0.861	0.31	**2.50**	0.40	
			50	122	1.0275	0.37	**2.985**	0.335	
Oak	0.65	40.55	20	68	0.58	0.2089	**1.686**	0.5934	Barratt
			100	212	0.61	0.2197	**1.772**	0.564	
Maple, across grain	0.71	44.3	30	86	0.38	0.1367	**1.1025**	0.907	Bureau of Standards
Maple, across grain; thickness of sample, 0.508 in.	0.72	44.9	20–80	68–176	0.434	0.1562	**1.26**	0.794	Taylor
Same, along grain, 0.733 in.	0.72	44.9	20	68	1.015	0.3654	**2.948**	0.3393	Taylor
			20–80	68–176	1.037	0.3733	**3.012**	0.332	
Lignum vitae	1.16	72.4	20	68	0.60	0.216	**1.743**	0.573	Barratt
			100	212	0.72	0.2592	**2.092**	0.478	
Greenhart	1.08	67.4	20	68	1.12	0.403	**3.25**	0.3073	Barratt
			100	212	1.10	0.396	**3.195**	0.3126	
Cellulose, compressed	1.425	88.9	15	59	0.583	0.210	**1.694**	0.59	Biquard
ARTIFICIAL WOODS									
Zenitherm C 28 (granulated cork, magnesite and binder, firm, fire resistive)	0.28	17.5	20	68	0.1528	0.055	**0.444**	2.25	Herter *c* estimated
Zenitherm S 75 (small wood chips, magnesite and binder, fire resistive; a substitute for Travertine stone)	1.10	68.6	20	68	0.448	0.0992	**1.3**	0.77	Herter *c* estimated
Composition board, dry ("Sperrholz")	0.588	36.7	0	32	0.2611	0.094	**0.7577**	1.32	Hencky
			20	68	0.2721	0.098	**0.790**	1.265	
Cement wood (sawdust and Portland Cement) dry	0.715	44.6	0	32	0.3057	0.11	**0.8875**	1.127	Nusselt
			20	68	0.333	0.12	**0.968**	1.033	
Cement wood, 11% by vol. moisture. Slabs 30x70 cm., 2, 4 and 6 cm. thick; fire resistive; made 1910 in Austria	0.824	51.4	20	68	0.4167	0.15	**1.210**	0.8265	Nusselt

THERMAL CONDUCTIVITY OF MATERIALS CONSISTING MAINLY OF VEGETABLE MATTER—*Continued*

A. S. R. E. Insulation Committee Report, Revised 1924

MATERIAL	Density		Temp. of Sample, mean or range		Thermal Conductivity			Resistance per inch thickness (R) 1 / Col. 8	Authority
	Grams per cu. cm. (Specific gravity)	Pounds per cu. ft.	°C.	°F.	Gram Calorie, sec., cm.², deg. C x 1000	Kg. Calorie hour, m², deg. C.	B.t.u. hour, sq. ft., 1 in. °F Commercial conductivity		
COLUMN 1	2	3	4	5	6	7	8	9	10
"Ebonize"	1.19	74.25	20	68	0.14	0.0504	**0.4063**	2.46	Barratt
			100	212	0.13	0.0468	**0.3776**	2.65	
Textan Rubber composition	1.3	81.0	30	86	0.40	0.144	**1.162**	0.861	Bureau of Standards
Rubber, hard; sample 0.38 in. thick	1.19	74.3	25–50	77–122	0.380	0.1368	**1.1035**	0.907	Taylor
Rubber, soft, vulcanized	...	...	...	...	0.34 to 0.54	0.1224 to 0.1944	**0.987 to 1.57**	1.013 to 0.637	H-L-D
Rubber, soft, vulcanized	1.1	68.6	30	86	0.42	0.1511	**1.218**	0.8215	Bureau of Standards
Linoleum, dry (0.29 in. thick)	1.183	73.8	0	32	0.4167	0.15	**1.21**	0.826	Groeber
			20	68	0.4443	0.16	**1.291**	0.775	
Celluloid, white	1.4	87.3	30	86	0.50	0.180	**1.452**	0.6886	Bureau of Standards
Fibre, white, sample 0.383 in. thick	1.22	76.2	20	68	0.663	0.2388	**1.926**	0.5195	Taylor
			20–80	68–176	0.695	0.2503	**2.018**	0.496	
Fibre, red	1.29	80.5	20	68	1.12	0.403	**3.25**	0.308	Barratt
			100	212	1.19	0.428	**3.452**	0.290	
Linen, coarse	...	...	...	below 32	0.0298	0.01073	**0.0865**	11.56	Forbes
Linen				...	0.21	0.0756	**0.610**	1.64	Lees & Chorlton

THERMAL CONDUCTIVITY OF MATERIALS COMPOSED MAINLY OF MINERAL MATTER

A. S. R. E. Insulation Committee Report, Revised 1924

"Calorox." Fluffy, finely divided mineral matter	0.064	4.0	30	86	0.076	0.02735	**0.2207**	4.533	Bureau of Standards, Washington, D. C. 1919
Lampblack, Cabot's No. 5	0.193	12.05	10–100 10–300 10–500	50–212 50–572 50–932	0.0755 0.0924 0.1088	0.0272 0.03325 0.0392	**0.2192** **0.2683** **0.316**	4.56 3.726 1.00	Randolph[1], 1912
Lava (Vulcanite)	....	....	....	below 32	0.0833	0.030	**0.242**	4.133	Forbes
Lava	....	....	16–99	61–210	2.01	0.7235	**5.83**	0.1716	F. Morano, 1898
"Poplox", made from $Na_2 Si O_3$ (water glass) by popping (twice over). Resembles popcorn. Size, pinhead. Settles	0.023	1.436	10–200 10–300	50–392 50–572	0.09715 0.134	0.03497 0.04823	**0.282** **0.389**	3.545 2.570	Randolph[1]
"Poplox." Dried at 932°F	0.093	5.80	10–200 10–300 10–400 10–500	50–392 50–572 50–752 50–932	0.0919 0.09975 0.1216 0.1718	0.03308 0.03592 0.0438 0.0584	**0.267** **0.2897** **0.3532** **0.4706**	3.743 3.453 2.831 2.124	Randolph[1]
Mineral (slag) wool. Loosely packed	0.192	12.0	30	86	0.090	0.0324	**0.2614**	3.824	Bureau of Standards
Mineral (slag) wool. Medium packed	0.20	12.5	30	86	0.095	0.0342	**0.2760**	3.62	Bureau of Standards
Mineral wool. Felted in blocks. Fibres perpendicular to heat flow	0.29	18.1	30	86	0.099	0.03562	**0.2875**	3.48	Bureau of Standards
Mineral wool. Firmly packed	0.34	21.2	30	86	0.102	0.03672	**0.2961**	3.377	Bureau of Standards
Mineral wool, from Eimer & Amend, N. Y. Dried at 662°F	0.427	26.66	10–500	50–932	0.1667	0.0600	**0.484**	2.064	Randolph[1]
Slag wool (British)—									
Sample No. 1	..	about 13	−16–18	4–64	0.104	0.03744	**0.302**	3.312	Griffiths
Sample No 2	..	about 21	−15–1	6–33	0.100	0.036	**0.290**	3.448	Griffiths
Sample No. 3, after 14 years service in warship	......	....	−6–+6	21–42	0.121	0.04356	**0.353**	2.833	Griffiths
Sample No. 4, greatly deteriorated by vibrations		...	−11–+8	10–48	0.145	0.0522	**0.422**	2.37	Griffiths
Sample No. 5, "felted to mats with organic binder"			−8–+6 21–33	18–42 70–92	0.105 0.112	0.0378 0.04033	**0.305** **0.327**	3.28 3.06	Griffiths
"Rock Cork" mineral wool, binder and waterproofing; rigid; high density	0.25	15.6	30	86	0.113	0.0407	**0.328**	3.067	Bureau of Standards
Silicate cotton	0.137	8.55	75.7	168.3	0.2009	0.0723	**0.583**	1.716	Desvignes
ASBESTOS									
Asbestos sponge—felt, asbestos, paper layers, 41 per inch thickness, enclosing finely ground sponge; for high prdssure steam. Dried at 302°F. before test	....	....	10–100 10–200	50–212 50–392	0.09364 0.1018	0.0337 0.0390	**0.272** **0.3143**	3.68 3.18	Randolph[1]
Same, without drying	0.38	23.7	70	158	0.1613	0.058	**0.468**	2.137	McMillan
"Sheet asbestos," 60 sheets $\frac{1}{64}$ in. thick; thickness tested, 1.1 in	0.7735	48.25	....	. .	....		**0.27** to **0.31**	3.705 to 3.227	Willard & Lichty

[1]The conductivities given by Randolph are the mean values between the given temperature and about 10° C. (50 deg. F.) Note effect of compression (density).

THERMAL CONDUCTIVITY OF MATERIALS COMPOSED MAINLY OF MINERAL MATTER—*Continued*

A. S. R. E. Insulation Committee Report, Revised 1924

MATERIAL	Density: Grams per cu. cm. (Specific gravity)	Density: Pounds per cu. ft.	Temp. of Sample, mean or range: °C.	Temp. of Sample, mean or range: °F.	Thermal Conductivity: Gram Calorie, sec., cm.³ deg. C. x 1000	Thermal Conductivity: Kg. Calorie hour, m², deg. C.	Thermal Conductivity: B.t.u. hour, sq. ft., 1 in. °F Commercial conductivity	Resistance per inch thickness (R) 1/Col. 8	Authority
Column 1	2	3	4	5	6	7	8	9	10
Asbestos paper, built up of thin layers, with organic binder	0.50	31.2	30	86	0.17	0.0612	**0.494**	2.024	Bureau of Standards
Asbestos paper	....	......		......	0.43	0.1549	**1.249**	0.8005	Lees & Chorlton
Asbestos fire-felt, very light, but self-sustaining	0.116	7.24	10–200	50–392	0.1085	0.03905	**0.3148**	3.174	Randolph[1]
			10–300	50–572	0.1601	0.0576	**0.4648**	2.151	
			10–400	50–752	0.1998	0.06837	**0.5513**	1.814	
Asbestos car lining— Thickness Nom. 1/8", Actual 0.221", Rated 0.36 lb. sq. ft.	0.434	27.1	....	......	0.143	0.0514	**0.415**	2.41	Bureau of Standards 1919, according to Sam Cabot, Boston, Mass.
Nom. 1/4", Actual 0.319", Rated 0.72 lb.					0.160	0.0576	**0.464**	2.156	
Nom. 3/8", Actual 0.437", Rated 1.06 lb.					0.170	0.0612	**0.494**	2.024	
Nom. 3/16", Actual 0.287", Rated 0.54 lb.					0.170	0.0612	**0.494**	2.024	
Nom. 1/2", Actual 0.543", Rated 1.40 lb.					0.172	0.0619	**0.499**	2.005	
"Zenitherm" boiler covering block (infusorial earth and asbestos fibres) made 1917 to 1920	0.26	16.2	30	86	0.17	0.0612	[1] **0.494**	2.026	Bureau of Standards
Magnesia, 85%, and asbestos (no forced drying)	0.216	13.48	10–100	50–212	0.162	0.0583	**0.47**	2.128	Randolph[1]
			10–400	50–572	0.1671	0.06016	**0.485**	2.061	
			10–600	50–1112	0.1983	0.714	**0.576**	1.737	
Magnesia	....	....	....	.	0.16 to 0.45	0.0575 to 0.162	**0.464** to **1.307**	2.155 to 0.765	Hutton-Blard
J-M Magnesia, 85%, covering, after 1915	0.279	17.4	70	158	0.172	0.062	**0.500**	2.00	McMillan A. S. M. E. Jour. Nov., 1918
Magnesia, 85%, and asbestos, 15%, rigid	0.31	19.3	30	86	0.175	0.063	**0.508**	1.969	Bureau of Standards
Magnesia board, thickness tested, 1.55 in	0.2163	13.5	....	......	....	....	**0.50** to **0.52**	2.00 to 1.923	Willard & Lichty

THERMAL CONDUCTIVITY OF MATERIALS COMPOSED MAINLY OF MINERAL MATTER—*Continued*

A. S. R. E. Insulation Committee Report, Revised 1924

Sall-Mo wool felt covering for low pressure steam and hot water pipes....	0.418	26.03	70	158	....	....	**0.510**	1.96	McMillan, L. B.—A. S. M. E. Dec., 1915 Reviewed in A. S. R. E. Journal Jan. 1916. (Steam pipe temp. 380 deg. F.; Room air Temp. 80°F.)
J-M wool felt for low pressure steam and hot water pipes	0.261	16.29	70	158	....	....	**0.521**	1.92	
Carey Carocel, plain and corrugated asbestos paper, corrugations ⅛ in. deep, run lengthwise of pipe; for medium and low pressure steam pipes	0.3445	21.5	70	158	....	....	**0.540**	1.852	
Nonpareil high pressure moulded pipe covering; contains diatomaceous earth and asbestos; for high pressure and superheated steam...	0.278	17.32	70	158	....	....	**0.543**	1.841	
Carey 85% (by weight) magnesia (15% asbestos) pipe covering for high pressure steam......	0.273	17.05	70	158	....	....	**0.546**	1.831	
J-M Eureka, low pressure and hot water pipe covering; layers of asbestos and wool felt.	0.46	28.67	70	158	....	....	**0.549**	1.821	
J-M 85% magnesia and asbestos covering for high pressure steam pipes. After 1915 this product was improved to c = 0.500 B.t.u. (McMillan)..	0.2977	18.56	70	158	....	....	**0.551**	1.815	
J-M plastic 85% Magnesia...	0.3573	22.28	70	158	....	....	**0.587**	1.703	
Air cell, corrugated asbestos paper, enclosing air spaces; ½ inch thick..........	0.14	8.74	30	86	0.15	0.054	**0.4355**	2.297	Bureau of Standards
Same, 1 inch thick....	0.14	8.74	30	86	0.17	0.0612	**0.494**	2.067	Bureau of Standards
Same, 1.00 inch thick..................	0.327	20.42	....	....	....	....	**0.43** to **0.48**	2.325 to 2.082	Willard & Lichty
Asbestos paper, corrugated................	0.260	16.23	15	59	0.20	0.072	**0.5805**	1.722	Biquard
J-M asbestocel pipe covering. Layers of plain and corrugated (⅛ in. deep, circular) asbestos paper around the pipe; for medium pressures.	0.1935	12.06	70	158	....	....	**0.596**	1.678	McMillan
Sall-Mo expanded asbestos pipe covering; small longitudinal air spaces. For high and low pressure steam...	0.353	22	70	158	....	....	**0.598**	1.671	McMillan
Carey Duplex, low pressure and hot water pipe covering. Layers of plain wool felt and corrugated asbestos paper. Corrugations run lengthwise...	0.208	12.98	70	158	....	....	**0.636**	1.572	McMillan
Carey Serrated. Layers of heavy asbestos felt with indentations. For high pressure steam pipes....	0.635	39.6	70	158	....	....	**0.682**	1.466	McMillan

[1]The conductivities given by Randolph are the mean values between the given temperature and about 10° C. (50 deg. F.) Note effect of compression (density).

THERMAL CONDUCTIVITY OF MATERIALS COMPOSED MAINLY OF MINERAL MATTER—*Continued*

A. S. R. E. Insulation Committee Report, Revised 1924

MATERIAL	Density		Temp. of Sample, mean or range		Thermal Conductivity			Resistance per inch thickness (R) 1/Col. 8	Authority
	Grams per cu. cm. (Specific gravity)	Pounds per cu. ft.	°C.	°F.	Gram Calorie, sec., cm.², deg. C. x 1000	Kg. Calorie hour, m², deg. C.	B.t.u. hour, sq. ft., 1 in. °F Commercial conductivity		
COLUMN 1	2	3	4	5	6	7	8	9	10
Air-cell asbestos (Chars at 572° F.)	0.250	15.6	10–100 10–200 10–300	50–212 50–392 50–572	0.2208 0.2369 0.266	0.0795 0.08524 0.0957	**0.641** **0.6875** **0.772**	1.849 1.455 1.295	Randolph
J-M indented covering for high pressure steam. Layers of asbestos felt with indentations	0.3382	21.11	70	158	...	...	**0.686**	1.457	McMillan
J-M air cell covering for medium steam pressures. Plain and corrugated asbestos paper. Air cells, ¼ in. deep, lengthwise of pipe	0.1728	10.76	70	158	......	...	**0.718**	1.392	McMillan
J-M moulded asbestos for low and medium steam pressures. Molded asbestos and other fireproof material	0.477	29.8	70	158	....	...	**0.778**	1.285	McMillan
Sall-Mo air cell, similar to J-M air cell	0.187	11.66	70	158	...	...	**0.802**	1.247	McMillan
Air cell asbestos (safe temp. 608° F.)	0.232	14.48	100 200 300	212 392 572	0.34 0.43 0.50	0.1224 0.1549 0.18	**0.9875** **1.25** **1.4525**	1.0125 0.800 0.713	Skinner
Insulex, blocks of asbestos and plaster; very porous	0.29	18.1	30	86	0.194	0.0698	**0.564**	1.772	Bureau of Standards
Same, more dense	0.47	29.4	30	86	0.31	0.1115	**0.900**	1.1111	Bureau of Standards
Asbestos, "fire roll"; pure long fibre asbestos cloth ¼-in. thick. Dried at 932°F. for 12 hours before testing	0.575	35.9	10–100 10–300 10–500	50–212 50–572 50–932	0.1962 0.1921 0.1958	0.0707 0.0692 0.0704	**0.57** **0.558** **0.568**	1.753 1.791 1.76	Randolph
Fire felt roll, asbestos sheet, soft, flexible	0.42	26.2	30	86	0.205	0.0738	**0.596**	1.678	Bureau of Standards
Fire felt sheet; asbestos sheet coated with cement; rigid	0.68	42.4	30	86	0.22	0.0792	**0.639**	1.565	Bureau of Standards
Asbestos, white fluffy fibres	0.057	3.56	15	59	0.150	0.054	**0.436**	2.293	Biquard, 1912
Asbestos, long fibre; dried at 662°F	0.293	18.3	Face temperatures 10–500	50–932	0.1719	0.06185	**0.499**	2.003	Randolph
Asbestos fibre, white, acid washed	0.201	...	10–500	50–932	0.19	0.0684	**0.5516**	1.814	Randolph
Asbestos fibre, white; dried at 662°F	0.279	17.42	10–500	50–932	0.196	0.07052	**0.569**	1.758	Randolph
Asbestos wool	0.200	12.48	10–500	50–932	0.217	0.07815	**0.63**	1.587	Randolph
Asbestos, fluffy	0.072	4.49	78.5	173.3	0.2206	0.0794	**0.640**	1.562	Desvignes, 1908

THERMAL CONDUCTIVITY OF MATERIALS COMPOSED MAINLY OF MINERAL MATTER—*Continued*

A. S. R. E. Insulation Committee Report, Revised 1924

Asbestos, packed loosely	0.383	23.9	0	32		0.096	**0.775**	1.29	Groeber, 1910 (Sphere)
			50	122		0.99	**0.798**	1.253	
			100	212		0.1025	**0.827**	1.209	
Asbestos, packed loosely	0.470	29.33	−200	−328		0.072	**0.58**	1.724	Groeber, 1910 (Sphere)
			−150	−238		0.102	**0.823**	1.215	
			−100	−148		0.117	**0.944**	1.06	
			− 50	− 58		0.127	**1.025**	0.975	
			0	32		0.133	**1.0725**	0.9325	
			+ 50	122		0.137	**1.105**	0.905	
			+100	212		0.140	**1.129**	0.886	
Asbestos, pure, dry, loose, discolors at high temperature	0.576	35.95	0	32		0.130	**1.048**	0.955	Nusselt, 1908 (Sphere)
			100	212		0.167	**1.347**	0.7425	
			200	392		0.180	**1.451**	0.689	
			300	572		0.186	**1.500**	0.6667	
			400	752		0.192	**1.550**	0.645	
			500	932		0.198	**1.598**	0.626	
			600	1112		0.204	**1.647**	0.6075	
Asbestos (not from same mine as preceding sample)	0.579	36.14	0	32		0.1715	**1.384**	0.723	Groeber, 1910 (Sphere)
			50	122		0.1770	**1.4275**	0.701	
			100	212		0.1825	**1.4725**	0.679	
			150	302		0.1870	**1.509**	0.663	
			200	392		0.1900	**1.533**	0.652	
Asbestos, hand packed, hard	0.702	43.8	−200	−328		0.136	**1.097**	0.912	Groeber, 1910 (Sphere)
			−150	−238		0.182	**1.468**	0.681	
			−100	−148		0.189	**1.524**	0.656	
			− 50	− 58		0.195	**1.573**	0.6355	
			0	32		0.201	**1.622**	0.6164	
			50	122		0.207	**1.670**	0.599	
			100	212		0.213	**1.719**	0.582	
Asbestos mill board; pressed asbestos, moderately flexible	0.97	60.5	30	86	0.29	0.1044	**0.843**	1.187	Bureau of Standards
Asbestos mill board, ⅜ inch thick					0.2766 to 0.388	0.0997 to 0.1398	**0.8035** to **1.1275**	1.245 to 0.887	Bacon
Same, actual thickness of sample, 0.344 in.	0.894	55.8	22–80	72–176	0.395	0.1422	**1.146**	0.873	Taylor
Asbestos paper, sheets 0.025 in. thick, total 0.306 in.	0.98	61.2	20–100	68–212	0.345	0.1242	**1.002**	0.998	Taylor
					0.375	0.135	**1.089**	0.918	
Asbestos paper, sheets 0.035 in. thick, total 0.356 in.			20	68	0.666	0.2398	**1.934**	0.517	Taylor
			20–80	68–176	0.685	0.2468	**1.99**	0.5023	
Asbestos sheet, ½ inch thick					0.694	0.2497	**2.014**	0.496	Bacon
J-M asbestos fire felt covering for superheated steam pipes	0.4214	26.28			0.3765	0.1355	**1.093**	0.915	McMillan

THERMAL CONDUCTIVITY OF MATERIALS COMPOSED MAINLY OF MINERAL MATTER—*Continued*

A. S. R. E. Insulation Committee Report, Revised 1924

MATERIAL	Density		Temp. of Sample, mean or range		Thermal Conductivity			Resistance per inch thickness (R) 1/Col. 8	Authority
	Grams per cu. cm. (Specific gravity)	Pounds per cu. ft.	°C.	°F.	Gram Calorie, sec., cm.³ deg. C. x 1000	Kg. Calorie hour, m³, deg. C.	B.t.u. hour, sq. ft., 1 in. °F Commercial conductivity		
COLUMN 1	2	3	4	5	6	7	8	9	10
J-M vitribestos, vitrified asbestos air cell, corrugations, ¼ in. deep, lengthwise of pipe. For superheated steam pipes, smoke stacks, etc.	0.474	29.6	70	158	0.3746	0.1348	**1.087**	0.92	McMillan
Vitribestos (safe temp. 600°C. or 1112°F.)	0.362	22.6	100	212	0.49	0.1764	**1.424**	0.7025	Skinner
			200	392	0.66	0.2378	**1.918**	0.5217	
			300	572	0.79	0.2845	**2.295**	0.436	
			400	752	0.90	0.324	**2.613**	0.3827	
			500	932	1.02	0.367	**2.96**	0.338	
Pipe covering plaster (Rohrverputz) ¾ inch, dry	......	......	0	32	0.389	0.14	**1.13**	0.885	Hencky
			20	68	0.417	0.15	**1.21**	0.826	
Asbestos slate	1.783	111.4	50	122	0.528	0.19	**1.532**	0.652	Groeber
Asbestos, compressed	1.240	77.4	15	59	0.611	0.220	**1.775**	0.5633	Biquard
Asbestos wood; asbestos and cement, highly compressed; very hard and rigid	1.97	123.0	30	86	0.93	0.3343	**2.70**	0.37	Bureau of Standards
Asbestos block and plaster	1.145	71.5	15	59	0.973	0.350	**2.824**	0.354	Biquard
Asbestos "board," sample 0.507 in. thick	1.93	120.4	20	68	1.780	0.641	**5.17**	0.1934	Taylor
			20–90	68–194	1.950	0.702	**5.66**	0.1768	
Plastic steam pipe covering, dry, to be applied with water in layers. Composition includes asbestos, diatomite, gran. cork, straw and binder. Tested in loose form	0.405	25.28	0	32	0.1668	0.060	**0.484**	2.068	Nusselt, 1908 (Sphere)
			50	122	0.1946	0.070	**0.564**	1.773	
			100	212	0.211	0.076	**0.613**	1.632	
			150	302	0.2194	0.079	**0.637**	1.57	
			200	392	0.225	0.081	**0.653**	1.531	
Same, compacted with water to a solid	0.690	43.05	150	302	0.278	0.10	**0.8064**	1.24	Nusselt, 1908 (Sphere)
			220	428	0.3335	0.12	**0.968**	1.033	
DIATOMITE									
"Sil-O-Cel" diatomite, in powder form	0.17	10.6	30	86	0.106	0.03816	**0.308**	3.245	Bureau of Standards
Diatomite (silicious earth)	0.150	9.36	15	59	0.12775	0.046	**0.371**	2.696	Biquard
Diatomic earth	......	......	......	......	0.13	0.0468	**0.377**	2.652	Hutton-Blard
Diatomaceous earth in powder form	0.270	16.86	0	32	0.139	0.050	**0.403**	2.48	Hencky
			20	68	0.1444	0.052	**0.4195**	2.384	

THERMAL CONDUCTIVITY OF MATERIALS COMPOSED MAINLY OF MINERAL MATTER—*Continued*

A. S. R. E. Insulation Committee Report, Revised 1924

Diatomaceous earth (Kieselguhr) powder "calcined pink," dry, (vegetable substances burnt out)	0.350	21.85	0	32	0.1444	0.052	**0.4195**	2.384	Nusselt, 1908 (Sphere)
			50	122	......	0.060	**0.484**	2.067	
			100	212	......	0.066	**0.532**	1.88	
			150	302	......	0.070	**0.564**	1.772	
			200	392	......	0.074	**0.597**	1.676	
			250	482	......	0.076	**0.613**	1.631	
			300	572	......	0.078	**0.629**	1.59	
			350	662	......	0.079	**0.637**	1.57	
Same, compacted with water, solid, and dried above 100°C	0.580	36.2	150	302	......	0.083	**0.669**	1.495	Nusselt, 1908 (Sphere)
			350	662	......	0.123	**0.992**	1.008	
Infusorial earth block, burnt, including a binder, porous, hygroscopic; boiler covering	0.200	12.48	0	32	0.178	0.064	**0.516**	1.939	Nusselt, 1908 (Sphere)
			50	122	......	0.071	**0.572**	1.749	
			100	212	......	0.078	**0.629**	1.59	
			150	302	......	0.085	**0.686**	1.458	
			200	392	......	0.092	**0.742**	1.348	
			250	482	......	0.099	**0.798**	1.253	
			300	572	......	0.106	**0.855**	1.17	
			350	662	......	0.113	**0.912**	1.096	
			400	752	......	0.120	**0.968**	1.031	
			450	842	0.353	0.127	**1.025**	0.975	
Diatomaceous earth brick, calcined (Gebrannter Kieselguhrstein)— No. 1	0.296	18.48	15	59	0.158	0.057	**0.452**	2.212	Poensgen, 1912
			50	122	......	0.066	**0.532**	1.88	
			100	212	......	0.075	**0.605**	1.653	
			200	392	......	0.089	**0.7177**	1.393	
			300	572	......	0.104	**0.839**	1.192	
No. 2	0.333	20.8	15	59	0.189	0.068	**0.548**	1.826	Poensgen, 1912
			30	86	......	0.070	**0.564**	1.773	
			50	122	......	0.072	**0.5805**	1.722	
			75	167	......	0.075	**0.605**	1.653	
			100	212	......	0.078	**0.629**	1.59	
			150	302	......	0.084	**0.677**	1.478	
No. 3	0.366	22.85	20	68	0.183	0.066	**0.532**	1.88	Poensgen, 1912
			50	122	......	0.071	**0.572**	1.749	
			100	212	......	0.078	**0.629**	1.59	
			200	392	......	0.090	**0.7255**	1.378	
			300	572	......	0.103	**0.831**	1.204	
No. 4	0.451	28.17	20	68	0.208	0.075	**0.605**	1.652	Poensgen, 1912
			50	122	......	0.080	**0.646**	1.548	
			100	212	......	0.087	**0.702**	1.425	
			150	302	......	0.093	**0.750**	1.334	
			200	392	......	0.100	**0.8064**	1.24	
Sil-O-Cel, infusorial earth; natural blocks	0.45	28.1	30	86	0.20	0.0720	**0.5805**	1.722	Bureau of Standards
Same, more dense	0.50	31.2	30	86	0.214	0.0771	**0.622**	1.608	Bureau of Standards

THERMAL CONDUCTIVITY OF MATERIALS COMPOSED MAINLY OF MINERAL MATTER—*Continued*

A. S. R. E. Insulation Committee Report, Revised 1924

MATERIAL	Density: Grams per cu. cm. (Specific gravity)	Density: Pounds per cu. ft.	Temp. of Sample, mean or range: °C.	Temp. of Sample, mean or range: °F.	Thermal Conductivity: Gram Calorie, sec., cm.², deg. C. x 1000	Thermal Conductivity: Kg. Calorie hour, m², deg. C.	Thermal Conductivity: B.t.u. hour, sq. ft., 1 in. °F Commercial conductivity	Resistance per inch thickness (R) 1/Col. 8	Authority
COLUMN 1	2	3	4	5	6	7	8	9	10
Diatomaceous earth	abt. 0.48	abt. 30	−11–9	9–49	0.193	0.0695	**0.560**	1.787	Griffiths
			14–32	58–89	0.215	0.0774	**0.624**	1.605	
			30–115	86–239	0.224	0.0806	**0.650**	1.539	
			23–64	74–146	0.228	0.0821	**0.662**	1.51	
Diatomite, dry	0.319	19.91	75.7	168.3	0.224	0.0807	**0.651**	1.537	Desvignes
Diatomaceous brick (burnt)	....	....	−15–+27	4–80	0.223	0.08025	**0.647**	1.545	Griffiths
Diatomaceous brick (crushed to powder)	....	....	−9–15	16–59	0.300	0.108	**0.870**	1.149	Griffiths
Diatomaceous earth and asbestos. No forced drying	0.33	20.6	10–100	50–212	0.244	0.0878	**0.718**	1.392	Randolph
			10–200	50–392	0.199	0.0716	**0.5777**	1.731	
			10–300	50–572	0.1796	0.0646	**0.5216**	1.918	
			10–400	50–752	0.1591	0.05725	**0.462**	2.163	
			10–500	50–952	0.206	0.07415	**0.598**	1.671	
Same, first dried 3 days at 572°F	0.33	20.6	10–200	50–392	0.172	0.06187	**0.499**	2.004	Randolph
			10–300	50–572	0.1745	0.0628	**0.5063**	1.973	
			10–400	50–752	0.1626	0.0585	**0.472**	2.118	
Diatomite (safe temp. 600°C or 1112°F.)	0.326	20.36	100	212	0.28	0.1008	**0.8135**	1.23	Skinner
			200	392	0.32	0.1152	**0.930**	1.075	
			300	572	0.37	0.1332	**1.075**	0.930	
			400	752	0.42	0.1511	**1.219**	0.820	
			500	932	0.46	0.1657	**1.336**	0.748	
Infusorial earth, natural	0.506	31.6	100	212	0.34	0.1224	**0.987**	1.013	Skinner
			200	392	0.32	0.1152	**0.930**	1.075	
			300	572	0.40	0.144	**1.162**	0.86	
Infusorial earth, hard pressed blocks (safe temp. 400°C. or 752°F.)	0.321	20.34	100	212	0.30	0.108	**0.8715**	1.1475	Skinner
			200	392	0.29	0.1044	**0.8425**	1.1865	
			300	572	0.33	0.1188	**0.9580**	1.055	
			400	752	0.36	0.1295	**1.045**	0.957	
PUMICE									
Rhenish pumice gravel pebbles ½ to ¾ inch; loose; dried by heat; air circulation in voids	0.292	18.23	20–65	68–149	0.556	approx. 0.20	**1.613**	0.62	Nusselt, 1908

THERMAL CONDUCTIVITY OF MATERIALS COMPOSED MAINLY OF MINERAL MATTER—*Continued*

A. S. R. E. Insulation Committee Report, Revised 1924

Material									Authority
Pumice gravel, Rhenish, grains 1/32 to 13/16 in. mixed grains reduce voids and improve insulating effect	0.301	18.8	20	68	0.216	0.079	**0.637**	1.57	Groeber (Sphere)
			30	86	0.225	0.081	**0.653**	1.531	
Rhenish insulating pumice	0.300	18.72	0	32	0.2083	0.075	**0.605**	1.652	Groeber (Sphere)
			20	68	0.2222	0.080	**0.645**	1.55	
Pumice stone, insulating (Rheinische Schwemmsteine, Rhenish alluvial stone) composed of pumice-sand and-gravel, and cement	0.630	39.3	20	68	0.361	0.13	**1.048**	0.9545	Groeber (Cube)
	......	......	30	86	0.3895	0.14	**1.130**	0.885	
	0.790	49.3	81.3	......	0.554	0.1997	**1.61**	0.6213	Desvignes
Pumice gravel, ordinary, dry	0.600	37.4	0	32	0.417	0.15	**1.21**	0.826	Hencky
			20	68	0.445	0.16	**1.291**	0.775	
Pumice stone	......	......	......	......	0.60	0.216	**1.743**	0.5735	H.-L.-D.
Fuller's earth, argillaceous powder	0.53	33.0	30	86	0.24	0.0864	**0.697**	1.448	Bureau of Standards
Blast furnace slag, dry, grains 0.08 to 0.20 in.	0.360	22.48	0	32	0.2444	0.088	**0.71**	1.408	Hencky
			20	68	......	0.090	**0.726**	1.378	
Grains, 1.18 in.	0.360	......	0	32	0.3333	0.12	**0.968**	1.033	Hencky
			20	68	......	0.13	**1.048**	0.954	
Both mixed	0.304	18.98	0	32	0.2775	0.10	**0.8064**	1.158	Hencky
			20	68	......	0.11	**0.8875**	1.126	
Blast furnace slag, porous, loose	0.360	22.48	20–120	68–248	0.264	0.095	**0.766**	1.306	Nusselt (Sphere)
Same, mixed 9 parts by vol., with one part cement (ratio by weight 1:0.61) age 2 months	0.550	34.32	20–90	68–194	0.528	0.19	**1.532**	0.652	Nusselt (Sphere)
Quartz sand, fine	......	......	......	......	0.131	0.0472	**0.3805**	2.628	Forbes
Quartz	......	......	......	......	0.36	0.1295	**1.045**	0.957	Hutton-Blard
Quartz, finely ground, thru 200 mesh screen; dried at 932°F.	1.05	65.5	10–500	50–932	0.24	0.0864	**0.697**	1.435	Randolph
Quartz, granular, about 1/16-in. diameter	1.64	102.4	10–500	50–932	0.623	0.2243	**1.81**	0.552	Randolph
Quartz, coarse, about 1/8-in. diameter	1.55	96.75	10–500	50–932	0.718	0.2585	**2.084**	0.4797	Randolph
"Patentgurit," German pipe covering cement, powder, mixed with water and applied in layers; tested in slab form	0.54 to	33.7	100	212	0.20	0.072	**0.581**	1.72	Groeber (Cube)
	.68	42.4	200	392	0.2444	0.088	**0.710**	1.408	
Magnesium carbonate (safe temp. 300°C or 572°F.)	0.450	28.10	100	212	0.23	0.0828	**0.668**	1.497	Skinner
			200	392	0.25	0.090	**0.7255**	1.378	
			300	572	0.25	0.090	**0.7255**	1.378	
Paraffine, "Parowax," melts at 52°C or 125.6°F.	0.89	55.6	30	86	0.55	0.1981	**1.598**	0.626	Bureau of Standards
Boiler clinkers, dry	0.750	46.8	0	32	0.361	0.13	**1.048**	0.954	Hencky
			20	68	0.389	0.14	**1.129**	0.8855	
Cement (flour)	......	......	......	below 32	0.162	0.0583	**0.47**	2.128	Forbes
Lime (powdered)	......	......	......	......	0.29	0.1045	**0.842**	1.188	Hutton-Blard
Coal dust; thickness of sample 0.476 in.	0.73	45.6	30	86	0.265	0.0954	**0.77**	1.298	Taylor
			30–150	86–302	0.298	0.10725	**0.865**	1.156	
Coke dust, dry	1.000	62.4	0	32	0.3332	0.12	**0.968**	1.033	Hencky
			20	68	0.361	0.13	**1.048**	0.954	

THERMAL CONDUCTIVITY OF MATERIALS COMPOSED MAINLY OF MINERAL MATTER—*Continued*

A. S. R. E. Insulation Committee Report, Revised 1924

MATERIAL	Density		Temp. of Sample, mean or range		Thermal Conductivity			Resistance per inch thickness (R) 1 / Col. 8	Authority
	Grams per cu. cm. (Specific gravity)	Pounds per cu. ft.	°C.	°F.	Gram Calorie, sec., cm.³ deg. C. x 1000	Kg. Calorie hour, m³, deg. C.	B.t.u. hour, sq. ft., 1 in. °F Commercial conductivity		
COLUMN 1	2	3	4	5	6	7	8	9	10
Iron dust and sand; thickness of sample 0.377 in.	1.14	71.2	30 30–150	86 86–302	0.460 0.517	0.1657 0.1862	**1.335** **1.501**	0.749 0.666	Taylor
Asphalt roofing; felt saturated with asphalt....	0.88	55	30	86	0.24	0.0864	**0.697**	1.434	Bureau of Standards
Roofing....	......	......	......	below 32	0.335	0.1205	**0.972**	1.028	Forbes
Roofing, 0.15 in. thick (1.34 lb. sq. ft.), covered with gravel (0.83 lb. sq. ft.), combined thickness assumed 0.25 in; c per inch thickness....	......	......	......	......	......	0.1646	**1.325**	0.755	Willard & Lichty, calculated from 2-in. tile tests.
Gypsum blocks containing granulated cork....	0.685	42.75	0 20 30	32 68 86	0.0639	0.21 0.23 0.24	**1.695** **1.857** **1.937**	0.59 0.5387 0.5162	Noell (Cube)
Gypsum plastered ceiling, moisture content 7.6 vol. %....	0.840	52.4	20	68	0.0611	0.22	**1.776**	0.563	Schenk
Same, with cyl. channels 7.6 vol. %.... (Note saving in weight by using air pockets.)	0.625	39.0	20	68	0.0611	0.22	**1.776**	0.563	Schenk
Keystone Plaster No. 100, 1 in. thick........	......	......	......	......	0.777	0.280	**2.23**	0.448	Bureau of Standards 1919, according to Sam. Cabot
Gypsum plaster....	0.74	46.2	30	86	0.80	0.288	**2.322**	0.4303	Bureau of Standards
Gypsum plaster board such as "Sheet Rock" and "Adamant," covered with paper about 0.02 in. thick. Thickness ¼ to ½ in. Called fire resistive wall board; 32 x 36 or 48 in..	0.97 to 0.99	60.5 to 61.8 net	......	......	0.895	0.322	**2.6**	0.3845	Herter c estimated
Gypsum fibrous plaster wall board, 32 x 36 in., ¼ to ½ in. thick; 3 layers plaster, total 4 sheets of paper....	1.04 to 1.09	64.9 to 68 net	......	......	0.947	0.341	**2.75**	0.3635	Herter c estimated
Gypsum (building), oven dried 3 weeks......	1.250	78.0	0 20 50	32 68	0.1027	0.36 0.37 0.38	**2.904** **2.987** **3.065**	0.3442 0.335 0.3262	Poensgen
Gypsum, artificial....	......	......	0	32	0.9	0.324	**2.615**	0.3813	R. Weber, 1895
Gypsum, natural....	......	......	0	32	3.1	1.115	**9.00**	0.1111	R. Weber, 1895
Gravel, fine, (0.16 to 0.35 in.)....	1.464	91.3	85	185	0.555	0.1999	**1.6125**	0.62	Desvignes

THERMAL CONDUCTIVITY OF MATERIALS COMPOSED MAINLY OF MINERAL MATTER—*Continued*

A. S. R. E. Insulation Committee Report, Revised 1924

Gravel, loose, dry	1.850	115.5	0	32	0.805	0.29	**2.34**	0.4273	Groeber
			20	68	0.888	0.32	**2.58**	0.388	
Gravel, washed, dry (stones, 1 to 3 in.)	1.850	115.0	0	32	0.805	0.29	**2.34**	0.4273	Groeber (Sphere)
			20	68	0.888	0.32	**2.58**	0.3878	
			40	104	0.9725	0.35	**2.823**	0.354	
Sand, fine, grains smaller than 0.08 in., dry	1.600	99.8	86.8	188.2	0.7385	0.2660	**2.146**	0.466	Desvignes
Sand, white, dry	......	......	......	......	0.93	0.3345	**2.7**	0.3703	H-L-D
Sand, river, fine grained, dried completely by heat	1.520	94.8	0	32	0.722	0.26	**2.098**	0.4768	Groeber (Sphere)
			20	68	0.778	0.28	**2.26**	0.4424	
			160	320	0.9165	0.33	**2.662**	0.3778	
Same, with normal moisture content (6.9% by weight or 11% by volume)	1.640	102.4	20	68	2.695	0.97	**7.825**	0.1278	Groeber (Sphere)
			50	122	2.75	0.99	**7.98**	0.12525	
Facing cement, as used for plastering cork slabs (magnesium oxychloride composition)	......	......	−8–2	16–36	0.38	0.1368	**1.010**	0.99	Griffiths
Portland cement	......	......	83–96	181–205	0.71	0.2557	**2.061**	0.485	Lees & Chorlton
Portland cement, neat, age 18 months	2.00	124.8	35	95	2.168	0.78	**2.265**	0.4416	Nusselt (Sphere)
Plaster of Paris	......	......	......	......	0.70	0.252	**2.033**	0.492	Lees & Chorlton
Plaster of Paris powder	......	......	......	......	2.6	0.936	**7.55**	0.1325	Lees & Chorlton
Plaster, ordinary, mixed, dry	1.339	83.55	89.6	193.3	0.834	0.3002	**2.422**	0.4127	Desvignes
Plaster, 12 parts sand (Schweiss sand) 4 parts lime	1.820	113.5	0	32	1.582	0.57	**4.6**	0.2173	Knoblauch
			20	68	1.611	0.58	**4.68**	0.2138	
Plaster ("Verputz") 1½ in. thick; of mortar; air dried for months	1.690	105.5	20	68	1.89	0.68	**5.48**	0.1826	Groeber (plate)
Soil, dry	......	......	......	......	0.33	0.1188	**0.958**	1.044	Lees & Chorlton
Soil, wet	......	......	......	......	1.6	0.576	**4.64**	0.2156	Lees & Chorlton
Soil, normal condition (excavated in Munich), including stones 1 to 3 in.	2.040	127.4	0	32	1.195	0.43	**3.467**	0.2883	Groeber (Sphere)
			20	68	1.25	0.45	**3.63**	0.2755	
			70	158	1.39	0.50	**4.03**	0.248	
Asphalt (for streets)	2.120	132.3	0	32	1.445	0.52	**4.195**	0.2384	Poensgen
			10	50	1.557	0.56	**4.52**	0.2212	
			20	68	1.668	0.60	**4.84**	0.2068	
			30	86	1.78	0.64	**5.16**	0.1938	
Bitumen composition (used for flooring and construction)	......	......	20–33	68–92	2.0	0.72	**5.9**	0.1696	Griffiths
Concrete: Pumice pebbles (0.20 to 0.39 in.), 9 parts, fine sand 2 parts, Portland cement 1 part	1.167	72.8	85.9	186.6	0.554	0.1994	**1.61**	0.621	Desvignes
Concrete: Granulated cork (0.087 sp. gr.) 3 parts, fine sand 2 parts, Portland cement 1 part	1.269	79.22	85.2	185.4	0.616	0.2218	**1.79**	0.5585	Desvignes
Cinder concrete, dry	0.870	54.3	0	32	0.666	0.24	**1.937**	0.516	Henckv
			20	68	0.694	0.25	**2.017**	0.496	
Concrete: Slag (0.08 to 0.39 in.), 9 parts; fine sand 2 parts, Portland cement 1 part	1.516	94.53	86.7	188	0.705	0.2540	**2.05**	0.488	Desvignes
Lime mortar (Beffes No. 3)	1.745	108.9	89.2	192.6	0.866	0.3118	**2.433**	0.411	Desvignes

THERMAL CONDUCTIVITY OF MATERIALS COMPOSED MAINLY OF MINERAL MATTER—*Continued*

A. S. R. E. Insulation Committee Report, Revised 1924

MATERIAL	Density		Temp. of Sample, mean or range		Thermal Conductivity			Resistance per inch thickness (R)	Authority
	Grams per cu. cm. (Specific gravity)	Pounds per cu. ft.	°C.	°F.	Gram Calorie, sec., cm.³ deg. C. x 1000	Kg. Calorie hour, m³, deg. C.	B.t.u. hour, sq. ft., 1 in. °F Commercial conductivity	1 / Col. 8	
Column 1	2	3	4	5	6	7	8	9	10
Cement mortar, pure Portland No. 1	1.715	107.0	88.6	191.5	0.803	0.2891	**2.331**	0.429	Desvignes
Cement mortar, pure Portland No. 2	1.886	117.6	89.6	193.3	1.278	0.4600	**3.71**	0.2695	Desvignes
Cement mortar, total thickness of layer 0.414 in., inclusive of reinforcing metal 0.157 in. thick (38%)	2.124	132.5	92.1	197.8	1.387	0.4995	**4.028**	0.248	Desvignes
Cement mortar, total thickness 0.472 in., including one layer of 0.043 in. galv. wire, 1 in. mesh, as reinforcement 0.118 in. thick (25%)	1.975	123.25	90.1	194.2	1.426	0.5137	**4.14**	0.2416	Desvignes
Concrete, gravel (0.16 to 0.35 in), 9 parts, fine sand 2 parts, Portland cement 1 part	1.985	123.9	90	194	1.531	0.5513	**4.444**	0.225	Desvignes
Concrete, 1 Portland cement, 2 parts washed sand, 2 parts washed gravel, 1½ in. thick Air dried 6 months	2.180	136.1	20 23	68 73.4	1.807 1.833	0.65 0.66	**5.24** **5.322**	0.191 0.1879	Groeber (plate)
Concrete 1:12, air dried 2 weeks	2.050	128.0	0 20 30	32 68 86	1.833 1.946 2.00	0.66 0.70 0.72	**5.32** **5.65** **5.80**	0.188 0.177 0.1724	Poensgen
Concrete, cinder, mixture 1-2-4	....	....	50*	122*	0.81	0.2916	**2.35**	0.4256	Chas. L. Norton, Boston, Mass., in Journal A. S. M. E. June, 1913 p. 1011-1021
Concrete, stone, mixture 1-2-4, not tamped	....	....	50*	122*	1.1 to 1.6	0.396 to 0.576	**3.195** to **4.65**	0.3133 to 0.2198	
Concrete, stone, mixture 1-2-5	....	....	35*	95*	2.16	0.7775	**6.27**	0.1596	
Concrete, stone, mixture 1-2-4	....	....	200* 400* 500* 1000* 1100*	392* 752* 932* 1832* 2012*	2.1 2.2 2.3 2.7 2.9	0.756 0.7922 0.8277 0.972 1.044	**6.10** **6.39** **6.68** **7.84** **8.42**	0.164 0.1566 0.1497 0.1276 0.1188	
Concrete wall, mixture 1-2-4, thickness 3.19 in.	**2.24**	**139.7**	....	....	....	....	**7.89** to **8.74**	0.1267 to 0.1145	Willard & Lichty

THERMAL CONDUCTIVITY OF MATERIALS COMPOSED MAINLY OF MINERAL MATTER—*Continued*

A. S. R. E. Insulation Committee Report, Revised 1924

Same, covered on one side with roofing 0.15 in. thick (1.34 lb. sq. ft.), and with gravel (0.83 lb. sq. ft.), total thickness of construction assumed 3.45 in.	......	......	......	......	......	......	**4.59** to **9.04**	0.218 to 0.1106	Willard & Lichty
Slate (ground)......	......	......	......	below 32	0.81	0.2917	**2.353**	0.425	Forbes
Slate......	......	......	94	201	3.57	1.285	**10.37**	0.0964	Lees & Chorlton
Slate, across cleavage......	......	......	......	......	3.15 to 3.60	1.134 to 1.296	**9.15** to **10.45**	0.1093 to 0.0957	Herschel-Ledebour-Dunn, 1879
Slate, along cleavage......	......	......	......	......	5.50 to 6.50	1.98 to 2.34	**15.98** to **18.88**	0.0626 to 0.053	Herschel-Ledebour-Dunn, 1879
Glass, crown......	......	......	10–15	50–59	1.63	0.587	**4.74**	0.211	H. Meyer, 1888
Glass, flint......	......	......	10–15	50–59	1.43	0.515	**4.16**	0.2404	H. Meyer, 1888
Glass, soda......	2.59	161.7	20	68	1.72	0.619	**4.99**	0.2004	Barratt
			100	212	1.82	0.655	**5.28**	0.1894	
Glass, plate, 0.252 in. thick......	2.49	155.5	20	68	1.785	0.6425	**5.18**	0.1930	Taylor
			20–100	68–212	1.945	0.70	**5.64**	0.1773	
Glass, plate, 0.289 in. thick......	2.60	162.3	20	.....	1.905	0.686	**5.53**	0.1809	Taylor
			20–120	68–248	2.016	0.7255	**5.85**	0.1710	
Porcelain (sevres)......	......	......	165	329	3.9	1.405	**11.34**	0.0882	Wologdine
			1055	1932	4.7	1.692	**13.65**	0.0733	
Chalk......	......	......	......	......	2.2	0.7922	**6.39**	0.1565	H-L-D
Boiler Scale No. 1......	......	......	51–82	124–180	3.13	1.127	**9.09**	0.1101	Ernst, 1902
Boiler Scale No. 2......	......	......	37–75	98–167	7.68	2.768	**22.32**	0.0448	Ernst, 1902
Seprentine (Cornwall red)......	......	......	......	......	4.41	1.589	**12.81**	0.078	H-L-D
MASONRY									
Peat blocks, dry......	0.840	52.4	0	32	0.389	0.14	**1.13**	0.885	Hencky
			20	68	0.417	0.15	**1.21**	0.826	
Same, masonry, dry, calculated, allowing for joints......			0	32	0.611	0.22	**1.776**	0.563	Hencky
			20	68	0.639	0.23	**1.857**	0.539	
Blast furnace slag stone, dry (Hochofen-Schwemmsteine)......	0.785	49	0	32	0.389	0.14	**1.13**	0.885	Hencky
			20	68	0.444	0.16	**1.29**	0.775	
Same, masonry, dry, calculated, allowing for joints......	......	......	0	32	0.611	0.22	**1.776**	0.563	Hencky
			20	68	0.666	0.24	**1.937**	0.516	
Rhenish alluvial stone, dry ("Schwemmsteine")	0.630	39.3	0	32	0.306	0.11	**0.887**	1.127	Groeber
			20	68	0.361	0.13	**1.048**	0.955	
			30	86	0.389	0.14	**1.129**	0.885	
Same, masonry, dry, calculated, allowing for joints......	......	......	0	32	0.555	0.20	**1.613**	0.62	Hencky
			20	68	0.611	0.22	**1.776**	0.563	

*Hot side of plate.

THERMAL CONDUCTIVITY OF MATERIALS COMPOSED MAINLY OF MINERAL MATTER—*Continued*

A. S. R. E. Insulation Committee Report, Revised 1924

MATERIAL	Density		Temp. of Sample, mean or range		Thermal Conductivity			Resistance per inch thickness (R) 1/Col. 8	Authority
	Grams per cu. cm. (Specific gravity)	Pounds per cu. ft.	°C.	°F.	Gram Calorie, sec., cm.² deg. C. x 1000	Kg. Calorie hour, m², deg. C.	B.t.u. hour, sq. ft., 1 in. °F Commercial conductivity	Col. 8	
COLUMN 1	2	3	4	5	6	7	8	9	10
Bricks very porous, dry	0.710	44.3	0	32	0.389	0.14	**1.13**	0.885	Henecky
			20	68	0.417	0.15	**1.21**	0.826	
Same, masonry, dry, calculated, allowing for joints	....		0	32	0.611	0.22	**1.776**	0.563	Henecky
			20	68	0.639	0.23	**1.857**	0.539	
Bricks, very porous, dry	0.812	50.6	0	32	0.444	0.16	**1.29**	0.775	Henecky
			20	68	0.472	0.17	**1.371**	0.729	
Same, masonry, dry, calculated, allowing for joints			0	32	0.666	0.24	**1.937**	0.5162	Henecky
			20	68	0.695	0.25	**2.018**	0.496	
Bricks, very porous, moisture 1.2 vol. %	0.739	46.1	20	68	0.403	0.145	**1.17**	0.855	Cammerer
Same, 5.8 vol. %	0.797	49.7	20	68	0.583	0.21	**1.695**	0.590	Cammerer
Same, 21.5 vol %	0.943	58.8	20	68	0.945	0.34	**2.743**	0.3645	Cammerer
Brick masonry (from old house)	1.850	115	0	32	0.912	0.328	**2.647**	0.378	Groeber (cube)
			20	68	0.9725	0.35	**2.823**	0.3542	
			47	117	0.056	0.38	**3.066**	0.326	
Bricks, hand made, dry (Munich)	1.536	95.8	0	32	0.917	0.33	**2.662**	0.3758	Poensgen
			15–35	59–95	0.945	0.34	**2.743**	0.3645	
Bricks, masonry, dry, calculated, allowing for joints			0	32	1.056	0.38	**3.066**	0.326	Henecky
			20	68	1.084	0.39	**3.147**	0.3177	
Clay, mixed with straw, dry	1.505	94.25	0	32	0.9725	0.35	**2.823**	0.354	Henecky
			20	68	1.056	0.38	**3.066**	0.326	
Slag brick	1.400	87.4	15	59	1.111	0.400	**3.225**	0.310	Biquard
Millstone, dry	1.258	78.5	80.8	177.4	1.156	0.4161	**3.36**	0.2976	Desvignes
Stone, soft	1.470	91.75	15	59	1.194	0.430	**3.47**	0.288	Biquard
Machine made bricks, dry	1.620	101.1	50.8	123.4	1.15	0.414	**3.34**	0.2994	Knoblauch
Same, 0.8 vol. % mixture	....	....	50.4	122.7	1.191	0.429	**3.46**	0.289	Knoblauch
Same, 1.81 vol. % mixture			43.3	110	2.287	0.823	**6.64**	0.1507	Knoblauch
Bricks, machine made, dry	1.672	104.4	0	32	1.2225	0.44	**3.55**	0.2817	Poensgen
			40	104	1.278	0.46	**3.71**	0.2697	
			80	176	1.306	0.47	**3.79**	0.264	
Same, masonry, dry, calculated, allowing for joints	....	....	0	32	1.306	0.47	**3.79**	0.264	Henecky
			20	68	1.334	0.48	**3.87**	0.2584	

THERMAL CONDUCTIVITY OF MATERIALS COMPOSED MAINLY OF MINERAL MATTER—*Continued*

A. S. R. E. Insulation Committee Report, Revised 1924

Bricks, American, machine made, in one-course wall, 3.79 in. thick	2.112	131.9	.....	.....	.....	.....	**3.73** to **4.55**	0.268 to 0.22	Willard & Lichty
Same, in two-course wall, 8.77 in. thick	2.112	131.9	.....	.....	.....	.....	**3.93** to **5.08**	0.2547 to 0.197	
Hollow-tile wall, American, with ½ in. thick cement plaster on both sides (c per inch of total wall thickness)	.....	.....	.....	.....	.....	.....	**2.538** to **3.08**	0.394 to 0.3247	Hollow masonry columns with electrically heated air inside, not agitated. Surface temperatures used.
2-inch tile, 2.02 in.	1.922	119.9	.....	.....	.....	.....	**2.86** to **3.24**	0.35 to 0.3087	
4-inch tile, 3.84 in.	2.035	127.0	.....	.....	.....	.....	**3.65** to **3.96**	0.274 to 0.2526	
6-inch tile, 6.77 in.	1.992	124.3	.....	.....	.....	.....	.....	.....	
2.02-inch tile covered with ½ in. plaster both sides, also with 0.15 in. roofing (1.34 lb. sq. ft.); and gravel (0.83 lb. sq. ft.) on one side. Total thickness of construction assumed 3.4 in.	.....	119.86	.....	.....	.....	.....	**2.79** to **2.86**	0.3584 to 0.35	
Hollow tile, dry, laid flat	.....	.....	0 20	32 68	0.472 0.528	0.17 0.19	**1.371** **1.533**	0.73 0.652	Knoblauch
Hollow tile masonry, dried 6 months	.....	.....	0 20 59	32 68 138	0.7225 0.7777 0.861	0.26 0.28 0.31	**2.10** **2.26** **2.50**	0.476 0.442 0.400	Groeber (cube)
Hollow tile ceiling. Heat flow upwards: Top tile 1.0 cm. air 2.5 cm. tile 1.0 cm. air 11.0 cm. tile 1.0 cm. air 2.5 cm. tile 1.0 cm. Total 20 cm. (7.87 in.)	.....	.....	Top Surface 2 Bottom surface 22.5	Top Surface 35.6 Bottom surface 72.5	1.64	0.59	**4.76**	0.21	Biquard, 1910

THERMAL CONDUCTIVITY OF MATERIALS COMPOSED MAINLY OF MINERAL MATTER—*Continued*

A. S. R. E. Insulation Committee Report, Revised 1924

MATERIAL	Density		Temp. of Sample, mean or range		Thermal Conductivity			Resistance per inch thickness (R) 1 / Col. 8	Authority
	Grams per cu. cm. (Specific gravity)	Pounds per cu. ft.	°C.	°F.	Gram Calorie, sec., cm.³ deg. C x 1000	Kg. Calorie hour, m³, deg. C.	B.t.u. hour, sq. ft., 1 in. °F Commercial conductivity		
COLUMN 1	2	3	4	5	6	7	8	9	10
Hollow tile ceiling. Heat flow upwards: Top tile . . . 0.85 cm. air . . . 0.80 cm. tile . . . 0.85 cm. air . . . 13.00 cm. tile . . . 0.85 cm. air . . . 0.80 cm. tile . . . 0.85 cm. Concrete . . . 3.00 cm. Total . . . 21. cm. (8.26 in.)	. . . . . .	. . . . . .	Top Surface 1 Bottom Surface 23	Top Surface 33.8 Bottom Surface 73.4	1.612	0.58	**4.68**	0.2137	Biquard, 1910
Same as a floor, heat flow upwards, the 13 cm. (5.11 in.) air space filled with concrete. (Note great increase in c.)	. . . . . .	. . . . . .	Top Surface 2 Bottom Surface 21	Top Surface 35.6 Bottom Surface 69.8	2.835	1.02	**8.235**	0.1215	Biquard, 1910
Brick. Vaugirard (French terra cotta), orange color	1.828	114	89.8	193.6	1.251	0.4505	**3.635**	0.275	Desvignes
Brick. Domont (French terra cotta), wineless color	1.804	112.6	91.2	196.2	1.591	0.5727	**4.62**	0.2163	Desvignes
Building and terra cotta	. . . . . .	. . . . . .	15 to 1100	59 to 1968	1.8 to 3.8	0.648 to 1.368	**5.22 to 11.035**	0.1917 to 0.0907	Wologdine
Concrete blocks, dry	1.660	103.6	0 20	32 68	1.584 1.668	0.57 0.60	**4.6** **4.84**	0.2174 0.2067	Hencky
Concrete blocks (used in construction)	. . . . . .	. . . . . .	16–46 tm. 31	60–115 tm. 88	2.8	1.008	**8.2**	0.122	Griffiths
Limestone, Villers-Adam (soft)	1.805	112.6	90.0	194	1.436	0.5167	**4.17**	0.2397	Desvignes

THERMAL CONDUCTIVITY OF MATERIALS COMPOSED MAINLY OF MINERAL MATTER—*Continued*

A. S. R. E. Insulation Committee Report, Revised 1924

			0	32	1.50	0.54	**4.36**	0.2293	
Limestone, fine-grained, dry	1.662	103.75	15	59	1.584	0.57	**4.60**	0.2173	Poensgen
			25	77	1.64	0.59	**4.76**	0.210	
			40	104	1.723	0.62	**5.00**	0.20	
Same, as masonry, dry, calculated, allowing			0	32	1.528	0.55	**4.44**	0.2252	Hencky
for joints			20	68	1.612	0.58	**4.68**	0.2137	
			0	32	2.0	0.72	**5.81**	0.1721	
Limestone, coarse grained, dry	1.987	124	25	77	2.222	0.80	**6.45**	0.155	Poensgen
			40	104	2.361	0.85	**6.86**	0.1458	
Same, as masonry, dry, calculated, allowing			0	32	1.945	0.70	**5.65**	0.1504	Hencky
for joints			20	68	2.083	0.75	**6.05**	0.1652	
	1.60	99.8	0	32	1.389	0.50	**4.03**	0.2481	
			20	68	1.25	0.45	**3.63**	0.2756	
	1.70	106.1	0	32	1.557	0.56	**4.518**	0.2216	
Lime sandstone masonry, dry; curves plotted			20	68	1.668	0.60	**4.84**	0.2068	Hencky
from tests. Influence of density and tempera-	1.80	112.4	0	32	1.75	0.63	**5.08**	0.1969	in his
ture is considerable			20	68	1.861	0.67	**5.40**	0.1852	book
	1.90	118.5	0	32	1.946	0.70	**5.64**	0.1773	1921
			20	68	2.056	0.74	**5.97**	0.1676	
	2.00	124.8	0	32	2.111	0.76	**6.13**	0.1631	
			20	68	2.222	0.80	**6.45**	0.155	
Limestone, Leronville (hard)	2.550	159.1	93.8	200.8	3.073	1.106	**8.92**	0.1121	Desvignes
Caen stone, limestone					4.3	1.549	**12.49**	0.080	H-L-D
			40	104	4.6 to 5.7	1.657 to 2.052	**13.35** to **16.56**	0.0749 to 0.0604	
Limestone			100	212	3.9 to 4.9	1.404 to 1.765	**11.32** to **14.23**	0.0883 to 0.0703	Poole, 1912
			350	662	3.2 to 3.5	1.152 to 1.26	**9.29** to **10.16**	0.1076 to 0.0984	
Trapp			22–64	72–147	3.6	1.295	**10.45**	0.0957	Peirce, 1903
Freestone, sandstone					2.1	0.756	**6.10**	0.164	H-L-D
Limestone, marbles, calcite, compact dolomite					4.70 to 5.60	1.6915 to 2.017	**13.65** to **16.28**	0.0733 to 0.06143	H-L-D
			10	50	3.695	1.33	**10.725**	0.0933	
Sandstone, gray, natural, freshly cut	2.259	141	20	68	4.0	1.44	**11.62**	0.0861	Poensgen
			40	104	4.39	1.58	**12.75**	0.0785	
			0	32	2.918	1.05	**8.47**	0.118	
Same, air dried 6 months	2.251	140.5	10	50	3.0	1.08	**8.715**	0.1147	
			20	68	3.083	1.11	**8.95**	0.1117	Poensgen
			30	86	3.17	1.14	**9.20**	0.1086	

THERMAL CONDUCTIVITY OF MATERIALS COMPOSED MAINLY OF MINERAL MATTER—*Continued*

A. S. R. E. Insulation Committee Report, Revised 1924

MATERIAL	Density: Grams per cu. cm. (Specific gravity)	Density: Pounds per cu. ft.	Temp. of Sample, mean or range: °C.	Temp. of Sample, mean or range: °F.	Thermal Conductivity: Gram Calorie, sec., cm.³ deg. C. x 1000	Thermal Conductivity: Kg. Calorie hour, m³, deg. C.	Thermal Conductivity: B.t.u. hour, sq. ft., 1 in. °F Commercial conductivity	Resistance per inch thickness (R) 1/Col. 8	Authority
COLUMN 1	2	3	4	5	6	7	8	9	10
Sandstone and hard grit, dry					5.45 to 5.65	1.9615 to 2.035	**15.83** to **16.41**	0.06315 to 0.0609	H-L-D
Granite			100	212	4.5 to 5.0	1.62 to 1.8	**13.06** to **14.5**	0.0765 to 0.069	Poole, 1912
			200	392	4.3 to 9.7	1.55 to 3.49	**12.5** to **28.2**	0.080 to 0.3546	
			500	932	4.0	1.44	**11.6**	0.0862	
Granite					5.10 to 5.50	1.837 to 1.980	**14.81** to **15.98**	0.0675 to 0.0626	H-L-D
Granite					7.5	2.700	**21.8**	0.0459	H. F. Weber, 1911
					8.0	2.878	**23.22**	0.04305	
					9.7	3.490	**28.18**	0.0355	
Marble, white				below 32	1.15	0.414	**3.34**	0.2995	Forbes
	2.706	168.9	95	203	3.10	1.116	**9.00**	0.1111	Desvignes
					7.8	2.807	**22.66**	0.04515	Hecht, 1903
					8.2	2.950	**23.8**	0.042	Weber
Marble, white, American			30	86	5.96	2.147	**17.32**	0.0577	Peirce & Willson
Marble, gray, Belgian	2.694	168.1	96.1	205	0.336	1.208	**9.75**	0.1025	Desvignes
Marble, black				below 32	1.77	0.637	**5.14**	0.1946	Forbes
Marble, black, American			30	86	6.85	2.467	**19.9**	0.05022	Peirce&Willson,1898
Marble, carrar			30	86	5.01	1.803	**14.55**	0.06873	Peirce&Willson,1898
Onyx (Mexico)			30	86	5.56	2.00	**16.14**	0.06194	Peirce&Willson,1898
Micaceous flagstone—									
Across cleavage					4.41	1.589	**12.8**	0.0781	H-L-D
Along cleavage					6.32	2.276	**18.36**	0.0545	H-L-D
Stoneware mixtures			70 to 1000	158 to 1832	2.9 to 5.3	1.044 to 1.91	**8.42** to **15.4**	0.11875 to 0.065	Wologdine, 1909

THERMAL CONDUCTIVITY OF MATERIALS COMPOSED MAINLY OF MINERAL MATTER—*Continued*

A. S. R. E. Insulation Committee Report, Revised 1924

Lime, hard	. . . .	. . . .	. . . .	. . . .	8.7	3.135	**25.27**	0.0396	H. F. Weber
Lime, with clay	. . . .	. . . .	. . . .	. . . .	7.8	2.807	**22.66**	0.04117	H. F. Weber
Lime, with much clay	. . . .	. . . .	. . . .	. .	6.7	2.410	**19.47**	0.0514	H. F. Weber
Soapstone, across cleavage. Thickness of sample 0.715 in	2.87	179.1	70–130	158 266	8.00	2.88	**23.22**	0.04307	Taylor
REFRACTORY BRICK									
Fire brick	1.73	108	20	68	1.10	0.396	**3.194**	0.3133	Barratt
			100	212	1.09	0.392	**3.16**	0.3165	
Fire brick	1.857	115.9	79.8	175.6	1.16	0.4177	**3.365**	0.297	Desvignes
			10	50	1.362	0.49	**3.95**	0.253	
Fire brick (Schamotte)	1.716	107	25	77	1.389	0.50	**4.03**	0.248	Poensgen
			40	104	1.417	0.51	**4.11**	0.2433	
			60	140	1.473	0.53	**4.27**	0.2342	
			200	392	1.417	0.51	**4.114**	0.2417	
Fire brick (Schamotte)	. . . .		600	1112	1.833	0.66	**5.322**	0.1879	Van Rinsum
			1000	1832	2.279	0.82	**6.615**	0.1512	
			200	392	1.557	0.56	**4.518**	0.2215	
Silica Brick	. .		600	1112	2.444	0.88	**7.10**	0.1408	Van Rinsum
			1000	1832	3.307	1.19	**9.60**	0.1042	
			200	392	2.057	0.74	**5.97**	0.1676	
Dinas brick	. . . .	. . . .	600	1112	2.583	0.93	**7.50**	0.1333	Van Rinsum
			1000	1832	3.140	1.13	**9.115**	0.10975	
			200	392	3.195	1.15	**9.275**	0.1078	
Magnesite brick	. . . .	. . . .	600	1112	3.584	1.29	**10.40**	0.0962	Van Rinsum
			1000	1832	3.974	1.43	**11.54**	0.0867	
			200	392	2.24	0.806	**6.5**	0.1539	
			400	752	. . . .	0.955	**7.7**	0.1298	
Fire brick, average values for various American bricks (Star Silica, Quartzite, Woodland) . . . Temperatures given are those on the hot side.		97.3 to 119	600	1112	. . . .	1.090	**8.7**	0.1150	B. Dudley, Jr., Pennsylvania State College, 1915
			800	1472	. . . .	1.203	**9.7**	0.1031	
			1000	1832	. . . .	1.352	**10.9**	0.0918	
			1200	2192		1.476	**11.9**	0.0840	
			1400	2552	4.48	1.612	**13.0**	0.077	
Silica brick	. . . .	. . . .	100 to 1000	212 to 1768	2.0 to 3.3	0.72 to 1.187	**5.8** to **9.575**	0.1724 to 0.1044	Wologdine
Silica, fused	2.17	135.1	20–100	68	2.37	0.853	**6.88**	0.1454	Barratt
				212	2.55	0.918	**7.41**	0.135	
			360	680	2.09	0.7525	**6.06**	0.165	Clement & Egy, University of Illinois, 1909
Fire clay	. . . .	. . . .	600	1048	2.21	0.795	**6.42**	0.1558	
			380	716	3.66	1.317	**10.64**	0.094	
			750	1318	3.62	1.303	**10.52**	0.0951	
Gas retort brick	. . . .	. . . .	100–1125	212–1963	3.8	1.368	**11.03**	0.0907	Wologdine

THERMAL CONDUCTIVITY OF MATERIALS COMPOSED MAINLY OF MINERAL MATTER—*Continued*

A. S. R. E. Insulation Committee Report, Revised 1924

MATERIAL	Density		Temp. of Sample, mean or range		Thermal Conductivity			Resistance per inch thickness (R) 1/Col. 8	Authority
	Grams per cu. cm. (Specific gravity)	Pounds per cu. ft.	°C.	°F.	Gram Calorie, sec., cm.^{3} deg. C. x 1000	Kg. Calorie hour, m^2, deg. C.	B.t.u. hour, sq. ft., 1 in. °F Commercial conductivity		
Column 1	2	3	4	5	6	7	8	9	10
Fire clay brick	. .	. . . . . .	125	257	3.2	1.152	**9.28**	0.1077	Wologdine
			1220	2164	5.4	1.944	**15.7**	0.0637	
Magnesia brick	. . . . . .	. . . . . .	50	122	2.7	0.972	**7.84**	0.1275	Wologdine
			1130	2003	7.2	2.59	**20.9**	0.04783	
Carborundum brick	. . . . . .	. . . . . .	150	302	3.2	1.152	**9.28**	0.1077	Wologdine
			1200	2128	27.	9.72	**78.4**	0.01276	
Graphite brick	. . . . . .	. . . . . .	300–700	572–1228	24.	8.64	**69.70**	0.01435	Wologdine
Gas Carbon	1.42	88.6	20	68	8.5	3.06	**24.7**	0.0405	Barratt
			100	212	9.5	3.42	**27.6**	0.0362	

THERMAL CONDUCTIVITY OF MATERIALS COMPOSED MAINLY OF ANIMAL MATTER—

A. S. R. E. Insulation Committee Report, Revised 1924

Hair cloth	...		...	below 32	0.0402	0.0145	**0.1167**	8.57	Forbes, 1872
Horse hair, pressed	0.172	10.74	0	32	0.042	0.01512	**0.122**	8.2	Nusselt, 1908
			20	68	0.043	0.0148	**0.1194**	8.38	
Hair felt, heat flowing across fibres	0.27	16.88	30	86	0.085	0.0306	**0.247**	4.05	Bureau of Standards
Felt	...	...		below 32	0.087	0.0313	**0.2525**	3.96	Forbes
Wool felt, dark grey, heat flowing across fibres; thickness of sample 0.98 in.	0.15	9.36	40	104	0.149	0.0536	**0.4327**	2.31	Taylor
			40–100	104–212	0.175	0.063	**0.508**	1.97	
Eiderdown; dried at 302°F. before test	0.00214	0.1335	10–100	50–212	0.112	0.0403	**0.3253**	3.077	Randolph
			10–150	50–302	0.1557	0.056	**0.452**	2.212	
	0.0788	4.92	10–150	50–302	0.0588	0.02116	**0.1707**	5.86	
	0.109	6.80	10–150	50–302	0.0471	0.01694	**0.1366**	7.32	
Feathers, with air	...	...	0–18	32–64	0.0574	0.0207	**0.1667**	6.00	Rubner, 1895
Mammal's hair, with air	...	...	0–18	32–64	0.0576	0.0208	**0.1672**	5.98	Rubner, 1895
Silk, with air	...	...	0–18	32–64	0.0613	0.02207	**0.178**	5.62	Rubner, 1895
Mammal's hair, without air	...	...	0–18	32–64	0.479	0.1725	**1.391**	0.7185	Rubner, 1895
Silk, without air	...	...	0–18	32–64	0.887	0.3193	**2.576**	0.3883	Rubner, 1895
"Keystone" hair felt (and other fibres), confined with building paper; flexible	0.30	18.72	30	86	0.093	0.0335	**0.2702**	3.703	Bureau of Standards
Silk	...	...			0.095	0.0342	**0.276**	3.623	Lees & Chorlton
Silk, scrap from spinning mill; for covering steam pipes	0.101	6.3	0	32	0.01055	0.038	**0.3067**	3.26	
			50	122	0.0125	0.045	**0.363**	2.754	Nusselt, 1908
			100	212	0.01416	0.051	**0.4117**	2.43	
Silk, braided	0.147	9.175	0	32	0.01083	0.039	**0.3147**	3.174	
			50	122	0.01305	0.047	**0.379**	2.64	Nusselt, 1908
			100	212	0.01445	0.052	**0.4195**	2.384	
Silk, scrap from spinning mill; for covering steam pipes	0.100	6.24	−200	−328	0.05555	0.020	**0.1614**	6.194	
			−150	−238	0.0075	0.027	**0.2179**	4.59	
			−100	−148	0.00889	0.032	**0.2583**	3.872	Groeber, 1910 (Sphere)
			−50	−58	0.010415	0.0375	**0.3027**	3.30	
			0	+32	0.0118	0.0425	**0.343**	2.916	
			+50	122	0.01334	0.0480	**0.387**	2.583	
Sheep's wool (impure, slightly greasy)	0.136	8.48	0	32	0.0917	0.033	**0.2662**	3.76	
			50	122	0.1166	0.042	**0.3387**	2.952	Nusselt, 1908
			100	212	0.139	0.050	**0.403**	2.48	
Sheep's wool, slightly greasy	0.084	5.24	76.3	169.4	0.1811	0.0663	**0.5348**	1.87	Desvignes
Leather, chamois	...		...	...	0.15	0.054	**0.4355**	2.297	Lees & Chorlton
Leather, sole	1.00	62.4	...	...	0.38	0.1368	**1.103**	0.907	Bureau of Standards
Leather, cowhide	...		72–97	162–207	0.42	0.1512	**1.22**	0.82	Lees & Chorlton
Flannel	...		...	below 32	0.0355	0.01278	**0.1031**	9.7	Forbes

THERMAL CONDUCTIVITY OF A FEW METALS

A. S. R. E. Insulation Committee Report, Revised 1924

MATERIAL	Density		Temp. of Sample, mean or range		Thermal Conductivity			Resistance per inch thickness (R)	Authority
	Grams per cu. cm. (Specific gravity)	Pounds per cu. ft.	°C.	°F.	Gram Calorie, sec., cm.², deg. C. x 1000	Kg. Calorie hour, m², deg. C.	B.t.u. hour, sq. ft., 1 in. °F Commercial conductivity	1 / Col. 8	
COLUMN 1	2	3	4	5	6	7	8	9	10
Steel Wool, No. 2	0.152	9.48	10–100	50–212	0.1919	0.069	**0.557**	1.794	Randolph
(Note influence of subdivision into more voids	0.101	6.30	10–100	50–212	0.209	0.07525	**0.607**	1.647	
containing confined air.)	0.076	4.74	10–100	50–212	0.2157	0.0776	**0.626**	1.597	
Mercury			0	32	14.8	5.33	**43**	0.02326	H. F. Weber
			50	122	18.9	6.8	**54.8**	0.01826	
Antimony			0	32	44.2	15.9	**128.35**	0.00779	Lorenz
			100	212	39.6	14.25	**115**	0.0087	
Lead			−183	−297.4	108	38.9	**313.8**	0.003187	Macchia
			−160	−256	92	33.1	**267**	0.003745	Lees
			−12	10.4	92.1	33.14	**267.3**	0.00374	Macchia
			0	32	83.6	30.1	**243**	0.004116	Lorenz
			18	64.4	83.	29.9	**241**	0.00415	Lees
			100	212	76.4	27.51	**222**	0.004503	Lorenz
Steel, Bessemer			15	59	96.4	34.7	**280**	0.003573	Kirchhoff & Hansemann
Steel, puddled			15	59	137.5	49.5	**399**	0.002507	Kirchhoff & Hansemann
Steel, carbon 1%			−160	−256	113	40.7	**328**	0.003048	Lees
			18	64.4	115	41.4	**334**	0.002995	Lees
			18	64.4	108.5	39.04	**315**	0.003173	Jaeger & Diesselhorst
			100	212	107.6	38.76	**312.5**	0.00320	
Nickel, 99%			−160	−256	129	46.44	**374.5**	0.00267	Lees
			18	64.4	140	50.4	**406.3**	0.00246	Lees
Wrought iron with 0.1% carbon; 0.2% silica; 0.1% manganese			18	64.4	143.6	51.7	**417**	0.002398	Jaeger & Diesselhorst
			100	212	142.0	51.1	**412**	0.002428	
Cast iron with 3.5% carbon; 1.4% silica; 0.5% manganese			30	86	149	53.6	**432.5**	0.00231	Hall & Ayres
Tin			0	32	152.8	55	**443.5**	0.002255	Lorenz
			100	212	142.3	51.2	**413**	0.00242	
Bronze with 85.7% copper; 7.15% zinc; 6.39% tin; 0.58% nickel			18	64.4	142.7	51.4	**414.3**	0.002412	Jaeger & Diesselhorst
			100	212	169.7	61.05	**492.2**	0.002031	

THERMAL CONDUCTIVITY OF A FEW METALS—*Continued*

A. S. R. E. Insulation Committee Report, Revised 1924

Brass, yellow			0	32	204.1	73.5	**592.5**	0.001688	Lorenz
			100	212	254	91.5	738	0.001355	
Brass, red			0	32	246	88.6	714	0.00140	Lorenz
			100	212	282.7	101.7	820	0.00122	
Zinc, pure			15	59	152.8	55	**443.4**	0.002257	Kirchhoff & Hansemann
			18	64.4	265.3	95.5	**770**	0.001299	Jaeger & Diesselhorst
			100	212	261.9	94.3	**760**	0.001316	
Magnesium			0–100	32–212	376	135.4	**1091**	0.000916	Lorenz
Aluminum			0	32	343.5	123.6	**997**	0.001003	Lorenz
			100	212	361.9	130.25	**1050**	0.000952	
Aluminum with 0.5% iron and 0.4% copper			18	64.4	480.1	173	**1395**	0.000717	Jaeger & Diesselhorst
			100	212	492.3	177.3	**1430**	0.000699	
Copper			0	32	719.8	259	**2090**	0.000478	Lorenz
			100	212	722.6	260	**2098**	0.000476	
Copper, pure			18	64.4	891.5	320.7	**2588**	0.000386	Jaeger & Diesselhorst
			100	212	877.1	313.2	**2547**	0.000393	
Copper			74	165.2	914	328.8	**2653**	0.000377	Child & Quick
			166.8	332.3	1024	368.7	**2974**	0.000336	
Copper, pure			—160	—256	1079	388.5	**3135**	0.000319	Lees
			18	64.4	916	330	**2660**	0.000376	
Silver (a metal often used as basis for comparison), 999.8 fine			0	32	1096	394.5	**3182**	0.000314	H. F. Weber
			18	64.4	1006	362	**2920**	0.000342	Jaeger & Diesselhorst
			100	212	991.9	356.5	**2880**	0.000347	

Section XI of "Heat Transmission of Insulating Materials," published by the American Society of Refrigerating Engineers, New York City, is a Bibliography of "References to articles and publications treating of heat insulation and heat transfer," compiled by Chas. H. Herter, with the cooperation of A. J. Wood and E. F. Grundhofer of the Pennsylvania State College. The source and year of publication, name of author and title are given in practically all listings.

Space does not permit the appending of this Bibliography, although its value in connection with the foregoing tables of thermal conductivity of various insulating materials will warrant its possession.

CORK INSULATION

Part III—The Insulation of Ice and Cold Storage Plants and Cold Rooms In General.

CHAPTER XI.

REQUIREMENTS OF A SATISFACTORY INSULATION FOR COLD STORAGE TEMPERATURES.

80.—Essential Requirements.—The widening knowledge of the use of refrigeration created a very definite demand for a suitable insulation for cold storage temperatures, which resulted in the introduction in 1893 of pure, compressed, baked corkboard, the superior qualities of which were apparent almost from the beginning; and its application became so general during the first quarter century of its use as to practically displace all competing materials, and strictly on its merits alone has become the accepted standard insulation for cold storage temperatures wherever refrigeration is employed.

It is by no mere chance, of course, that cork bark is the foundation for the one satisfactory insulating material for cold storage temperatures; and the reason for its universal acceptance and extensive use is easily, though not generally, understood.

Pure corkboard, as an ideal insulating material for cold storage temperatures, excels in every single particular; but it possesses one inherent quality without which it could not have been used for cold storage work at all—it is inherently nonabsorbent of moisture, that is, does not possess capillarity, the property that causes a blotter to suck up ink; for cold storage temperatures very definitely involve moisture conditions, through the medium of the condensation of water against cold surfaces, and any material that is to retain its initial insulating efficiency in the almost continuous presence of moisture, must be impervious to moisture, must be inherently free from capillarity, else it will become saturated with water and lose its insulating worth entirely.

A satisfactory insulation for any purpose whatever must be able to retard the flow of heat to an unusual degree. Many materials will do this, but a satisfactory insulation for cold storage temperatures must combine with such insulating property the ability to retain its insulating efficiency for an indefinite period under the adverse conditions of the constant presence of moisture. Pure corkboard meets this very exacting combination of these two major requirements to a degree never yet approximated under actual operating conditions by any other insulation.

Then, too, the delicacy of many foodstuffs makes them peculiarly susceptible to tainting, and the insulation must keep free from rot, mold and offensive odors, and be germ- and vermin-proof; economical building construction requires an insulation that possesses ample structural strength and in such form that it can be installed easily in all types of buildings; conservation of valuable space requires an insulation that is compact and occupies minimum space; the reduction of fire hazard calls for an insulation that is slow-burning and fire-retarding; and in the interests of economy, the insulating material must be easily obtained and reasonable in cost. Pure corkboard also meets these secondary but nevertheless important requirements better than any other insulating material that has ever been offered commercially.

81.—**A Good Nonconductor of Heat.**—It has been seen that heat transference is accomplished by conduction, convection and radiation; and that when the problem of insulating a cold room, for example, is under consideration, the heat transfer by *conduction* is the most important, consisting of ninety per cent or more of the total heat leakage into the room when a suitable insulating material is employed.

It will be recalled that the heat conductivity of dense substances, such as metal, is high; that of lighter materials, such as wood, is less; while that of gases is very low. Thus air, the most available gas, is the poorest *conductor* of heat, if a vacuum is excepted, but air is a good *convector* of heat, unless it is broken up into great numbers of minute particles, so small in size that the effect of convection currents is reduced to a negligible quantity.

Consequently, in an efficient insulating material, air must be present in the very smallest possible units, such as atoms, so that convection is reduced to a minimum; and since these atoms of air must each be confined, the use of a very light encompassing material having little density and thus very low conduction, is essential. Such an insulator will be as efficient from the standpoint of heat transfer as it is possible to obtain;

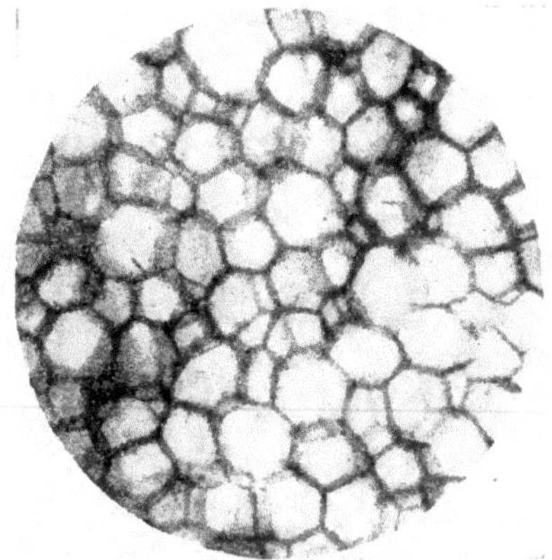

FIG. 47.—CORKBOARD UNDER POWERFUL MICROSCOPE, SHOWING CONCEALED AIR CELLS.

that is, a very light material containing myriads of microscopic air cells, each one sealed unto itself.

The outer bark of the cork oak was evidently provided by nature to prevent the sun's rays and the hot winds from drying up the life-sustaining sap that courses through the inner bark of this peculiar and remarkable tree; and an examination under the microscope reveals the reason why cork is such an excellent nonconductor of heat. It is found to be composed of countless air cells, so tiny and infinitesimal that it takes many millions of them to fill a cubic inch of space. Flow of heat by convection is therefore reduced to the lowest conceivable minimum, because the velocity that can be obtained by air in so small a space is virtually *nil*. Again, these cells are separated from each other by thin walls of tissue of very low density. Thus the flow of heat by conduction is as low as is reasonable to expect in any material extant.

FIG. 48.—BOILING TEST ON CORKBOARD INSULATION.

It would therefore be but natural to find this outer bark an excellent nonconductor of heat, and the experience of many years with pure corkboard has amply confirmed this deduction.

82.—Inherently Nonabsorbent of Moisture.—A satisfactory insulation, however, for any purpose, must retain its insulating efficiency indefinitely. That is, it must not pack down and lose its original "dead-air" content; and it must not become saturated with moisture, since water is a relatively good conveyor of heat. Suitable materials for the insulation of warm or hot surfaces may possess the property of absorbing water, for under normal conditions of service they are rarely subjected to severe moisture conditions and are almost constantly undergoing a drying out process; but cold storage temperatures, on the other hand, involve moisture conditions, through the precipitation of moisture from air in contact with cold surfaces, and any material that is to retain its original insulating efficiency in the almost continuous presence of moisture and in the absence of appreciable heat, must be impervious to moisture. In a word, a satisfactory insulation for cold storage temperatures must be inherently free from capillarity, as otherwise it will, in the presence of moisture, become saturated and of no further value as an insulating material.

At least as early as the reign of Augustus Cæsar, cork was used as stoppers for wine vessels, and has been used during the intervening 2,000 years, practically unchallenged, as stoppers for liquid containers, thus amply demonstrating its inherent imperviousness to moisture. And this important property of cork—its entire freedom from capillarity—is in no way impaired by the manufacturing process followed in the production of pure corkboard. On the contrary, the inherent or natural qualities of cork that makes it the basis for the best cold storage insulation yet discovered or developed on a commercial scale, are enhanced by the baking of the granules of pure cork bark in metal molds under pressure at moderate temperature; for such manufacturing process brings out the natural resin of the cork, which cements the particles firmly together and makes the use of an artificial binder unnecessary, and by coating the entire surface of each separate granule with a thin film of the natural waterproof gum affords an additional barrier against the possible entrance of moisture.

The "Navy Test" was designed by the United States Navy Department some years ago to concentrate in a short period of time those destructive forces to which all cold storage insulation is subject during its term of actual service. The test consists of boiling a piece of insulation completely submerged for three hours at atmospheric pressure without its disintegrating and without its expanding more than two per cent in any direction. Pure corkboard of standard quality easily meets the requirements of this test, merely demonstrating in a simple laboratory way that corkboard insulation is proof against deterioration in service from the destructive action of moisture that is ever present at cold storage temperatures.

83.—Sanitary and Odorless.—Any insulating material employed at cold storage temperatures usually encounters foodstuffs, and should therefore be perfectly sanitary and free from mold, rot, appreciable odor or vermin. For these reasons any insulation in which binders are used, especially pitch, is dangerous, since the delicacy of many foodstuffs makes them peculiarly susceptible to tainting and contamination.

Pure corkboard contains no foreign binder of any character and the cork bark of which it is composed is inherently moisture-proof. Therefore it will not rot, mold or give off offensive odors; and if corkboard is properly erected, it is vermin-proof. Cold storage rooms insulated with pure corkboard, and finished with Portland cement troweled smooth, as recommended by the United States Department of Meat Inspection, are easily and indefinitely kept in sanitary and hygienic condition by ordinary washing and cleansing methods.

The sanitary and odorless qualities of an insulation for cold storage temperatures are of very real importance, and pure corkboard is easily the standard by which all cold storage insulating materials are judged.

84.—Compact and Structurally Strong.—It has been noted that a particle of cork bark is made up of a myriad of tiny sealed air cells, separated from each other by thin walls of tissue of very low density, each cell containing a microscopic bit of air. In the manufacture of pure corkboard, of standard specifications, the particles of cork bark are sufficiently compressed in the molds to eliminate the voids between the particles, which produces a finished material of maximum compactness in relation to weight and insulating value.

This compactness is an essential quality of pure corkboard, a quality not possessed in proportionate degree by other insulating materials. In fibrous materials, or materials not of cellular structure, the insulating value is dependent on air spaces, which are not independent of each other. The air content is merely entrapped between closely matted or interlaced fibres, such interstices or voids being connected one with another; and when moisture contacts with such materials

FIG. 49.—PURE CORKBOARD INSULATION IN MODERN FIBRE CARTON CONTAINING 72 BOARD FEET.

it is readily communicated, not alone by capillarity but also by gravity, from one air space to another.

The inherent ruggedness and toughness of cork bark is one of its outstanding and well-known qualities; and after it has been properly processed into sheets of pure corkboard, the resultant product is sufficiently strong to permit of its being transported, handled and used as readily as lumber, its strength in compression being sufficient to take care of loads many times greater than ordinarily encountered. The remarkable strength of such an excellent nonconducting material is simply another of the very important reasons for its universal use for all cold storage purposes.

85.—Convenient in Form and Easy to Install.—The standard sheet of pure corkboard, 12 inches wide and 36 inches long, which all American and most foreign manufacturers follow as a standard, is the most convenient in form for every purpose. It may be handled, sawed, and applied as readily as lumber, or put up in Portland cement or hot asphalt cement with the same ease as any common building material. Its characteristics are such that there need be little, if any, waste from sawing and fitting, because the fractional sheets may be neatly and tightly assembled to give as efficient an installation as could be had with the full size standard sheets.

FIG. 50.—APPARATUS FOR SIMPLE FIRE TEST ON PURE CORKBOARD.

86.—A Fire Retardant.—In the manufacture of pure corkboard, partial carbonization of the raw cork bark is accomplished without destruction of tissue, that is, the baking process, at moderate temperatures, dissolves the resins (inherent in cork bark) sufficiently to everlastingly bind the particles into a good, strong sheet of insulation, while at the same time producing a protection of carbon that a flame penetrates with much difficulty.

A simple experiment to show the slow-burning and fire-retarding properties of pure corkboard as compared with other materials can be made by anyone by means of an iron rack and a gas burner. Place the sample of insulation on the rack and record the time it takes to burn a hole clear through and carefully note the condition of each sample at the conclusion of each test. A piece of pure corkboard two inches thick will not burn through under about four hours if subjected in this way to a 1500° F. gas flame; and when this is compared with the condition of other kinds of cold storage insulating materials at the end of similar tests, it will be clear why the underwriters have given their approval to pure corkboard and to no other form of cold storage insulation.

FIG. 51.—CORKBOARD INSULATION ON BRICK WALL—APPROVED BY NATIONAL BOARD OF UNDERWRITERS.

Many examples of the remarkable value of pure corkboard as a fire retardant could be selected from the fire records of the past thirty years or so, if it were any longer necessary in the minds of insulation users to offer proof of this well-known fact; but possibly it will serve a double purpose to make specific mention here of a fire that lasted nine hours in the grocery of A. Weber of Kansas City, Missouri, on December 3, 1914, and which consumed everything of value in the basement except the corkboard insulated cold storage room. Fifty hours after the fire started the frost still remained on the pipes in this room, which was then found to be only 38° F., a rise in temperature of but 10° from the time the fire started. Thus not only the fire retarding property of pure corkboard was spectacularly demonstrated,—the Portland cement finish having been destroyed but the corkboard having escaped almost unharmed,—but the remarkable insulating value of pure corkboard was most effectively demonstrated as well.

FIG. 52.—BASEMENT OF WEBER'S STORE AFTER THE FIRE.—NOTE CORKBOARD WALLS OF THE COLD STORAGE ROOM IN BACKGROUND.

Other demonstrations† of what pure corkboard will do in actual fires have been so numerous as to attract considerable attention. In cold storage plants in particular, total destruction of buildings and equipment has often been prevented solely by the corkboard walls of the cold storage rooms.

87.—Easily Obtained and Reasonable in Cost.—Pure corkboard can today be classed as merchandise, and is carried in stock in every city of any importance in the United States. In addition, large supplies are always on hand in storage warehouses at New York and New Orleans, and at the four facto-

†See Appendix for "How Insulation Saved a Refinery."

ries that manufacture corkboard in the United States. Consequently, pure corkboard insulation is almost as easily obtained in this country as is any approved building material in common use; and considering its permanent insulating worth and general utility, is fairly priced and often to be had at a cost that makes its purchase an unusually attractive investment.

88.—Permanent Insulating Efficiency.—Thus it will be noted that the requirements of a satisfactory insulation for cold storage temperatures cover a wide range indeed, and may be summed up briefly in the statement that such insulation must be of such permanent thermal resistivity, obtainable in such form, structurally suitable in such degree, readily available in such quantity and at such price, as to make that insulating material one of permanent insulating worth and efficiency.

There are, perhaps, a number of insulating materials of various kinds and in various forms, that show, under laboratory tests, when such materials are new and dry and unused, a heat resistivity, or an insulating value, as high as, or higher than, pure corkboard insulation; but for many years it has been the actual experience of countless insulation users that pure corkboard of proper thickness applied in the proper manner is the only cold storage insulation for which, from every consideration, permanent efficiency can be claimed.

CHAPTER XII.

PROPER THICKNESS OF CORKBOARD TO USE AND STRUCTURAL SUGGESTIONS.

89.—Economic Value of Insulating Materials.—During the past fifteen years or so there has been considerable time and attention given to the study of insulating materials, both theoretical and practical; but the results have taken the form of the determination and comparison of the thermal efficiency of many materials, and the best methods of erecting and caring for them in service, rather than having dealt with the determination of the range of profitable expenditure which is the real aim and end of industrial research. In the absence of any concrete information of generally recognized worth on the subject of how much money it is advantageous to expend for cold storage insulation, the users of such materials have divided into two main classes: First, those who came to believe that it was not profitable to employ as much insulation as generally recommended by responsible manufacturers, or who came to believe that cheaper materials in the same thicknesses would suffice; and, secondly, those whose experience and judgment taught them that increased thicknesses of only the best insulating materials were profitable to install.

Those in the first class are much in the minority, yet their numbers justify careful consideration of their policy. It might be expected that a third class exists, consisting of those who have not changed their insulation ideas and practices during the period of time mentioned; but it is believed that these are now so few in actual numbers as to be of no real importance with respect to a discussion of this subject.

The true economic value of an insulating material must, of course, follow rather closely a consideration of the monetary return on the initial insulation investment for the period of the useful expectancy of such insulation. The factors to which it is possible to assign definite values are:

(a) Value of heat loss through insulation in terms of total cost to remove it.
(b) Interest on the insulation investment.
(c) Insurance on the insulation investment.
(d) Cost of insulation repairs and depreciation.
(e) Value of building space occupied by insulation.

In addition, there are certain factors for or against more and/or better insulation, the value of which it is often difficult to determine or predict, as follows:

(f) Term of useful expectancy for insulation, or probable obsolescence period.
(g) Improvement in product from better temperature conditions due to insulation.
(h) Advertising value of better cold storage equipment.
(i) Saving in cost of bringing product and/or room to temperature.
(j) Saving resulting from ability to anticipate with reasonable accuracy the drop in thermal efficiency of the insulation in service.
(k) Type and character of structure to which insulation is to be applied.
(l) Ability to obtain proper application of insulation.
(m) Effect of type, temperature and continuity of refrigeration applied.
(n) Effect of outside atmospheric conditions.
(o) Effect of air humidity maintained in insulated rooms.
(p) Effect of the arrangement of product stored and its influence on air circulation over insulation.
(q) Effect of anticipated abuse of insulation and failure to make repairs.
(r) Funds available.

Mr. P. Nicholls*, Pittsburgh, Pa., working along these lines and taking the general case of a flat surface with insulation applied to it, developed the formula:

$$X = 1.74\sqrt{\left\{\frac{A(T_a - t)F + \dfrac{0.327P}{K(C - t_1)}\left\{I' + R' + \dfrac{100}{Y'}\right\}(T_m - t)}{B\left\{I + R + \dfrac{100}{Y}\right\} + 8.3S} \times C\right\}} - \frac{C}{U}$$

in which

X = economic thickness of insulation in inches, that is, the thick-

*P. Nicholls, Supervising Engineer, Fuel Section, Bureau of Mines Experiment Station, U. S. Dept. of Commerce, Pittsburgh, Pa.

ness that will reduce to a minimum the sum of the expenses due to the heat leakage through the insulation plus the expenses of preventing the additional heat leakage.

C = average thermal conductivity coefficient of insulation during its life, in B.t.u. per square foot, per inch thickness, per hour, per degree temperature difference F.

B = cost of insulation installed, in dollars per square foot, per inch thickness, or in dollars per board foot. (Note: $B = (\frac{H}{X} + B')$ where H = the fixed square foot cost to cover wall finish, plaster, starting the insulation job, etc., and B' = cost of insulation per square foot that is proportional to the thickness.)

I = per cent interest allowed on insulation investment, plus per cent insurance cost.

Y = years of life allowed insulation.

R = yearly repair cost, as per cent of investment in insulation.

F = fraction of year room is in operation.

T_m = maximum temperature during the period of yearly operation of the outside air adjacent to cold storage room wall, in degrees F.

t = cold room temperature, in degrees F.

t_p = mean temperature of cooling coil piping.

K = surface transmission coefficient of pipe surface in B.t.u., per square foot, per hour, per degree F.

A = average cost over period of yearly operation, in dollars, of one ton of refrigeration (cost per B.t.u. × 288,000) delivered to the room under consideration, exclusive of cooling piping.

P = cost in dollars of the pipe per square foot of its surface, including installation and accessories.

G = investment in refrigerating equipment, of whatever nature, in dollars per ton of refrigeration per day. This excludes machinery, the cost burden of which is included in A.

$$(\text{Note: } G = \frac{288{,}000\ P}{24\ K\ (t_p - t)})$$

I' = per cent interest allowed on refrigerating equipment investment covered by G.

Y' = years of life allowed refrigerating equipment covered by G.

R' = yearly repair cost, as per cent of investment in refrigerating equipment covered by G.

S = yearly value of one cubic foot of space occupied by insulation.

U = the over-all thermal coefficient of heat transmission from air to air for the given thickness of the entire wall, other than insulation, and including the surface transmission coefficients of the outside wall surface and the inside insulated wall surface.

By substituting:

C = 0.35 B.t.u.

$$B = \left\{\frac{0.04}{X} + 0.16\right\} \text{dollars}$$

I = 6 per cent.
Y = 15 years.
R = 3 per cent.
F = 1 year.

$T_a = 50°$ F. average temperature outside wall.
$T_m = 90°$ F.
$t =$ cold room temperature, degrees F., as assigned.
$(t - t_p) = 10°$ F.
$K = 2.0$ surface transmission coefficient.
$A = \$1.00$ per ton.
$P = \$4.35$ per square foot.
$I' = 6$ per cent.
$Y' = 8$ years.
$R' = 3$ per cent.
$S = 0$.
$U = 0.303$.

the economical thickness, X, of insulation was readily obtained for a range of cold room temperatures, t, and curve B of Fig. 53 was platted.

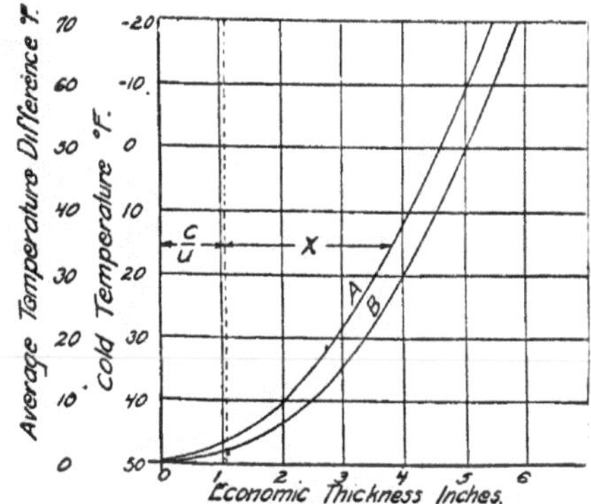

FIG. 53.—WALL INSULATION—ECONOMIC THICKNESS AGAINST TEMPERATURE.

With the same set of conditions and a cold room temperature of 20° F., the true yearly cost, per square foot, based on various thicknesses of insulation, were computed and curve B of Fig. 54 was platted.

According to the definition, the economic thickness of insulation occurs when the yearly cost is a minimum, which thickness is (3.99—1.06) 2.93 inches on the curve in Fig. 54; and the shape of the curve shows that *the refrigeration cost per square foot increases at a more rapid rate with a given decrease below the economic thickness than it does for a similar increase.* It will also be noted that such curve is comparatively flat on each side of the economic thickness, indicating that *a small change in insulation thickness, either above or below the true point of maximum economy, will not materially affect the cost of refrigeration per square foot.*

The real value of the work of Mr. Nicholls is summarized in the two deductions just set forth in italics, rather than in the numerical results obtained for economic thicknesses of insulation as shown by the curves, because values for factors (f) to (r) could not be assigned and made a part of the formula.

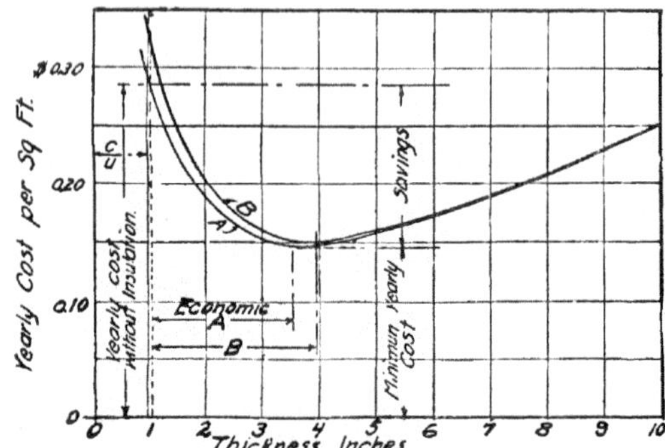

FIG. 54.—YEARLY WALL COST PER SQUARE FOOT AGAINST THICKNESS OF INSULATION.

90.—Tendency Toward More and Better Insulation.—Many years ago a responsible manufacturer of pure corkboard* pointed out that:

The proper thickness of . . . corkboard to install, in order to maintain a given temperature economically, depends, as with every other type of insulation, upon several factors, which vary in the case of each plant:

(a) The character of the building—whether brick, stone, concrete, hollow tile or frame;
(b) The thickness of the walls, floors and ceilings;
(c) The temperature to be maintained;
(d) The climatic conditions;
(e) The character of the material to be stored or the purpose for which the rooms are to be used;
(f) The cost of producing refrigeration.

*Armstrong Cork Company, Insulation Department, Pittsburgh, Pa.

Each case that arises must be considered on its own merits. Generally speaking, however, it may be said that under average conditions, the thicknesses of . . . corkboard that can be economically installed for the several temperatures noted, are as follows:

ORIGINAL RECOMMENDATIONS FOR CORKBOARD THICKNESS

Temperatures	Thickness
—20° to — 5° F.	8 inches
— 5° to + 5° F.	6 inches
5° to 20° F.	5 inches
20° to 35° F.	4 inches
35° to 45° F.	3 inches
45° and above	2 inches

For the bottom of freezing tanks, five inches or preferably six inches of . . . corkboard should be employed; around the sides the same thickness of corkboard, or twelve inches of granulated cork securely tamped in place.

The method of arriving at these recommendations might not now conform with the data and information available, but the experience of many years has taught that these recommendations for pure corkboard were then sound to a remarkable degree.

Reference has previously been made to a class of insulation users who came to believe that it was not profitable to employ as much insulation as recommended by responsible manufacturers, or who came to believe that cheaper materials in about the same thicknesses would suffice. It was pointed out that they were much in the minority, yet their numbers justified consideration of their policy.

The factors that influence this class of buyers are:

(a) Uncertainty as to the success of the undertaking.

(b) Building on leased property, or building on owned property the value and/or utility of which is subject to quick change.

(c) Excess refrigerating machine capacity available.

(d) Insufficient initial funds available for best equipment.

(e) Expansion as part of plan to prepare business for sale, consolidation or refinancing.

(f) Work in charge of an architect, engineer or contractor who follows the practice of specifying materials and labor of but average quality for the sake of wide competition and the lowest price.

(g) Influence of the practices of the business being conducted, such as one offering average or indifferent quality product at average or low prices, upon the purchase of products, supplies and equipment.

(h) Lack of true knowledge of the importance of adequate refrigeration and insulation equipment.

91.—Proper Thickness of Corkboard to Use.—The original recommendations for pure corkboard insulation need be changed only slightly to bring them up to date, as follows:

PROPER THICKNESS OF CORKBOARD.

Temperatures	Thickness
—20° to —10° F.	12 inches
—10° to — 5° F.	10 inches
— 5° to 0° F.	8 inches
0° to 10° F.	7 inches
10° to 20° F.	6 inches
20° to 30° F.	5 inches
30° to 40° F.	4 inches
40° to 50° F.	3 inches
50° and above	2 inches

This table is predicated on a useful expectancy for corkboard insulation of about fifteen years†, an ideal condition of prod-

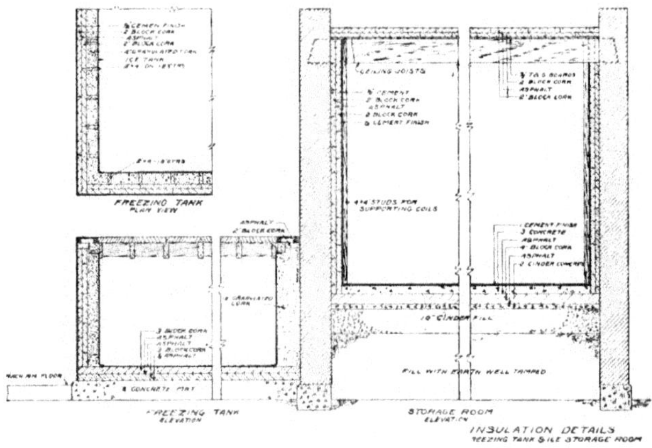

FIG. 55.—VOGT INSULATION DETAILS FOR NEW FREEZING TANK AND ICE STORAGE ROOM.

uct stored, and a depreciation in thermal insulation efficiency of not to exceed 10 per cent for the useful expectancy period. Such table follows very closely the general practice of today, by the majority of insulation users, whose experience and judgment has taught them that generous thicknesses of only the best insulating materials are profitable in the long run to install.

†This time limit fixed by anticipated obsolescence, rather than by the probable life of the corkboard insulation.

92.—Importance of Proper Insulation Design.—It is now customary, when planning an ice or a cold storage plant, to treat the entire project as a whole, so that location, building, cold rooms, mechanical equipment, and complete cost are all properly balanced and correlated, to the end that the purpose and intent of the undertaking can be fully and satisfactorily carried out. Such a project should be entrusted only to reliable architects and engineers competent to handle cold storage work; and if so entrusted, the design of the insulation should have that major attention that its importance and cost entitles it to receive.

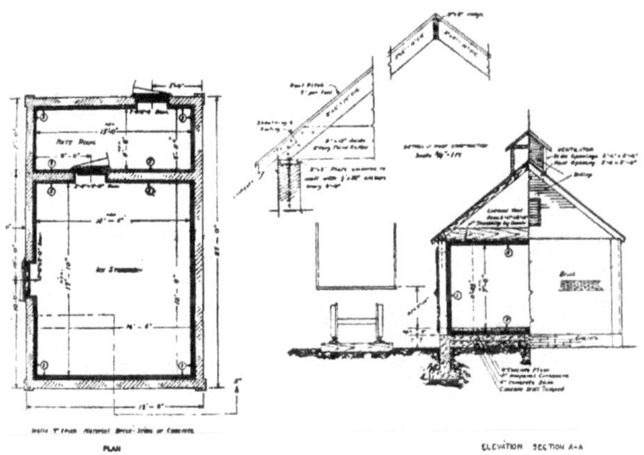

FIG. 56.—TYPICAL SUB-STATION FOR STORAGE AND HANDLING OF ICE, INSULATED WITH 4-IN. CORKBOARD.

Each new ice plant and each new cold storage plant will present its own peculiar problems in design and equipment; but the field of insulation experience is now so very broad and has yielded up so many lessons, especially lessons in what not to do, that no architect and engineer who is really experienced in the design and operation of such plants need longer be in doubt as to the proper insulating material to use and the proper insulation specifications to employ. It must never be forgotten, however, that insulation is a branch of engineering and construction that is highly specialized, and an architect's license alone is in no sense a sufficient recommendation for the handling of an ice or cold storage project. Here, as in most cases of specialized building construction, it will pay to engage the architect and engineer who has had considerable experience in cold storage work.

But in addition to the insulation that is built into ice and cold storage plants as part and parcel of their original design, there are innumerable small insulated cold storage rooms and groups of rooms designed and built for use in connection with commercial refrigerating machines, which units are installed as adjuncts to businesses usually handling food products in one form or another. Such installations are made to serve the local needs of the individual business,—such as creameries, dairies, fruit storages, produce houses, poultry and egg plants, meat markets, groceries, hotels, clubs, hospitals, oil refineries, candy factories, ice cream factories, and so forth,—and in connection with the installation of which no architect or engineer is usually employed. Among such rooms there is a great variety of shape and size, design and arrangement, method of cooling, and so forth; because a variety of purposes must be served by rooms built into every sort of structure, under many different conditions; and such rooms can here be discussed first as a class and then special features treated separately as they may apply in certain cases.

For many years the order for planning such a cold storage room, after deciding on its location and size, was to consider first its refrigeration and then how it was to be designed and insulated. The order is now reversed, in most cases, with excellent results; because it is today better understood that the efficiency of the insulation determines in great degree the amount of refrigeration that is required and how it should be applied. It has been seen how the kind of insulation that goes into a cold storage room has a direct bearing not only on the amount of the initial investment, but also on the everyday cost of operation, yearly repairs, etc. The design of the room, however, is equally important; because the very best insulation will be ineffective and short lived unless it is properly installed, following correct design. Thus in planning cold storage rooms, provision must first be made for their adequate insulation, for on this feature more than any other will depend their permanence and the economy and efficiency of their operation.

93.—Types and Design of Cold Storage Rooms.—It is well known that cold storage rooms and groups of rooms are required for ice making and ice storage, creameries and dairies, fruit and produce houses, poultry and egg plants, fish and meat markets, groceries and provisioneries, candy and ice

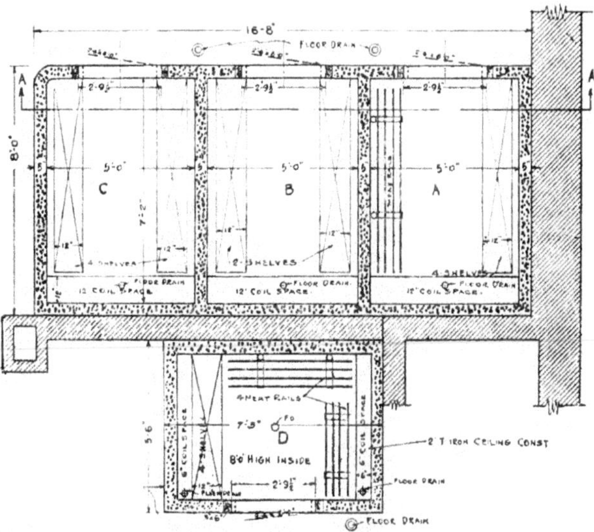

FIG. 57.—BAKER PLAN FOR INSULATED ROOMS IN OLD BUILDING.

cream factories, hotels and clubs, hospitals and sanitariums, precooling and canning plants, oil and gasoline refineries, waxed paper and paraffin coating establishments, fur and garment storages, brewing and bottling plants, battery and ignition testing rooms, serum and vaccine rooms, sharp freezers and hardening rooms, and so forth. These rooms may readily be divided into two main classes; that is, those operating above freezing temperature, and those operating below freezing.

In new structures, cold storage rooms to operate at any desired temperature can be made the exact shape and size desired, and in every way suited to their purpose; but the majority of cold storage rooms operating above freezing—usually serving the purpose of the storage or handling of food products—are erected in existing buildings, and must be conformed to structural limitations. The design of cold storage rooms employing pure corkboard insulation is so very adaptable, however, in experienced hands, that there are virtually no restrictions on the construction of such rooms. Space, shape, height, location, kind of building, single room or a group of rooms; it is all "grist for the mill" when the basic, underlying principles of insulation design are understood.

The two chief points to be kept in mind in the design of cold storage rooms are: First, the principle of no voids or air spaces in or back of the insulation; and, secondly, the principle of ample air circulation within the cold room. The principle of no air spaces in or back of the insulation is of primary importance when rooms are to operate below freezing, and the principle of ample air circulation is of primary importance when rooms are to operate above 32° F., although both principles are of major importance in either case.

The first principle, that of no voids or air spaces in or back of the insulation, is especially important where cold storage rooms are to operate below freezing, because of the greater likelihood of colder temperatures back of the insulation and the consequent greater likelihood of condensed water. If there are no voids in the insulation itself, no voids in the finish applied to the surface of the insulation, no voids in the material used to bond the insulation to the surfaces to which it is applied, no voids or open cracks between the sheets of corkboard, no voids or air pockets in the construction of the building walls themselves, no voids anywhere, the result will be a perfect insulation job, assuming such perfect conditions obtainable; for all such voids and air spaces are likely to fill up with water, through condensation of moisture from the air against chilled surfaces, and deterioration and lowered insulation efficiency will be the certain result.

In practice, the aim is for that which is as near perfection as is consistent with a variety of conditions, costs, and so forth. If possible, walls, floors and ceilings should be of solid construction, that is, without voids or air spaces, as solid brick or concrete in preference to hollow tile or sheathed studs and joists. The air in such spaces contains moisture in suspension, which is likely to be condensed on the cool surfaces next to the cold temperature room*; and as the water contained in the air in such spaces condenses, it occupies as a liquid less

FIG. 58.—SAUSAGE COOLER WITH STATIONARY AND PORTABLE RACKS, TRACKING AND OVERHEAD BUNKERS.

space than it did as a vapor, an uneven pressure is set up or partial vacuum created, more air containing moisture of proportion indicated by its humidity is drawn in, more precipitation takes place, and if there is then no opportunity for such water deposits to quickly evaporate away again, all such spaces will be the source of "moisture trouble." Such moist-

*Dirty lath streaks on ceilings of offices, residences, etc., furnish a good example of the precipitation of moisture from the air against cool surfaces. In winter the air above the wood lath and plaster is often cooler than the air of the room; and, as a result, moisture is condensed on the cool strips of plaster between the lath, and minute particles of dust are caught in this moisture.

ure, in closed-in spaces, may be the cause of all sorts of building construction troubles, such as rotting, and bulging and cracking from uneven expansion; but our thought will be primarily for the damage to the insulation itself. In the case of ceilings especially, the water slowly finds its way into the insulation underneath, and failure of that ceiling insulation will be the certain result. Where such construction cannot be avoided, all such spaces should be left as open as

FIG. 59.—ICE CREAM HARDENING ROOM WITH PERFORATED PLATES OVER PIPE SHELVES.

possible so that air may circulate freely through them and thus carry off by evaporation any condensed moisture.

The second principle, that of ample air circulation, is even more important in cold storage rooms operating above freezing than it is in rooms maintaining lower temperatures; because refrigeration in its simplest terms is the extraction and removal of heat from the goods stored, which is done not by immediate contact between the goods and the refrigerant but through the medium of the air, and in rooms operating above freezing the moderately cooled air does not drop to the floor of the room as swiftly as if it were chilled to a lower temperature. That is, in rooms operating above freezing, the air circulation is naturally sluggish, although the process of heat interchange, by means of the positive circulation of the air, is essential. Room design must therefore promote air circulation as much as possible, to keep it positive and active, especially in rooms used for products containing much moisture, such as butter, poultry and meats, particularly if such products are put in warm for quick chilling; because such moisture must be taken up by the circulating air and carried quickly to the coils and there deposited as frost. Otherwise, with poor circulation, moisture will condense on the finish of the insulated surfaces, on the goods stored, or remain in the air of the room to make it damp and mouldy.

94.—Types of Bunkers and Details of Construction.—The one positive way to guarantee a definite circulation of air throughout a cold storage room is to construct a separate cooling room, or coil bunker room, install air conveying ducts from the coil room to and into the cold storage room, and by means of blower equipment circulate or pass the air of the cold storage room through the system and over the cooling coils at a predetermined rate. This method of positive circulation, or cold air distribution, is frequently employed in fur rooms, candy dipping rooms, freezing rooms, or wherever the demand justifies the initial expense for such extra equipment and the cost of its subsequent operation.

By far the most effective natural means of insuring active circulation is the overhead bunker. Air, cooled over such bunker by contact with the cooling coils or ice, falls over the low side of the bunker and to the floor, due to the fact that cold air is heavier than the warmer air it displaces; and as this cold air absorbs the heat of the goods stored as well as the heat that leaks into the room through the insulation, doors, etc., such air rises over the high side of the bunker, circulates through the coils or over the ice, gives up its excess of heat to the refrigerant, and begins the cycle over again. Thus the circulation follows its natural course, and as the bunker extends the length of the room, the air circulation reaches every corner of the room and maintains a fairly uniform temperature in practically all parts.

Single overhead bunkers are the most common type, but should not be used for rooms over 16 feet in width. For rooms wider than 16 feet, double bunkers should be installed. The bunker construction serves to guide the circulating air, and this function is greatly assisted by proper bunker design. First, the warm air up-take and the cold air down-flow must

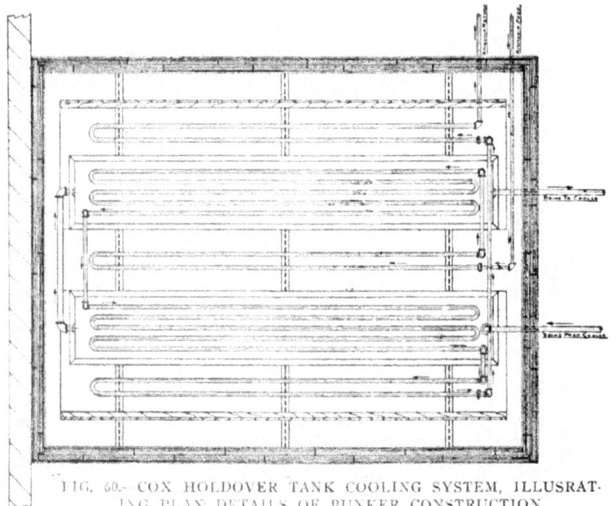

FIG. 60.—COX HOLDOVER TANK COOLING SYSTEM, ILLUSRATING PLAN DETAILS OF BUNKER CONSTRUCTION AND CORKBOARD INSULATION.

be adequate; a "rule-o'-thumb" method that has given excellent results in rooms operating above freezing is to make the total width of these duct openings equivalent to one-third of the total width of the room, and then divide that one-third equally between the warm and the cold air ducts. Care should then be exercised not to "choke" the circulation at any point in the bunker construction between the warm air entrance and the cold air exit, either by restricting the passage by decreased dimensions, or by obstructing it by a crowded arrangement of coils or ice, or by counter air currents set up by failure to use sufficient insulation on the bottom* and baffle of the bunker.

The overhead bunker, single or multiple type, requires considerable head room, a 10-foot height before the insulation is erected on floor and ceiling being necessary for a maximum head room of 6 feet under bunker and a coil loft maximum height of 2¼ feet. A minimum height of 12 feet before insulation is applied is much better, especially if ice, which re-

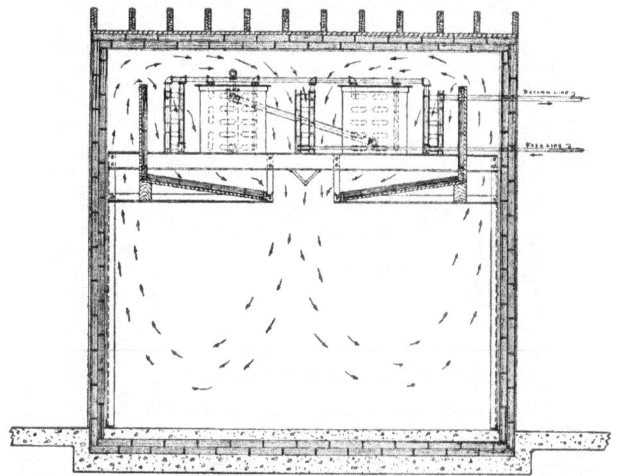

FIG. 61.—COX HOLDOVER TANK COOLING SYSTEM, ILLUSTRATING ELEVATION DETAILS OF BUNKER CONSTRUCTION AND CORKBOARD INSULATION.

quires more head room than coils, is to be used. If the room is to contain overhead tracking, additional height will be necessary. The natural arrangement of double bunkers is to place each warm air up-take next a side wall and the cold air down-flow in the center of the room; because the warmest air in the cold storage room is likely, on account of the heat leakage, to be a layer adjacent to the walls. In certain cases, however, such as chill rooms for fresh killed poultry or precoolers for fresh beef, this warm and cold air duct order

*Sufficient insulation on the bottom of bunker will also prevent sweating.

should be reversed; because the greater temperature will then come from the fresh goods stored in the room, away from the walls, and the natural circulation will be through a warm air up-take in the center of the room and down at either side.

In the case of a single bunker, the warm air up-take should be on the entrance door side of the cold storage room, so that the in-flow of warm air occasioned by the opening of the cold storage door will be carried up and over the bunker before coming in contact with the goods stored in the room.

Where the available ceiling height does not permit of overhead bunkers, the side or wall bunker may be used, though it is much less effective, except in narrow rooms, a width of 12 feet probably being the ultimate limit for a single wall

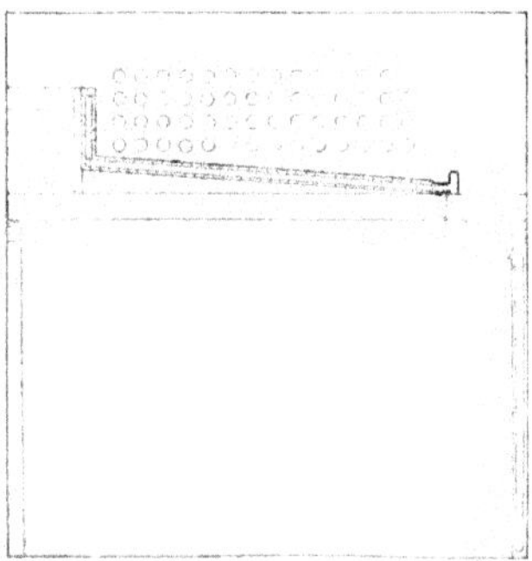

FIG. 62.—SECTION OF TYPICAL SINGLE OVERHEAD COIL BUNKER.

bunker. Wider rooms of limited ceiling height should have wall bunkers along both sides, but not along one side and one end.

Low rooms employing mechanical refrigeration, frequently use ceiling or wall coils, or both, instead of the side bunker, provided the cold storage room does not contain too much moisture requiring an active and positive circulation to dispose of it as frost on the cooling coils. Drip pans under ceiling coils and open drain spouting under wall coils should be provided to care for the water of meltage. Very wide rooms and rooms used for long storage, more often use ceiling coils than bunkers, regardless of the height available; such ceiling coils are grouped and the groups spaced at proper distances, each group equipped with an *insulated* drip pan, a modified form of overhead bunker. The arrangement, when both ceiling and wall coils are used, should never include an installation of piping on ceiling, one side wall and one end wall; but should be limited to ceiling and one or both side walls, so as to avoid cross or counter currents and consequent poor air circulation and "pockets." Where wall coils only are used, the coils should be located on opposite side walls, or equally dis-

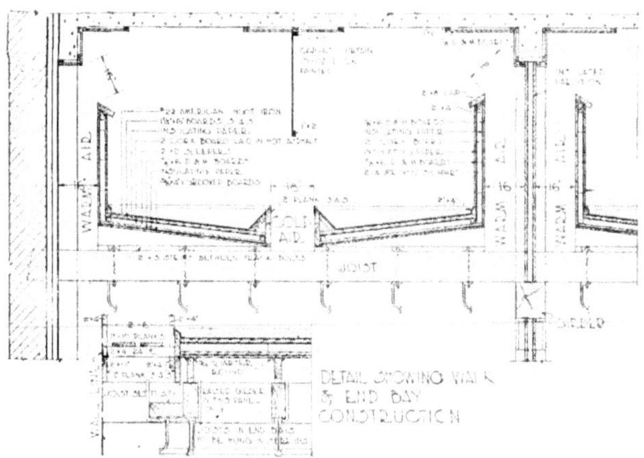

FIG. 63.—DETAIL OF HENSCHIEN PIPE LOFT FOR HOG COOLER.

tributed on all four walls, the shape of the room as it may or may not depart from a square being the governing factor.

95.—Circulation, Ventilation and Humidification.—A good deal has previously been said about the necessity for air circulation in cold storage rooms, but the subject shall now be briefly considered in conjunction with the ventilation and humidification of rooms used for the handling and storage of certain products.

The question of the hygrometric condition of the air in

cold storage rooms, especially in refrigerated warehouses, is of much importance for satisfactory results in the preservation of various kinds of foods, such as fruits, meats, eggs, etc. Humidity is now believed by many to be almost as important as temperature itself; and this conviction coupled with the further recognition of the desirability, if not the necessity, for the ventilation of rooms containing certain products, makes circulation, ventilation and humidification of cold rooms an important, and it may be said an involved, subject.

It is a well-known fact that meat cannot stand a higher temperature than the freezing point, without it undergoes a continuous evaporation through its surface, unless the humidity of the cold room is kept sufficiently low. For eggs, the

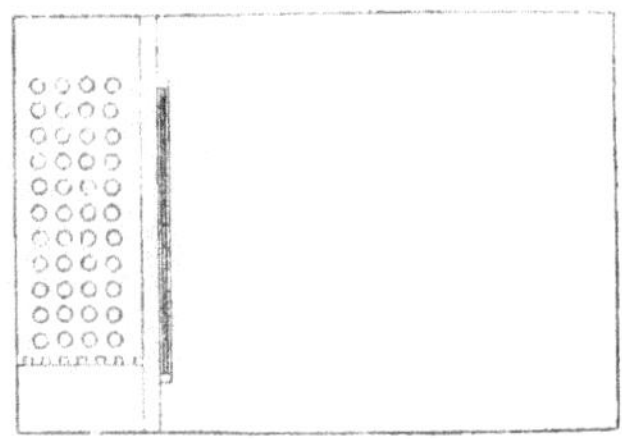

FIG. 64.—SECTION OF TYPICAL SIDE BUNKER ARRANGEMENT FOR SMALL ROOM OF RESTRICTED HEIGHT.

air must be kept at a higher degree of moisture than for meat. For fresh fruits, the air must be moist enough to prevent the drying out of the fruit due to excessive surface evaporation, while at the same time the air must not be too moist if decay is to be avoided.

Thus with some products it is essential for best results that some form of ventilation and humidification, or air conditioning, be provided in cold storage rooms to prevent evaporation and spoilage; and the proper design and insulation of such rooms is even more important than that of the regular run of cold storage rooms. The question of the proper method and equipment to use for the air conditioning of cold storage rooms will not be treated in this text, although permission has been given for the partial reproduction of an article, which should be of general interest at this point, on the subject of "Temperature, Humidity, Air Circulation and Ventilation," by M. R. Carpenter, Architect and Refrigerating Engineer, 72 W. Washington St., Chicago, Illinois:

During the past ten years, or thereabout, the subject of air conditions in cold storage has been receiving considerable attention from those who are in a position to recognize the shortcomings of the average cold storage plant as a means of holding and preserving edible products, during the time of storage.

FIG. 65.—INSULATED MEAT COOLER ON BLUE STAR LINE S. S. ALAMEDA, SHOWING INSTALLATION OF PIPING ON CEILING AND ALL WALLS.

Many things are involved in the successful preservation of such commodities and it is for the purpose of calling attention to these various items that this paper is written.

As a rule, cold storage plants represent the expenditure of large sums of money and are owned and operated by conservative business men, who have to be shown before they will adopt any new system, or attempt to maintain any condition in their cold storage rooms which has not been proved to them to be desirable in practical use. This is good business policy, as failure would mean the loss of enormous sums in spoiled goods, which they would have to assume, due to such experiments.

In the early days of cold storage, the first consideration was temperature, and the designers of such plants gave little thought to other features. This is still true, for that matter, with a large majority, as may be noted by examination of many storages, and by the fact that practically all contract forms issued by manufacturers of refrigerating machinery guarantee temperatures and nothing further, inside of the rooms; but practice soon proved that other things were important, especially as some storages were damp and musty, which was disastrous to the goods, due to the growth of fungi or mould; therefore, it was found desirable to adopt measures to avoid this condition, and the next step was in the direction of obtaining cold, dry rooms; this was accomplished either by properly locating the refrigerating coils

FIG. 66.—CORKBOARD INSULATED CHOCOLATE DIPPING ROOM WITH COLD AIR DUCT CIRCULATING SYSTEM.

or by some method of drying the air, by means of lime or calcium chloride; the various methods for accomplishing this are familiar to all, especially the older heads.

Experience showed that the design of the refrigerating coils and the location of them in the rooms to be cooled had a material bearing, both on the efficiency of the cooling effect and on the humidity of the air; this was to have been expected as it follows out a simple law of nature which, when adhered to consistently, results in an extremely dry atmosphere.

This dry condition naturally leads to shrinkage, or evaporation of the moisture from the goods, which, if it was allowed to proceed beyond a certain point, caused trouble of another type; therefore, it was found desirable to maintain a certain amount of humidity; and many practical experiments were, and still are, being made, to determine to just what extent relative humidity can be carried before it becomes objectionable and dangerous in other respects; this led to many differences of opinion, as each example of practical results was modified by specific conditions pertaining particularly to the individual room; these conditions were not fully understood or taken into consideration in the conclusions; therefore, a certain relative humidity, which proved correct or beneficial in one room, or house, proved incorrect in another; then, too, the method and manner employed for

FIG. 67.—MEAT STORAGE COOLER WITH OVERHEAD TRACKING AND COIL ROOM ABOVE.

determining humidity was often open to question, as was also the correctness of the determination.

Humidity determinations taken in a room are often of no value in fixing the relative humidity immediately surrounding the goods, due to sluggish air movement or definite pocketing of the surrounding air, such as, for instance, goods contained in tight barrels or other tight or semi-tight packages, goods wrapped in paper, or goods piled tight, without channels between them.

As a rule, there is very little trouble encountered in securing humidity; the difficulty lies in controlling it and maintaining it constant; therefore, the tendency is to proceed very carefully and not overdo it.

Until comparatively recent years, there has been no reliable data on which to proceed in a practical way. It is true that experiments have been made for years; some along the line of best temperatures for particular goods, some for humidity in relation to shrinkage, humidity in relation to mould, etc., and these experiments have been made by individuals fully qualified and capable of carrying on such work. Especially is this true of the experiments made by the United States Department of Agriculture; however, in most cases there has been a lack of some certain conditions, or combination of conditions, either through lack of knowledge of new factors entering into the experiment, or through a lack of efficient apparatus to fully cover all requirements. No criticism of these experiments is implied, for every one, when made with care, has brought us nearer to a solution, and a step-by-step advancement in this art is a surer way than to try everything at once.

It probably is universally conceded that all vegetable products have a definite life limit, during which time they function as living organisms, absorbing or breathing in certain gases and exhaling, or giving off certain other gases or esters, during which period they continue to develop and change until their physical development is complete and their life span is ended, after which, especially in the case of fruits, they are spoken of as being dead ripe.

Assuming the foregoing facts to be true, one may readily appreciate how necessary it is to have definite air circulation to supply fresh air to absorb the heat, as well as to remove the gases given off, or ejected, by the goods.

No vegetable products, in the natural state, are of the same food value after becoming dead ripe, as they are at some stage prior to reaching that state, after which no temperature or other cold storage condition will prevent them from deteriorating at a rapid rate.

Animal products, on the other hand, are dead and any change is either chemical or due to plant or animal organisms.

Granting that the foregoing statements are correct, let us consider what means will best serve to prolong the life of fruits, vegetables and animal products. In answering this, there need be no hesitancy in stating that there are just two factors—correct temperature, and pure, conditioned air. By conditioned air, is meant air containing the correct amount of moisture for the particular goods under consideration. This sounds rather simple; yet, to secure these two conditions requires a knowledge of and a scientific appreciation of nature's laws. To even approach a state of perfection in a practical way, involves about all that is known at the present time regarding correct design, equipment, and operation of cold storage warehouses; so it is not as simple as it seems.

It may be well to consider, at this time, briefly, the subject of temperature. What is its function? And pure, conditioned air; what part does it play?

Temperature affects the growth of living organisms, both vegetable and animal, and, when below the temperature level best suited to this growth, or development, has the effect of slowing them up, rendering them dormant or destroying them entirely; depending upon the decreasing temperature to which they are subjected; therefore, in the case of vegetables or fruit products, their life span is increased, and, in respect to attack from the outside, they are again protected by the dormant condition of their enemies.

Animal products, which are dead substances, can only be preserved by the prevention of changes due to attack by living organisms, either contained in but not a part of them, or by attack from the outside; again, as in the case of the vegetable kingdom, these enemies are rendered less active as the temperature decreases.

Our problem may then be divided into two parts. The first is to determine the correct temperature and relative humidity of the air, for each particular product; and this division may best be left in the hands of scientists, who have the proper knowledge and apparatus for making scientific tests and determinations for solution. The second involves the application of the conditions first found, and naturally leads to the designing engineer, with the co-operation of the scientist, in providing such construction, apparatus and operation as will secure the correct temperature and air conditions.

Having been instructed regarding the proper temperatures and relative humidity, how shall we proceed to secure them?

Temperature.

We shall first consider temperature. It is self-evident that if a product is to be held at a certain specified temperature, it is the temperature of the product and not necessarily the temperature of the room which is important.

This being the case, how are we to insure the temperature of the product? In answer to this, it is necessary to consider the transfer of heat. Heat must be taken from the goods and delivered into the refrigerant, which is circulating through the refrigerating coils, and this heat can only be transferred in two ways—by conduction, or by convection.

Heat transfer by conduction through air is a slow process, and altogether out of consideration for practical results; therefore, transfer by convection is the only practical method, and this involves a definite air movement, and the rapidity with which the heat is transferred is in direct proportion to the rapidity of the air movement through the goods, to and over the refrigerating coils and back to the goods.

There are two methods of circulating air, one way being to take advantage of what is called natural circulation, that is, air movement in a vertical direction, due to the difference in temperature, or specific gravity, which method is slow, uncertain, and with little power to overcome obstacles, to reach out into pockets and crevices, or to move through piled goods in any direction.

The other method is by means of mechanically moved or forced air circulation, which is powerful and active in entering into all crevices, pockets, etc., and which moves through goods in any direction, thereby taking up the heat from the interior of packages, as well as from the outside, and is therefore efficient in securing quick transfer of heat.

From the foregoing it will be noted that the only practical method of insuring the proper temperature of goods in storage appears to be to subject them to a forced air circulation, due consideration to be given to proper piling, ventilated crates, etc., and with means of controlling the intensity of the air movement.

Air and air movement are considered in the foregoing only as a medium for holding, and a method of conveying the heat units from the goods to the refrigerating coils; later we shall utilize this same air and air movement for another purpose.

Pure Conditioned Air.

The second condition essential for the preservation of goods is to surround them with air which is free from all foreign gases, dust, germs, spores, bacteria, etc., but with sufficient moisture content to prevent the absorption of the natural moisture content of the goods, as otherwise they would be caused to shrink, which is not only objectionable in itself, but, in the case of vegetable products, also causes them to become more susceptible to attack from other sources, and hastens the breaking down of the whole organic structure.

Pure air not only insures against contamination from the exterior, but has a decided purifying effect in itself.

To surround goods with pure air and correct moisture content, it is not sufficient to merely maintain this condition in the open parts of the room; because, as in the consideration of temperature, it is the products themselves which must be considered, and the air in the room is only an approximate indication, depending largely upon the circulation of the air.

As in the example under temperature, natural circulation is very slow and without the power to penetrate deeply; therefore, air becomes pocketed, in which condition it absorbs moisture from the goods until it becomes fully saturated; it also absorbs gases or esters and, as a result, becomes foul, the natural effect of which is to provide a condition suitable for the growth of moulds, fungi, or other destructive agents, which, also due to the lack of proper temperature, as shown before by sluggish or stagnant air, are not materially retarded in their growth.

The other method—that of forced air circulation—is positive, penetrating, and scrubbing in its action. It prevents any accumulation of dead air, and therefore maintains an ideal condition immediately in contact with the goods, assuming, of course, that the method of packing and storing the goods is in keeping with the idea of thorough and efficient air circulation.

It will have been noted that use of the term ventilation has not been made in any of the foregoing, the term being considered as a description covering another process.

In the foregoing subject of pure, conditioned air, it is assumed that the air being circulated is pure and of the correct relative humidity; in practice, this is, of course, impossible, unless there is provided some means of keeping it pure and of the right moisture content. The air is continuously taking up gases and odors from the goods, as well as changing in moisture content, due to absorption

FIG 68.—INSULATED EGG STORAGE WITH OVERHEAD BUNKERS AND PATENTED VENTILATING SYSTEM.

of moisture from the goods or depositing it on the refrigerating coils, thereby becoming impure and with the wrong moisture content, which will, in the course of time, cause the air to become foul and dangerous and, in the case of forced air circulation, increasingly so, due to the ability to distribute dangerous organisms, spores of disease germs, quickly and effectively, unless some provision is made for keeping it pure; this is where use is made of ventilation.

Starting out with the storage space clean and free from mould or objectionable odors, and with the goods in a clean and altogether suitable condition, the preservation is dependent more upon preventive measures than upon corrective ones, and it is a very simple matter to offset or rectify the slight contamination of the circulated air, due to eliminations from the goods, by some system of ventilation, that is, by introducing pure, fresh air, in sufficient quantities, while discharging an equal amount of stale air, thereby keeping the percentage of impurities down to a low point. Naturally the amount of fresh air introduced will depend entirely upon the amount required to rectify the foul condition of the old air.

Where forced air circulation is employed, providing the equipment is properly designed, the introduction of fresh air is a simple matter.

Normal Humidity.

The control of moisture content of the circulating air is difficult unless proper provision is made for adding or subtracting moisture, as occasion demands.

At this point, the privilege is taken of using one word to indicate the proper moisture content of the air for a specific commodity, and it is *normal*; normal may mean any relative humidity, but when used in connection with a specific commodity it is a definite percentage; if it is above this percentage, it is normal-plus, if below, it is normal-minus.

Therefore, what may be normal humidity for one class of goods may be normal-plus or normal-minus for another.

To determine what is normal in each instance is the work of the scientist, or it may be determined by practical experience, extending over a period of years, but in this case it may only apply to a particular room or warehouse, as the amount of moisture which may be maintained in the air of any room is absolutely dependent on the efficiency of the air circulating system and its ability to penetrate to all parts of the goods, thereby maintaining the proper temperature and air condition.

As before explained, the air, in circulating through the various channels, is ever subjected to conditions which have a tendency to vary the moisture content. The most severe conditions are: First, the goods in storage; and, second, the refrigerating coils; the first in adding to the moisture content and the second in reducing the moisture content, and, where ventilation is utilized to purify the air, another condition is encountered, which may either increase or decrease the humidity.

It has been proved by scientific research, as well as by practical experience, that a certain amount of moisture in the air is not only beneficial, but is absolutely necessary to the preservation of goods; also, that under certain conditions, especially with forced air circulation, it is absolutely necessary to maintain a high moisture content in the air.

Assuming, therefore, that we carry a relatively high humidity, which will prevent the air from taking up moisture from the goods, we have eliminated, to a large extent, interference from that source; we have then left the drying effect of the refrigerating coils and, with forced air circulation, this is sufficient, practically all of the time and under almost all conditions, to produce normal-minus humidity; therefore, in order to keep the air up to normal, it is usually necessary to introduce moisture, either with the fresh, ventilating air, or with the recirculated air. In either case, a fully saturated air may be introduced when necessary, without danger of depositing moisture on the goods, due to the fact that it will be mixed with a much greater volume of normal-minus air before coming into contact with the goods.

At certain seasons of the year, namely, during periods of low temperature, when the refrigerating coils are not being used, except to a very limited extent, if at all (and therefore their drying effect is greatly reduced or stopped entirely), nature still provides ample means

FIG. 69.—INSULATED BANANA ROOM EQUIPPED WITH OVERHEAD BUNKERS AND PATENTED CONTROL SYSTEM.

of controlling the humidity, by furnishing cold air which, when raised to the temperature requirements of the room, will be comparatively dry and may be introduced in sufficient volume to offset other conditions, and thus maintain the circulating air in normal condition.

Theoretically, the system which would maintain ideal air conditions would be one which circulated fresh, pure, conditioned air, at the proper temperature, through the goods in ample volume, and discharged it after one passage through the goods, but this is impracticable, due to the great expense of purifying, conditioning and cooling such a volume, and the enormous loss occasioned by discarding the air at such a temperature, and unnecessarily, as practically the conditions may be secured in another manner, that is, by introducing a small amount, comparatively, of pure air, which will rectify the air consumed or contaminated by the goods.

Pure air is difficult to secure, especially in or adjacent to thickly populated communities or manufacturing districts; however, various means may be employed to assist in this respect; to enter into discussion of this subject would be beside the point at this time, yet it may be well to call attention to one agent, which has been utilized to some extent and found beneficial under some conditions, but due to poor design or mechanical faults, and to apparatus not adapted to use in air with even a low relative humidity, the benefits have not been secured in full measure; this agent is "ozone" or "ionized air." Equipment for the production of ozone is now perfected and being installed under a guarantee, which safeguards the purchaser.

This agent and the equipment for producing the same is mentioned here, as it is particularly well adapted for use with forced air circulation, and gives just the teeth with which we wish to endow our air in order to make it function as a purifier.

In consideration of all that has been brought out heretofore, there is but one conclusion possible. In order to secure proper conditions for the preservation of food products there must be correct temperature and air conditions, in and around the products, which can be assured in one way only, that is, by mechanically circulated air.

Air conditions can only be secured by proper humidity control and efficient means of ventilating or rectifying, or both.

96.—Preparation of Building Surfaces to Receive Insulation.—Perhaps the greatest change in insulation practice during the past ten years has occurred in connection with the method of applying the initial course of insulation to wall surfaces, especially to concrete, brick, tile or stone.

To erect corkboard in any manner against plaster over wood or over metal lath, has never been approved; such lath and plaster must be removed and replaced by ⅞-inch T. & G. sheathing boards, solidly secured; and whether the insulation of a cold storage room should be erected against studs closed in by sheathing, will depend entirely upon the conditions surrounding each case. The dangers from confined air spaces back of insulation have already been pointed out; but the purpose, utility, cost, allowable investment, etc., should be the final determining factor for each project.

In the case of stone, concrete, brick and tile surfaces in existing buildings, it is necessary to take such surfaces as they come along, carefully inspect them, and then properly prepare them to receive insulation. Usually such surfaces have been whitewashed, painted, or otherwise coated; and if so, they must be carefully and thoroughly cleaned before it is possible to apply corkboard insulation to them successfully. Such cleaning must usually take the form of hacking, which is a difficult job in most instances, and considerable care must be exercised if the finished work is to be satisfactory.

After the complete area of such walls has been hacked, or otherwise prepared as required, it will often be found that their surfaces are sufficiently irregular to require pointing up, unless the first layer of insulation is to be erected in a bedding of Portland cement mortar, and sometimes even then. On the other hand, if the purpose of the insulated room or structure makes it imperative that the first layer of insulation be erected in hot asphalt to walls that have first been primed with suitable asphaltic material, then the pointing up work must take the form of a complete leveling and smoothing up of the areas to be insulated; because the thickness of the hot asphalt that clings to the sheets of corkboard when they are dipped, is quite insufficient to be relied upon for anything except a bond, and a uniformly full bond is not possible except against reasonably smooth, flat surfaces. Furthermore, if the primed surface to which the sheets of corkboard are applied is uneven, the surface of the finished cork work will be just as much, or possibly more, uneven, and may seriously interfere with the making of tight insulation joints and with the proper interior room finish over insulation, not to mention the air pockets behind the corkboards. Consequently, the cost of proper preparation for insulation to be applied in existing structures and following the most approved specifications, is sometimes prohibitive, and an insulation specification less expensive must be selected or the project altered or abandoned.

The preparation of surfaces in new structures to receive insulation frequently does not have the forethought and attention that its importance justifies. Preparation should begin with the drafting of the plans and specifications for the building itself; but smooth, even, brick walls on the architect's drawings are not necessarily smooth, even, brick walls when actually erected, unless thought is given to the functioning of those walls other than their load-carrying and encompassing capacity. It costs more to make both sides of a building wall equally straight and smooth; but if the latest, approved insulation specifications are to be carried out, this point must be given necessary advance attention.

The insulation specification usually followed for many years was to apply the first layer of corkboard to the new, clean building wall in a bedding of Portland cement, then apply the second layer to the first in a bedding of Portland cement, or in hot, odorless asphalt, and then finish the insulation off with Portland cement plaster, applied in two coats. Thus surfaces to receive insulation had to be only reasonably smooth; but failures of insulation applied in this way, especially in ice storage houses, became sufficiently numerous, as the years passed, to finally justify active investigation of the subject by manufacturers and important users; and the failures of insulation, aside from those due to poor materials and workmanship at the time of installation, were traceable to moisture in the insulation, which collected after the corkboard had been in service for some time and which in time caused disintegration of the corkboard through the decomposition of the resin binder in contact with water or which caused more rapid disintegration from alternate freezing and thawing of moisture in the insulation. These investigations conclusively demonstrated that this moisture found its way into the cork insulation through two distinct and different sources.

When water is precipitated on the plastered surface of an insulated cold storage room, by the condensation of moisture out of the air against a cool surface, a part of such water is absorbed by the plaster by capillarity, which tends slowly to disintegrate the plaster while placing a portion of this moisture on the surface of the insulation directly behind the plaster. The cork, unlike other materials, will not take up this water by capillarity, as previously explained, but such water may find its way into the corkboards by gravity, traveling through small interstices or voids between the particles of cork bark used in the manufacture of the corkboard. While manufacturers now understand and appreciate that the modern corkboard product of maximum worth must be compact and free from voids to the greatest possible extent, yet it would appear that in the manufacturing process all voids, especially surface voids, cannot be eliminated. Thus water in contact, as just explained, has been known to penetrate corkboard insulation to a depth of an inch or so toward the outside building walls.

Water may also find its way into corkboard insulation through an entirely different source, that is, from the outside of the building. When the temperature of a cold storage room is lowered by refrigeration, the air in that room contracts with cooling, because cold air occupies less space than the same original volume of warm air. Thus the cooling of the air in a cold storage room creates in that room a temporary partial vacuum, or an unequal pressure between the inside and the outside of the room. If the room is tightly closed, air will be sucked through the building walls and the insulation, to balance the unequal pressures, and this air, carrying with it water in suspension, the quantity measurable by the humidity of the air, will precipitate its moisture in the insulated wall where the dew point is reached.

The discovery of these two distinct ways in which moisture is placed in corkboard insulation has been of great value in revising insulation specifications. The air-proofing of the surfaces to which the insulation of cold storage rooms is applied, to be carried out as best as possible under each set of conditions, is now done wherever possible or feasible, so that instead of air being drawn through the building walls and the insulation to compensate a partial vacuum, such air will be supplied through some other channel or in some other way. For example, it is now frequently the practice in large ice storage houses to install a small air compensating vent door or opening in or near the ceiling.

It will be noted that surfaces to receive insulation are recommended to be air-proofed, not water-proofed; and the necessity for air-proofing is believed to increase with decrease of cold storage room operating temperature, and in a general way with the size of the room, that is, the greater the cubical content of the room the greater will be the vacuum effect produced by the refrigeration. Again, the choice of the kind of materials used in the building construction, for instance, will decrease or increase the resistance of the passage of air.

A hard, repressed brick is to be preferred. If monolithic concrete, it should contain a so-called water-proofing material to close up the pores as much as possible and provide just that much more resistance to the infiltration of air.

Reasonably smooth and level inside building surfaces must be left to receive insulation, if it is to be erected in hot asphalt instead of the usual half-inch bedding of Portland cement mortar; because there is no appreciable thickness to hot asphalt

FIG. 70.—MILK STORAGE ROOM WITH CEILING OF IRONED-ON-AT-THE-FACTORY MASTIC CORKBOARD AND WALL INSULATION PLASTERED.

to compensate uneven wall surfaces, as previously noted. To air-proof building walls, two good coats of a suitable "asphalt primer"—not ordinary asphalt paint—should be applied, by brush or spray gun, as reason dictates. A suitable priming material is a good grade of unfluxed petroleum asphalt cut to the proper consistency with a solvent. The corkboards should then be erected in hot, odorless asphalt against the primed surface of the building walls, and the second course of insulation erected to the first in the same material and additionally secured with hickory skewers. If the building surfaces provided in the first place are not reasonably smooth, the second layer of insulation may have to be erected to the first layer in a bedding of mortar, instead of in hot asphalt, to effect a general leveling up of the last course of insulation in preperation for the finish over insulation. But hot asphalt between the layers of corkboard is preferable, because it gives just that much additional air-proofing. Detailed information relative to asphalts will be found in a later Article in this Chapter; and detailed specifications and directions for applying asphalts will be found in their proper order in Chapters XIII and XIV, respectively.

It must not be inferred that the greater proportion of moisture in corkboard insulation comes in from the outside through the building construction. It is but one of two ways, and it will be recalled that the other way in which moisture finds entrance is through the Portland cement plaster finish that it has been for so many years the universal custom to apply; but the proper preparation of building surfaces to receive insulation is one of the most important single contributing items to the high efficiency and long life of cold storage room insulation.

97.—Insulation of Floors, Columns, Ceilings and Beams.— Probably because a cold storage room is colder at the floor than at the ceiling, even though the floor insulation may be wholly inadequate, some have been tempted to specify either very light floor insulation, or none at all. The importance of adequately insulating the bottoms of ice-making tanks and the floors of all ice storage houses and cold storage rooms, especially when such floors are located on the ground, is probably not as fully appreciated as is the necessity for proper insulation of other surfaces.

The fact that a cold storage room is colder at the floor than at other vertical points, even though it has no insulation on the floor, is due to the weight of cold air as compared with warm air, rather than to the possibility of the heat leakage being less through such uninsulated floor than it is through the insulated walls and ceiling. This fact, of course, is very elemental; but it evidently persists in the minds of some, and should be disposed of before proceeding to the consideration of the proper insulation of all floors that rest on the ground.

The average temperature of the earth varies for different years and localities between about 50° and 60° F. If a cold storage room is operated throughout the year, the loss of refrigeration per unit area through an uninsulated floor resting on the ground is surprising; and if such room is operated during the warm and hot seasons only, when the average temperature of the earth for such period is somewhat higher than the average for the year, then the loss of refrigeration through such uninsulated floor in contact with the ground is even a more serious item. Where temperatures below freezing are maintained, failure to adequately insulate ground floors is quite likely to entail serious losses other than those of unnecessary heat leakage, as the freezing of the earth has been known to disturb entire building structures with consequent heavy loss to property and business.

The insulation of floors should have the same careful consideration as would be given to the insulation of any other building surface. Sharp freezer rooms in cold storage plants should always be located on the top floor, or floors, not in the basement, and not between floors that are to operate at higher cold storage temperatures. If sharp freezers are located in the basement, there is unnecessary risk of the freezing of the ground underneath, even though the floor is heavily insulated, with consequent heavy losses; and if they are located between floors that are to operate at higher temperatures, goods stored on the floor directly above, even though the building slab between is well insulated, are likely to freeze.

The complete arrangement of cold storage rooms—their size, height, location, purpose, and general utility—should be most carefully thought out in advance, with the idea of adequate safeguard and maximum economy in construction and operation; and the degree of success obtainable with cold storage rooms is directly dependent on the degree of intelligence and care that is put into such planning.

Columns and pilasters, of concrete or steel, especially those in cold storage rooms situated in basements and lower floors, must be adequately insulated, primarily as a safeguard against disastrous results to the stability of the entire building structure caused by the freezing of the earth at their base. The proper insulation of columns and pilasters for the prevention

the ceiling construction, as floor insulation, and the insulation of the walls can be made continuous, without breaks at floor (ceiling) levels, by providing an interior building structure of concrete and steel to carry the load of the cold storage section of the building and its contents, and casing it in with self-sustaining curtain walls, of brick or concrete, entirely independent of the interior structure except for a few small metal ties. The insulation of *outside* building walls is then applied against the inner surface of the curtain walls in a continuous sheet, without breaks at floor lines and connecting with the

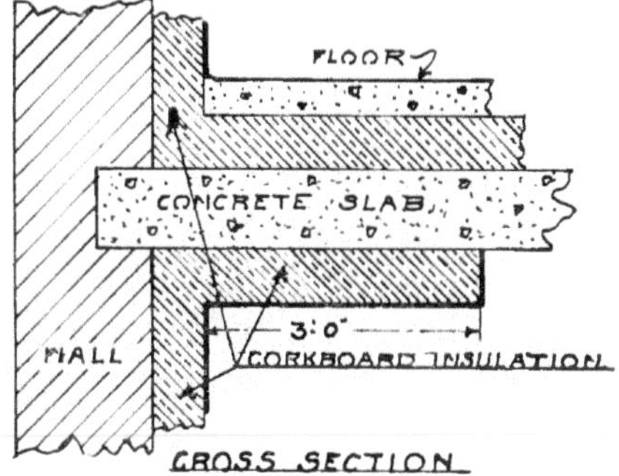

FIG. 73.—DETAILS OF BROKEN WALL INSULATION WITH 3-FOOT CORKBOARD RETURN ON CEILING BELOW (SEE TEXT).

proper floor (ceiling) insulation wherever it may occur; but where insulated *interior* dividing walls are required, such as those walls that may divide the cold storage section of the building from the dry storage section, provision frequently need be made only for self-sustaining cork walls unsupported by interior building walls of any kind. In this way the cold storage section of the building is literally enveloped with insulation, loss of refrigeration is reduced to a minimum, and all ceiling insulation disappears in favor of floor or roof insulation next above.

In old buildings of mill construction, it is frequently possible, and if so, highly desirable, to remove the ceiling and floor coverings at all wall lines where insulation will occur, and make such insulation *continuous* through and between the joists of such ceiling and join it with floor (ceiling) insulation above. In old buildings containing concrete ceiling slabs so supported as to make cutting through for continuous insulation impossible or not feasible, the wall insulation is sometimes carried out on the underside of ceiling a distance of 3 feet and then the entire floor area above is insulated.

The effect of this is to obtain an insulating value at the uninsulated perimeter of the concrete slab of something in excess of 36 inches of concrete, which will suffice for normal temperatures, and places much the greater part of the ceiling insulation on the floor above.

In old buildings of such design that *continuous* insulation is not possible or feasible, then the insulation must be applied to the underside of wood sheathed joists, or to the underside of concrete slab and around all beams and girders. Great care should then be taken to properly prepare the surfaces for such insulation, to properly apply it, and then finally to finish such insulation off in accordance with the most approved modern practice. Especial care should be taken to carry the insulation around all beams and girders, it never being permissible to construct any kind of false ceiling at the bottom line of beams or girders and apply insulation to such false work, leaving closed air spaces above, because such spaces will fill with water and the insulation will fail. If the height between floors of the building is greater than required for the cold storage rooms, then false ceilings hung from above are permissable if they leave enough space between for good ventilation. For rooms of moderate width, under the same conditions, where there will never be extra weight applied on top of the cold storage room ceiling construction, T-irons are frequently supported on the side wall insulation, 12 inches apart, to support two layers of corkboard, one above and one below, to form a self-supporting cork ceiling of satisfactory utility.

98.—Doors and Windows.—The three principal heat losses that occur in the average cold storage room, after it has been brought to temperature, are:

(a) Heat leakage through the insulated floor, walls and ceiling.

(b) Heat entrance permitted by the opening of doors, allowing warm air to pass in and cold air to pass out.

(c) Heat brought into the room in goods placed in storage, through the medium of the thermal capacity of such goods.

The relation of these, or the importance of any one with respect to another, in the case of any given cold storage room, is dependent on too many variables to permit of comparisons; but it is now generally recognized that the modern cold storage door plays an important part in reducing "door losses"

FIG. 74.—VICTOR STANDARD INSULATED FRONT FOR CORK-AND-CEMENT SERVICE REFRIGERATORS.

to a very low point. The fact is that the use of special door equipment, consisting of door and frame and hardware assembled complete, and built by reliable manufacturers, for cold stores, is now so universal in the United States as to be standard, the time-honored, ill-fitting, home-made cold storage door having been completely discarded in favor of the modern cold storage door that is well braced and heavily constructed of seasoned lumber to withstand years of hard special service, corkboard-insulated for highest permanent thermal efficiency, and delicately fitted to heavy frame on special and reliable hardware for quick and easy opening and air-tight closing. Cold storage windows, except for retail display purposes, were also discarded, following the advent of modern electric lighting equipment. Where windows must be used, they should be specially manufactured, with multiple panes and sealed air spaces and equipped with modern improved hardware.

With the use of modern cold storage door equipment, the entrance of heat permitted by the opening of doors cannot be further reduced except through the employment of such de-

FIG. 75.—STEVENSON "CAN'T STAND OPEN" TRACK DOOR—RIGHT HAND SWING.

vices as anterooms, vestibule or "flapper" doors, automatic door closers, etc., which will reduce the amount of warm air that would otherwise enter the cold room.

Cold storage doors may swing either "right-hand" or "left-hand"; and since there is often confusion as to the exact meaning of these terms, an explanation shall be given. When standing so as to squarely face the front of a cold storage door, a *right-hand* door will have the hinges on the right hand side, and when opened with the right hand will swing past the right hand side of the body; and a *left-hand* door will have the hinges on the left side and when opened with the left hand will swing past the left hand side of the body. Cold storage doors may have any one of three kinds of sills, namely, (1) beveled or threshold or beveled threshold, (2) high or overlapping, and (3) no-sill or angle iron or concrete. Specifications for cold storage doors to be equipped with automatic

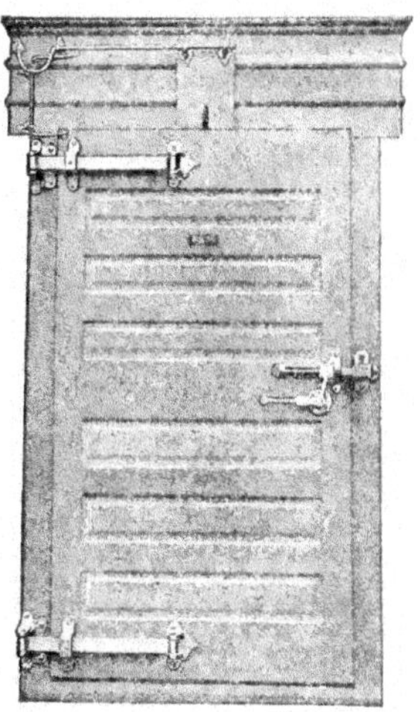

FIG. 76.—JAMISON STANDARD TRACK DOOR—LEFT HAND SWING.

trap door to accommodate overhead track, must include *the height of the top edge of track above the finished floor of the*

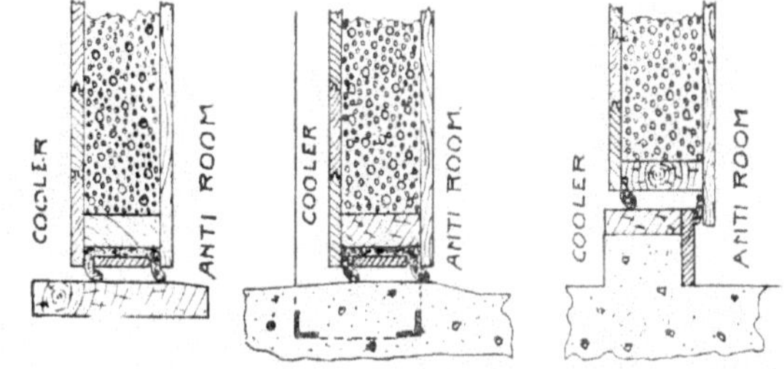

FIG. 77.—TYPES OF SILLS FOR COLD STORAGE DOORS—(LEFT) BEVELED THRESHOLD; (CENTER) NO-SILL; (RIGHT) HIGH SILL.

room just inside doorway, and the depth of rail. (Allowance is provided by manufacturers for any bevel of sill and any slight variation in the height of track rail.) The width and height of cold storage doors are always specified as "the dimensions inside of frame" or "door in the clear." In the case of the no-sill type, the height of the "door in the clear" is understood to be the dimension measured from the lowest point of frame at top of door to the concrete floor level in doorway. (Consult manufacturers for detailed cold storage door specifications.)

99.—**Interior Finishes for Cold Storage Rooms.**—It has been noted that when water is precipitated on the plastered surface of an insulated cold storage room, by the condensation of moisture from the air upon a cool surface, a part of such water is absorbed by the plaster by capillarity, which slowly disintegrates the plaster while placing a portion of such moisture on the surface of the insulation directly behind the plaster. Cork, unlike other materials, will not take up this water by capillarity, but such water may by gravity find its way into the corkboards through possible small interstices or voids between the particles of cork bark that comprise the sheet of insulation.

It has also been noted that the modern corkboard product of maximum worth must be compact and free from voids to the greatest possible extent, although the nature of the raw material, and the manufacturing process that must be followed, do not permit of the elimination of all voids, especially surface voids. Water in contact with corkboard on the walls of buildings can be expected to penetrate the insulation to some extent at least, such penetration having been known in extreme cases to reach a depth of as much as an inch or so.

Thus it should be evident that the finish over the corkboard insulation on cold storage room walls should have more than passing attention, but the subject has long been neglected and not until comparatively recently has it had serious attention.

Portland cement plaster troweled smooth and hard for the finish coat over the last layer of insulation is much better than plaster floated; because the troweled plaster is less porous and possesses less capillarity. This fact does not seem to be appreciated by many, however, for plaster floated has long been the universal practice, although for many years the United States Government has not permited floated plaster in government-inspected meat rooms because of its porosity and consequent tendency to take up water and become foul.

Materials not possessing capillarity, for the finish coat over cold storage room insulation, are coming into much favor. Factory ironed-on mastic finish coated corkboards for the sec-

FIG. 78.—CORKBOARD INSULATED ICE STORAGE HOUSE WITH PORTLAND CEMENT PLASTER FINISH.

ond course, with all joints effectively sealed at point of erection with the point of a hot tool, are much better where moisture is encountered in cold storage rooms than is any kind of plaster; while a finish having an emulsified asphalt base, which may be troweled on at the job, in two coats, in much the same way as plaster, is gaining in use, although it has probably not yet been tried over a sufficient period of time, and its formula has not yet been sufficiently standardized, to permit of an unqualified general approval.

If good troweled plaster on walls is finished off first with a filler and then with a good *elastic* enamel, such surface will present an efficient barrier to the entrance of moisture. An elastic enamel is required, to withstand the contraction and expansion of the room surfaces due to changes in temperature. The Portland cement plaster, however, is of such nature as to expand and contract a considerable amount, under cold storage room conditions, so much so that it has long been the practice to score the surface of such plaster finish in four foot squares to confine the checking and cracking to such score marks, or, if you wish, to provide expansion joints, similar to the expansion joints in concrete sidewalks. The weak points in enameled troweled plaster are these score marks, or expansion joints, and especial care must be taken to keep all such cracks so well closed with filler and enamel that little, if any, moisture will contact with the insulation through that source. To do this is not as difficult as it may sound, or as some would have us believe; for it is, in many cold storage rooms, entirely feasible and practical to use enameled troweled plaster on walls with entire success, and if to the plaster mix a small portion of some good and suitable integral waterproofing compound is added, the value of the plaster as a protective coating will be enhanced.

The service in cold storage rooms of cold storage buildings is not usually as severe, from the standpoint of moisture, as is the service in daily ice storages, milk rooms, poultry chill rooms, and a host of small cold storage rooms in small plants; because in cold storage buildings the rooms are not, as a rule, entered nearly as often as are the cold storage rooms in small plants, and when the rooms in a cold storage building are entered it is invariably through anterooms that keep the warm, outside air from rushing directly into the cold storage room and precipitating its moisture upon cool surfaces of every kind. Consequently, the need for the most efficient protective finish for the interior of cold storage rooms will be in rooms operating at moderate temperatures, such as from 28° to 35° or 40° F., in which rooms the moisture precipitated upon cold surfaces is not converted into frost crystals, or not so quickly converted but that there is an opportunity for some of it to be absorbed.

If insulation is applied to the underside of ceilings in rooms where the height is limited and cooling coils are either hung near the ceiling or placed close to the ceiling in bunkers, as is usual in the small cold storage rooms to be found outside of cold storage buildings, the finish over the corkboards should always be something more vulnerable than plaster. Either factory ironed-on mastic finish, with all joints carefully sealed upon application, or the very best emulsified asphalt prepara-

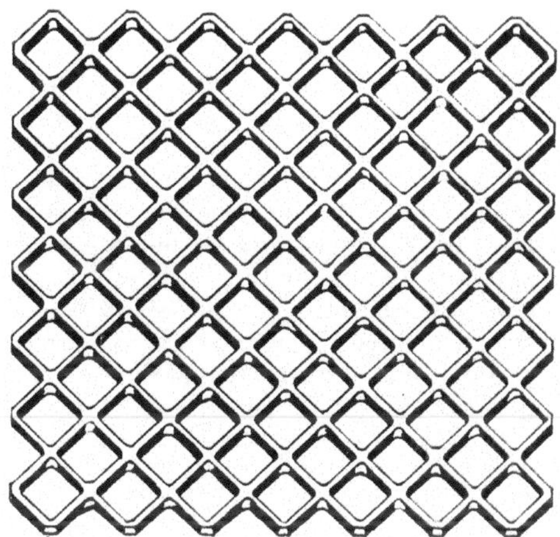

FIG. 79.—BARDES METAL FLOOR GRIDS.

tion, troweled on in two coats, should be used on all such insulated ceiling areas; and where coil bunkers are used, such special asphaltic waterproof finish should also be used on all walls down at least to the lower line of bunker construction, and often preferably on the entire wall areas of the room. (Plaster should never be applied in rooms to be used for the storage or handling of ice.)

Wall finishes containing asphalt will discolor most paints of lighter color unless a continuous coating of orange shellac is first applied to the asphaltic surface, but aluminum paint can be applied directly over asphalt without fear of discoloration. Aluminum painted surfaces have the advantage of radiating less heat than non-metallic surfaces, although since not over 10 per cent of all heat normally entering an insulated cold storage room through its surfaces is traceable to radiation and convection combined, the insulating effect of the aluminum paint is of negligible importance, and the finish should be valued alone for its utility as a coating and preserving material.

On floors, it is customary and very satisfactory to use concrete over insulation, such concrete troweled hard and smooth and sloped to drain. In ice storage houses the concrete should be of increased thickness, or contain reinforcing mesh, or both, on account of the weight to be supported. In fur storages, the desire is often for a wood floor of maple, which is satisfactory in dry rooms if properly laid. In milk rooms, and generally wherever metal containers must be moved over floors, metal grids should be imbedded flush in the concrete; in fact the use of such metal grids is increasing rapidly in cold storage rooms of every kind.

Lumber in cold storage rooms, as exposed ceiling construction where insulation is applied above, or as bunker construction, or as spacing strips on the floors and walls of ice storage houses, or as bumper plates around the walls to protect the finish from boxes and barrels, should not be creosoted before installation, because of the danger from odors, but should be properly painted immediately afterwards and before the cold storage room is put in service.

100.—Asphalt Cement and Asphalt Primer.—Authentic evidence exists that asphalt was known for its useful and valuable properties almost as far back as our knowledge of civilization extends. The earliest recorded use of asphalt was by the Sumarians, inhabitants of the Euphrates Valley before the ascendency of the Babylonians. Unearthed relics demonstrate that as early as 3000 B. C., asphalt was used by these people as a cement for attaching ornaments to sculptures, carvings and pottery. An asphalt mastic cast excavated at Lagash, near the mouth of the Euphrates, dates back to 2850 B. C., and as early as 2500 B. C. the Egyptians utilized melted asphalt as a preservative coating for the cloth wrappings of their mummies.

The famous towers of Babylon were protected for some twelve stories with a coating consisting of crushed brick mixed with bitumen, to effectually retard the encroachments of both damp creeping up from the earth and of the flood waters of the Euphrates. Arthur Danby says that there is no doubt but that the sole reason why the remaining tower of Babylon (Birs Nimrod) has stood for such a great length of time, is that the builders used bitumen as an admixture in its construction. Nebuchadnezzar's father, as king of Babylon, about 500 B. C., is believed to have first used asphalt as a mortar for brick pavements, and Nebuchadnezzar continued the practice, as recorded by an inscription on a brick taken from one of the streets.

Thus asphalt, instead of being a product of modern use, as may be commonly supposed, has a useful record behind it of thousands of years, handed down from the oldest civilization; but prior to about 1900 A. D. the term asphalt was restricted almost exclusively to certain semi-solid or solid bitumens found in natural deposits, often mixed with silt or clay and thus known as asphaltic-sand or rock-asphalt. Trinidad natural asphalt since about 1880, and Bermudez Lake natural asphalt since about 1890, have been imported into the United States and used for paving purposes. Deposits of asphaltic sands and rock asphalt have been found in the United States, but they appear to be somewhat unsuited for present industrial purposes. Small deposits of hard and nearly pure asphalts, commonly known as Gilsanite, Grahamite, and so forth, have also been discovered in the United States and are well suited for the manufacture of certain asphalt specialties.

Practically all natural or native asphalt is too hard for direct use in the manufacture of asphalt products; and after a simple refining process, which consists in heating the crude material until water, gas and other volatile material is driven off, native asphalt must be softened to suitable consistency by combining it with the proper amount of a residual petroleum known as flux oil. Petroleum probably always served as an important integral part of all asphalt used for industrial purposes; in fact, it is now generally believed that all natural asphalt originated in petroleum.

The first petroleum known and used in the United States was of the paraffin type and occurred in Pennsylvania, Ohio and Indiana. Distillation of this petroleum, to remove the more volatile matter, yielded a thick, greasy oil residue which proved quite satisfactory as a flux for natural asphalt, but which upon further distillation produced coke; whereas, later, with the discovery and refining of California petroleum, further distillation of California residual oil produced, before coke was formed, a semi-solid, sticky or tacky asphaltic material resembling native asphalts. Refinements in distillation processes improved the California petroleum asphalt until it was demonstrated that if recovered by suitable means it was essentially the same as certain native asphalts.

FIG. 86.—CORKBOARD INSULATED ICE STORAGE HOUSE WITH IRONED-ON-AT-THE-FACTORY MASTIC FINISH.

Appreciable quantities of petroleum asphalt were being used in the United States for paving, by about 1900. However, it was received on trial for over ten years until experience with it in service demonstrated that it was equally as good for paving purposes as the natural or lake asphalts. By about 1911, the asphalt produced from domestic petroleum exceeded the Trinidad and Bermudez asphalt importations; and since then the production of petroleum asphalt has continued to grow rapidly, stimulated by large available quantities of Mexican petroleum highly asphaltic in character.

Statistics of the United States Geological Survey for 1919* show the following:

UNITED STATES GEOLOGICAL SURVEY STATISTICS FOR 1919.

Asphalt from domestic petroleum	614,692	tons	41.4%
Asphalt from Mexican petroleum	674,876	tons	45.5%
Domestic native asphalt (bituminous rock)	53,589	tons	3.6%
Other domestic native bituminous substances	34,692	tons	2.3%
Asphalt imported from Trinidad and Tobago	51,062	tons	3.5%
Asphalt imported from Venezuela	47,309	tons	3.2%
Other imported asphalts including bituminous rock	7,277	tons	0.5%
TOTAL ASPHALT	1,483,497	tons	100.0%
Asphalt exported from U. S.†	40,208	tons	2.7%
Approximate consumption of asphalt in U. S.	1,443,289	tons	97.3%

These figures indicate that approximately 87 per cent of all asphalt produced by or imported into the United States that year was obtained from the distillation of petroleum, and since then this ratio has continued to increase in favor of the petroleum asphalts.

Asphalt would appear to be the oldest waterproof adhesive known to man; and since the manufacture of asphalt from petroleum has made it readily available in almost unlimited quantities, it has been adapted to a great many industrial purposes, of which the paving industry leads and the roofing industry is second, consuming together some 85 or 90 per cent of the entire asphalt output. The remainder of the output is used for waterproofing, flooring, insulating, and some asphalt finds its way into the manufacture of rubber goods, paints, varnishes, bituminous putty, emulsions, sealing compounds, floor coverings, etc.

As the general term "asphalt" is commonly applied to a great variety of asphalts and asphaltic products, the asphalt

*Asphalts and Related Bitumens in 1919, by R. W. Cottrell.

NOTE—See also "Asphalt," by Prévost Hubbard, in "The Mineral Industry during 1925," Volume 34, McGraw-Hill Book Co.

†This does not include manufactures of asphalt valued at approximately one-half the value of the tonnage of asphalt exported.

to be used in applying cold storage insulation shall be termed "Asphalt cement" and should be carefully selected for certain properties and characteristics that are highly desirable where foodstuffs are stored and where the success of the installation depends to a marked degree on the permanent air-proofing and cementing qualities of the Asphalt cement selected. These properties are substantially as follows:

(a) Purity.
(b) Durability.
(c) Flexibility.
(d) Adhesiveness.

Tests to determine the presence of these properties are reflected in the specifications of the American Concrete Institute, the American Society for Testing Materials and the United States Bureau of Standards, which specifications are much the same; and by the aid of these specifications, supported by the practical knowledge of the requirements of a suitable asphalt for use in applying cold storage insulation to building or other surfaces, a specification has been prepared, as follows:

Specification for Asphalt Cement for Cold Storage Insulation.

Impurities.—The Asphalt cement shall contain no water, decomposition products, granular particles, or other impurities, and it shall be homogeneous. (Ash passing the 200-mesh screen shall not be considered an impurity; but if greater than 1 per cent., corrections in gross weights shall be made to allow for the proper percentage of bitumen.)

Specific Gravity.—The specific gravity of the Asphalt cement shall not be less than 1.000 at 77° F. (25° C.).

Fixed Carbon.—The fixed carbon in the Asphalt cement shall not be greater than 18 per cent.

Sulphur.—The sulphur and sulphur compounds in the Asphalt cement shall not be greater than 1¾ per cent., by the ash free basis of determination.

Solubility in Carbon Bisulphide.—The Asphalt cement shall be soluble to the extent of at least 98 per cent. in chemically pure carbon bisulphide (CS_2).

Melting Point.—The melting point of the Asphalt cement shall be greater than 165° F. and less than 190° F., by the Ring and Ball method.

Flash Point.—The flash point of the Asphalt cement shall be not less than 425° F. (218.3° C.), by the Cleveland Open Cup test.

Penetration.—The Asphalt cement shall be of such consistency as to show a penetration of more than 15 when tested at 32° F. (0° C.) and less than 70 when tested at 115° F. (46.1° C.). (0.2 millimeter shall be added for each 1.0 per cent. of ash, to give the true penetration.)

Volatilization.—The loss by volatilization on heating of the Asphalt cement shall not exceed 1 per cent., the penetration after heating shall be not less than 80 per cent. of the original penetration, and the ductility after heating shall have been reduced not more than 20 per cent.

Ductility.—When pulled vertically by a motor at a uniform rate of 5 c.m. per minute in a bath of water, a cylinder of Asphalt cement 1 c.m. in diameter at a temperature of 77° F. (25° C.) shall be elongated not less than 15 c.m. before breaking, and at a temperature of 40° F. (4.5° C.) shall be elongated not less than 3 c.m. before breaking.

Outline of the Purpose of Specifications for Asphalt Cement for Cold Storage Insulation.

Impurities are a measure of the care with which the Asphalt cement has been refined and handled. Usually the presence of impurities in large quantities indicates a poor grade of asphalt. Water as an impurity would act as a diluent and would cause foaming in the kettle. Ash, or mineral matter, is not considered an impurity if it is a natural constituent of the Asphalt cement, but the cementing value must be figured on the bitumen alone.

Specific Gravity of the Asphalt cement should be over 1.000 because Asphalt cements of a pentration satisfactory for cold storage insulation work always have a specific gravity greater than 1.000, whereas paraffin base and air-blown products frequently have a specific gravity less than 1.000.

Fixed Carbon is to some extent a measure of the chemical constitution of an Asphalt cement, and is largely used to determine the source and uniformity of an asphalt. Fixed carbon is not free carbon, which latter is practically absent in Asphalt cement, but fixed carbon includes free carbon.

Sulphur and sulphur compounds are ordinarily the cause of the odor in oils and asphalts, particularly upon heating. An Asphalt cement that is low in sulphur compounds is necessary for cold storage insulation work.

Solubility in Carbon Bisulphide is a measure of the purity of an Asphalt cement; and the cementing value, other things being equal, is proportional to the CS2 solubility. Any carbonaceous material, such as coal tar or pitch, is detected by this test.

Melting Point is a measure of the temperature at which the Asphalt cement will flow readily. The melting point desired is determined by the workability of the Asphalt cement on corkboards when dipped, and should have a melting point somewhat higher than the highest temperature to which it will be subjected in place with insulation.

Flash Point is a measure of the amount of volatile hydrocarbons that are present in the Asphalt cement, and of the readiness of the asphalt to decompose by heat.

Penetration is a measure of the consistency of the Asphalt cement. It is merely a quick, convenient test for checking up numerous samples. The penetration is expressed in degrees, and 1/10 m.m. equals one degree. The penetration to be desired will depend upon the climate, the ductility and adhesiveness of the Asphalt cement.

Loss by Volatilization is a measure of the amount of light hydrocarbons that are present in Asphalt cement, which indicates its tendency to oxidize and to lose its ductility and penetration.

Ductility is a measure of the ability of an Asphalt cement to expand and contract without breaking or cracking. The same asphalt at a higher penetration should have a higher ductility, so all ductility tests should be based on a certain definite penetration regardless of temperature, or should be based on a temperature of 32° F. (0° C.). Ductility is also a measure of the cementing strength.

Viscosity is a measure of the ability of the Asphalt cement to impart plasticity and malleability.

The methods of testing to be followed in connection with *Specification for Asphalt Cement for Cold Storage Insulation*, are those of the American Society for Testing Materials, as follows:

(a) Determination of Bitumen in Asphalt Products (Deducted from 100 per cent. equals Purity) A. S. T. M., D4-23T.
(b) Softening Point of Bituminous Materials (Ring and Ball Method) A. S. T. M., D36-24.
(c) Flash and Fire Points of Bituminous Materials (by the Cleveland Open Cup Method) A. S. T. M., D92-24.
(d) Penetration of Bituminous Materials, A. S. T. M., D5-25
(e) Loss on Heating of Oil and Asphaltic Compounds, A. S. T. M., D6-20.
(f) Ductility of Bituminous Materials, A. S. T. M., D113-22T.
(g) Sulphur in Bituminous Materials (Ash Free Basis) A. S. T. M., D29-22T.

The Kansas City Testing Laboratory, in its Bulletin No. 15, publishes values for the composition of natural and petroleum asphalts, as follows:

1.—COMPOSITION OF NATURAL ASPHALTS.

	Natural Trinidad	Bermudez	Gilsonite	Grahamite
Bitumen	56.0%	94.0%	99.4%	94.1%
Mineral Matter	36.8%	2.0%	0.5%	5.7%
Specific Gravity	1.400	1.085	1.045	1.171
Fixed Carbon	11.0%	13.5%	13.0%	53.3%
Melting Point, °F.	190	180	300	Cokes
Penetration (77° F.)	0.5	2.5	0	0
Free Carbon	6.0%	4.0%	0.1%	0.2%
Sulphur (ash free basis)	6.5%	5.6%	1.3%	2.0%
Petroleum ether soluble	65.0%	70.0%	30.0%	0.4%
Total Carbon (ash free)	82.6%	82.5%	.....	87.2%
Hydrogen (ash free)	10.5%	10.3%	.....	7.5%
Nitrogen (ash free)	0.5%	0.7%	.....	0.2%

2.—COMPOSITION OF PETROLEUM ASPHALTS.

	Mexican	Mid-Continent Air Blown	California	Stanolind*
Bitumen	99.5%	99.2%	99.5%	99.8%
Mineral Matter	0.3%	0.7%	0.3%	0.3%
Specific Gravity	1.040	0.990	1.045	1.060
Fixed Carbon	17.5%	12.0%	15.0%	17.5%
Melting Point °F.	140	180	140	135
Penetration (77° F.)	55	40	60	50
Free Carbon	0.0	0.0	0.0	0.0
Sulphur (ash free basis)	4.50%	0.60%	1.65%	0.35%
Petroleum Ether Soluble	70.0%	72.0%	67.0%	70.0%
Cementing Properties	good	poor	good	good
Ductility (square mold)	45 cm	2 cm	70 cm	100+
Loss at 32° F. 5 hrs.	0.2%	0.1%	0.2%	0.1%
Heat test	adherent	smooth	adherent	scaly

These values were obtained by methods of testing as published by the K. C. T. L., Bulletin No. 15, which are in many particulars slightly different from the methods adopted by the American Society for Testing Materials, and consequently the values of the K. C. T. L. are given here for general information only and are in no way to be confused with the values called for in a *Specification for Asphalt Cement for Cold Storage Insulation*, or with an *Asphalt Primer for Use with Asphalt Cement.*

The "Heat Test" mentioned in the K. C. T. L. Table No. 2, should be of interest, as follows:

Resistance of Asphalt Cement to Oxidation, K. C. T. L., 1919

A strip of thin sheet iron 2 inches wide and 6 inches long is covered on its lower 4 inches with the melted asphaltic cement. This strip is placed in an oven at 275° F. for 15 minutes and allowed to thoroughly drain.

It is removed from the oven and allowed to cool, then placed in an electrically heated oven at a temperature of 450° F. for one hour. At the end of the hour, the door of the oven is opened and the heat is turned off, the specimen being allowed to remain in the oven.

The oven shall be one having outside dimensions of 12 x 12 x 12 inches with an opening in the top 1 c.m. in diameter, the heating elements being in the bottom of the oven. The resistance shall be so distributed that the heat is uniform throughout the oven. The lower end of the strip shall be suspended so that it is at least 3 c.m. from the bottom of the oven.

The resistance is preferably so arranged that three different heats can be maintained with a snap switch such that the lowest heat is 325° F., the medium heat is 400° F. and the highest heat is 450° F.

After being subjected to these tests, the film of asphalt should be brilliant and lustrous, should not be scaly and fragile, should adhere firmly to the metal and should not be dull and cheesy in texture.

*(Cracked-pressure tar residue.)

A suitable *Asphalt Primer* for initial application to concrete and masonry surfaces as preparation for the erection of cold storage insulation in Asphalt cement, is as follows:

Asphalt Primer for Use With Asphalt Cement

The asphalt used in preparing the primer shall be homogeneous and free from water, and shall conform to the following requirements:

(a) Melting point (R & B)......140 to 225° F. (60° to 107.2° C.)
(b) Penetration at 77° F. (25° C.) 100 grams pressure for 5 seconds ....20 to 50
(c) Flash point (Open Cup)....Not less than 347° F. (175° C.)
(d) Loss on heating 50 grams at 325° F. (163° C.) for 5 hours ....Not more than 1%
(e) Penetration at 77° F. (25° C.) 100 grams pressure for 5 seconds, of the residue after heating 50 grams at 325° F. (163° C.) for 5 hours as compared with penetration of asphalt before heating ....Not less than 60%
(f) Ductility at 77° F. (25° C.).............Not less than 15 c.m.
(g) Insolubles in Carbon disulphide...........Not more than 2%

The solvent used in cutting the asphalt (in preparing the primer) shall be a hydrocarbon distillate having an end point on distillation of not above 500° F. (250° C.), of which not more than 20 per cent shall distill under 248° F. (120° C.).

The finished Asphalt Primer shall be free from water* and shall conform to the following requirements:

(a) Sediment* ....Not more than 1%
(b) Asphaltic base by weight.........................25 to 35%

101.—**Emulsified Asphalt.**—Emulsified asphalt and emulsified asphalt plastic, for the interior finish of cold storage rooms, and sometimes for the priming of surfaces in preparation for insulation to be applied in hot Asphalt cement, has had enough publicity—favorable and unfavorable—to justify a very careful look into the general subject of asphalt emulsions.

"Colloid chemistry is the chemistry of grains, drops, bubbles, filaments, and films," according to Bancroft; but colloid chemistry actually deals with grains, drops, and bubbles only when they are sufficiently small, of diameters ranging from 100 millimicrons to 1 millimicron†, and when such particles are surrounded by, or dispersed in, some other substance, as dust in air (smoke), water in butter, oil in water (milk), air

*To test for Water and Sediment, use A.S.T.M. Method D95-23T.

†A millimicron, 1 $\mu\mu$, is one millionth of a millimeter, 100 $\mu\mu$ just barely being visible with the aid of the best microscope, and the largest molecules approach a diameter of 1 $\mu\mu$.

in water (foam), etc. "The colloidal realm ranges from the lower limit of microscopic visibility to the upper limit of molecular dimensions," says Holmes, and adds that most colloidal particles are aggregates of hundreds or even thousands of molecules.

Water, wood, paper, clothing, glass, cement, paints, inks, asphalt, cheese, oils, and countless other materials in common

FIG. 81.—INSULATED ICE STORAGE HOUSE WITH PLASTIC MASTIC FINISH APPLIED OVER CORKBOARD AT POINT OF ERECTION.

use are colloidal, that is, may be *dispersed* in or surrounded by some other substance.

A small quantity of oil may, for example, be dispersed in water, by vigorous shaking or stirring; but to maintain the dispersion, or keep the emulsion, is the problem. Aside from the unequal specific gravities of the two substances, the fact of the unequal surface tensions of water and oil assists in causing the microscopic drops of oil to form together, separating from the water, the surface tension of any given liquid being that tension by virtue of which it acts as an elastic enveloping membrane tending always to contract the surface of the liquid to the minimum exposed area.* When a substance is colloidally dispersed, the effect of gravity is considerably counteracted, while surface tension, electric (ionic) charge, and other forms of energy increase greatly.

Thus by lowering the surface tension of water, by the introduction of an alkali, an oil-in-water emulsion should keep longer. But water molecules are always in constant motion when above absolute zero temperature, and bombard the suspended colloids of oil from all sides, tending to move them about, and thus to coagulate or unite upon touching due to the surface tension of oil. Then, too, particles in the colloidal state bearing unlike electric charges, tend to attract each other, and thus coagulate; while particles similarly charged, tend to repel, and thus move about, and coagulate upon touching.

It will be seen that lowering the surface tension often exerts considerable influence in emulsification, but the concentration of a film of some non-adhesive gelatin substance around the suspended colloids, so that they have difficulty in touching, is usually of more importance.

There are several methods of subdividing common substances so that they may be colloidally suspended, some methods being purely mechanical and others chemical; but in connection with proposed chemical methods, it must be remembered that colloidal suspensions are not true solutions, colloid aggregates often being thousands of times as large as a molecule while molecules only are found in true solutions.

Colloid particles have an ability to *adsorb* other substances, that is, hold other substances to their surfaces, and it is this property that makes it possible to coat or cover such colloids with a non-adhesive substance, such as starch or geletin or clay, so that the colloids will not coalesce or unite when they touch each other. On the other hand, if the particles in suspension were originally of too great size to fall within the range of the colloidal realm, and thus are beyond the help of

*A cube 1 cm. on edge has a surface of 6 sq. cm. If subdivided in much smaller cubes 100 $\mu\mu$ on edge, the total surface is 600,000 sq. cm If further subdivided into the colloidal realm of cubes 10 $\mu\mu$ on edge, the total surface is 6,000,000 sq. cm. Surface tension tends to reduce the colloidal particles to the cube 1 cm. on edge, or, more properly, to a sphere.

the bombardment of the water molecules (Brownian movement) to keep them suspended, such aggregates will settle. Emulsoids are dehydrated and coagulated by excessive amounts of salts, by nitric acid, sometimes by heat and by shaking. Thus if it is necessary to shake an emulsion a great deal, in handling, or shipping, or stirring to counteract settling, the particles (having lost their full protective coats by disturbance) may coagulate an amount sufficient to destroy the emulsion.

It is the non-adhesive substance used to coat the dispersed colloidal particles that is known as the emulsifying agent, and such agent must be capable of being colloidally dispersed also. The emulsifying agent selected, however, must be such that the *adsorptive* power of its colloids is less than that of the colloidally dispersed basic substance being emulsified, else the dispersed *protective* colloids of the emulsifying agent will not be held to the surface of the colloidal particles of the basic material, but the reverse will occur, and the colloidal particles of the emulsifying agent will become coated by the dispersed colloids of the basic material. The adsorptive power of an adhesive type of colloidal particle, for colloidal particles of a non-adhesive and protective character, is apparently increased by the simple addition of a flocculating agent that will tend to coagulate or unite the protective colloids in larger aggregates about the basic colloids and thus give the basic colloids a certain measure of greater protection or isolation one from another.

If even a faint conception of colloid chemistry, and particularly the preparation and holding of emulsions, is possible from the foregoing paragraphs, then a consideration of the preparation, handling, shipping and application of asphalt emulsions can follow.

Asphalt, as has been noted, is a colloidal substance; it is one that may be colloidally dispersed in water by admixture of the molten material with a hot aqueous alkaline solution; it is a material that is capable of being *mechanically* dispersed in a colloidal state in water that has had its high surface tension relieved. But to emulsify asphalt, that is, hold it in colloidal suspension, requires the addition of a suitable emulsifying agent, one that is non-adhesive, capable of colloidal dispersion and of inferior *adsorptive* power in the presence of the basic asphalt colloids. In a word, the colloids of the emulsifying agent must be such as to be held to the surface of the dispersed asphalt colloids in sufficient quantity and with sufficient bond to prevent the colloidal particles of asphalt from sticking together as they touch each other during propulsion about through the aqueous alkaline solution by the forces that make colloidal suspension possible.

U. S. Letters Patent No. 1,582,467, for example, sets forth as one of its claims the following:

> A process for producing an aqueous bituminous emulsion which consists in melting solid bitumen of the type artificially prepared from petroleum, adding thereto with agitation a proportion less than 10% of an emulsifying agent comprising a substance of the starch-dextrin type, and then separately adding a dilute aqueous solution of alkali, and maintaining the heating and agitation of the mixture until emulsification has been effected.

U. S. Letters Patent No. 1,567,061 sets forth certain claims relating to the admixture of a flocculating agent* to an asphalt emulsion to increase the degree of protection to the suspended asphalt colloids by causing the colloids of the emulsifying agent to more tenaciously cling to the suspended colloidal asphalt, as follows:

> A process of forming a non-adhesive emulsion, consisting in emulsifying an adhesive bituminous substance with colloidal clay in an aqueous vehicle, adding aluminum sulphate to the emulsion to cause the emulsifying particles to more tenaciously gather about the bituminous substance.

The colloidal dispersion of asphalt in water is usually accomplished by heating the asphalt to about 225° F. and adding it to a hot aqueous alkaline solution under vigorous and intimate agitation; and there have been a number of patents issued covering mechanical equipment for many ways of accomplishing such dispersion. It would therefore appear that the equipment used and the care exercised in the manufacturing process may have considerable to do with the worth of the finished product. For instance, if the asphalt were not actually broken up into microscopic particles sufficiently small to place them in the colloidal realm, then the tendency of that

*Ammonia salts are frequently used in emulsions as flocculating agents.

"emulsion" would be to settle in the container, the particles of asphalt simply being held apart by their coatings of non-adhesive material; and the disturbances of handling, shipping, and stirring to counteract settling may sufficiently dislodge the protective coatings from the asphalt particles to cause enough coagulation to make the emulsion unfit for practical use. The use of an unsuitable emulsifying agent, or incorrect proportions of ingredients, or insufficient heat, or other errors of omission or commission, may conceivably be responsible for an unsatisfactory emulsified asphalt product.

Back of it all, too, is this important fact: If a good grade of a suitable asphalt is used as the basic material to be emulsified, then when dehydrated on the walls of a building, or on cork insulation, there will remain the same good grade of a suitable asphalt as a protective coat; otherwise, not; if a poor asphalt is emulsified, it remains a poor asphalt, always.

Emulsified asphalt is, of course, subject to freezing, which is a serious objection to the shipping and handling of the material in cold weather.

The exact determination of the constituents of an asphalt emulsion is usually attended with considerable difficulty and no predetermined scheme can be made applicable to all materials of this character. The following methods, however, are used by the United States Office of Public Roads and Rural Engineering, according to Prévost Hubbard, and have yielded reasonably satisfactory and fairly accurate results:

Special Tests for Emulsions.

Fatty and Resin Acids.—In order to break up the emulsion, a 20-gram sample is digested on a steam bath with 100 cubic centimeters of N/2 alcoholic potash. The digestion is carried out in a flask with a reflux condenser for about 45 minutes. The solution is filtered and the precipitate washed with 95 per cent alcohol. The filtrate is evaporated to dryness, after which the residue is taken up with hot water and any insoluble matter is filtered off. The aqueous solution, which contains the potassium soaps of the fatty acids, is acidified with dilute sulphuric acid and then shaken in a separatory funnel with petroleum ether. The aqueous portion is drawn off and the ethereal layer shaken up with cold water and washed twice, after which it is evaporated in a weighed platinum or porcelain dish to constant weight, first over a steam bath and then in a drying oven at 105° C. The residue consists of the fatty and resin acids present in the emulsion.

Water.—The percentage of water in the emulsion is determined by distilling a 100-gram sample in the retort used for dehydration. The distillation is carried out in exactly the same manner as described under this test until the volume of water in the receiver shows no further increase. Any oils that come over are thoroughly mixed with the material remaining in the retort.

Ammonia.—Many emulsions contain ammonia, and when this is present a second distillation of the material is necessary. This is carried out on a 100-gram sample in exactly the same manner as described for the determination of water, except for the fact that 40 cubic centimeters of a 10 per cent. solution of caustic potash is added to the contents of the retort before beginning the distillation. The distillate is collected in a measured volume of N/2 sulphuric acid. When the distillation is completed the excess acid is titrated with N/2 caustic potash, and the ammonia thus determined.

Ash.—A one-gram sample of the dehydrated material is ignited in a weighed platinum or porcelain crucible. The ash will contain any inorganic matter from the bitumen as well as the fixed alkali present in the soap. The results are, of course, all calculated on the basis of the original material.

Total Bitumen.—A two-gram sample of dehydrated material is extracted with carbon disulphide as described in the method for the determination of total bitumen, flask method, and in this manner the organic matter insoluble in carbon disulphide can be determined.

Having determined all constituents as above noted, it is assumed that the difference between their sum and 100 per cent. is bitumen, which amount is reported accordingly.

It will be seen that with emulsified asphalt, as with many "prepared" products, the average purchaser must rely on the manufacturer for the quality and fitness of the emulsion for the work in hand.

The advantage offered by a suitable emulsified asphalt as a priming material for masonry surfaces, as compared with an Asphalt primer, is that emulsified asphalt is non-inflammable; and the advantage of the Asphalt primer over the emulsion is that the asphalt that is cut with a solvent can be handled with an air-gun at much higher pressures, and thus with greater penetration, than the emulsion can be handled. If too great pressure is used with the emulsion, the air-gun is liable to foul in the nozzle and clog; because the excessive pressure tends to force too much water out of the emulsion and coagulate the asphalt in the nozzle.

Emulsified asphalt plastic is simply emulsified asphalt mixed by mechanical means in suitable proportion with asbestos fibre and fine sand or other more suitable mineral aggregates, to form a plastic material resembling Portland cement mortar in consistency and suitability for application with trowel over corkboard surfaces. The advantage offered by a suitable emulsified asphalt plastic as a protective coating for corkboard insulation, as compared with factory ironed-on mastic finish corkboard, is found in the versatility of the plastic emulsion. Except for the contingency of freezing weather, emulsified asphalt plastic may be applied on the job much like plaster, to any areas desired, at any time; and, furthermore, a suitable emulsified asphalt plastic may be applied so as to present a continuous surface that is sufficiently elastic to withstand without cracking the contraction and expansion incident to cold storage rooms, while it may be difficult to have the joints between factory ironed-on mastic finish corkboards effectually sealed against the same forces. However, the factory ironed-on mastic joints can be properly sealed, under adequate supervision and with reasonable care.

The choice between the factory finish and the plastic emulsion should rest entirely upon all the facts surrounding each case.

CHAPTER XIII.

COMPLETE SPECIFICATIONS FOR THE ERECTION OF CORKBOARD.

102.—Scope and Purpose of Specifications.—These specifications and illustrations are intended to show corkboard insulation adapted to practically every type of construction to be found in old buildings or to be employed in new structures, which specifications long experience has demonstrated to be practical. In many instances, however, more than one specification is given for the erection of corkboard to a given surface, and no recommendation is made as to preference; because the use of each and every one of these specifications is a matter of selection based on experience and a knowledge of all the conditions of the case, as previously elaborated.

The thickness of corkboard to use must be suited to the temperatures to be maintained, and to a less degree to several other factors that will vary in each case, all as noted in Chapter XII.

These specifications comprise the following:

103.—Walls.—Stone, concrete or brick:
- (1) Single layer, in Portland cement.
- (2) Single layer, in Asphalt cement.
- (3) Double layer, first in Portland cement, second in Asphalt cement.
- (4) Double layer, both in Portland cement.
- (5) Double layer, both in Asphalt cement.

104.—Walls.—Wood:
- (6) Single layer, in Asphalt cement.
- (7) Double layer, both in Asphalt cement.

105.—Ceilings.—Concrete:
- (8) Single layer, in Portland cement.
- (9) Double layer, both in Portland cement.
- (10) Double layer, first in Portland cement, second in Asphalt cement.

(11) Single layer, in forms before concrete is poured.
(12) Double layer, first in forms before concrete is poured, second in Portland cement.
(13) Double layer, first in forms before concrete is poured, second in Asphalt cement.

106.—Ceilings.—Self-supported:
(14) Double layer, T-irons and Portland cement core.

107.—Ceilings.—Wood:
(15) Single layer, in Asphalt cement.
(16) Double layer, both in Asphalt cement.

108.—Roofs.—Concrete or wood:
(17) Single layer, in Asphalt cement.
(18) Double layer, both in Asphalt cement.

109.—Floors.—Wood:
(19) Single layer, in Asphalt cement, concrete finish.
(20) Single layer, in Asphalt cement, wood finish.
(21) Double layer, both in Asphalt cement, concrete finish.
(22) Double layer, both in Asphalt cement, wood finish.

110.—Floors.—Concrete:
(23) Single layer, in Asphalt cement, concrete finish.
(24) Single layer, in Asphalt cement, wood finish.
(25) Double layer, both in Asphalt cement, concrete finish.
(26) Double layer, both in Asphalt cement, wood finish.

111.—Partitions.—Stone, concrete or brick:
(See 103.—Walls.—Stone, concrete or brick.)

112.—Partitions.—Wood:
(27) Single layer, between studs, joints sealed in Asphalt cement.
(28) Double layer, first between studs with joints sealed in Asphalt cement, second in Asphalt cement.

113.—Partitions.—Solid cork:
(29) Single layer, joints sealed in Asphalt cement.
(30) Double layer, first with joints sealed in Asphalt cement, second in Portland cement.
(31) Double layer, first with joints sealed in Asphalt cement, second in Asphalt cement.

114.—Tanks.—Freezing:
(32) Double layer on bottom, both in Asphalt cement, granulated cork fill on sides and ends.
(33) Double layer on bottom, both in Asphalt cement; double layer on sides and ends, both in Asphalt cement.
(34) Double layer on bottom, both in Asphalt cement; single layer on sides and ends against studs, with granulated cork fill.

115.—Finish.—Walls and ceilings:
(35) Portland cement plaster, in two coats.
(36) Factory ironed-on mastic finish, joints sealed.
(37) Glazed tile or brick, in Portland cement.
(38) Emulsified asphalt plastic, in two coats.

116.—Finish.—Floors:
(39) Concrete.
(40) Wood.
(41) Galvanized metal.

117.—Miscellaneous Specifications:
(42) Ends of beams or girders extending into walls.
(43) Rat proofing.
(44) Portland cement mortar.
(45) Asphalt cement.
(46) Asphalt primer.

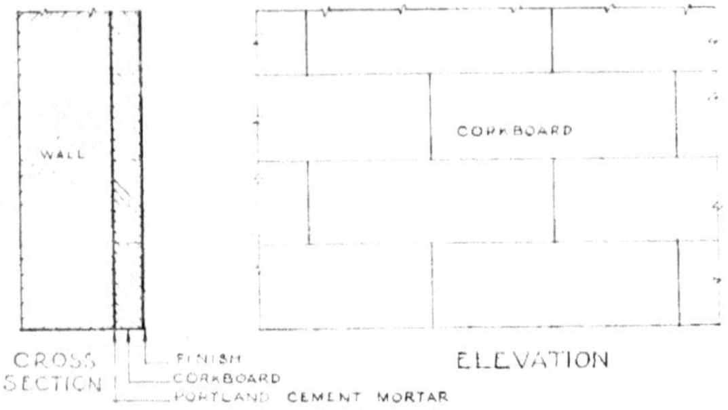

FIG. 82.—WALLS: STONE, CONCRETE OR BRICK. ARTICLE 103 (1).

103.—Walls.—Stone, concrete or brick.

(1) Single layer, in Portland cement.

To the reasonably smooth and clean . . . walls to be insulated, one layer of . . .-inch pure corkboard shall be erected in a ½-inch bedding of Portland cement mortar, with all vertical joints broken and all joints butted tight. To the surface of the insulation shall then be applied a finish as selected.

103.—Walls.—Stone, concrete or brick (continued).

(2) Single layer, in Asphalt cement.

To the reasonably smooth and clean . . . walls to be insulated, shall first be applied with brush or air-gun two uniform, continuous coats of Asphalt primer, to consist of one gallon per 75 square feet for brick surfaces or per 100 square feet for concrete surfaces for the first coat, and one gallon per 125 square feet for brick or concrete for the second coat. To this prepared surface, one layer of . . .-inch pure corkboard shall be erected in hot Asphalt cement, with all vertical joints broken and all joints butted tight and sealed in the same compound. To the surface of the insulation shall then be applied a finish as selected.

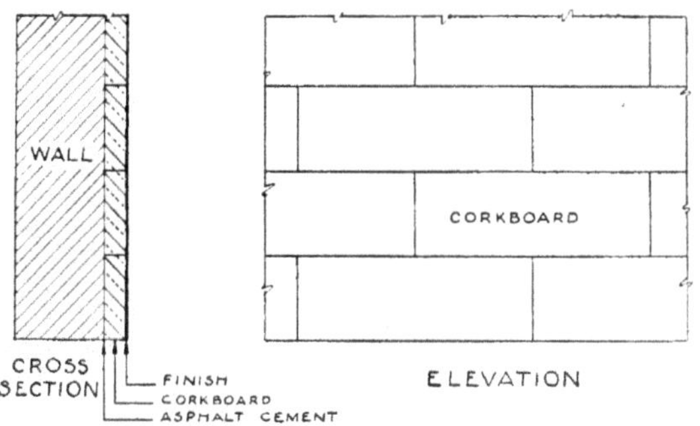

FIG. 83.—WALLS; STONE, CONCRETE OR BRICK. ARTICLE 103 (2).

103.—Walls.—Stone, concrete or brick (continued).

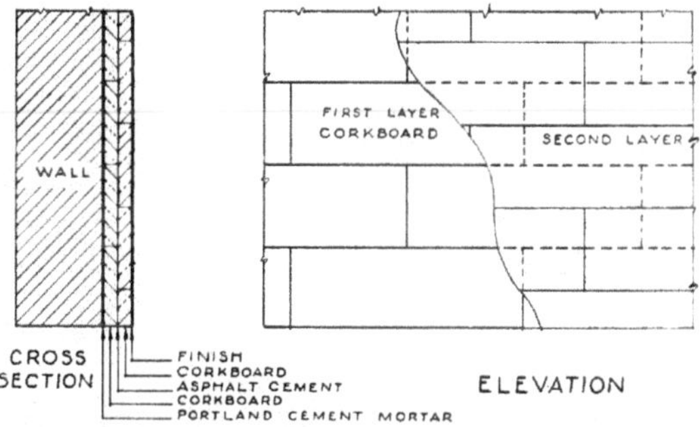

FIG. 84.—WALLS; STONE, CONCRETE OR BRICK. ARTICLE 103 (3).

(3) Double layer, first in Portland cement, second in Asphalt cement.

To the reasonably smooth and clean . . . walls to be insulated, one layer of . . .-inch pure corkboard shall be erected in a ½-inch bedding of Portland cement mortar, with all vertical joints broken and all joints butted tight. To the first course, a second layer of ...-inch pure corkboard shall be erected in hot Asphalt cement, additionally secured to the first with wood skewers, with all joints in the second course broken with respect to all joints in the first course and all joints butted tight and sealed in the same compound. To the surface of the insulation shall then be applied a finish as selected.

103.—Walls.—Stone, concrete or brick (continued).

(4) Double layer, both in Portland cement.

To the reasonably smooth and clean . . . walls to be insulated, one layer of ...-inch pure corkboard shall be erected in a ½-inch bedding of Portland cement mortar, with all vertical

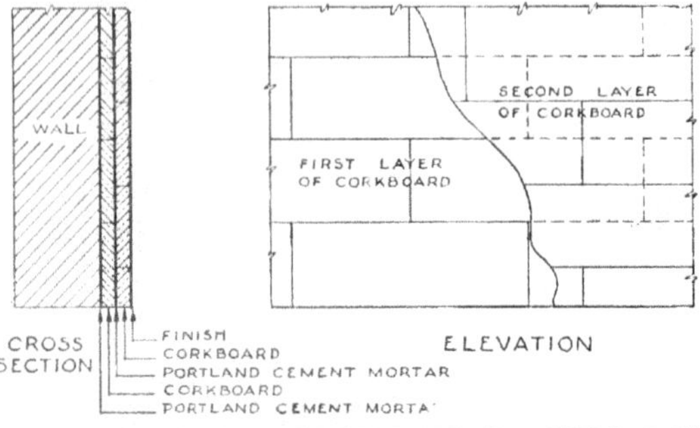

FIG. 85.—WALLS; STONE, CONCRETE OR BRICK. ARTICLE 103 (4).

joints broken and all joints butted tight. To the surface of the insulation shall then be applied a finish as selected.

103.—Walls.—Stone, concrete or brick (continued).

(5) Double layer, both in Asphalt cement.

To the reasonably smooth and clean . . . walls to be insulated, shall first be applied with brush or air-gun two uniform, continuous coats of Asphalt primer, to consist of one gallon per 75 square feet for brick surfaces or per 100 square feet for concrete surfaces for the first coat, and one gallon per 125 square feet for brick or concrete for the second coat. To this prepared surface, one layer of ...-inch pure corkboard shall be erected in hot Asphalt cement, with all vertical joints broken and all joints butted tight and sealed in the same compound. To the first course, a second layer of ...-inch pure corkboard shall be erected in hot Asphalt cement, additionally secured to the first with wood skewers, with all joints in the second course broken with respect to all joints in the first course and all joints butted tight and sealed in the

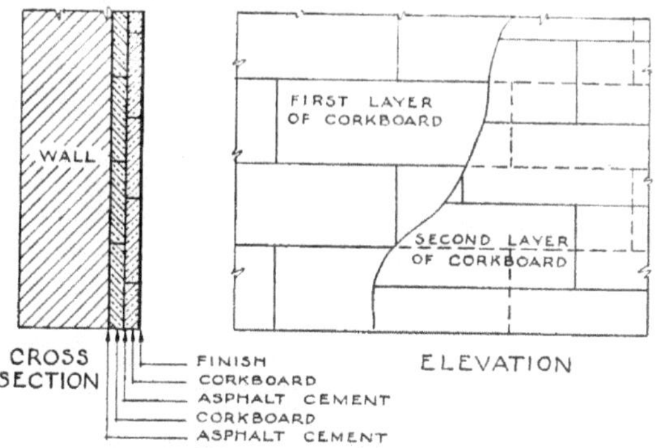

FIG. 86.—WALLS; STONE, CONCRETE OR BRICK. ARTICLE 103 (5).

same compound. To the surface of the insulation shall then be applied a finish as selected.

104.—Walls.—Wood.

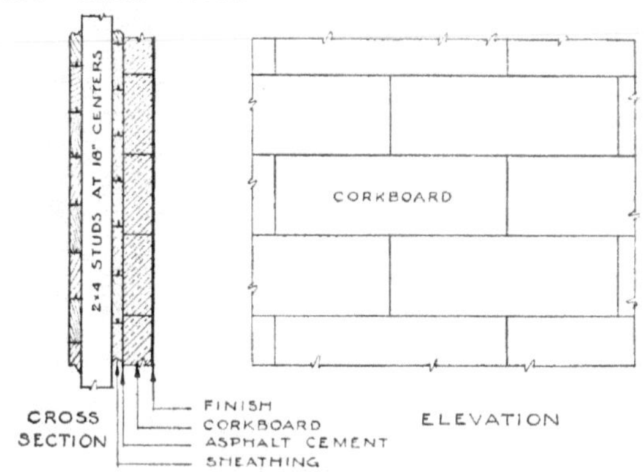

FIG. 87.—WALLS; WOOD. ARTICLE 104 (6).

(6) Single layer, in Asphalt cement.

To the reasonably smooth and clean walls to be insulated (consisting of ⅞-inch T. & G. sheathing over wall studding), one layer of ...-inch pure corkboard shall be erected in hot Asphalt cement, additionally secured with galvanized wire nails, with all vertical joints broken and all joints butted tight and sealed in the same compound. To the surface of the insulation shall then be applied a finish as selected.

104.—Walls.—Wood (continued).

(*7*) Double layer, both in Asphalt cement.

To the reasonably smooth and clean walls to be insulated (consisting of ⅞-inch T. & G. sheathing over wall studding), one layer of ...-inch pure corkboard shall be erected in hot

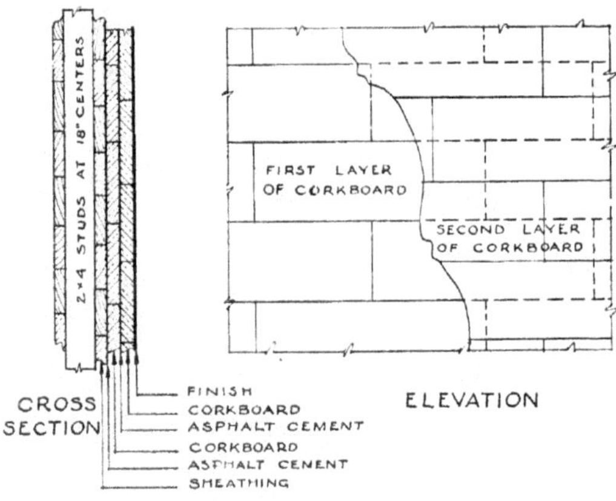

FIG. 88.—WALLS; WOOD. ARTICLE 104 (7).

Asphalt cement, additionally secured with galvanized wire nails, with all vertical joints broken and all joints butted tight and sealed in the same compound. To the first course, a second layer of ...-inch pure corkboard shall be erected in hot Asphalt cement, additionally secured to the first with wood skewers, with all joints in the second course broken with respect to all joints in the first course and all joints butted tight and sealed in the same compound. To the surface of the insulation shall then be applied a finish as selected.

105.—Ceilings.—Concrete.

(8) Single layer, in Portland cement.

To the reasonably smooth and clean concrete ceiling surface to be insulated, one layer of . . .-inch pure corkboard shall be erected in a ½-inch bedding of Portland cement mortar, with all transverse joints broken and all joints butted tight,

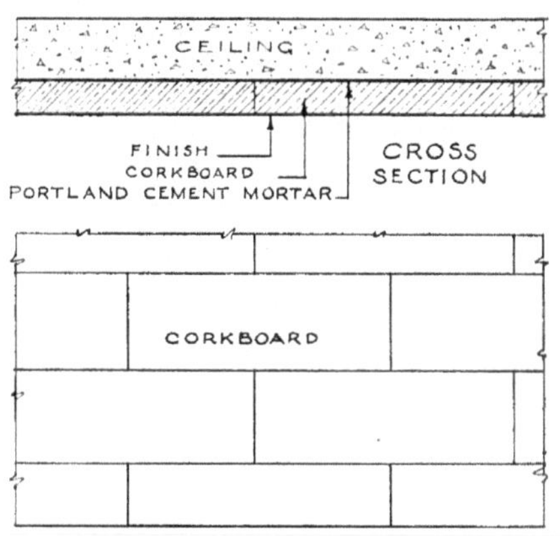

FIG. 89.—CEILING; CONCRETE. ARTICLE 105 (8).

and the corkboards propped in position until the cement sets. To the surface of the insulation shall then be applied a finish as selected.

105.—Ceilings.—Concrete (continued).

(9) Double layer, both in Portland cement.

To the reasonably smooth and clean concrete ceiling surface to be insulated, one layer of . . .-inch pure corkboard shall be erected in a ½-inch bedding of Portland cement mortar with all transverse joints broken and all joints butted tight, and the corkboards propped in position until the cement sets. To the first course, a second layer of . . .-inch pure corkboard shall be erected in a ½-inch bedding of Portland cement mortar, additionally secured to the first with wood skewers, with all joints in the second course broken with respect to all joints in the first course and all joints butted tight. To the surface of the insulation shall then be applied a finish as selected.

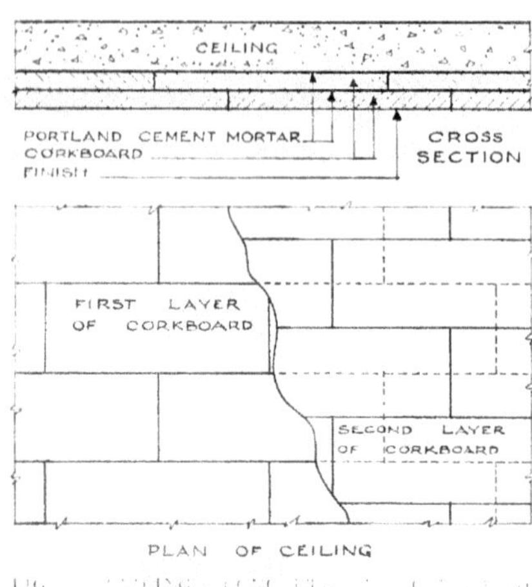

FIG. [illegible]

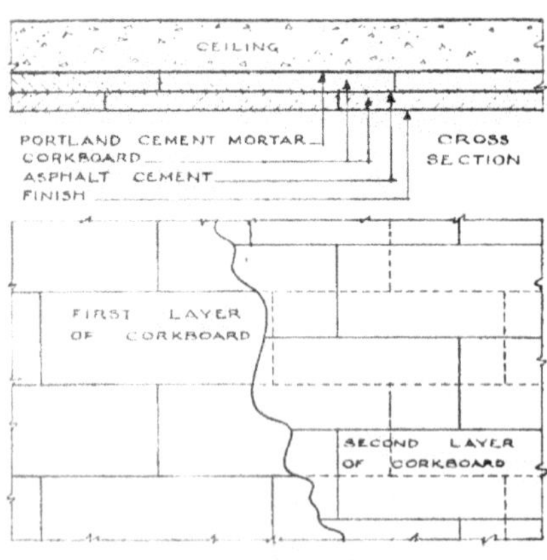

FIG. 91.—CEILINGS; CONCRETE. ARTICLE 105 (10).

105.—Ceilings.—Concrete (continued).

(10) Double layer, first in Portland cement, second in Asphalt cement.

To the reasonably smooth and clean concrete ceiling surface to be insulated, one layer of . . . -inch pure corkboard shall be erected in a ½-inch bedding of Portland cement mortar, with all transverse joints broken and all joints butted tight, and the corkboards propped in position until the cement sets. To the first course, a second layer of . . . -inch pure corkboard shall be erected in hot Asphalt cement, additionally secured to the first with wood skewers, with all joints in the second course broken with respect to all joints in the first course and all joints butted tight and sealed in the same compound. To the surface of the insulation shall then be applied a finish as selected.

105.—Ceilings.—Concrete (continued).

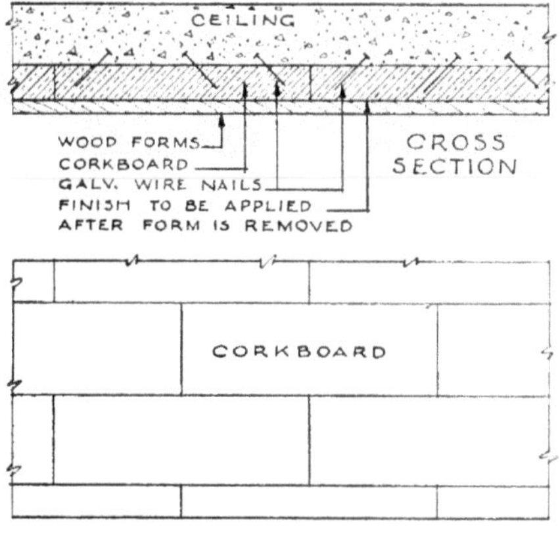

FIG. 92.—CEILINGS; CONCRETE. ARTICLE 105 (11).

(11) Single layer, in forms before concrete is poured.

In the concrete ceiling forms, constructed by another contractor . . . inches deeper than would otherwise be necessary, one layer of . . . -inch pure corkboard shall be laid down, with all transverse joints broken and all joints butted tight, and into which corkboard long galvanized wire nails shall be driven obliquely. Into these forms and over this insulation the concrete contractor shall pour the concrete. To the under surface of the insulation, after the concrete contractor has removed the forms, shall then be applied a finish as selected.

105.—Ceilings.—Concrete (continued).

(12) Double layer, first in forms before concrete is poured, second in Portland cement.

In the concrete ceiling forms, construed by another contractor ... inches deeper than would otherwise be necessary,

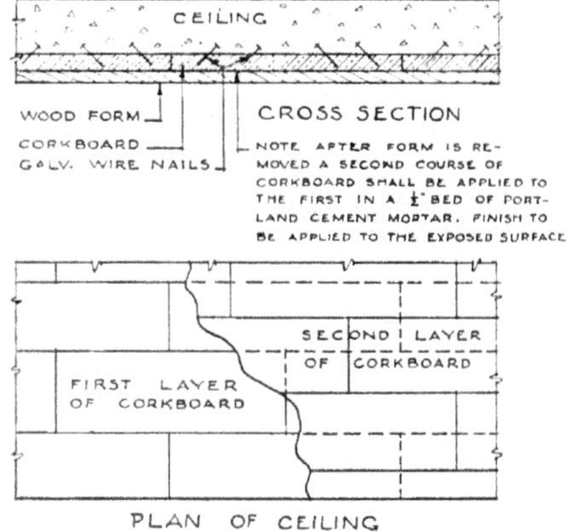

FIG. 93.—CEILINGS; CONCRETE. ARTICLE 105 (12).

one layer of ...-inch pure corkboard shall be laid down, with all transverse joints broken and all joints butted tight, and into which corkboard long galvanized wire nails shall be driven obliquely. Into these forms and over this insulation the concrete contractor shall pour the concrete. After the forms have been removed by the concrete contractor, a second layer of ...-inch pure corkboard shall be erected to the underside of the first course in a ½-inch bedding of Portland cement mortar, additionally secured with galvanized wire nails, with all joints in the second course broken with respect to all joints in the first course and all joints butted tight. To the surface of the insulation shall then be applied a finish as selected.

105.—Ceilings.—Concrete (continued).

(13) Double layer, first in forms before concrete is poured, second in Asphalt cement.

In the concrete ceiling forms, constructed by another contractor ... inches deeper than would otherwise be necessary, one layer of ...-inch pure corkboard shall be laid down, with

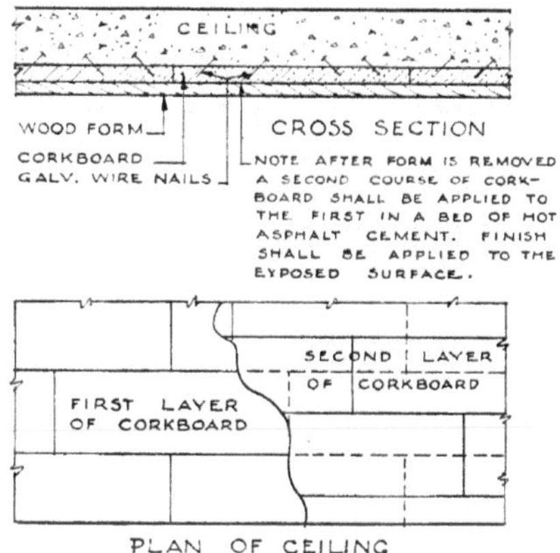

FIG. 94.—CEILINGS; CONCRETE. ARTICLE 105 (13).

all transverse joints broken and all joints butted tight, and into which corkboard long galvanized wire nails shall be driven obliquely. Into these forms and over this insulation the concrete contractor shall pour the concrete. After the forms have been removed by the concrete contractor, a second layer of ...-inch pure corkboard shall be erected to the underside of the first course in hot Asphalt cement, additionally secured with galvanized wire nails, with all joints in the second course broken with respect to all joints in the first course and all joints butted tight and sealed in the same compound. To the surface of the insulation shall then be applied a finish as selected.

106.—Ceilings—Self-supported.

(14) Double layer, T-irons and Portland cement core.

Upon the top edges of the side wall insulation shall be placed, running the short way of the room,* 2x2x¼-inch,

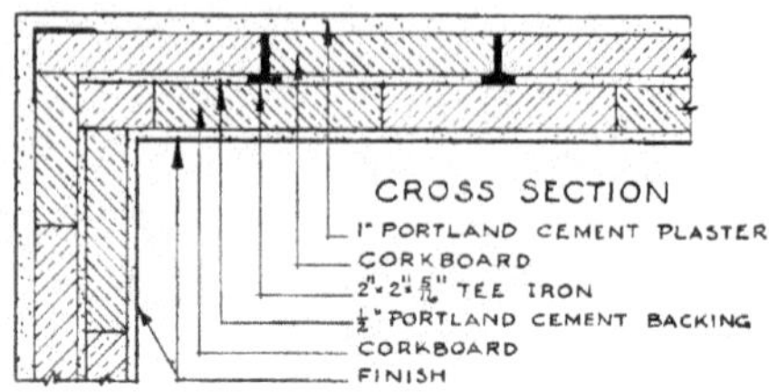

FIG. 95.—CEILINGS; SELF-SUPPORTING. ARTICLE 106 (14).

or 2x2x5/16-inch T-irons, spaced at a distance of 12 inches between the vertical sections of the T-irons (not from center to center). Upon the flanges, or horizontal sections, of the T-irons, one layer of ...-inch pure corkboard shall be carefully put in place, with all joints butted tight. To the top surface of the insulation shall then be applied a 1-inch thick Portland cement finish, mixed in the proportion of one part Portland cement to two parts clean, sharp sand.

To the under side of the first course, a second layer of ...-inch pure corkboard shall be erected in a ½-inch bedding of Portland cement mortar, additionally secured to the first with galvanized wire nails, all joints in the second course broken with respect to all joints in the first course and all joints butted tight. To the surface of the insulation underneath shall then be applied a finish as selected.

107.—Ceilings.—Wood.

(15) Single layer, in Asphalt cement.

To the reasonably smooth and clean ceiling surface to be insulated (consisting of ⅞-inch T. & G. sheathing to joists), one layer of ...-inch pure corkboard shall be erected in hot

*About 10 feet is the maximum width that may be spanned safely by T-irons carrying double layer of corkboard, and following this specification. It is not permissable to double the span and center-support the T irons by rods fastened to ceiling of building above; because water will be condensed on the cool surfaces of these rods and will follow through into ceiling insulation below, tending to destroy it or otherwise make it unfit for service within a year.

Asphalt cement, additionally secured with galvanized wire nails, with all transverse joints broken and all joints butted

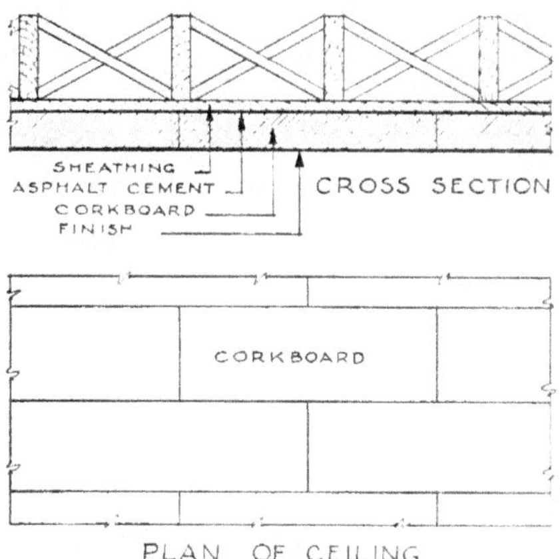

FIG. 96.—CEILINGS; WOOD. ARTICLE 107 (15).

tight and sealed in the same compound. To the surface of the insulation shall then be applied a finish as selected.

107.—Ceilings.—Wood (continued).

(16) Double layer, both in Asphalt cement.

To the reasonably smooth and clean ceiling surface to be insulated (consisting of ⅞-inch T. & G. sheathing to joists), one layer of . . .-inch pure corkboard shall be erected in hot Asphalt cement, additionally secured with galvanized wire nails, with all transverse joints broken and all joints butted tight and sealed in the same compound. To the first course, a second layer of . . .-inch pure corkboard shall be erected in hot Asphalt cement, additionally secured to the first with wood skewers, with all joints in the second course broken with respect to all joints in the first course and all joints butted tight and sealed in the same compound. To the surface of the insulation shall then be applied a finish as selected.

108.—Roofs.—Concrete or wood.

(17) Single layer, in Asphalt cement.

To the reasonably smooth and clean . . . roof area to be

insulated, one layer of . . .-inch pure corkboard shall be laid down in hot Asphalt cement, with all transverse joints broken

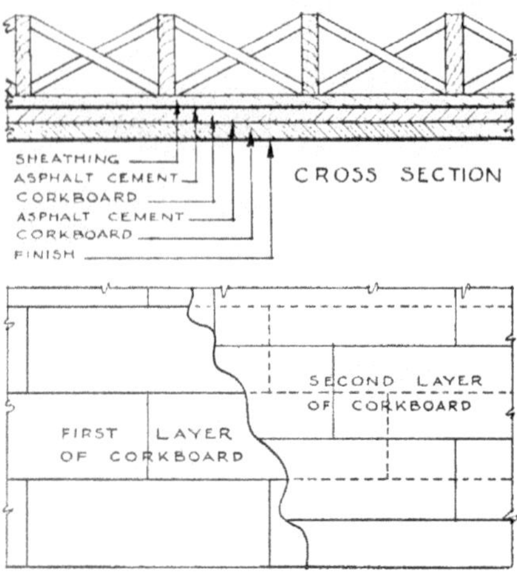

FIG. 97.—CEILINGS; WOOD. ARTICLE 107 (16).

and all joints butted tight and sealed in the same compound.* The roofing contractor shall then apply, to the surface of the insulation, a roofing as required.

108.—Roofs.—Concrete or wood (continued).

(18) Double layer, both in Asphalt cement.

To the reasonably smooth and clean . . . roof area to be insulated, one layer of . . .-inch pure corkboard shall be laid down in hot Asphalt cement, with all transverse joints broken and all joints butted tight and sealed in the same compound. To the first course, a second layer of . . .-inch pure corkboard shall then be laid down in hot Asphalt cement, with all joints in the second course broken with respect to all joints in the first course and all joints butted tight and sealed in the same

NOTE—The wall insulation should be carried up so as to connect with the roof insulation, wherever possible; and in such cases, insert the following sentence at the point starred (*) in the above specification: "The roof insulation shall connect with the wall insulation, the joint being sealed with hot Asphalt cement."

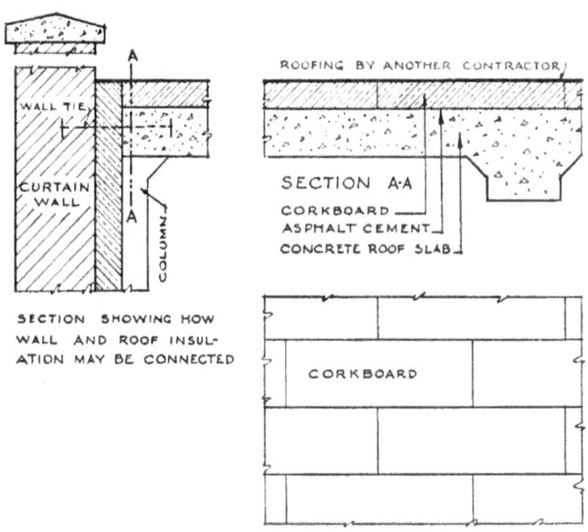

FIG. 98.—ROOFS; CONCRETE OR WOOD. ARTICLE 108 (17).

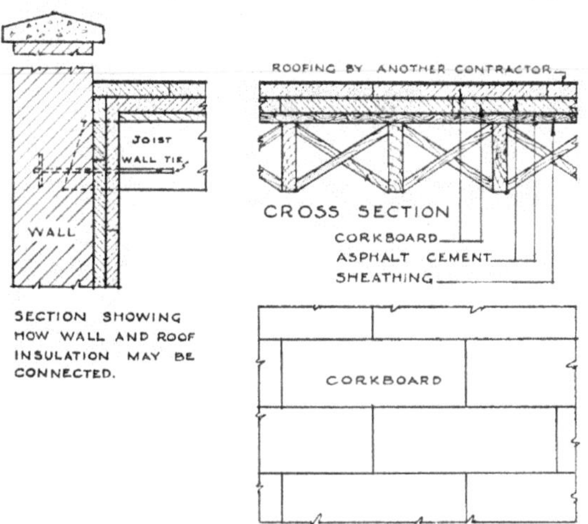

FIG. 99.—ROOFS; CONCRETE OR WOOD. ARTICLE 108 (18).

compounds.* The roofing contractor shall then apply, to the surface of the insulation, a roofing as required.

109.—Floors.—Wood.

(19) Single layer, in Asphalt cement, concrete finish.

To the reasonably smooth and clean wood floor to be insulated (consisting of 1⅜-inch T. & G. flooring over joints),

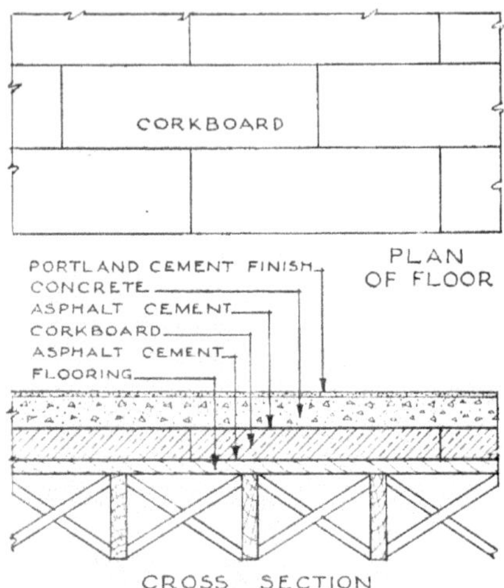

FIG. 100.—FLOORS; WOOD. ARTICLE 109 (19).

one layer of . . .-inch pure corkboard shall be laid down in hot Asphalt cement, with all transverse joints broken and all joints butted tight, and the top surface then flooded with hot Asphalt cement. Over the surface of the insulation shall then be applied a concrete floor finish as selected.

109.—Floors.—Wood (continued).

(20) Single layer, in Asphalt cement, wood finish.

To the reasonably smooth and clean wood floor to be insulated (consisting of 1⅜-inch T. & G. flooring over joists),

NOTE—The wall insulation should be carried up so as to connect with the roof insulation, wherever possible; and in such cases, insert the following sentence at the point starred (*) in the above specification: "The roof insulation shall connect with the wall insulation, the joint being sealed with hot Asphalt cement."

2-inch x ...-inch sleepers shall be put in place on edge on 38-inch centers. Between these sleepers, one layer of ...-inch pure corkboard shall be laid down in hot Asphalt cement, with all joints butted tight, and the top surface then flooded

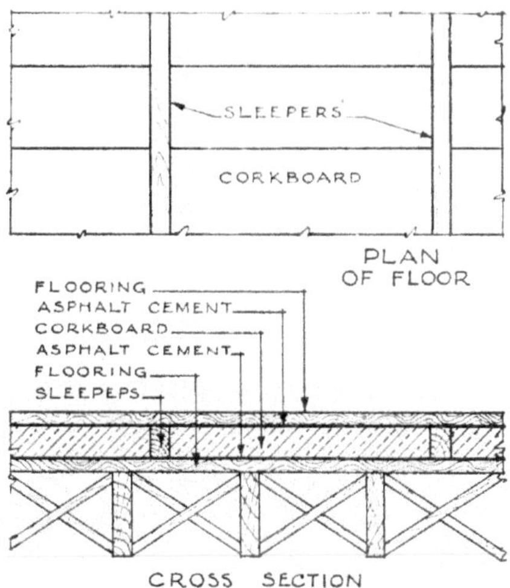

FIG. 101.—FLOORS; WOOD. ARTICLE 109 (20).

with the same compound. Over the surface of the insulation shall then be applied a T. & G. flooring as selected, securely fastened to the sleepers.

109.—Floors.—Wood (continued).

(21) Double layer, both in Asphalt cement, concrete finish.

To the reasonably smooth and clean wood floor to be insulated (consisting of 1⅜-inch T. & G. flooring over joists), one layer of ...-inch pure corkboard shall be laid down in hot Asphalt cement, with all transverse joints broken and all joints butted tight. To the first course, a second layer of ...-inch pure corkboard shall be laid down in hot Asphalt cement, with all joints in the second course broken with respect to all joints in the first course and all joints butted tight, and the top surface then flooded with the same compound

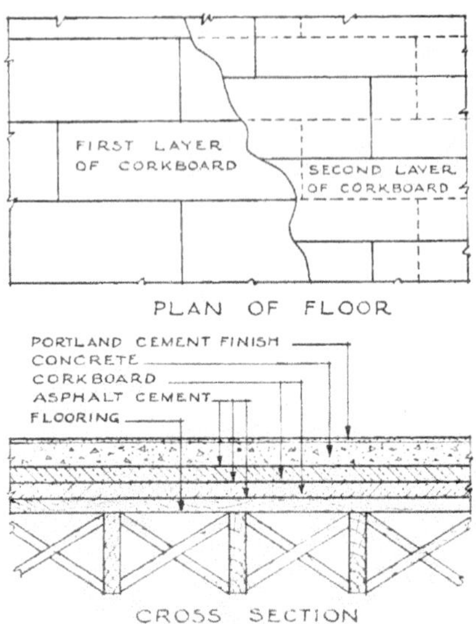

FIG. 102.—FLOORS; WOOD. ARTICLE 109 (21).

Over the surface of the insulation shall then be applied a concrete floor finish as selected.

109.—**Floors.**—Wood (continued).

(22) Double layer, both in Asphalt cement, wood finish.

To the reasonably smooth and clean wood floor to be insulated (consisting of 1⅜-inch T. & G. flooring over joists), one layer of ...-inch pure corkboard shall be laid down in hot Asphalt cement, with all vertical joints broken and all joints butted tight. Over this insulation, 2-inch x ...-inch sleepers shall then be put in place on 38-inch centers. Between these sleepers, the second layer of ...-inch pure corkboard shall be laid down in hot Asphalt cement, with all joints in the second course broken with respect to all joints in the first course and all joints butted tight, and the top surface then flooded with the same compound. Over the surface of the insulation shall then be applied a T. & G. flooring as selected, securely fastened to the sleepers.

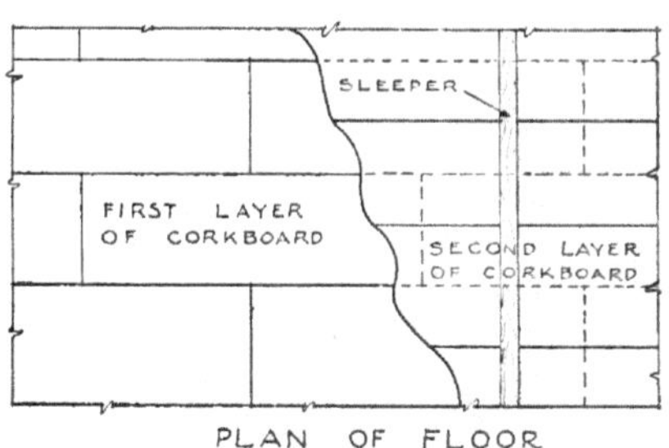

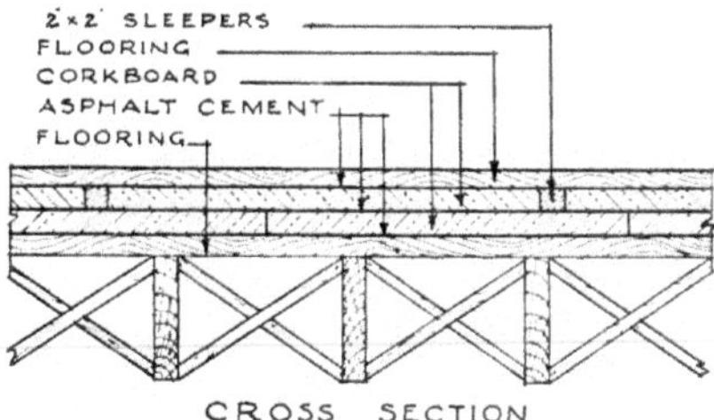

FIG. 103.—FLOORS; WOOD. ARTICLE 109 (22).

110.—Floors.—Concrete.

(23) Single layer, in Asphalt cement, concrete finish.

To the reasonably smooth and clean concrete floor to be insulated, one layer of ...-inch pure corkboard shall be laid down in hot Asphalt cement, with all transverse joints broken and all joints butted tight, and the top surface then flooded with the same compound. Over the surface of the insulation shall then be applied a concrete floor finish as selected.

110.—Floors.—Concrete (continued).

(24) Single layer, in Asphalt cement, wood finish.

To the reasonably smooth and clean concrete floor to be insulated, 2-inch x ...-inch sleepers shall be put in place on edge on 38-inch centers. Between these sleepers, one layer of

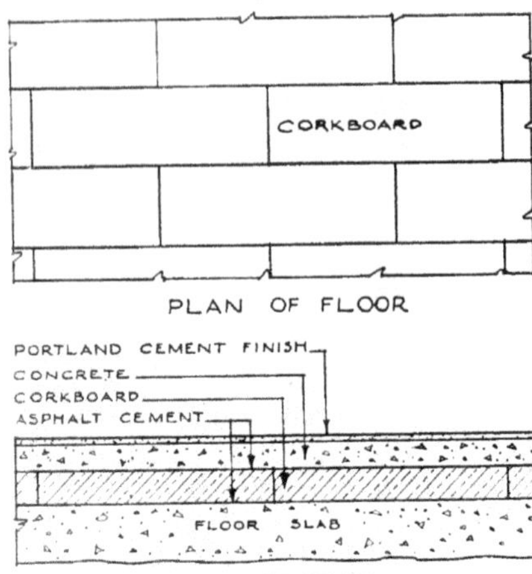

FIG. 104.—FLOORS; CONCRETE. ARTICLE 110 (23).

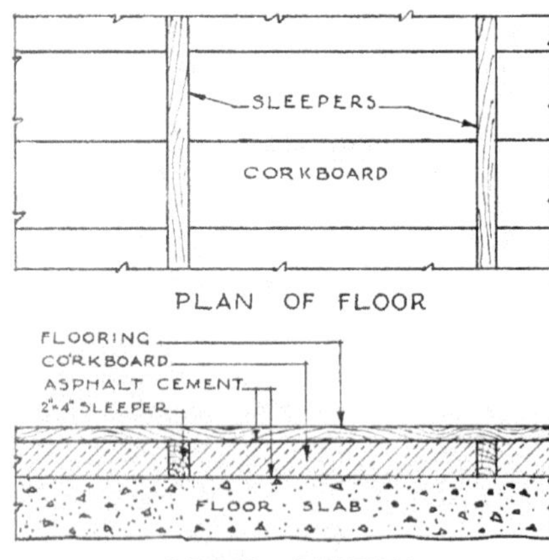

FIG. 105.—FLOORS; CONCRETE. ARTICLE 110 (24).

...-inch pure corkboard shall be laid down in hot Asphalt cement, with all transverse joints broken and all joints butted tight, and the top surface then flooded with the same compound. Over the surface of the insulation shall then be applied a T. & G. flooring as selected, securely fastened to the sleepers.

110.—Floors.—Concrete (continued).

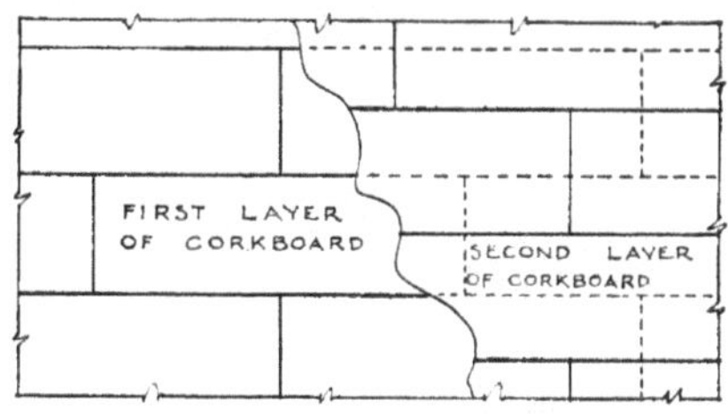

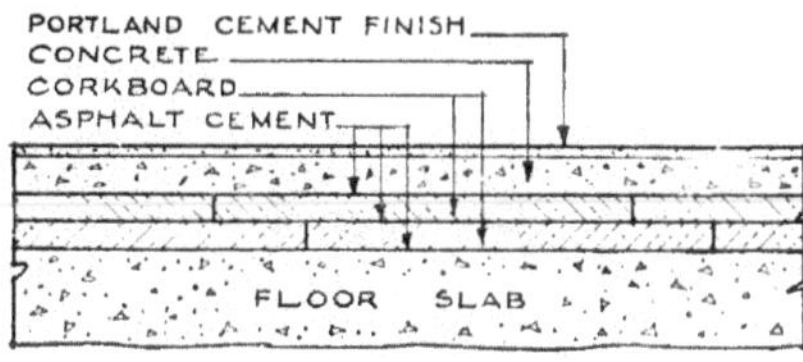

FIG. 106.—FLOORS; CONCRETE. ARTICLE 110 (25).

(25) Double layer, both in Asphalt cement, concrete finish.

To the reasonably smooth and clean concrete floor to be insulated, one layer of ...-inch pure corkboard shall be laid down in hot Asphalt cement, with all transverse joints broken and all joints butted tight. To the first course, a second layer of ...-inch pure corkboard shall be laid down in hot Asphalt cement, with all joints in the second course broken with respect to all joints in the first course and all joints butted tight, and the top surface then flooded with the same compound. Over the surface of the insulation shall then be applied a concrete floor finish as selected.

110.—Floors.—Concrete (continued).

(26) Double layer, both in Asphalt cement, wood finish. To the reasonably smooth and clean concrete base floor to be insulated, one layer of ...-inch pure corkboard shall be laid down in hot Asphalt cement, with all vertical joints broken

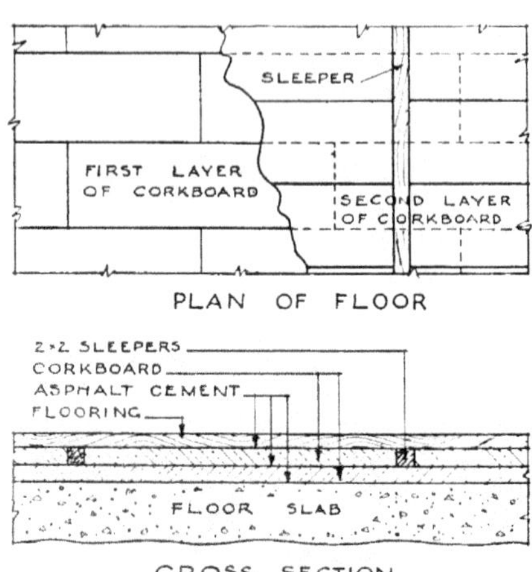

FIG. 107.—FLOORS; CONCRETE. ARTICLE 110 (26).

and all joints butted tight. Over this insulation, 2-inch x ... -inch sleepers shall then be put in place on 38-inch centers. Between these sleepers, the second layer of ...-inch pure corkboard shall be laid down in hot Asphalt cement, with all joints in the second course broken with respect to all joints in the first course and all joints butted tight, and the top surface then flooded with the same compound. Over the insulation shall then be applied a T. & G. flooring as selected, securely fastened to the sleepers.

111.—Partitions.—Stone, concrete or brick.

(See 103.—Walls: Stone, concrete or brick; specifications (1), (2), (3), (4) and (5).

NOTE: It is not always necessary to divide the total thickness of insulation and put half of it on either side of partition walls; instead, it is sometimes sufficient to apply the total thickness of insulation to one side or the other, finish it off as desired, and then apply the same finish to the uninsulated side of the wall.

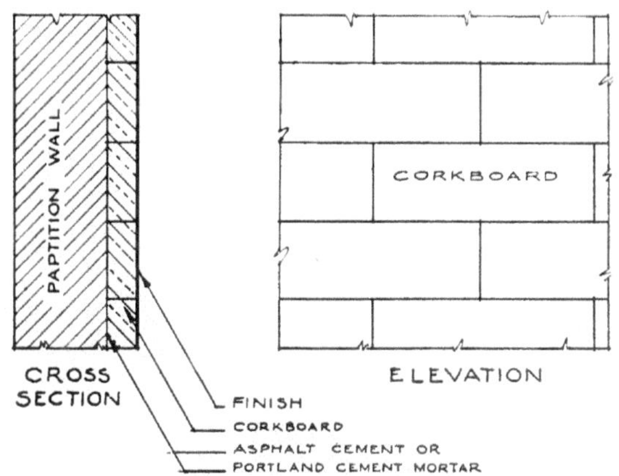

FIG. 108.—PARTITIONS; STONE, CONCRETE OR BRICK. ARTICLE 111.

112.—Partitions.—Wood.

(27) Single layer, between studs, joints sealed in Asphalt cement.

Two-inch x 4-inch studding shall be erected 36 inches apart, the studs secured so that the 2-inch dimension runs with the wall thickness. Between studs, one layer 2-inch corkboard shall be erected edge on edge, with all joints butted and sealed with hot Asphalt cement, and each corkboard secured to the studs and additionally to the adjacent corkboard with galvanized wire nails. Over the exposed area of the studding shall be put in place 12-inch wide strips of galvanized wire square-mesh screen, No. 18 gauge, 3 mesh (1/3-inch), securely stapled to the studs and nailed to the insulation on both sides of studs. Where cold storage doors are to be set, 4-inch x ...-inch permanent studs, with a lintel between them, shall be securely anchored to the floor and ceiling in the line of the partition so as to form an opening the size of the cold storage door frame; and after the partition has been constructed, the permanent studs and lintel shall be covered on both sides with ...-inch pure corkboard secured with galvanized wire nails. To the surface of the

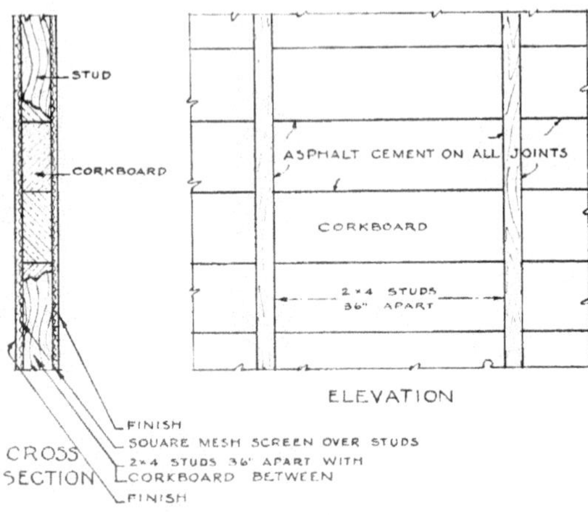

FIG. 109.—PARTITIONS; WOOD. ARTICLE 112 (27).

insulation and over the wire mesh shall then be applied a finish as selected.

112.—Partitions.—Wood (continued).

(28) Double layer, first between studs with joints sealed in Asphalt cement, second in Asphalt cement.

Two-inch x 4-inch studding shall be erected 36 inches apart, the studs secured so that the 2-inch dimension runs with the wall thickness. Between the studs, one layer 2-inch pure corkboard shall be erected edge on edge, with all joints butted and sealed with hot Asphalt cement, and each corkboard secured to the studs and additionally to the adjacent corkboard with galvanized wire nails. To the first course, a second layer of ...-inch pure corkboard shall be erected in hot Asphalt cement, additionally secured with wood skewers, with all joints in the second course broken with respect to all joints in the first course and all joints butted tight and sealed in the same compound. Over the exposed area of the studding shall be put in place 12-inch wide strips of galvanized wire square-mesh screen, No. 18 gauge, 3 mesh (1/3-inch), securely stapled to the studs and nailed to the insulation on both sides of studs. Where cold storage doors are to be set,

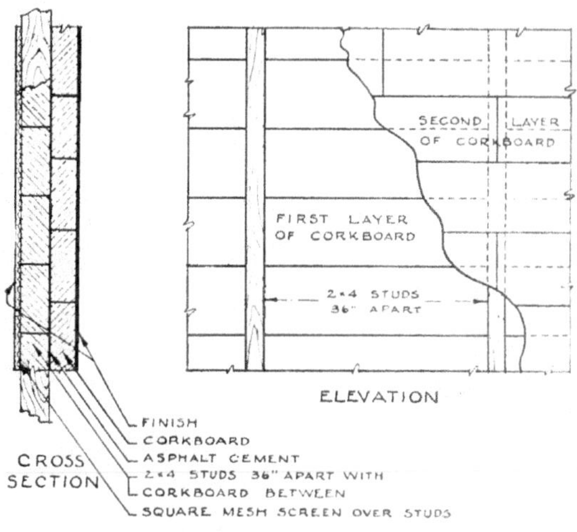

FIG. 110.—PARTITIONS; WOOD. ARTICLE 112 (28).

4-inch x ...-inch permanent studs, with a lintel between them, shall be securely anchored to the floor and ceiling in the line of the partition so as to form an opening the size of the cold storage door frame; and after the partition has been constructed, the permanent studs and lintel shall be covered on both sides with ...-inch pure corkboard secured with galvanized wire nails. To the surface of the insulation and over the wire mesh shall then be applied a finish as selected.

113.—Partitions.—Solid cork.

(29) Single layer, joints sealed in Asphalt cement.

To form the partition wall, there shall be built up edge on edge one layer of ...-inch pure corkboard, with all vertical joints broken and all joints butted tight and sealed in hot

Asphalt cement. Each corkboard shall be additionally secured to the abutting corkboards and, where possible, to the wall, floor and ceiling insulation, with long wood skewers. Where cold storage doors are to be set, 4-inch x ...-inch permanent studs, with a lintel between them, shall be securely anchored to the floor and ceiling in the line of the partition so as to form an opening the size of the cold storage door frame; and after the partition is constructed, the permanent

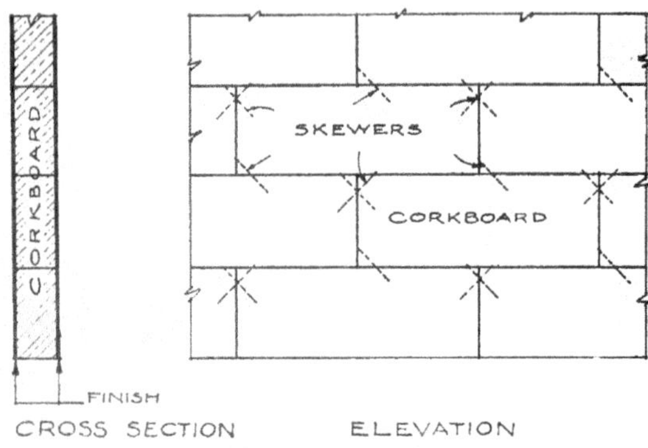

FIG. 111.—PARTITIONS; SOLID CORK. ARTICLE 113 (29).

studs and lintel shall be covered on both sides with ...-inch pure corkboard secured with galvanized wire nails. To the surface of the insulation shall then be applied a finish as selected.

113.—**Partitions.**—Solid cork (continued).

(30) Double layer, first with joints sealed in Asphalt cement, second in Portland cement.

To form the partition wall, there shall be built up edge on edge one layer of ...-inch pure corkboard, with all vertical joints broken and all joints butted tight and sealed in hot Asphalt cement. Each corkboard shall be additionally secured to the abutting corkboards and, where possible, to the wall, floor and ceiling insulation, with long wood skewers. To the first course, a second layer of ...-inch pure corkboard shall then be erected in a ½-inch bedding of Portland cement mortar, additionally secured to the first with wood skewers, with all joints in the second course broken with respect to all joints in the first course and all joints butted tight. Where cold storage doors are to be set, 4-inch x ...-inch permanent studs, with a lintel between them, shall be securely anchored to the floor and ceiling in the line of the partition so as to form an opening the size of the cold storage door frame; and after the partition is constructed, the permanent studs and

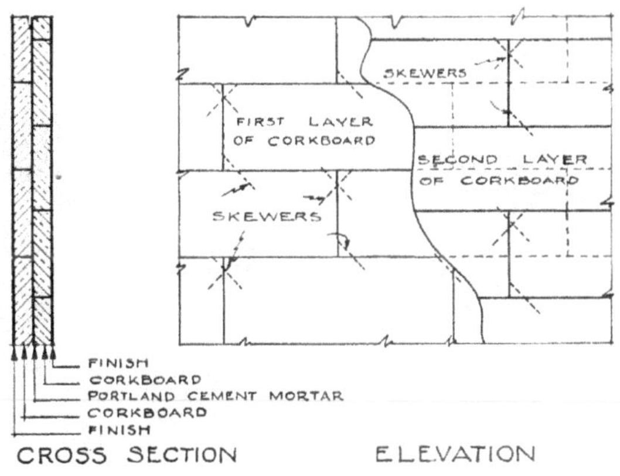

FIG. 112.—PARTITIONS; SOLID CORK. ARTICLE 113 (30).

lintel shall be covered on both sides with ...-inch pure corkboard secured with galvanized wire nails. To the surface of the insulation shall then be applied a finish as selected.

113.—Partitions.—Solid cork (continued).

(31) Double layer, first with joints sealed in Asphalt cement, second in Asphalt cement.

To form the partition wall, there shall be built up edge on edge one layer of ...-inch pure corkboard, with all vertical joints broken and all joints butted tight and sealed in hot Asphalt cement. Each corkboard shall be additionally secured to the abutting corkboards and, where possible, to the wall, floor and ceiling insulation, with long wood skewers. To the first course, a second layer of ...-inch pure corkboard shall then be erected in hot Asphalt cement, additionally secured to the first course with wood skewers, with all joints in the second course broken with respect to all joints in the first course and all joints butted tight and sealed in the same compound. Where cold storage doors are to be set, 4-inch x ...-inch permanent studs, with a lintel between them, shall be securely anchored to the floor and ceiling in the line of the partition so as to form an opening the size of the cold storage

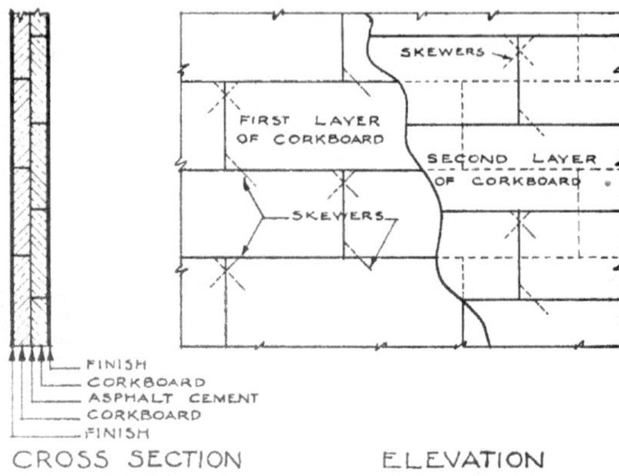

FIG. 113.—PARTITIONS; SOLID CORK. ARTICLE 113 (31).

door frame; and after the partition is constructed, the permanent studs and lintel shall be covered on both sides with ...-inch pure corkboard secured with galvanized wire nails. To the surface of the insulation shall then be applied a finish as selected.

114.—Tanks.—Freezing.

(32) Double layer on bottom, both in Asphalt cement, granulated cork fill on sides and ends.

To the reasonably smooth and clean concrete base, of dimensions 2 feet wider and 2 feet longer than the size of the freezing tank, one layer of ...-inch pure corkboard shall be laid down in hot Asphalt cement, with all transverse joints broken and all joints butted tight. To the first course, a second layer of ...-inch pure corkboard shall be laid down in hot Asphalt cement, with all joints in the second course broken with respect to all joints in the first course and all joints butted tight, and the top surface then flooded with the same compound and left ready for the tank to be set down directly on top.

After the tank has been properly set by others, retaining walls of lumber shall be constructed so as to leave a space 1 foot all around the four* sides of the tank, by erecting

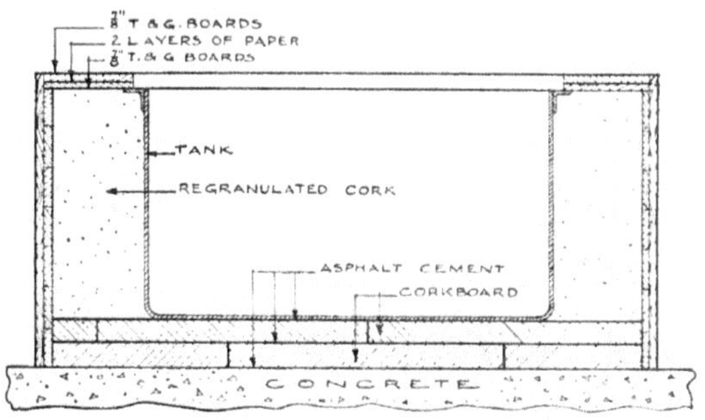

CROSS SECTION OF TANK

FIG. 114.—TANKS; FREEZING. ARTICLE 114 (32).

2-inch x 12-inch studding on suitable centers at right angles against the sides of the tank and then sheathing the studs with double layer ⅞-inch T. & G. boards having two layers of waterproof paper between. The studs shall be carefully anchored by dropping them into depressions in the concrete base and then wedging them under and securing them with metal clips to the flange at top of tank. The space between the retaining walls and the tank shall be filled with regranulated cork well temped in place, and a curbing consisting of double layer ⅞-inch T. & G. boards with two layers of waterproof paper between shall then be installed so as to rest on the flange of the tank and cover the space filled with regranulated cork.

114.—Tanks.—Freezing (continued).

(33) Double layer on bottom, both in Asphalt cement; double layer on sides and ends, both in Asphalt cement.

*If the tank is to be set in a corner so that masonry walls of the building act as two retaining walls, they should be damp-proofed in a suitable and thorough manner.

To the reasonably smooth and clean concrete base, of dimensions enough wider and longer than the size of the freezing tank sufficient to overlap the thickness of insulation on ends and sides, one layer of ...-inch pure corkboard shall be laid down in hot Asphalt cement, with all transverse joints broken and all joints butted tight. To the first course, a second layer of ...-inch pure corkboard shall be laid down in hot Asphalt cement, with all joints in the second course broken

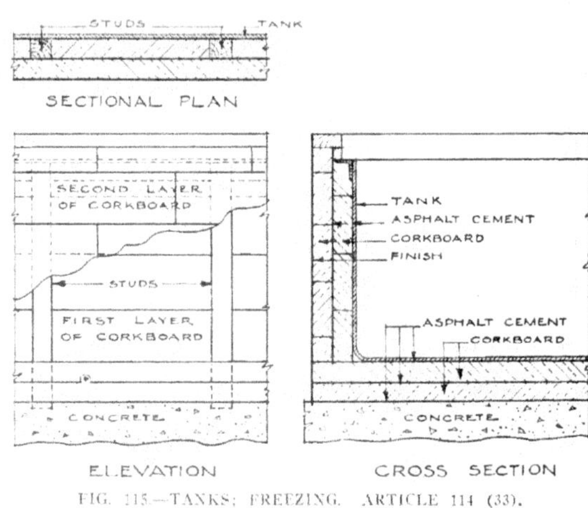

FIG. 115—TANKS; FREEZING. ARTICLE 114 (33).

with respect to all joints in the first course and all joints butted tight, and the top surface then flooded with the same compound and left ready for the tank to be set down directly on top.

After the tank has been properly set by others, suitable studding, 2-inch x a dimension equivalent to the thickness of the first course of corkboard to be applied, shall be set 36 inches apart at right angles against the sides and ends of the tank, and shall be carefully anchored by dropping them into depressions in the concrete base and then wedging them under and securing them with metal clips to the flange at the top of tank. Between the studs, one layer of ...-inch pure corkboard shall then be erected with all joints butted and sealed with hot Asphalt cement, and each corkboard secured to the studs and additionally to the adjacent corkboards with galvanized wire nails. To the first course, a second layer of ...-inch pure corkboard shall be erected in hot Asphalt cement with all joints in the second course broken with respect to all joints in the first course and all joints butted tight and sealed in the same compound. To the surface of the insulation shall then be applied a finish as selected.

114.—Tanks.—Freezing (continued).

(34) Double layer on bottom, both in Asphalt cement; single layer on sides and ends against studs, with granulated cork fill.

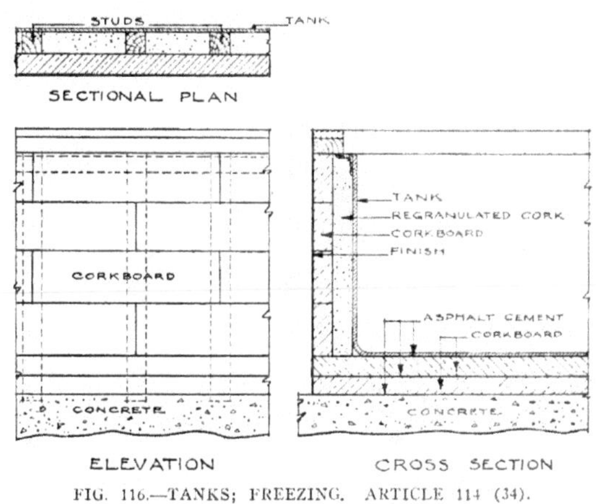

FIG. 116.—TANKS; FREEZING. ARTICLE 114 (34).

To the reasonably smooth and clean concrete base, of dimensions enough wider and longer than the size of the freezing tank sufficient to overlap the thickness of insulation on ends and sides, one layer of ...-inch pure corkboard shall be laid down in hot Asphalt cement, with all transverse joints broken and all joints butted tight. To the first course, a second layer of ...-inch pure corkboard shall be laid down in hot Asphalt cement, with all joints in the second course broken with respect to all joints in the first course and all joints butted tight, and the top surface then flooded with the same compound and left ready for the tank to be set down directly on top.

After the tank has been properly set by others, 4-inch x 4-inch studding shall be set on 18-inch centers at right angles against the sides and ends of the tank, and shall be carefully anchored by dropping them into depressions in the concrete base and then wedging them under and securing them with metal clips to the flange at the top of tank. Against the studs, one layer of ...-inch pure corkboard shall be secured with galvanized wire nails, with all joints butted and sealed with hot Asphalt cement. The space between the studs, the sides and ends of the tank, and the corkboard, shall then be filled with regranulated cork well tamped in place. To the surface of the insulation shall then be applied a finish as selected.

115.—Finish.—Walls and ceilings.

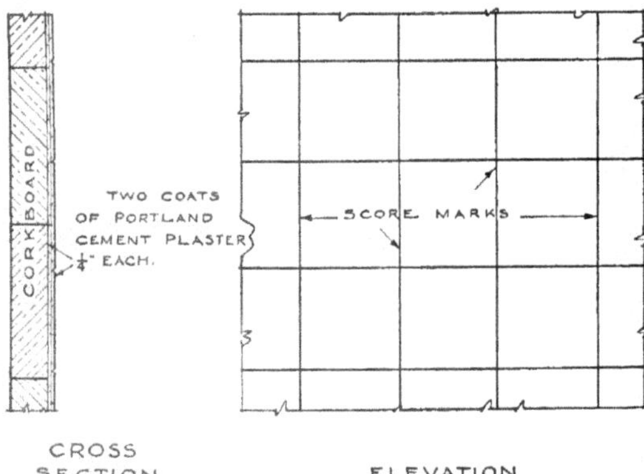

FIG. 117.—FINISH; WALLS AND CEILINGS. ARTICLE 115 (35).

(35) Portland cement plaster, in 2 coats.

To the exposed surface of the corkboard insulation, a Portland cement plaster finish approximately ½-inch in thickness shall be applied in two coats. The first coat shall be approximately ¼-inch in thickness, rough scratched, and mixed one part Portland cement to two parts clean, sharp sand. To the first coat, after it has thoroughly set, a second coat, mixed in the same proportion, shall be applied approximately ¼-inch in thickness, and troweled to a hard, smooth finish. The surface shall then be scored in ...-foot squares to confine any checking and cracking of the plaster to such score marks.

115.—Finish.—Walls and ceilings (continued).

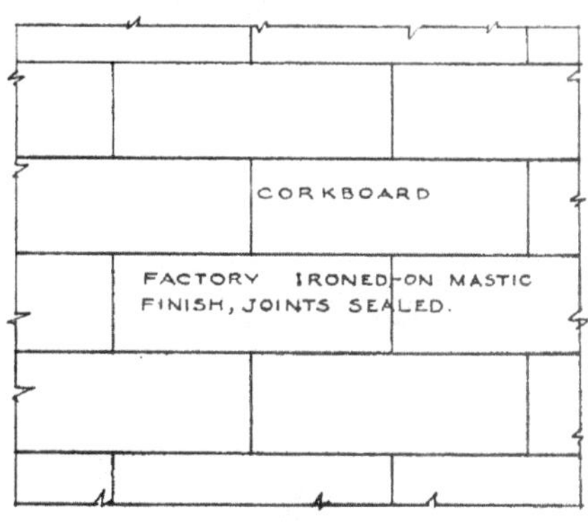

FIG. 118.—FINISH; WALLS AND CEILINGS. ARTICLE 115 (36).

(36) Factory ironed-on mastic finish, joints sealed.

The exposed surface of the corkboards, used on the second or exposed course of insulation, shall be coated to a thickness of approximately ⅛-inch with an asphalt mastic* finish ironed on at the factory, the mastic coating having beveled (V) edges; and after the corkboard is erected, all joints shall be sealed with suitable plastic asphalt mastic put carefully in place and gone over with the point of a hot tool, hot enough to melt the mastic and the plastic and seal the joints and render them tight.

115.—Finish.—Walls and ceilings (continued).

(37) Glazed tile or brick, in Portland cement.

To the exposed surface of the corkboard insulation, a Portland cement plaster finish approximately ⅜-inch in thickness,

*Each manufacturer presumably follows its own formula for the particular brand of ironed-on mastic finish offered, and its probable worth in service must be judged accordingly.

mixed one part Portland cement to two parts clean, sharp sand, shall be applied in one coat, floated to a reasonably true

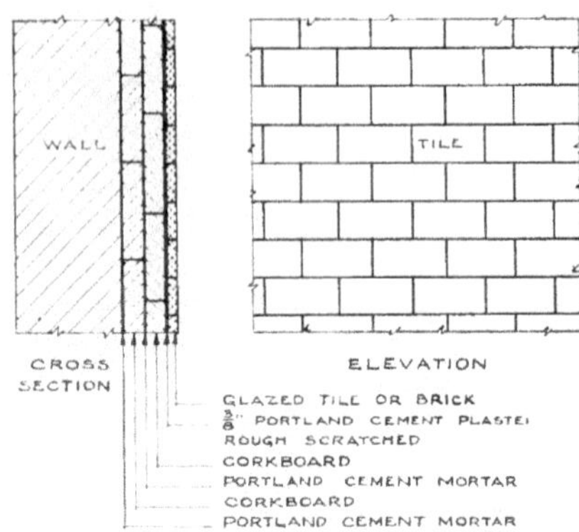

FIG. 119.—FINISH; WALLS AND CEILINGS. ARTICLE 115 (37).

surface and left rough scratched. A glazed tile or glass brick finish, as specified, shall then be installed by another contractor.

115.—**Finish.**—Walls and ceilings (continued).

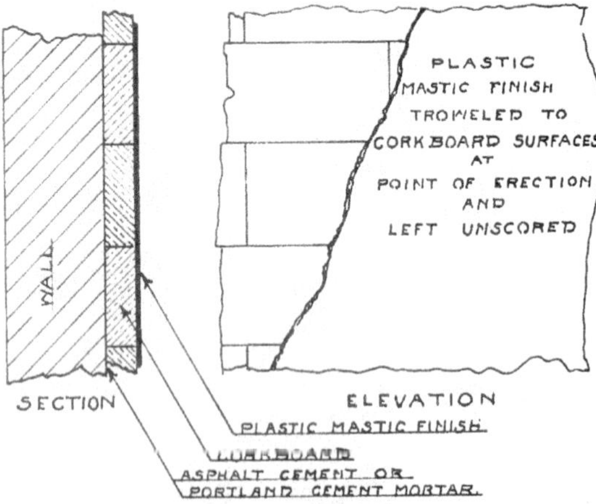

FIG. 120.—FINISH; WALLS AND CEILINGS. ARTICLE 115 (38).

(38) Emulsified asphalt plastic, in 2 coats.

The surface of the corkboards to receive the asphalt plastic finish shall be made reasonably even and true by trimming off any slight projections.

To the corkboard surface thus prepared, shall be applied two coats of approved Emulsified Asphalt Plastic. The first coat, approximately 3/32-inch in thickness, shall be applied under a wet trowel, care being taken to press the material firmly into the surface irregularities of the corkboard. When this coat has set, a second coat shall be applied under a wet trowel, making the total thickness for the two coats not less than 1/8-inch. The second coat shall be troweled smooth after it has begun to set but before it has hardened. Its surface shall not be scored.

116.—Finish.—Floors.

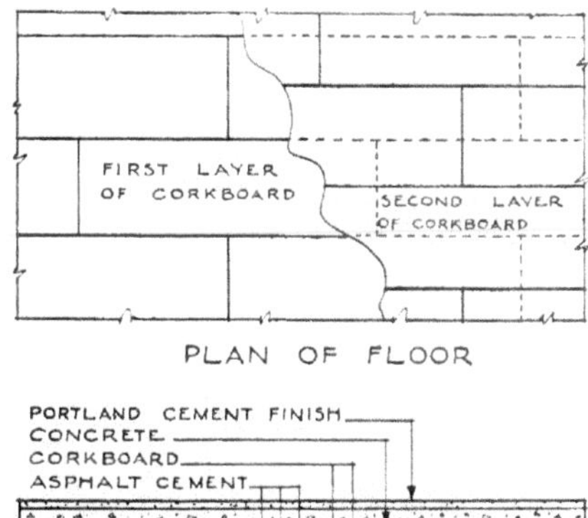

FIG. 121.—FINISH; FLOORS. ARTICLE 116 (39).

(39) Concrete.

A ...-inch concrete wearing floor shall be laid down directly on top of the asphalt flooded surface of the corkboard, consisting of . . . inches of rough concrete, mixed one part Portland cement to two and a half parts clean, sharp sand and five parts clean gravel or crushed stone, well tamped in place until the water comes to the surface, and then followed by a 1-inch troweled smooth top finish composed of one part Portland cement and one part clean, sharp sand. The concrete wearing floor shall be sloped to drain as desired.

116.—Finish.—Floors (continued).

(40) Wood.

The finished wood floor shall be of thoroughly dry and

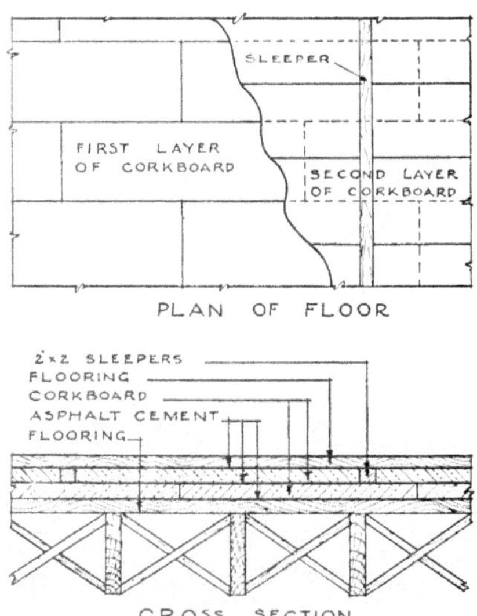

FIG. 122.—FINISH; FLOORS. ARTICLE 116 (40).

seasoned ⅞-inch T. & G. . . . lumber, laid with approximately 1/32-inch between the boards, to eliminate as much as possible the tendency of the floor to expand and warp, and secret nailed to the sleepers that were provided in the insulation underneath, and the floor left perfectly smooth and even.

116.—Finish.—Floors (continued).

(41) Galvanized metal.

Over the asphalt flooded surface of the corkboard on the floors and baffles of bunkers, there shall be installed a floor

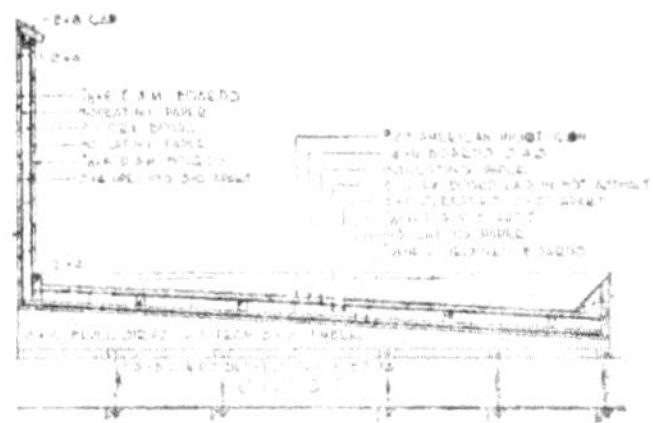

FIG. 123.—FINISH; FLOORS. ARTICLE 116 (41).

or cover of . . . gauge galvanized iron. The metal shall extend over all edges of the bunker at least two inches and be securely anchored, and all joints and nail heads in the finished work shall then be carefully soldered.

117.—Miscellaneous Specifications.

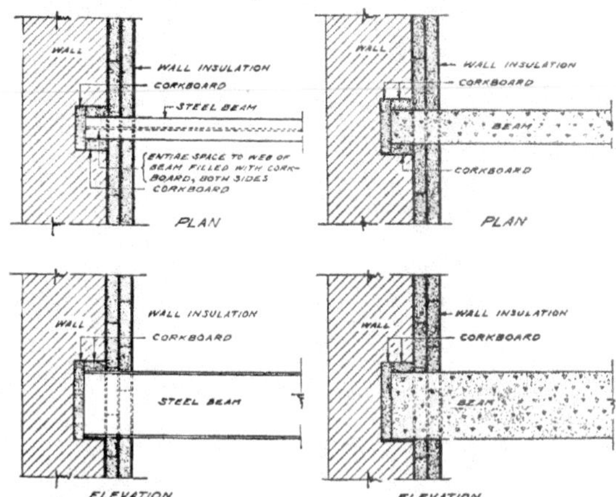

FIG. 124.—MISCELLANEOUS SPECIFICATIONS. ARTICLE 117 (42).

(42) Ends of beams or girders extending into walls.

All beams and girders extending into the building walls shall be insulated on the ends, tops and sides with one layer of ...-inch pure corkboard cut accurately and joints sealed tightly with hot Asphalt cement, the corkboard extending beyond the inside face of the wall so as to join and seal with the wall insulation. The insulation contractor shall furnish the material required for this purpose, but the installation shall be made by the general contractor.

117.—Miscellaneous Specifications (continued).

(43) Rat proofing.

As a barrier against rats and mice entering this cold storage room, there shall be installed over all areas of the room and securely stapled in place, with all joints carefully butted or lapped, galvanized wire square-mesh screen, No. 18 gauge, 3 mesh (1/3-inch). The screen shall be located as near as possible to the point of expected attack, that is, the screen shall be laid across ceiling joists and wall studding before the sheathing is applied, fastened to the surface of soft brick or laid down over wood floor before the first layer of insulation is applied, and similarly used elsewhere as required.

117.—Miscellaneous Specifications (continued).

(44) Portland cement mortar.

The Portland cement mortar (not the Portland cement plaster) used in connection with the corkboard insulation on *walls and partitions* shall be mixed in the proportion of one part Portland cement to two parts clean, sharp sand.

The Portland cement mortar used in connection with the corkboard insulation on *ceilings* shall be mixed in the proportion of one part Portland cement to one part clean, sharp sand.

(45) Asphalt cement.

NOTE: See specification given in Article 100, under heading entitled, "Specification for Asphalt cement for cold storage insulation."

(46) Asphalt primer.

NOTE: See specification given in Article 100, under heading entitled, "Asphalt primer for use with Asphalt cement."

CHAPTER XIV.

COMPLETE DIRECTIONS FOR THE PROPER APPLICATION OF CORKBOARD INSULATION.

118.—General Instructions and Equipment.—For many years it was considered necessary, or at least highly desirable, that all corkboard surfaces to be erected in Portland cement mortar and all corkboard surfaces to be finished with Portland cement plaster, should be *scored* on the side against which the mortar or plaster was specified to be applied. This scoring had to be done at the factory and consisted of several parallel saw grooves running the length of the corkboards, and which were put there as a key or bond for the cement. Experience has demonstrated, however, that the plain surface of corkboard is of such character as to permit an intimate and satisfactory bond with Portland cement, as with Asphalt cement, and score marks are no longer considered essential. The plain corkboard may be scored on the job, if scoring is preferred, before being erected in Portland cement mortar, by roughening the surface slightly with any pronged tool, such as a few wire nails driven through a piece of wood. If it is desired to roughen the surface to receive Portland cement plaster, then the work is done after the corkboard has been put in place and just before the first coat of plaster is applied.

The *Portland cement mortar*, in which corkboard is frequently erected to masonry walls, and the like, should be prepared by mixing* one part (by volume) of any standard grade of Portland cement with two parts of clean, sharp sand. Be sure the sand is clean, and be sure that it is sharp. It will require 5.0 barrels of Portland cement* and 2.1 cubic yards of

*The Portland Cement Association, 33 West Grand Avenue, Chicago, Illinois, with branches in many cities, gladly furnish complete data relating to the proper mixing of Portland cement for any purpose. Also see Appendix of this text.

sand* for each thousand square feet of surface. Do not mix too much mortar at a time, make it fairly stiff, and do not add any lime.

Portland cement mortar, or "backing," should be uniformly one-half inch in thickness over the whole surface of the corkboards and none should be allowed on the sides and ends. This cement backing is never applied directly to the area to

FIG. 125—CORKBOARD ERECTED TO CONCRETE WALLS AND COLUMNS IN PORTLAND CEMENT MORTAR.—NOTE THE SIMPLE MORTARBOARD AND HOPPER DEVICE FOR APPLICATION OF THE "BACKING" DESCRIBED IN THE TEXT.

be insulated, as some might suppose, but to the surfaces of the individual corkboards before they are set in place. To facilitate the application of the cement backing to the corkboards, a mortar board about 4 feet square is equipped with a simple runway and hopper attachment that is entirely practical and very satisfactory. Across the top of the mortar board nail two strips parallel to each other and exactly 12 inches apart,

*1 barrel cement = 4 sacks = 4 cubic feet = 400 pounds; 1 cubic yard sand = approximately 2,400 pounds—based on tables in "Concrete, Plain and Reinforced," by Taylor and Thompson.

so that one standard sheet of corkboard (12 inches wide x 36 inches long) may be laid down between them. Make the height of these strips one-half inch more than the thickness of the corkboards to be coated. Construct a simple wooden hopper about two feet high, having an opening at the top about 2 feet x 2 feet and one at the bottom exactly 12 inches by 12 inches. Mount the hopper on the two strips so that a

FIG. 126.—ERECTING CORKBOARD IN ASPHALT CEMENT TO ASPHALT PRIMED CONCRETE WALL SURFACES—NOTE THE ASPHALT PAN AND OIL STOVE ARRANGEMENT FOR HOLDING ODORLESS ASPHALT AT THE CORRECT TEMPERATURE AT POINT OF ERECTION.

corkboard can be pushed through the runway (formed by the two strips) and under the hopper. Then fill the hopper with Portland cement mortar; and by pushing one board through ahead of another, butted end to end, the individual boards are uniformly coated to a thickness of one-half inch and without the liklihood of the mortar getting on the sides and ends of the corkboards.

To prepare *Asphalt cement* for use with corkboard to walls and ceilings requires a large kettle, several small kettles and an equal number of gasoline torches, and several buckets. Set up the large kettle outside the building and melt down sufficient Asphalt cement, or odorless asphalt, computed at three-quarters of a pound for each square foot of corkboard surface to be coated, using wood as fuel under the kettle, and the fire protected from possible wind by a sheet-iron shield. Do not overheat the asphalt. Transfer the molten asphalt in buckets to the small kettles, or pans, located close to where the corkboard is being erected. The pans should be about 18 inches wide, 42 inches long and 8 inches deep, should be rigidly constructed, and should be kept hot by the gasoline torches.* To the molten asphalt in these pans, add approximately 8 per cent. (by weight) of cork dust, or cork flour, and stir in thoroughly. The admixture of the cork dust stiffens up the molten asphalt just enough so that the proper quantity clings to the corkboards when dipped.

To prepare Asphalt cement for use with corkboard on floors and bottoms of freezing tanks, proceed as outlined in the foregoing paragraph, except no pans are ordinarily needed and no cork dust is mixed with the molten asphalt.

Ordinary wire nails should never be used in erecting corkboard insulation, because they will soon rust away, although they are sometimes employed by careless and disinterested erectors. *Galvanized wire nails* having large heads and of proper length should always be used where specified, but do not use galvanized wire nails where *wood skewers* are specified and can be employed instead. Wood, even hard hickory, is a far better thermal insulator than metal, and consequently galvanized wire nails should never be used where wood skewers will serve the purpose, for there is always danger of frost following in along nails or forming on wall finishes over nail heads underneath. Hickory skewers should be used in preference to softer woods, to diminish the chances for damage to the hands of workmen from splintering and breaking of the skewers when being driven into the insulation.

*CAUTION—Gasoline torches have been known to explode if not properly constructed, not kept in proper condition, or not properly operated. Charcoal pots are less applicable, but safer. See Appendix for description of Oil-Burning Cork Dipping Pan.

If masonry surfaces are to be primed with *Asphalt primer* before the corkboard is applied in Asphalt cement, the work should be done with an air-gun, if possible. The complete equipment for such application consists of a suitable air-gun of approved make and the necessary supply of compressed air.

Extension cords, electric light guards, sand screens, metal mortar boxes, hods, hoes, shovels, trowels, rope and tackle, hand saws, hatchets, hammers, salamanders, metal wheelbarrows, water buckets, rubber hose, big asphalt kettle on wheels with firebox and stack, these and possibly other utensils constitute some of the *additional equipment* that may be required to properly handle a corkboard insulation job.

Where *cold storage doors* are to be installed, it is necessary that the outside dimensions of the door frames be known in advance, so that if necessary or desirable the door bucks and lintels may be properly placed in the line of insulated walls or partitions in advance of the actual arrival, or of the uncrating, of the door equipment.

Unnecessary and sometimes very expensive delays in the prosecution and completion of a given job of cork insulation may be brought about through failure of the job superintendent to check first of all the actual size of rooms and tanks to be insulated against the measurements as originally planned, and then, as the materials, supplies and equipment are delivered, to check them carefully against the requirements of the work. The superintendent must, in a word, *anticipate his needs* well and sufficiently in advance.

119.—First Layer Corkboard, Against Masonry Walls, in Portland Cement Mortar.—See that the walls present a reasonably smooth and level surface, remove all dirt, plaster, loose mortar, whitewash, paint, or other foreign material, and if the walls are very smooth concrete, roughen them by hacking the surface with a hatchet or hacking hammer, or arrange to have these several items taken care of by those responsible for such preliminary work, before making preparations to erect corkboard to masonry walls in Portland cement mortar.

Now see that the floor at the base of the wall is free from obstruction, and is level; because the first row of corkboards must be applied to the wall at the floor, on a level line, so that the corkboards on the entire wall area are kept in perfect alignment and all vertical and transverse joints in the upper rows are made to fit close and tight.

Prepare suitable Portland cement mortar in reasonable quantity, sprinkle the wall to be insulated with clean water, coat one side of each corkboard with a half-inch of Portland cement mortar, by the hopper method, put each in proper position against the wall, slightly press into place and hold for a few moments until the mortar begins to set. Keep cement backing off edges of corkboards. Do not "vacuum cup" the backing before setting the corkboards, by hollowing out the mortar with the point of a trowel, because it is impossible to spread out the mortar again in setting the corkboards, and air pockets behind insulation, with disastrous results, will be inevitable.

FIG. 127.—ERECTING FIRST LAYER CORKBOARD AGAINST MASONRY WALL IN PORTLAND CEMENT MORTAR.

Cut a corkboard half-length and with it start setting the second row on top of the first, thus breaking vertical joints. As each corkboard is set, butt it tightly at all points of contact against the adjoining boards, but do not loosen boards already in position. Join the wall insulation tightly with the ceiling, cutting pieces of corkboard neatly to fit and never using Portland cement mortar to fill in openings between corkboards or pieces of corkboard.

Give the cement backing ample time to set, say 48 hours,

before erecting another layer of corkboard against the first, or before applying a finish over the insulation.

120.—First Layer Corkboard, Against Masonry Walls, in Asphalt Cement.—See that the walls present a reasonably smooth and level surface, remove all dirt, plaster, loose mortar, whitewash, paint, or other foreign material, or arrange to have these several items taken care of by those responsible for such preliminary work, before making preparations to erect corkboard to masonry walls in Asphalt cement.

FIG. 128.—ERECTING FIRST LAYER CORKBOARD AGAINST CONCRETE WALLS, COLUMNS AND COLUMN CAPS IN ASPHALT CEMENT TO SUITABLY PRIMED SURFACES.—NOTE PRIMED BUT UNINSULATED WALL AND COLUMN SECTION AT TOP LEFT.

With suitable Asphalt primer and proper air-gun equipment, apply evenly under a minimum air pressure of 50 pounds, to the entire masonry wall surfaces to be insulated, two uniform, continuous coats of the priming liquid, using approximately 1 gallon per 75 square feet for brick or per 100 square feet for concrete surfaces for the first coat, and 1 gallon per 125 square feet for brick or concrete for the second coat. If the Asphalt primer thickens because of exposure to the air, or during very cold weather, it may be thinned with suitable solvent to permit an even flow through the air-gun nozzle. The first coat is to become hand-dry before the second is applied, and the second is to become hand-dry before cork-board is applied.

See that the floor at the base of the wall is free from obstruction, and is level; because the first row of corkboards must be applied to the wall at the floor, on a level line, so that the corkboards on the entire wall area are kept in perfect alignment and all vertical and transverse joints in the upper rows are made to fit close and are sealed tight.

FIG. 129.—ERECTING DOUBLE LAYER CORKBOARD TO ASPHALT PRIMED CONCRETE WALL SURFACE IN ASPHALT CEMENT, AS CONTINUOUS INSULATION THROUGH CONCRETE FLOOR SLAB.

Prepare suitable Asphalt cement in reasonable quantity, distribute it to heated pans, add the proper proportion of cork dust and mix, dip one flat side, one end and one edge of each corkboard in the molten material, put the boards in proper position against the wall, slightly press into place and hold for a few moments until the Asphalt cement begins to cool.

Cut a corkboard half-length and with it start setting the second row on top of the first, thus breaking vertical joints. As each corkboard is set, butt and seal it tightly at all points of contact against the adjoining boards. Join and seal the wall insulation tightly with the ceiling, cutting pieces of corkboard neatly to fit.

Give the Asphalt cement ample time to cool and set, say 12 hours, before erecting another layer of corkboard against the first, or before applying a finish over the insulation.

121.—First Layer Corkboard, Against Wood Walls, in Asphalt Cement.—See that the walls present a smooth, continuous, solid surface, free from open cracks and loose or warped boards, remove all dirt, plaster, loose mortar, paper or other foreign material, or arrange to have these several items taken care of by those responsible for such preliminary work, before making preparations to erect corkboard to wood walls in Asphalt cement.

See that the floor at the base of the wall is free from obstruction, and is level; because the first row of corkboards must be applied to the wall at the floor, on a level line, so that the corkboards on the entire wall area are kept in perfect alignment and all vertical and transverse joints in the upper rows are made to fit close and are sealed tight.

Prepare suitable Asphalt cement in reasonable quantity, distribute it to heated pans, add the proper proportion of cork dust and mix, dip one flat side, one end and one edge of each corkboard in the molten material, put the boards in proper position against the wall, slightly press into place and securely nail in position to sheathing with galvanized wire nails driven obliquely, two nails per square foot.

Cut a corkboard half-length and with it start setting the second row on top of the first, thus breaking vertical joints. As each corkboard is set, butt and seal it tightly at all points of contact against the adjoining boards. Join and seal the wall insulation tightly with the ceiling, cutting pieces of corkboard neatly to fit.

Give the Asphalt cement ample time to cool and set, say 12 hours, before erecting another layer of corkboard against the first, or before applying a finish over the insulation.

122.—Second Layer Corkboard, Against First Layer on Walls, in Portland Cement Mortar.—See that the first layer of corkboard on the walls is solidly attached, and presents a reasonably smooth and level surface,* then remove all dust, dirt or loose mortar, before making preparations to erect a second layer of corkboard in Portland cement mortar.

Now see that the floor at the base of the wall is free from obstruction, and is level; because the first row of corkboards in the second layer must be applied to the first layer at the floor, on a level line, so that the corkboards on the entire second layer are kept in perfect alignment and all vertical and transverse joints in the upper rows are made to fit close and tight.

Prepare suitable Portland cement mortar in reasonable quantity, saw sufficient corkboards lengthwise down the center so as to have enough half-width pieces to make one row around the room, coat the half-width corkboards on one side with a half-inch of Portland cement mortar, cut a piece 6 inches wide and 27 inches long and with it start putting the half-width pieces of corkboard in proper position against the first layer of insulation, slightly press into place and additionally secure with wood skewers driven obliquely, two skewers per square foot.

Then start with a full-width and 9-inch long piece of corkboard and set the second row of full-size corkboards on top of the first row, thus breaking vertical joints in the second layer, and all joints in the second layer with respect to all joints in the first layer. As each corkboard is set, butt it tightly at all points of contact against the adjacent boards and additionally secure to the first layer with wood skewers driven obliquely, two skewers per square foot. Join the wall insulation tightly with the ceiling, cutting pieces of corkboard neatly to fit and never use Portland cement mortar to fill in openings between corkboards or pieces of corkboard.

Give the cement backing ample time to set, say 48 hours, before applying a finish over the insulation.

---

*If necessary, cut off any protruding corners or edges of corkboard with a suitable tool.

123.—Second Layer Corkboard, Against First Layer on Walls, in Asphalt Cement.—See that the first layer of corkboard on the walls is solidly attached, and presents a reasonably smooth and level surface,* and then remove all dust, dirt or loose mortar, before making preparations to erect a second layer of corkboard in Asphalt cement.

Now see that the floor at the base of the wall is free from obstruction, and is level; because the first row of corkboards in the second layer must be applied to the first layer at the floor, on a level line, so that the corkboards on the entire second layer are kept in perfect alignment and all vertical and transverse joints in the upper rows are made to fit close and are sealed tight.

Prepare suitable Asphalt cement in reasonable quantity, distribute it to heated pans, add the proper proportion of cork dust and mix. Saw sufficient corkboards lengthwise down the center so as to have enough half-width pieces to make one row around the room, cut a piece 6 inches wide and 27 inches long and with it start putting the half-width pieces of corkboard in proper position against the first layer of insulation, first dipping one flat side, one end and one edge of each piece in the molten material, slightly pressing into place and additionally securing with galvanized wire nails or wood skewers, as specified, driven obliquely, two per square foot.

Then start with a full-width and 9-inch long piece of corkboard and set the second row of full-size corkboards on top of the first row, thus breaking vertical joints in the second layer, and all joints in the second layer with respect to all joints in the first layer. As each corkboard is set, butt it tightly at all points of contact against the adjacent boards and additionally secure to the first layer with galvanized wire nails or wood skewers, as specified, driven obliquely, two per square foot. Join and seal the wall insulation tightly with the ceiling, cutting pieces of corkboard neatly to fit.

Give the asphalt cement ample time to cool and set, say 12 hours, before applying a finish over the insulation.

*If necessary, cut off any protruding corners or edge of corkboard with a suitable tool.

124.—First Layer Corkboard, to Concrete Ceilings, in Portland Cement Mortar.—See that the ceiling presents a reasonably smooth and level surface, remove all dirt, plaster, loose mortar, whitewash, paint, or other foreign material, and if the ceiling is very smooth concrete, roughen it by hacking the surface with a hatchet or hacking hammer, or arrange to have these several items taken care of by those responsible for such preliminary work, before making preparations to erect corkboard to ceiling in Portland cement mortar.

FIG. 130.—ERECTING FIRST LAYER CORKBOARD TO CONCRETE CEILING IN PORTLAND CEMENT MORTAR.—NOTE METHOD OF PROPPING UNTIL CEMENT SETS.

Prepare suitable Portland cement mortar in reasonable quantity, sprinkle the ceiling to be insulated with clean water, coat one side of each corkboard with a half-inch of Portland cement mortar, by the hopper method, put each in proper position against the ceiling, press firmly into place and prop until the cement sets. Keep cement backing off edges of corkboards. Do not "vacuum cup" the backing before setting the corkboards, by hollowing out the mortar with the point of a trowel, because it is impossible to spread out the mortar again in setting the corkboards, and air pockets behind insulation, with disastrous results, will be inevitable.

Apply the first row of corkboards against the ceiling along one side of the room, in a straight line. Keep the sheets in perfect alignment, so that the joints in the rows to follow may fit close and tight.

Cut a corkboard to half-length and with it start setting and propping a second row of full-size corkboards adjacent to the first row, thus breaking transverse joints. As each corkboard is set, butt it tightly at all points of contact against the adjacent boards, but do not loosen boards already in position. Join the ceiling insulation tightly with the wall, cutting pieces of corkboard neatly to fit and never using Portland cement mortar to fill in openings between corkboards or pieces of corkboard.

Give the cement backing ample time to set, at least 48 hours, before erecting another layer of corkboard against the first, or before applying a finish over the insulation.

125.—First Layer Corkboard, in Concrete Ceiling Forms.—See that the wooden forms for the concrete ceiling slab have

FIG. 131.—PLACING FIRST LAYER CORKBOARD IN CEILING FORMS BEFORE CONCRETE IS POURED.

been lowered the proper distance to allow for the thickness of the layer* of corkboard specified to be placed in forms, and see

*Never put two layers of corkboard in ceiling forms.

that the forms are reasonably even. Lay down the first row of corkboards on the forms, along one side of the ceiling area, in a straight line. Keep the corkboards in perfect alignment, so that the joints in the rows to follow may fit close and tight.

If the surface of the forms should be slightly uneven, secure the corkboards to the forms with a few headless finishing nails, which will easily pull out of the corkboard when the forms are removed. Break all joints between the different rows, by starting alternate rows with half-length boards, and see that all joints are butted close and made tight, so that none of the concrete can run down between the corkboards and pieces of corkboard when the concrete is poured. When the opposite end and the opposite side of the ceiling area is reached, cut pieces of corkboard neatly to fit the outline of the forms.

Drive three galvanized wire nails per square foot obliquely into the corkboard and leave the heads protruding about 1½ inches to afford an additional key for the concrete, and leave the insulation in readiness for the concrete contractor to pour the ceiling slab.

After forms have been removed, permit this layer of corkboard on underside of concrete ceiling to dry out thoroughly, not less than an additional 48 hours, before erecting another layer of corkboard against the first, or before applying a finish over the insulation.

126.—First Layer Corkboard, to Wood Ceiling, in Asphalt Cement.—See that the ceiling presents a smooth, continuous, solid surface, free from open cracks and loose or warped boards, remove all dirt, plaster, paper, or other foreign material, or arrange to have these several items taken care of by those responsible for such preliminary work, before making preparations to erect corkboard to wood ceiling in Asphalt cement.

Prepare suitable Asphalt cement in reasonable quantity, distribute it to heated pans, add the proper proportion of cork dust and mix, dip one flat side, one end and one edge of each corkboard in the molten material, lay up the first row of corkboards to the ceiling surface and against the edge of the wall, in a straight line, slightly press the corkboards into place and securely nail in position to sheathing with galvanized wire nails driven obliquely, three nails per square foot. Keep the corkboards in perfect alignment, so that the joints in the rows to follow may fit close and seal tight.

Break all joints between the different rows, by starting alternate rows with half-length boards, and see that all joints are butted close and sealed tight. When the opposite end and the opposite side of the ceiling area is reached, cut pieces of corkboard neatly to fit and seal with the wall lines of the room.

Give the Asphalt cement ample time to cool and set, say 12 hours, before erecting another layer of corkboard against the first, or before applying a finish over the insulation.

127.—Second Layer Corkboard, to First Layer on Ceiling, in Portland Cement Mortar.—See that the first layer of corkboard on the ceiling is solidly attached, and presents a reasonably smooth and level surface,* and then remove all dust, dirt, or other foreign material, before making preparations to erect a second layer of corkboard in Portland cement mortar.

Saw sufficient corkboards lengthwise down the center so as to have enough half-width pieces to make one row along one side of the ceiling. Cut a piece 6 inches wide and 27 inches long with which to start setting the half-width pieces in proper position to the ceiling area, in a straight line, against the edge of the wall.

Prepare suitable Portland cement mortar in reasonable quantity, coat one side of each piece of corkboard with a half-inch of Portland cement mortar, put each in proper position against the ceiling, press firmly into place and additionally secure with galvanized wire nails or wood skewers, as specified, driven obliquely, three per square foot. Keep the pieces of corkboard in perfect alignment, so that the joints in the rows to follow may fit close and seal tight.

Then start with a full-width and 9-inch long piece of corkboard and set the second row of full-size corkboards adjacent to the first row, thus breaking all joints in the second layer,

*If necessary, cut off any protruding corners or edges of corkboard with a suitable tool.

and all joints in the second layer with respect to all joints in the first layer. As each corkboard is laid up, butt it tightly at all points of contact against the adjacent boards, and additionally secure to the first layer with galvanized wire nails or wood skewers, as specified, driven obliquely, three per square foot. Join the second layer of ceiling insulation tightly with the opposite wall, cutting pieces of corkboard neatly to fit and never using Portland cement mortar to fill in openings between corkboards or pieces of corkboard.

Give the cement backing ample time to set, at least 48 hours, before applying a finish over the insulation.

128.—Second Layer Corkboard, to First Layer on Ceiling, in Asphalt Cement.—See that the first layer of corkboard on the ceiling is solidly attached, and presents a reasonably smooth and level surface*, and then remove all dust, dirt, or other foreign material, before making preparations to erect a second layer of corkboard in Asphalt cement.

Saw sufficient corkboards lengthwise down the center so as to have enough half-width pieces to make one row along one side of the ceiling. Cut a piece 6 inches wide and 27 inches long with which to start setting the half-width pieces in proper position to the ceiling area, in a straight line, and against the edge of the wall.

Prepare suitable Asphalt cement in reasonable quantity, distribute it to heated pans, add the proper proportion of cork dust and mix; dip one flat side, one end and one edge of the special corkboard pieces in the molten material, lay up the first row to the surface of the first layer of insulation, slightly press into place and additionally secure with galvanized wire nails or wood skewers, as specified, driven obliquely, three per square foot. Keep the pieces of corkboard in perfect alignment, so that the joints in the rows to follow may fit close and seal tight.

Then start with a full-width and 9-inch long piece of corkboard and set the second row of full-size corkboards adjacent to the first row, thus breaking all joints in the second layer, and all joints in the second layer with respect to all joints

*If necessary, cut off any protruding corners or edges of corkboard with a suitable tool.

in the first layer. As each corkboard is laid up, butt and seal it tightly at all points of contact against the adjacent boards, and additionally secure to the first layer with galvanized wire nails or wood skewers, as specified, driven obliquely, three per square foot. When the opposite end and the opposite side of the ceiling area is reached, cut pieces of corkboard neatly to fit and seal with the wall lines of the room.

Give the Asphalt cement ample time to cool and set, say 12 hours, before applying a finish over the insulation.

129.—Double Layer Corkboard, Self-supporting T-iron Ceiling, Portland Cement Mortar Core.—Before starting the construction of this self-supporting, or "false," ceiling, see that the wall insulation rises above the line of the under side of the finished ceiling to be constructed, a distance equal to the thickness of the under layer of corkboard. Cut the T-irons to a length equal to the width of the room plus the total thickness of the two walls, set and space the T-irons on the top edges of the side wall insulation, spanning the room, parallel to each other and 12 inches between vertical sections (not 12 inches from center to center), and then anchor the T-irons with large head galvanized wire nails driven obliquely into the top edges of the wall insulation.

Place one layer of full-size corkboards between the vertical sections of the T-irons and resting on the flanges or horizontal sections of the T-irons, butting the ends of adjacent boards tight. Apply a 1-inch thick Portland cement finish over the corkboard and the T-irons, mixed one part Portland cement to two parts clean, sharp sand, and give the cement time to set, at least 48 hours, before applying the second layer of ceiling insulation.

Prepare a suitable Portland cement mortar in reasonable quantity, coat one side of each corkboard with a half-inch of Portland cement mortar, by the hopper method, lay up a row to the under side of the first layer, in a straight line, against the long wall of the room, pressing the boards firmly into place and additionally securing with galvanized wire nails, driven obliquely, three per square foot. Keep the corkboards in perfect alignment, so that the joints in the rows to follow may fit close and seal tight.

Break all joints between the different rows, by starting alternate rows with half-length boards, and break all joints in the second layer with respect to all joints in the first layer.

FIG. 132.—APPLYING FIRST LAYER CORKBOARD OVER CONCRETE ROOF IN ASPHALT CEMENT.—NOTE THE EQUIPMENT USED AND THE METHOD FOLLOWED.

As each corkboard is laid up, butt it tightly at all points of contact against the adjacent boards, and additionally secure to the first layer with galvanized wire nails, driven obliquely, three per square foot. Join the second layer of ceiling insulation tightly with the opposite wall, cutting pieces of corkboard neatly to fit and never using Portland cement mortar to fill in openings between corkboards or pieces of corkboard.

Give the cement backing ample time to set, at least 48 hours, before applying a finish to the under surface of the insulation.

130.—First Layer Corkboard, over Concrete or Wood Floor or Roof, in Asphalt Cement.—See that the concrete or wood surface to be insulated presents a smooth, continuous solid surface, free from pits or open cracks and loose or warped boards, remove all dirt, plaster, paper, loose mortar, or other foreign material, or arrange to have these several items taken care of by those responsible for such preliminary work, before making preparations to apply corkboard over a flat surface in Asphalt cement.

Prepare suitable Asphalt cement in reasonable quantity, transfer it to the point of erection in buckets, flood the surface to be insulated with the molten material, uniformly over a small area or strip at a time, lay* down quickly in the hot Asphalt cement, first a row of corkboards against the edge of the wall, in a straight line, and closely follow with a second and a third row of corkboards, each row lagging behind the preceding one, in the laying, by the length of one-half board. Keep the corkboards in each row in perfect alignment, so that the joints in the rows to follow may fit close and seal tight.

Break all joints between the different rows, by starting alternate rows with half-length boards, and see that all joints are butted tight. When the opposite end and the opposite side of the floor or roof area is reached, cut pieces of corkboard neatly to fit and seal with the wall lines.

When completed, if the corkboard was laid as an only layer of floor insulation, flood the top surface with the molten material to an even thickness of approximately ⅛-inch, and leave in readiness for the concrete* wearing floor; if the corkboard was laid as roof insulation, or as the first layer of a double layer floor insulation, leave the surface of the cork-

---

*If wood floor is desired over single layer of insulation, instead of concrete, then sleepers must be embedded in the single layer of corkboard, as outlined in Article 144.

board uncoated and in readiness for the roofing contractor to lay the roof, or in readiness for the insulation contractor to lay down the second layer of corkboard.

131.—Second Layer Corkboard, over First Layer on Floor or Roof, in Asphalt Cement.—See that the first layer of corkboard is solidly laid, and presents a reasonably smooth and level surface*, and then remove all dirt, loose mortar, or other

FIG. 133.—APPLYING FIRST AND SECOND LAYERS CORKBOARD SIMULTANEOUSLY OVER CONCRETE ROOF IN ASPHALT CEMENT.

foreign material, before making preparations to lay a second layer of corkboard in Asphalt cement.

Saw sufficient corkboards lengthwise down the center so as to have enough half-width pieces to make one row along one wall of the area to be insulated. Cut a piece 6 inches wide and 27 inches long with which to start laying the half-

*If necessary, cut off any protruding corners or edges of corkboard with a suitable tool.

width pieces in proper position to the floor or roof area, in a straight line, in the first row against the edge of the wall.

Prepare suitable Asphalt cement in reasonable quantity, transfer it to the point of erection in buckets, flood the surface to be insulated with the molten material, uniformly over a small area or strip at a time, lay down quickly in the hot Asphalt cement first the row of half-width corkboards against the edge of the wall, follow with a second row of full-size corkboards starting off with a full-width and 9-inch long piece, and then with a third row of full-size corkboards starting off with a half-length board, each row lagging behind the preceding one, in the laying, by the length of one-half board. In this way, all joints in the second layer of insulation will be broken with respect to all joints in the first layer. Keep the corkboards in each row in perfect alignment, so that the joints in the rows to follow may fit close and seal tight. When the opposite end and the opposite side of the floor or roof area is reached, cut pieces of corkboard neatly to fit and seal with the wall lines.

When completed, if the corkboard was laid as floor insulation, flood the top surface with the molten material to an even thickness of approximately 1/8-inch, and leave in readiness for the concrete* wearing floor; if the corkboard was laid as roof insulation, leave the surface of the corkboard uncoated in readiness for the roofing contractor to lay the roof.

132.—Single Layer Corkboard, Between Partition Studs with Joints Sealed in Asphalt Cement.—Erect 2-inch x 4-inch permanent studs, in a vertical position, 36 inches apart, in the line of the partition, so that the 2-inch dimension runs with the wall thickness. Place permanent studs, with a lintel between them, where cold storage doors are to be set, so as to form an opening the size of the cold storage door frame. Use door bucks and lintels 2 inches in thickness, and anchor securely to the floor and ceiling in such manner that they may take up and withstand any shock from the operation of the cold storage door.

Prepare suitable Asphalt cement in reasonable quantity, on the basis of one-quarter pound per square foot of partition

*If wood floor is desired over double layer of insulation, instead of concrete, then sleepers must be embedded in the second layer of corkboard, as outlined in Article 144.

area (one face only), distribute it to heated pans, add the proper proportion of cork dust and mix, dip both ends and one edge of the 2-inch thick corkboards in the molten material, erect the first row on the floor between the permanent studs, on a level line, so that the corkboards in the entire partition wall are kept in perfect alignment, and all vertical joints

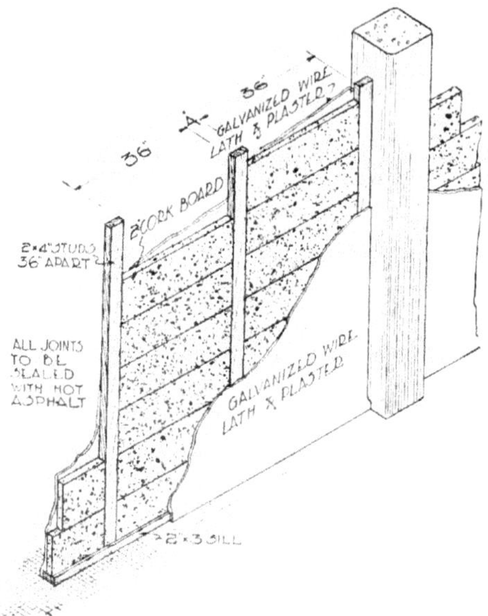

FIG. 134.—DIAGRAMMATIC ILLUSTRATION OF SINGLE LAYER CORKBOARD ERECTED BETWEEN PARTITION STUDS WITH JOINTS SEALED IN ASPHALT CEMENT.

between corkboards and studs, and all transverse joints between corkboards in all rows, are made to fit close and are sealed tight. Toe-nail the first or bottom row of corkboards securely to the floor, if the floor be of wood, using galvanized wire nails, and drive galvanized wire nails through the corners of each corkboard into the adjoining studs.

Join and seal the partition insulation tightly with the ceiling, cutting pieces of corkboard neatly to fit, additionally toe-nailing if the ceiling be of wood. Cover the permanent door bucks and lintels with corkboard, as specified, nailed in place. Cover the exposed edges of the permanent partition studs with 12-inch wide strips of galvanized wire square-mesh screen, No. 18 gauge, 3 mesh ($\frac{1}{3}$-inch), securely stapled to the studs and nailed to the insulation on both sides of the studs.

FIG. 135.—ERECTING FIRST LAYER CORKBOARD OF SELF-SUPPORTING PARTITION WITH JOINTS SEALED IN ASPHALT CEMENT—NOTE TEMPORARY STUDS, WHICH ARE REMOVED WHEN PARTITION IS COMPLETED TO THE POINT OF RECEIVING FINISH ON SIDE STUDS APPEAR.

Give the Asphalt cement ample time to cool and set, say 12 hours, before applying a finish over the insulation.

133.—First Layer Corkboard, Self-supporting Partition, Joints Sealed in Asphalt Cement.—Erect temporary studding on 18-inch centers on a line with one side of the proposed partition. The studs must be erected in a vertical position and in perfect alignment. Erect permanent studs, with a lintel between them, in the line of the partition, where cold storage doors are to be set, so as to form an opening the size of the cold storage door frame. Use studs and lintels of the same thickness as the total thickness of corkboard to be erected, and anchor the permanent studs securely to the floor and ceiling in such manner that they may take up and withstand any shock from the operation of the cold storage door.

Prepare suitable Asphalt cement in reasonable quantity, on the basis of one-quarter pound per square foot of partition area (one face only), distribute it to heated pans, add the proper proportion of cork dust and mix, dip but one end and one edge of the corkboards in the molten material, erect the first row against the temporary studs, end to end on the floor, on a level line, so that the corkboards in the entire partition wall are kept in perfect alignment and all vertical and transverse joints in the upper rows are made to fit close and are sealed tight. Toe-nail the first or bottom row of corkboard securely to the floor, if the floor be of wood, using galvanized wire nails; and drive long galvanized wire nails obliquely through the corners of each corkboard into the abutting corkboards.

Cut a corkboard half-length and with it start setting the second row on top of the first, thus breaking vertical joints. As each corkboard is set, butt and seal it tightly against the adjacent boards and drive long galvanized wire nails obliquely through the corners of each corkboard into the abutting corkboards, and at the lower corner of the exposed end of each board drive one of these galvanized wire nails obliquely into the corkboard of the row below.

To insure the corkboards being kept in perfect alignment, as the rows are erected edge on edge, drive small headless nails obliquely through the upper edge of each row of corkboards into the temporary studs at occasional points. These nails will readily pull through the corkboards when the temporary studs are later removed.

Join and seal the partition insulation tightly with the ceiling, cutting pieces of corkboard neatly to fit, and additionally toe-nailing if the ceiling be of wood. Cover the permanent studs and lintels, on the side away from the temporary studding, with corkboard, as specified, nailed in place.

Before removing the temporary studs, and after the Asphalt

cement has had ample time to cool and set on all corkboard joints, apply the finish to the free side of the corkboard partition, as specified. After such finish has had ample time to set, take down the temporary studs and apply the finish to the other side of the corkboard partition, or leave it in readiness to receive a second layer of corkboard insulation.

134.—Second Layer Corkboard, Against First Layer of Self-supporting Partition, in Portland Cement Mortar.—See

FIG. 136.—ERECTING SECOND LAYER CORKBOARD AGAINST FIRST LAYER OF SELF-SUPPORTING PARTITION IN PORTLAND CEMENT MORTAR. —NOTE ALSO THE METHOD OF INSULATING COLUMNS AND CAPS AND METHOD OF SETTING DOOR BUCKS AND LINTEL.

that the first layer of corkboard of the self-supporting partition is solidly erected, and presents a reasonably smooth and level surface*, and then remove all dust, dirt, or loose mortar, before making preparations to erect a second layer of corkboard in Portland cement mortar.

Now see that the floor at the base of the wall is free from obstruction, and is level; because the first row of corkboards in the second layer must be applied to the first layer at the floor, on a level line, so that the corkboards on the entire second layer are kept in perfect alignment and all vertical and transverse joints in the upper rows are made to fit close and are sealed tight.

Prepare suitable Portland cement mortar in reasonable quantity, saw sufficient corkboards lengthwise down the center so as to have enough half-width pieces to make one row along the partition, coat the half-width corkboards on one side with a half-inch of Portland cement mortar, cut a piece 6 inches wide and 27 inches long and with it start putting the half-width pieces of corkboard in proper position against the first layer of insulation, slightly press into place and additionally secure with wood skewers driven obliquely, two skewers per square foot.

Then start with a full-width and 9-inch long piece of corkboard and set the second row of full-size corkboards on top of the first row, thus breaking vertical joints in the second layer, and all joints in the second layer with respect to all joints in the first layer. As each corkboard is set, butt it tightly at all points of contact against the adjacent boards and additionally secure to the first layer with wood skewers driven obliquely, two skewers per square foot. Join the wall insulation tightly with the ceiling, cutting pieces of corkboard neatly to fit and never use Portland cement mortar to fill in openings between corkboards or pieces of corkboard.

Give the cement backing ample time to set, say 48 hours, before applying a finish over the insulation.

135.—Second Layer Corkboard, Against First Layer of Self-supporting Partition, in Asphalt Cement.—See that the first layer of corkboard of the self-supporting partition is solidly erected, and presents a reasonably smooth and level sur-

*If necessary, cut off any protruding corners or edges of corkboard with a suitable tool.

face, and then remove all dust, dirt, or loose mortar, before making preparations to erect a second layer of corkboard in Asphalt cement.

Now see that the floor at the base of the wall is free from

FIG. 137.—ERECTING DOUBLE LAYER CORKBOARD SELF-SUPPORTING PARTITIONS TO FORM CORRIDOR WALLS OF UNUSUAL HEIGHT.—NOTE TEMPORARY STUDS, WHICH ARE LATER REMOVED.

obstruction, and is level; because the first row of corkboards in the second layer must be applied to the first layer at the floor, on a level line, so that the corkboards on the entire second layer are kept in perfect alignment and all vertical and transverse joints in the upper rows are made to fit close and are sealed tight.

Prepare suitable Asphalt cement in reasonable quantity, distribute it to heated pans, add the proper proportion of cork dust and mix. Saw sufficient corkboards lengthwise down the center so as to have enough half-width pieces to make one row along the partition, cut a piece 6 inches wide and 27

FIG. 138.—ERECTING SECOND LAYER CORKBOARD TO FIRST LAYER IN PORTLAND CEMENT MORTAR TO WALLS, CEILING AND BEAMS.—NOTE SCAFFOLDING, SHORING, EXTENSION CORD, MORTAR BOARD AND OTHER EQUIPMENT REQUIRED.

inches long and with it start putting the half-width pieces of corkboard in proper position against the first layer of insulation, first dipping one flat side, one end and one edge of each piece in the molten material, slightly pressing into place and additionally securing with wood skewers driven obliquely, two skewers per square foot.

Then start with a full-width and 9-inch long piece of corkboard and set the second row of full-size corkboards on top of the first row, thus breaking vertical joints in the second layer, and all joints in the second layer with respect to all joints in the first layer. As each corkboard is set, butt it tightly at all points of contact against the adjacent boards and additionally secure to the first layer with wood skewers driven obliquely, two per square foot. Join and seal the wall insulation tightly with the ceiling, cutting pieces of corkboard neatly to fit.

Give the asphalt cement ample time to cool and set, say 12 hours, before applying a finish over the insulation.

136.—Double Layer Corkboard, Freezing Tank Bottom, in Asphalt Cement.—See that the concrete base is well adapted to the purpose and presents a reasonably smooth and level surface, remove all dirt, loose mortar, or other foreign material, or arrange to have these several items taken care of by those responsible for such preliminary work, before making preparations to apply corkboard over the surface of the freezing tank foundation.

Prepare suitable Asphalt cement in reasonable quantity, transfer it to the point of erection in buckets, flood the surface to be insulated* with the molten material, uniformly over a small area or strip at a time, lay down quickly in the hot Asphalt cement, first a row of corkboards in a straight line against the outer edge of the area of the tank bottom insulation, closely follow with a second and a third row of corkboards, each row lagging behind the preceding one, in the laying, by the length of one-half board. Keep the corkboards in each row in perfect alignment, so that the joints in the rows to follow may fit close and seal tight.

Break all joints between the different rows, by starting alternate rows with half-length boards, and see that all joints are butted tight. Carry the insulation on both ends and both sides to the outer limits of the end and side insulation of the tank, cutting pieces of corkboard as required to finish out such dimensions.

*The dimensions of the tank bottom area to be insulated shall be enough wider and longer than the size of the freezing tank, so as to overlap the insulation to be installed on the vertical ends and sides of the tank.

See that the first layer of corkboard is solidly laid, and presents a reasonably smooth and level surface. Saw sufficient corkboards lengthwise down the center so as to make one row along the one side of the insulated area, laying the half-width pieces in the first row of the second layer, in a straight line, starting off with a piece 6 inches wide and 27 inches long, then lay a second row of full-size corkboards, starting off with a full-width and 9-inch long piece, and then lay a third row of full-size corkboards, starting off with a

FIG. 139.—LAYING SECOND LAYER CORKBOARD ON FLOOR IN ASPHALT CEMENT—TANK BOTTOM INSULATION IS APPLIED IN SAME MANNER.

half-length board, following the same method of laying as described for the first layer of insulation. In this way, all joints in the second layer will be broken and made tight, and all joints in the second layer will be broken with respect to all joints in the first layer. When completed, flood the top surface with the molten material to an even thickness of approximately 1/8-inch, and leave in readiness for the tank to be set.

137.—Regranulated Cork Fill, Freezing Tank Sides and Ends, With Retaining Walls.—See that the tank has been properly set, having its bottom edges the proper distance in from the edges of the insulation underneath. Erect 2-inch x 12-inch studs on suitable centers (from 24 to 36 inches) at right angles against the sides and ends of the tank*, anchoring carefully by cutting slots through tank bottom insulation,

*If the tank is to be set in a corner, so that masonry walls of the building act as two retaining walls, such walls must be damp-proofed before the tank is set and the loose fill insulation is placed.

chiseling slight depressions in the concrete base, dropping the studs into these slots and depressions and wedging their tops under and securing them with suitable metal clips to the flange at the top of the tank. Sheath the studs with double layer ⅞-inch T. & G. boards, having two layers of waterproof paper between, and securely nail to the studs.

Fill the space between the retaining walls and the sides and ends of the tank with regranulated cork (by-product from the manufacture of pure corkboard), and tamp well until there is sufficient in place to avoid future settling. Then install a curbing, as and if specified, over the regranulated cork fill.

138.—Single Layer Corkboard and Regranulated Cork Fill, Freezing Tank Sides and Ends.—See that the tank has been properly set, having its bottom edges the proper distance in from the edges of the insulation underneath. Erect 4-inch x 4-inch studs on 18-inch centers at right angles against the sides and ends of the tank*, anchoring carefully by cutting slots through tank bottom insulation, chiseling slight depressions in the concrete base, dropping the studs into these slots and depressions and wedging their tops under and securing them with suitable metal clips to the flange at the top of the tank.

Prepare suitable Asphalt cement in reasonable quantity, on the basis of one-quarter pound per square foot of corkboard area (one face only), distribute it to heated pans, add the proper proportion of cork dust and mix, dip both ends and one edge of the corkboards in the molten material, erect the first row against the studs, end to end, on a level line, so that the corkboards are kept in perfect alignment, and all vertical and transverse joints in the upper rows are made to fit close and are sealed tight. Break all joints between the different rows, by starting alternate rows with half-length boards, and as the rows are erected edge on edge, securely fasten the corkboards to the studs by nailing with galvanized wire nails, two per square foot. Carry the insulation to the

*If the tank is to be set in a corner, so that masonry walls of the building act as two retaining walls for regranulated cork fill on one side and one end of the tank, such walls must be damp-proofed before the tank is set and the loose fill insulation is placed.

line of the flange at the top of the tank, cutting pieces of corkboard neatly to fit.

Fill the space between the insulation and the sides and ends of the tank with regranulated cork (by-product from the manufacture of pure corkboard), and tamp well until there is sufficient in place to avoid future settling. Then install a curbing, as and if specified, over the side and end insulation.

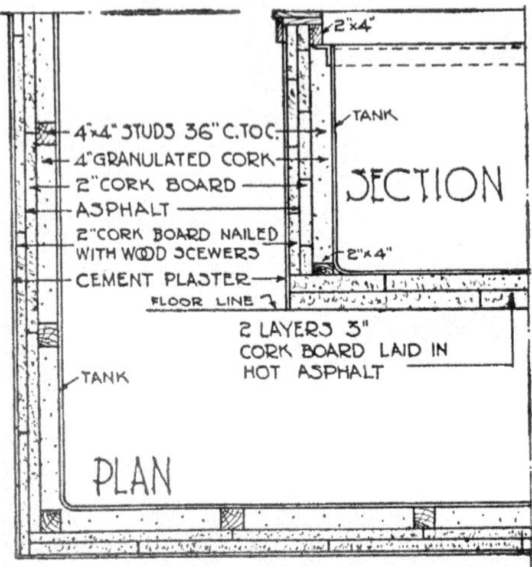

FIG. 140.—PLAN AND SECTION OF FREEZING TANK INSULATION.

139.—Double Layer Corkboard, Freezing Tank Sides and Ends.—See that the tank has been properly set, having its bottom edges the proper distance in from the edges of the insulation underneath. Erect studs (2-inch by a dimension equivalent to the thickness of the first layer of corkboard specified to be applied to tank sides and ends) at right angles against the sides and ends of the tank*, and 36 inches apart, anchoring carefully by cutting slots through tank bottom insulation, chiseling slight depressions in the concrete base, dropping the studs into these slots and depressions and wedging their

*If the tank is to be set in a corner, so that masonry walls of the building act as two retaining walls for regranulated cork fill on one side and one end of the tank, such walls must be damp-proofed before the tank is set and the loose fill insulation is placed.

tops under and securing them with suitable metal clips to the flange at the top of the tank.

Prepare suitable Asphalt cement in reasonable quantity, on the basis of one pound per square foot of corkboard area (one face only), distribute it to heated pans, add the proper proportion of cork dust and mix, dip one flat side, both ends and one edge of the corkboards in the molten material, erect the first row between the studs and against the tank, on a level line, so that the corkboards are kept in perfect alignment, and all vertical joints between corkboards and studs, and all transverse joints between corkboards in the upper rows to follow, are made to fit close and are sealed tight. Drive galvanized wire nails through the corners of each corkboard and into the adjacent studs. Carry the insulation to the line of the flange at the top of the tank, cutting pieces of corkboard neatly to fit.

Saw sufficient corkboards lengthwise down the center so as to have enough half-width pieces to make one row in a second layer around the tank, cut a piece 6 inches wide and 18 inches long and with it start putting the half-width pieces of corkboard in proper position against the first layer of insulation, first dipping one flat side, one end and one edge of each piece in the molten material, slightly pressing into place and additionally securing with wood skewers driven obliquely, two skewers per square foot.

Then start with a full-width and 9-inch long piece of corkboard and set the second row of full-size corkboards on top of the first row, thus breaking vertical joints in the second layer, and all joints in the second layer with respect to all joints in the first layer. As each corkboard is set, butt it tightly at all points of contact against the adjacent boards and additionally secure to the first layer with wood skewers driven obliquely, two skewers per square foot. Carry the insulation to the line of the flange at the top of the tank, cutting pieces of corkboard neatly to fit. Then install a curbing, as and if specified, over the side and end insulation.

140.—Portland Cement Plaster.—See that the exposed surface of the corkboard to receive the Portland cement plaster presents a reasonably smooth and level surface* and that all

*If necessary, cut off any protruding corners or edges of corkboard with a suitable tool.

corkboards are butted tight, score the surface of the corkboard (if preferred) by roughening slightly with a pronged tool, such as a few wire nails driven through a piece of wood, so as possibly to increase the bond for the cement plaster, and then remove all dust, dirt, or other foreign material, or arrange to have these several items taken care of by those responsible for such preliminary work, before making preparations to apply a Portland cement plaster finish to the exposed surface of corkboard insulation.

Prepare suitable Portland cement mortar in reasonable

FIG. 141.—CORKBOARD INSULATED COLD STORAGE ROOM FINISHED WITH PORTLAND CEMENT PLASTER SCORED IN 4-FT. SQUARES.

quantity, mixed one part Portland cement to two parts clean, sharp sand, with no lime added. Be sure the sand is clean and free from loam, and that it is sharp.

Apply the first coat of plaster approximately ¼-inch in thickness, rough scratch, and leave until thoroughly dried out. Then apply the second coat to the first, also approximately ¼-inch in thickness, and trowel to a hard, smooth finish. Score the surface of the finished plaster in squares, as specified, using suitable scoring tool only, so as to confine any checking or cracking† of the plaster to such score marks.

141.—Factory Ironed-on Mastic Finish.—See that the exposed surface of the factory ironed-on mastic finish is reasonably level, and that all joints between the coated corkboards are butted tight.

Prepare suitable mastic filler for the V joints of the coated corkboards, by following the directions furnished by the manufacturer, which directions frequently, but not always, consist in heating the mastic filler until plastic by immersing in hot water and working up a small quantity at a time in the hand like putty*.

Fill the joints between the mastic coated corkboards with the prepared mastic material in such practical manner as will eliminate all voids. Then follow with an electric iron, or heated pointing trowel, applying sufficient heat to melt the edges of the coating on the corkboards so that it will flow into and amalgamate with the mastic filler in the joints, making a continuous and permanent seal.

142.—Emulsified Asphalt Plastic.—See that the exposed surface of the corkboard to receive the emulsified asphalt plastic presents a reasonably smooth and level surface§, and then remove all dust, dirt, or other foreign material, or arrange to have these several items taken care of by those responsible for such preliminary work, before making preparations to apply emulsified asphalt plastic finish to the exposed surface of corkboard insulation.

Shake or roll the barrel or cylinder in which the emulsified asphalt plastic is supplied, before opening; and if water is found standing on the surface, work it into the mass before using. After a container is opened, it should be kept covered, to prevent the drying out of the material and coalescence of the asphalt particles. The emulsified asphalt plastic, if a ready

†Cracks frequently develop in plaster at the top corners of door frames, which can usually be prevented by setting and stapling pieces of galvanized wire square-mesh screen (No. 18 gauge, 3 mesh) to the corkboard over such corners and at an angle of 45 degrees before the plaster is applied.

*It is essential that the material furnished by the manufacturer for the sealing of the joints be prepared and used as directed by the manufacturer.

§If necessary, cut off any protruding corners or edges of corkboard with a suitable tool.

mixed product*, should be applied exactly as received, without adding sand or any other material whatever. If, by reason of evaporation, the product is too heavy to work easily under a trowel, add as little as possible of clean water, working it well through the mass.

Apply the first coat of emulsified asphalt plastic approximately 3/32-inch in thickness, keeping the trowel wet, and working the material well into the surface voids of the corkboard. Then apply the second coat to the first, after the first coat has set up, approximately 1/32-inch in thickness, and trowel as smooth as the material will permit. After the second coat has taken its initial set, sprinkle with water and trowel again, to obtain a smooth, hard surface.

Do not score the surface of the emulsified asphalt plastic finish, unless specified.

143.—Concrete Wearing Floors.—See that the exposed surface of the corkboard has been flooded to a thickness of approximately ⅛-inch with hot odorless asphalt, so that the entire surface of the insulation is thoroughly protected.

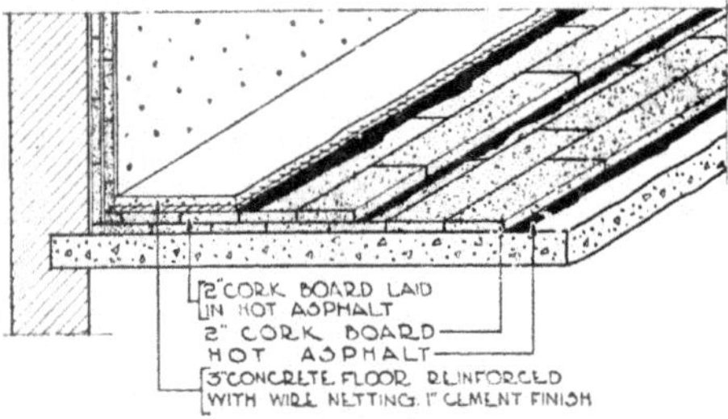

FIG. 142.—DIAGRAMMATIC ILLUSTRATION OF CONCRETE WEARING FLOOR (REINFORCED) OVER DOUBLE LAYER CORKBOARD ON COOLER FLOOR.

Prepare suitable concrete in reasonable quantity, mixed one part Portland cement to two and one-half parts clean, sharp sand, and five parts clean gravel or crushed stone. Cover the corkboard to a depth of 3 inches with the concrete, tamp until the water comes to the surface, and let stand until

*If the emulsified asphalt plastic material is not a ready mixed product, then prepare the material for use only as directed by the manufacturer.

thoroughly dry, about 48 hours, before applying the finish coat.

Prepare suitable Portland cement mortar in reasonable quantity, mixed one part Portland cement to one part clean, sharp sand, and then apply a top coat, of minimum depth of 1 inch, over the rough concrete base, slope to drain as specified, and trowel to a smooth, hard surface.

144.—Wood Floors Secured to Sleepers Embedded in Insulation.—Embed wood sleepers, 2 inches wide and of suitable thickness, in the single or the second layer of corkboard, as the case may be, by putting the sleepers in place, parallel to

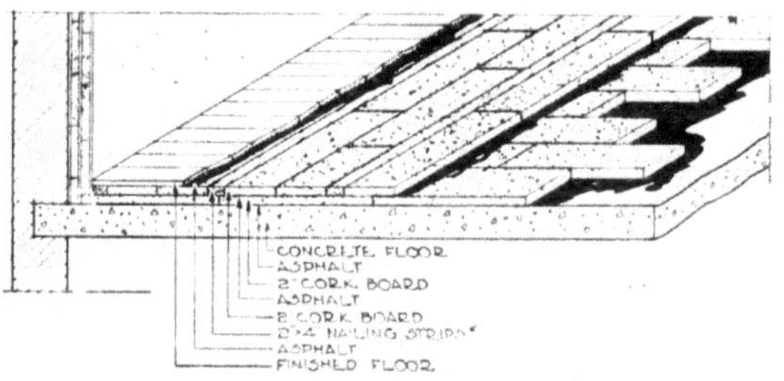

FIG. 143.—DIAGRAMMATIC ILLUSTRATION OF WOOD FLOOR OVER DOUBLE LAYER CORKBOARD APPLIED OVER CONCRETE SLAB.

each other, on 38-inch centers, and lay down a layer of corkboard in suitable hot Asphalt cement between the sleepers with all joints carefully butted and sealed tight. The top surface of the corkboards and the sleepers shall then be flooded with the same compound to a uniform thickness of approximately ⅛-inch.

Lay a finished wood floor of thoroughly dry and seasoned ⅞-inch lumber, as specified, with approximately 1/32-inch between the boards, to eliminate as much as possible the tendency of the floor to expand and warp, secret nail securely to the sleepers embedded in the corkboard underneath, and leave the surface of the floor perfectly smooth and even.

145.—Galvanized Metal Over Corkboard.—Embed wood sleepers, 2 inches wide and of suitable thickness, in the single or the second layer of corkboard, as the case may be, on the floors and baffles of bunkers, on such centers as to permit lapping the galvanized metal joints 1 inch, over such sleepers, and anchoring thereto by securely nailing.

Apply the metal of specified gauge and suitable width, extending it over all edges of the bunker at least 2 inches and lapping all joints 1 inch over sleepers, and then anchor at all points by securely nailing.

Carefully and permanently solder all joints and nail heads in the finished work, and leave the surface of the metal perfectly smooth and even.

CORK INSULATION

Part IV—The Insulation of Household Refrigerators, Ice Cream Cabinets and Soda Fountains.

CHAPTER XV.

HISTORY OF REFRIGERATION EMPLOYED TO PRESERVE FOODSTUFFS.

146.—Early Uses of Refrigeration.—Preservation of food through the use of snow and ice undoubtedly was practised several centuries before the Christian era in those climates and regions where the preservation of the snow and ice in turn during the short summer season was accomplished by Nature through natural storage in caves. During the long winters, large quantities of snow and ice accumulated in sheltered spots and never entirely melted away during the warmer season of the year that followed. Such crevices and caves afforded natural cold storages, for fish and meat, and there is every reason to believe that they were so employed. Later, perhaps as early as 1000 B. C., snow was artificially stored in caves, and used for cooling and preserving. At any rate, Simonides, the early Greek poet, who lived about 500 B. C., when made angry by observing other guests at the board treated to snow poured into their liquor, while he sipped warm wine, enscribed the ode that concludes "for no one will commend the man who gives hot water to a friend." It is also known that Alexander the Great, King of Macedon (336-323 B. C.) had trenches dug and filled with snow to cool hundreds of kegs of wine to be given to his soldiers on the eve of battle, and Nero, Roman Emperor (37-68 A. D.), had his wines cooled by snow brought down from the mountains by slaves. It may therefore be assumed that by the first century the luxury of drinking cooled liquors was enjoyed rather generally by kings and emperors and their friends.

History also shows that the ancient Egyptians, on the other hand, knew the secret of cooling liquids by evaporation, which method of cooling is practised today by the natives of India, as well as by the desert traveller, and quite probably by many others. The ancient Egyptians placed shallow trays, made of porous material and filled with water, on beds of straw, and left them exposed to the night winds. Through the resultant evaporation, the water became chilled sometimes

FIG. 144.—ARTIST'S CONCEPTION OF ANCIENT EGYPTIANS PREPARING WATER FOR CHILLING BY EVAPORATION.

to the extent of a thin film of ice on the surface. Today, in the upper provinces of India, water is made to freeze during cold, clear nights by leaving it overnight in porous vessels, or chilled in containers that are wrapped in moistened cloth. In the first instance, the water freezes by virtue of the cold produced by its own evaporation; and in the second instance, the water is rapidly cooled by the drying of the moistened wrapper. In Bengal the natives resort to a still more elaborate plan. Pits are dug about two feet deep and filled three-quarters full with dry straw, on which are set flat, porous pans containing water. Exposed overnight to a cool, dry, gentle wind from the northwest, the water evaporates at the expense of its own heat with sufficient rapidity to overbalance the slow influx of heat from above through the cooled dense air, or from below through the badly conducting straw, and the water freezes. The desert traveller carries water in a porous canvas water bag so as to have, through slow evaporation, a supply of drinking water sufficiently palatable to dampen his parched lips and cool his throat.

The use of saltpetre mixed with snow for cooling and freezing liquids was known and employed at a remote period in India. In 1607 Tancrelus mentioned the use of this mixture to freeze water, and in 1626 Santono mentioned the use of common salt and snow to freeze wine. At about that same time, in Italy, iced fruits put in an appearance at table, and during the 17th century a method of congealing cream was discovered.

Lord Francis Bacon, English scientist, philosopher and statesman (1561-1626), appreciated what a useful thing it would be if man could have the same command of cold as of heat, and undertook experiments into its possibilities that terminated in his death. Among his notes there is this:

> Heat and cold are Nature's two hands whereby she chiefly worketh, and heat we have in readiness in respect of the fire, but for cold we must stay till it cometh or seek it in deep caves or high mountains, and when all is done we cannot obtain it in any great degree, for furnaces of fire are far hotter than a summer's sun, but vaults and hills are not much colder than a winter's frost.

History is filled with interesting references to the early use of snow and natural ice, especially by the French, Spaniards and Italians, devotees of better living. In England, the sale of natural ice from the wagons of fishmongers was an early practice that continues to this day. In the United States a cargo of natural ice was sent from New York to New Orleans in 1799, the first delivery of natural ice to an American home was made in 1802, and Frederick Tudor exported natural ice from the United States to the West Indies in 1805 to help stay the ravages of yellow fever.

147.—The Formation, Harvesting and Storing of Natural Ice.—The formation of ice is a very common phenomenon of Nature, but the exact process followed in converting water into natural ice is not generally understood by those who make use of the resultant product.

That water freezes at 32° F. at a pressure of one atmosphere is generally understood. When the air above a body of water is chilled to a temperature below that of the water, heat is transferred from the water to the air, the top layer of water is chilled, it becomes denser than the water underneath, drops to the bottom, and is replaced by other water rising to

FIG. 145.—LOADING A CARGO OF NATURAL ICE AT NEW YORK FOR SHIPMENT TO NEW ORLEANS IN 1799.

be similarly chilled. But this chilling process continues only until the entire body of the water is cooled to 39.1° F., which is the point of the greatest density of water, the temperature at which water is heaviest, but a temperature not yet low enough to cause the water to freeze. Further cooling of the water on the pond, lake or stream will no longer cause the top layer of water to drop, by convection, and the chilling effect is thereafter concentrated on the surface of the water instead of being applied generally to the entire body of the water. When the temperature of the top layer of water reaches 32° F., ice forms, and increases in thickness as the water in contact underneath is chilled, by conduction, to the freezing point.

Each particle of water, in freezing, sets free the air that was contained in that water, and the tiny bubbles of air cling to the newly frozen ice crystals, unless dislodged. If these bubbles are not dislodged, by agitation, then other ice crystals forming adjacent to the first ones entrap the clinging air bubbles to form opaque, or "milky," ice. Opaque ice is usually found on ponds where the water is not in motion, or on sluggish streams; while clear, hard ice is frozen on bodies of water that are in motion sufficiently to free the newly formed ice crystals of all clinging air particles.

FIG. 146.—HARVESTING NATURAL ICE FROM A NORTHERN LAKE.

The development of the scientific harvesting of natural ice is an interesting chapter in itself, and second in importance only to the development of the use of natural ice as a refrigerant for the preservation of foodstuffs. It must be sufficient to mention here that during the latter half of the 19th century enormous quantities of natural ice came to be harvested and stored in huge ice houses, ice houses of moderate size and little ice houses, located almost in every community in the United States where the temperature dropped low enough at some time during the winter to freeze ice on the ponds, lakes and streams. The very large ice houses were scientifically constructed and equipped, and were insulated between wood walls with shavings and sawdust well tamped. The smaller ice houses, especially those in the rural communities, were often crudely built, simply of wood slabs nailed to one side of the timber framing. In the well-built and insulated ice houses, straw was frequently used between layers or tiers of ice blocks, and sometimes sawdust was thus employed, to insulate the several layers from each other and to keep them from freezing together; but the insulation between the double walls of the structure was relied upon for the reasonable preservation of the ice during the warmer months, while the house was being emptied of its valuable contents. The ice was stored in the smaller uninsulated structures in such fashion that a space of approximately two feet was left all around the house between the walls and the pile of ice blocks. This space was filled with sawdust as the tiers of ice were

FIG. 147.—TYPICAL ICE STORAGE HOUSES FOR NATURAL ICE, SITUATED AT SOURCE OF SUPPLY.

laid, and sawdust was sometimes placed between layers to a thickness of several inches. Over the top layer, sawdust was piled to a depth of several feet; and louvre-windows at different levels in either end of the house served to ventilate the space over the ice and directly under the uninsulated roof, to prevent superheating of the air in that space on summer days with consequent excessive meltage of the ice in the top layers.

The business of harvesting, storing and dispensing large quantities of natural ice was built on the constantly growing demand for the use of such ice by brewers, packers and large dealers in food products, the trade gradually extending to the

FIG. 148.—GIFFORD-WOOD ICE STORAGE HOUSE EQUIPMENT.

smaller establishments, then to the retail stores, and finally to countless homes, especially in the congested, large city areas. This trade had extended gradually each year and had grown to enormous proportions, but its real size and scope was not fully appreciated, and the necessity for ice was not generally understood, until the summer of 1890, when the greatest shortage in the crop of natural ice that has ever occurred in the United States resulted from the exceptionally mild preceding winter season. This unusual shortage gave mechanical refrigeration an impetus such as it never had before, and marks the real beginnings of the use of ice as a necessity of life.

148.—The Development of the Ice Machine.—The earliest machine to produce ice by purely mechanical means was of the "vacuum" type, built by Dr. William Cullen in 1755. In this class of "liquid" machine, since the refrigerating liquid is itself rejected, the only agent cheap enough to be employed is water. The boiling point of water varies with pressure; and at a pressure of one atmosphere (14.7 pounds per square inch) the boiling point is 212° F., whereas at a pressure of 0.085-pound per square inch it is 32° F., and at lower pressures there is still further fall in temperature. Water at ordinary temperature is placed in an air-tight, insulated vessel, and when the pressure is reduced by means of a vacuum pump it begins to boil, the heat necessary for evaporation being taken from the water itself. The pressure being still further reduced, the temperature is gradually lowered until the freezing point is reached and ice formed, when about one-sixth of the original volume has been evaporated. Dr. Cullen is said to have produced the vacuum by means of a pump alone.

In 1810, Sir John Leslie combined with the air pump a vessel containing strong sulphuric acid for absorbing the vapor from the air, and is said to have produced several pounds of ice in a single operation. Vallance of France, in 1824, produced another machine for the same purpose.

Several suggestions had been made with regard to the production of ice by the evaporation of a more volatile liquid than water, but the first machine actually constructed and operated on that principle was built in 1834 from the designs of Jacob Perkins, an American living abroad, who that year took out patents in England on an ether machine. This machine, though never actually used commercially, is the parent of all modern compression machines. James Harrison, of Geelong, Victoria, later worked out the Perkins principle in a more complete and practical manner and in 1861 had his machine adopted successfully in England for the cooling of oil to extract paraffin.

FIG. 149.—EARLY TYPE REFRIGERATING MACHINE.

Meanwhile, Michael Faraday, English chemist and physicist (1791-1867), succeeded in condensing ammonia gas to a liquid by applying pressure and then cooling it. When the pressure was removed, the liquid boiled off rapidly as a gas, absorbing heat, as any liquid will do when it turns into a gas. Faraday's discovery, made in about 1826, proved of the greatest importance, both practically and theoretically.

Professor A. C. Twining, of New Haven, Connecticut, and Dr. John Gorrie, of Appalachicola, Florida, also contributed to the successful development of the ice machine, Dr. Gorrie taking out the first American patent in 1850 for a practical process of manufacturing ice.

In 1858, E. C. Carré adopted the same principle as Sir John Leslie, but used a solution of ammonia and water in his vacuum machine to make ice. The first one of these Carré machines to reach the United States ran the blockade of New Orleans in 1863. Dr. A. Kirk invented an air machine, in 1862, which was fully described by him in a paper on the "Mechanical Production of Cold," being simply a reversed Sterling air engine, the air working in a closed cycle instead of being actually discharged into the room to be cooled, as is the usual practice with compression machines. It is said that Kirk's machine was used commercially with success on a fairly large scale, chiefly for ice making, producing about 4 pounds of ice per pound of coal.

In 1870, the subject of refrigeration was investigated by Professor Carl Linde, of Munich, Germany, who was the first to consider the question from a thermodynamic point of view. He dealt with the coefficient of performance as a common basis of comparison for all machines, and showed that the compression vapor machine more closely reached the theoretical maximum than any other. Linde also examined the physical properties of various liquids, and, after making trials with methylic ether in 1872, built his first ammonia compression machine in 1873. In the next two years, these machines were introduced into the United States by Professor Linde, and David Boyle of the United States. From then until the ice shortage of the summer of 1890, many new forms of apparatus were produced and certain important improvements were made, following which the rapid development and practical utilization of the art of ice making and refrigeration grew by leaps and bounds, until today ice and refrigeration may be had at any time and anywhere that power can be obtained.

149.—Early Methods of Utilizing Ice as a Refrigerant.— Just as snow was used in ancient times to cool the cup that cheered, so harvested natural ice was probably first employed in later times to cool wines and preserve beer. Deep cellars were dug, walled with heavy masonry, and divided longitudinally by arched stone ceilings into top cellars and sub-cellars. The goods to be preserved were placed in the lower or sub-cellars and the ice was filled into the top cellars just above, an ingenious and effective arrangement that permitted the storing of sufficient quantities of natural ice, as harvested, to carry the sub-cellars through the warm summer months at temperatures cool enough for many purposes. Such cellars were probably the first man-made cold storage houses or refrigerating plants, the suggestion having no doubt come down from the early days of the utilization of snow and ice found in the summer months in deep rocky crevices and natural caves of the mountains.

These underground masonry caverns were not insulated, except naturally by the earth, but their heavy masonry walls, once cooled, acted as enormous reservoirs of cold. Many of these storage cellars were constructed in Europe, especially

FIG. 150.—SAWDUST INSULATED NATURAL ICE HOUSE.

in Germany, and many more of them were built later in the United States, particularly in connection with breweries, in the early days when a simpler and cheaper method of guaranteeing summer refrigeration was unknown. However, as time passed, ice storages and cooling rooms were arranged in single tier cellars, by locating the cold room within the ice storage, so to speak, and having less height, so that the ice could be piled, as harvested, around and over the cold room. Another type of cold storage and ice storage combined was constructed by digging a cellar into the side hill and building the four walls of thick masonry, as the food storage compartment, with a double layer plank ceiling laid over heavy joists, and then building a double-thick plank-walled ice house over such structure. Then boards and air spaces took the place of the double layer plank walls above ground, and holes were cut in the floor to let the cold through. It was only a step, of course, from the cutting of holes in the floor alongside of the ice to permit the cold air to drop into the room below, to a practical bunker arrangement and an efficient air circulation, which was the forerunner of the present indispensible overhead bunker. The sawdust insulated natural ice house next came into being along the shores of northern rivers and lakes, the first large ice house in the United States having been built on the shores of the Hudson river in 1805; and from then on the development of the use of natural ice as a refrigerating medium was rapidly extended. Farmers, for instance, put up ice in cheaply constructed ice houses, surrounded the ice stores with sawdust as insulation, kept fresh meats in sacks buried among the blocks of ice, used the ice to cool milk, to keep butter, and otherwise to serve useful purposes incident to farm life. Simultaneously, in the cities, insulated coolers were being constructed in certain retail establishments, and in the better homes portable ice chests were installed, natural ice delivery service having been established in the larger cities, which functioned as far into the summer as the supply of natural ice lasted.

It may now appear to be a curious fact, but a fact it remains nevertheless, that the breweries had equally as much to do with the extension of the use of natural ice, and later of manufactured ice, as had any other single agency. For, first of all, the brewing of beer was a profitable business, and the industry attracted capital. Some of the finest plants in the world were breweries. They could afford to harvest and store ice in their cellars, to be among the very first to install ice machines for the manufacture of ice, to re-equip their plants for mechanical cooling, and to experiment with different kinds of insulation. As a means of widening the market for beer, especially after the advent of manufactured ice, portable coolers in large quantities were built by the breweries and loaned out to inns, hotels, saloons and a variety of establishments, ice being delivered daily in generous quantities, often at no extra cost whatever, with which to cool the boxes and their contents. Perishable foods soon found their way into those refrigerators, where it was kept cool with the beer, at the expense of the brewery. The conveniences and benefits accruing, however, from the consistent use of ice-cooled, insulated boxes created a demand on the part of others, in other lines of business, for a like refrigeration service for the handling of perishable foodstuffs, and the breweries were the first, in many instances, to provide the public with such service and at a very nominal cost indeed.

150.—Early Methods of Insulating Cold Stores.—Hollow walls, or air chambers or spaces, were the very first artificial barriers used in cold stores to retard the influx of heat, some of the first installations being made on ships, to permit of the exporting and importing of perishables, particularly fresh meats, from one country to another. Later it became the practice, especially in cold storage structures, to lay up double walls and fill the space between with a light-weight, loose material. Powdered charcoal, sawdust, diatomaceous earth and similar materials were thus employed, and except for the gradual loss of the insulation from settling and sifting out, the loss of storage space due to the bulkiness of the insulation, the fire hazard, and so forth, such insulated cold stores proved satisfactory in service, using ice as the refrigerant and operating at temperatures sufficiently high to obviate the condensation of enough moisture within the insulation to seriously interfere with its heat retarding qualities.

But with the real advent of mechanical refrigeration in ice and cold storage plants, following the summer of 1890, and the gradual use of temperatures lower than were ever obtained with ice, or with salt and ice mixtures, serious difficulties began to be experienced with insulated structures. If the insulation was boards and air spaces, or double wall frame construction with loose fill insulation, the wood frequently became soaked with water, and rotted away, or the loose fill insulation became water-logged and of no further value as an insulator, meanwhile throwing a heavy extra load on the refrigerating apparatus and equipment, and of course increasing the cost of operation excessively. At such points in the insulation where the wood remained perfectly dry, there was great danger of dry-rot, consequent weakening of supporting members, and danger to the safety of the structure. It was not at all uncommon to have the entire over-head bunker structure drop to the floor because of dry-rot or wet-rot of the supporting timbers at the points where the members pierced the thick walls of insulation to gain support in the outer walls of the building. If the construction consisted of double walls of masonry, with inside surfaces pitched, and the intervening space filled with a loose insulating material, the loose fill material settled and packed down and frequently became thoroughly water-logged and of no further value whatever as an insulator.

Every possible precaution was taken to waterproof the walls between which the loose fill insulation was placed, such as coating them with expensive pure resin pitch, imported from afar, probably on the theory that water got into the insulation by penetrating such walls. However, water continued to be condensed out of the air in the countless voids between particles of the insulation, from the fact of the cold storage rooms operating at temperatures low enough to throw the dew point within the insulation, fresh air carrying more water was automatically drawn in, the insulation sucked up the precipitated water by capillarity and soon became completely water-logged, as formerly.

Meanwhile, in Europe, cork, possessing no capillarity but high in insulating value because of its sealed air cell structure, was being formed into slabs by gluing the cork particles together with a hot mixture of certain clays and asphalt, and these slabs were applied to the walls of cold storage rooms as insulation, and the results were heralded as being very satisfactory. The Armstrong Cork Company subsequently acquired the United States patent rights for this "impregnated" type of corkboard insulation, and constructed a factory at Beaver Falls, Pennsylvania, for its production. Large quantities of this impregnated corkboard were purchased and installed, especially by the breweries; but it was later discovered that such "composition" corkboard was inferior in structural strength and insulating quality to pure corkboard manufactured under the patents of John T. Smith, and with the purchase of the Nonpariel Cork Manufacturing Company and the Smith patents, by the Armstrong Cork Company, composition corkboard virtually disappeared from the market. In competition with pure corkboard, however, there was offered very early a great variety of insulating boards or slabs, made from fibrous materials of one sort or another and possessing marked affinity for water; but experience in service with all such substitutes for pure corkboard clearly and conclusively demonstrated wherein they were unsuited for cold storage temperatures, and they have virtually disappeared from the market as cold storage insulating materials.

CHAPTER XVI.

DEVELOPMENT OF THE CORKBOARD INSULATED HOUSEHOLD REFRIGERATOR.

151.—Early Forms of Household Coolers.—Probably the first household "cooler" was a crude box anchored in a nearby stream, in which in turn several tall earthen jars or pieces of crockery were placed, the ends of the box provided with slatted openings to permit the fresh water to pass through,

FIG. 151.—THE FIRST METHOD OF KEEPING FOOD COOL—A BOX IN A NEARBY STREAM SERVED THE PURPOSE OF THE MODERN REFRIGERATOR.

and the top of the box covered with a strap-hinged lid. If a spring of water was available, the box was of course anchored just below the overflow and probably in a slight excavation made to accommodate it. In either case, perishable foods, such as milk, butter, eggs and meat, were placed within the jars or crocks, to be cooled and preserved as best as possible.

The objection to this simple type of household cooler was

that the mid-day sun often beat down upon the low, flat lid of the box with telling effect on the perishable foodstuffs just underneath, and at night the lid was sometimes disturbed and the food stolen by prowling marauders of the field and forest. So here, as elsewhere, necessity being the mother of invention, the next step in the development of the present household refrigerator was the construction of a rude shelter over the box to protect the food from the elements and from unwelcome guests. This shelter was made of logs, as a miniature log cabin, and was usually spoken of as the "milk house," or the "spring house."

FIG. 152. THE SPRING HOUSE—A RUDE SHELTER BUILT OVER SPRING OR STREAM TO PROTECT THE FOOD STORED.

Long before cellars were excavated under dwellings, some provision had to be made for the storing of fruits and, more particularly, vegetables in a uniformly cool atmosphere sufficiently dry to preserve the stores as far into the next season as possible. Natural caves were occasionally available, but more often artificial caves were dug out of the side of a hill, lined with timbers and equipped with shelves, bins and a strong door. Again, where a hillside was not conveniently near, a low, log room was constructed, similarly equipped, and completely surrounded and covered with earth thrown up in the form of a mound. The mound was then tamped and covered with thick sod, which made a suitable storage conveniently nearby and which was commonly spoken of as the "root house," the name borrowed from still earlier times when similar provision was made for the storing of roots for medicine. When cellars were first excavated under dwellings, they

FIG. 153.—THE "ROOT HOUSE," COVERED WITH HEAVY SOD—A COOL THE YEAR 'ROUND VEGETABLE STORAGE.

were installed as a substitute for the outside provision cave or root house, and the only entrance was through an outside cellar door so as to avoid direct communication between the

FIG. 154.—ENTRANCE TO CELLAR—A MORE CONVENIENT STORAGE THAN THE "ROOT HOUSE."

heated dwelling above and the cool cavern underneath. These original cellars were provision storages only and as such were little more than pits dug in the ground.

It has been seen how, in ancient times, trenches were dug and filled with snow to cool kegs of wine. At a later time, pits were dug, filled with ice and roofed over, which was probably the earliest form of ice storage or ice house. About the middle of the 16th century the rich in America harvested and stored ice in private ice houses built of logs and padded inside between the logs and the pile of ice with straw packed tight, and later with sawdust. The blocks of ice were then used in a heavy, wooden chest, about three feet wide by three feet high and possibly ten or twelve feet long, resting on the floor, usually in an out-building adjacent to the kitchen, in which chest earthen containers were used in very much the

FIG. 155.—FOREFATHER OF THE MODERN HOUSEHOLD REFRIGERATOR—A HEAVY CHEST CONTAINING RECEPTACLES FOR FOOD SURROUNDED BY NATURAL ICE AND WATER.

same way as they were in the earlier crude box anchored in the stream or spring. This heavy, water-tight, wooden chest, filled with ice and with vessels for liquids and provisions to be cooled and preserved, having as a drain for the water of meltage merely a hole in the end of the chest about half way up, and equipped with a heavy, hinged lid, was the predecessor of the household ice-box and the crude forefather of the modern household refrigerator.

152.—The Household Ice-box.—It has been seen that hollow walls, or air spaces, were the very first artificial barriers used in cold stores to retard the influx of heat, which method of insulating cold temperatures from the higher temperatures of the surrounding atmosphere followed upon the use of thick masonry walls underground and of walls of heavy timbers or planks in structures above ground. Following the same development, and true to tradition,* the ice chest in time became an ice-box, smaller in length, made of oak, chestnut or other hard wood, with hollow walls lined inside with sheet zinc, standing upon raised feet formed from prolongations of the side posts, a hole in the bottom for the water to drain

FIG. 156.—SLIDING-TOP HOUSEHOLD ICE CHEST.

away, with perhaps a shallow pan underneath to catch the drip. The very first of these ice-boxes had wood pieces laid in the bottom to keep the ice and food from contacting with the metal lining, but there was no provision for the separation of the food from the ice. The lid, usually of double layer boards with no air space between, was at first hinged, and later, in some instances, built in two sections and made to slide. As time passed, these convenient household ice-boxes were provided with a vertical division across the box at the

*The box, whatever its shape or purpose or the materials of which it is fashioned, is the direct descendent of the chest, one of the most ancient articles of domestic furnishings.

center to separate the food from the ice, but it was at that time in no sense a baffle for the promotion of air circulation, the idea not then having been adapted to such purpose.

In due course, it became the practice in cold stores to construct double walls and fill the intervening space with flaked charcoal, silicate cotton, small pumice, sawdust, and similar loose or granular materials; and the principle of the over-

FIG. 157.—LIFT-LID HOUSEHOLD ICE BOX.

head bunker was at about the same time being fast developed to a point of efficiency that opened up new avenues of usefulness for cold stores employing ice, or salt and ice mixtures, as the refrigerant. This influence was quickly reflected in the large beer and meat coolers of retail establishments and in turn in the household ice-box, flaked charcoal becoming the preferred type of loose fill insulation between ice-box walls, followed later by silicate cotton, or mineral wool. Then for the first time the household ice-box was elevated, so to speak, to a new position; its length was somewhat decreased in favor of a much greater height, and the division between the ice and the food changed from a vertical one to a horizontal one. In a word, the household ice-box became a household "refrigerator," of the kind now known as a lid type top-icer, by virtue

FIG. 158.—LID TYPE TOP-ICER HOUSEHOLD REFRIGERATOR.

of the location of the ice on an overhead support of such design as to utilize the fact of the greater weight of cold than of warm air to cause a natural circulation to be set up throughout the refrigerator. Then came the top-icer with a side ice-chamber door; and, later, the side-icer completed the interesting evolution of the form our modern household refrigerator finally came to take.

Except for the gradual loss of the insulation from settling and sifting out, those early household refrigerators proved much more satisfactory in service, using ice as the refrigerant, than did the cold storage rooms in plants cooled by mechanical means and insulated in exactly the same manner. Of course the rooms cooled by mechanical means could be, and were, held at lower temperatures than were the household refrigerators chilled with ice; and this fact was responsible for the different degrees of success experienced with the same

FIG. 159.—SIDE-DOOR TOP-ICER HOUSEHOLD REFRIGERATOR.

type and kind of insulation under those different conditions of service; for it will be recalled that with the gradual use in cold stores of temperatures lower by mechanical means than were possible with ice, serious difficulties began to be experienced with insulated structures from condensation of water within the insulation.

153.—The Era of Multiple Insulation in Household Refrigerators.—Pliny, writing in the first century, said: "The natives who inhabit the west of Europe have a liquid with which they intoxicate themselves, made from corn and water. ..The people in Spain in particular brew this liquid so well that it will keep good a long time. So exquisite is the cunning of mankind in gratifying their vicious appetites that they have thus invented a method to make water itself produce intoxication." It has been seen how that same "exquisite cunning" of which Pliny wrote also provided means of making that *ceria* more palatable and soothing by cooling with snow, and later with ice; how the physicist working in the laboratory formulated certain laws which apply to the condensation of gases; how the engineer, in his workshop, utilized these fundamental principles to develop machines to make ice on a hot summer's day; and it only remained for the practical business man of the 20th century to so organize the ice industry that ice is no longer a luxury, to be obtained only by the wealthy, but is today within the reach of almost everyone. Sixteen million tons of natural ice are harvested and forty-two million tons are manufactured each year in the United States alone. And of this total ice production of fifty-eight million tons (1923), American households used the enormous total of twenty-five million tons.

So from practically nothing at the beginning of the 19th century, the ice industry of the United States has become ninth in the list of great commercial activities, with a monetary involvement of over one billion dollars, which may be accounted for by the increased cost of foods, a better knowledge of the value of very fresh foods in the diet, a more thorough understanding of the danger of stale or decomposed foods, and the means on the part of countless numbers of people not only to purchase fresh foods the year 'round but also to provide facilities in the home for the care of such perishables.

The many industries that use refrigeration in their routine business have been benefited by careful scientific research begun many years ago; and only by correctly utilizing the findings of engineers, chemists, physicists and bacteriologists have they been able to reach their present high efficiency. But similar studies applicable to the problems of the home were never undertaken in similar concerted fashion by either the ice manufacturers or the refrigerator manufacturers, and even those principles worked out and established for the benefit and guidance of the ice and refrigerating and allied industries, and which are directly applicable to the household, often have been overlooked, ignored or misapplied.

For instance, careful scientific research established the fact that the flow of heat through a given insulating material was retarded by an external or surface resistance as well as by an internal resistance, but that its surface resistance virtually disappeared if the surfaces of the material were no longer in contact with the surrounding atmosphere, as elaborated in the section of this book on "The Study of Heat." But this scientific fact was either misunderstood, or its true significance ignored, because many manufacturers of household refrigerators re-designed their product on the basis of multiple insulation on the incorrect theory that each layer of material in the walls of a refrigerator sets up or offers its own individual surface resistance to the transfer of heat, even though these layers are laid one against another or in positions of intimacy and their surfaces are not exposed to the surrounding atmosphere. In other words, in theory, the surface resistances of many layers of material were incorrectly combined to arrive at a wholly fictitious high total resistance of a given wall to the infiltration of heat. The claim of superiority based on multiple walls of insulation was a familiar one, and for too many years unsuspecting householders counted the layers in comparing prices.

With the growth of the ice industry, the refrigerator industry expanded proportionately, and competition became keen and difficult. Little real attention was paid to the actual insulating qualities of a household refrigerator; for, as some have said, "the ice man wanted to sell ice, the refrigerator manufacturer wanted to sell refrigerators, and the householder wanted something low in cost and high in hopes." It is probably more to the point, however, that the real need for better insulation in household refrigerators had never been made clear to the ice man, the refrigerator builder, or the householder. In a word, the *necessity* did not exist, and the ***need*** was not understood.

Nevertheless, the more progressive refrigerator manufacturers and the more progressive producers and distributors of ice, often in cooperation with various United States Governmental agencies, State Universities, and a few private experimental laboratories, kept up a constant if not intensive search for more practical and accurate information on the application of refrigeration principles and appliances in the home New and better sanitary refrigerator linings were developed, air circulation was vastly improved, shelves were rearranged to accommodate various foods in the position in the refrigerator where they would keep best, better hardware was adopted, doors were sealed with improved wick gasket, drain pipes were placed so as to permit of ready removal and cleaning, ice compartments were enlarged to an adequate size, outside icing doors were provided for the discriminating, and better exterior finishes were offered. Very little attention, however, was paid to the insulation of what would otherwise have been a perfect masterpiece of craftsmanship. A few manufacturers, among them those using solid porcelain linings, adopted granulated cork as the insulating medium; but as refrigerators were not then sold on the basis of comparative permanent efficiency of operation in service, the added value of the ground cork insulation was not generally appreciated even by those manufacturers who used it.

154.—The Advent of the Household Refrigerating Machine and Early Trials with Pure Corkboard in Household Refrigerators.—It has been seen that the practice of cooling food and drink below the temperature of the atmosphere by the use of snow and ice was followed for many centuries before natural ice came to be stored in caves, in ice pits, and then in ice houses, and that within the present generation means were perfected for the manufacture of ice in commercial quantities for refrigeration purposes. Now we observe that within scarcely the past dozen years attention has been directed to ways and means of producing refrigeration in the home by mechanical means directly; but it is only since the World War that the household machine has been manufactured in quantities and proven a success, the production during recent years having been about as follows:

Prior to	1923	20,000
Year	1923	25,000
Year	1924	50,000
Year	1925	100,000
Year	1926	500,000
Estimated	1927	750,000

At present the subject of household refrigeration is receiving the attention of many inventors and engineers, as well as

FIG. 160.—TYPICAL AIR-COOLED HOUSEHOLD REFRIGERATING MACHINE.

of several hundred manufacturers. New and improved mechanical devices and processes are being developed almost constantly, several editions of a complete treatise on "the principles, types, construction, and operation of both ice and mechanically cooled domestic refrigerators, and the use of ice and refrigeration in the home," having already been published,* under the title of "Household Refrigeration," by H. B. Hull, Refrigeration Engineer.

Mr. Hull, in introducing his subject, says that, "mechanical household refrigeration is having an important influence on refrigerator cabinet construction; it is necessary to have better constructed and insulated refrigerators to operate satisfactorily, with the lower food-compartment temperatures produced by the mechanical unit"; and Mr. Hull drew extensively on his experience as a refrigeration and research engineer, and in turn upon the work and experience of many others in allied industries, in setting forth his conclusions with respect

*Nickerson & Collins Co., Publishers, 5707 West Lake Street, Chicago, Illinois.

to the insulation of mechanically cooled household refrigerators.

It was little suspected, perhaps, in the beginnings of mechanical refrigeration for the home, that serious trouble would be experienced with the operation of the household refrigerator itself; because there was then enough real and potential trouble with the mechanical unit, without contemplating trouble from a coordinated product manufactured by others, especially since household refrigerators had been successfully produced, sold and used in the home for a great many years. Yet serious trouble there was, and it took a lot of time and much money to eliminate it.

A dozen years or so ago (about 1915), there was need for better insulation in household refrigerators, but the necessity for it did not then exist; and it was not until a serious attempt was made to cool such refrigerators by mechanical means that the subject of enough permanently efficient insulation was made a research and engineering consideration. The cost of operating one of the early makes of mechancially cooled domestic refrigerators, original investment ignored, was frequently somewhat greater than the cost of cooling the same refrigerator with ice. The much lower temperature that could be maintained by the mechanical unit was consequently featured as its greatest advantage, and the plant was adjusted and sold on that basis. Thereupon the refrigerator usually began to leak, and frequently to smell, and then the motor was observed to operate a greater number of hours per day, until it was sometimes said to operate almost continuously, and general dissatisfaction with the installation on the part of the purchaser was, under such conditions, the inevitable result.

Examination of these "leakers" and "smellers" usually revealed the fibrous insulation in the hollow walls of the refrigerator water-soaked and odor-saturated; whereupon, after a considerable lapse of time and following much investigation, the insulation specifications were changed, and, borrowing a page from the experience and practice of commercial cold storage plants, pure corkboard was directed to be used. The permanent insulating efficiency of corkboard in cold storage structures was a known quantity, and its well-known freedom from capillarity was expected to rid the correctly insulated mechanical refrigerator of the water conditions so consistently encountered theretofore. Unfortunately, however, the question of the manner and method of installing the corkboard, with respect to the refrigerator as a finished unit, was virtually left to the discretion of the superintendent of the plant producing the refrigerators; and it was but natural for him to cut the corkboards to fit easily into generous wall spaces, and in other respects to do with the corkboard just about as had always been done with other kinds of insulation in the many years preceding the advent of the household refrigerating machine.

The results were almost as unsatisfactory as they had been with other kinds and forms of insulation. Leakers and smellers continued to be the order of the day, and the insulating efficiency was below that to be expected with corkboard as the insulating material. Perhaps the refrigerator did not leak half as much, or smell quite as badly, or run nearly as long, as formerly, with other kinds of insulation; but it leaked, and it gave off odors, and it cost too much to operate; and these things, coupled with the usual run of mechanical troubles incident to the development of a new device, were enough to discourage much less courageous manufacturers than those who blazed trails for the present-day mechanical unit.

If a glass pitcher of ice water is placed on a kitchen table, it will "sweat," under usual conditions of humidity, such an amount that the water of condensation will sometimes run on to the table top, although usually it will evaporate away almost as rapidly as it forms; and just as water vapor in suspension in the surrounding air of the kitchen would be precipitated on the cool, outer surface of the glass pitcher, so would water vapor have been precipitated or condensed at the same rate on the outer, exposed surface of the interior lining of a refrigerator cooled to the same degree by ice and located in the same kitchen.

If salt is added to the pitcher of ice water and stirred, to reduce the temperature of the mixture, the sweating will usually exceed the evaporation by such an amount as to quickly form a puddle of water on the table top; and just as water vapor in suspension in the surrounding air of the kitchen would be precipitated on the cold, outer surface of the pitcher containing the low temperature mixture, at a rate too rapid to permit of its being evaporated away as fast as it formed, so would water vapor have been condensed at the same rate on the outer, exposed surface of the interior lining of a refrigerator chilled to the same degree by a mechanical household refrigerating machine.

FIG. 161. THE SWEATING PITCHER OF ICE WATER POINTED THE WAY TO THE PROPER APPLICATION OF CORKBOARD IN HOUSEHOLD REFRIGERATORS.

In either case, the only difference between the action of the pitcher and that of the refrigerator would be in the rate of evaporation of the condensed water; evaporation from the surface of the pitcher would be more rapid than from the exposed surface of the interior lining of the refrigerator, because there would be greater freedom of air currents about the pitcher than there would be about the confined interior refrigerator lining.

The foregoing explains why the mechanically cooled household refrigerator frequently "leaked," and why the former ice-cooled domestic refrigerator rarely if ever gave evidence of the same defect; the rate of condensation of water vapor in the case of the mechanical refrigerator was considerably greater than the rate of evaporation, whereas the rate of condensation in the case of the ice-cooled refrigerator was usually no greater and was frequently less than the rate of evaporation. Then, too, in the case of an ice-cooled refrigerator, moisture condensed out of air entrapped within the walls of the refrigerator would usually be in intimate contact with the insulation in such walls, and would be absorbed by it if the insulation possessed capillarity in any degree whatever.

Water, as is well known, is very susceptible to tainting; a glass of water standing on a dining-room table will pick up odors at a rapid rate, and become unfit for human consumption. Place a glass of water on a kitchen table during the preparation of a meal, and two hours later the water will have an odor. The water of meltage coming from an iced refrigerator has an odor; because as the air in the refrigerator circulates over the melting ice, the water of meltage extracts the food odors and carries them away through the refrigerator drain. Condensed water on the back of an exposed interior lining of a refrigerator will quickly become foul, by absorption of odors from the air; and thus we have the explanation for the so-called "cork odor" in the structure of the early mechanically cooled household refrigerator insulated with corkboards so loosely installed as to leave the exterior surface of the interior lining exposed. For unless some material with a certain heat insulating value is in intimate contact with the entire outer surface of a refrigerator lining, such surface must be thought of and dealt with as being exposed to the surrounding atmosphere, at least in so far as the condensation of moisture on its face is concerned.

Odors within the food compartment of a mechanical refrigerator are usually accounted for by the foods stored, or by odors coming in through dry bell-trap or goose-neck of the drain pipe from which all water has evaporated. An ice-cooled refrigerator is constantly at work to keep its air purified, by absorption of odors by the water of meltage and discharge to drain; but a mechanically-cooled refrigerator frequently has little or no water of meltage, and other provision must be made for the purification of its air. This has been variously accomplished by ventilation through dry drain pipe, where such pipe terminates low enough to escape the odors from the refrigerating machine, by ventilation through loosely fitted doors, and by still other means entirely. These items do not come within the scope of the subject of the proper insulation of a refrigerator, but they are touched upon here because insulation was frequently and erroneously blamed for such interior odors in the days of the early trials at insulating household refrigerators with corkboard.

155.—The Modern Corkboard Insulated Household Refrigerator.—Early ice storages, ship's cold stores, cold storage houses and breweries were insulated with air spaces and loose fill materials in hollow walls with reasonable success, all things considered, during the days when ice was employed as the refrigerant. The advent of mechanical refrigeration and lower temperatures in cold stores increased the condensation of moisture within the air spaces and the loose fill insulating materials to such a degree, however, as to frequently destroy the insulating capacity of the walls entirely. For it will be recalled, from an elaboration of the subject in the chapter on "Measurement of Heat, Change of State, and Humidity," that the capacity of air to absorb and hold moisture, or water vapor, in suspension, varies with its temperature; and, warm air being capable of holding more moisture than cold air, when warm air is cooled, its moisture capacity is lowered until a temperature is reached at which the air can no longer hold all of its moisture in suspension, which point is the point of saturation, or the dew point. By insulating the exposed surfaces of cold stores with a sufficient thickness of a material having its air content, upon which it must depend for its heat retarding properties, divided into an infinitesimal number of microscopic or colloidal particles dispersed throughout the material in hermetically sealed cells, *so that such air loses its normal properties as air,* the precipitation of water vapor within such insulation or within the building structure back of the insulation, due to exposure of chilled surfaces to the atmosphere, was eliminated. Pure corkboard was the insulating material that met these conditions, both in theory and practice, when properly manufactured and when properly applied in intimate contact with the surfaces to be insulated.

Borrowing another page from the experience and practice of commercial cold storage plants, through the advice of a trained insulation engineer* of recognized experience and responsibility, pure corkboard was directed to be applied in mechanically chilled household refrigerators in a manner that would absolutely eliminate air pockets or air spaces of any kind between the corkboard and the outside surface of the

FIG. 162.—SEEGER MODEL SHOWING PURE CORKBOARD APPLIED IN ASPHALT CEMENT TO INTERIOR ONE-PIECE ENAMELED STEEL REFRIGERATOR LINING, WITH ALL AIR EXCLUDED.

interior refrigerator lining; for otherwise water vapor in that air would be condensed, due to its contact with the cold exterior surface of the lining, the partial vacuum created by such cooling and condensing would be balanced by the infiltration of additional air carrying water vapor in suspension, which fresh supply of air would in turn be cooled and give up

*PUBLISHER'S NOTE—The author of this book is credited with formulating the suggestions that led to a solution of the problems touched upon here.

water, and the cycle continued so long as the refrigerator was in service. A certain type of refrigerator, having an opal glass panel lining, and usually produced by skilled cabinet-makers, escaped almost completely the difficulties with mechanical household refrigeration that were experienced by manufacturers of refrigerators having the one-piece enameled steel linings. The wall construction of such refrigerators consisted of exterior oak, paper, corkboard tightly compressed

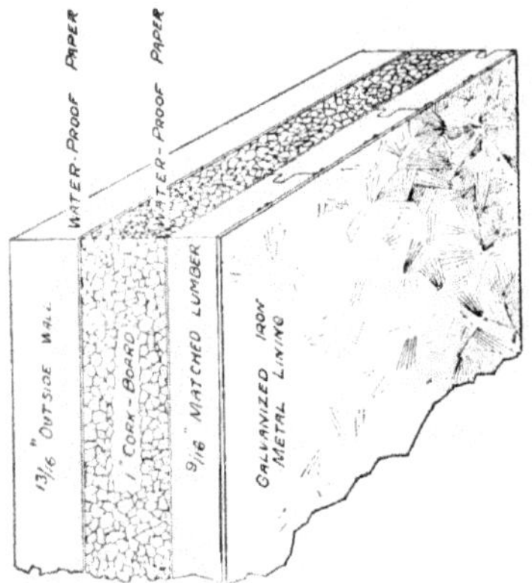

FIG. 163.—CABINETMAKER'S INSULATION DETAILS FOR REFRIGERATOR.

into position in intimate contact at every point, paper, wood sheathing, and a thin pad of builder's felt against which the opal glass paneled interior lining was secured. One of the first demands placed on the mechanical household refrigeration industry, however, was for a very much reduced cost of the assembled refrigerator units; and the cabinet type of corkboard insulated refrigerator with opal glass paneled lining, which was virtually a cabinetmaker's product and which did not readily lend itself to quantity production, was soon abandoned in favor of the one-piece enameled-steel lining type of refrigerator.

The outside or back of an enameled steel lining does not present a level surface, and from desire to have sanitary corners within the food compartment the corners were rounded. Early types of enameled steel linings were L-shaped, necessitating a separate galvanized iron section or lining to accommodate the mechanical cooling unit and to be fitted into

FIG. 164.—CABINETMAKER PLACING CORKBOARD IN STILES AND RAILS BETWEEN DOOR OPENINGS.

the crook of the L as best as possible and insulated from it. The corkboard insulation had to be built around the lining, obviously, instead of the insulation being installed in the refrigerator walls and the lining fitted in place afterwards. Therefore, the use of some waterproof, odorless, elastic, highly cementatious material, plastic at workable temperatures and solid at ordinary temperatures, a material reasonable in cost and easily obtained, had to be found in which to lay up or set the corkboards in position against the exterior of the refrig-

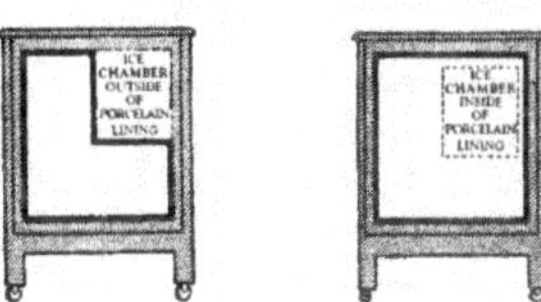

FIG. 165.—(LEFT) L-SHAPED REFRIGERATOR LINING, DIFFICULT TO INSULATE.—(RIGHT) RECTANGULAR REFRIGERATOR LINING, EASY TO INSULATE.

erator linings. After repeated trials with many materials, an unfluxed petroleum asphalt of suitable characteristics and mixed with a certain preparation of cork flour, as described in the Articles on "Asphalt Cement and Asphalt Primer" and "General Instructions and Equipment," came to be used with success, and such method of application of corkboard in household refrigerators and ice cream cabinets came to be known as the *"hydrolene process"**.

The equipment for the proper preparation and handling of hot Asphalt cement, in the refrigerator manufacturing plant, must of course be a separate consideration with each manufacturing organization, and for that reason no attempt will be made here to give any of the details whatever. A word of caution would probably not be out of place, however, with respect to the danger from fire. This is probably the only serious manufacturing objection to the Asphalt cement process of installing corkoard in household refrigerators, but the benefits have been of so great an importance to the household refrigeration industry as to put such objection, for the present at least, in the class of "necessary manufacturing evils." The properties of asphalt are at least briefly outlined elsewhere in this book, and additional information should be available from reliable sources. There is just one simple rule to follow with respect to the asphalt to use; namely, start with the correct material (not necessarily the most expensive), and if it is not damaged by overheating in the process of applying the insulation, the finished refrigerator construction will contain the correct Asphalt cement as a bonding and sealing material.

Thus it has been seen how corkboard came to be adapted to, and adopted for, the insulation of household refrigerators by the mechanical household refrigeration industry, through the desirability of using a more efficient insulating material to reduce costs of mechanical operation, and an insulating material which when properly applied in a unit to be mechanically cooled would obviate the condensation of moisture within the insulation. Also, competition between the enormous ice industry and the fast growing mechanical household refrigeration industry had the usual effect of directing attention to the comparative cost and efficiency of the two systems of preserving foodstuffs in the home. Research on the part of the ice industry is said to have made the important discovery that with adequate and proper corkboard insulation, with improved air circulation, with proper placement of foods, and other considera-

*Registered by Delco-Light Company, subsidiary of General Motors Corporation, Dayton, Ohio, manufacturers of Frigidaire Electric Refrigeration.

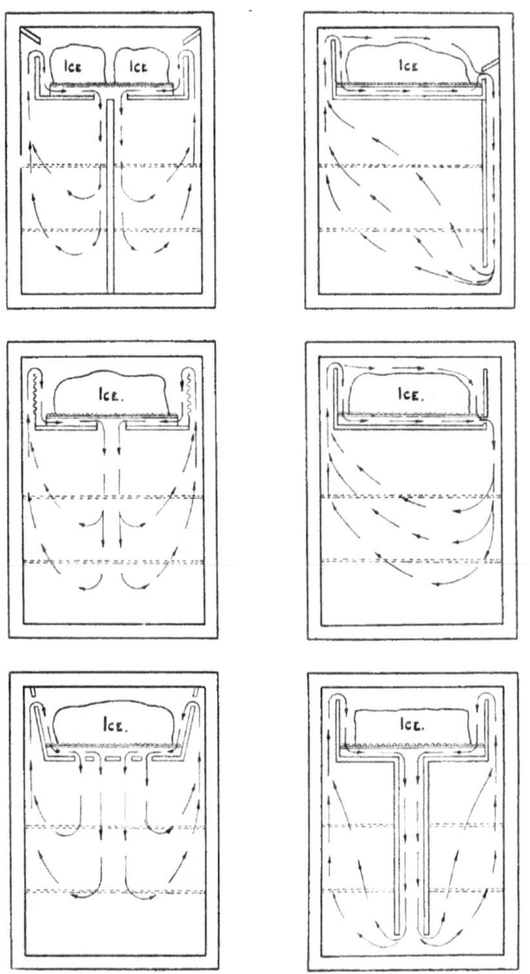

FIG. 166.—AIR CIRCULATION IN HOUSEHOLD REFRIGERATORS.

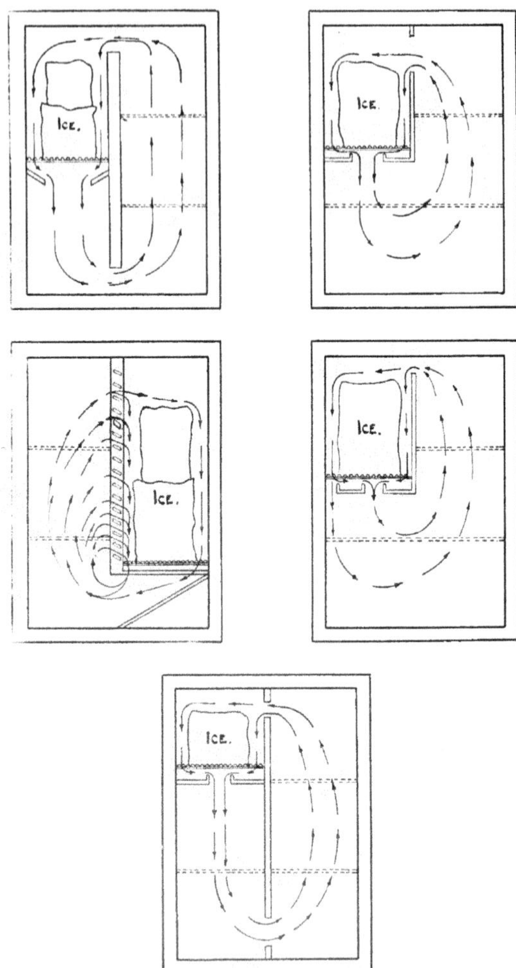

FIG. 167.—AIR CIRCULATION IN HOUSEHOLD REFRIGERATORS.

tions, an ice cooled refrigerator will give results in the correct preservation of foods in the home that cannot be expected with mechanically cooled refrigerators. Then, too, some of that great fraternity of refrigerator manufacturers not identified with the mechanical household refrigeration industry, wished, for the most part, to have their products adaptable to either system of refrigeration,—ice or mechanical,—and therefore adjusted their insulation specifications to meet the most exacting requirements.

Household refrigeration and the proper insulation of the household refrigerator are today important correlated subjects, and their importance promises to continue to increase so long as food is consumed in the home. The National Association of Ice Industries, 163 West Washington Street, Chicago, Illinois, has equipped* to give the subject of refrigeration in the home every attention and consideration. From one of its many interesting and valuable publications and pamphlets, this is extracted:

WE GO SHOPPING FOR A REFRIGERATOR

A clever woman once said that it was a wise girl who knew good "husband-material" when she saw it! And it is a wise woman who knows a good refrigerator when she meets one, for here beauty is only skin deep with a vengeance and it's the inside, not the outside, of an ice box that counts. A woman's intuition won't help her much in looking at it. Nor do white enamel and nickel finishings make the refrigerator, any more than clothes make the man.

Rule one, in a case like this, is to go to a reliable, intelligent dealer and buy a box that bears the name of an established builder of refrigerators. When a man signs his output with his own name, he is apt to be proud of it and to do a good job.

The main points to look out for in choosing a refrigerator to live with are these:

1. Insulation: How are its walls built?
2. Circulation: Can the air flow freely?
3. Size: Not only of the whole box in relation to the size of the family, but of the ice compartment in relation to the box itself.
4. Drain pipes and shelves: Are they easy to adjust and hard to rust?
5. Handles and corners: Are they easy to turn and easy to clean?

What and Why Is Insulation?—To insulate anything is to cut it off from its surroundings, make an island of it. And the walls and

* Household Refrigeration Bureau of the National Association of Ice Industries. Dr. Mary E. Pennington, Director.

interlinings of a good refrigerator, the doors and top, should cut it off from the warm outside air. It's not fair to expect 100 pounds of ice to cool the whole outside world! So a poorly insulated refrigerator, however handsome to look upon, is largely an ice-melting plant that wastes ice and does not maintain sufficiently low temperatures.

The ideal is to have a hard-wood case about ⅞-inch thick (oak is best) with the equivalent of at least two inches of corkboard between this and the inside lining of porcelain. The "reason why" for this is that such an interlining not only keeps heat out, but it will not absorb moisture, and is rigid so that it will not sag leaving air spaces.

FIG. 168.—WISE WOMEN KNOW GOOD REFRIGERATORS.

Merely wood, paper and air will not keep the heat out of the refrigerator, such walls leave the ice badly handicapped in its war with outside heat! Ask to see a cross-section of the refrigerator walls. If the makers are proud of their box, they will be glad to "show" you.

On these protecting walls and well-insulated and tightly closing doors depends largely the coolness of the food compartments. They should average 20 to 26 degrees colder than outside the refrigerator when the room thermometer reads 70 to 75° F. As the weather grows colder, this difference grows less. Under the ice, the coldest place, the thermometer should read not more than 45° F., and on the top shelf of a side-icer or on the bottom of a top-icer, the temperature should not be much more than 50° F. when the room is 70 to 75° F.

Circulation Means "Air Move On."—"Side-Icer or Top-Icer"? That is a question, too.

It's the cold circulating air that cools the foods. To be sure that you are getting good circulation, look to see that there is a broad unobstructed drop from the ice chamber into the food compartment.

In a side-icer there should be a solid insulated partition between the ice chamber and the food compartments. In this way the cold air is "baffled" in any attempt to sneak out into the food compartment. It must go down and around, collecting heat and odors from the food and traveling all the way back to the ice chamber to be re-cooled and deodorized. Good circulation is necessary to dryness and absence of odors, as well as to evenness of temperature.

Both side- and top-icers are good if well designed. The side-icer is often more convenient to ice; and the top-icer has the advantage of a broader drop for the cold air and less difference between the coldest and warmest place in the box, but the average temperatures are about the same.

Size, Too, Is Important.—Be sure that the refrigerator is big enough for the family needs, not only in winter, but in the good old summer time when more perishable foods are used, when the refrigerator must work harder to keep the temperatures down and when week-end guests are abundant. Almost, then, you need elastic, rubber refrigerators! So buy the refrigerator for your greatest need, not your smallest one, remembering it won't stretch.

Also, it is important that the ice chamber be the right size in proportion to the remainder of the box. It should occupy about one-third of the whole inner space and the smaller the box, the larger the relative size of the ice chamber.

Generally speaking, a family of two can get along with a refrigerator taking fifty pounds of ice. For the average family of four, 100-pound capacity is required.

Drain Pipes and Shelves.—"I've missed all the best advantages that came my way," said the blonde spinster, "because I had to go home and empty the pan under the refrigerator." Don't have a pan! Be sure there is a drain pipe, well fitted and easily disconnected, with a good water seal at the floor so that it lends itself gracefully both to cleaning and readjustment without danger of leakage. This small point means much to the housekeeper's serenity, and keeps her temper down, though not so important in lowering refrigerator temperature!

Again, the blonde spinster needed an automatic ice man. She got him by having an outside door into the ice chamber. No longer did she need to be at home when the ice man came!

Shelves should be of woven steel wires, well welded to steel bars, so that they, too, are easy to clean, hard to rust, and will neither slip nor sag.

Handles and Corners.—Round corners are easier to clean than square ones, but if you have more time than money, the more expensive round construction may be foregone. It is worth the money, however, to be sure that handles are heavy and close the doors easily and tightly. No use to buy a refrigerator and let it stand open.

Always the more you invest, the more interest you draw. The money invested in a really good, efficient refrigerator draws big interest in appetizing, wholesome food, economically stored.

HOW TO BRING UP A REFRIGERATOR IN THE WAY IT SHOULD GO.

Refrigerators must be properly fed and taken care of if you want them to do you credit. Long life and good service from a refrigerator are dependent on points like these:

Location.—Set your refrigerator in as cool a place as possible. It is hard on the refrigerator's efficiency to put it for your convenience too near the stove, or in the sun for the ice man's pleasure. Give it a fair location—no ice box craves a place in the sun. Fill it full of ice and allow it twenty-four hours to get the heat out of the box before you start to cool foods.

Feed It Plenty of Ice.—It costs less in the end, and you get more for your money, if you keep the ice chamber full. Never let it get more than half empty. When there is only a small piece of ice, it has more to overcome, melts more quickly and you pay more to get back to the necessary low temperatures again.

Cleanliness.—Cold and Cleanliness are the two slogans of food preservation. Keep dirt from getting into the box and you won't need to work to get it out. An ounce of prevention is worth several pounds of cure here. This means washing the ice, if necessary, before it goes into the refrigerator, wiping off milk bottles, washing lettuce, etc.

Have the proper kind of containers to put the food in, to save space, permit proper circulation and prevent spoilage and "spillage." There are enamel and glass containers, with and without tops, and attractive nests of bowls to be had at varying prices to suit all purses. The many glass bottles with screw tops that foods come in these days make perfect and economical containers for food storage.

With these precautions there will be no need to heat up the refrigerator by giving it hot baths. Wipe it out with cold water and sal soda (one tablespoon to four quarts) once a week. Monday morning, when food and ice are low, is a good time for this, or Friday before loading with ice and food for the week-end.

Dry with a clean cloth. Work rapidly and use a double strength washing soda solution of cold or tepid water to pour down the drain to remove slime. There will be little need of extreme measures, of long brushes or the use of hot water, if foods are carefully stored.

Clear the Way for the Cold Air.—Note the places where the cold air drops from the ice and where, when warmed, it goes back to the ice, and do not shut them off by stacking food in these spots. Also, do not shut off the air passages where the warmed air goes up and into the ice chamber again. Air currents (good circulation) are just as necessary to efficient refrigeration as is insulation. In other words, leave air spaces between everything and everything else, so that the cold air can be on its way. When the inside of the refrigerator begins to look like a sardine can, it is a reproach to you.

A False Economy.—Don't wrap the ice in a mistaken effort to make it last. Ice must melt in order to cool. It takes up the heat and sacrifices itself to serve you. Hoard it and like a miser's money it can do you no good.

Fair Play.—Never put hot foods into the refrigerator. This is taking an unfair advantage. Cool jellies, soups, custards, etc., to room temperature before putting them in the ice box.

Go in and out of the refrigerator quickly and close the door behind you every time. Take a tray and remove several things at once. Every time you carelessly open the door of a refrigerator into a hot room, you cause an appreciable increase in ice meltage.

156.—Typical Details of Household Refrigerator Construction.—It would be impossible to illustrate in this book even a fractional part of the many makes and types of refrigerators manufactured in the United States, and for that reason but a very few of them, selected at random, are illustrated and described* in this Article:

RHINELANDER "AIRTITE" REFRIGERATORS.

Lining.—One piece patented porcelain lining. All surfaces are beautiful, snow white porcelain as smooth as glass—no cracks or seams, with broadly rounded corners at top and bottom, greatly simplifying cleaning. The inside linings of all doors are full porcelain, pan shaped, in keeping with the beautiful, snow-white interior.

Hardware.—Heavy brass, nickel plated, hand buffed hardware used throughout, made oversize to insure extra wear. Self-acting type lock takes immediate action and holds door air-tight.

Equipped for Ice or Mechanical Refrigeration.—Ice or coil chamber is placed *inside* of the porcelain lining, instead of outside, to insure free, unobstructed circulation of cold air around the compartment as well as through it. Many models are equipped for ready installation of electric refrigerating unit. Hanger bolts, and capped openings in the rear near top of ice chamber, are standard equipment on these models; suitable either for ice or mechanical refrigeration. Other

*Descriptions are those of the manufacturer, and are to be accepted only for what they may prove to be worth.

models, for ice only, have extra-sturdy ice racks, more than twice as strong as necessary, made from heavily coated galvanized steel, with galvanized iron baffles in ice compartment to direct air circulation.

Shelves.—Rhinelander shelves are woven in our factory, electrically welded, and then heavily coated with tin giving a clean, bright and lasting finish. Shelves designed to insure free circulation of air.

Casters.—Ball bearing lignum-vitae casters.

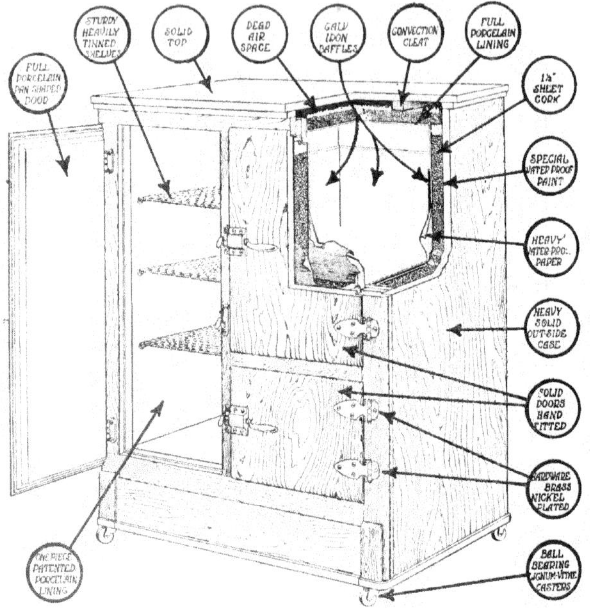

FIG. 169.—DETAILS OF RHINELANDER REFRIGERATOR CONSTRUCTION.

Insulation.—One and one-half inch pure sheet cork compressed in position in intimate contact with waterproof, saturated-felt covered lining surface, and sealed in with special waterproof compound.

Exterior.—Heavy Airtite solid hardwood construction. No thin, set-in, sunken panels. Triple coated porcelain or natural hardwood finish.

Manufactured by Rhinelander Refrigerator Company, Rhinelander, Wisconsin.

McCRAY RESIDENCE REFRIGERATORS.

Compartments.—Compartments to be as per manufacturer's standard for each size.

General Construction.—The general construction shall be of cork and wood; two inches of 100% pure cork-board. Both sides sheathed to approximate thickness of four inches.

Exterior Finish.—Exterior finish to be as per manufacturer's standard for model selected. (a) Exterior front, top and two ends shall

FIG. 170.—McCRAY HOUSEHOLD REFRIGERATOR.

be covered with No. 20 gauge sheet steel finished in white lacquer. Back and bottom covered with No. 24 gauge galvanized sheet iron. (b) Exterior front, top and two ends shall be finished in quarter-sawed oak, well filled and varnished. Back and bottom to be finished with 13/16-inch matched yellow pine, well painted.

Interior Finish.—The interior finish of food compartments shall be lined with highest grade of one-piece porcelain fused on steel. Ice or coil compartment shall be lined with No. 24 gauge sheet iron, finished with white refrigerator enamel.

Doors.—Door fronts to be as per manufacturer's standard for model selected. (a) Door fronts shall be covered with lacquer finished pressed steel to match exterior front finish of refrigerator. (b) Door fronts shall be of five-ply veneered wood, flush panel type, finished to match exterior front of refrigerator.

Shelves.—All refrigerators shall be equipped with bar steel shelving, electrically welded, heavily tinned and easily removable for cleaning.

Hardware.—All hardware shall be of substantial pattern nickel plated bronze. All fasteners shall be of self-closing bar or roller type.

Circulation System.—Ice or coil compartment shall be on left top side of refrigerator, well baffled to insure good circulation of cold air, and to have suitable water-sealed drain pipe to outside of unit.

Base or Foundation.—Refrigerators to have wood base approximately four inches high. Ball bearing casters to be supplied where necessary.

Special Equipment.—Special base for enclosure of automatic refrigeration machine to be furnished on order and same to be finished to conform with body of refrigerator. Hasps for locks to be furnished on order, but locks will be furnished by others.

Detailed Specifications.—All refrigerators shall be constructed of 100% pure compressed cork-board insulation and thoroughly kiln-dried lumber, especially selected and well adapted to the service required. The cork-board insulation shall be inserted in a substantial and well braced wood framing, all seams of the cork-board to be sealed with odorless, hot asphalt cement, each side then covered with heavy, waterproof, odorless insulating sheathing, forming sections in which the insulation has been hermetically sealed, ready to receive finishing sheathing on both sides of the sections. The thickness of cork-board insulation shall be as indicated.

The finishing sheathing on the exterior of all refrigerators shall be approximately 13/16-inch thick and consist of suitable material to give desired exterior finish.

All wood surfaces exposed to view, which are to be finished in natural wood or stained to match other trim, shall be well sanded and finished with one coat of filler, one coat of shellac and two coats of best refrigerator varnish.

Refrigerators for All Purposes.—There is a McCray Refrigerator for every purpose, the result of 37 years of experience.

Manufactured by McCray Refrigerator Co., Kendallville, Indiana.

GIBSON "ALL PORCELAIN" REFRIGERATORS.

General Description.—The Gibson "All Porcelain" refrigerators are, without doubt, the finest in the country. The beautiful exteriors and interiors of dazzling white porcelain are immaculate, sanitary and durable. The new Gibson cast aluminum door frame construction (patent pending) is one of the greatest advances that has been made in refrigerator construction in years. It prevents warping or swelling of the doors and insures many years of added life to the refrigerator.

Interior.—Three models are equipped with galvanized iron lined ice compartments and seamless porcelain provision compartments. All other

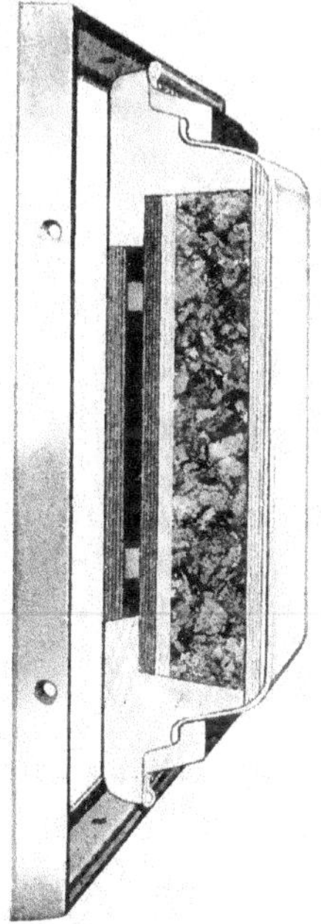

FIG. 171.—GIBSON REFRIGERATOR DOOR CONSTRUCTION, SHOWING CORKBOARD INSULATION.

models have porcelain lined ice compartments. All doors are lined with porcelain door plates.

Insulation.—The Gibson "All Porcelain" refrigerators are insulated with 100 per cent. pure cork-board, sealed air-tight with hydrolene cement and, in addition, have many layers of waterproof asphalt saturated charcoal sheathing, insulating felt, and polar board. The insulation and wall construction is unexcelled for economy of ice consumption or efficiency when used in connection with electric refrigeration.

Hardware.—The locks and hinges are heavy cast manganese bronze, triple nickel-plated and highly polished. The doors are all equipped with Wirf's air-tight cushion gaskets.

Shelves.—The new Gibson flat wire shelves (patent pending) are used in all models. They are easier to clean and dishes slide on them without tipping.

Electric Refrigeration.—Leading manufacturers of electric ice machines have approved the "Gibson" for use with their machines. Ice machine bases are carried in stock for Gibson "All Porcelain" refrigerators. The Gibson "All Porcelain" refrigerators are equipped with hangar bolts and sleeve outlets, so they are suitable for present ice needs and future electric refrigeration requirements.

All Metal Refrigerators.—A line of Gibson "All Metal" refrigerators have an outside case of heavy galvanized steel finished in white enamel, with other attractive features. Gibson's "One-Piece" porcelain line of white porcelain lined refrigerators has merited great favor.

Manufactured by Gibson Refrigerator Co., Greenville, Michigan.

SEEGER ALL-PORCELAIN REFRIGERATORS.

Circulation.—A major feature of efficiency in the Seeger refrigerator a remarkable food, ice and power conserving device, whether ice or electrical refrigeration is used—is the Seeger system of air circulation, the original "Siphon System." It is installed only in Seeger refrigerators and accomplishes the successful preservation of foods and the necessary low temperature with a minimum consumption of ice or electricity.

The Seeger original siphon system, briefly, continuously keeps in circulation, throughout the interior, a vigorous current of air that is dry and clean, and keeps the refrigerator's every nook and corner pure and sweet at all times.

The siphons form a partition between the ice or cooling unit chamber and the food chambers. The cold air—heavier in the ice or cooling unit chamber than in the food compartments—continuously sinks to and through the grate beneath the ice block or cooling unit, then to the slanting deflector plate that is seen beneath the grate. Next the deflector plate projects the air into the food chamber. In the food chambers the air expands, and in so doing consumes any and all heat atoms that are existent there, and picks up all odors, moisture and impurities.

Finally, the siphons draw the air back into the ice or cooling unit chamber where all the odors and impurities that have been gathered up are condensed and drained off with the water from the melting ice or cooling unit. So long as any ice remains the circulation continues.

Insulation.—Seeger all-porcelain refrigerators are insulated with pure sheet corkboard, 2 inches thick laid between four sheets of waterproof paper.

Interior.—The new seamless, one-piece porcelain interior is made in our own factories, of vitreous porcelain on Armco iron and is in one entire piece, including food chambers, ice chamber and drip pan. The corners are round and the surface is guaranteed non-chippable. A new improvement is the providing of fastenings, as part of the interior lining, for the hanging of electrical refrigeration units.

Exterior.—The exterior is of the same vitreous porcelain as the interior and is finished with nickel-silver (German silver) trimmings. The porcelain exterior surface, like that of the interior, is guaranteed non-chippable.

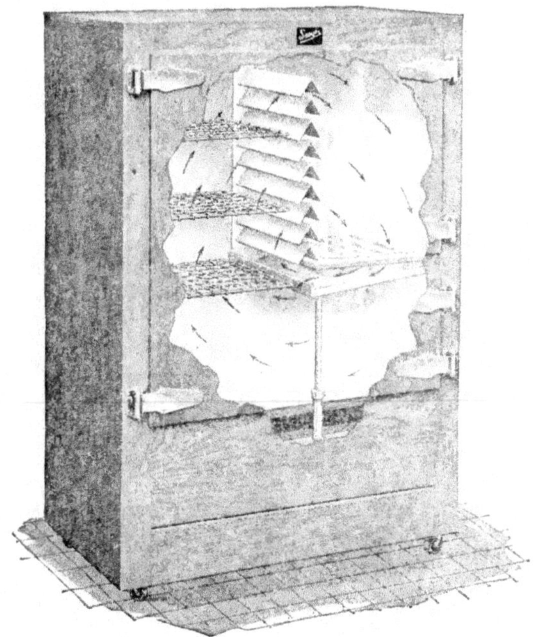

FIG. 172.—SEEGER ORIGINAL SYPHON SYSTEM CORK INSULATED REFRIGERATOR.

Hardware.—Each door, large or small, is fitted with locks and hinges exactly suited for each refrigerator's requirements. All locks are of solid brass and of roller type, fitted with non-breakable springs. Where rubber covered compression gaskets are used, the hinges are of spring brass and are fitted with steel bushings, washers and pins. Where no gaskets are used, the hinges are solid brass.

Manufactured by Seeger Refrigerator Company, St. Paul, Minnesota.

JEWETT SOLID PORCELAIN REFRIGERATORS.

Refrigerator Principles.—Jewett Solid Porcelain refrigerators combine all four basic essentials by which the true value of any refrigerator may be judged: (1) Absolute sanitation, without which no refrigerator, regardless of its other features, is safe as a storage place for food; (2) Efficient insulation, an unseen essential which really determines the cost of operating the freezing unit and the number of years of service it will render; (3) Perfect circulation, which produces dry, crisp air in the refrigerator instead of a damp, mouldy atmosphere; and (4) Durable construction, without which a refrigerator soon wears out and is a poor purchase no matter how cheap its initial price.

The Famous Solid Porcelain Interiors.—It is unfortunate that the descriptions of refrigerator linings have never been standardized like the nomenclature of bathroom equipment. "Jewett" solid porcelain linings are moulded from selected clays with a highly glazed china finish fused on the surface in our pottery. All other so-called "porcelain" linings are made of thin sheet metal with a coating of enamel painted or baked on them. There is just as vast a difference between them and "Jewett" linings as between a *solid porcelain* bathtub and an *enameled iron* one.

These solid porcelain linings are an inch and a quarter thick and even without the super-insulation that surrounds them, these crocks alone would store up the cold and maintain low temperatures more uniformly than most complete refrigerators.

Insulation.—The illustration shows the construction of the walls, floors and ceilings of "Jewett" solid porcelain refrigerators. The aggregate thickness is 5-3/8 inches, which is almost double the thickness of the wall construction used in any other refrigerator.

The exterior case is of solid ash, carefully doweled and glued; next come two courses heavy waterproof insulating paper, then a 1-inch sheet of pure cork, then two more courses heavy waterproof insulating paper, then a course of 7/8-inch tongued and grooved lumber, then 1¼ inches more of pure cork, then a course of waterproof insulating paper, then the solid porcelain lining 1-¼ inches thick.

Outside of the two courses of lumber necessary to give the proper strength and rigidity, the insulation of the "Jewett" solid porcelain refrigerator consists entirely of *pure cork*, which is the most efficient form of insulation known.

Circulation.—A dry atmosphere in a refrigerator is essential for the preservation of food. In a refrigerator with poor or no ciculation, all things are damp, moist and moldy. Then there is an odor. Dryness prevents all these things.

The cold air ducts and warm air flues in the "Jewett" solid porcelain refrigerators are designed to take advantage of the well-known principle that cold air falls and warm air rises. On account of its greater weight, the cold air descends from the ice compartment into the food compartment below, and forces the warmer air in the upper part

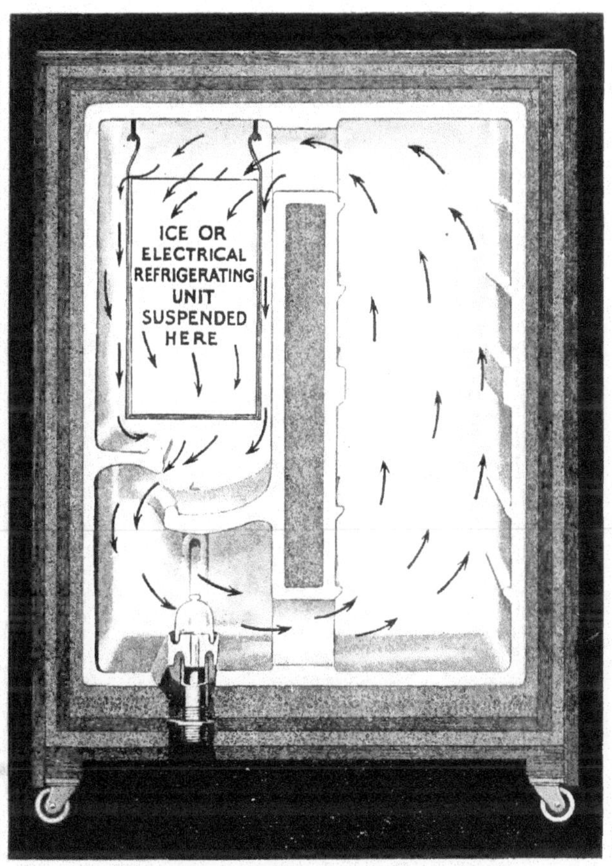

FIG. 173.—SECTION OF JEWETT SOLID PORCELAIN REFRIGERATOR SHOWING CORK INSULATION.

of the opposite compartment over on to the freezing unit where the heat, moisture and odors are absorbed by condensation. After being cooled and purified, the air again descends and passes through the refrigerator back to the ice chamber, thus forming a vigorous and continuous rotation of the entire atmosphere in the refrigerator.

The design of the "Jewett" ice compartment is radically different from the type prevailing in ordinary refrigerators. Being suspended in the metal rack, the freezing unit is constantly surrounded by air and the cold air falls easily from all the sides as well as from the bottom.

Exterior Finish.—The outer case is made of thoroughly seasoned brown ash carefully doweled and glued. Solid ash is particularly adapted for refrigerator purposes because it is less affected by changes of temperature and humidity than almost any other wood.

"Jewett" refrigerators are made in three standard finishes. Finish A—exterior of natural color, carefully selected, straight grain, brown ash with three coats of varnish. Finish B—exterior painted with five coats of white enamel. Finish C—exterior of white opaque glass 7/16-inch thick, secured with heavy, solid nickel-silver (not nickel plated) trim, highly polished.

When special finishes are desired, we can furnish the cases with three coats of flat white which can be enameled to match surrounding woodwork. Or we can build the exterior of any wood desired and finish to sample or ship without stain for finish upon installation.

Hardware.—"Jewett" refrigerators have always been famous for the quality and durability of their hardware. The doors are secured by lever fasteners that close automatically with the slamming of the door, preventing the condensation (commonly called "sweating"), swollen jambs, etc., which result when doors are not tightly closed.

The hardware on natural or grey finish "Jewetts" is solid brass, highly polished; on white enamel or opaque glass finish it is solid nickel-silver (not nickel plated), and is much heavier and more substantial than the hinges and latches on any other make of refrigerator.

Doors.—No matter how well the rest of a refrigerator is built if the doors are light and poorly insulated or do not fit tight it cannot be a safe and efficient storage chest for your food. The doors on a "Jewett" are heavy, substantial and well insulated. They are made of solid ash with plain exterior faces; no veneer to peel off; no moldings or panels to catch dust; no chance that they will warp or sag. They have heavy 7/8-inch overlaps on all sides instead of the usual 3/8-inch or 1/2-inch overlap on ordinary refrigerators and this permits the use of a heavy, live-rubber (not fabric) compression gasket which makes the doors absolutely air tight.

Shelves are constructed of 1/4-inch rod spot welded to 5/16-inch cross-bars heavily coated with pure block tin after fabrication. These shelves rest on ribs moulded into the porcelain lining and are easily removable for cleaning.

Manufactured by Jewett Refrigerator Co., Buffalo, New York.

REOL "LIFETIME" REFRIGERATORS.

Construction.—Custom-built to endure. Solid frame-work of ash posts, with cross-members of equal strength and durability. Vertical posts run the full height of the box reinforced at bottom with pressed steel angles. Heavy piano-type casters are set into lower end of these posts. Interlocking joints, rigidly securing the cross members to

FIG. 174.—DETAILS OF CONSTRUCTION OF REOL CUSTOM BUILT REFRIGERATOR—ARROWS (3) POINT TO CORKBOARD INSULATION AND (4) TO ASPHALT CEMENT.

the vertical members. Glued and screwed into a rigid solid foundation to hold the balance of the structure. Cores for doors milled from one solid piece of ash, made so that they will fit closely and not warp. Rabbits on the doors, fitting into ledges on the framework, effectually diminishing leakage.

Insulation.—Two inches of solid sheet cork, fastened securely to the framework. Fits close at all sides, forming an effective and permanent barrier against the passage of heat, and protected with heavy waterproof coating. Solid insulated doors, with extra insulation filling out air space formed by vitreous porcelain lining. Insulation extends through front stiles and rails, thus eliminating, to a large degree, one of the points where heat leakage is most evident in ordinary refrigerator construction. Insulated baffle board, directing downward the flow of cold air, and affording complete circulation and even temperatures in all sections of the food compartment.

Interior.—Extra heavy, one-piece vitreous porcelain crock fused on heavy rustless Armco iron, with corners rounded and curved lips provided at front, making the inside sanitary and easy to clean. Extra heavy interwoven steel wire shelves, rust-proof.

Exterior.—Flush hardwood exterior, with sections firmly joined together to form one solid piece. Top set flush, making a smooth finish. Rounded corners at top. Heavy and substantial hardware that is solidly fastened to the framework, operates easily and amply supporting doors when open or closed. Springless latches that are self-closing, without effort or slamming.

Manufactured by Reol Refrigerator Co., Baltimore, Maryland.

BELDING-HALL "ALL PORCELAIN EXTERIOR" REFRIGERATORS.

Description.—Belding-Hall all porcelain refrigerators are constructed with porcelain exterior and one-piece seamless porcelain lined ice and provision chambers. Insulated especially for mechanical refrigeration.

FIG. 175.—CORNER SECTION OF CORKBOARD INSULATED BELDING-HALL REFRIGERATOR.

Materials.—The best grade of 18-gauge Armco Rust Resisting Ingot Iron is used throughout. The lumber used in the construction of the walls of these cases, also in the doors, has been chosen with care to avoid swelling from climatic changes.

Insulation.—The corner section illustration shows our 2-inch corkboard insulation, and all joints and corners are filled with an odorless pitch which prevents air leakage as it seals all the crevices where the cork cannot fit absolutely tight. The door construction is identical with the walls of the refrigerator.

Hardware.—All locks, strikes and hinges, as well as all screws, are heavy solid brass, nickel-plated, of the latest and most efficient design. The trimming around the doors and corners of the refrigerator is heavy aluminum, nickel-plated.

Metal Ice Rack.—One of the greatest improvements is our solid metal ice rack for which we claim, and the trade concedes, many points of excellence. Also, our new air trap.

Manufactured by Belding-Hall Electrice Corporation, Belding, Michigan.

SCHROEDER "THERMO FLO" REFRIGERATOR.

Refrigerating Unit.—The Inman Thermatic unit which operates on nature's thermo-syphon principle is described in detail as follows: Tank

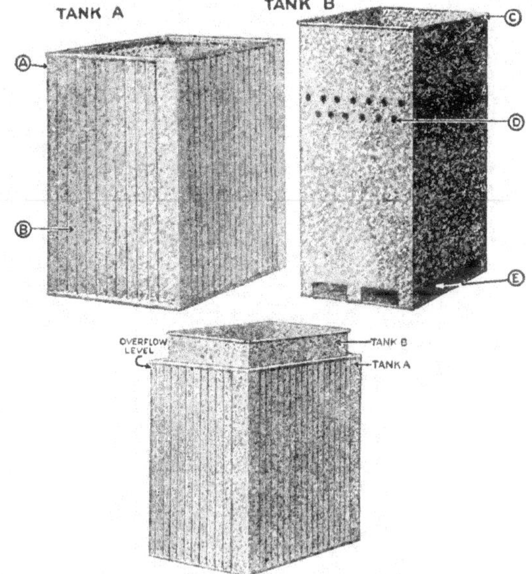

FIG. 176.—SCHROEDER THERMO FLO REFRIGERATOR TANKS.

B fits inside of tank A as shown in the illustration. The ice is placed in tank B and cold water is poured over the ice until it reaches the level of the lower row of holes in Tank B. As the colder water seeks the

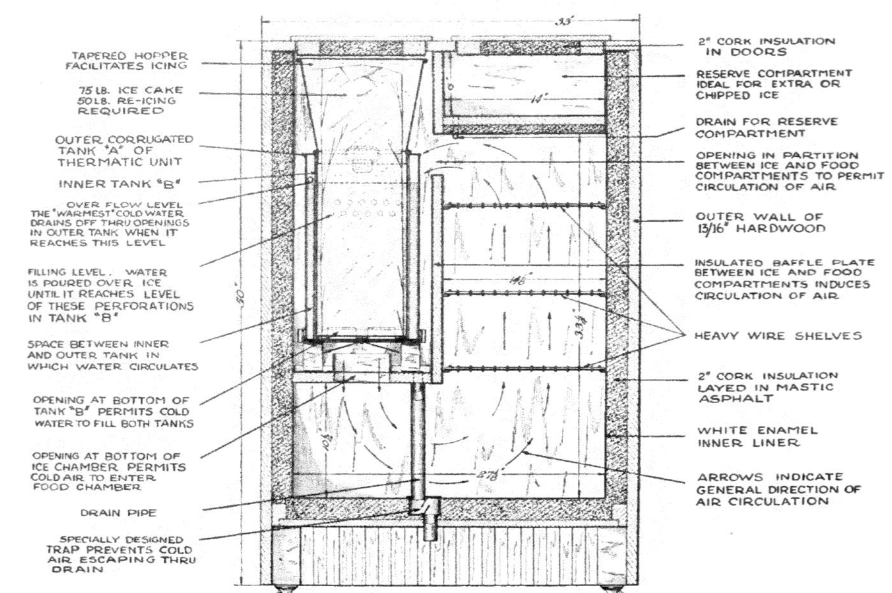

FIG. 177.—DETAILS OF CONSTRUCTION OF SCHROEDER THERMO FLO 50-LB. RE-ICER.

lower levels this immediately creates a circulation of water from top to bottom of ice chamber. This circulation is maintained as long as there is even a small piece of ice in the tank. Tank B has ¾-inch corrugations which increase the cooling area of the ice compartment from 2550 to 7072 square inches—or nearly three times the area of a flat surface. As the ice melts the over-flow is carried off through a row of holes near the top of one side of tank A. Inasmuch as the warmer water rises to the top and is carried off through these holes, the coldest water always remains in the refrigerating unit. The over-flow is carried off through

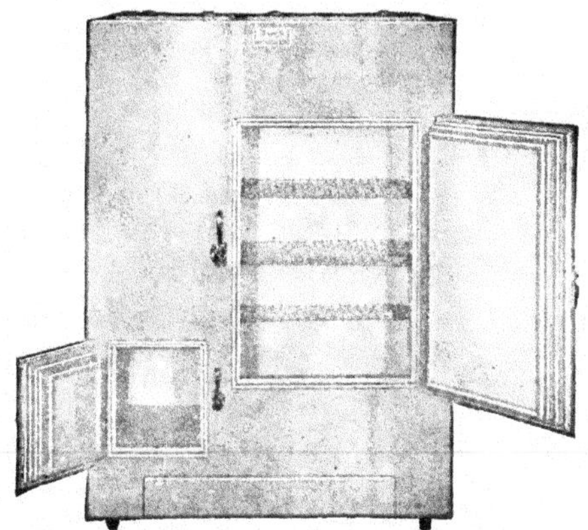

FIG. 178.—SCHROEDER THERMO FLO REFRIGERATOR.

a drain at the bottom of the ice chamber. The fact that it utilizes water as a refrigerant in addition to the ice, results in: (1) Uniform low temperature; (2) Practically 100% efficiency out of every piece of ice; (3) Economical consumption of ice.

Circulation of Air.—The circulation of air within the refrigerator is always at the maximum because the refrigerant is always above the insulated baffle plate which separates the ice and food compartments. When ice alone is used as the refrigerant, the circulation of air diminishes as the ice melts away below the top of the baffle plate. The circulation of air is a highly important factor in maintaining constant, low temperatures.

Insulation.—In order that the thermatic unit may function at its highest efficiency, the influence of outside temperatures and air currents must be held to a minimum. For this reason 2-inch sheet cork, laid in mastic asphalt is used in all walls and doors.

Top Icer.—The Thermo Flo is a top icer due to the thermatic unit. This feature eliminates the customary abuse, by the housekeeper, of putting all kinds of foods in the ice compartment.

Reserve Compartment.—The reserve compartment above the food chamber is entirely separate from the rest of the refrigerator. It is designed to hold reserve ice, chipped ice, or for special cooling purposes. Its drain connects with the main drain pipe.

Exterior Finish.—The outer cabinet of the Thermo Flo refrigerator is built of selected ash, and reflects the skill of master cabinetmakers. A variety of finishes including white and gray lacquer are furnished as specified. Only high grade fittings and hardware are used. Self-locking door handles are standard equipment.

Interior.—The interior is finished in white enamel of highest quality. Three shelves in the food compartment are made of heavily tinned wire.

Humidity.—The fact that the Thermo Flo uses both ice and water results in just the right amount of humidity for proper food preservation.

Size.—The Thermo Flo refrigerator is made in two sizes, the 50-lb. re-icer and the 75-lb. re-icer, requiring 75 lbs. and 100 lbs. original icing, respectively. The 50-lb. re-icer has outside dimensions of 33¼x22⅞x52½ inches and a food compartment capacity of 6 cubic feet. The 75-lb. re-icer has outside dimensions of 38⅞x22⅞x52½ inches and a food compartment capacity of 8 cubic feet.

Manufactured.—The Thermo Flo refrigerator is manufactured by the same organization which introduced the JaSeL ice box and the National ice chest—The J-S Refrigeration Division of the John Schroeder Lumber Co., Milwaukee, Wisconsin.

SERVEL ELECTRIC REFRIGERATION FOR HOUSEHOLD USE.

Exterior.—The Servel new steel cabinets are constructed of especially selected "Armco" steel carefully lead-coated as an absolute protection against rust. The steel shell is given two applications of oil base primer coat, after which the ground coat is slowly and carefully baked on under a low temperature, producing a finish which will neither peel nor scale. Next, several coats of genuine white Duco are applied, which are each allowed to air dry. The slow process of air drying, while it creates an additional factory cost, produces a much better appearing and more lasting finish than can ever be expected under artificial or forced drying.

Interior.—The porcelain liners are of the box type, and are so constructed, with double lock flanges, that bolt holes or screw holes are entirely eliminated except those required for tank and shelf supports.

This produces an absolutely sanitary liner and eliminates all chance of flaking of the porcelain finish, due to uneven strain such as results from the use of screws or bolts.

Chilling Unit.—The chilling units are of tinned copper and have front panels and ice cube tray-fronts of genuine porcelain.

Insulation.—The insulation is, of course, pure compressed corkboard thoroughly impregnated with hydrolene, 1½ inches thick on top and sides on the S-5, 2 inches thick top and sides on the S-7 and S-10; with a 3-inch bottom thickness on all models.

FIG. 179.—SERVEL ELECTRIC CORKBOARD INSULATED REFRIGERATOR.

All seams in the corkboard are filled with hydrolene. Waterproof paper is then applied over the corkboard as added seal against air leaks. The insulation is applied against the liner, and there is an air space of from ¼-inch to ½-inch between the insulation and the exterior metal.

Manufactured by the Servel Corporation, Evansville, Indiana.

COPELAND "DEPENDABLE" ELECTRIC REFRIGERATORS.

Model.—No. C-5-P; 60¼ inches high, 22 inches deep, 28 inches wide. (One of 5 models for small homes and apartments. Also two styles of model No. 215, with machine overhead and covered with hood; also four Copeland-Seeger models.) Construction, rugged and accurately mortised.

Interior.—White, vitreous porcelain, with rounded coves. Ice cube drawers have bright metal finish. Ice cube capacity, 90 cubes, or 6 pounds at one freezing. Shelf space, 7.64 square feet; shelves, woven

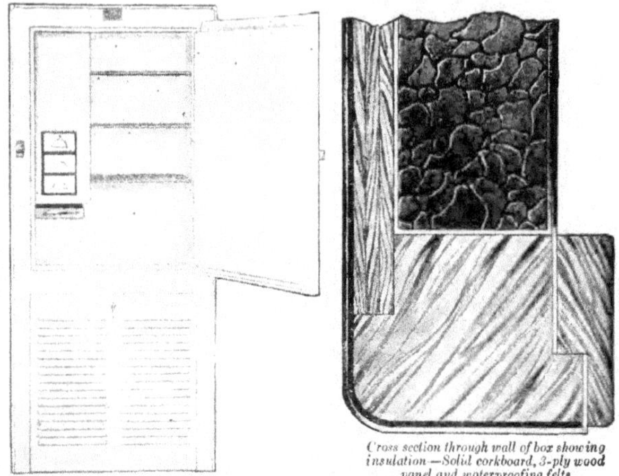

Cross section through wall of box showing insulation—Solid corkboard, 3-ply wood panel and waterproofing felts

FIG. 180.—EXTERIOR VIEW AND WALL SECTION OF COPELAND ELECTRIC REFRIGERATOR.

wire, retinned. Food storage capacity, 5 cubic feet. Defrosting receiver eliminates drain pipe.

Insulation.—Two inches solid corkboard, walls, top, door and bottom, hermetically sealed and moisture-proofed by special hydrolene treatment and protected by all-metal sheathing, prevents odors and deterioration.

Exterior.—Exterior finish, white pyroxylin lacquer on steel. Trim, bright metal molding. Hardware, extra-heavy automatic.

Refrigeration.—Efficient ⅙ horsepower motor; quiet operation, well-designed valves, accurately fitted bearings, high grade materials, skilled workmanship, exceptionally fine inspection, most efficient of its kind Connects with electric light socket.

Manufactured by Copeland Products Co., Detroit, Michigan.

157.—Notes on the Testing of Household Refrigerators.— While there are no generally accepted and approved methods for the testing of either ice or machine cooled household refrigerators, and virtually all tests made thus far are subject to considerable interpretation as to the results obtained, yet much progress has been made and there is reason to expect that some suitable and satisfactory *standard* method of testing household refrigerators may soon be arrived at and be generally accepted by those most interested in the subject.

The Chicago Tribune originally published some data and suggestions by Dr. W. A. Evans for a practical "Refrigerator Score Card," for refrigerators using ice, which Forest O. Rick later combined with data from various sources, including the U. S. Bureau of Standards and the Good Housekeeping Institute, to produce a refrigerator score card substantially as follows:

REFRIGERATOR SCORE CARD

Name of manufacturer..
Name or other method of designating refrigerator..

	Test Items	Perfect	Score
1.	Temperature of food chamber	45%	%
2.	Ice economy	20	
3.	Humidity	8	
4.	Circulation	7	
5.	Interior finish	12	
6.	Drainage	3	
7	Exterior finish	5	
	Total	100%	%

EXPLANATION OF SCORE CARD

1. *Temperature Test*—Standard conditions for test demand refrigerator to be in a room free from drafts and at an even temperature. Box should not contain food. Door should not be opened except when taking readings. Refrigerator should be thoroughly chilled for 48 hours before making test. Have the ice chamber full. Place thermometer in the center of the food chamber. Make twelve readings at intervals of one hour. Take room temperature simultaneously. Score as follows:

SCORE FOR TEMPERATURE

Temperature, F	Rate
40°	45
45	43
50	36
55	23
60	9
over 60	0

2. *Ice Economy.*—Refrigerator should be thoroughly chilled for 48

hours before starting test. Weigh ice at the start of test proper. Weigh ice left at termination of test proper. Obtain data:

(a) Temperature of food chamber (t).
(b) Temperature of room (T).
(c) Square feet of surface exposure (S), calculated on exterior dimensions.

To determine Ice Economy, substitute in the following formula:

$$R = \frac{I \times 144}{S \times (T - t)}$$

where R is the rate of heat transmission, which may be defined as the number of B.t.u. that pass through one square foot of surface daily when the difference between the surface is 1° F.; I is the number of pounds of ice melted daily; 144 is the B.t.u. required to melt one pound of ice; S is the surface exposure; T is the average atmospheric temperature; and t is the average temperature of food chamber. Score as follows:

SCORE FOR HEAT TRANSMISSION

Value for R	Rate
1.13	20
1.63	18
2.00	16
2.33	14
2.66	12
3.00	10
3.33	8
3.66	6
4.00	4
4.33	2
4.66	1
5.00	0

3. *Humidity.*—In making humidity tests, a wet and dry bulb thermometer should be used. Take twelve readings at intervals of one hour. See U. S. Bureau of Standards' tables* for readings calculated upon differences in temperatures of wet and dry bulb thermometers. Score as follows:

SCORE FOR HUMIDITY

Humidity	Rate
55 to 65%	8.0
65 to 76	7.5
45 to 55	7.5
40 to 45	7.2
75 to 80	6.4
30 to 40	6.0
80 to 85	4.8
20 to 30	4.8
85 to 95	2.4
90 and over	0.0
20 and under	0.0

4. *Circulation of Air.*—Credit a maximum of 5 for probability that cold air will readily pass from the ice compartment to and through the food compartment and back again to the ice. If ice compartment is ample, credit 2. If doors do not fit snugly, subtract 1. If any wall is moist, subtract 3.

5. *Interior Finish.*—Ease of cleaning refers to cleaning of food chamber, all shelves therein, and the drain pipes. If ease of cleaning is ideal, credit 5. If interior finish is hard and non-absorbent, credit 2. If color is white, credit 5.

*See Appendix for tables mentioned.

6. *Drainage.*—See that the trap in the drain pipe works. If there is proper trapping, credit 2. If there is proper tubing, credit 1.

7. *Exterior Finish.*—If exterior, including doors, has solid surface, easily cleaned, credit 1. If finish is durable and lasting, instead of easily flaked or chipped, credit 2. If hardware is simply constructed, durable and easily handled, credit 2.

John R. Williams, M.D., carried on considerable research into refrigeration in the home to obtain data for a paper to be presented before the Third International Congress of Refrigerating Industries. Dr. Williams obtained considerable interesting information in reference to the construction and performance of household refrigerators in actual use, the room temperatures under which they operate, the box temperatures at which food is stored, the relative amounts of ice used, and so forth. He points out most emphatically that the weakness of most "ice boxes" is in poor insulation, having found that very few refrigerators in common use have an efficiency above 25 per cent. He says:

> Indeed the low priced boxes used in the homes of working people are probably less than 15 per cent. efficient. This means that of 100 pounds of ice put into a refrigerator, at least 80 pounds were used in neutralizing the heat which percolates through the walls. It is worthy of note that the market is flooded with these shoddy ice boxes. No less than 75 different makes were found among the 243 examined.

The U. S. Bureau of Standards, the New York Tribune Institute, the University of Illinois, the Good Housekeeping Institute, the National Electric Light Association, the Armour Institute of Technology, the Geo. B. Bright Engineering Laboratory, and probably many others, have performed interesting and valuable tests on ice and mechanically cooled refrigerators. The methods of testing have varied so widely, however, that the results of one laboratory are not safely comparable with the results of another; and it is in the direction of standardization of method of testing, so as to make the results of all properly conducted tests readily and safely available for comparison, that attention should be given.

Household refrigerators, as at present produced, may be divided into three main classes:

(a) Ice cooled.
(b) Ice or mechanically cooled.
(c) Mechanically cooled.

It is not, in general, satisfactory to design and build refrigerators for dual service; that is, a refrigerator correctly designed for mechanical cooling may possibly be adjusted to ice, but the average ice refrigerator, though satisfactory with ice, usually is not satisfactory when mechanically cooled, for reasons having to do with temperature and insulation, as elaborated throughout this Chapter, and for still other reasons to be noted. The ice cooled refrigerator, on the one hand, aims to fulfill one major function:

1. To maintain at a suitable and reasonably uniform temperature a compartment for the storing of perishable foodstuffs.

The mechanically cooled refrigerator, on the other hand, must fulfill an additional major function:

2. To supply at all times cube-ice for table use.

These functions are sufficiently unrelated, or require sufficient correlation, as to make the two types of refrigerators somewhat dissimilar in design. Consequently, for the present, all tests on household refrigerators should be made from the standpoint of either ice cooling or mechanical cooling.

Considering first the ice cooled refrigerator, it is well understood that a "suitable" temperature must of necessity fall within a higher zone than would be possible with mechanical refrigeration, which higher zone of temperatures has both its advantages and its disadvantages. It imposes a narrow limit of safety for temperature fluctuations from the zone of satisfactory temperature operation; but it provides a temperature zone in which miscellaneous "moist foods" may be stored in the same compartment with the minimum loss of weight and natural flavor, and, because of the air purifying process constantly carried on by the absorption of odors by the water of ice meltage, it guarantees against the tainting of one food from the odors of another.

The temperature of melting ice being 32° F., the coldest air dropping into the food compartment will range from about

40° to 50° F., depending on the amount of ice in the ice chamber, the rate of air circulation, the room temperature and humidity, and the insulation of the refrigerator. The rise in temperature of the air in passing through the food compartment may range from 10 to 20 degrees, circulation, room temperature and insulation being the determining factors. United States Government tests* on a number of standard refrigerators show that the comparative rate of air flow in nine different refrigerators varied as much as 100 per cent under identical operating conditions. A wide range of temperature between the coldest and the warmest points in the food compartment indicates sluggish air circulation, if ice supply is adequate, not active air circulation. The variation in the food compartment temperature of an ice refrigerator should not be more than about 10 degrees; because since 40° F. is about the lowest temperature to be reasonably expected, 50° F. would then be the highest temperature, and 50° F. is near the temperature limit at which many perishable foodstuffs can be safely preserved.

The refrigerator using ice may be expected to have an average temperature in the food compartment from 20, or 25, to 35 degrees lower than the room temperature, but only the better types of refrigerators will approach the 35 degree temperature difference with a good supply of ice in the ice compartment and the room temperature at about 90° F. The average temperature of the food compartment of the better refrigerators under such conditions would then be about 55° F., and in the poorly constructed ones the average temperature would be 65° F. or more.

The average temperature of the food compartment of an ice cooled refrigerator may be reduced in three ways:

1. By breaking up the ice in the ice compartment so as to expose more surface to the circulating air.
2. By increasing the air circulation.
3. By increasing the insulation in the walls of the refrigerator.

If the ice is broken up to expose more surface to be melted and thus cause more heat to be absorbed from the circulating air of the refrigerator, a lower temperature will be produced

*U. S. Bureau of Standards Circular No. 55.

at the daily expense of labor and ice; and some improvement may be effected by the manufacturer through a change in the interior design of the refrigerator that will locate the ice compartment in a top-center position, and at no additional expense; but by increasing the thickness of *permanently efficient* insulation in the walls of the refrigerator, at a low percentage of increase in manufacturing cost, the food compartment may be so effectively isolated from outside heat influences as to make the maintenance of correct temperatures by the melting of ice a practical matter even on the hottest and the most humid days of the year. Experience has safely fixed this insulation at three inches of pure corkboard, when properly incorporated in the construction of the refrigerator.

From these few observations, it would appear to be of but limited value to test poorly designed and badly constructed refrigerators that are to be cooled with ice. Consequently, the first point to cover in planning for a test of an ice refrigerator should be a careful investigation into the design and construction of the unit; and if this research reveals a lack of reasonable consideration for basic principles of design and construction, as they are then generally known and understood, there probably will be good reason to abandon the intention to perform the test. Otherwise, the following test conditions should be observed:

(a) Refrigerators of identical shape and size must be selected for comparative test purposes. It is suggested that standard sizes be determined upon for a top-icer apartment refrigerator, a side-icer small residence refrigerator and a center-icer large residence refrigerator, and that all future tests be run on refrigerators as near those sizes as possible.

(b) A constant temperature room should be used, the temperature held uniform to within one degree Fahr. by electric heater placed within hollow walls of the test room and controlled by thermostat. A room temperature of at least 85° F. is suggested for test purposes.

(c) Control of the humidity of the constant temperature room should be effected by suitable means, tests having demonstrated that a considerable increase in the percentage of ice melting is effected by increasing the percentage of relative humidity in a constant temperature room from a low to a high point.

(d) The ice should be carefully regulated on the basis of weight, and of one piece, of size or shape suitable for the ice compartment of the class of unit tested.

(e) The ice should be only hard, "black" ice.

(f) The ice should be prepared outside the test room, and placed in the refrigerator during a fixed period, at the same hour, every day (24-hour icing), old ice to be removed and weighed simultaneously.

(g) The food compartment of the refrigerator should be empty, it being known that over 90 per cent. of refrigerator losses are caused by the heat leakage through the walls of the refrigerator, and less than 10 per cent. in cooling food and opening doors, under normal household operation.

(h) Record of refrigerator temperatures should be made every hour, by suitable means, such record to be taken at three designated points in

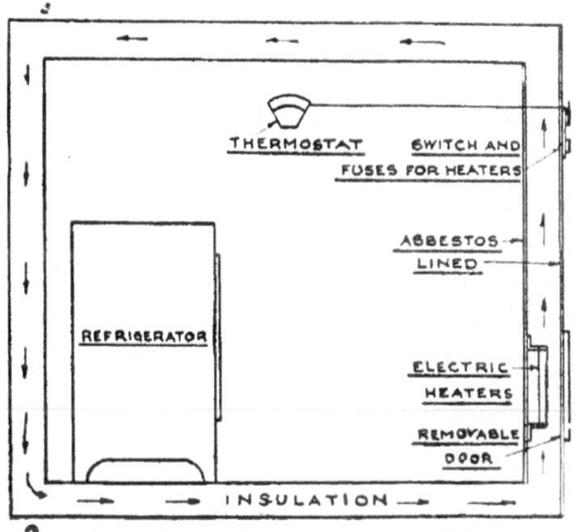

FIG. 181.—CONSTANT TEMPERATURE TESTING ROOM—HOLLOW WALL TYPE.

the food compartment of the apartment refrigerator, at four points in the small residence refrigerator and at five points in the large residence refrigerator.

(i) Record of the relative humidity of the food compartment should be made simultaneous with temperatures, by suitable means.

(j) Drip water should be weighed every hour, and the record used as a check on the actual weight of ice melted during the test.

(k) Three days preliminary operation should be allowed to establish a temperature equilibrium in the walls of the refrigerator before the test proper should be started, and the test should then continue for 30 more days.

Tests performed under standardized conditions, values for such standards to be fixed upon a practical basis for test purposes and a basis most nearly conforming to the practices of the ice industry as regards service to the household, should be comparable, as to ice consumption, food compartment temperatures and humidity. And if to such test results is appended a record of the exact condition of the refrigerator wall construction, as to moisture, observed immediately after the conclusion of the 30-day test by cutting all the way through the wall construction to the interior lining, the ability of the refrigerator to maintain its efficiency will be more easily predicted.

Considering next the mechanically cooled refrigerator, the operation of the apparatus is intended to be automatic but conditions arise at times that make the simultaneous carrying on of its two major functions, previously mentioned, almost impossible. In designing the automatic control, a compromise is therefore effected in order to obtain the best all 'round performance possible.

By pressure or thermostatic control, the temperature of the cooling element is held at a more or less constant temperature at all times, because of the necessity of producing cube ice, instead of the machine being automatically controlled directly by the temperature of the food compartment.

It is thus apparent that the commonly used method of control is not capable, without readjustment, of maintaining a constant temperature in the food space under wide variations in room temperatures, such as are occasioned by the hour of the day or the season of the year. In general, there may reasonably be expected a three degree change in refrigerator temperature for each ten degrees alteration of room temperature, which will give some idea of the probable temperature fluctuation in the food compartment of a fair quality refrigerator under any given adjustment of automatic control. If the unit operates in a heated room where the temperature is subject to but slight variation day or night, winter or summer, its regulation is likely to be fairly good, without making seasonal adjustments of the regulating device; but under conditions not approaching such an ideal, foods are likely to be either frozen or insufficiently cooled.

These observations are based on a refrigerator cabinet of fair quality, as respects insulation; but as the permanent insulating qualities of mechanically cooled household refrigerators are improved, so the difficulties of food compartment temperature control are reduced. The well insulated unit, such as a cabinet containing three inches of pure corkboard set tightly against the interior lining at all points, is not sensitive to room temperature fluctuations to any appreciable degree, and consequently may easily perform its two major functions with that degree of accuracy required by a discriminating owner. At the same time, such a mechanical unit can be operated at a cost that will be low enough to justify the extra investment.

In testing mechanical units, the same test conditions should be observed as outlined for ice refrigerators, with but a few changes. The kilowatt-hours power consumption is measured instead of ice melted. A given quantity by weight of water at say 70° F. temperature is filled into standard cube trays that have been cooled to the same temperature, and the trays are placed in the refrigerator once every day for the cubes to be frozen, the frozen cubes from the day before being simultaneously removed. If it is desired to put a normal "food load" on either the ice cooled or the mechanically cooled refrigerators, same should amount to 8 B.t.u. per hour, per cubic foot of cabinet contents, same being introduced electrically by an immersion heater in a container of oil placed at a given point in the food compartment.

On account of the lower temperatures in general desired by owners and maintained in mechanical units, especial attention must be paid to the subject of condensed moisture within the wall construction of the mechanically cooled cabinet at the end of the 30-day test period.

CHAPTER XVII.

DEVELOPMENT OF THE CORKBOARD INSULATED ICE CREAM CABINET.

158.—Growth of the Ice Cream Industry.—Ancient records reveal that Saladin, Sultan of Egypt and Syria, sent Richard I, King of England, a frozen sherbet in the 12th century; that Marco Polo, the great Italian navigator, brought recipes for water and milk ices from Japan and China in the 13th century; and that Catherine d'Medici when leaving Florence, Italy, for France, in the 16th century, took with her certain chefs skilled in the preparation of frozen creams and ices.

Frozen desserts were, however, regarded as luxuries, to be indulged in only upon occasion, until comparatively recent times. In the United States, ice cream became popular as a table dessert among the colonists. The first public advertisement of ice cream appeared in *The Post Boy*, a New York paper, in 1786; but it was not until about 1851 that an attempt was made to manufacture ice cream in wholesale quantities. In that year John Fussell, a milk dealer in Baltimore, Maryland, became interested in ice cream in an effort to find a profitable outlet for surplus sweet cream that he had on hand from time to time. The manufacture of ice cream was undertaken as a side line, and sold at wholesale, but the business proved so profitable that Fussell disposed of his entire milk business and devoted his whole attention to the new industry. His remarkable success may be judged from the fact that he later established ice cream factories in Washington, Boston and New York City.

Perry Brazelton, of Mt. Pleasant, Iowa, studied the wholesale ice cream business in Fussell's Washington plant; and later established his own plant in St. Louis, Missouri, followed by still others in Cincinnati, Ohio, and Chicago, Illinois, which is indicative of the success that attended his efforts in the new industry in the Middle West. From then on there was a steady growth in this branch of the dairy industry, but rapid expansion did not begin until the shortage of natural ice in 1890 gave the art of ice making and refrigeration the impetus necessary to establish that industry on a successful commercial basis. Then great improvements in machinery, and methods of ice cream manufacture, were rapidly introduced during

FIG. 182.—CORKBOARD INSULATED LONG-DISTANCE REFRIGERATED ICE CREAM TRUCK.

the next two decades, until by the end of 1912 there was a reported total output of 154 million gallons of ice cream valued at 160 million dollars.

The National Association of Ice Cream Manufacturers was organized in 1906, to more effectively promote the interests of ice cream manufacturers by assisting the industry to develop along permanent, substantial lines, through standardization of factory operations, pure food laws, and so forth. Trade associations and trade papers did much to promote the welfare of the industry, by teaching a common-sense code of ethics and by acting as a clearing house for its numerous activities. Many schools and colleges took up the teaching of the principles and practices pertaining to the manufacture of ice creams and ices. Through the cooperation of these useful agencies, the public was enabled to receive such ample protection against impure and unsatisfactory ice cream products as to so solidly establish the industry that by the end of 1926 the output was 325 million gallons valued at 300 million dollars (wholesale).

159.—Ice and Salt Cabinets.—It has been noted that saltpetre mixed with snow was used for cooling liquids centuries ago in India, but the 17th century saw probably the first serious attempt to utilize that method of refrigeration to produce ice and frozen desserts. The low temperature produced by mixing ice and salt is due of course to the fact that salt lowers the melting point of ice to about 5° F. (−15° C.) and keeps it there until all the ice is melted by heat rapidly absorbed from surrounding objects, which explains why a can of freshly made ice cream placed in an insulated cabinet and surrounded with cracked ice and salt will harden by giving up its heat to the low temperature mixture at the expense of melting the ice, all as elaborated in the section of this book on "The Study of Heat." Since the ice is melted by heat extracted from the ice cream, and from the walls of the cabinet, which gets its heat from the surrounding atmosphere, it is necessary to set up in those cabinet walls an efficient barrier against the infiltration of heat from the warm air of the room.

The ice cream industry was founded upon the fact of the melting point of ice being lowered in the presence of salt. A mixture of ice and common salt was the only refrigerant used to congeal cream, and to keep the frozen mass in a satisfactory state of preservation for palatable consumption, for many years before and after the advent of mechanical refrigeration. Low temperature brine produced by a mixture of cracked ice and salt, or low temperature brine produced by adding salt to water and cooling the mixture by mechanical means, differ, in so far as the manufacture, hardening and storage of ice cream in the plant is concerned, only in that the salt and ice mixture is more difficult to handle and its temperature is not as easily controlled. In either case, about equally good manufacturing results were possible, although mechanical refrigeration in the plant effected a very great saving in cost of production by placing all manufacturing operations under the complete and accurate control of relatively few workmen.

Outside the plant, however, on delivery wagons and trucks, on railway cars, in retail cabinets and soda fountains, the salt and ice mixture was depended on exclusively, until the last few years, for necessary refrigeration for the preservation of ice cream until consumed. Early cabinets were built of heavy tongued and grooved planks of wood, with no insu-

FIG. 183.—ARTIST'S CONCEPTION OF THE OLD UNINSULATED ICE CREAM CABINET.

lation other than the wood itself, just about as the early household ice chest was constructed; but cabinets with hollow walls, filled usually with sawdust, came into early use and remained a long time. They left much to be desired, however, because the low temperature necessary for the holding of ice cream caused heavy condensation of moisture within the air entrapped between the sawdust particles, and the cabinet walls became ice laden and water-soaked. Granulated cork was next tried as the loose fill insulating material, with better success, but still with much to be desired both from the standpoint of insulating efficiency and a dry condition of the walls of the cabinet.

In those days it was necessary, in summer, for the ice

cream manufacturer to service or ice his cabinets in retail stores twice daily. In an effort to cut this expensive service to one daily icing, the Rieck ice cream interests, of Pittsburgh, Pennsylvania, undertook experiments with ice cream cabinets insulated with sheets of pure corkboard, an insulation specification for retail ice cream cabinets almost unheard of up to that time (about 1912), and an extravagance thought to be wholly unjustified. The experiments started with cabinets

FIG. 184—MODERN CORK INSULATED ICE CREAM SHIPPING CONTAINER; REPLACES ICE PACKED TUB.

containing one inch thick corkboard, which thickness was then increased little by little until satisfactory results were obtained, in conjunction with the use of a suitable ice and salt mixture. The results of these experiments did much to establish pure corkboard as the standard insulation for retail ice cream cabinets, and it has so remained, the only improvement being in the methods followed in putting the corkboard in place and in an economical distribution throughout the cabinet of the thickness of corkboard used. In general, the details of cabinet assembly, with respect to insulation, should be predicated on a thorough understanding of the basic principles pertaining to the insulation of walls and structures to be subjected to low temperatures, as previously elaborated in this text, to the end that ice cream cabinets may contain adequate insulation installed so as to insure *permanent* cabinet efficiency.

160.—Mechanical Ice Cream Cabinets.—The trend in the development and applications of mechanical refrigerating machinery was slowly but constantly from large many-ton plants toward smaller units, much as in the development of electric power the large-motor main-shaft drive gave way a little at a time to individual drive by small motors. But the high pressures at which ammonia compression refrigerating machines operate, placed restrictions on the smallness, the lightness, and the cost of production of the ammonia units of fractional-ton capacity, past which it was not practical for the manufacturer to go. And that minimum cost was too high for general application to small refrigeration duty, such as the cooling of household refrigerators and retail ice cream cabinets, when in competition with ice, and ice and salt mixtures.

The use of a refrigerant that could be effectively operated at relatively low pressures, such as sulphur dioxide, proved to be the solution of the problem, which development established the small fractional-ton refrigerating machine as a practical and economical refrigerating unit through much lighter and simpler construction and greatly reduced cost. However, in the practical application of such household refrigerating units, as they quickly came to be known, it was determined that their successful operation, as well as their low manufacturing cost, depended on a certain restriction of the unit refrigerating capacity.

Thus the efforts to reduce the cost of production of the fractional-ton ammonia compression machine to the point of successful competition with ice and salt mixtures were, in general, unsuccessful; while the efforts to economically raise the unit refrigerating capacity of the sulphur dioxide type of machine enough to handle the heavier duty cabinets were, in general, unavailing. But virtually by the simple expedient of increasing the thickness of the corkboard insulation in ice cream cabinets to be mechanically cooled, and by so setting the insulation in the walls of the cabinet as to guarantee the permanent thermal efficiency of the cabinet, the small low pressure carbon dioxide type of machine was adapted to retail ice cream cabinet refrigeration loads, and took the field from the fractional-ton high pressure ammonia machine.

These considerations are briefly set forth here, emphasized in their relation to insulation, merely to show the part corkboard played in the preliminary research and engineering development work incident to the beginnings of what is now a large industry—the mechanical ice cream cabinet industry, which the Crouse-Tremaine interests, of Detroit, Michigan, are given considerable credit for having pioneered.

161.—Typical Details of Ice Cream Cabinet Construction.—It would serve little purpose to illustrate in this book all the different makes and types of ice cream cabinets—ice and salt cabinets and mechanical cabinets—manufactured in the United States, and for that reason but a very few of them, selected at random, are shown and described* in this Article:

BROOKS NEW DOUBLE ROW TWO-TEMPERATURE DRYPAK CABINET.

Frame.—Built of 2 x 2 long leaf heart pine lumber, possessing great tensile strength and durability, without excessive weight. This material contains a large amount of turpentine and rosin that prevents decay.

The Bottoms.—Made of 1-inch gulf cypress are strong and securely fastened to the frame, reinforced with skids made of long leaf heart pine. The bottoms of the Brooks Drypak Cabinets are made to hold their weight. They can never sag or be pushed out.

Pure Corkboard Insulation.—The insulation is extra heavy pure corkboard, consisting of 6 inches in the bottom and 4 inches in the sides and ends. We do not attempt to save cork by tapering the insulation in the side walls, as it is just as necessary to keep the heat out at the top of the side walls as it is at the bottom of the side walls. We therefore use 4 inches of pure corkboard in the sides and ends all of the way up to the top of the cabinet.

Hermetically Sealed.—Besides the precaution taken to have all joints lapped, or perfectly butted, the entire corkboard insulation is *sealed* by flowing on a thick layer of hot asphaltum. This assures the filling and closing up of all pores, joints and cracks, which prevents the leakage of refrigeration or the penetration of heat.

*Descriptions are those of the manufacturer, and are to be accepted only for what they may prove to be worth.

No Substitutes for Corkboard.—There are no substitutes for corkboard used in any part of these cabinets. The insulation will remain in place and retain its efficiency during the entire life of the cabinet. Buy plenty of insulation once and save icing expenses daily. There is no better investment for ice cream manufacturers than plenty of pure corkboard insulation in ice cream cabinets. It pays big dividends every day the cabinets are in use.

The Corners.—Nickel zinc angles protect the corners and add a pleasing appearance to these cabinets. They are fastened with brass nails and will not rust or corrode.

Tops.—The tops are made from heavy, straight grain gulf cypress lumber, the corners are rigidly secured and the construction throughout

FIG. 185.—BROOKS CORKBOARD INSULATED DRYPAK ICE CREAM CABINET.

strong and substantial. These tops are arranged to make filling easy, without undue loss of time or refrigeration.

The Lids.—The lids are large enough to remove empty cans and replace them with full cans of cream without removing the top of the cabinet and exposing other compartments. The lids are also insulated with pure corkboard. A "hand grip" is carved into the one-piece cover, so that there are no metal handles to break off or rust, no knobs to obstruct an even surface. The edges are designed to seal against loss of refrigeration and yet make opening and closing easy.

The Finish.—Solid, laminated, three-ply, waterproof panels, selected for graining and durability, are used on all sides and ends. The finish is rich old mahogany, four-coat work, giving a smooth, hard surface that resists wear.

Sheet Metal Work.—The linings and cans are made from genuine Armco Ingot iron. This well-known brand of copper-bearing metal, heavily galvanized, is further assurance of the definite and dependable values built into Brooks Drypak Cabinets.

Ice Compartments.—The Brooks Drypak Cabinet ice compartments are large enough to provide ample capacity to care for exceptional conditions during the summer months. These cabinets will keep cream in perfect condition for forty-eight hours or more.

Drains.—One-piece, leak-proof and non-corrosive Smith and Mann valves are used. They are of ample size to perfect quick drainage and are threaded for three-quarter inch hose connection.

Mounted on Skids.—For a sanitary base and to facilitate moving, Brooks Drypak Cabinets are mounted on sturdy skids; there are no legs to break off.

Workmanship.—The workmanship throughout the cabinets is first class in every particular. The design is the result of long experience with the problems of ice cream manufacturers, by the men who actually manufacture Brooks Drypak Cabinets.

Manufactured by Brooks Cabinet Co., Norfolk, Virginia.

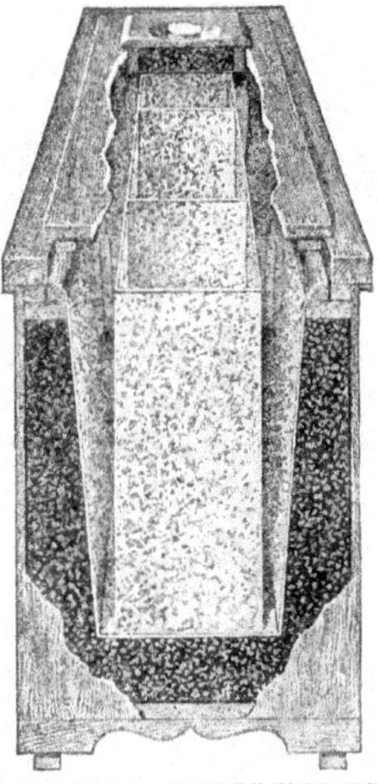

FIG. 186.—SECTION OF NELSON DUPLEX-ZERO DRY-PACK CABINET.

NELSON DUPLEX-ZERO DRY-PACK CABINETS.

Insulation.—A cabinet can be no more efficient than its insulation. The high efficiency of Duplex-Zero cabinets is guaranteed by the perfect design and the massive insulation of solid slabs of sheet cork, tapering from 3 inches on sides and ends at the top to 5 inches at and on bottom, heat treated with a special asphaltum base formed into a solid, continuous, air-tight, moisture-proof and settle-proof wall around and under the ice chamber. This construction insures maximum refrigerating results—48 to 72 hours on one icing.

Lining.—The metal lining is of 22-gauge copper bearing iron, heavily galvanized, fitting snugly against the corkboard, giving maximum wear, yet easily removed and replaced.

Finish.—Added insulation and durability are assured by the use of California redwood on all Nelson cabinets.

Corners.—Duplex-Zero Dry-Pack cabinets are equipped with bright metal corner irons.

Drain.—Drains quickly with Nelson patented brass drain.

Manufactured by C. Nelson Manufacturing Co., St. Louis, Missouri.

FIG. 187.—SECTION OF GRAND RAPIDS CABINET CO. TRAY-PACK ICE CREAM CABINET. (PATENTED JAN. 25, 1926.)

GRAND RAPIDS CABINET CO. "TRAY-PACK" ICE CREAM CABINETS.

Description.—The accompanying figure shows the position of the trays, the abundance of scientifically distributed corkboard insulation, and the individual servicing covers for each side of cabinet. These covers permit servicing without exposing ice cream—a decidedly worthwhile sanitary feature.

Operaton.—The "Tray-Pack" service method simply consists of the removal of the trays by the service man from the Tray-Pack cabinet, the dumping of the brine at the curb or other suitable place, the repacking of the trays at the truck, and the replacement of the trays in the Tray-Pack cabinet. That's all. No drip, no dirt, no muss in the dealer's store. Just a few minutes' work, and all is set for two days or more of perfect refrigeration.

Sizes.—Made in standard 2-, 3-, 4-, 5-, and 6-hole "Tray-Pack" sizes. Finish is rich walnut color. Also, obtainable with two separate compartments, suitable for: (1) two temperatures for ice cream; (2) one compartment shut off during dull season; (3) one compartment for milk or bottled goods.

Insulation.—Only the best insulation obtainable is used in "Tray-Pack" ice cream cabinets—pure compressed corkboard, it being more impervious to water than any other known insulating material. Asphaltum and other products are applied hot on both sides of the corkboard as assembled in the cabinet, so as to exclude all air from between the insulation and the inner cabinet tank and from between all joints in the corkboard sheets and thus exclude all condensed water from the insulation and obviate destruction of the insulation by the expansion of freezing.

Manufactured by Grand Rapids Cabinet Co., Grand Rapids, Michigan.

FIG. 188.—SECTIONAL VIEW OF NIZER SELF-CONTAINED WATER COOLED ELECTRIC ICE CREAM CABINET.

NIZER WATER-COOLED SELF-CONTAINED ELECTRIC ICE CREAM CABINET.

General.—The figure shows a sectional photograph of one of the many Nizer ice cream cabinets, which illustrates particularly the corkboard insulation.

Insulation.—There are 3 inches of pure compressed corkboard on the bottom, 2 inches on the sides and 1 inch on top. The insulation is not composed of single thicknesses of corkboard, but, with the exception of the top, of two thicknesses, separated by sheets of heavy waterproof paper. There are also several sheets of this paper between the insulation and the brine tank, as well as on the outside surface of the insulation. Such places as cannot be effectively sealed with corkboard (around the gas line for example) are packed tightly with cork plastic insulation.

Assembly.—The method of assembly of the insulation in the cabinet, consists in using sheets of cork made slightly oversize and pressed firmly into position, thus making perfectly tight joints without the use of sealing material. All joints in one layer of corkboard are staggered with respect to the joints in the other layer, so as to further prevent the passage of heat.

Manufactured by Kelvinator, Inc., Nizer Division, Detroit, Michigan.

FIG. 189.—UNIVRSAL COOLER CORP. ELECTRICALLY REFRIGERATED ICE CREAM CABINET.

UNIVERSAL COOLER CORPORATION ELECTRICALLY REFRIGERATED ICE CREAM CABINET.

Requirements.—In undertaking to supply the trade with an acceptable electrically refrigerated ice cream cabinet, there were two problems which presented themselves. The first had to do with creating a machine for producing a low temperature within the cabinet of such a degree as would keep the ice cream in the best possible condition, and the second having to do with the maintenance of this temperature.

The Machine.—The Universal Cooler Corporation were readily able to satisfy this first requirement, with a unit that was both simple, compact and economical, and could produce the low temperature required.

The Cabinet.—The second problem which attached to the maintenance of this low temperature was one which depended entirely upon the construction of the cabinet.

Low Power Cost.—If the cabinet was properly built and correctly insulated, it meant that the mechanical cooling unit was only called upon to operate for the shortest possible time, with a consequent low current consumption, and, of course, a longer life for the machine.

The Insulation.—Therefore, they undertook to devise a cabinet which employed corkboard as the insulating material. The cork employed in the ice cream cabinet adopted by the Universal Cooler Corporation is in solid slabs, which lap at corners, top and bottom, and are treated with a hot asphaltum base product known as "Hydrolene," so that the interior of the box is a solid, continuous, air-tight, moisture-proof, and settle-proof wall around and under the ice chamber.

Corkboard.—The necessity for having the cork in continuous slabs is for the purpose of eliminating cracks and voids which would permit ordinary atmospheric humidity to creep in, become solidified when the cabinet is in operation and thus dissipate some of the effectiveness of the box, and when the cabinet is not in use this moisture would melt, run down into the bottom of the box, become stagnant, and cause unpleasant odors.

Manufactured by the Universal Cooler Corporation, 18th and Howard streets, Detroit, Michigan.

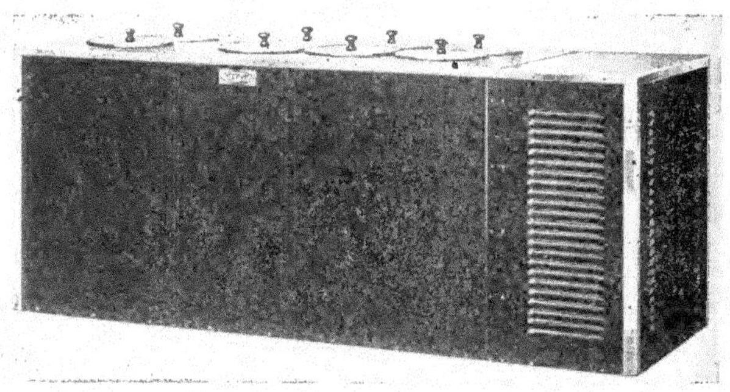

FIG. 190.—SERVEL 8-HOLE, DOUBLE ROW, TWO TEMPERATURE ELECTRICAL ICE CREAM CABINET.

SERVEL ALL-STEEL ICE CREAM CABINETS.

Insulation.—The Servel line of ice cream cabinets is considered the best insulated cabinet on the market. For the single row, two layers of

3-inch thick sheet cork is used on the bottom, two layers 2-inch thick sheet cork on the ends and sides, and one layer 2-inch sheet cork on the top. The double row cabinets, however, in order to stay within the 30 inches width, have one layer 2-inch and one layer 1½-inch sheet cork on the ends and sides.

Manufactured by Servel Corporation, Evansville, Indiana.

ABSOPURE ELECTRIC ICE CREAM CABINET.

Description.—The accompanying photograph shows the covering removed from the ice cream can section of an Absopure 4-hole, in line, self-contained, air-cooled electric ice cream cabinet, display-

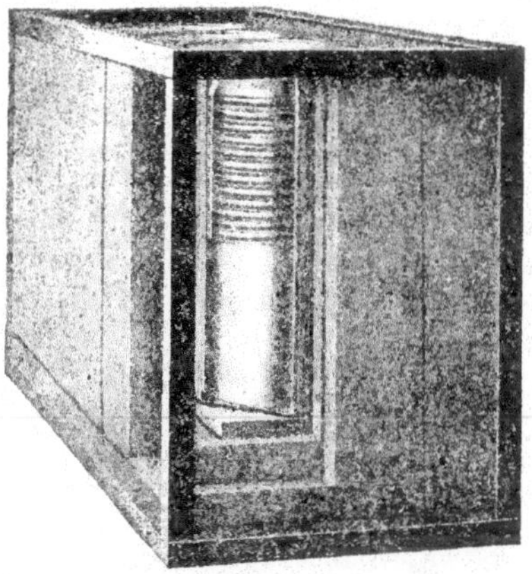

FIG. 191.—ABSOPURE 4-HOLE, IN LINE, SELF-CONTAINED, AIR-COOLED ELECTRICAL ICE CREAM CABINET (COVERING REMOVED SHOWING CORKBOARD INSULATION).

ing the sturdy framework of steel, the solidly placed pure compressed corkboard insulation and the position of the refrigerating coils.

Insulation.—The insulation of this unit consists of two layers 3-inch thick pure compressed corkboard on the bottom of the cabinet, two layers 2-inch thick pure compressed corkboard on the ends and sides of the cabinet, and one layer 2-inch thick pure compressed corkboard in the cabinet top. This insulation is carefully pressed into position, using a waterproof sealing material on all joints and surfaces to obviate the possibility of the collection and freezing of water within the cabinet construction, due to the condensation of moisture from concealed air spaces or pockets, and the consequent disintegration of the insulation, damage to the cabinet and serious loss of efficiency in operation. Such spaces that cannot be effectively sealed with corkboard sheets, are packed tight with a special waterproof sealing material combined with a suitable proportion of prepared cork particles.

Maintenance Cost.—It is believed that the construction of this cabinet is an effective guarantee of lowest power and maintenance costs, when operated in conjunction with the Absopure refrigerating unit.

Manufactured by the General Necessities Corporation, Detroit, Michigan.

162.—Notes on How to Test Ice Cream Cabinets.—There are no generally accepted and approved methods for the testing of either ice and salt cabinets or mechanical ice cream cabinets, and most all tests made thus far are subject to more or less inaccuracies and interpretation as to the meanings of the results obtained. For instance, as mentioned for household refrigerators, it has been for years a well-understood fact in the cold storage industry that the efficiency of a new cold storage room is in itself of very minor importance, if of any real importance at all. What is important to the owners and operators of large cold storage plants, is what the efficiency of that room will be one year or ten years after it has been in operation; for it is possible to construct hollow walls of wood, fill the space with chimney soot and show under accurate test an initial cold room insulating efficiency far greater than could probably be shown with any commercial insulating material procurable, yet the soot would retain its remarkable efficiency for a very short time only. Glass wool, fluxed limestone, wood flour, medicinal cotton, nail polish, and many other materials* in common use, are very efficient thermal insulators, but quickly lose their heat retarding properties by settling and packing down and by saturation with condensed water vapor, if used in connection with cold temperatures.

The first point to cover in planning for tests of any ice

---

*In a number of the "Berichte" (1899), Prof. Hempel describes a series of experiments undertaken by him, in order to determine which substance was best suited for isolating freezing mixtures in experimental work in the laboratoty. Starting with a temperature of about -75° to -80° C. (-103° to -112° F.) produced by solid carbon dioxide and ether, the rate of rise of temperature with time was measured, and, as a result, eiderdown was found to be the best insulator, wool, carefully dried at 100° C. (212° F.) being nearly as good, and having the advantage of cheapness. Thus with eiderdown a rise of 12° C. occurred in eighty-eight minutes, with dry wool a rise of 20° to 24° C. in the same time.

cream cabinet must therefore be a careful investigation and research into the ability of the insulating material to retain its initial insulating efficiency under the conditions of its application in the walls of the cabinet and for an indefinite period of time under known or anticipated conditions of service. If such research reveals that the insulation cannot be expected to stand up under the conditions to be imposed, there probably will be fewer reasons for going ahead with the plans to test out the cabinet.

Ice cream cabinet service is much more severe than the service that household refrigerators receive. Thus the proper insulation to use and the correct specifications to be followed in installing it, are of much more importance in the ice cream cabinet than they are in units that operate at considerably higher temperatures. The experience of the dairy and ice cream industries for the past several decades in the insulation and operation of refrigerated milk rooms, cream rooms, ice storage rooms, hardening rooms, and cold rooms in general, is of value as research into the fitness or lack of fitness of any insulating material for ice cream cabinet construction and temperatures. Pure corkboard is the standard material for all such rooms in countless plants all over the United States, the reason for which was elaborated in the section of this text on "The Insulation of Ice and Cold Storage Plants and Cold Rooms in General," and which amounts to the fact that corkboard is the only suitable material employed for such purpose that when intelligently installed will retain approximately 90 per cent of its initial insulating efficiency for ten years or more.

In testing various kinds and sizes of corkboard insulated ice and salt cabinets, assuming that virtually the same or equally satisfactory specifications were followed in installing the corkboard in the cabinets, and assuming that the results are to be made available for general comparison with the results of other tests made at different times and places, the following conditions should be observed:

(a) A constant temperature room should be used, the temperature held uniform to within one degree Fahr. by electric heater placed within hollow walls of the test room and controlled by thermostat.

(b) Control of the humidity of the constant temperature room should be effected by suitable means, tests having demonstrated that a considerable increase in the percentage of ice melting is effected by increasing the percentage of relative humidity in a constant temperature room from a low to a high point.

(c) The mixture of ice and salt should be carefully regulated on the basis of weight.

(d) The salt should be of standard specifications.

(e) The ice used should be only hard, "black" ice, and should be crushed to uniform size. The finer the ice is crushed and the more salt used, the lower, within limits, will be the resultant temperature.

(f) Ice and salt should be mixed thoroughly in suitable mixing box located outside the test room, and packed in the ice cream cabinet during a fixed period, at the same hour, every other day (48-hour icing), no ice and salt to be put on top of cans and brine to be drained off cabinet before each re-icing.

(g) The ice cream to be used for test purposes should be a product of rigid specifications, because different mixtures and flavors require different temperatures to keep them in satisfactory condition, and the volume of ice cream in the cabinet should be a fixed quantity.

(h) Special long-bulb thermometers should be used in ice cream cabinets, of such length as to obtain average temperature readings for the total depth of the ice cream and for the empty can of each cabinet.

(i) Four days preliminary operation should be allowed to establish a temperature equilibrium in the walls of the cabinet before the test proper should be started, and the test should then continue for 30 more days.

Tests performed under standardized conditions thus suggested, values for such standards to be fixed upon a practical basis for test purposes and a basis most nearly conforming to the practices of the ice cream industry, should be comparable, as to ice consumption, cabinet air temperature, ice cream temperature, and condition of the ice cream throughout the test.

An electric ice cream cabinet may be tested in much the same fashion, the electric power consumption by the cabinet machine, instead of the ice consumption, being comparable with results of other electric cabinet tests.

CHAPTER XVIII.

THE REFRIGERATED SODA FOUNTAIN

163.—Automatic Operation of an Intricate Unit Made Possible with Corkboard Insulation.—Soda fountain design has kept well abreast of all modern trends and developments in automatic carbonation, mechanical refrigeration, scientific insulation, pure food preservation, efficient operation, and rapid dispensation of popular delectation. And as a result the "fountain" is popular. Few of its patrons probably realize, however, that the modern soda fountain is an intricate and delicate assembly of beautiful store fixture, refrigeration plant, cold storage, chemical plant, and food and drink dispenser. Five different temperature zones must be automatically established and accurately maintained; and all in a space often less than a dozen feet long and a quarter as high and wide! The modern soda fountain deserves admiration; its successful operation is made possible by permanently efficient corkboard insulation, scientifically adjusted to the service desired.

For it is one thing to produce refrigeration, and another thing to conserve it and apply it to good purpose. When a quarter-score temperatures must be maintained and controlled within such narrow confines as twenty cubic feet, the cold storage problem takes on a new interest and importance indeed. Corkboard insulation, properly utilized, permits of the most delicate and accurate operation of the most modern soda fountain, just as it has been of so much use and assistance wherever temperatures below that of the atmosphere are artificially produced, efficiently maintained and advantageously utilized.

164.—Extracts from Manufacturers' Specifications* for

*Descriptions are those of the manufacturer, and are to be accepted only for what they may prove to be worth.

Modern Mechanically Refrigerated Soda Fountain with Typical Details of Construction.—The following excerpts from a manufacturer's complete soda fountain specification are presented to illustrate the scope of the work of designing and building such equipment, in which corkboard insulation plays such an important part; by courtesy of The Bastian-Blessing Company, Chicago, Illinois, and Grand Haven, Michigan:

DETAILS OF SODA FOUNTAIN CONSTRUCTION.

Note the heavy construction throughout and the unexcelled cork insulation. There are 4-inch walls all around, front, bottom, back and two ends. These walls are provided with 3-inch pressed pure corkboard insulation. To correctly understand this construction is to appreciate the superiority of the material and workmanship, and the correctness of the fundamental principles employed in the construction of the Guaranty fountains.

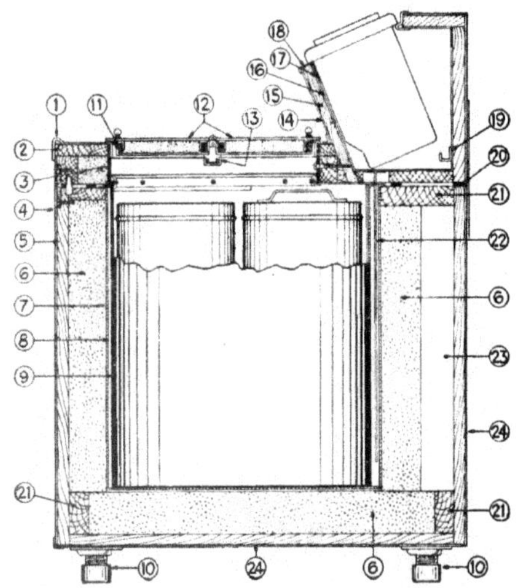

FIG. 192. SECTIONAL VIEW OF FOUNTAIN CABINET.

1. Raised edge creamer capping and top in one piece, 16-gauge nickel silver.
2. 3-inch removable top insulated with 2-inch pressed pure corkboard.
3. Fabric base special non-conductor practically prevents all refrigeration loss.
4. No. 18 porcelain white enamel Armco iron front; can also be faced with 7/16 vitrolite or marble, when specified.
5. 1-inch waterproof cypress wall.
6. 3-inch pressed pure corkboard insulation.

7. 20-ounce hot rolled copper lining of brine compartment.
8. Brine solution.
9. 32-ounce hot rolled tinned copper ice cream tanks with galvanized copper steel sleeve.
10. Strong adjustable legs, screwed in brass flanges bolted through creamer bottom.
11. Special non-conductor frame practically eliminates all sweating.
12. Double acting nickel silver hinged lid insulated with 1-inch pressed pure corkboard.
13. Removable gutter easily cleaned.
14. No. 18 porcelain white enamel Armco iron facing for syrup jar enclosure.
15. 1-inch waterproofed cypress wall.
16. 16-ounce cold rolled tinned copper lining in syrup unit.
17. Special non-conductor, breaking all metal to metal contact with the outside.
18. Nickel silver syrup unit capping.
19. Open gutter, to take off draft arm spillage, easily cleaned.
20. Waterproof airtight seal.
21. Solid 2x3 inches interlocking frame.
22. Metal conductor strips insure positive and constant refrigeration of syrup unit.
23. Dead air space forming additional insulation.
24. Heavy copper bearing steel facing bottom, back and ends.

Complete Refrigeration With One Frigidaire Unit.

The application of mechanical refrigeration to soda fountains required considerable study, many experiments and much caution. Mechanical refrigeration in itself was nothing new and had been in commercial use for many years. However, its application to the soda fountain at once brought out the difficulty of supplying the many temperatures needed for the successful operation of these fountains with one refrigerating unit.

In designing the Guaranty fountain in its simple and practical way to secure the five necessary temperatures, the engineers have scored a complete triumph.

The many months spent in experimenting, simplifying and in other ways adding to the all-around efficiency of this type of fountain, resulting in the 100 per cent. mechanically refrigerated Guaranty, was well worth while. The operation of thousands of these fountains in every-day use has completely demonstrated not only Guaranty's ability to serve supremely well and economically, but also to deliver many years of continuously satisfactory service.

Maintaining Five Correct Temperatures Automatically.

The Guaranty soda fountain is constructed in a simple and practical way to secure the five necessary soda fountain temperatures.

The soda and city water coolers and the Frigidaire boiler, located in the first, or cooling chamber, are immersed in a water bath as shown more clearly in the sectional view, Fig. 199. The temperature is automatically maintained at approximately 33° F. by a regulating control valve.

The dry storage refrigerator is located second from the left in which a temperature ranging from 40° to 45° F. is maintained. This compartment is equipped with a sliding shelf, thus providing double-deck arrangement for bottle goods. Refrigeration for this compartment is secured through a semi-insulated partition from the cooling compartment.

On the extreme right is located the brick compartment, where a

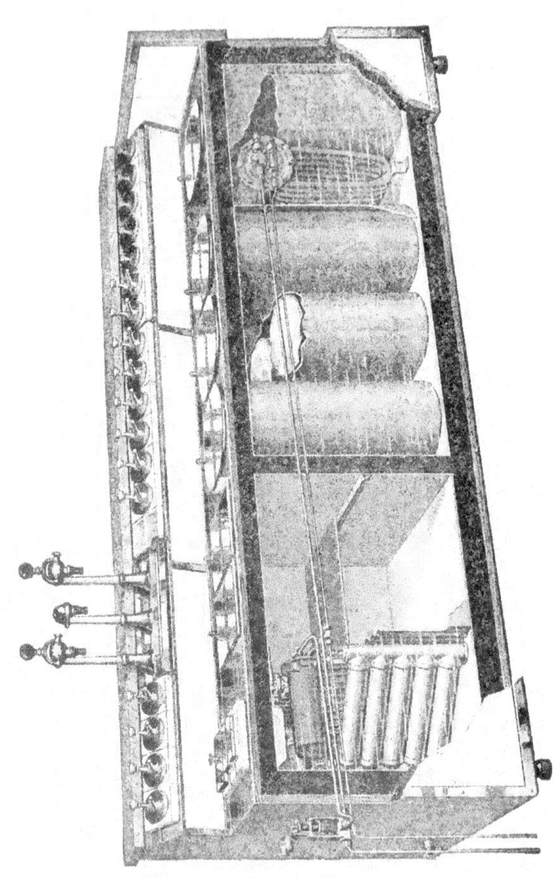

Left to right—1.—Soda and Plain Water, 33° to 40°. 2.—Refrigerator, 40° to 45°. 3.—Bulk Ice Cream, 10° ot 12°. 4.—Brick Ice Cream, 0° to 5°. Top.—Syrups, 20° to 30° under room temperature.

FIG. 193.—FOUNTAIN CABINET WITH FRONT REMOVED—NOTE LOCATIONS OF FIVE DIFFERENT TEMPERATURES MAINTAINED AUTOMATICALLY.

temperature of 0° to 5° F. is maintained. The Frigidaire boiler producing this temperature is automatically controlled by the compressor itself.

Separating the brick compartment from the bulk compartment at its left is a correctly proportioned baffle partition which permits the exact amount of refrigeration in order that the bulk cream may be kept at a temperature of from ten to twelve degrees above zero.

The syrup unit secures its refrigeration through copper conductor plates attached to the bottom of the syrup unit lining and extending down into the brine of the bulk compartment. The refrigeration necessary to produce a temperature of from twenty to thirty degrees under the room temperature of from ten to twelve degrees above zero. The bulk compartment and storage refrigerator are separated by a 2½-inch corkboard partition.

Study well the illustrations in Fig. 193. Take note of the arrangement and the method and system of operation of the refrigerating unit, and remember that continuous operation and efficient functioning requires the utmost in simplicity and practicability of construction, all so clearly shown in Fig. 193.

FIG. 194.—CORKBOARD INSULATED CREAMER.

Creamer.

Frame—Constructed of genuine Louisiana red cypress, a product of the Southern swamps, inured to all kinds of weather, accustomed to moisture and exposure and, above all, possessing a long life. Front and rear paneled, tenoned, glued and nailed to a chestnut supporting frame, all thoroughly impregnated with preservative paint, making it truly the "box eternal."

Insulation.—In addition to the 1-inch cypress walls the insulation consists of 3-inch pressed pure corkboard, all joints cemented with a specially prepared cork cement, making a jointless wall. Insulating qualities of corkboard are based on the natural quality of the cork plus the dead air space so long in use as a barrier of heat. The cork is pressed into a board under heat and the natural resin cements the cork together, imprisoning millions of tiny dead air cells forming a veritable deadline against the entrance of heat into the soda fountain.

Ice Cream Compartment Linings.—All materials that enter into the construction of the Guaranty are selected with a view to securing the best for the use intended. Tests and experiments have fully and clearly demonstrated that copper is the most practical and durable for soda fountain linings. The Guaranty fountain is lined with 20-ounce hot rolled copper, front, bottom and back in one piece. Ends are double seamed, interlocked and soldered. The bottom is reinforced with 20-gauge Keystone copper-bearing steel to insure greater strength and resistance.

Tank and Sub-Covers.—Water-tight tanks and sub-covers are required to hold the ice cream cans. Tank bodies are made of 32-ounce hot rolled tinned copper and have one vertical double seam soldered on the outside. Tank bottom is also 32-ounce hot rolled tinned copper and is double seamed and soldered to the bodies. A galvanized copper-bearing steel sleeve extending 6 inches down into the tank is soldered to it. This sleeve protects the copper and prevents dents, or perhaps punctures from carelessness in removing or inserting the ice cream cans. The complete tanks are sweated to a sub-cover made of 32-ounce hot rolled copper.

The sub-cover has the proper number of oval openings carefully machine stamped and also has an opening through which the coil can be removed should it ever become necessary.

In the bottom of each tank there is placed a 20-gauge galvanized copper-bearing steel plate as additional reinforcement to prevent the tank bottom from being dented when the ice cream cans are dropped into place.

After the tank and sub-cover unit have been assembled as described, it is placed into the creamer box and the sub-cover is sweated to the lining. The Frigidaire boiler is then installed and the entire unit is filled with water and tested for leaks.

Cooler and Dry Storage Refrigerator.—An integral part of the creamer, separated from the ice cream compartment by 2½-inch cork partition; lined with 16-ounce cold rolled copper tinned one side, front, bottom and back in one piece, ends double seamed, interlocked and soldered. This compartment is divided by a semi-insulated partition. One side contains a water bath and refrigerating coil for cooling soda and city water and the other side is a dry storage compartment which secures its refrigeration through the semi-insulated partition. An outlet with an overflow pipe topped with a funnel is provided to drain the syrup unit and cooler compartment when necessary.

Brick Compartment.—This compartment is separated from the bulk cream compartment by a metal baffle partition. This compartment contains the boiler which is regulated to maintain a temperature of approximately zero. All *Guaranty* standard plans are shown with one rectangular brick compartment with a capacity of 50 one-quart bricks.

Bulk Compartment.—The correctly proportioned metal baffle which separates the brick and bulk compartments retards refrigeration sufficiently to produce a temperature of from 8 to 12 degrees above zero in the bulk compartment.

Frigidaire Coils.—In order to supply 100 per cent. mechanical refrigeration under positive automatic control, two coils and one regulating valve, in addition to the compressor suitable for the refrigeration of the creamer, are required in all cases.

The standard installation consists of one coil for supplying refrigeration to the cooler and cold storage compartment, and one coil for the refrigeration of the ice cream compartments. They are installed at the factory in a neat and workmanlike manner and the entire tank is tested for leaks before it leaves the plant. All Guaranty interiors are equipped at the factory with the standard installation of coils and shipped complete with the regulating valve.

Facings.—Front is faced with No. 18 Armco Iron with three coats of white porcelain enamel fired at a temperature above 1700° F. All facings are made to exact dimensions before coating, and there are never any crazed edges so often found when sheared to size after being enameled. Both ends, bottom and back are covered with 20-gauge copper-bearing galvanized steel, coated with aluminum bronze paint.

Bindings.—The bindings are 20-gauge nickel silver, neatly made up, attached with brass nickel plated screws.

Adjustable Legs.—Creamer units are equipped with heavy metal legs adjustable to allow for ordinary irregularities in the floor without resorting to the use of wedges.

The legs are fitted with rounded caps which provide a smooth sliding surface, and are turned in heavy solid brass flanges, securely fastened to the creamer box with bolts, which pass through the entire thickness of the creamer bottom.

FIG. 195.—CORKBOARD INSULATED CREAMER TOP.

Creamer Top.

Frame.—Like the creamer box, the frame of the top is constructed of genuine Louisiana Red Cypress, the "wood eternal," thoroughly impregnated with a wood preservative.

Insulation.—Pure corkboard 2 inches thick is used for insulation. The surface of the cork is effectively sealed against moisture by a heavy coating of hydrolene.

Capping.—One solid piece of 16-gauge Grade A 18% nickel silver (weighing approximately two pounds to the square foot) forms the covering for the top. The front edge is raised and beveled to prevent water from dripping on the floor. Machine cut oval openings provide access to the ice cream cans and a rectangular opening to the cooler and cold storage compartment. A raised rim in each oval opening prevents seepage into tanks and ice cream cans.

Non-Conductor.—Great care was exercised in the selection of Guaranty Non-Conductor. After countless experiments had determined that Bakelite with a fabric base possessed the needed strength, ability to withstand moisture and above all, had the required insulating property, it was chosen for use with Guaranty soda fountains and the actual operation of these fountains in daily use has fully justified this selection.

Removable Gutter.—Leakage through the hinge of the twin packer lid has not been overcome nor completely eliminated by anyone. In some cases the covers have been built up to such a height that most of the water can be carried off to the top of the creamer. The height of this projection or of the complete cover itself, hinders ease in operating and cleaning, besides which it is unsightly. The Guaranty solution of the problem consists of a removable gutter attached to lugs directly underneath the hinge, as shown in Fig. 192. What little water has occasion to seep through the lid is caught by this gutter and its removal and subsequent cleaning is both simple and easy. At the same time, a beautiful smooth and even creamer top is maintained.

Twin Packer Cover.—An ingenious hinged cover divided in the center provides access to both ice cream cans, making each can a dipping can. This cover folds back completely either way so that both cans can be emptied completely without removing the front can and bringing the rear can forward as is necessary in so many other types.

FIG. 196.—CORK INSULATED TWIN PACKER COVER.

Non-Conductor Lid.—The operation of the twin packer cover is shown above, and the accompanying illustration shows this lid in complete detail. It is made with a frame of special insulating material, strong, durable and non-absorbent. The lid top is 14-gauge nickel silver, fastened to the non-conductor frame with nickel silver brackets electrically welded to the underside of the top. It is insulated with one inch of pressed pure cork-board, and a nickel silver bottom, binding the entire cover together, is sprung into a groove in the non-conductor frame. The front and rear half are each provided with rubber tipped knobs, doing away with the old thumb nip, thus eliminating the slight opening, and providing additional precaution against refrigeration loss, at the same time making the operation of these covers easy and noiseless. The illustration shows clearly that all metal to metal contact is broken practically eliminating all refrigeration loss.

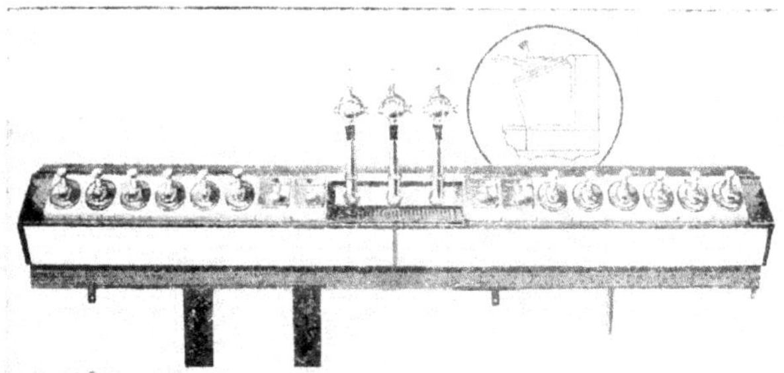

FIG. 197.—INSULATED SYRUP UNIT.

Syrup Unit.

Frame.—The usual unbeatable Louisiana red cypress is used in the construction of the syrup unit frame. The bottom is 5-ply, ½-inch Haskelite panel board, which gives the necessary strength to insure that quality of endurance.

Non-Conductor.—Wherever it has been necessary Guaranty soda fountains are equipped with special non-conductor to practically eliminate all refrigeration loss. The syrup unit is so constructed, and special non-conductor strips, completely breaking all metal-to-metal contact with the outside, are provided in the construction, as shown by the accompanying illustration.

Drain for Draft Arm Spillage.—All Guaranty interiors are constructed with an open drain, leading from the drip pan to the creamer outlet. This is attached to the rear syrup unit wall, a convenient and out of the way location. No spillage resulting from mixing drinks at draft arms reaches the syrup jar enclosure bottom, making it easy to keep dry and clean.

Lining.—16-ounce pure cold rolled tinned copper forms the lining, made of one piece with ends double seamed and soldered.

Capping.—The front rail and top capping are heavy Grade A 18% nickel silver.

Adjusting Plates.—The product of the best porcelain manufacturers in the country is used, but it is impossible to guarantee absolute, precise uniformity in jar sizes.

In order to insure a perfect fit, adjusting plates are provided at each end of the syrup unit to take up any excess opening. These are stamped of 18-gauge nickel silver.

Facing.—The ends are faced with No. 18 porcelain white enamel Armco iron, the back with galvanized copper-bearing steel painted with aluminum bronze.

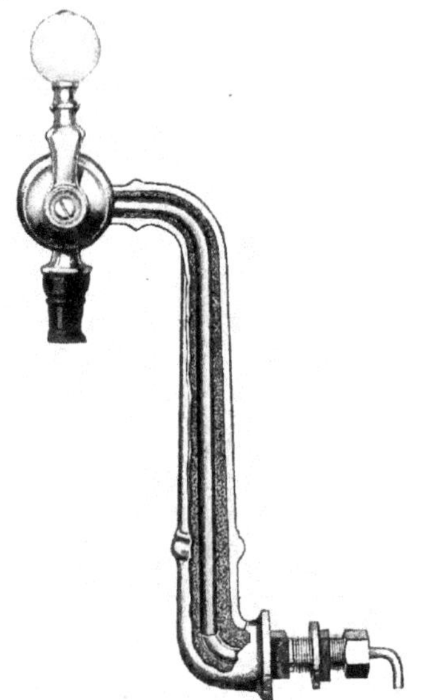

FIG. 198. CORK INSULATED DRAFT ARM.

Filler Inlets.—In the bottom of the syrup unit and directly to the rear of the boiler, provision is made for filling the outfit with brine or for inserting a siphoning hose should it ever become necessary to remove the brine. These consist of heavy brass ¾-inch filler tubes just long enough to extend through the sub-cover. The upper end is threaded on the inside to fit a brass plug. Convenient and out of sight.

Workboards.

Clear Counter Service Cork Insulated Draft Arms.—The draft arms used in all Guaranty interiors are as shown in the accompanying illustration. They are made of bronze, heavily silver plated, hand burnished, and are supplied with block tin tubing for the passage of the carbonated water through the draft arm to the head. Refrigeration loss is reduced to a minimum by the cork insulation which is used. The soda and city water after it leaves the coolers travels through the refrigerated syrup unit and is connected directly to this cork insulated Guaranty draft arm. In the design of these draft arms all sharp lines are eliminated, thus avoiding the premature wearing of silver plating through the ordinary process of polishing.

The soda leader pipes running from the coolers to the draft arms are equipped with individual shut-off valves for each draft, thereby making it possible to replace a tumbler or washer when necessary without turning off the entire service supply. These valves are located at a convenient point in the syrup unit, and are readily accessible.

Cooling System.

Soda and city water in all Guaranty interiors are cooled by what was formerly known as the Iceless system, or since the advent of mechanical refrigeration as the 100% method. This consists of coolers submerged in a fresh water bath, cooled by a boiler used in connection with the refrigeration unit which is used to refrigerate the ice cream.

FIG. 199.—COOLER AND BOILER ARRANGEMENT, 56-IN. AND 64-IN. GUARANTY BOXES.

The refrigerator section is divided into two compartments by a semi-insulated partition; one for cooling soda and city water, known as the cooler compartment; the other provides cold storage facilities for bottled goods, etc., known as the cold storage compartment. In the 56-inch and 64-inch tall and squat and 77-inch and 82-inch squat creamers, the coolers are located at the rear of the cooler compartment with the Frigidaire boiler exactly in front center. In all of the other creamers, the coolers are placed on each side of the cooler compartment with the Frigidaire boiler between them. The boiler and coolers are submerged in a water bath; ice forms around the boiler cooling the water bath and in turn the soda and city water.

The refrigeration is controlled by an automatic regulating valve located at the end of the creamer, directly under the drainboard. A temperature sufficiently low is maintained, but controlled to prevent freezing.

The balance of the refrigerator compartment furnishes dry cold

FIG. 200 - COOLER AND BOILER ARRANGEMENT, ALL OTHER GUARANTY BOXES.

storage for bottled goods, etc. It secures its refrigeration through the semi-insulated wall from the cooler compartment, and there is no difficulty in maintaining the correct temperature for this compartment.

Coolers.—In the 56-inch and 64-inch creamer boxes is provided a 6-cylinder upright soda cooler installed to the rear of the Frigidaire boiler. In all other creamers is provided a 5-cylinder soda cooler 19 inches long. Either of these coolers has ample capacity to assure cold water. The outside wall of these coolers is heavily tinned, seamless copper tubing; the inside lining is of pure seamless block tin tubing with die cast tin ends. All coolers are thoroughly tested under heavy pressure before they leave the factory. There are absolutely no flexible connections to become twisted, choked or broken. Carbonated water passes through the series of cylinders and is finally drawn from the top cylinder. The Guaranty iceless coolers reduce wear and tear to a minimum and are properly designed and constructed to insure cold soda water.

The water cooler used is the same style and capacity as that for the soda, except that it is tinned inside instead of being lined with block tin tubing. This large capacity water cooler insures plenty of cold water and is a feature not found in many other makes of fountains.

Syrup System.—The syrup unit is one of the most important features of the soda fountain, the effectual operation of which adds materially to the right kind of service, sanitation and cleanly appearance of the fountain itself. It is just as necessary to supply adequate refrigeration for this unit as it is in the balance of the fountain.

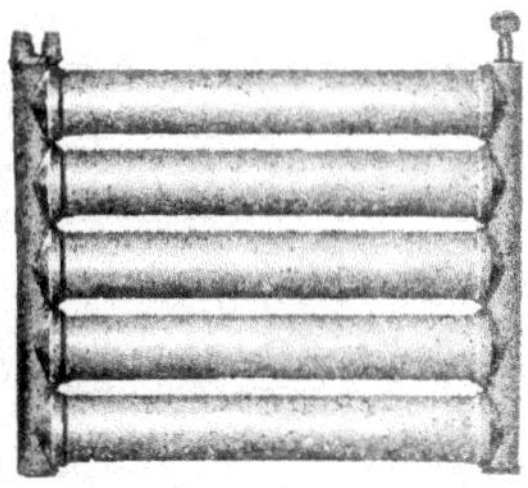

FIG. 201.—COOLER.

The Guaranty fountains' refrigeration is provided by means of metal contacts between the syrup unit lining and the lining of the bulk cream compartment. Wide copper conductor strips are attached to the bottom of the syrup unit lining, the other end of which is submerged in the cold brine. This metal contact is a positive conductor, and heat is absorbed from the syrup unit, just as certain as the flow of electricity over copper wire. A temperature of from 20 to 30 degrees less than the room temperature is maintained, and fruits and syrups never sour.

To conserve all of the refrigeration supplied, a special non-conductor breaks all metal to metal contact with the outside, as fully described and illustrated previously.

This method of supplying refrigeration to the syrup has been successfully used by Guaranty for years, and the application of it when used with mechanical refrigeration is not only highly approved by prominent refrigeration engineers but has proven an outstanding success in actual use.

Compressor Installation under Drainboard.—Standard Guaranty plans shown contemplate installation of the Fridigaire compressor in the basement or other convenient place, removed from the soda fountain. Where this is impossible and it is necessary to keep the refrigerating unit in the same room with the soda fountain, installation can be made under the drainboard, as shown in Fig. 202.

These compressor enclosures are made of paneled cypress, contain a floor for the machine and are vented to allow free circulation of air, which not only insures a dry enclosure, but permits the operation of the compressor to its fullest efficiency. They are faced with porcelain white enamel Armco iron to conform to the rest of the fountain. Minimum plain drainboard space required is 38 inches.

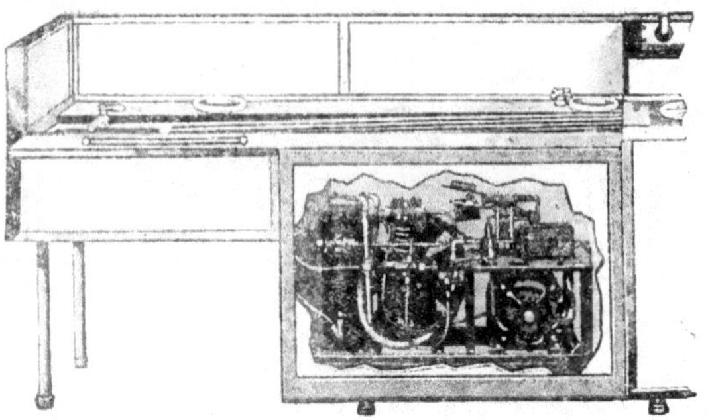

FIG. 202.—COMPRESSOR UNDER DRAINBOARD.

Backbar Bases.

Refrigerator Bases.—Where cold storage in addition to that provided in the interior is desired, bases can be supplied either partially or wholly refrigerated. Bases of this construction are metal lined and equipped with hardwood racks. The bottom, back, top and both ends are insulated with 2-inch thick pressed pure corkboard, as are the doors which are of heavy refrigerator construction with stainless vitrolite panels. Bases constructed as above are 22 inches wide overall.

The installation of the Frigidaire cooling coils is a simple matter and consists of placing one of the ordinary ice box coils in the base. The unit required depending on the number of cubic feet it is intended to refrigerate. The local Delco Light dealer can give the desired information and recommend the coil to be used.

Three Door Refrigerator including Biological Drawer Section.—Fig. 203 illustrates a standard cabinet base with a section refrigerated by a Frigidaire remote installation as shown. A standard drawer section for storage of biologicals is included. This is a handy arrangement for use in drug stores. The two end cabinets are not refrigerated, but these also can be included if so desired.

Three Door Refrigerator Section.—The base shown in Fig 204 is designed to accommodate the installation of the necessary compressor in the base. A compact arrangement where no basement space is available.

The doors of the compressor enclosure are metal with ventilating openings, finished in baked white enamel. Ventilator holes are also provided thru the back and end.

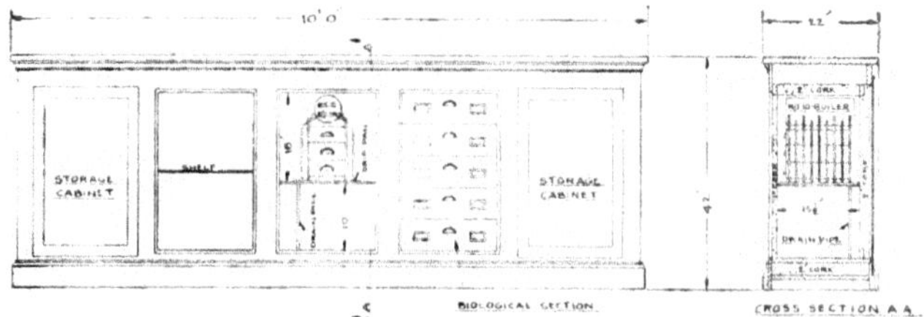

FIG. 203.—REFRIGERATOR BASE WITH BIOLOGICAL DRAWER SECTION.

A convenient auxiliary for those soda fountain owners who require much space for storage of bottled goods.

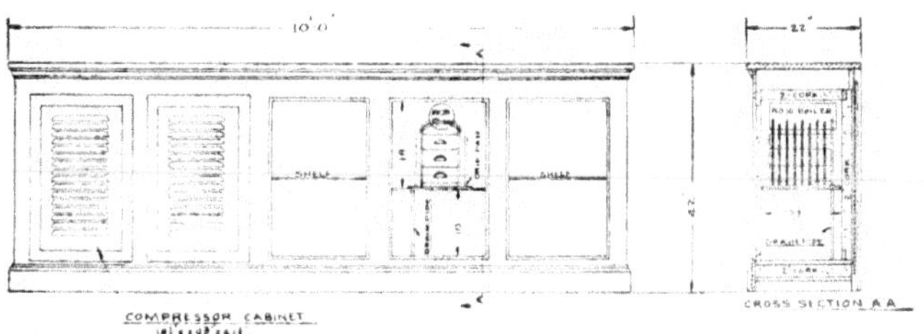

FIG. 204.—REFRIGERATOR BASE WITH FRIGIDAIRE MACHINE COMPARTMENT.

Cubical contents of refrigerated sections in backbar bases with size of Frigidaire coil recommended:

DIMENSIONS OF REFRIGERATED SECTIONS AND COIL RECOMMENDED.

Size	Depth	Height	Length	Cubic Feet	Coil
3 Door	15½ inches	29 inches	63 inches	16.4	No. 10
4 Door	15½ inches	29 inches	85½ inches	22.25	No. 12
5 Door	15½ inches	29 inches	108 inches	28.1	No. 14
6 Door	15½ inches	29 inches	130½ inches	34.0	No. 14

Backbar Bases With Recessed Ice Cream Cabinet.

When it is not practical to put sufficient ice cream cabinets in the interior, the use of this base will be found desirable. The standard size is made to take six 5-gallon ice cream packing cans (twin packer style construction). The width overall of this base is 30 inches. It is regularly built with cabinet base ends but may be built with full refrigerator ends at an additional price if so specified.

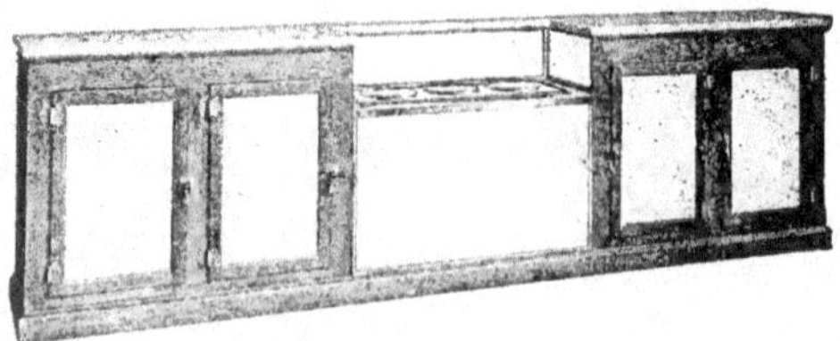

FIG. 205.—BACKBAR BASES WITH RECESSED ICE CREAM CABINET.

The overall dimensions of the standard recessed ice cream cabinet are 29 inches high, 28⅛ inches deep from front to back and 46⅛ inches long. A standard 30-gallon capacity recessed ice cream cabinet as illustrated, occupies the same space as is required for three regular standard door compartments.

If squat cans are used the overall width of the base is 32 inches and the overall dimensions of the cabinet are: Height, 29 inches; depth, 30⅛ inches; length, 49⅛ inches.

The following specifications have been extracted, through the courtesy of the manufacturer, from the literature of The Liquid Carbonic Corporation, Chicago, Illinois:

UNIVERSAL MECHANICOLD SODA FOUNTAIN.

Fig. 206 is a marble constructed cooler box, insulated throughout with pure corkboard. The top capping is one piece 18-gauge nickel silver with a beaded or rolled edge.

Two boilers and a control valve are supplied and a ½ h.p. Frigidaire compressor is required to operate

The box has two openings for bulk ice cream storage. Each opening is equipped with a double hinged black insulating cover and is capable of holding two 5-gallon bulk ice cream cans. This gives a capacity of four 5-gallon cans of bulk ice cream or 20 gallons, all of which is maintained at a uniform temperature from the top to the bottom of the cans.

The extreme left hand opening is a package storage compartment which has a storage capacity of 10 gallons with an insulating cover the same as those over the bulk ice cream compartments. It is maintained at a special low temperature, around zero to insure proper storage for package ice cream.

NOTE—All references to positions in illustration and diagrams are made as if standing in front of counter.

A dry cold storage compartment is located next to the attemperating chamber. This compartment is extra large and roomy being 24x24 inches. There is ample room for the storage of milk, grape juice and other bottled goods. No ice is used in this compartment; it is maintained at a low temperature by means of the ice formation in the attemperating chamber.

In the top of this compartment is a large size chipped ice pan, the drip from which is carried into an outlet pipe, keeping the interior of the cold

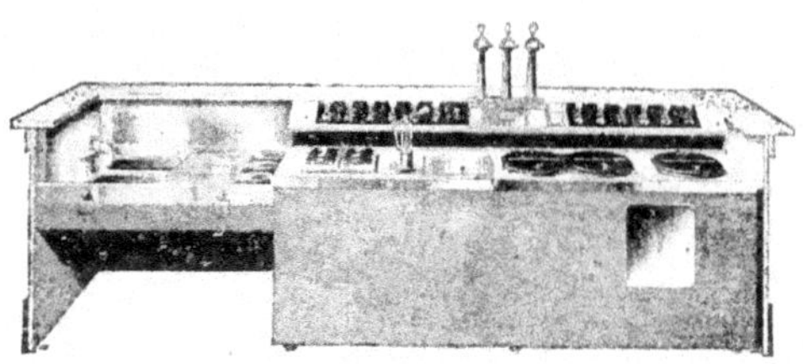

FIG. 206.—UNIVERSAL MECHANICOLD SODA FOUNTAIN (ONE STATION COOLER BOX).

storage compartment dry. If desired this pan may be used as a container for whipped cream.

There are three octagonal pattern stamped silver, silver-plated, cork insulated, draft arms in the center of the box. The box is also equipped with 14 "Mechanicold" double support, silver-plated pumps with black insulating tops and 14 white vitreous syrup jars. In place of any of the syrup pumps a white vitreous two compartment spoon holder can be supplied.

If additional crushed fruit jars are required a short jar can be supplied to take the place of the regular syrup jar. This jar is equipped with a black insulating hinged cover in which is fitted a porcelain name plate. These covers are similar to those used on the crushed fruit jars in the cooler box.

A double capacity Coca-Cola jar can be furnished in place of two regular jars. This double capacity jar can be equipped with either two syrup pumps or one syrup pump and one crushed fruit cover; permitting the filling of the jar without the removal of the pump.

In the cooler box are three crushed fruit bowls and ladles. These are placed between the storage compartment and the attemperating chamber. In place of two of these crushed fruits a double capacity jar may be supplied at no additional cost which can be used as a whip cream container. A milk pump may be substituted for all three jars if desired. An additional charge is made if the milk pump is wanted.

The cooler box may also be equipped with six crushed fruit bowls over the attemperating chamber in place of the corrugated drain cover which is regularly supplied. If the crushed fruits are desired, there will be an additional charge. All of these crushed fruit jars are equipped with black insulating hinged covers in which are fitted porcelain name plates. Ladles are supplied for each jar.

FIG. 207.—X-RAY VIEW OF THE UNIVERSAL MECHANICOLD, SHOWING CORKBOARD INSULATION.

Insulation.—It is not possible to build a perfectly insulated box. The best that can be done is to take every possible precaution against permitting unnecessary losses through faulty insulation or construction.

FIG. 208.—PURE CORKBOARD INSULATION USED BY MECHANICOLD.

Pure cork board is the best insulator known, other than a perfect vacuum and it is not possible to obtain a vacuum in building a fountain. Therefore, the next best thing is used, pure cork board as shown in Fig. 208.

A minimum thickness of three inches of cork is used in front, ends, bottom, and top, and there are five inches in the back. This 3-inch minimum of pure cork board is supplemented with additional ground cork, which fills every inch of space in the interior of the box around the brine tank.

Insulated Draft Arm.—This is another exclusive Liquid feature that helps to produce the wonderful results certified to by Prof. Gebhardt of The Armour Institute.

Metal is a thermal conductor, that is, it conducts heat just as a wire conducts electricity. An uninsulated metal draft arm will pick up heat from room temperature and raise the temperature of the water drawn from the coolers.

The Liquid draft is made of stamped nickel silver, silver plated, and is filled with cork, insulating the block tin tube which carries the water from the coolers to the head of the draft arm.

Aside from its actual value in conserving refrigeration, the draft is worth while by reason of its attractive appearance.

The old stereotyped design is gotten away from and the new type outfit adds materially to the appearance of the fountain.

There is also provided a perfectly sanitary channel for the flow of soda water from where it leaves the coolers up to the time it is dispensed into a glass for service to a customer.

Block tin is the only sanitary metal impervious to the chemical action of soda water or carbonic gas.

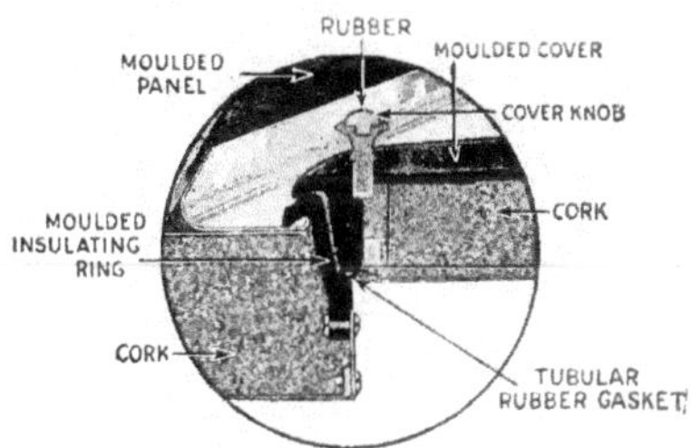

FIG. 209.—SECTION THROUGH COVER AND LID, SHOWING CORKBOARD INSULATION.

Breaking Metal Contacts.—Metal is a thermal conductor, that is, it conducts heat or cold. Fig. 209 shows how all metal contacts between the top cappings nad the linings are broken.

If this was not done the heat from the room temperature would be communicated to the metal capping and carried into the box through contact with the metal linings. This would result in putting an unnecessary load on the refrigerating unit, soft ice cream, and loss through shrinkage.

Completely Insulated Syrup Enclosure.—The illustration shows some very radical changes in the construction of the Syrup Enclosure, all made to conserve refrigeration.

The syrup jars are completely enclosed and the enclosure is insulated with slabs of pure cork board at front, ends, top and back.

The front of the enclosure is faced with Bakelite panels, mahogany color, which add to the appearance and afford additional insulation.

The bottom lining in the enclosure is contacted with the walls of the brine tank. Metal is a thermal conductor, i.e., heat units flow through it as does an electric current. The contact between the walls of the brine tanks, with their zero temperature, and the tinned copper lining of the syrup enclosure, serves to carry the cold to this enclosure.

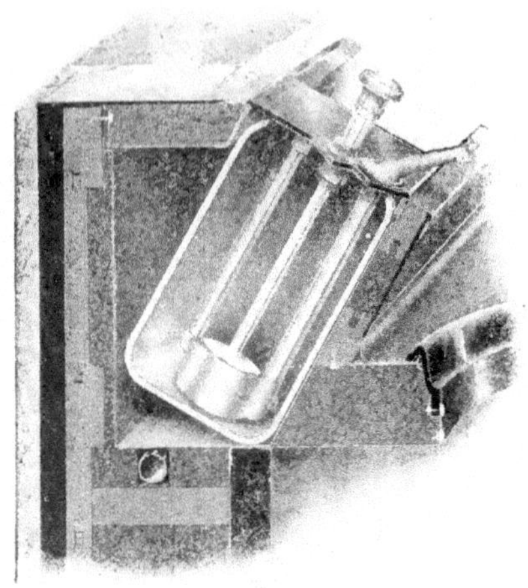

FIG. 210.—SECTION OF CORKBOARD INSULATED SYRUP ENCLOSURE.

Metal contacts between the enclosure linings and the capping around the top of the enclosure are broken by strips of non-conducting material, so that this capping will not conduct heat into the enclosure. See also, in description of Bakelite pump plate, the additional precaution exercised at this point.

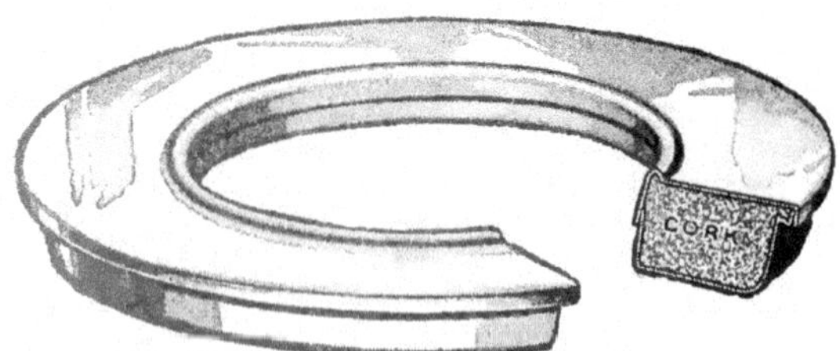

FIG. 211.—CORK INSULATED COVER RING.

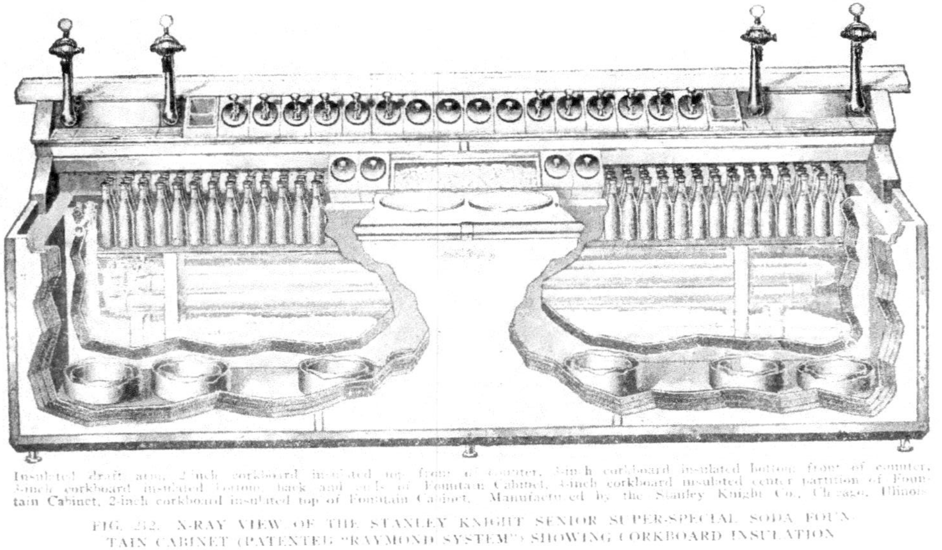

Insulated draft arm, 2-inch corkboard insulated top front of counter, 3-inch corkboard insulated bottom front of counter, 3-inch corkboard insulated bottom, back and ends of Fountain Cabinet, 4-inch corkboard insulated center partition of Fountain Cabinet, 2-inch corkboard insulated top of Fountain Cabinet. Manufactured by the Stanley Knight Co., Chicago, Illinois.

FIG. 252. X-RAY VIEW OF THE STANLEY KNIGHT SENIOR SUPER-SPECIAL SODA FOUNTAIN CABINET (PATENTED "RAYMOND SYSTEM") SHOWING CORKBOARD INSULATION

Covers for Junior Box.—As there is but a single opening on the Junior type Mechanicold, the full opening cover is supplied with double point hinges.

These lids are made of 16-gauge nickel silver (weighing 2½ pounds to the square foot). The linings, also of nickel silver, are formed so as to fit inside the turned down edges of the top. This is known as telescoping and the joint is flooded with solder, making what amounts to one piece construction.

Between the top and lining is insulation of pure cork board.

The double point hinge permits of the full opening of the lid.

The raised edge around the opening in the capping which received the lid, is die stamped and will not break down. It prevents moisture on the cover getting into the ice cream can.

CORK INSULATION

Appendix

REFRIGERATION IN TRANSIT.*

By Dr. M. E. Pennington,

Chief, Food Research Laboratory, Bureau of Chemistry,
United States Department of Agriculture.

The people of the United States are as dependent upon refrigerator cars for their food supply as are the people of England upon her ships. The English refrigerated food ship is the result of a systematic evolution; the American refrigerator car, like Topsy, has "just growed." The United States has now well over one hundred thousand refrigerator cars belonging to railroads. It costs at least $1,500.00 to build a refrigerator car, and most of them are in need of rebuilding after five years of service. With such an investment and cost of maintenance, and with the responsibility of transporting fresh food to the people, we may well inquire into the efficiency of the car for the work it is performing, and into the expense involved.

The United States Department of Agriculture, through the Bureaus of Plant Industry and Chemistry, has for some years been studying the temperatures required to preserve perishable produce in transit. The Department has obtained definite information on fruits, vegetables, dressed poultry and eggs. It is now determining the most efficient and economical means of transporting these perishables. The problem is of great importance to the shippers, to the railroads, and to the consumer as well.

The efficiency of the refrigerator car depends upon such factors as the quantity and kind of insulation, the type and the capacity of the ice bunkers, the size of the car, the temperature of the entering load, the manner of stowing the packages, the circulation of cold air from the ice bunkers, and the freedom of the insulating material from moisture. The economy of operation depends on such factors as the weight of the car in relation to the weight of the load, the amount of ice required to cool the product in transit or to maintain the initial temperatures of the precooled load, and the length of life of the car. All these, and other questions are the

*Address before the Chicago Traffic Club, October 5th, 1916. **Reprint from the Waybill, October, 1916. Volume No. 7.**

subject of investigation in the Department of Agriculture in connection with the study of the preservation of the good condition of perishables while in transit.

Apparatus and methods of investigation had to be developed to obtain the necessary data. Gradually there has been evolved an arrangement of electrical thermometers which can be installed not only in appropriate locations in the car, but within the packages, and even inside an orange, peach, chicken or fish. The wires from these thermometers run out between the packings of the door, and the terminals are permanently or temporarily attached to the indicators installed in an accompanying caboose.

Fundamental Facts Established.

To complete this investigation will require years of detailed study. Certain fundamental facts, however, have been established and are outlined in this paper. For example, the distribution of the cold air from the ice bunker throughout the car is vital to the preservation of the lading. The circulation of the air is produced and maintained by the difference in weight of warm and cold air. The actual difference between the weight of a cubic foot of air at 65° F. (1.18 oz.) and 32° F. (1.27 oz.) is only 0.09 ozs. Experiments with stationary precooling plants, cooled by ice or by ice and salt, have shown that the best and most economical results are obtained by hanging a basket of suitable ice capacity close to, but actually free from the walls of the room, and closing off the basket by an insulated bulkhead open about twelve inches, both at the top and bottom, to permit entrance and exit of air. In this way a large surface of ice is exposed to air contact and the air is compelled to travel over the entire column of ice before it escapes. The insulated bulkhead prevents the absorption of heat from the commodity and from the car, varying in quantity according to the distance from the ice. The bulkhead also facilitates a steady ascent and progression of the warm air in the car toward the top of the bunker. To further facilitate the distribution of cold air throughout the space, floor racks four inches high have been installed.

Now let us see what practical results such a combination produces when applied to a refrigerator car which is, in other respects, of the usual type. Chart I* shows the average temperature in three cars of oranges in the same train in transit between Los Angeles and New York, each car containing 462 boxes of fruit. Car "A" had the box bunker and open or slatted bulkhead so commonly seen in present day refrigerators. The lading was placed directly on the floor. Car "B" had a basket bunker, insulated solid bulkhead, and a rack four inches off floor. Car "C" was of the same construction as car "B" but the ice was mixed with nine per cent salt

*The study of fruits and vegetables is being conducted by the Bureau of Plant Industry, under the supervision of Mr. H. J. Ramsey. I am indebted to him for the data on oranges and also such other facts concerning the transportation of fruits and vegetables as are brought out in this paper.

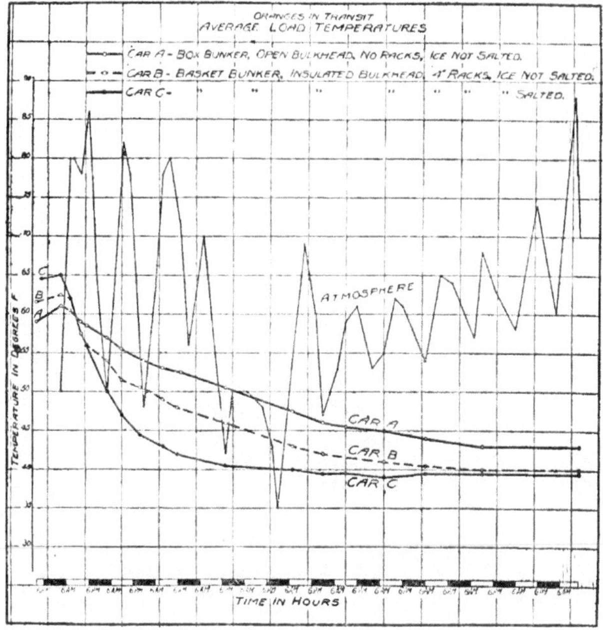

CHART I.

the first day and five per cent of the added ice on the second. The temperature of the load in the car "A" averaged 54.4° F. The temperature of the load in the car "B" averaged 49.5° F., while car "C," in which salt had been added to the ice, not only cooled the oranges more quickly but reduced the average temperature of the load to 45.5° F., a gain of 9° F. as compared with car "A." The amount of ice placed in the bunkers in car "A," including that remaining in them at destination, was approximately 23,200 pounds. In car "B" the ice amounted to 18,675 pounds, a saving of more than two tons. Car "C," which had been salted, had 22,750 pounds of ice, still a little less than car "A."

The results obtained with car "C" open up great possibilities in the better distribution of such extremely perishable products as strawberries, raspberries and cherries, widely produced under conditions which generally preclude proper precooling before loading into the car. The insulated bulkhead prevented the frosting of the lading next to the bunker, and the floor rack provided a quick runway for the very cold air, which soon lost its temperature of 20° F., or even less, by the absorption of the heat of the lading and of the car.

Such results with the basket bunker, insulated bulkhead and floor rack, combined, naturally raise the question of the relative value of each of the three factors in producing and maintaining circulation, and gaining the available refrigeration from the ice. Experimentation shows that a rack on the floor of the car hastens the cooling of the load, and affords very decided protection to the lower layer of goods against both frost and heat. The floor rack, alone, however, is far less efficient than the combination of the basket bunker and insulated bulkhead with the floor rack. The addition of insulation to bulkhead increases circulation and the lading is more rapidly and completely cooled than when the bulkhead is either not insulated or is open. For example, Chart II shows two cars of similar size and construction, one of which was provided with a floor rack and an insulated bulkhead, the other as commonly used. Both were loaded with eggs. The car with the insulated bulkhead and the floor rack reduced the average temperature of the load 17° F. in sixty-four hours. The load in the ordinary car showed a reduction of 7.5° F. during the same period. The average temperature of the car with the insulated bulkhead and the floor racks was 5.5° F. lower than the ordinary car. That it is not advisable to cease improvements with the floor rack and the insulated bulkhead is indicated by experiments which show that quick cooling by ice and salt safely performed with basket insulated bulkhead and floor rack is not possible without it. The pocketed cold air at the box bunker, which is always observed with bunkers of the box type, causes frosting of the goods against the bulkhead even when that is insulated.

The failure of refrigerator cars to maintain even temperatures throughout the load has been a serious menace to extremely perishable products. In order to produce temperatures at the top of the load between the doors—commonly the warmest place in the car—low enough to carry dressed poultry safely, it has been necessary to freeze the birds at the bunker. While freezing in transit does not injure the food value of dressed poultry, it does lower its money value at certain seasons or in some markets. Better air circulation tends to equalize temperatures, as shown in Chart III. In the car with the box bunkers and open bulkhead (car B), where the load was placed on floor strips, the package at the bunker on the floor froze solidly (23° F.) during a four-day haul, although the package on the top of the four foot load was 35.4° F. A similar car (car A), except that it had a basket bunker with insulated bulkhead and a floor rack, maintained an average temperature of 29.3° F. at the bunker and 34.1° F. in the package on the top of the load between the doors. In the one case, the average difference between the

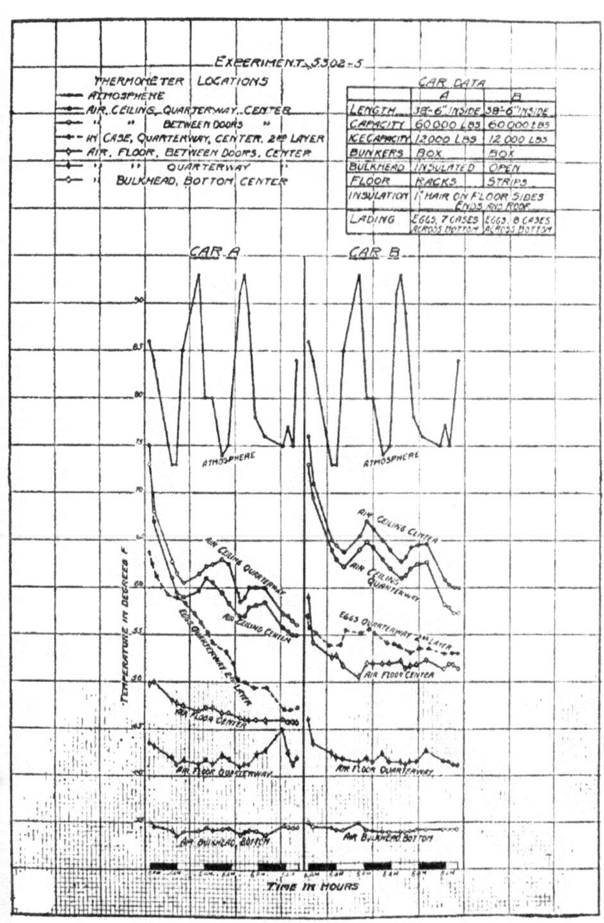
EXPERIMENT 5302-5
THERMOMETER LOCATIONS
ATMOSPHERE
AIR, CEILING, QUARTERWAY, CENTER
" " BETWEEN DOORS "
IN CASE, QUARTERWAY, CENTER, 2ND LAYER
AIR, FLOOR, BETWEEN DOORS, CENTER
" " QUARTERWAY "
" BULKHEAD, BOTTOM CENTER
CAR DATA
A
B
LENGTH 38'-6" INSIDE 38'-6" INSIDE
CAPACITY 60000 LBS 60000 LBS
ICE CAPACITY 12000 LBS 12000 LBS
BUNKERS BOX BOX
BULKHEAD INSULATED OPEN
FLOOR RACKS STRIPS
INSULATION 1" HAIR ON FLOOR SIDES ENDS AND ROOF
LADING EGGS, 7 CASES ACROSS BOTTOM EGGS, 8 CASES ACROSS BOTTOM
CAR A
CAR B
ATMOSPHERE
AIR CEILING CENTER
AIR CEILING QUARTERWAY
EGGS QUARTERWAY 2ND LAYER
AIR FLOOR CENTER
AIR FLOOR QUARTERWAY
AIR BULKHEAD BOTTOM
TEMPERATURE IN DEGREES F
TIME IN HOURS

CHART II.

warmest and the coldest points in the car was 12.3° F., in the other 4.8° F.

The reduction of the temperature on top layers can be increased by better and more judiciously applied insulation, especially in the roof of the car. Most of the cars in service have the same amount of insulation throughout, regardless of the additional strain on the roof during the heat of summer, and on the floor when frost protection is necessary. Experiments are now under way to determine just how much insulation it is advisable to have in roof and floors as well as in the body of the car. At present the work indicates that there is scarcely a refrigerator in the country which is sufficiently well insulated to be an economical as well as a safe carrier of perishables. A large proportion of the refrigerator cars now in service have one inch of insulating material over the entire car. Some have two inches throughout, and a few, comparatively, have had special care bestowed on the insulation of the roof and the floor. The lack of sufficient insulation, especially on the roof of the car, has been responsible for the fact that the top layers of such fruits as peaches, strawberries and cherries are so different in quality from the rest of the carload that they must be sold as separate lots. The higher temperature of the upper half of the car has led the shippers to urge longer cars, that they might extend rather than heighten the stacks of packages. As a result of this, and also in line with a general increasing of capacity of all cars, the refrigerator has been lengthened regardless of the fact that heat transmission increases directly as the number of square feet of surface enclosing the car space. For example, a car whose roof, walls and ends aggregate 1170 square feet and which is 33 feet between linings, has the same amount of temperature protection with two inches of insulation as a car with 2.5 inches of insulation whose surfaces aggregate 1407.5 square feet, and whose length between lining is 40 feet 6 inches.

To determine the economical size of a refrigerator car in relation to the height of the lading, the consumption of ice, the total weight of the car and its initial cost, is an economic problem of importance. Studies to obtain such information are now in progress.

The most obvious results due to increased insulation are, first better protection to the lading against both heat and cold, and second, a saving in the use of ice. The modern trend in the handling of perishables is to include precooling as a preparation for shipment, and it is a highly desirable practice from all viewpoints.

When the goods enter the car at a temperature conducive to preservation, it is the business of the car to maintain that temperature. The goods need no further refrigeration, and the ice in the bunkers is required only to overcome the heat leakage through the walls. The difference in performance of a car with one inch of insulation as compared with a similar car, except that the latter was provided with two inches, is shown in Charts IV and V. Both cars were loaded with eggs and closed without putting any ice in the bunkers.

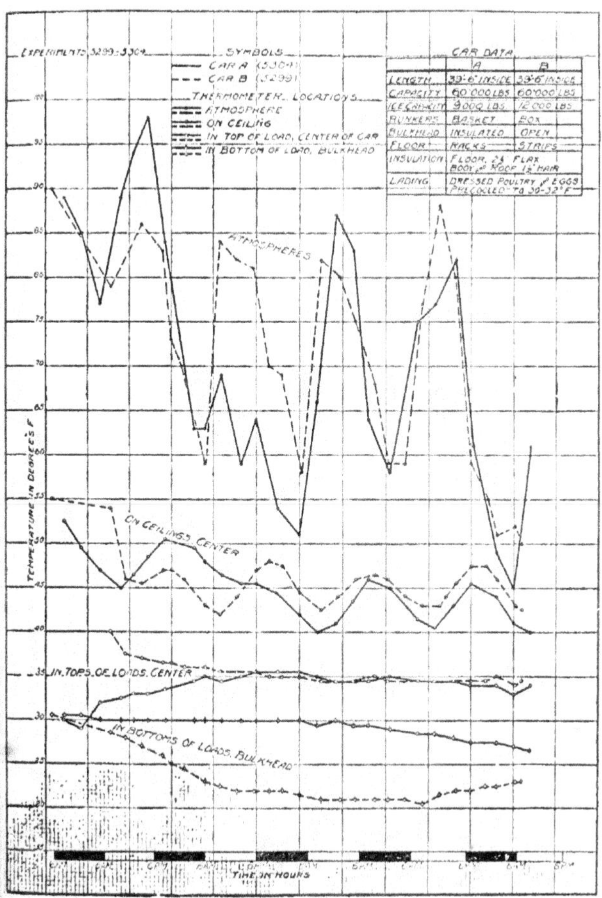
EXPERIMENTS 3299-3304
SYMBOLS
CAR A (3304)
CAR B (3299)
THERMOMETER LOCATIONS
ATMOSPHERE
ON CEILING
IN TOP OF LOAD, CENTER OF CAR
IN BOTTOM OF LOAD, BULKHEAD
CAR DATA
A
B
LENGTH
39'-6" INSIDE
39'-6" INSIDE
CAPACITY
60 000 LBS
60 000 LBS
ICE CAPACITY
9000 LBS
12 000 LBS
BUNKERS
BASKET
BOX
BULKHEAD
INSULATED
OPEN
FLOOR
RACKS
STRIPS
INSULATION
FLOOR, 2" FLAX
BODY AND ROOF 1½" HAIR
LADING
DRESSED POULTRY AND EGGS
PRECOOLED TO 30-32° F
ATMOSPHERES
ON CEILINGS, CENTER
IN TOPS OF LOADS, CENTER
IN BOTTOMS OF LOADS, BULKHEAD
TEMPERATURE IN DEGREES F
100
95
90
85
80
75
70
65
60
55
50
45
40
35
30
25
20
TIME IN HOURS
6PM

CHART III.

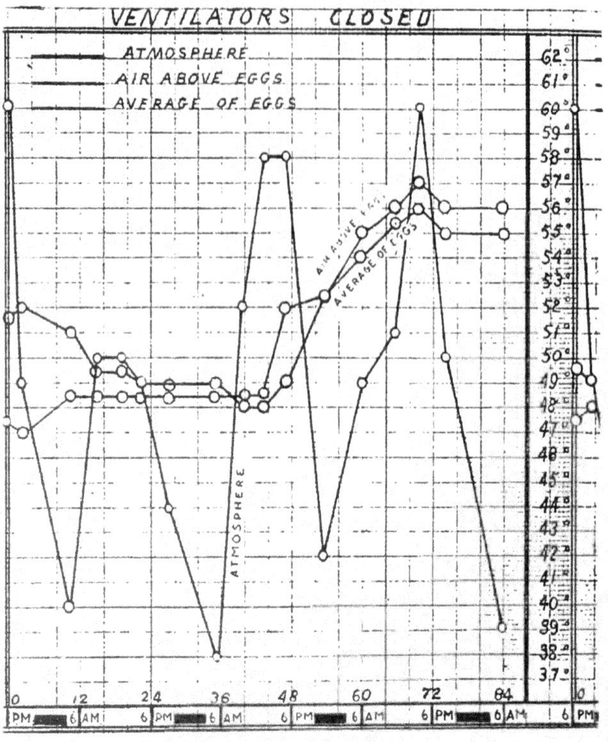

CHART IV.

The weather at the loading point was cool enough to ensure a cool car. The possible dangers—against which the insulation was to protect—lay ahead. Chart IV, showing the performance of the car with one inch of insulation, indicates very plainly that it could not protect the eggs. Chart V, on the other hand, shows that two inches of insulation, even with higher atmospheric temperatures, delivered the eggs at destination at practically the same temperature as they entered the car, and the maximum variation was but four degrees.

The one inch car needed 10,000 pounds of ice—the two inch car needed none. Is it any wonder that wide-awake shippers are picking out their refrigerator cars more and more carefully?

Experimentation indicates that marked economies can be effected

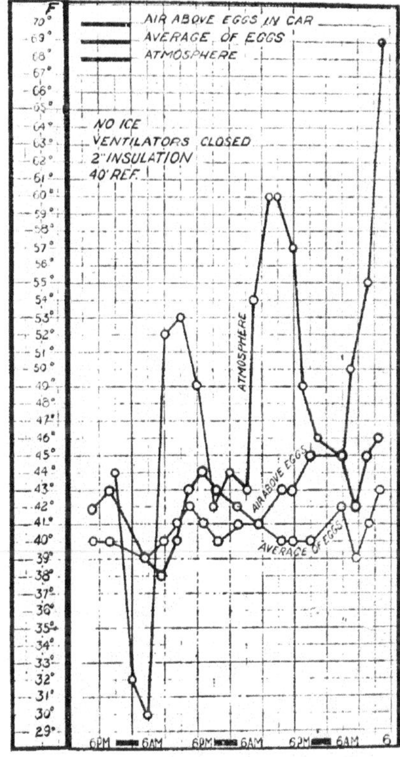

CHART V.

in the consumption of ice in transit aside from the question of insulation. Raising the load off the floor, inducing a circulation of air in the car, and bringing a large surface of ice into contact with the air, tends to reduce the amount of ice used. As stated in another connection in this paper, a carload of oranges in a car having box bunkers with open bulkheads, and without a rack on the floor, had 23,200 pounds of ice put into the bunkers between Los Angeles and New York. A similar car provided with basket bunkers, insulated bulkheads, and a floor rack, had 18,675 pounds. Neither load was precooled.

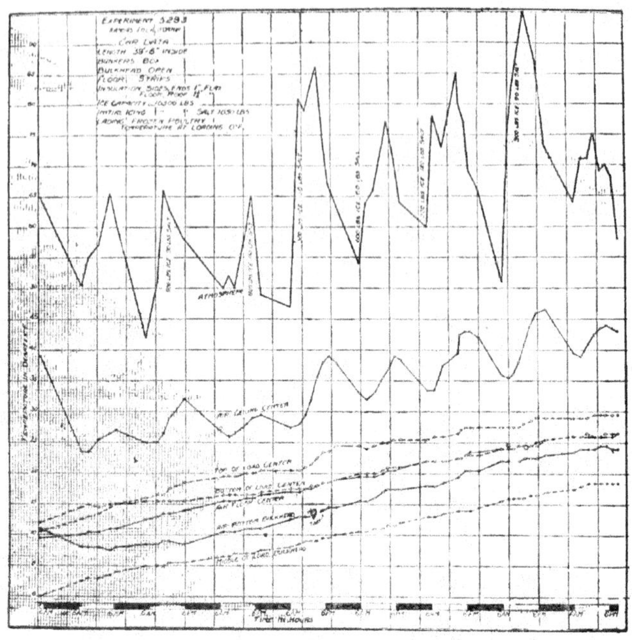

CHART VI.

That precooling of the lading means fewer icings in transit is a matter of common knowledge. That hard freezing of the goods, whereby they not only do not require additional chilling in transit, but actually furnish refrigeration to the car, is not so commonly recognized. Chart VI shows the temperatures in transit of 20,000 pounds of poultry which went into the car at 0° F. The railroad icing record shows that 4,700 pounds of ice was added during the eight-day haul, and 470 pounds of salt. Other experiments, under comparable conditions, show that nearly 5,000 pounds of ice is used by cars carrying 20,000 pounds of poultry chilled to 30-32° F. during a four-day haul, or approximately twice as much.

The temperature records show that the poultry grew gradually warmer, faster on the top and bottom of the load, where the heat leakage from the roof and floor was most pronounced, and most slowly in the center of the load, where the packages protected one another. The chart also shows that the amount of salt added during transit is insufficient to maintain the temperature produced on the initial salting, when the full ten per cent of the weight of the ice was present. It must be remembered that the salt bores through the ice and escapes as brine more rapidly than the bulk of the ice melts, hence it is in constantly decreasing proportion. Icing and salting rules take no account of the fact. It is quite obvious that different rules must be formulated if efficiency is to be secured.

This problem, like all the other problems confronting the shipper and the carrier who are engaged in getting perishables to market in good condition, can be solved only on the basis of exact knowledge. That knowledge the United States Department of Agriculture, in co-operation with the shippers and the railroads, is now endeavoring to acquire and to pass on to all whom it may benefit.

THE ABILITY OF REFRIGERATOR CARS TO CARRY PERISHABLE PRODUCTS.*

By Dr. M. E. Pennington.

Chief, Food Research Laboratory, United States Department of Agriculture, Bureau of Chemistry, Philadelphia, Pa.

Mr. Herman J. Pfeifer (Terminal R. R. Ass'n, St. Louis): Mr. President, ladies and gentlemen: At our last meeting, Mr. Aishton, President of the Chicago & Northwestern Railroad, made the remark that on the advice of Dr. Pennington, his road appropriated the sum of $200,000 for improvements in the matter of refrigerator cars in a shorter time than an equal sum of money had ever been appropriated by that railroad.

The question of food conservation is intimately connected with its transportation, and a great deal of our food being of a perishable nature, which must be transported in refrigerator cars, makes the consideration of this subject a very vital one at this time. The subject, therefore, about which Dr. Pennington is to speak, namely, the ability of refrigerator cars to transport perishable products safely, is one of vital interest, under present conditions.

Dr. Pennington is recognized throughout the country as an authority on food conservation and preservation, and it now gives me great pleasure to introduce to you Dr. M. E. Pennington, Chief of the Food Research Laboratory of the United States Department of Agriculture. (Applause.)

*Reprint from the Official Proceedings, St. Louis Railway Club, October 12th, 1917, Vol. 22, No. 6. Address delivered before the St. Louis Railway Club, October 12th, 1917.

Mr. President, Members and Guests of the St. Louis Railway Club:

It is with a great deal of embarrassment that I undertake to address you railroad men upon a subject dealing with facts with which so many of you are already well acquainted.

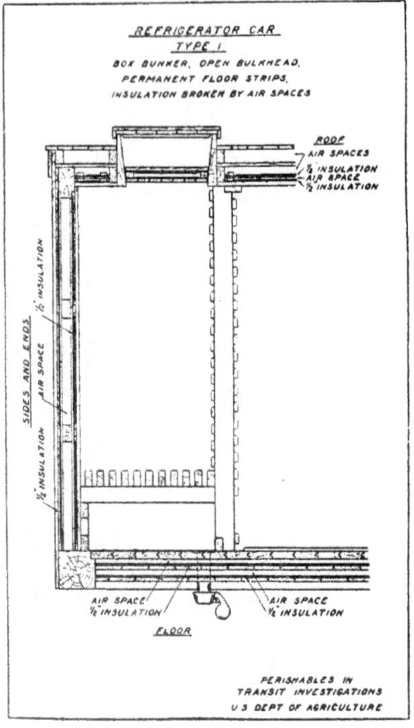

FIG. I.

The responsibility of appearing before you is great, dealing, as I shall, with matters which are of daily occurrence in your own line of business, and inasmuch as I come here, talking to you in your own bailiwick, the only excuse that I can plead is that we are at war, that we need food, and that food must be saved. Anything that we can do to save the chicken, the egg, the fish, no matter to how small an extent, we must do, as a part of the work that we all have in hand, to the end that we may win this war.

If I can do just a very little bit by placing before you some of the results of the investigations of the Department of Agriculture in the matter of saving foodstuffs, I will be more than glad, and I know that you, as patriotic American citizens, will rejoice, also.

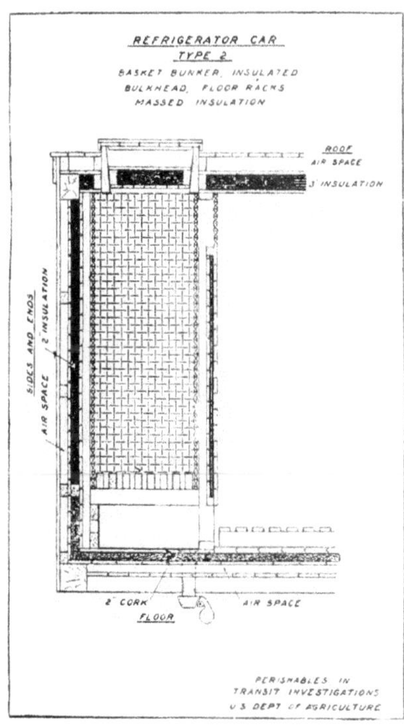

FIG. II.

We are being daily more and more impressed with the evidence to show that this war will be won by food.

The task of feeding the Allies and ourselves becomes more important as it becomes more difficult. The President urges increased production and agriculture is fostered as never before—yet we know that the calling of men to the colors and to the many activities of war means greater and greater difficulty in the production of the foodstuffs necessary to win the war. Therefore, conservation and the elimination of food waste and spoilage has become a world question of vital interest.

The question of transportation has also become of overwhelming importance. Our railroads are taxed to their utmost, and, as in the food question, the future seems to hold problems even harder to solve than those now at hand. Every rail, locomotive and car must be utilized for maximum service. The refrigerator car, especially, becomes an object of renewed interest, because upon it depends very largely our ability to render available the crops produced and food animals raised. It must carry a full load, yet we must not, in our zeal to transport perishables, permit any spoilage or damage in transit that can possibly be avoided.

The investigation of the transportation of perishables which is now under way in the United States Department of Agriculture has shown that the refrigerator equipment on the various lines differs widely in ability to protect against heat and cold. This variation depends to a certain extent upon the size and character of the load as well as upon the construction of the car. It is my purpose to discuss with you some of the results of these investigations, comparing the performance of cars of varying types when loaded with varying quantities of the commodity to be transported. First, however, let me very briefly outline the major differences in the construction of the cars used in these experiments. In the general purpose refrigerator car we find two types of bunker—one known as the "box bunker," illustrated in Fig. I, in whhich the ice rests directly against the end and sides of the car—and the other, known as the "basket bunker" in which the ice is held in a wire container two inches away from walls and bulkhead (see Fig. II). The box bunker usually has an open bulkhead of wood or metal. Sometimes we find a solid wooden partition open at top and bottom. The basket bunker commonly has a solid, wooden bulkhead, open twelve inches at the bottom and fourteen inches at the top, and in the new cars this bulkhead is insulated with one inch of a recognized insulator. The new cars, also, have a rack, on the floor, four inches in the clear, made of 2x4 runners and 1x3 cross slats, 1½ inches apart. These racks are fastened to the sides of the car with hinged bolts. They are divided in the middle so that they can be turned up against the walls when the car is cleaned. They are absolutely necessary for the safe carrying of perishable loads. Most of the cars now on the lines are without racks. Some have permanent strips on the floors one or one and one-half inches in height. These strips are practically valueless. The insulation varies from a few layers of paper to three inches of some recognized insulator. In some cars the layers of insulation are broken by spaces—in others the insulation is massed. The cars in the experiments were from approximately twenty-nine feet between bulkheads to approximately thirty-three feet.

The majority of the experiments used as illustrations are taken from the investigations on the transportation of eggs, because that

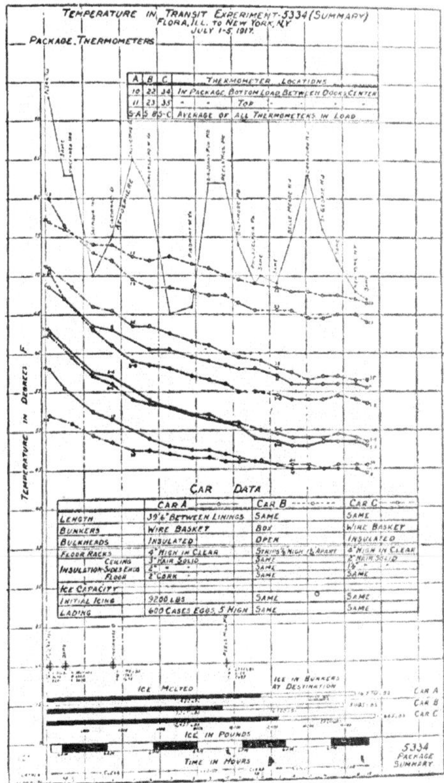

CHART VII.

field of work is under my charge. Whenever the shipment of fruits or vegetables is used to emphasize a fundamental, the facts have been furnished me by Mr. H. J. Ramsey, of the Bureau of Plant Industry, under whose direction all such commodities are being investigated. Of course, all temperatures were taken by means of electrical thermometers inserted when the cars were loaded, and the mechanism was such that neither the doors nor the hatches were opened to take records nor was the car modified in any way.

Now let me proceed to the work done by such classes of cars as above indicated.

The car factors which determine the size of the load which can be safely carried are insulation, bunkers and floor racks. Each exer-

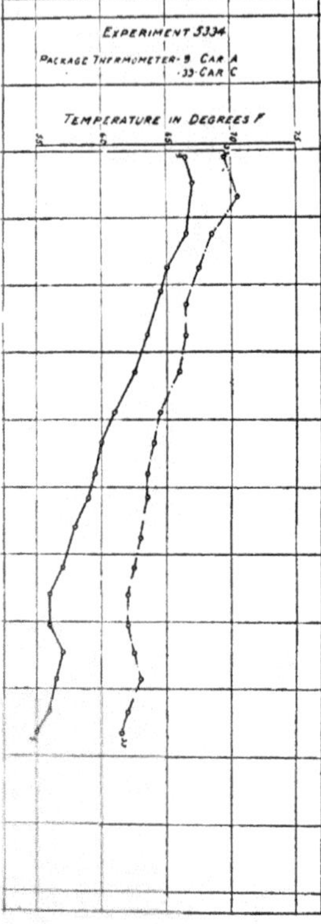

CHART VIII.

cises a specific influence as indicated in Chart VII. This experiment consisted of three cars which had been in experimental service for about ten months. As shown on the chart, cars A and C were provided with basket bunkers and floor racks; car B had a box bunker and strips on the floor. Cars A and B had three inches of insulation in the roof, two inches in side walls and ends and two inches of cork in the floor. Car C had one and one-half inches in the walls and two inches in the roof and floor. Each was loaded with six hundred cases of eggs consolidated from pickup cars, and each re-

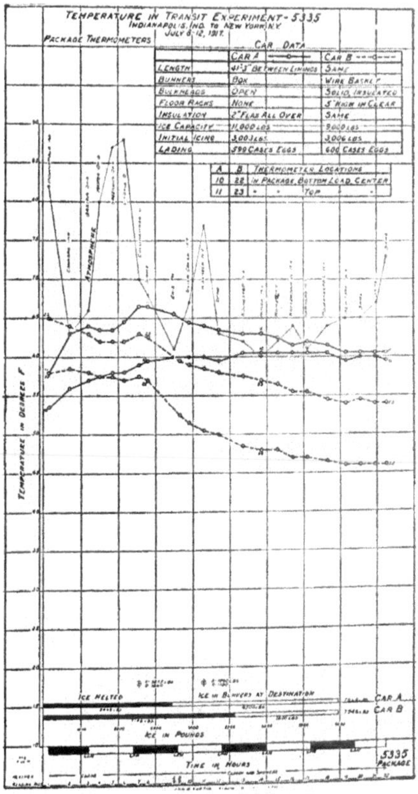

CHART IX.

ceived the same amount of ice accurately weighed into the bunkers. About twelve thermometers were put into each car. For our purposes the temperatures in the cases of eggs on the bottom and top of the load are especially significant, and indicate very plainly the amount of work which the car can do. For example, the temperature of the eggs on the floor of car B, between the doors, was 66.5° F. on arrival; car C, in the same location, was 45.5° F. and car A, 44.5° F. The packages between the doors on the top of the load—in this case five layers high—showed for car B, 64°, for car C, 56.5°, and for car A, 55.5° F.

The behavior of the packages on the floor of car B between the doors is especially noteworthy. They were continuously higher in temperature than the packages on the top of the load, a condition

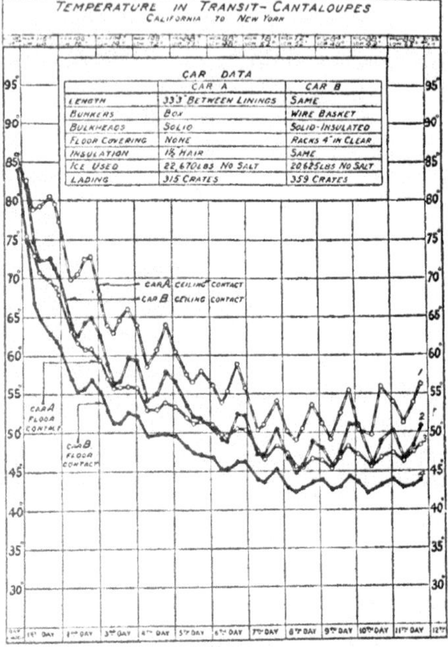

CHART X.

quite contrary to the generally held idea that the coolest place in a refrigerator car is its floor. That is only true when the construction is such that the cold air from the bunkers can travel along the car floor. This experiment, and many others that we have made, shows conclusively that a rack 4 inches above the floor is necessary if the goods on the bottom of the load in the two middle quarters of the car are to be refrigerated. It is of interest to note, also, that the insulation in cars A and B is unusually heavy, in fact, more than twice as much as in most of the refrigerator cars now in service, yet, because of the construction of the bunkers in car B and the absence of a rack on the floor, there was practically no refrigeration except near the bulkheads.

Manifestly, car B is not a satisfactory carrier for a heavy load of eggs. Car A, on the other hand, has done its work well, and at first sight car C, having less insulation, appears to be efficient for a

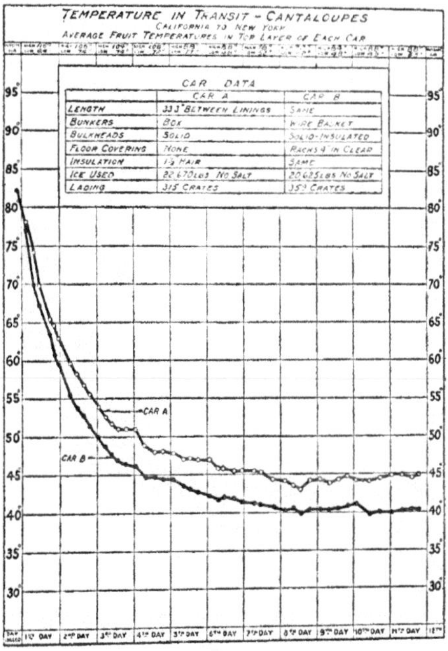

TEMPERATURE IN TRANSIT – CANTALOUPES
CALIFORNIA TO NEW YORK
AVERAGE FRUIT TEMPERATURES IN TOP LAYER OF EACH CAR

CAR DATA

	CAR A	CAR B
LENGTH	33 3" BETWEEN LININGS	SAME
BUNKERS	BOX	WIRE BASKET
BULKHEADS	SOLID	SOLID-INSULATED
FLOOR COVERING	NONE	RACKS 4" IN CLEAR
INSULATION	1½" HAIR	SAME
ICE USED	22,670 LBS NO SALT	20,625 LBS NO SALT
LADING	315 CRATES	352 CRATES

CAR A
CAR B

CHART XI.

load of 600 cases of eggs during hot summer weather. Further study, however, shows that the packages around the walls of car C came into destination over 6° higher than the corresponding packages in car A (Chart VIII), though when loaded they were but 3° apart.

Car C used about 1,000 pounds more ice than car A and, on the whole, did less satisfactory work, especially around the walls, where actual deterioration due to heat undoubtedly occurred.

It may be said that in the experiment cited, car B, having the box bunker and open bulkhead, was unfairly treated in that the temperature of the entering load was distinctly higher. The facts illustrated in Chart IX tend to nullify the significance of such an argument. In this experiment, the cars had two inches of insula-

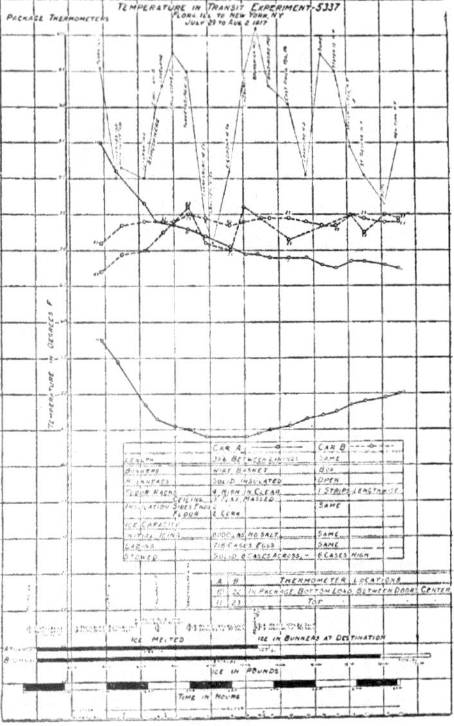

CHART XII.

tion throughout, but car A was of the box bunker type, while car B had a basket bunker and its adjuncts. Here the eggs entering car A were cooled to between 50 and 60° F., while those in car B ranged between 55 and 65° F. However, car A could not even maintain the initial temperature. At destination the packages in the middle of the car on the floor were nearly 5° warmer than when they entered the car and those in the top layer were over 2° higher. Car B, on the contrary, brought in the load from 6 to 14° lower than car A. These two cars were loaded with 600 cases of eggs and, so long as the atmospheric temperatures were above 80° F., refrigeration was of doubtful efficiency. The third and fourth days of the trip were unseasonably cool and also rainy, which compensated for the lack of insulation in the roof and permitted the load in the car B to drop below 55° F. before the end of the fourth day.

The performance of a poorly built car, said to contain an inch and a half of insulation throughout, as compared with a well built car known to have one and a half inches of insulation, is well illustrated in Charts X and XI, where cantaloupes were hauled for eleven days across a hot territory. The top layer in car A, loaded six wide and four high at the bunkers, was in such bad condition on arrival that claims were filed for damage in transit. Car B, on the other hand, was in good condition, although the load was seven cases wide and four cases high. In car A the combination of a lack of cold air circulation and of insulation proved disastrous, even though the load was light and open in character, and much easier to refrigerate than a load of eggs. In fact, we know that eggs can not be safely loaded more than three layers high in summer weather in cars having one inch of insulation. Cars having one and one-half inches of insulation, if provided with a basket bunker and a floor rack, can carry four layers. To load five high, we must have three inches in the roof and two inches in the walls, ends and floors, and good air circulation. Beyond five layers of egg cases we have not succeeded in getting good refrigeration.

This is illustrated in Chart XII, showing top and bottom layer temperatures in two cars stowed six layers high, making 700 cases to the load. Car A is of the same type as was used in Chart VII, where with 600 cases it did good work. With 700 cases there was practically no refrigeration except in the bottom layer. The companion car, B, with the same insulation but having a box bunker, did not even refrigerate the lower layers. The packages on the floor, middle of the car, were often warmer than the top of the load, which was only 12 inches from the ceiling. It varied more than 5° with the daily rise and fall of the atmosphere and arrived at destination showing an increase of 7.5°.

Encouragingly good results have been obtained in refrigerating heavy loads of fruit in the basket bunker cars by adding salt to the ice in the bunkers. On a long haul across a hot territory salt has been added to the ice at the first three icing stations. By that time (the third day) the load was cooled and very frequently no more ice was needed, even though the haul continued for five to eight days. The air issuing from the bunkers is far below 32° F., but the circulation is so rapid that there is no pocketing at the bulkhead. The insulated bulkhead also protects the load so that frosting does not occur. Salting ice in a box bunker, open bulkhead, merely freezes the load next to the bulkhead. The packages in the middle of the car are not benefited because of a lack of air circulation.

We have used salt to assist in refrigerating heavy loads of eggs and with some success, but we have not succeeded in refrigerating

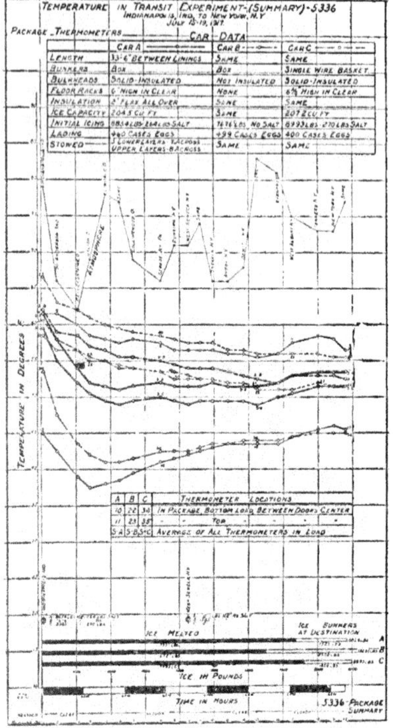

CHART XIII.

700 cases in a car 33 feet between bulkheads. The records of car A, in Chart XII, bring out this fact. Three per cent of salt was added after the load had been placed in this car and salt was again put into the bunkers at three icing stations. While the car was not able to handle so heavy a load during the very hot weather prevailing, it nevertheless did rather remarkable work and furnished valuable information on which to develop a more economical and efficient icing

system. Car A, which brought the sixth layer of eggs from 85° down to 66.5° F., used 12,660 pounds of ice and 540 pounds of salt; car B, which did not refrigerate either the top or bottom of the middle part of the load, used 19,755 pounds of ice.

A great many experiments have been made with fruits and eggs,

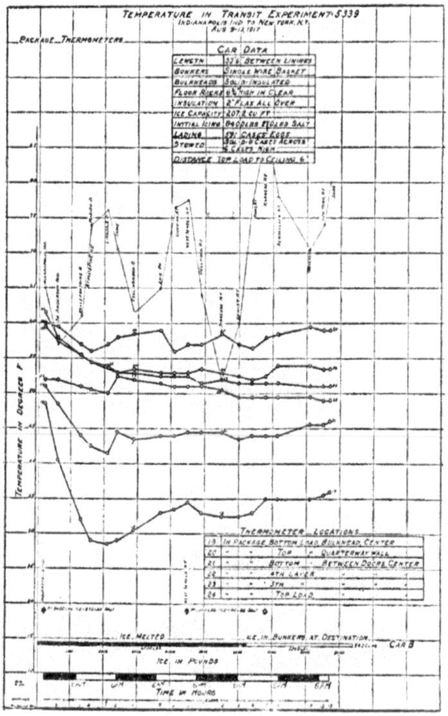

CHART XIV.

all of which confirm the foregoing; namely, that a suitable use of salt saves ice on a long haul and greatly increases the efficiency of the work done on both short and long hauls.

The experiment recorded in Chart XIII adds still further to our knowledge of car construction and car performance when salt is used with the ice. In this case we had short cars, so that by comparison the two inches of insulation became nearly 2.5 inches, and the air circulation was more rapid because of lessened distance. Car B was of the usual box type; car A had a box bunker with an insulated bulkhead and a floor rack; car C was of the standard basket type. Cars A and C received salt on the initial icing. They were neither iced nor salted in transit on an 88-hour haul. Car B was iced once. All contained from 400 to 500 cases of eggs. The three lower layers were seven cases wide, spaced for air circulation, and the upper layers were eight cases across. The average of all the thermometers in the packages in various parts of car B showed that it was far above cars A and C until the last day of the trip. An analysis of temperatures in different locations shows, further, that the floor of car B paralleled the top layer of car C. Car C did much the best work of the three. Car A, having the rack and the insulated bulkhead, but not the basket bunker, did not succeed in maintaining a sufficiently rapid air circulation to cool the top layer more than 5°. The packages on the floor, on the contrary, were exaggeratedly chilled because of the pocketing of the cold air. The conclusion follows that even with an openly stowed load, the car must be provided with a basket bunker, an insulated bulkhead, a floor rack and ample insulation, if our present loads are to be materially increased with safety to the commodity.

Car C (Chart XIV) of the foregoing experiment, was again used with a load of about 600 cases, stowed eight across. The ice was salted at the start and 40 pounds was added on the second day. Thermometers in the first, fourth, fifth and sixth layer packages give an instructive picture of the rise in temperature with the height of the load. Without salt, the fourth layer would be the stopping point. The fifth layer cases around the walls of the car would suffer if the weather were hot, if salt were not used. With the salt, as this experiment shows, we can load five high with impunity, but not six, because of damage to wall cases. A study of the chart shows that the 40 pounds of salt added at the first icing station was enough to cause a drop in temperature in all except the sixth layer wall packages. Had another charge of 40 pounds been added the next day, the rise shown in the lower layers would have been avoided and the fourth and fifth layers would have continued to cool instead of remaining practically stationary.

The investigation has convinced us that in the future ice and salt will be used for more commodities than fresh meats, poultry and fish. Indeed, it is the only way that we now see by which very perishable small fruits can be transported in good condition throughout the entire car. Of course, a definite routine for its application must be worked out. The experiments for the summer just ending have yielded much information. We hope that by the end of another summer we can bring you specific instructions for a number of commodities.

Such instructions must, however, be based on the type of car used. Far too many cars now on our lines would be useless no matter what treatment they received. For example, we still have

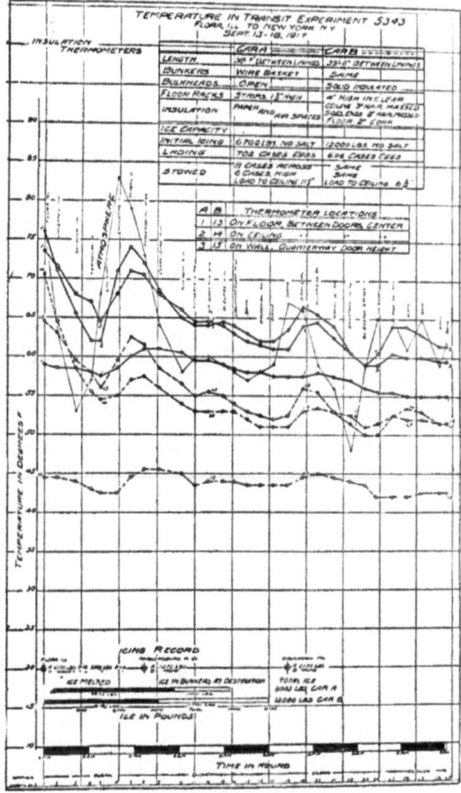

CHART XV.

cars with one-half inch of some insulator posing as refrigerators, and we still have cars, the walls of which contain only paper and air spaces. Considering the relation of foodstuffs to the winning of this war, I cannot look upon the use of such cars to transport perishables as anything short of a wasteful practice and should be discontinued.

Look at Chart XV. One of the cars represented is of the paper

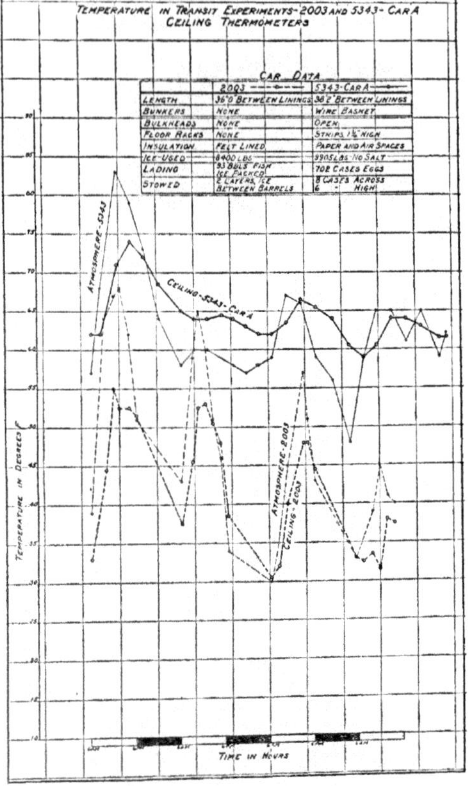

CHART XVI.

variety, the other well insulated. There is a variation of more than 15° between the two cars. The floor of the one is often six or more degrees warmer than the ceiling of the other. The paper car follows the atmospheric temperature and the refrigerant in the bunkers is almost powerless. Yet again and again this summer, eggs, fruit, vegetables and dressed poultry have been shipped in these cars and sometimes they have been loaded almost to their cubical capacity!

The relative value of the air space and paper as an insulator may be further emphasized by comparing a car built with what is termed, especially in the south, "a double-felt-lined" car. Such a car is considered to be a greater protection than a box car but in no wise is it a refrigerator. Indeed, it is not provided with ice bunkers. Chart XVI shows how the temperatures on the ceiling of such a car follow the atmosphere. Compare its performance with that of the paper car on the same chart, and I think you will agree with me that there is a decided similarity between the two.

Summary

Summing up the results of such experiments as these we are led to the following conclusions:

1. A combination of basket bunker, insulated bulkhead and floor rack, produces a circulation of air which is not obtained in a car having a box bunker, open bulkhead and bare floor or permanent strips.

2. Such a basket bunker car, approximately 33 feet between bulkheads, can refrigerate the top and bottom of the load in the two middle quarters of the car, provided it is sufficiently well insulated and not overloaded.

3. Cars which depend for insulation on paper and air spaces should not be used for the transportation of such perishables as fruit, delicate vegetables, poultry, eggs and fish.

4. Cars having one inch of insulation will not carry eggs successfully during hot weather when loaded more than three layers high.

Cars having one and one-half inches of insulation in the side walls and two inches in the roof and floor will not carry eggs successfully during hot weather when loaded more than four layers high.

Cars having three inches of insulation in the roof, two in the side walls and ends, and two inches of cork in the floor will carry eggs five cases high, but not six.

The box bunker car, regardless of quantity of insulation, does not refrigerate the two middle quarters of the load when it is tightly stowed. Even with an open load the performance is unsatisfactory.

5. The use of salt with the ice in a well insulated basket bunker car will permit an increase in the load of from 25 to 40 per cent.

6. While each commodity must be studied separately in order to determine the maximum load, the principles of the relation between car efficiency and tonnage of eggs as indicated in this discussion can be applied to perishables in general.

We are continuing, of course, such work as I have outlined to you this evening; it will be a long study before all of the many questions which have come to your minds, and which have come to our minds, can be answered. It is only by co-operation of the railroads and the shippers that we can come anywhere near solving the many questions that we will have to answer. You railroad men have abundantly furnished the co-operation, and we of the Department of Agriculture feel ourselves very greatly your debtors.

If we can be of any further service to you, please call upon us. We want to be of service, of course, that is what the money is appropriated for, and that is what we are all working for.

THE DEVELOPMENT OF THE STANDARD REFRIGERATOR CAR.*

By Dr. M. E. Pennington.

Chief, Food Research Laboratory, United States Department of Agriculture, Bureau of Chemistry, Philadelphia, Pa.

A short time ago the Railroad Administration issued a circular the opening paragraph of which reads as follows: "In order to insure the greatest possible degree of efficiency in refrigeration and conservation of food stuffs, refrigerator cars having trucks of 60,000 pounds capacity or over, will, when receiving general repairs or being rebuilt, be made to conform to the following United States Standard refrigerator car requirements." Then follow specific details and references to blue prints for the construction of the car in general, its insulation, its ice boxes and the many details which go to make up a refrigerator car. Throughout one finds that the railroads are instructed to build in conformity with the "United States standard refrigerator car."

Knowing the difficulties which attach to obtaining agreement among car builders, the desire of the financiers of the railroads to minimize the outlay for equipment and the great variety of perishables to be transported, one may well ask how such an order has come about, and upon what it is based.

Considering the fact that we have in this country more than one hundred thousand refrigerator cars, and that ultimately all will probably conform to the essentials just laid down by the Railroad Administration, it may not be amiss to review the circumstances which have led to the issuance of "Mechanical Department Circular No. 7."

In the latter part of the '90's and early 100's the difficulties in

*Reprint from the American Society of Refrigerating Engineers Journal, July, 1919, Vol. 6, No. 1, presented at the fourteenth annual meeting, New York, Dec. 2nd, 3nd and 4th, 1918.

the distribution of our perishables attracted an increasing amount of attention because the length of the hauls increased as more distant markets demanded supplies, and the losses from decay in transit kept pace with the distance traveled. Some of the shippers applied to the United States Department of Agriculture for assistance, among them the Georgia peach growers. These growers were in trouble; they could not successfully ship their product to northern markets because of the losses from decay. So in 1903 Mr. G. Harold Powell and his associates undertook to investigate the matter. They studied the effect on ripening of cooling the fruit quickly after picking and before loading in the car as well as the development of decay in transit. Precooling, however, was not a reliable remedy because the insulation of the refrigerator car of the south was, and is, insufficient to retain the chill imparted to the fruit and the air circulation in the cars was, and is, inadequate to transfer the refrigeration from the ice bunkers to the center and top of the load. This is a handicap which limits the distribution of the Georgia peach crop and from which the industry has never been able to escape. So universal is the failure of the cars to refrigerate the top layers and the middle of the car, that receivers expect to market the load as at least two grades, though the pack may have been uniform when shipped. To anticipate the story somewhat, I may say here that when carloads of peaches in adequate refrigerator cars came into the market during the summer of 1918, with top, bottom, middle and ends all in like condition, the astonishment of the trade was interesting to contemplate. The higher prices to the shippers, likewise, were gratifying in the extreme, and the railroads had no claims to pay.

From Georgia peaches the investigators were called to California oranges. The industry was severely handicapped because of decay in transit. Again the inadequacies of the refrigerator cars were apparent. The investigations of the temperature in cars in transcontinental trips brought out the differences in the different parts of the car and their relation to the excessive decay in the middle of the load and its upper portion. With oranges which ripen slowly after picking, careful handling in orchard and packing house to eliminate decay could go much farther toward ensuring preservation than with quick ripening peaches. It is interesting to observe, too, the improvements in insulation and general construction undergone by the far western refrigerator cars, in response to the definite information furnished and the demands of the great western fruit business. However, these improvements were practically all based on the requirements of citrus fruits, which are, as we now know, extremely easy to refrigerate if they are well picked, graded and packed. The needs of deciduous fruits, poultry, eggs, butter, fish and delicate vegetables were still little known and uncared for.

In 1908 the Food Research Laboratory, which had been studying the effect of long cold storage on poultry, extended the work to the handling of the fresh goods in the packing houses and in transit.

Our object was to prevent deterioration, and to that end the best packing house methods available were sought. However, we soon found that standardized methods at the packing house did not give standardized results at the market; in other words the refrigerator cars were a variable factor. This was proven, not only by the chemical and bacteriological analysis of the poultry, but by the temperature records on the thermographs placed in various parts of the load. Again we found the packages on the top of the load and those in the middle of the car more or less injured by lack of refrigeration. Indeed, it was not and is not uncommon to find chickens on the floor at the bunker hard frozen, those quarterway of the car in a good chilled condition, and between the doors green struck, and this in spite of the fact that the condition of the packages was practcially uniform when they were loaded.

After several years of such work, during which shipments had been made from various poultry packing houses in the corn belt both west and east of the Mississippi to eastern markets and a number of car lines had been used, a tabulation of the data showed, among other things that deterioration in transit was increased when the cars of certain lines were used.

Then began the study of the construction of these cars, using the blue prints showing the plans on which the cars were built, and as a resultant further confirmation of the close relation between the condition of the goods on arrival and the quantity and placing of the insulation and the type of ice bunker. In 1913 the results were published as Bulletin No. 17 of the United States Department of Agriculture. The conclusions presented in that bulletin outline fairly well the lines of work since followed by the investigators and which have led to the information on which the construction of the standard refrigerator car is based. The concluding paragraph of the bulletin says, "It is eminently necessary that such questions as the most efficient and economic size of the refrigerated car, the exact amount of insulation required to insure the maintenance of low temperatures, or, conversely, to protect the contents of the car against frost, the equalization of temperatures in all parts of the car, and many others, be pressed for more exact and far reaching answers." The bulletin points out the importance of roof and floor construction in relation to insulation efficiency, especially the waterproofing of the floor. It also calls attention to the efficiency of the wire basket bunker which permits of abundant air access to the refrigerant.

Throughout the period between 1908 and 1913 the investigators of the transportation of dressed poultry and eggs were in constant touch with the men of the Bureau of Plant Industry who were performing a like service for fruits and vegetables. Their field of operations had rapidly widened and data was being assembled on apples, pears, berries, cantaloupes, lettuce, celery and many other products. It is needless to state that the defects found in the cars hauling plant products were identical with those hauling animal products. It was obvious, too, that no amount of work to teach better field, orchard and packing house methods would have the desired result—namely, freedom from decay at the market—until the construction of the refrigerator cars was suited to the work which they were expected to perform. To determine in detail what that construction must be, opened a new phase of the problem.

In the first place the thermograph was relegated to the garret. It was no longer sufficiently exact for our purposes nor could its information be made sufficiently specific. We substituted the resistance thermometer, so constructed that it might be plunged into the orange, chicken or fish, as well as hung in the air of the car or placed firmly against the car body. These thermometers were sensitive to a tenth of a degree Fahrenheit. They were attached to long wires which were passed between the packing of the door and the jamb without admitting air and were collected into cables with terminals on top of the car, or which extended from car to car and so into a caboose, or living car, where all the thermometers in the cars under observation might be read by plugging into a switch board attached to an indicator. In this manner the environment of all cars was kept the same and, if the variables in each car were reduced to one, a direct comparison of the temperatures observed furnished valuable information.

The number of cars under observation in the same train, loaded with the same commodity, has varied from two to fourteen. The hauls have been from one hundred to three thousand miles, during which the cars were not opened. Readings of the thermometers were made, on the average, once every four hours. The ice and salt which went into the bunkers were weighed by the investigators and in some experiments the water issuing was measured. When salt was used with the ice, the specific gravity of the issuing brine was taken at frequent intervals.

Gradually a uniform plan was developed for the placing of the thermometers in the commodity and in the car, as key positions were located. Ordinarily twelve thermometers are used in each car, distributed as follows:

(1) On the floor, midway between the doors, middle of car.
(2) On the ceiling midway between the doors, middle of car.
(3) On the wall, quarter way of car, door height.
(4) In air, bottom bulkhead opening, midway between walls.
(5) In air, floor, midway between doors, middle of car.
(6) In air, ceiling, midway between doors, middle of car.
(7) In package, bottom layer, first stack, middle row.
(8) In package, top layer, quarter way stack, wall row.
(9) In package, bottom layer, middle stack, middle row.
(10) In package, top layer, middle stack, middle row.
(11) In package, quarter way stack, middle layer, middle row.
(12) In package, top layer, first stack, middle row.

As air circulation is one of the most important items to be studied, it was necessary to adopt uniformity in the placing of the air thermometers. Results which are comparable and practical have been obtained by mounting each air thermometer on a block of cork board, two inches thick and long enough to extend well beyond the ends of the instrument. These blocks of cork were fastened to the floor and ceiling beside the thermometers which were intended primarily to register the differences in heat leakage and which were fastened down tightly by two staples. The thermometers in the commodity were imbedded between four and five inches whenever possible. Every effort was made by the cooperating shippers to furnish comparable lading, and the placing of the loads was supervised by the investigators.

It must not be inferred that the railroads were either indifferent or antagonistic toward this research work. On the contrary, they had almost without exception cordially assisted the investigators. As the facilities for the acquisition of information became more exact, and as closer correlation between car building and temperature was shown, it was evident that cars must be built with insulation and bunkers of varied construction, and, so far as possible, the cars to be compared must be duplicates except for the one variable on which information was desired. This need was explained to certain cooperating roads, and they were also given just as much information concerning the performance of their own refrigerator cars as we possessed. A number of them were willing to build a few experimental cars, and a few practically put their shops at our disposal. What was quite as advantageous to the work, was the better understanding on the part of the railroads of the aims of the Department and the methods employed. These were personally explained to the Vice Presidents of Traffic and Operation of practically every large system in the country and in many cases to the Presidents as well. Members of the Interstate Commerce Commission were also informally kept in touch with the progress of the work. The fact that the study of commodities in transit had shown that the same kind of car was necessary to carry fruits, vegetables, dairy freight and fish, and that the building of specialized cars for certain products was unnecessary, was, of course, greeted with approbation by everyone interested in the economics of railroading.

One of the favorable happenings in the doing of this transportation work was the fact that the men engaged upon it were also in close touch or actually engaged upon cold storage investigations and were familiar with many phases of the precooling and storage problems. In the course of the fruit and vegetable precooling work, the investigators had observed the increase in efficiency when a slatted rack, a few inches above the floor, was used. The addition of such a rack to a refrigerator car seemed eminently desirable. Accordingly, we asked the railroads to add them to certain cars for trial purposes.

The studies already reported in Bulletin No. 17 had shown the desirability of the basket bunker. To this we asked the roads to add an insulated, solid, bulkhead, open top and bottom for air inlet and outlet. We had found such a bulkhead to be an essential in maintaining air circulation in small, ice cooled chill rooms designed especially for dressed poultry and eggs with bunkers of either the overhead or the upright type, and had worked out the details of the construction in such rooms. We also asked for cars containing varying amounts of insulation and we suggested that it be installed with and without air spaces.

By the early spring of 1916 we had ready quite a number of experimental cars built by four roads in as many shops. The details of construction varied widely. This we considered advisable because we first had to establish the fundamentals of construction, such as the type of bunker and the action of floor racks, regardless of the size or particular desirability of the car itself. In every case the principle of one variable, only, was maintained, hence the cars were built and used in series. For example, in order to test the bunker of the basket type with solid insulated bulkhead, such a car had for comparison another, built at the same time and identical in every respect except that it was provided with a box bunker and an open bulkhead. To reduce the information to still simpler terms, a third car had a box bunker with an insulated bulkhead, and a fourth car had a basket bunker with an uninsulated bulkhead. When this series was loaded with the same commodity and run in the same train to the same destination, with resistance thermometer equipment as previously described, variations in temperature could be referred with a fair degree of certainty to the one variation in construction.

A similar series was used to determine the relative value of the floor rack and also the details of its construction, such as height, width of slats and width of space between the slats. The insulation series contained cars having one, two and three inches, respectively, of hair felt, flaxlinum and linofelt. In order to determine the points of heavy strain on the insulation roofs, floors and walls were given unequal amounts.

Of course, these experimental cars were not all built at once, and, as we were in close co-operation with the shop superintendents, the facts, as gleaned, were at once incorporated into the building.

To go into the details of the many experiments, with various products, in various parts of the country and under varied weather conditions, will be a lengthy task even for a government bulletin. What concerns us here are the broad facts and the deductions which have been drawn from them, especially those concerning air circulation and the amount and distribution of insulation. Let us begin with air circulation.

It did not take long to decide that the basket bunker, insulated bulkhead and a rack four inches off the floor, with lengthwise stringers and cross slats about three inches wide and about two inches apart, are essentials for the distribution of the refrigerated air. The wire basket hanging free in the end of the car permits the warm air entering at the top to flow without obstruction over the entire surface of the ice and, as it cools, to fall to the floor. At the floor it is not pocketed, but finds a ready exit under the rack, and so along the car floor and up through the load, gathering heat as it goes and carrying it to the upper bulkhead opening where again the ice has a chance to absorb it.

If we place thermometers in the air of the car to determine its temperature at the lower bunker opening, again at the middle between the doors, then at the ceiling midway of the car, then at the ceiling quarter way, and finally about ten inches in front of the upper bunker opening, we find a steady rise in temperature, the upper bunker opening thermometer being the highest. Generally, we find from two to four degrees difference between the air in the upper, middle part of the car and that at the upper bunker opening. If the thermometers are similarly placed in a car equipped with a box bunker with open bulkhead and without the floor rack the graduations of temperature in the upper part of the car are just reversed. Here the temperature at the upper bunker opening is ordinarily from two to four degrees lower than at the middle of car. This observation has been made again and again and is further confirmed by the performance of a box bunker combined with solid bulkhead and a floor rack, with which there is good cooling in the top of the load at the bunkers, but unsatisfactory results in the upper, middle parts of the load. In other words, we have only a partial air circulation. Even more striking are the results obtained when salt is added to the ice in the basket bunker combined with the insulated bulkhead, and floor rack, or the "standard type" bunker, as it is now termed. So rapid is the removal of the very cold air from the bottom of the bunker that fruit and eggs may be rapidly cooled throughout the car without frosting the packages at the bulkhead. Of course, the bulkhead, insulated with one or two inches of a standard insulator, is an essential if the packages against it are to be protected from the frigid air close to the ice and salt; but, that this protection is not due entirely to the bulkhead, is proved by the pocketing of the cold at the bottom of the bunker when the box bunker with an insulated bulkhead is salted. Then the packages at the bottom of the load, next to the bunker, are frosted. In other words, there is no force to the air movement and it cannot be distributed with sufficient rapidity to prevent the intensive chilling of itself. With the standard bunker and floor rack and a lading such as cantaloupes or oranges, as much as 9 per cent of salt may be safely used in the initial icing, and the same percentage, or a little less, may be used on the two successive days, by which time the load is cooled throughout. It is unnecessary to point out the great advantages accruing to the transportation of such perishables as berries, peaches and cherries by this ability to cool them rapidly while rolling. It is also of benefit to eggs, which because of the character of the commercial package and the tight load are exceedingly slow to cool in the ordinary car. Indeed, the top and middle of the load is but little affected by the refrigerant.

The question of insulation has been more complex. We have not only a compound wall, but one which is continually in vibration and which is moving constantly. To this constant movement of the insulator must be added the difficulties of making it continuous because of the framing of the car and the habitual use of tie rods and bolts which offer runaways for heat. The sills as usually placed in the floor, the belt rails and the carlines were very real obstacles to the efficient placing of the insulation. The thickness of the insulator was by no means the only question to be answered; how it should be attached to the framing was almost as important. It was also necessary to determine the most vulnerable parts of the car and guard them accordingly.

The thermometers which were fastened tightly against the lining of the car very promptly and consistently indicated that roofs and floors must be better protected than the walls and, in the case of the floor and the lower part of the walls, it is imperative to waterproof. Comparisons of cars having varying amounts of insulation, loaded with representative commodities, showed that for the safety of the load, as well as economy in loading and in refrigerant, it is necessary to have the equivalent of two inches of pure cork board in the sidewalls and ends, at least two and one-half inches in the roof, and at least two inches in the floor, the insulation in the floor to be continuous from side to side and end to end. In other words, the insulation on the floor must not be broken by sills and it must be at least two inches of pure cork board.

It has not been possible, heretofore, to waterproof the floor. Consequently there has been wet insulation and a serious loss of efficiency. Therefore, the findings of the Department emphasize the need of cork board in the floor.

Such essentials of a refrigerator car as an adequate amount of insulation and air circulation, had been agreed upon by the investigators prior to government control of the railroads, and certain lines had incorporated some or all of the findings into their new cars and rebuilds. When the Railroad Administration took up the matter of the standardizing of equipment, it appointed a committee to draw plans and specifications for a United States standard refrigerator car. This committee first met on March 13, 1918, and appointed a subcommittee of six members, who were ordered to prepare plans in accordance with certain definite instructions given by the general committee. Within six weeks these plans and specifications had been presented to and accepted by the Director General's Mechanical Committee. So far as possible, the trucks, draft gear, framing and other general construction features, are standardized with the United

States standard double wall box car. The essentials upon which rest efficiency in protecting perishables against heat and cold have followed very closely the findings of the investigators of the Department of Agriculture. The committee's plans include unbroken insulation on both floor and roof. On the walls the insulation is continuous from door post to door post. It was not possible to devise a scheme by which the insulation could be run over the belt rails, but the exposed surface was reduced. All the insulation is applied in a solid mass, unbroken by air spaces. It is supported by pressure and not by direct nailing. The excess space afforded by the framing is left on the inner side, under the lining, to receive such nails as the shipper cannot be prevented from driving into the walls and which have played havoc with the insulation. Bolt heads and tie rod exits are protected by insulation. The bunker is a woven wire basket holding approximately ten thousand pounds of ice, surrounded by a two inch space and separated from the body of the car by a bulkhead carrying at least one inch of insulator; and last, but far from least, is a floor rack, four inches in the clear, built of 2x4 runners with 1x3 cross slats 1½ inches apart. This rack is hinged to the side walls. Each half may be turned up and the doorway section folds back to facilitate cleaning the car. The length of the car over end sills should be approximately 41 feet, and the loading space should be 33 feet; it must not be more than 33 feet 3 inches.

The foregoing is a very brief description of the essentials of the car designed to protect perishables in transit which the Railroad Administration has designated as "standard" and to which the lines when rebuilding must conform. Such instructions to the railroads should insure quick results in an increase of reliable refrigerator cars. Of course, there should, and doubtless will be, a program covering the building of new cars to replace at least ten thousand so-called refrigerator cars now in the service which are camouflaged box cars and a menace to every pound of foodstuff loaded in them.

On the basis of a standard car, the Department is now predicating a standard icing service which should save foods and money. It is also working on standardized methods of stowing loads and the standardization of packages. The ability to quickly cool certain commodities in transit by the use of salt with the ice has given a new impetus to orchard, field and packing house handling, while the reasonable assurance of proper care in transit of such products as dressed poultry lends a stability to the industry which is much needed. There has been much discontent on the part of shippers of products requiring intensive refrigeration because they could not obtain such cars as the large meat packers are using. The United States standard refrigerator car will carry meat hung from rails quite as successfully as the cars built especially for meat. In addition it will carry package loads on the floor under the meat better than the meat cars. An important difference in the standard car as compared with the meat car is the reserve of ice in the bunkers which are often amply supplied when the tanks of the meat cars need replenishing. Neither is there visible in practical results the advantages supposed to accrue from the retention of the brine, provided coarse rock salt is placed *on top of the ice* and so forced to bore its way through the whole mass before finding an exit. We have wasted much salt, in the past, as well as ice and foodstuff for lack of knowledge of car requirements.

For every standard car turned out of the shops there will follow a saving of food, a saving of money and a saving of labor. To that end the Department of Agriculture has worked long and patiently, and to that same end the Railroad Administration has now issued "Mechanical Department Circular No. 7" and has also indicated its intention of reminding the railroads of the instructions.

Truly, facts, faith, and friends, by co-operation have brought about a consummation long and earnestly desired.

SPECIFICATIONS FOR REFRIGERATOR CAR INSULATION.

THE ATCHISON, TOPEKA AND SANTA FE RAILWAY SYSTEM.

(No. C-52—Insulation for cars—nonpareil cork board)
Adopted January 1, 1923.

1. *Scope:* These specifications cover an insulation material for freight and passenger cars.

I. Manufacture.

2. *Material:* This insulation material shall consist entirely of pure ground compressed cork, properly baked and held together by the natural resinous matter of the cork, without the use of any foreign binder, and shall be capable of providing adequate insulation.

II. Physical Properties and Tests.

3. *Tests:* (a) The thermal efficiency of the material shall be determined by the "Hot Box" method with air to air flow. The sections to be tested shall truly represent the material as used and disposed in the car.

(b) In following this method, a calorimeter as illustrated and described in R.M.S. Drawing, Sheet 18, Proceedings of Master Car Builders' Association, 1918, shall be used. It shall be carefully constructed and of the materials indicated and before used must be standardized for its thermal loss factor. The heat must be supplied by direct electric current of constant voltage, measured by standardized instruments. The difference between the inside and outside temperatures must be held as nearly 70° F. as possible. Readings of temperature and current shall not be recorded until 48 hours after heat is turned on and test begins, in order to insure thorough heat saturation of calorimeter and test sections. The duration of actual test shall be eight (8) hours, during which time temperature and electric readings shall be made and recorded each hour or more frequently if considered necessary. The average of all readings thus recorded shall be taken as the final result.

4. *Conductivity:* Cork board one square foot in area and one thickness of one inch (1 in.), shall not transmit heat to exceed 6.4 B.t.u. per degree Fahr. difference in temperature per 24 hours.

5. *Weight:* The weight of one square foot of this cork board shall be as follows:

¼ in. thick—4 oz.
⅜ in. thick—6 oz.
½ in. thick—8 oz.
¾ in. thick—12 oz.
1 in. thick—15½ oz.
1½ in. thick—1 lb. 5 oz.
2 in. thick—1 lb. 11 oz.
3 in. thick—2 lb. 7½ oz.

with a permissible variation allowed in weight of 10 per cent either above or below the weights given above.

6. *Compression Test:* A sample of this cork board, two-inches thick and one-foot square, when subjected to a compressive load of 2,000 lbs. shall not show a decrease in thickness of more than 0.164 inches.

7. *Expansion Test:* Representative samples of the cork shall be submerged in boiling water at atmospheric pressure for three hours without disintegrating. Immediately upon removal from the boiling water, samples shall be measured for lineal expansion, which shall not exceed two per cent in any direction. The pounds of water retained in insulation, after being boiled three hours and then drained twenty-four (24) hours, shall not exceed 12 per cent of light weight of sample.

8. *Dimensions:* The material will be furnished to the dimensions specified on order and will be cut perfectly square and true to dimensions.

9. *Permissible Variations:* The thickness of the material shall be determined by placing a sample between two flat smooth boards or plates, at least 6 in. wide, the ends of which shall project about ⅛ in. beyond the edge of the cork board. Upon hand pressure being applied to the top board or plate, the measurement as taken between the inner faces of the two boards or plates between which the sample is compressed, shall not be more than 1/32 in. per inch over or under the thickness specified. It is desired, however, to secure the material to the exact thickness specified.

III. Inspection and Rejection.

10. *Inspection:* (a) The inspector representing the purchaser shall have free entry at all times while work on the contract of the purchaser is being performed, to all parts of the manufacturer's works which concern the manufacturer of the material ordered. The manufacturer shall afford the inspector free of charge, all reasonable facilities and necessary assistance to satisfy him that the material is being furnished in accordance with these specifications. Tests and inspection at the place of manufacture shall be made prior to shipment.

(b) The purchaser may make the tests to govern the acceptance or rejection of the material in his own laboratory or elsewhere. Such tests, however, shall be made at the expense of the purchaser.

(c) The manufacturer must notify the General Material Inspector, Chicago, Ill., or his representative at the plant, at least three days before the material is ready for inspection.

11. *Rejection:* (a) Material represented by samples, which fail to conform to the requirements of these specifications, will be rejected.

(b) Material which, subsequent to test and inspection at the factory or elsewhere and its acceptance, shows defects or imperfections will be rejected and shall be replaced by the manufacturer.

12. *Rehearing:* Samples tested in accordance with these specifications, which represent rejected material, shall be held for fourteen days from date of test report.

13. All specifications of previous date for this material are hereby annulled.

(Signed) M. J. Collins,
General Purchasing Agent.

CORK PAINT.*

For all surfaces, except ceiling and insulation, the surface of the metal, in addition to the priming coats already applied, will be given a thick coat of "under cork" or cork size (Formula No. 15). The ground cork, which should be fairly large grained (large enough to pass through a No. 8 sieve and be held on a No. 12), will then be sifted and applied, and left until the paint is slightly set, when, if required to efficiently cover the surface, a second coat of "under cork" and ground cork will be applied in a similar manner to the first coat in order to secure the adherence of the maximum amount of cork. Over this will be applied two or more coats of white paint, the first coat of which may be either applied by compressed-air spray or by hand, the other coats to be applied by hand. The coating of cork paint to be continuous and of substantial thickness. The above method will be applied also to the outboard surface of metal plates of ceiling and insulation, except that this plating will be laid flat to receive the application of ground cork, and that the final average thickness of cork paint is to be about $\frac{3}{64}$-inch.

The inboard surface of all metal ceiling will be finished white (not cork painted) glossed in officers' quarters. Cork painting should be limited to the minimum absolutely required to prevent excessive sweating, but where for instance, a part of the deck overhead would require to be cork painted, the remainder of the deck, if of metal, within the same compartment should be so painted in order to obtain a uniform appearance. In a compartment generally finished in white, glossed, where a portion of the surface is cork painted, the cork paint will also be glossed.

AUTHOR'S NOTE: Formula No. 15.—"Under cork," for one gallon, consists of: (a) Whiting, 10 pounds; (b) Hard Oil, ⅜-gallon; and (c) Japan Drier, ⅛-gallon. One gallon of "under cork" will cover approximately 20 square yards, at the weight of 2¼ pounds per 100 square feet of surface. Ground cork, "Newport Special," consists of natural cork bark ground to such size as to pass a screen having 8 meshes per inch and be caught on a screen having 12 meshes per inch.

PULVERIZED CORK—SUBIRINE.†

It is said that considerable use is now being made of the newly introduced French article to which the name of "subirine" has been given. The substance consists of pulverized cork of different degrees of fineness, known as impalpable, fine, medium and coarse, the pulverization being effected by very simple means, such as a horizontal grindstone. Among these the medium powders have for some time been employed in the French navy and by various navigation companies for painting the sheet iron and partitions of the insides of

*Extracted from specifications of the United States Navy Department for "cork paint" to reduce sweating of metal surfaces.

†Extracted from Ice and Refrigeration, January, 1894.

vessels; the effect of such coatings is said to be to considerably diminish the conductibility of the sheet iron, and the vibrations so unpleasant, which are produced as soon as the sea becomes a little rough. Another use for these cork powders is in the preparation of a substance called "liegine," which consists of the powder mixed with fine plaster in the proportion of about ten per cent. This liegine composition is turned out in all shapes and sizes, and is stated to be specially useful as a protection alike from heat or cold, or for partitions, roofs, lofts, ceilings, and coatings of all descriptions; also as packing for boilers, ice houses, conservatories, coverings for wagons, steam pipes and similar uses—in short, for the large number of cases where it is desirable to maintain an equal temperature.

CORK AS A BUILDING MATERIAL.*

By S. Sampolo.

Cork is one of the lightest and the worst conductors of heat and sound substances. It is also somewhat elastic, and when moderately compressed does not absorb water. These evident properties have for a long time given a great extension to the use of cork for industrial purposes, principally for the manufacture of stoppers for any kind of vessels containing liquids which do not attack organic substances.

Everybody knows that cork is the bark of a particular oak growing, not in America, but on the coasts of northern Africa and southern Europe. After being deprived of its hard, nonelastic and useless elements, this cork bark is cut into square pieces and turned on a special lathe, where the stopper shape is acquired. In this manufacture the waste should, theoretically, be about 20 per centum; in fact, how much larger is the quantity of scraps thrown away by the machine? It is an interesting industrial problem to try and make the best use of them in a judicious way.

So far, the only important application of this refuse material has been made in the manufacture of linoleum, which can utilize but a small percentage of the waste. Render possible the introduction of cork refuse for building purposes, and at once all scraps and cuttings will find an important application. If, at first, the idea may not appear realizable on account of the little resistance of cork, we may say that thousands and thousands of bricks and tile have already been made in France with pulverized cork refuse, and have worked satisfactorily. Labor and patience have not been spared, and

*Extracted from Ice and Refrigeration, June, 1895.

strengthening cements, which can be poured into any shape, size and thickness, have been in use.

Two kinds of cements can be manufactured; the first containing powder or small pieces of cork, plaster of Paris, dextrine and sesquioxide of iron. The second, besides all those substances, also contains an oxychloride such as the oxychloride of zinc, which makes that composition perfectly waterproof. Like cork itself, these cements are non-conductors of heat and sound; they carbonize without giving any flame when exposed to a high temperature, do not decay, and absorb very little or no water. Moreover, this product is better than cork, because of its great resistance to compression. Experiments have been made, and it is now demonstrated that the bricks begin only to crack under a pressure of 190 pounds per square inch. Therefore, if, with the cements, bricks and tiles are molded or concrete is poured off, we will obtain very valuable building materials, the main applications of which we will examine here.

First. Every time heat or cold is to be kept in a room, or a heated or cool pipe or other recipient, cork refuse may be used with advantage. The coefficient of conductibility of heat determined by Pictet for cork is 0.143 in French measures, which will be used now for convenience sake. To demonstrate how comparatively small is this figure, and therefore how efficient would be the use of that material for such a purpose, we will calculate the quantity of steam condensed per hour in a steam pipe insulated with a 1-inch thick covering (0.025 gramme).

For example, let us assume a pipe 0.10 in diameter, the live steam being at a temperature of 125° C., and circulating at a speed of forty meters per minute, the temperature of the room being supposed to be 15° C. The quantity of steam passing through that pipe for one meter of length is per hour:

$$1.25 \times \frac{3.14}{4} \times 0.10^{2} \times 1 \times 40 \times 60 = 23.40 \text{ kilos.}$$

If we neglect the radiation and convection, the quantity of heat lost for that surface of pipe will be:

$$\frac{3.14 \times 0.125 \times 1 \times 0.143(125^\circ - 15^\circ)}{0.025} = 24 \text{ calories and } \frac{6}{10}$$

And as one kilo of steam gives out by being condensed 600 calories, in round numbers, the percentage of steam lost will evidently be:

$$\frac{24.6}{600 \times 23.40} \text{ about } \frac{1}{600} \text{ or } \frac{1}{6} \text{ of 1 per cent.}$$

These figures show all the benefit we can derive from using cork refuse for boilers and pipe coverings, and also for building purposes.

Many a time, in a light construction, the loft is not habitable on account of the difference of temperature which tenants would have to support. Cork tile nailed on inclined joists and on ceiling boards would make this loft as comfortable as any other story of the flats. In hot countries, for instance in Algeria, where heat is considerable during the summer, they use now cork tiles to coat the walls inside, and Russians are also protected in the same way from cold. In a word, there are numerous applications of this material as a protection against heat and cold.

Second. As has been already mentioned, cork material does not conduct sound. We will give you an example of this, as we had occasion to observe it in Paris. It was in the Menier house Festival hall. That house, six stories high, was occupied by different tenants, and the use of the hall for meetings and private parties was quite objectionable to them on account of the disturbing noise at night. By replacing the plaster ceiling by cork concrete, all objections were removed. This fact proves how much sound deadening is a cork concrete floor, and how useful it will prove to have such a material where quietness is required, as in library reading rooms, telephone closets, etc.

Third. A third important property of cork compositions is to attenuate the vibrations to a great extent; for instance, when near engine or dynamo rooms are located places where vibrations can be troublesome, as in drawing rooms or offices, and especially in rooms where crystallization of certain salts is carried on. In fact, crystallization is always disturbed and sometimes prevented by a constant trepidation; and we quote a circumstance in which, having to produce chrome crystals, the manufacturer had to leave the town and go to a quiet country place to carry on his work. A cork floor would have saved all that trouble.

In regard to elasticity of cork, I will mention here the following happy application of that material. To prevent dampness in a gunpowder factory, all walls had been protected by a cork brick coat, and all partitions had been made with cork tiles. One day they had a terrible explosion, as dangerous as they are sure to be in such cases. If the walls and partitions had been in stones or bricks, the loss of life would have been serious. The cork product (after having greatly slackened the vibrations) crumbled to powder, and only a shower of small pieces of harmless cork dropped on workingmen, and no one was injured.

Fourth. Lightness and waterproof quality have not to be spoken of. In a country like the United States, where high buildings are getting in favor, light partitions are a very desirable device. Everything has been tried in that line, and a quantity of materials have been worked on. Among all these, porous brick is as yet probably the best. But cork tile is a great deal lighter. The specific gravity of porous brick is represented by 0.70 when that of cork brick is only 0.38; that is to say, that nearly half of the weight is saved. I will merely mention here again the importance of waterproof material in cellars, basement walls, bath rooms, etc.

Fifth. Is cork fireproof? That is the question of today. Insur-

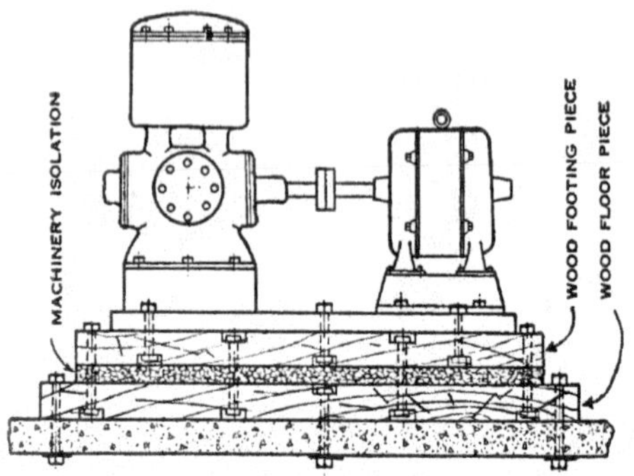

FIG. 213.—MODERN APPLICATION OF PURE COMPRESSED BAKED CORK SHEETS FOR THE REDUCTION OF VIBRATION AND SOUND IN BUILDING STRUCTURES.

ance companies will not take any risk for the highest stories on account of the difficulty of extinguishing fire; and of course, fireproof material is carefully looked for. Positively, there is no entirely fireproof material. Brick partitions crack and flames can spread out in every direction. What should be required from a partition is that it shall not propagate fire. Cork cement answers the purpose, as it carbonizes very slowly and gives out smoke but no flame.

SOME USES OF CORKBOARD INSULATION.*

Cold Storage Rooms
- Apple storage
- Banana storage
- Battery testing
- Berry storage
- Butter storage
- Candy storage
- Cheese storage
- Chocolate dipping
- Commissaries
- Daily ice storage
- Dough, mixing and proving
- Ducts, cooling
- Ducts, ventilating
- Egg storage
- Fever (clinical)
- Fish freezer
- Fish storage
- Flower storage
- Fruit pre-cooling
- Fruit storage
- Fur storage
- Garment storage
- Ice cream hardening
- Ice stations
- Ice storage
- Meat freezers
- Meat pickling
- Meat pre-cooling
- Meat storage
- Paraffin
- Potato storage
- Poultry pre-cooling
- Poultry storage
- Public auditoriums
- Sausage
- Serum storage
- Scientific
- Syrup storage
- Testing
- Tobacco humidor

Boxes and Refrigerators
- Apartment house refrigerator
- Bottle box
- Confectioners' refrigerator
- Dairy products refrigerator
- Fish box
- Florists' refrigerator
- Meat box
- Mortuary box
- Oyster box
- Pie refrigerator
- Residence refrigerator
- Vegetable box

Display Counters and Cases
- Candy
- Cut flower
- Delicatessen
- Meat
- Milk, butter and eggs

Cars
- Passenger railway
- Refrigerator
- Street railway
- Tank

Cabinets
- Bottled goods
- Chocolate cooler
- Ice cream dispensing
- Ice cream storage
- Soda fountain

Tanks
- Brine storage
- Gasoline storage
- Ice making
- Ice water
- Milk cooling
- Milk storage
- Railway
- Steel tempering
- Water cooling

Trucks
- Fish
- Ice
- Ice cream
- Meat
- Milk

Miscellaneous
- Bank vaults
- Bee hives
- Incubators
- Industrial buildings
- Humidifiers
- Machine base
- Residence insulation
- Roof insulation
- Sound deadening
- Vibration absorption

---

*Cork Pipe Covering is employed as permanent insulation for refrigerated lines and tanks and drinking water systems.

RELATIVE HUMIDITY TABLE, PER CENT. (PRECISION THERMOMETER AND INSTRUMENT CO.)

AIR TEMPERATURES	DIFFERENCE BETWEEN THE DRY AND WET BULB THERMOMETERS																																					AIR TEMPERATURES
	0	1	2	3	4	5	6	7	8	9	10	11	12	13	14	15	16	17	18	19	20	21	22	23	24	25	26	27	28	29	30	31	32	33	34	35	36	
30	100	89	78	67	57	47	36	26	17	7																												30
35	100	91	82	73	65	54	45	37	28	19	12	3																										35
40	100	92	84	76	68	60	53	45	38	30	22	16	8	1																								40
45	100	92	85	78	71	64	58	51	44	38	32	25	19	13	7	1																						45
50	100	93	87	80	74	67	61	55	50	44	38	33	27	22	16	11	6	1																				50
55	100	94	88	82	76	70	65	59	54	49	43	39	34	29	24	19	16	10	6	1																		55
60	100	94	89	84	78	73	68	63	58	53	48	44	39	34	30	26	22	18	14	10	6	2																60
65	100	95	90	85	80	75	70	65	61	56	52	48	44	39	35	31	28	24	20	17	13	10	6	3														65
70	100	95	90	86	81	77	72	68	64	60	55	52	48	44	40	36	33	29	26	23	19	16	13	10	7	4	1											70
75	100	95	91	87	82	78	74	70	66	62	58	55	51	47	44	40	37	34	31	27	24	21	19	16	13	10	7	5	2									75
80	100	96	92	87	83	79	75	72	68	64	61	57	54	51	47	44	41	38	35	32	29	26	23	20	18	15	13	10	8	6	3	1						80
85	100	96	92	88	84	80	77	73	70	66	63	60	56	53	50	47	44	41	38	36	33	30	28	25	22	20	17	15	13	11	9	6	4	2				85
90	100	96	92	88	85	81	78	75	71	68	65	62	59	56	53	50	47	44	41	39	36	34	32	29	26	24	22	20	17	15	13	11	9	7	5	3	2	90
95	100	96	93	89	86	82	79	76	72	69	66	63	60	58	55	52	49	47	44	42	39	37	35	32	30	28	25	23	21	19	17	15	13	11	10	8	6	95
100	100	97	93	90	86	83	80	77	74	71	68	65	62	59	57	54	51	49	47	44	42	39	37	35	33	31	29	27	25	23	21	19	17	15	14	12	10	100
105	100	97	93	90	87	84	81	78	75	72	69	66	64	61	58	56	53	51	49	46	44	42	40	38	35	33	31	30	28	26	24	22	20	19	17	15	14	105
110	100	97	94	90	87	84	81	78	76	73	70	67	65	62	60	57	55	53	50	48	46	44	42	40	38	36	34	32	30	28	27	25	23	22	20	19	17	110
115	100	97	94	91	88	85	82	79	76	74	71	69	66	64	61	59	57	54	52	50	48	46	44	42	40	38	36	34	33	31	29	28	26	24	23	21	20	115
120	100	97	94	91	88	85	83	80	77	75	72	70	67	65	62	60	58	56	54	51	49	47	45	44	42	40	38	36	35	33	31	30	28	27	25	24	22	120
125	100	97	94	91	88	86	83	80	78	75	73	70	68	66	64	62	59	57	55	53	51	49	47	45	43	42	40	38	37	35	33	32	30	29	27	26	24	125
130	100	97	94	91	89	86	83	81	78	76	74	71	69	67	65	62	60	58	56	54	52	50	49	47	45	43	42	40	38	37	35	33	32	31	29	28	27	130
135	100	97	94	92	89	86	84	81	79	77	74	72	70	68	65	63	61	59	57	55	53	51	50	48	46	45	43	41	40	38	37	35	34	32	31	30	28	135
140	100	97	95	92	89	87	84	82	79	77	75	73	71	68	66	64	62	60	58	56	55	53	51	49	48	46	44	43	41	40	38	37	35	34	33	31	30	140
	0	1	2	3	4	5	6	7	8	9	10	11	12	13	14	15	16	17	18	19	20	21	22	23	24	25	26	27	28	29	30	31	32	33	34	35	36	

HEAT TRANSMISSION: A NATIONAL RESEARCH COUNCIL PROJECT.*

By F. E. Matthews.

Member Engineering Division National Research Council; Official Representative of the American Society of Refrigerating Engineers.

Heat transmission, than which there is no subject more basically important to so many lines of engineering, has been made the subject of a recently authorized project of the Engineering Division of the National Research Council,[1] with two main sub-committees dealing specifically with heat transfer—viz., heat transmission through building and insulating materials, and heat transmission between fluids and solids. The refrigerating industry, with its numerous refrigerating media, primary and secondary, the former occurring in both the liquid and gaseous phases, is vitally interested in both of these subjects.

Just how inadequate and generally chaotic present information bearing on heat transmission really is, is most frankly admitted by those engineers most vitally interested and most familiar with such data. There seem to be two generally admitted outstanding facts regarding heat transmission data: that they are fundamentally important and shamefully inadequate. The responsibility of providing himself with reliable data in order that he may turn out accurate results (impossible without them), is the engineer's and his alone. Rough rules have been employed for determining necessary areas of the heat transmitting members of refrigerating systems, such as evaporators and condensers of refrigerating media, based on certain conditions, but not necessarily on the most advantageous conditions realizable. Similar rules have been employed for determining the amount of insulation employed for the conservation of the refrigeration produced at the expense of the fuel by the refrigerating machine. Rare indeed are the instances in which due recognition is given to the fact that the more it costs to develop refrigeration the more one can afford to spend for its conservation.

Numerous sporadic efforts have been made to procure better heat transmission data, but the results have fallen far short of the objective which the time and money expended should have insured, due largely to poor physical equipment, unscientific procedure, and incomplete description, which should be eliminated by the standardization of method, procedure, and specification proposed for building and insulating materials, heat transmission investigations, and made

*Extracted from Proceedings of the Fourth International Congress of Refrigeration, London, 1924, Volume 1.

[1] Means for carrying on research work in America under governmental supervision was originally provided for in 1863, when the Charter of the National Academy of Science was approved by President Lincoln. The National Research Council was established in 1916 by the National Academy of Science for war purposes, and perpetuated by executive order of President Wilson in 1918, for the "promotion of scientific research and the dissemination and application of scientific knowledge." It was organized with the cooperation of over seventy major scientific and technical societies, in thirteen major divisions of which Engineering is one of the most important.

possible through the correlation of scattered efforts by means of the machinery of a national organization such as that of the National Research Council.

AIR INFILTRATION.

Following are some of the air infiltration values obtained on erection materials from investigations and tests conducted in the labora-

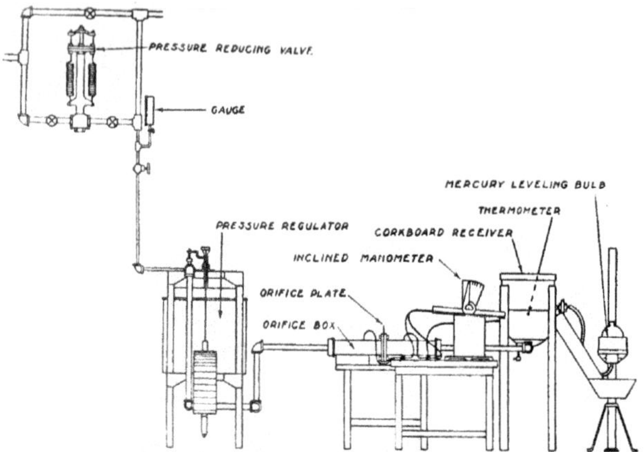

FIG. 214.—ARMSTRONG'S INFILTRATION APPARATUS—ARGO LABORATORY, GLOUCESTER, N. J.

tory of the Armstrong Cork & Insulation Co. Illustration of the apparatus used in making the determinations is shown.

AIR INFILTRATION VALUES ON ERECTION MATERIALS

		Cu. ft./sq. ft./hr. 10 lbs. pressure	Cu. ft./sq. ft./hr. 40 pct. pressure
(1)	13-in. brick wall ½-in. cement plaster cracks in plaster between bricks	..	115
(2)	13-in. plastered brick wall two spray coats Armstrong's asphaltic paint	0	0
(3)	⅛-in. film erection asphalt. No cracks	0	0
(4)	178 Samples Armstrong's corkboard 2-in. thick	335	..
(5)	2:1 Portland cement plaster ⅜-in. thick. No cracks	..	22
(6)	Same. 10 pct. added lime	..	2
(7)	2:1 Portland cement plaster ⅝-in. thick. No cracks	..	..
(8)	2:1 Portland cement plaster ½-in. thick. Fine cracks	..	19
(9)	22 Samples sprayed on asphalt emulsion from skin coat to ⅛-in. thick, nine showed tight, other 13 varied from 2.75 to 5.60 cu. ft./sq. ft./hr./40 lbs.		
	Values of (3) and from (5) to (9) inclusive taken by applying the material to two inch corkboard.		

Another series of tests were conducted on the relative infiltration of corkboard in respect to thickness. Following is a typical average of these tests:

DENSITY OF CORKBOARD 0.854 LBS. PER BD. FT. AIR INFILTRATION VALUES GIVEN IN CU. FT./SQ. FT./HR./40 POUNDS PRESSURE.

Thickness of Corkboard	Cu. Ft.
1 inch	485
2 inch	343
3 inch	239
4 inch	186
5 inch	163
6 inch	150
7 inch	132
8 inch	124
9 inch	105
10 inch	98
11 inch	97
12 inch	95

The following specifications cover an oxidized asphalt obtained from an asphaltic base crude oil, usually Mexican:

SPECIFICATIONS FOR 180/200° F. STANDARD OXIDIZED ASPHALT

	Minimum	Maximum
Specific gravity at 60° F.	1.045	1.065
Melting point (ball and ring)	180° F.	200° F.
Flash point (open cup)	460° F.	..
Penetration: 32° F. 200 gram 60 seconds	6	25
77° F. 100 gram 5 seconds	15	..
115° F. 50 gram 5 seconds	..	45
Volatility, 50 grams 5 hrs. at 325° F.	..	1%
Bitumen soluble in CS_2	99.5%	..

CORK DIPPING PAN.

Specifications.—This oil-burning cork dipping pan is used for melt-

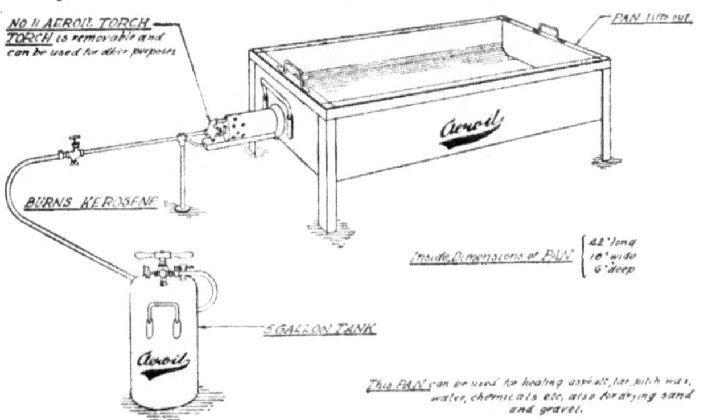

FIG. 215.—MODERN CORKBOARD DIPPING PAN, MANUFACTURED BY AEROIL BURNER CO., UNION CITY, N. J.

ing and heating asphalt in connection with cork insulation work. A standard size slab of cork can be easily dipped into the hot asphalt and permits rapid application of the cork. Being smokeless, the pan can be used indoors, right close to the job.

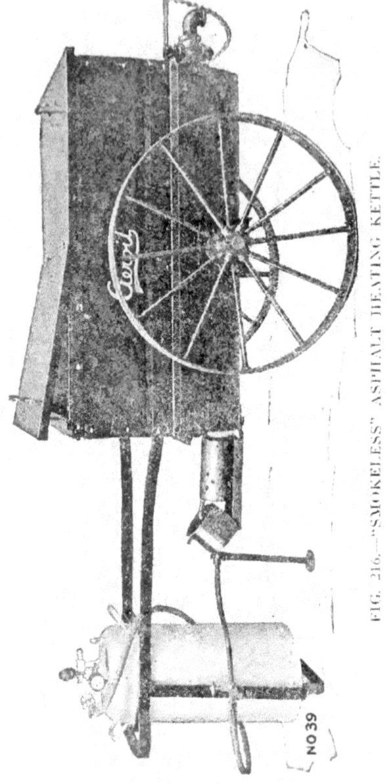

FIG. 216.—"SMOKELESS" ASPHALT HEATING KETTLE.

The pan is 42 inches long, 16 inches wide and 6 inches deep, inside measurements. It is made of No. 14 gauge steel throughout properly braced and reinforced with 1¼x1¼x3/16-inch angle iron all around and equipped with four handles.

The burner is removable and can be used for many other heating purposes, such as drying out wet spots in concrete or brick walls or floors, melting ice and snow, etc. Shipping weight about 175 pounds.

PROTECTION OF INSULATION AGAINST MOISTURE.*

By Charles H. Herter.

This paper is to record the latest methods used in safeguarding cold storage insulation against the entrance of moisture. Corkboard, which is now being employed almost exclusively, has been erected and finished off with Portland cement motar and plaster for so many years now (March, 1927) that this method continues to be specified by those who have not been informed of improvements made in the art.

Manufacturers of corkboard declare that their material is moisture resistant of itself, that it can be boiled for hours and yet remain dry inside. However, in actual use, where the material is exposed to the influence of moisture for months and years, it does lose its insulating value, and decays. This applies to all insulating materials, because all depend upon minute air cells for their ability to retard heat flow, and as condensed moisture (water) is denser than air, the air is gradually being crowded out by the water.

Moisture Detrimental.—In the wall of a cold storage room the corkboard lining is exposed to moisture from both outside and inside. A 12-inch brick wall may be rain tight, and yet it is not moisture tight even if all joints between the brick are filled solid with mortar. Both the brick and the mortar are porous and allow moisture to penetrate by capillary attraction, as has often been verified by actual tests. Under the influence of wind the exposed surface of a brick wall will dry very soon, but this drying action does not reach the water already drawn in, especially if the room is being refrigerated, the temperature within the wall getting lower and lower toward the inside.

At 90° F. a cubic foot of air can hold up to 14.79 grains of moisture; at 60°, 5.745 grains, and at 30°, 1.935 grains. As the air and moisture become cooled, the excess moisture will be precipitated. At the room side of the insulation we have this condition: When the door is opened, or if people are present, moisture at relatively high temperature mixes with the air; and the goods in the room, such as meat or other perishables, also lose moisture. Very soon the air is fully saturated, and whatever moisture is not gathering as frost upon the refrigerating pipes will be precipitated as condensation upon any cold surface or wall. These phenomena were studied years ago and the conclusion was reached that special efforts must be made to prevent the entry of moisture into the insulation.

The detrimental effect of moisture on insulation has been investigated to some extent. In the Insulation Committee Report of the American Society of Refrigerating Engineers, 1924, p. 78, it is shown

*Paper presented before New York Chapter, No. 2, N. A. P. R. E., at its meeting of March 4, 1927. Reprinted by permission from the April, 1927, "Ice and Refrigeration," Chicago.

that for each one per cent moisture absorbed the heat conduction increases four to forty per cent, depending upon the material used.

In most branches of engineering progress is being made by degrees only. When, over thirty years ago, corkboard first came into use, it was being protected against air and moisture by means of waterproof insulating paper on both sides. Also the pure corkboard used to be more dense; it weighed fully fourteen pounds per cubic foot as against nine or eight pounds now. The lighter board is a better insulator, but is, of course, not so strong and durable as the dense board. Formerly the finish for floors, walls and ceilings used to be one or two layers of ⅞-in. tongued and grooved sheathing, nailed with galvanized nails against furring strips imbedded between the corkboards. This construction when varnished looked well, but was rather expensive. It was not fire resistive, and at low temperature the boards dried out, shrank, and allowed moisture to enter the cracks, which caused rotting to take place.

The next step was the erection of corkboard in hot asphalt. Walls on the inside have to be pointed up with cement mortar so as to be reasonably flat, to avoid hollow spaces behind the corkboard because these would hold moisture and might freeze, forcing off the insulation. The wall was mopped with hot asphalt, although with the rapid chilling on the bare wall the resulting surface could not be air-tight. The corkboard also was mopped over with hot asphalt and thus cemented against the wall. The second layer of corkboard was again dipped in hot asphalt, and wooden skewers used to pin the various slabs together. The exposed face of insulation also might have been mopped over with hot asphalt, but this was not done because fire insurance companies prefer a Portland cement plaster finish, at least ½-in. thick, the 1/16-in. thick coat of asphalt being incapable of withstanding abuse and contact with trucks and packages, although wood fenders might be erected for this purpose.

Insulation asphalt necessarily has to be odorless so as to impart no foreign odor to the products stored. It is difficult to employ hot asphalt in ceiling work due to hot drippings. The heating of the asphalt by maintaining fires in the building is a nuisance, and so the insulation contractors soon avoided the use of asphalt and recommended Portland cement mortar and plaster in nearly all cases. Simple home-made boxes of wood were designed facilitating the rapid coating of cork slabs with a uniform thickness of cement mortar. Thus mortar exclusively was used next to the wall, between courses, and cement plaster finish in two ¼-in. coats, applied to the erected insulation.

The moisture in cement mortar occupies a certain amount of space, one cubic foot for every 62.4 pounds of water. In due time all this moisture disappears and causes shrinkage cracks. When the air is saturated, moisture re-enters every pore in the plaster, and the open cracks especially. In an effort to hide these cracks plastered surfaces are usually marked off in 3-foot squares or scores, the plaster naturally breaking first in these grooves. Evidently a plastered surface of this kind is but an imperfect moisture protection for insulation.

Keep Cork Out of Wet Forms.—In concrete construction, which method came into vogue at the same time, it was deemed good practice and economy to place the ceiling cork right into the form, and to pour the wet mixture on top of it, this being the recommendation of the insulation contractor. It was hoped that the corkboard would bond perfectly and securely with the concrete, and as corkboard had been declared immune against moisture, no one suspected that the insulating effect would diminish under this method. However, the writer knows of many cases where such corkboard continues to drop off the ceiling, consequently this method must be condemned as very unsatisfactory. The rule that insulation should always be kept out of contact with moisture must ever be borne in mind.

In ceiling work it is frequently possible to apply the insulation above the ceiling, where there is no danger of its coming loose. The work there is cheaper and better than at the underside of ceiling, especially if girders and beams have to be covered.

The cement mortar construction has now been in use for about twenty years, but since about 1920 its shortcomings have been recognized by many users. Cement mortar in the thin layers used with insulation is porous and not only imparts the initial quantity of moisture to the corkboard, but it cracks readily and thereby permits moisture from the air to enter day after day. Now that a far better bonding material which is strictly waterproof is available, the use of cement mortar is to be avoided whenever possible.

Asphalt for Damp-proofing.—The modern protection of all sorts of insulating materials is an asphalt emulsion, equivalent to a pulverized pure asphalt mixed with a certain amount of cold water, prepared in accordance with a process first developed in Germany and covered by a number of United States patents. Under this method the asphalt is broken up into minute particles averaging 0.001 to 0.005 in in the presence of an inert mineral colloid such as asbestos fibres. At the factory the asphalt flows into a high speed emulsifying machine whose propellers whip the stream of asphalt into the most minute particles and at the same time combine it with the water and the colloid. In this way the particles of asphalt are held in suspension until after the emulsion has been applied on the job, when the water disappears by evaporation, leaving the mixture of asphalt and asbestos fibres behind, in the form of a homogeneous coating. This emulsion can be applied cold with a brush by hand or by means of a spraying machine.

This emulsified asphalt is being marketed under various trade names such as Korkseal; Krodeproof; Rex Flintkote—emulsion and mortar; Stonewall Plastic; Par-Lock Bond; Vorco Waterproofing Cork Mastic, etc. There must be differences among these as in the case of other goods of different manufacture, but so far as we can see the main difference is in their water content and consistency. The *liquid emulsion* flows like cream and can be applied like a paint to metal, stone and wood surfaces with a cheap fibre brush or a spray, while the *thick emulsion*, or asphalt mortar, simply contains less water. It is plastic and can be troweled on, successfully taking the place of cement or gypsum plaster and forming one continuous waterproof sheet, requiring no scoring.

Securing Air Tightness.—Tests have been made to ascertain the degree of air tightness obtained with various cork coatings. When exposed to forty pounds per square foot excess air pressure on one side of an insulated wall, the rate of air leakage was in one case, unprotected, 240 cubic feet of free air, 75 cubic feet when the first coat had been applied, and 10 cubic feet after the second coat (presumably plaster) had been applied. When Korkphalt (asphalt) was used in joints the leakage without finish was 222 cubic feet air; 0.036 cubic feet after a coat of Krodeproof asphalt emulsion had been applied, and no loss whatever after this had been covered with a coat of Korkseal asphalt mortar. This type of asphalt finish is therefore indispensable in dry ice cream hardening rooms and other places where an excess air pressure is being created by forcing air with a fan over the cooling coils in the bunker.

Modern Construction.—This approved method of erecting corkboard insulation will be best understood by describing the various operations required when insulating masonry walls:

In the first place the surface to be insulated must be made as flat as possible because no crevices or hollow spaces can be allowed behind the smooth flat corkboard. Such cavities are apt to hold water of condensation, freezing to ice, which requires more space and thus breaks the bond between cork and surface. Concrete walls may be smooth enough, but other constructions usually require trueing up with cement mortar or plaster.

Next apply over the flat wall that has been freed of all dirt and dust at least one coat of asphalt emulsion for the purpose of filling every pore and providing a base for the asphalted corkboard. Spraying the emulsion on under an air pressure of fifty pounds or more will drive in the asphalt more effectively and cheaper than can be done by hand. Two coats will be better than one. Also the wall need not be dry because the emulsion contains water, while hot asphalt should not be laid direct against any cold wall because it will chill and contract at once; leaving pin holes, and it will not bond well with the wall. The emulsified asphalt also should be kept from freezing during application, and it will flow much better if the air tempterature is not below 45° F.

The first course of corkboard is to be erected in a dip coat of hot asphalt, starting this course level and breaking all joints. The second layer is again erected in hot asphalt and preferably secured with wood skewers, breaking joints in both directions.

One brand especially adapted for sticking up corkboard is known as Korkphalt, its melting point being 180° F. This is relatively soft at low temperature, rigid at high temperature, very adhesive at normal temperature, and serves to thoroughly air-proof and damp-proof the insulation at the weatherside.

Asphaltic Plaster.—Then comes the surface protection, which is very important. Spray or trowel onto the cork surface one thorough application of pure asphalt emulsion; one brand is called Korkseal, say 1/16-in. thick, which will completely fill all small holes and cracks. Allow to get dry, then finish with a layer of thick emulsified asphalt mortar a full 3/16-in. thick, floated to an even surface and then troweled.

Where it is intended to follow up with a white enamel finish, the black asphalt surface can be allowed to toughen up and then be troweled extra smooth by being sprinkled with clean water and again troweled.

After this has thoroughly dried, the entire surface can be given two or three coats of white enamel. One odorless enamel is known as Korkseal Enamel. If a less expensive coating is desired, Korkseal Aluminum may be applied in one coat directly to the black surface, but this is not equal in illuminating effect to the beautiful white enamel. The cost of material for white enamel is about one cent per square foot of coat. The aluminum paint costs about half as much because one coat is used. These paints stand washing with hot water, insuring a strictly sanitary cold storage room.

Most white paints or enamels will in time get yellowish, especially in dark rooms. Some enamels containing acetone or solvents used in the manufacture of celluloid will keep their whiteness, but they also keep their strong celluloid odor, which is very objectionable in refrigerators. A white glossy paint is quite popular with some users.

Asphalt Paint.—The thin creamy asphalt emulsion, such as Krodeproof, comes in the proper consistency for painting or spraying, and is recommended as a positive protective coating against weather, water, acids, gases, brine and all corrosive substances. It may be used on steel and other metals, on wood, concrete, cement or brick. It is also used for dampproofing masonry, foundations and walls, and for coating prepared and built-up roofings. If it is to be thinned at all, add but a little clean water and always stir well.

For best results, surfaces should be clean and free from all loose particles, oil or grease. Steel brush metal surfaces, whether dry or damp, down to bright metal, but masonry surfaces should be wetted with water before applying. Daub it on thick. Brushes (of white vegetable fibre) to be cleaned with soap and water after using. Do not apply at lower air temperatures than 45° F., and not during rain because it will be washed off. It must be given time to set. With sunshine it will dry in two to three hours. A man will soon learn to give 350 to 400 square feet surface per hour one coat. The quantity of the various materials required per 100 square feet of surface may be obtained from the manufacturers. The following data were obtained from the Lewis Asphalt Engineering Corp.:

Karnak Korkphalt......70 lb. per layer of corkboard
Korkseal (or Krodeproof), first coat..........4 gal.
Korkseal Mortar (finish coat).................5 gal.
Korkseal Enamel, white, per coat...........1/3 gal.
Korkseal Aluminum, per coat................1/6 gal.

Strength.—Tests have been made for the United Cork Companies, New York, to determine the tenacity of adhesion of a 3-in. thick slab of corkboard cemented to concrete. When a pull was exerted of 1,360 pounds per square foot cork, the cork yielded, but not the asphalt emulsion, which proves conclusively that the emulsified asphalt furnishes a very reliable bond. In fact, the adhesive strength of Par-Lock asphalt alone was found by the Investigating Committee of Architects and Engineers, New York, to exceed 125 pounds per square inch, equivalent to 18,000 pounds per square foot. Its ductility is rated at four to five centimeters at 77° F. The penetration of a needle bearing a 200 gram weight is twenty-five to thirty millimeters per minute at 77° F. The re-melting point of these surfacing asphalts is between 200° and 215° F. when tested by Bureau of Standards ring and ball method. The re-melting point of the hot asphalt used for dipping one face and two edges of corkboard should be between 180° and 200° F. It should be heated to the consistency of molasses, the slabs firmly pressed against the surface asphalt, such as Krodeproof, until the asphalt in the joints chills.

Mastic Asphalt Facing.—The Korkseal or asphalt mastic finish, 1/8-in. thick, above described, is an improvement over the method of ironing on the asphalt plaster at the factory to each slab of cork, because the subsequent patching up of the many lineal feet of joint is a difficult and expensive task, and the result is not equal in air and water tightness to that of a continuous troweled facing. Not to chip off readily, a tough grade of asphalt is used which is hard on the saw when fitting slabs into place. This asphalt becomes very brittle at low temperature. It has to be a hard variety so as not to run during shipping in summer.

Some insulation manufacturers do not urge the use of the Korkseal asphalt plaster where the cork is exposed to injury from the handling of goods. There they recommend again the old Portland cement plaster finish, at least 1/2-in. thick; but even here the advantage of moisture proofing should not be sacrificed. One can erect suitable fenders, rails and baseboards to prevent truck wheels from damaging the wall, or one can provide a cement wainscoat ¾-in. thick over the asphalt dampproof emulsion.

Detailed instructions for waterproofing and dampproofing in building construction are contained in circulars issued by manufacturers.

Asphalt emulsion, like Korkseal, is also effective for sealing pipe coverings and is greatly to be preferred to the black crude oil paint or tar commonly employed for this purpose.

HOW INSULATION SAVED A REFINERY.*

An interesting example of how material installed for one purpose may render valuable service in a quite unexpected way occurred last summer at the plant of the Island Petroleum Co., Neville Island, Pittsburgh, Pa.

The company had recently completed three steel cold settling tanks, 20 feet in diameter by 25 feet high, for bright stock. Being operated part of the time at low temperature produced by brine refrigeration, these tanks were insulated with three inches of Nonpareil corkboard furnished and installed by the Armstrong Cork & Insulation Co. At the time of this incident they were practically filled with oil.

On August 25, 1921, during a violent electrical storm accompanied by unusually heavy rain, lightning struck one of the crude oil tanks. The resulting explosion released a large quantity of burning oil which spread out over the partially flooded yard and practically surrounded the nearest settling tank; hastily constructed dikes shut it off from immediate contact with the others.

For nearly three hours the fire raged around this tank, and for almost an hour, the flames were leaping directly against its sides, while the officials and employees, striving to stop the spread of the fire, momentarily expected the big tank to "let go" with consequent disaster to the entire plant. Three times the hatch on the roof lifted to allow the escape of accumulated gas, but the remarkable heat retarding quality of the corkboard insulation kept the temperature below the danger point, and the fire finally burned itself out with no further loss of property or damage to the insulated tank beyond a slight charring of the outer surface of the corkboard insulation.

The Island Petroleum Co. officials are unanimous in the opinion that nothing but the protection afforded by the insulation prevented the destruction of all three tanks and the heavy loss such an explosion would have entailed.

Though insulation may seldom be called upon to withstand so severe a test, the record of this performance is convincing proof of the nonconducting property and fire resistance of corkboard.

*Extracted from *Ice and Refrigeration*, June, 1922, Page 460.

ECONOMY OF GASOLINE STORAGE TANK INSULATION.

In a paper prepared by the Armstrong Cork and Insulating Co., of Pittsburgh, Pa., in April, 1918, an interesting detailed description is given of various methods of manufacturing gasoline from both gas well and oil well products, on the distillation, compression and absorption methods of gasoline separation from gas and oil.

By permission the following reproduction of that portion of the paper referring particularly to the economical results secured through cork insulation of gasoline storage tanks in three separate refining plants, has been extracted:

Early in March, 1917, the United Fuel Gas Company, of Charleston, West Virginia, requested quotations on insulation for a number of gasoline storage tanks located at their various stations. Upon calling on the above company at Charleston, West Virginia, it was learned that they were losing by evaporation approximately 600 to 1,800 gallons of gasoline per day at each of their several plants in operation. Before proceeding further the reason for this loss shall be explained.

The temperature of the gasoline as it passes from the coolers and condensers to the storage tanks is much lower than the temperature of the air, due to the cooling methods employed. This product is of low boiling point and readily evaporates even at the low temperature at which it leaves the condensers. As the temperature increases, the evaporation becomes more pronounced and for this reason it is desirable that the gasoline be kept at as low a temperature as possible. The tanks in which the material is stored are, as a rule, located outside of buildings and exposed to the weather. If the tanks are not insulated the gasoline contained therein soon acquires the same temperature as the outside air and in the summer months when the hot sun constantly beats down upon the tanks the temperature of the gasoline becomes very high. The gasoline evaporating freely increases the pressure in the tanks, which are equipped with safety valves to permit of the vapors passing off whenever the pressure exceeds that at which the valve is set.

In cool or cloudy weather the valve does not "blow off" as often as in hot weather and the evaporation loss past the man-hole cover is reduced. The evaporation loss in the summer months is naturally considerably more than in the cooler months of the fall and winter.

At the Cobb Station of the United Fuel Gas Company the evaporation loss early in the spring averaged close to 600 gallons of liquid gasoline per day, and at the Sandyville Station of the same company the loss ran as high as 1,500 gallons per day. The gasoline lost by evaporation is valued at 20c per gallon by the company producing the material, and it was obviously necessary for the United Fuel Gas Company to take steps to reduce their evaporation loss which amounted to approximately $300.00 per day at each plant.

Armstrong secured contracts for insulating the gasoline storage tanks at three of the United Fuel Gas Company's six absorption plants—Cobb Station, Sandyville Station and Leach Station. The first two stations are owned and operated by the United Fuel Gas Company, while the Columbia Gas and Electric Company, of Cincinnati, Ohio, own the Leach Station and lease it to the United Fuel Gas Company for operation. These tanks were insulated throughout with Armstrong's Corkboard, whereas the tanks at the other three stations, contracted for by a competitor, were insulated with felt on the cylindrical surfaces and Impregnated Corkboard on the tops and ends. It might be in order to state that Armstrong's prices were higher than the prices on felt and Impregnated Corkboard.

The specifications followed in erecting the Armstrong's Corkboard Insulation were briefly as follows:

The cylindrical surface and ends of all horizontal tanks were insulated with two layers of 1½-inch Armstrong's Corkboard. Both layers were applied in hot asphalt and both securely wired in place with copper-clad steel wire. The second layer was additionally secured to the first layer with galvanized wire nails.

The vertical tanks were insulated in practically the same manner. As they rested directly upon the ground, no bottom insulation was used. The cylindrical surfaces received two layers of 1½-inch Armstrong's Corkboard, applied as specified on the horizontal tanks, while the tops were insulated with two layers of 2-inch Armstrong's Corkboard, both applied in hot asphalt with the top surface flooded with the same material.

As the tanks were located outside of buildings, the insulation was protected against the weather by the application of one layer of 2-ply (the very best grade) roofing paper. Weatherproofing was applied with all edges lapped and the seams securely sealed with Nonpareil Waterproof Cement. Bands of copper-clad steel wire were used to hold the paper in place.

The melting of asphalt at one of these gasoline plants is dangerous business if a fire of any kind is used and it is necessary, therefore, that the owners provide live steam for this operation. If live steam is not obtainable, Nonpareil Waterproof Cement instead of hot asphalt should be used in erecting the Armstrong's Corkboard.

To give some idea of the tank insulation requirements, the following is submitted: At the Cobb Station two horizontal tanks each 8 feet in diameter x 32 feet long and one vertical tank 20 feet in diameter x 20 feet high, were insulated, at a contract price of $2,270.00. At the Leach Station two vertical tanks each 8 feet 6 inches in diameter x 9 feet 11 inches high and one vertical tank 20 feet in diameter x 20 feet high were insulated at a contract price of $1,447.50. At the Sandyville Station the same number and size tanks as at the Leach Station, were insulated at a price of $1,440.00. The total for the three installations amounted to $5,157.50.

That this amount of money was well spent shall be seen upon reading the following paragraphs:

The manager of the Cobb Station advises that the saving effected directly through insulating the tanks averages close to 600 and runs as high as 900 gallons of gasoline per day. These figures are true for the 1917 summer months, and as the capacity of this plant is 5,500 gallons per day, over 10% is saved. At the Sandyville Station losses reported as high as 1,500 gallons per day in the cooler weather of early spring with the tanks uninsulated, were reduced to 18 gallons per day during the hot summer months after the insulation was applied. The storage capacity at this plant runs about 40,000 gallons. It is understood that the temperature in the insulated tanks does not vary more than two or three degrees F. during the operating day of 24 hours.

From the figures given above, estimating the loss at 20c per gallon, it can readily be seen that the insulation paid for itself at each station in less than ten days. As the insulation will last for years, it is a wonderful investment. The foregoing is conclusive proof that all gasoline manufacturing stations using storage tanks should have them properly insulated when erected.

A comparison between felt and Armstrong's Corkboard insulated tanks can be secured from a letter written by Mr. R. N. Parks, of the United Fuel Gas Company to Mr. C. C. Reed of the Hope Natural Gas Company. This letter, which follows, is in answer to an inquiry regarding the experience of the United Fuel Gas Company with insulated tanks:

> "I enclose blue print showing evaporation losses from 100-barrel tanks standing side by side, one insulated and the other non-insulated.
>
> "Both were filled with 87.4 degrees Baumé gasoline on March 17th, and on April 7th the loss from the insulated tank was 88 gallons while the non-insulated tank showed a loss of 423 gallons.
>
> "One of our stations has reported evaporation as high as 1500 gallons under cooler weather conditions than we are having now, but showed on their last report evaporation loss of only 18 gallons with over 40,000 gallons in stock.
>
> "Three of our stations were insulated with cork entirely by the Armstrong Cork & Insulation Co. of Pittsburgh. We insulated two 100-barrel run tanks and one 40,000-gallon stock tank at each station."

In explanation of the above letter, paragraphs one and two refer to felt insulated tanks while paragraph three refers to Armstrong's Corkboard insulated tanks. Felt insulated tanks show a saving of 423 minus 88 gallons, while the cork insulated tanks show a saving of 1500 minus 18 gallons. It is not very difficult to choose the better insulation with these figures at hand.

The insulation on these tanks is exposed to the rain, sleet, snow and all kinds of weather; consequently, only insulation that is non-absorptive of moisture should be used, even though an attempt is made to waterproof it. The Armstrong's Corkboard applied at the stations mentioned above remains in excellent condition. The felt at one of the stations already appears to be coming loose. This work was installed about eleven months ago, May, 1917. Provided care is exercised to keep the weatherproofing in good condition, the Armstrong's Corkboard will long out-last the felt and although the first cost is slightly greater, its superior insulating value alone makes it by far the best money investment.

INTERIOR FINISH OF COLD STORAGE ROOMS IN HOTELS.

The proper construction of cold storage rooms for hotels is a highly important matter. The rooms must not only be efficient from an insulation standpoint when they are new, but they must retain this efficiency over a period of many years. Then, too, the design must be correct in order that the rooms give satisfactory and economical service in the proper handling of perishable foods.

These items involve proper insulation, proper placing of cooling coils and correct bunker construction. Positive circulation of air at all times is necessary to maintain temperatures sufficiently low to protect the stores, and to prevent condensation of moisture on walls and ceilings which would soon result in damp, moldy conditions so fatal to many items included on the hotel menu.

Aside from these considerations, however, practical experience has taught that some interior finishes over cork insulation are satisfactory for hotel conditions, and some are not. It must be borne in mind that these cold storage rooms receive a great deal of abuse, so to speak, and the interior finish that would be quite satisfactory for a cold storage warehouse, for example, is entirely unsatisfactory in hotels where rooms are small and doors are opened and closed repeatedly throughout the entire day. The influx of warm air each time doors are used carries with it a certain proportion of water held in suspension. As it comes in contact with chilled surfaces this water condenses. Unless this warm air is carried directly up over cooling coils by an active air circulation in the room, it will condense on walls and stores. While correct design of the interior arrangement of hotel cold storage rooms is a reasonable safeguard against damp, moldy conditions, yet some little moisture is always likely to form on walls and ceiling and the interior finish must be such that it will successfully resist such temporary conditions and permit of sanitary and hygienic conditions at all times through proper cleansing.

To tile the entire interior of hotel cold storage rooms in white is the most satisfactory way, but is expensive. An alternate specification, considerably less expensive, is now in use with satisfactory results. It consists of two coats of Portland cement plaster troweled smooth and hard for the walls, ironed-on at the factory mastic finish[1] corkboard for the ceilings, and hard concrete wearing floor over floor insulation, with metal floor grids embedded flush in the 1-inch cement top finish. The plaster is marked off in suitable squares to confine hair line check cracks to the score marks, and the joints in the ironed-on mastic finish corkboard are sealed flush with a mastic filler, by ironing with a hot tool. This ironing process causes the filler to combine with the mastic material so that the finished surface is a continuous sheet, sufficiently elastic at low temperatures to eliminate the possibility of cracking and absolutely impervious to moisture.

The walls and ceiling can then be painted two coats of white prime and one good coat of white elastic enamel. Two coats of orange shellac should be applied to the mastic surface before the prime is applied, as otherwise the oils in the mastic material will cause the white prime and enamel to stain.

In quite a few instances, ironed-on mastic finish corkboard has been used on walls, as well as ceiling, with excellent results. It, unquestionably, is superior to Portland cement plaster but does not finish off as smoothly unless unusual care is taken in erection and sealing of the mastic joints.

It is quite difficult to obtain concrete wearing floors hard enough to successfully withstand hotel service. For that reason the use of metal floor grids is essential, and a cold storage room floor so constructed will outlast steel plates.

These items, naturally, make the cost of a strictly modern hotel cold storage room somewhat more than the cost of *ordinary* equipment, but the first cost is practically the last cost and is far cheaper in the long run.

---

[1] Since this article was written in 1918, plastic mastic finish, hand troweled to corkboard surfaces at point of erection, has been developed to a satisfactory standard by the use of a high grade emulsified asphalt mixed and handled according to proven formula and tested method.—*The Author.*

CONCRETE.*

Anyone who is careful to observe the simple rules for doing concrete work such as that outlined herewith can make and place concrete satisfactorily, even though he may have had no previous experience.

What Concrete Is.—Concrete is made by mixing portland cement, sand, pebbles or broken stone and water in certain definite proportions according to the kind of work for which the concrete is to be used, and then permitting the mixture to harden under proper conditions in forms or molds. As soon as concrete has been mixed, if left undisturbed, it begins to harden and soon becomes like stone. The hardening process, which is a chemical change that takes place in the cement when mixed with water, continues for a long time after the concrete has acquired sufficient strength for the purpose intended. This continual increase of strength is the quality by which concrete differs from all other materials. Concrete grows ever stronger, never weaker by age.

Theory of Mixing Concrete.—Pebbles, sand and cement must be mixed together in correct proportions in order to make a dense, strong concrete.

For this reason, in mixing concrete, stone and sand are used in such proportions that the amount of spaces or voids between them is as small as possible, and all the surfaces of the sand and pebbles are coated with a film of cement. The smaller the voids are, the stronger and more dense will be the concrete. A dense concrete is also watertight; if the voids are not all completely filled, the concrete will be porous and will not be impervious to water.

It is very important that no dirt or finely powdered sand be used, as the use of such material interferes with the action of the cement in hardening. The strength of the concrete depends upon the adhesion of the cement mixture to the clean surfaces of sound, hard particles of sand or stone.

Portland Cement.—Portland cement is a uniform, reliable product. Any of the standard brands produced by members of the Portland Cement Association are tested and guaranteed and will produce good concrete when properly combined in correct proportion with the other materials necessary for a concrete mixture.

Portland cement is packed and shipped in standard cloth sacks or in paper bags holding 94 pounds net weight. For convenience in determining the necessary quantity of the several materials entering into a concrete mixture, a sack of portland cement may be considered as one cubic foot.

*Courtesy of Portland Cement Association.

Practically all building material dealers handle portland cement. Cloth sacks are charged to the cement purchaser. When empty they should be returned to the cement dealer, who will buy them back if they are fit for further use as cement containers. Cement sacks which have been wet, torn or otherwise rendered unfit for use are not redeemable.

Paper bags are not returnable.

Cement should always be kept in a dry place until used.

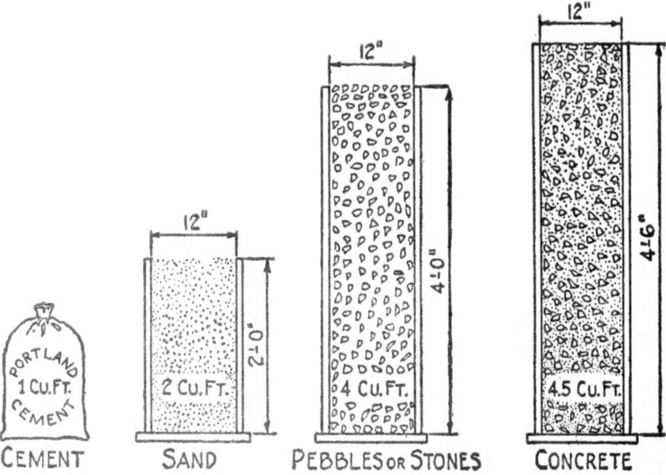

FIG. 217.—CEMENT, SAND AND PEBBLES IN THE PROPER PROPORTIONS WHEN MIXED WITH WATER HARDEN INTO THE SOLID MASS THAT IS CONCRETE.—NOTE THAT 7 CU. FT. OF MATERIALS MAKE BUT 4.5 CU. FT. OF CONCRETE.

Aggregates.—Sand and pebbles or broken stone are usually spoken of as "aggregate." Sand is called "fine aggregate" and pebbles or crushed stone "coarse aggregate." Sand or other fine aggregate, such as rock screenings, includes all particles from very fine (exclusive of dust) up to those which will just pass through a screen having meshes ¼-inch square. Coarse aggregate includes all pebbles or broken stone ranging from ¼-inch up to 1½ or 2 inches. The maximum size of coarse aggregate to be used is governed by the nature of the work. In thin slabs or walls the largest pieces of aggregate should never exceed one-third the thickness of the section of concrete being placed.

Sand should be clean and hard, free from fine dust, loam, clay and vegetable matter. These "foreign" materials are objectionable because they prevent adhesion between the cement and sound, hard particles of sand aggregate, thereby reducing the strength of the concrete and increasing its porosity. Concrete made with dirty sand or pebbles hardens very slowly at best and may never harden enough to permit the concrete to be used for its intended purpose.

Sand.—Sand should be well graded, that is, the particles should not all be fine nor all coarse, but should vary from fine up to those particles that will just pass a screen having meshes ¼-inch square. If the sand is thus well graded the finer particles help to occupy the spaces (voids) between the larger particles, thus resulting in a denser concrete and permitting the most economical use of cement in filling the remainder of the voids or air spaces and binding the sand particles together.

Coarse Aggregate.—Pebbles or crushed stone to be used in a concrete mixer should be tough, fairly hard and free from any of the impurities that would be objectionable in sand. Stone containing a considerable quantity of soft, flat or elongated particles should not be used.

Bank-run Gravel.—The natural mixture of sand and pebbles as taken from a gravel bank is usually referred to as bank-run material. This is not suitable for concrete unless first screened so that the sand may be separated from the pebbles and the two materials reproportioned in correct ratio. Most gravel banks contain either more sand or more pebbles than desirable for concrete mixture. Usually there is too much sand.

Water.—Water used to mix concrete should be clean, free from oil, alkali and acid. In general, water that is fit to drink is good for concrete.

Proportioning Concrete Mixtures.—In order to obtain a strong, dense, durable concrete, the materials entering into it must be definitely proportioned. For a given purpose, a certain quantity of portland cement with a certain quantity of sand, pebbles or crushed rock and water will make the best concrete. The several materials entering into concrete must be so proportioned that the cement will fill the voids or air spaces in the sand and when combined with the correct quantity of water will coat every particle of sand, thus making a volume of cement-sand mortar slightly in excess of the volume required to fill the air spaces or voids in the volume of broken stone or pebbles to be used. Some concrete work requires denser concrete than other kinds, so it is good practice to vary the mixture according to the job.

A 1:2:3 mixture means 1 sack (1 cubic foot) of cement, 2 cubic feet of sand and 3 cubic feet of pebbles or crushed stone. The first figure stands for the cement, the second for the sand and the third for the pebbles or broken stone. A 1:2 mixture means 1 sack (1 cubic foot) of portland cement and 2 cubic feet of sand. A 1:2 mixture would be called a mortar, since it contains no pebbles or broken stone (coarse aggregate).

The following table shows the usual proportions recommended for several classes of construction:

Table of Recommended Mixtures and Maximum Aggregate Sizes.—

Mixture	Use	Max. Size Agg.
1:1:1½—Mixture for:		
	Wearing course of two-course pavements	¾ in.
1:2:3 —Mixture for:		
	One-course walks, floors, pavements	1½ in.
	Basement walls exposed to moisture	1½ in.
	Sills and lintels without mortar surface	¾ in.
	Tanks	1 in.
1:2:4 —Mixture for:		
	Foundations for light machinery	2 in.
	Concrete work in general	1½ in.
1:2½:4—Mixture for:		
	Building walls above ground	1½ in.
	Walls of pits or basements	1½ in.
	Base of two-course floors or pavements	1 in.
1:2 —Mixture for:		
	Wearing course of two-course floors and pavements	¼ in.

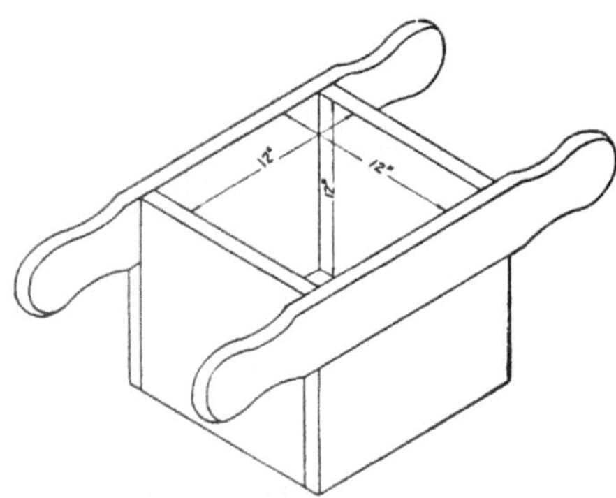

FIG. 218.—BOTTOMLESS MEASURING BOX OF 1 CU. FT. CAPACITY FOR DETERMINING THE EXACT BATCH PROPORTIONS.

Don't Guess at Quantities.—All materials should be accurately measured. This can be done easily by using a measuring box made to hold exactly 1 cubic foot, 2 cubic feet or any other volume desired. Such a box is in reality a bottomless frame. An illustration of a measuring box is shown here. To measure the materials the box is placed on the mixing platform and filled. When the required amount of material has been placed in it, the box is lifted off and the material remains on the platform. Cement need not be measured because, as already explained, one sack can be considered as 1 cubic foot in volume. A pail might also be used in proportioning concrete. For example, a 1:2:3 batch of concrete would be measured by taking 1 pail of portland cement, 2 pails of sand and 3 pails of pebbles or stone.

FIG. 219.—SIMPLE TOOLS FOR MAKING AND PLACING CONCRETE—WATER BARREL AND BUCKET; STEEL-PAN WHEELBARROW FOR HANDLING DRY AGGREGATE, AND CONCRETE TO FORMS; SAND SCREEN FOR PROPER GRADING OF AGGREGATES; SQUARE POINTED SHOVEL FOR TURNING AND MIXING CONCRETE; WOODEN FLOAT FOR FINISHING.

Mixing the Materials.—Concrete may be mixed either by hand or by machine. Machine mixing is to be preferred as in this way thorough mixing is easier to obtain and all batches will be uniform. However, first-class concrete can be mixed by hand. Whichever way mixing is done, it should continue until every pebble or stone is completely coated with a thoroughly mixed mortar of sand and cement.

Mixing Platform.—For hand mixing a watertight platform at least 7 feet wide and 12 feet long should be provided. A platform of this size is large enough to permit two men using shovels to work upon it at one time. Such a platform should preferably be made of boards at least 1½ inches thick, tongued and grooved so that the joints will be tight and the platform rigid. These planks may be nailed to three or more 2 by 4's set on edge. Two sides and one end of the platform should have a strip nailed along the edge and projecting 2 inches above the mixing surface of the platform to prevent materials from being washed or shoveled off while mixing.

Hand Mixing.—The usual procedure in mixing concrete by hand is as follows:

The measured quantity of sand is spread out evenly on the platform. On this the required amount of cement is dumped and evenly distributed. The cement and sand are then turned over thoroughly with square pointed shovels enough times to produce a mass of uniform color, free from streaks of brown and gray. Such streaks indicate that the sand and cement have not been thoroughly mixed. The required quantity of pebbles or broken stone is then measured and spread in a layer on top of the cement-sand mixture and all of the material again mixed by turning with shovels until the pebbles have been uniformly distributed throughout the mixed cement and sand. At least three turnings are necessary. A depression or hollow is then formed in the center of the pile and water added slowly while the materials are turned with square pointed shovels, this turning being continued until the cement, sand and pebbles have been thoroughly and uniformly combined and the desired consistency or wetness obtained throughout the mixture.

It is very important that no more water be used than necessary, as too much will reduce the strength of the concrete. Too little water will also reduce its strength and make it porous. For general use, concrete, after thorough mixing, should be wet enough to form a mass of pasty or jelly-like consistency, but never so wet as to flow easily or be soupy.

Placing Concrete.—Concrete should be placed into forms as soon as possible after mixing and in no case more than 30 minutes after mixing. It should be deposited in layers of uniform depth, usually not exceeding 6 inches. When placed in the forms it should be tamped and spaded so as to cause it to settle thoroughly everywhere in the forms and produce a dense mass. By "spading" is meant the working of a spade or chisel-edge board in the concrete and between it and the side of the forms, moving the spading tool to and fro and up and down. This working of the concrete next to the forms forces the large pebbles or stone particles away from the form face into the mass of the concrete and insures an even, dense surface when forms are removed.

Finishing Concrete.—The surface of a floor or walk should be finished by using a wood float. A metal trowel should be used sparingly, if at all, because its use brings a film of cement to the surface, which lacks the wearing quality of the cement and sand combined and may cause the surface to develop "hair cracks" after the concrete hardens. A trowelled surface is smoother, but does not wear so well as a floated surface and is likely to be slippery.

Protecting Newly Placed Concrete.—If concrete is left exposed to sun and wind before it has properly hardened, much of the water necessary to hardening will evaporate and the concrete will simply dry out. Moisture is necessary to the proper hardening of concrete because, as already mentioned, the hardening process is a chemical change which takes place in the cement when mixed with water.

Concrete floors, walks, pavements and similar large surfaces can be protected by covering with moist earth, sand, or other moisture-retaining material as soon as the concrete has hardened sufficiently to permit doing so without marring the surface. This covering should be kept moist in warm weather by frequent sprinkling during a period of ten days or so. Walls or other sections which cannot con-

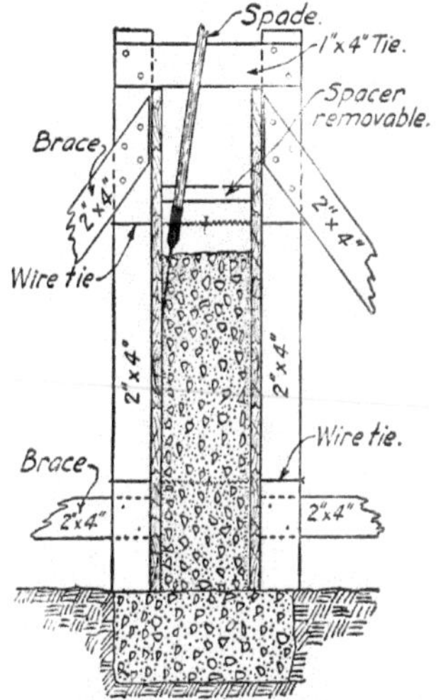

FIG. 220.—"SPADING" OF CONCRETE IN WALL FORMS FORCES THE COARSE AGGREGATE BACK FROM THE FACE AND PRODUCES A SMOOTH SURFACE ON THE FINISHED WALL.

veniently be covered in the manner suggested can be protected by hanging moist canvas or burlap over them and wetting down the entire work often enough to keep it always moist for ten days after placing. During cold weather protection is equally important, but the concrete need not be kept moist as evaporation is not so rapid.

Concrete in Winter.—There is no difficulty in doing concrete work in cold weather if a few simple precautions are taken. The booklet "Making Concrete and Cement Products in Winter" describes the rules to be followed. A copy may be obtained free by addressing the Portland Cement Association, Chicago, Ill.

QUANTITIES OF CEMENT, FINE AGGREGATES AND COARSE AGGREGATES REQUIRED FOR ONE CUBIC YARD OF COMPACT MORTAR OR CONCRETE.

MIXTURES			QUANTITIES OF MATERIALS				
Cement	F. A.	C. A. Gravel or Stone	Cement in Sacks	Fine Aggregate		Coarse Aggregate	
				Cu. Ft.	Cu. Yd.	Cu. Ft.	Cu. Yd.
1	1.5	.	15.5	23.2	0.86	..	.
1	2.0	.	12.8	25.6	0.95	..	.
1	2.5	..	11.0	27.5	1.02	.	..
1	3.0	..	9.6	28.8	1.07	..	..
1	1.5	3	7.6	11.4	0.42	22.8	0.85
1	2.0	3	7.0	14.0	0.52	21.0	0.78
1	2.0	4	6.0	12.0	0.44	24.0	0.89
1	2.5	4	5.6	14.0	0.52	22.4	0.83
1	2.5	5	5.0	12.5	0.46	25.0	0.92
1	3.0	5	4.6	13.8	0.51	23.0	0.85

1 Sack Cement = 1 cu. ft.; 4 sacks = 1 bbl.
Based on Tables in "Concrete, Plain and Reinforced," by Taylor and Thompson.

MATERIALS REQUIRED FOR 100 SQ. FT. OF SURFACE FOR VARYING THICKNESSES OF CONCRETE OR MORTAR.

Proportion	1 : 1½			1 : 2			1 : 2½			1 : 3		
Thickness in Inches	C.	F.A.	C.A.	C.	F.A.	C.A	C.	F.A.	C.A.	C.	F.A.	C.A.
⅜	1.8	2.7		1.5	3.0		1.3	3.2		1.1	3.4	
½	2.4	3.6		2.0	4.0		1.7	4.3		1.5	4.4	
¾	3.6	5.4		3.0	6.0		2.5	6.3		2.2	6.8	
1	4.8	7.2		4.0	7.9		3.4	8.4		3.0	8.9	
1¼	6.0	9.0		4.9	9.9		4.2	10.5		3.7	11.1	
1½	7.2	10.8		5.9	11.9		5.1	12.7		4.4	13.3	
1¾	8.4	12.6		6.9	13.9		5.9	14.7		5.2	15.7	
2	9.6	14.4		7.9	15.8		6.8	16.9		5.9	17.7	
	1 : 2 : 3			1 : 2 : 4			1 : 2½ : 4			1 : 2½ : 5		
3	6.5	13.0	19.3	5.6	11.2	22.4	5.2	12.9	20.6	4.6	11.5	23.0
4	8.6	17.2	25.8	7.5	14.9	29.8	6.9	17.1	27.5	6.2	15.4	30.7
5	10.8	21.6	32.2	9.4	18.7	37.4	8.6	21.5	34.3	7.7	19.2	38.3
6	12.9	25.8	38.6	11.2	22.4	44.7	10.3	25.8	41.2	9.2	23.0	45.9
8	17.2	34.4	51.6	15.0	29.8	59.7	13.7	34.3	54.9	12.3	30.7	61.3
10	21.5	43.2	64.4	18.7	37.4	74.8	17.2	43.0	68.6	15.3	38.3	76.6
12	25.8	51.6	77.2	22.4	44.7	89.4	20.6	51.6	82.4	18.4	45.9	91.8

C. = Cement in Sacks.
F. A. = Fine Aggregate (sand) in Cu. Ft.
C. A. = Coarse Aggregate (pebbles or broken stone) in Cu. Ft.
Quantities may vary 10 per cent either way depending upon character of aggregate used.
No allowance made in table for waste.

How to Use Materials Table for Calculating Quantities.

Problem 1:—What quantities of materials are required for a monolithic concrete foundation wall 34 feet square, outside measurements, 12 inches thick, 7 feet high, with a footing 12 inches thick and 18 inches wide, using a 1:2:4 mixture in both the wall and footing?

Solution:—The wall contains 924 square feet of surface, 12 inches thick, deducting for duplication at corners.

Referring to table under 1:2:4 mixture for 12 inch walls, 22.4 sacks of cement are required for each 100 square feet of surface. Dividing 924 by 100 gives the number of times 100 square feet are contained in the total wall surface and multiplying by 22.4 gives the total number of sacks of cement required. Similar calculations are made for the fine aggregate and the coarse aggregate in both the wall and the footing, noting that the width of the footing, 18 inches, is 1½ times the 12 inches thick.

$$\frac{924 \times 22.4}{100} = 207 \text{ sacks of cement.}$$

$$\frac{924 \times 44.7}{100} = 413 \text{ cu. ft. fine aggregate.}$$

$$\frac{924 \times 89.4}{100} = 826 \text{ cu. ft. coarse aggregate.}$$

The footing contains 132 square feet of surface, 18 inches thick (1½ x 12 inches), deducting for duplication at corners.

$$\frac{132 \times 22.4 \times 1\frac{1}{2}}{100} = 44.4 \text{ sacks cement.}$$

$$\frac{132 \times 44.7 \times 1\frac{1}{2}}{100} = 88.5 \text{ cu. ft. fine aggregate.}$$

$$\frac{132 \times 89.4 \times 1\frac{1}{2}}{100} = 177.0 \text{ cu. ft. coarse aggregate.}$$

Total materials required for footing and wall: 251.4 sacks cement, 501.5 cu. ft. fine aggregate, 1003 cu. ft. coarse aggregate.

Probem 2:—What quantities of material are required for a 1:2 cement plaster coat, one inch thick on the lower four feet of the above foundation?

Solution:—Perimeter of foundation: 4 x 34 feet = 136 feet. This multiplied by height of plaster coat, 4 ft., equals 544 square feet.

$$\frac{544 \times 4.0}{100} = 21.8 \text{ sacks of cement.}$$

$$\frac{544 \times 7.9}{100} = 42.5 \text{ cu. ft. sand.}$$

EXAMPLE OF PURCHASER'S INSULATION SPECIFICATIONS.*

Furnish and erect pure corkboard and sundry materials necessary to construct cold storage rooms, of arrangement, location and size as outlined by drawings, dated . . . and as per the following specifications:

REFRIGERATED BANANA ROOMS.

Floor Insulation.—It is understood that the base floor is depressed 7" below the general level of the floor of the building, which base is reasonably smooth and level and in readiness to receive insulation.

Upon such reasonably smooth and level concrete base, the contractor shall furnish and apply one layer 2" Pure Corkboard in hot asphalt with the top surface flooded with the same compound, and left in readiness to receive 5" concrete wearing floor to be put in place by owners or others.

Ceiling Insulation.—To the underside of concrete ceiling surface, in proper condition to receive insulation, the contractor shall furnish and erect two layers 2" Pure Corkboard. The first layer shall be erected in a ½" bedding of Portland cement mortar and propped in position until the cement sets, following which the second layer shall be erected to the underside of the first in hot asphalt and additionally secured with galvanized wire nails driven obliquely, three to the square foot. The exposed surface of such insulation shall then be finished as hereinafter specified.

Tile Wall Insulation.—To a tile wall surface running the length of one Banana Room, in place for the contractor and in proper condition to receive insulation, the contractor shall furnish and erect two layers 2" Pure Corkboard. The first layer shall be erected in a ½" bedding of Portland cement mortar, following which the second layer shall be erected to the first in hot asphalt and additionally secured with wood skewers driven obliquely, two to the square foot. The exposed surface of such insulation shall then be finished as hereinafter specified.

Pilaster, Column and Caps Insulation.—To the concrete surfaces of pilasters, columns and caps, wherever insulation is required as indicated by drawings, the contractor shall furnish and erect one layer 3" Pure Corkboard in a ½" bedding of Portland cement mortar and prop in position or otherwise secure in position until the cement sets. The exposed surface of such insulation shall then be finished as hereinafter specified.

*Insulation specifications for The Kroger Grocery & Baking Co., Charleston, W. Va., Warehouse.

Outside Cork Wall Insulation.—To construct the self-sustaining outside cork walls, the contractor shall furnish and erect two layers 2" Pure Corkboard, with the sheets in the first layer set edge on edge in hot asphalt and toe-nailed to each other with galvanized wire nails, following which the second layer shall be erected to the first in hot asphalt and additionally secured with wood skewers driven obliquely, two to the square foot. The exposed surfaces of the insulation shall then be finished as hereinafter specified.

Cork Partition Wall Insulation.—To construct the self-sustaining cork partition walls, the contractor shall furnish and erect one layer 3" Pure Corkboard, with the sheets set edge on edge in hot asphalt and toe-nailed to each other with galvanized wire nails. The exposed surfaces of the insulation shall then be finished as hereinafter specified.

Cold Storage Doors.—The contractor shall furnish and set, where indicated by drawings, six standard cold storage doors, 4′6″ wide x 6′6″ high, three right hand swing and three left hand swing, no sill type, and three standard bunker doors, 4′6″ wide x 2′0″ high, left hand swing, high sill type.

REFRIGERATORS AND EGG ROOM.

Floor Insulation.—It is understood that the base floor under Refrigerators in the basement, is depressed 7" below the general level of the floor of the building, which base is reasonably smooth and level and in readiness to receive insulation. It is understood that the base floor under Egg Room, on second floor, is not depressed below the general level of the floor but is reasonably smooth and level and in readiness to receive insulation.

Upon such reasonably smooth and level concrete base floors, the contractor shall furnish and apply two layers 2" Pure Corkboard in hot asphalt with asphalt between the layers and the top surface flooded with the same compound, and left in readiness to receive 4" concrete wearing floor to be put in place by owners or others.

Ceiling Insulation.—To the underside of concrete ceiling surfaces, in proper condition to receive insulation, the contractor shall furnish and erect two layers 2" Pure Corkboard. The first layer shall be erected in a ½" bedding of Portland cement mortar and propped in position until the cement sets, following which the second layer shall be erected to the underside of the first in hot asphalt and additionally secured with galvanized wire nails driven obliquely, three to the square foot. The exposed surface of such insulation shall then be finished as hereinafter specified.

Tile Wall Insulation.—To a tile wall surface running the short way of the Egg Room, in place for contractor and in proper condition to receive insulation, the contractor shall furnish and erect two layers 2" Pure Corkboard. The first layer shall be erected in a ½" bedding of

Portland cement mortar, following which the second layer shall be erected to the first in hot asphalt and additionally secured with wood skewers driven obliquely, two to the square foot. The exposed surface of such insulation shall then be finished as hereinafter specified.

Building Wall Insulation.—To the brick building wall extending along one long side of the group of Refrigerators, and to the brick building wall extending the length of the Egg Room, in place for the contractor and in proper condition to receive insulation, the contractor shall furnish and erect two layers 2" Pure Corkboard. The first layer shall be erected in a ½" bedding of Portland cement mortar, following which the second layer shall be erected to the first in hot asphalt and additionally secured with wood skewers driven obliquely, two to the square foot. The exposed surface of such insulation shall then be finished as hereinafter specified.

Pilaster, Column and Caps Insulation.—Same as specified for Refrigerated Banana Rooms.

Outside Cork Wall Insulation.—Same as specified for Refrigerated Banana Rooms.

Cork Partition Wall Insulation.—Same as specified for Refrigerated Banana Rooms.

Cold Storage Doors.—The contractor shall furnish and set, where indicated by the drawings, four standard cold storage doors, 4' 6" wide x 6' 6" high, right hand swing, no sill type.

Coil Bunkers.—It is understood that the owners shall provide in proper locations in concrete ceiling slabs in advance of the insulation work being done, a suitable number and kind of expansion anchors to receive ½" hanger bolts as supports for coils and coil bunkers.

After the insulation work has been completed, the contractor shall provide, on the floor of each of these rooms, an insulated coil bunker with all necessary material for supporting it at the proper distance below the ceiling, but it is understood that another contractor shall raise the bunkers into place after adjusting coils in position thereon.

The bottoms of the bunkers shall be insulated with one layer 2" Pure Corkboard on ⅞" T&G lumber, while the baffles of the bunkers shall be double layer T&G lumber with insulating paper between the layers. The floors of the bunkers shall be covered with No. 24 gauge galvanized iron, flashed at all edges, with all joints and nail heads soldered. Galvanized iron drain pipe shall be provided to carry drip from low point of each bunker to the floor of the room.

CORKBOARD FINISH.

Where mentioned hereinbefore, except ceiling areas, the contractor shall furnish and apply to the exposed insulation surfaces a ½" Portland cement plaster finish, in two coats, each approximately ¼" thick, mixed in the proportion of one part Portland cement to two parts clean sharp sand, the second coat brought to a float finish and scored in suitable squares to reduce and confine checking to such score marks.

Where mentioned hereinbefore for ceiling areas, the contractor shall furnish and apply by hand with trowel to the exposed insulation surfaces one uniform coat of Plastic Mastic Primer, mixed one bag asbestos fibre to one drum approved asphalt emulsion. Over this coat the contractor shall then furnish and apply a uniform coat of Plastic Mastic Finish, mixed one bag asbestos fibre and three bags hard silica grits to one drum approved asphalt emulsion, such finish troweled to as smooth a surface as the material will permit and left unscored. The contractor may furnish Pure Corkboard for the second layer on the ceiling having an asphalt mastic finish approximately ⅛" thick ironed on at the factory, in which case all mastic joints in the finished work shall then be filled in with suitable Plastic Mastic material and thoroughly sealed in approved manner.

GENERAL.

Owners shall assume all risk of any damage to, or destruction or loss of, all goods furnished whether by fire or otherwise after they, or any part of them, shall have been delivered on or about owner's premises, though the erection or installation of the same has not been begun or completed by the contractor. Owner will have building in readiness and all surfaces left in proper condition, so that the work once begun may be pushed to completion without delays. Owner will supply satisfactory storage room under cover and protection at point of erection for the materials called for, allow the contractor the use of elevator and such additional facilities as may be available for handling materials, and shall furnish all scaffolding, electric current, artificial light, heat and water required. It is understood that there is a side track at the building so that materials shipped in carlots need not be drayed by the contractor, but it is understood that the contractor shall handle all his own materials at the building.

FREIGHT CLASSIFICATIONS, CLASS RATES, C/L MINIMUMS IN THOUSANDS OF POUNDS, ETC.

Pure Corkboard and Sundries

Material	Railroad Description	Containers	Official LCL	Official CL	Official MIN	Western LCL	Western CL	Western MIN	Southern LCL	Southern CL	Southern MIN
Corkboard, no binder	"Granulated cork compressed in sheets without binder," or "cork sheets compressed without binder"	Crates or cartons	2	4	20	2	4	20	2	4	20
Granulated cork	"Granulated cork"	Bags	1	3	12	1	3	12	1	3	12
Asphalt	"Asphalt, solid"	Drums or bbls.	4	6	40	4	D	40	6	A	40
Galvanized wire nails	"Galv. wire nails"	Kegs or boxes	4	5	36	4	5	36	6	6	30
Wooden skewers	"Wooden skewers"	Boxes or cartons	3			2					
Insulating paper	"Building paper, plain or saturated"	Rolls	R26	5	30	3	5	30	5	A	30
Cold storage doors	"Doors or windows, insulated, cold storage, not glazed"	Crates	3	5	24	3	B	24	4	6	24
Kettles, over 100 lb. wt.	"Kettles, iron or steel, other than steam jacket"	Bulk	1	5	30	1	A	30	2	5	30
Emulsified asphalt	"Asphalt, liquid, other than paint, stain or varnish"	(a) Metal cans, in bxs. or crates	3	6	40	3	D	40	3	A	40
		(b) Barrels	4	6	40	4	D	40	6	A	40
Elastic enamel	"Paint (no label required)"	(a) Pails or metal cans, in bbls., or boxes; or bulk in kits or pails	3	5	36	4	5	36	4	5	36
		(b) Barrels		5	36		5	36		5	36
Mixed C/L Corkboard and gran. cork	(See descriptions above)	Bulk, cork board; bags, gran. cork. Corkboard may be in packages, also	x	4	20	x	4	20	x	4	20

FREIGHT CLASSIFICATIONS, CLASS RATES, C/L MINIMUMS IN THOUSANDS OF POUNDS, ETC.

Cork Pipe Covering, Cork Lags, Cork Discs and Sundries

Material	Railroad Description	Containers	Official LCL	Official CL	Official MIN	Western LCL	Western CL	Western MIN	Southern LCL	Southern CL	Southern MIN
Cork cov'g.	"Cork pipe covering with or without binder"	Crates or boxes	2	4	20	2	4	20	2	4	20
Cork lagging and discs	"Cork pipe or tank covering without binder"	Crates or boxes	2	4	20	2	4	26	2	4	20
Waterproof cement	"Cement paste (no label required)"	Pails or metal cans, in bbls. or boxes; or bulk in kits or pails	2	2		1	1		2	2	
Asphaltic paint	"Asphaltum paint (no label required)"	Do	3	5	36	4	5	36	4	5	30
Brine putty	"Putty"	Do	3	5	36	4	5	36	4	5	30
Seam filler	"Asphaltum, liquid other than paint, stain or varnish"	(a) Metal cans, in boxes or crates	3			3			3		
		(b) Barrels	4	6	40	4	D	40	6	A	40
Copper clad steel wire	"Copper clad steel wire"	Bbls., boxes, coils, bdls., crates, tubs, or on reels	3	4	30	2	4	30	2	4	30
Gal. band iron and clips and bolts	"Band or hoop iron"	Loose or in packages	4	5	36	4	5	36	6	6	36
Plastic cork, no sundries	"Cork pipe covering with or without binder"	Cartons or boxes	2	4	20	2	4	20	2	4	20
Plastic cork and sundries	"Plastic cork with sundries"	Cartons or boxes	1			1			1		
Plastic cork sundries	"Plastic cork sundries"	Cartons or boxes	1			1			1		
Mixed C/L											
Cork covering	(See description above)	Crates or bxs.									
& Corkboard	"Granulated cork compressed in sheets without binder"	Bulk or crates or cartons	x	4	20	x	4	20	x	4	20

CORK PIPE COVERING SPECIFICATIONS.

Brine and Ammonia Lines Operating Between 0° and 25° F.— Cover all brine and ammonia lines operating at from 0° to 25° F., after they have been tested, cleaned and approved, with Brine Thickness cork pipe covering having a mineral rubber finish ironed on at the factory.

Use sectional covering on all pipe lines up to and including 8-inch nominal pipe size. On all larger sizes use segmental covering, beveled to the proper radius. Cement all joints with waterproof cement, all end joints being broken by making one-half of the first section 18 inches long and the other half the full length of 36 inches. Place all longitudinal joints on top and bottom. Wire the covering in place with copper clad steel wire, applying not less than six wires per section or its equivalent of three feet. Draw wires up tight all around the covering and not just at the point of twist.

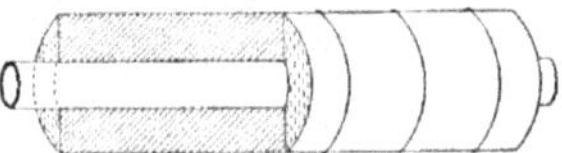

FIG. 221.—METHOD OF APPLYING SECTIONAL CORK PIPE COVERING TO BREAK END JOINTS.

Use cork fitting jackets on all screwed fittings up to and including 6-inch, and on all flanged fittings up to and including 6-inch. On all larger sizes use cork segments, beveled to the proper radius. Cement all joints with waterproof cement and wire securely with copper clad steel wire, applying not less than six wires per fitting. Fill all spaces between the cork jackets and/or the cork segments with brine putty, so applied as to leave no void spaces whatever behind the insulation.

After the insulation is thus applied, fill all seams and broken edges with seam filler so as to leave a smooth, workmanlike surface. Paint the entire exposed surfaces of the insulation with one good coat of asphaltic paint, or finish as otherwise specified.

Carry all insulated lines on hangers fitted to the outside of the covering, which shall be protected by a 6-inch wide sheet iron shield shaped to fit the covering and extending halfway up the sides of the covering.

Brine and Ammonia Lines Operating Below 0° F.—NOTE: Follow same specifications as given for Brine Thickness cork pipe covering, except:

(a) Substitute *Special Thick Brine* for "Brine Thickness."

(b) Use sectional covering on all pipe lines up to and including 6-inch nominal pipe size, and segmental covering on larger sizes.

(c) Use cork fitting jackets on all screwed fittings up to and including 5-inch, and on all flanged fittings up to and including 4-inch. On all larger sizes use cork segments.

Ice Water and Cold Lines Operating Above 25° F.—NOTE: Follow same specifications as given for Brine Thickness cork pipe covering, except:

(a) Substitute *Ice Water* for "Brine."

(b) Use sectional covering on all pipe lines up to and including 10-inch nominal pipe size, and segmental covering on larger sizes.

(c) Use cork fitting jackets on all screwed fittings up to and including 6-inch, and on all flanged fittings up to and including 4-inch. On all larger sizes use cork segments.

Cylindrical Tanks Operating at Various Temperatures.—

Below 5° F. use one layer 6-in. cork lags.
5° to 20° F. use one layer 5-in. cork lags.
20° to 32° F. use one layer 4-in. cork lags.
32° to 55° F. use one layer 3-in. cork lags.
55° F. and up use one layer 2-in. cork lags.

Cover the cylindrical tank operating at from ....° to ....° F., after it has been tested, cleaned and approved, with .... inch thick cork lags and discs weighing approximately 1.25 lbs. per board foot and having a mineral rubber finish ironed on at the factory on both the inner and outer surfaces.

Insulate the cylindrical surface of the tank with one layer of cork lags beveled to the proper radius. Insulate any and all flanges of the tank with one layer of cork lags projecting beyond the heads of the tank the equal of the thickness of the discs and applied so as to have a bearing of at least one foot on the lags of the body of the tank. (If either head of the tank has no flange, extend the body lags beyond the end of the tank the equal of the thickness of the disc.)

Apply body and flange lags with waterproof cement on all joints, and secure in place with 1-inch bands (or 1½-inch bands) of not lighter than No. 26 gauge brass drawn up tight by means of bolts and clips riveted to the ends of the bands. Space these bands not more than one foot apart for body lags and use not less than three for lags on each flange.

Apply discs directly against the heads of the tanks, and hold in place by means of flange or body lags as the case may be. Fill all spaces between the tank heads and the discs with regranulated cork well packed.

Build boxes of tongued and grooved boards around the supports on which the tank rests, so as to leave from four to six inches of space on all sides, and fill these spaces with regranulated cork well packed. (To obviate the necessity of boxing in the tank supports and to give a better insulation job, it is preferable, where weight permits, to carry a horizontal tank on saddles outside the body lags, so that the insulation will be continuous between the tank and the saddles.)

FIG. 222. CORK PIPE COVERING, LAGS AND DISCS ERECTED IN APPROVED MANNER TO VARIOUS SURFACES

After the insulation is thus applied, fill all seams and broken edges with seam filler so as to leave a smooth, workmanlike surface. Paint the entire exposed surfaces with one good coat of asphaltic paint, or finish as otherwise specified.

INSTRUCTIONS FOR THE PROPER APPLICATION OF CORK PIPE COVERING.

The service that cold pipe insulation encounters is the most severe service that insulation of any kind or character is called upon to withstand. Therefore, it is important:

1. That only the very best cold pipe insulation should be selected for use.
2. That it should be intelligently chosen as to the proper thickness for the service encountered.
3. That it should be very carefully erected in conformity with proven specifications and methods of application.
4. That it should have attention at least once each year.

Basic Fitness.—Experience of many years has taught that the most satisfactory results have been obtained by the use of an insulation that does not possess capillarity (the inherent property of certain materials that causes them to absorb water, as a blotter sucks up ink), and this experience in service with coverings for brine, ammonia and ice water lines has limited the materials that are entirely suitable for cold pipe insulation to those composed of cork, having no foreign binder used in the manufacturing process.

The "cork of commerce" is the outer bark of the cork oak tree—native of Spain. The air cell structure of cork and its freedom from capillarity, in combination, are the two properties provided by Nature to make this remarkable material, when put through the proper manufacturing processes, the best cold pipe insulation known.

Description.—Cork pipe covering is made of pure granulated cork, compressed, molded and baked in sectional form to fit the different sizes of pipe and fittings. It is coated inside and out with a mineral rubber finish. Properly applied, it is a thoroughly satisfactory insulation, which is impervious to moisture and which will last longer than the pipe if given reasonable care in service.

Advantages.—Cork pipe covering possesses maximum insulating efficiency, due to the clean cork waste used in its manufacture and to the manufacturing processes employed; is remarkably durable in service, is clean and neat in appearance and is easy to apply. Under average conditions, on brine and ammonia lines, it will pay for itself in one year.

Three Thicknesses.—Cork pipe covering is manufactured in three thicknesses, to meet different service conditions, as follows:

1. Brine Thickness, from two to three inches thick, is designed for brine and ammonia gas lines, and generally where the refrigerant ranges from 0° to 25° F.
2. Heavy Brine Thickness, or Special Thick Brine, from three to four inches thick, is for brine lines where the temperature runs below 0° F.

3. Ice Water Thickness, approximately one and one-half inches thick, is intended for use on refrigerated drinking water lines, liquid ammonia lines and generally where temperatures of 25° F. and higher are carried.

It is important, if satisfactory results are to be obtained, that the correct thickness of cork pipe covering be used in every instance.

Must Be Properly Applied.—But it is also essential that cork pipe covering be properly applied if satisfactory results are to be obtained over a long period of years, and the following points must be kept firmly in mind when erecting the material.

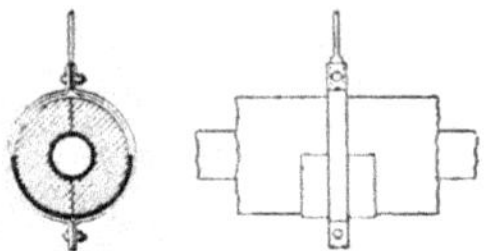

FIG. 223.—TYPE OF PIPE HANGER FOR CORK PIPE COVERING.

Spacing of Lines.—All pipe lines and fittings should be erected and spaced so as to permit of the free application of cork pipe covering without the necessity for the cutting away of the insulation in any way. Dimensions required for the proper spacing of pipe lines and fittings to receive cork pipe covering are as follows:

Thickness of Covering	Space Required Between Parallel Pipes	Space Required Between Pipes and Adjacent Surfaces
Brine Thickness		
Screwed Fittings up to and including 6 inch	8	6
Screwed Fittings larger than 6 inch.......	14	8
Flanged Fittings	14	8
Special Thick Brine		
Screwed Fittings up to and including 3 inch	10	8
Screwed Fittings larger than 3 inch........	18	12
Flanged Fittings	18	12
Ice Water Thickness		
Screwed Fittings up to and including 6 inch	6	4
Screwed Fittings larger than 6 inch........	10	5
Flanged Fittings	10	5

Preparation of Lines.—Cork pipe covering must never be erected until all lines have been tested, made tight, cleaned of foreign matter, freed of frost and made perfectly dry.

Pipe Hangers and Shields.—All pipe hangers must be placed on the outside of the cork pipe covering, and the insulation should be protected from each hanger by a sheet iron shield shaped to fit the curvature of the covering and extending at least four inches on each side of the hanger and up the sides to the center of the pipe.

Branch Lines, By-pass Lines, Rods, Etc.—All unused or infrequently used branch or by-pass lines leading off from lines being covered must be insulated to a distance of not less than three feet from the main insulated pipe line. Where this section of insulation ends it must be carefully sealed off with seam filler. No uninsulated pipe, rod or metal of any kind must be allowed to remain near enough to an insulated pipe line so that such metal enters or cuts into the cork pipe covering at any point.

Insulation Sundries.—In order that cork pipe covering and cork fitting jackets may be properly applied, the following sundry materials are supplied by the manufacturer without extra cost:

1. Waterproof Cement for the cementing of all lateral and end joints.
2. Brine Putty for the filling of any and all spaces between the covering and the pipe or the fittings.
3. Copper Clad Steel Wire for the holding of the covering in place. (Ordinary copper wire or galvanized wire is unsatisfactory in service.)
4. Seam Filler for the finishing up of seams and broken edges.
5. Asphaltic Paint for the painting of the outside surfaces of the insulation so as to give it a neat and finished appearance and to enhance its value.

The quantity of these insulation sundries shipped is intended to be sufficient if used as directed.

Waterproof Cement.—Waterproof cement sets quickly when exposed to the air. Consequently, it must not be applied to any surface until the joint is ready to be made, as otherwise a film forms that prevents a proper bond. Coat only as much of a surface as is to be placed immediately in contact with another surface. Use cement on but one of two adjoining surfaces—the last to be applied. *Do not coat both surfaces with waterproof cement.* Stir the cement thoroughly before applying it, and keep cover of the container on tight when not in use.

Screwed Fitting Jackets.—*Apply cork fitting jackets to all screwed fittings before the sectional covering is installed on the pipes incident thereto.* This is necessary because the cork jackets extend beyond the beads of the screwed fittings. By installing the sectional covering last, tight end joints can be made with the cork jackets by slightly wedging the sectional covering in place. Eliminate all voids between the fitting and the cork jacket by filling with brine putty. Use waterproof cement on all joints of the cork jackets, and then wire securely in place using not less than four wires to each jacket.

Sectional Covering.—Waterproof cement must be used on all lateral and end joints of sectional covering. All joints must be brought tightly together before a film has had a chance to form on the cement. All end joints must be broken by making one-half of the first section 18 inches long and the other half the full length of 36 inches. Place all lateral or longitudinal joints on the top and bottom.

The slightest opening through either the lateral or end joints of the covering will allow moisture to condense and frost to form to damage or destroy the insulation. Thus exceptional care must be taken to use waterproof cement properly, and the cork pipe covering must be secured in place with copper clad steel wire, using not less than six wires for each section of covering. These wires must be drawn up tight all around the covering—not just at the point of twist—tight enough so that the wire is embedded in the mineral rubber finish around the whole circumference. *Never use any kind of wire except copper clad steel wire, as other kinds are not satisfactory.*

Flanged Fitting Jackets.—Cork fitting jackets for flanged fittings rest on the outside of the sectional covering. *For this reason, it is necessary to apply the sectional covering first on pipe lines having flanged fittings incident thereto.* Butt the sectional covering against the flanges of the fittings, wedging it slightly between them, following instructions just given.

Then insulate the flanged fittings by first applying one-half of the cork jacket in a temporary manner and carefully filling the space between the fitting and the half jacket with brine putty packed tight. Remove this half jacket and repeat the process with the other half jacket on the other side of the fitting. Now put both in place to test the workmanship as to the elimination of all voids between the insulation and the fitting. When satisfactory, use waterproof cement on all joints and wire in place securely with not less than six wires to each jacket.

Mitered Bends.—Pipe bends should be insulated by mitering sectional covering to fit the bend. Insulate the straight pipe on both sides of the bend up to the points where the bend starts. Determine the radius of the bend and the angle of the mitre, and cut pieces sufficiently short to give practically straight pipe contact between the pipe and the mitered covering. Cut the center piece for a good tight fit. *After all mitered pieces are ready,* put them in place with waterproof cement on all joints, using two wires to each mitered section, working from each end of the bend toward the middle. The last or key section should be applied while the cement is still soft on all other mitered joints, to insure perfection of the finished work.

Seams and Chipped Edges.—Smooth up all seams and chipped edges along the lateral and end joints of the covering and the fitting jackets with seam filler, so applied as to leave a smooth surface.

Painting.—After the seam filler has been applied, give the exposed surfaces of the completed insulation work one good coat of asphaltic paint. This is the only finish that is required on inside lines; but outside lines, or lines passing through cold rooms, tunnels, pipe shafts, etc., must be further protected by weather-proofing.

Weather-proofing.—Wrap with one layer of 2-ply roofing paper, with a 3-inch lap on side and ends. Point the exposed end of the side lap down. Apply asphaltic paint on all laps to cement them in place, and additionally secure lateral laps with copper staples. Paint the finished work with one good coat of asphaltic paint.

White Finish Over Mineral Rubber.—If white finish, or color other than black, is desired for cork pipe covering, it may be obtained by painting the mineral rubber finish with two good coats of orange shellac followed by any selected paint or enamel. Some enamels, specially prepared, are suitable without the use of orange shellac.

Segmental Covering.—Piping and fittings larger than the sizes for which sectional covering and sectional fitting jackets are furnished are insulated with segmental covering. Instructions for proper application are supplied by the manufacturer with every such shipment, and should be followed carefully.

Lags and Discs.—Brine coolers, tanks, accumulators, etc., are insulated with cork lags and discs. Separate sheets sent by the manufacturer with every shipment of lags give complete and detailed instructions for proper application. See that they are received, and follow such instructions carefully.

Care and Maintenance.—*The service that cold pipe insulation encounters is the most severe service that insulation of any kind is called upon to withstand. Therefore, it is important that it should have care and attention if it is to be kept in good condition. Properly applied and properly cared for, cork pipe covering will last longer than the pipe.*

Inspect the installation at regular intervals for:

1. Loose or broken wires.
2. Joints opening up.
3. Cracks in mineral rubber finish and seam filler coming loose.

If a loose or broken wire is found, replace it without delay. If any open joints are found, the section of covering or the fitting jacket should be removed the very next time the refrigeration is off, dried out and replaced, or new insulation installed.

Close up any cracks that may have developed in the mineral rubber finish with seam filler. At least once each year give the entire exposed surface of the cold pipe insulation one good coat of asphaltic paint.

Such attention is inexpensive and will add materially to the long life and the high efficiency of cold pipe insulation.

A GOOD DRINK OF WATER.*

Speaking of Values.—Years ago an authority on economics pointed out that *values* were of two different kinds: Value in exchange, and value in use. Gold, for example, was mentioned as possessing a relatively high exchange value, due to its scarcity and the demand for it for ornamentation; but as having practically no real value in use, as it was in no sense necessary to mankind. Water, on the other hand, was referred to as having no exchange value, as it was never sold; but as possessing an extraordinary high value in use because it was an absolute necessity to mankind.

While these examples can still be used today for the purpose of illustrating the difference between these two classes of values, yet the *real* value of gold and the *exchange* value of water have both increased immeasurably since about the 15th century. Gold is today considered necessary as the basis of our monetary exchange; and good water has a very definite monetary value to those who are in position to dispense it.

A Good Drink of Water.—Especially is this true of good drinking water. But good water and good drinking water may be two wholly different things; especially in the industries and in most public buildings. While water may be pure, it is not necessarily fit for human consumption. It must be available at the proper temperature. If it is too warm it does not satisfy and workers complain or seek employment elsewhere. If it is too cold the health of the consumer is very vitally impaired. Medical science has conclusively demonstrated that at 45° to 50° F. pure drinking water is best; in fact, extremely essential to the health and well-being of all classes of workers.

Thus, pure drinking water of the proper temperature has a high exchange value today, considering that the efficiency or productiveness of workers depends so very much upon the condition of their minds and bodies. And if such wholesome drinking water is easily available in adequate quantity, procurable without risk of contamination, and does not cost too much to provide, it can easily be a source of large monetary profit to the individual or concern supplying it. While this profit is an indirect one, yet it is a real profit notwithstanding in that it constitutes a saving over old methods of supplying workers with drinking water.

Consider the Facts.—In too many factories, mills and public buildings, the worker, in order to obtain his daily requirement of drinking water, must be away from his employment for a considerable period of time each day. He must usually walk an appreciable

*Advertisement, copyright, 1923, Armstrong Cork & Insulation Company, Pittsburgh, Penna. Reprinted by permission.

distance to a faucet or tank; perhaps he must wait his turn there, and while he waits, he gossips a bit, usually to no good purpose. If the supply is city reservoir water, he runs off a certain quantity in the belief that he can get it cool; if it is tank water, it is either too warm to be satisfying or, if iced, too cold to be healthful.

It is a well-established fact that the usual methods of drinking water supply are wasteful to a high degree—wasteful of time and water, conducive to ill health, and frequently responsible for a good share of the peevishness and unrest so manifest among workers in the warmer months of the year.

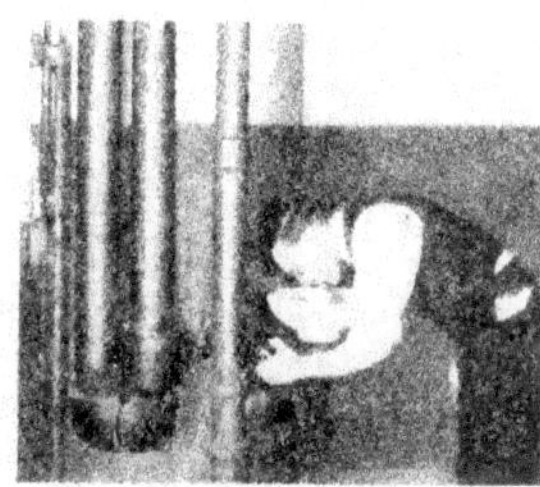

FIG. 224. CORK PIPE COVERING ON THE LINES OF A REFRIGERATED DRINKING WATER SYSTEM.

The Solution.—Progressive and well-informed managements are in complete agreement with doctors on the important part that drinking water plays in maintaining health, morale and efficiency under modern working conditions. And thus the refrigerated drinking water distribution system has come into extensive use. It has been found not only completely practical and satisfactory from the hygienic and the production standpoints, but actually cheaper to operate than the cruder methods previously used.

This modern system is very simple both in principle and operation. It consists of refrigerating equipment, an insulated water tank located at the correct point, and properly insulated distributing lines connected to sanitary drinking fountains conveniently and correctly placed throughout the plant or building. It is readily adaptable to any industrial requirements, and is elastic enough to be expanded or contracted as future needs may require. With it a constant supply of properly cooled water is instantly available, without waste or effort, with no slop or muss, and at no risk of contamination from dirt or communicable disease. Its operation vastly simplifies a problem that has become more and more troublesome with the passing of time, and which in many mills, factories and public buildings is today crying for solution.

The Cost and the Return.—Most of these modern installations show a marked reduction in operating cost as compared with the superseded method. One plant, for example, kept a careful record of the cost of supplying drinking water by the bucket-and-dipper method and, later, for refrigerated water through a modern distribution system and fountains. The results showed a saving of over 60% in the cost of distribution in favor of the improved system. But the actual saving in money was not all. There were also the less-tangible but none-the-less real factors of safety, health and improved morale.

Design Is Individual.—Of course, a refrigerated drinking water system is not a standard piece of equipment. It must be designed for each individual plant or building, and its cost depends upon local conditions. The number of employees and the nature of their work determines the amount of water required. The size of the refrigerating machine, velocity of flow, pipe sizes, proper insulation of lines and equipment are technical matters that are not fully covered by ordinary engineering books.

Realizing the need for making such information available to architects, engineers and plant executives, this Company's Engineering Department has made a thorough study of the subject over a long period of time, the results of which have been compiled in a 48-page book, "Drinking Water Systems." This book will be gladly sent on request and without charge to all who are seriously interested in learning more about the benefits and economies of this method of handling the drinking water supply.

Engineering Assisistance.—The drinking water problem being a specific one for each individual plant or building requires a careful survey of conditions and an estimate of the complete cost. For the purpose of preliminary investigation as well as for practical engineering assistance, the experience and resources of the Armstrong Cork & Insulation Co., Pittsburgh, Pennsylvania, are at the service of architects, engineers and executives, without charge or obligation.

FUNDAMENTAL CONTRACT LAW.*

Cost of Litigation.—It should be and usually is the policy of every servant corporation to avoid litigation so far as possible. Lawsuits are very costly, not only in attorneys' fees, the taking of evidence, the court proceedings, the loss of time of salaried employees and officials, but also in the loss of "good-will," which alone amounts to more than the gain through litigation, if the cost incident to litigation is ignored.

As it is very rarely necessary to resort to litigation, or to make concessions or render credits to avoid litigation, if the original contract is properly drawn and having been so drawn is executed or carried out in a spirit of fairness and a business-like manner, it is highly important that the sales engineer, who must draft such contracts, understands the enormous cost of litigation and the fundamentals of contract law to guide him in avoiding resort to the courts.

The law of contracts is as simple and as readily understood as any department of the law. Nevertheless, the average engineer is usually unable to avoid complications and weaknesses in the preparation of specifications and other documents pertaining to contracts. The importance of understanding and knowing the contents of the following paragraphs of this chapter can not, therefore, be exaggerated, and the sales engineer can do well to make them the basis of much thought and study.

Kinds of Contracts.—A contract is a promise to do or refrain from doing some act or series of acts that law will enforce. There are, in general, two kinds of contracts:

(1) Sealed contracts, or specialties.

(2) Parol contracts.

A sealed contract, or specialty, is a contract made under seal; while a parol contract is a simple oral or written agreement not made under seal.

A sealed contract may be described in greater detail as a written agreement signed by the parties with a seal appended to the signatures. Formerly a seal consisted of "an impression on wax, or paper, or some other tenacious substance capable of being impressed." Now, however, an impression of a seal on the paper itself is construed as a proper seal, and in many states by statute a scroll enclosing the word *seal* made opposite the name of the signer is quite sufficient. Engineering contracts are now very rarely executed under seal; although the bond which holds the sureties for the faithful performance of the work by the contractor must be under seal, be-

*Chapters on "Fundamental Contract Law" and "Engineering Contracts," reprinted by permission from SALES ENGINEERING, by P. Edwin Thomas.

cause the agreement of the bondsmen to become responsible is not often supported by a valuable consideration.

While any contract may be executed under seal, and thus become a sealed contract, under the *common law* the following must be executed under seal to become binding:

(1) Gratuitous promises.
(2) Contracts with corporations.
(3) Conveyances of real estate.
(4) Bonds.

We are interested here only with contracts with corporations. The *common law* rule that contracts with corporations must be executed under seal no longer obtains in the United States of America. In this country a contract entered into with the proper officers of a corporation is valid without being sealed, the same as though made with an individual, unless the charter of the corporation specifically requires all contracts to be made under seal.

All contracts, either oral or written, not executed under seal are called simple or parol contracts. An oral contract has all the force of a written contract; but an oral contract is subject to difficulties in the way of establishing or proving its terms, from which a properly written contract is practically, if not entirely, free. A large part of the litigation arising from the non-fulfillment of contracts is caused by a failure to reduce the terms of the contract to writing; and the rest of the litigation, in connection with written contracts, is caused by weaknesses of various kinds in such written documents.

A written contract has another advantage over an oral contract. An oral contract can be modified by subsequent oral agreements; while a written contract is presumed in law to embody all the understandings and agreements made at the time of or prior to the signing of the contract. No oral evidence, therefore, can be admitted as to agreements or understandings made at the time of or previous to a written agreement that would modify its terms or conditions, except for the purpose of establishing proof of fraud, duress, deception, mistake in the drafting of the contract, or to explain any latent ambiguity, unusual phraseology or technical words.

Essentials of a Legal Contract.—The law will not enforce an agreement or contract unless:

(1) The parties are competent to make the agreement.

(2) The subject matter is lawful.

(3) The parties have mutually agreed to the conditions set forth, or they were of the same mind and intention concerning the subject matter.

(4) There is, excepting sealed contracts, a valuable consideration.

The four essentials of a legal contract are, therefore:

(1) Competency.
(2) Legality.
(3) Agreement.
(4) Consideration.

Competency—A sane person who has attained his majority is considered competent to make any legal agreement or contract. The disabilities of married women in the matter of contracts are too numerous to touch upon here. Without intent to cast aspersion on married women, we shall also omit reference to those disabilities pertaining to aliens, convicts, infants, insane persons, and drunkards.

The Federal or any state government may become a party to a contract, and may sue on their contracts and enforce them; but the reciprocal of this is not true. Neither the United States nor any state of the union can be sued without its consent. However, all public corporate governments subservient to that of the state can be sued on their contracts.

A corporation has no powers for entering into or performing contracts beyond those given it by the state in its charter, because officers of corporations are not in such case held to be personally liable. Its capacity for transacting business, however, is not limited by the specific privileges granted in its charter, but by implication is necessarily extended to include such other powers as may be required for the complete consummation of its specific purposes.

A contract by an agent or representative is not valid unless the principal is himself competent to enter into a contract. Nevertheless, a contract by an agent is valid if the principal is competent even though the agent be incompetent to enter into a contract as principal. The legality of the acts of an agent or representative is similar to the legality of the acts of a corporation. As a corporation receives its authority from the state for the conduct of a particular kind of business, so an agent receives his authority from his principal. Should the agent exceed his express and implied authority, the principal is privileged to repudiate his acts; and the other party to the contract has no recourse except against the agent himself. In order that an agent may relieve himself from all responsibility in the signing of a contract, the documents must reveal, either in its body or in the signature, who the principal is; as a mere signing of a contract by a person as agent will not relieve the one so signing from personal responsibility unless the document does reveal the principal. The eminently satisfactory way is to have the document specifically state that it is not to be construed as a contract until approved by some officer of the corporation, unless the corporation elects to delegate unusual authority to the agent and the other party to the agreement is willing to trust the agent not to exceed his express and implied authority.

Legality—In general, no contract is legal, and can not be enforced in the courts, that involves an agreement to perform an act that is:

(1) Forbidden by statutory law.
(2) Contrary to the rules of common law.
(3) Opposed to public policy.

It will not be necessary for us to elaborate upon the first and second, but in connection with the third there is a class of agreements frequently entered into by the principals to all engineering contracts that are often construed in the courts as against the public policy. An agreement that provides that matters which may arise between the parties shall be referred to an arbitrator or arbitrators —such as the engineer or architect—is not binding, and either party may have recourse to the courts notwithstanding it[1].

Agreement—In order that a contract shall be binding on both parties to an agreement, it must have been understood and accepted by both in the very same sense. However clear the agreement may appear to be on its face, if evidence can be introduced to show that it was not mutually understood in the same sense, it can not in general be enforced. The inference must not be drawn, however, that all claims of having misunderstood the plain and express provisions of a written contract will relieve the party making such claim from liability under it. That is to say, the mental agreement is evidenced by the language used in expressing such agreement and the law will presume that such words were understood, provided only that their meaning is plain and evident to the court.

A person or corporation making an offer, bid or proposal whether orally, by messenger, by mail, by telegraph, or by public advertisement, must allow a *reasonable time* for its acceptance, provided no time limit is stated in the proposal or provided meanwhile it is not withdrawn. Any proposal may be withdrawn at any time before it is accepted, unless a consideration has been paid for the privilege of acceptance for a definite time. It is presumptuous to say what the law will consider a reasonable time. Such time period might depend upon the nature of the transaction and the construction of the particular court. For that reason a majority of corporation letterheads, used in quoting prices, contain this printed clause: "All quotations subject to immediate acceptance or withdrawal without notice."

Whenever a proposal made by one party is accepted by another with any kind of qualification or change of the conditions or wording of the original proposal, such an acceptance is simply the making of a counter proposal to the first party; and does not constitute an agreement until such first party has in turn assented fully to the en-

[1] Since this was originally written, some states have passed commercial arbitration laws fostered by the American Arbitration Association, which legalize arbitration by prior agreement, under certain conditions.

tire proposal as amended—which makes of it a new proposal to the second party—and it is again accepted by the second party: then only does it become binding. The assent which finally makes of the proposal a binding contract is the full, absolute and unconditional acceptance of its terms as presented.

The party making an offer has the right to stipulate in it the time, place, form and other conditions of acceptance, in which case such offer can be accepted only in the manner prescribed. This privilege on the part of the bidder does not permit him to impose the condition, however, that a failure to receive an acceptance within a certain time will be construed as an acceptance. In other words, he may not impose the condition of refusal.

As a general rule, fraud vitiates all contracts.

Consideration—All engineering, or parol, contracts must in every instance be supported by a valuable consideration; as otherwise they are not enforceable. However, in the case of a money consideration, it is not necessary that the amount named shall be adequate to support the promise. A contract under seal, as previously stated, does not require a consideration to enforce it.

Subsequent Changes and Agreements.—In general it can be said that any oral or written agreement may be altered at pleasure after such agreement has been entered into, if done by mutual consent. Any such change makes a new contract out of the original, and because of this fact a surety or a third party to the agreement not consenting to the change is automatically released from all obligation. In all cases where sureties or bondsmen guarantee faithful performance, they must always be consulted and their consent obtained to any material change in the original contract. As "material change" is likely to be a subject for dispute and as changes are invariably made in engineering contracts without thought of consulting the bondsmen, said bondsmen are as a rule thereby released from all obligations, and the bond becomes of no effect, unless the following type of clause is added: "And the said surety does hereby stipulate and agree that no change, extension, alteration or addition to the terms of the contract or specifications shall in anywise affect obligation on this bond".

Even though a written contract has a clause stipulating that no change shall be made in it except in writing, thus forbidding oral alterations of any kind, such a provision is void and the contract may be altered by oral agreement notwithstanding. This is because in law oral and written contracts are of the same class, both being parol contracts, and consequently are of equal force and effect. No one may forfeit his legal rights even by agreement. Where contracts are illegal except when they are in writing, as under the Statute of Frauds, then such written contracts can not be modified except by agreement in writing.

In general, unless every change entered into or agreed upon after the contract has been consummated is supported by some kind of legal consideration, the contract can not be enforced.

Discharge of Contracts.—Any contract entered into under any of the methods mentioned may be discharged and the parties to the contract freed from all obligations involved, in any one of the following ways:

(1) By performance.
(2) By impossibility of performance.
(3) By agreement.
(4) By operation of Law.
(5) By breach.

The usual method of discharging a contract is, of course, by each party fully performing the duties prescribed for him in the agreement. In such case the performance by each party must be strictly in accordance with all of the terms of the contract. However, in engineering work it is seldom that the fulfillment is in all details strictly in accordance with the plans and specifications; but while in law the contract requires a strict and full compliance, yet in equity a substantial compliance is accepted in place of a full and complete performance.

Some contracts are based on the specifications of an engineer or architect that contain the unfair provision that the work must be done to the *complete satisfaction* of some party named. The court in every such case will construe this meaning *reasonable satisfaction.*

A common example of the operation of a *condition precedent,* with reference to a third party, is where a contractor binds himself to receive payments only on the certificate of the engineer or architect. Without such certificate he must prove that the engineer or architect has acted fraudulently in withholding the certificate, or has acted under gross mistake and in bad faith, or has negligently refused to honestly examine the work. It is always extremely difficult to establish such proof; and, consequently, it is very bad policy to operate under such a condition.

ENGINEERING CONTRACTS.

Specific Provisions.—An engineering contract consists of a number of specific provisions, each one of which defines some one element of the contract. These provisions are usually grouped under the following headings, and in the order indicated:

(1) Scope and purpose, including plans, if any.
(2) Specifications relating to and describing the work in detail.
(3) Business relation of the parties to the contract.

Thus the first essential of a good engineering contract is to make clear the scope and purpose of the "work to be done"; then describe the work in detail; and follow these specific clauses quite naturally with the general clauses setting forth the business relation of the parties to the contract, such as price, terms of payment, delivery, time of completion, guarantee, and other provisions which shall be touched upon later.

Scope and Purpose.—Too much care can not be exercised in setting forth as briefly, yet as clearly as possible, the extent and intent of the work to be performed under the terms of the contract. It has been pointed out that the first principle of the successful management of any project is a thorough analysis of the job. That is to say, it is necessary to know what is expected to be accomplished before it is possible to work out an effective and proper plan for doing it. The general clauses referred to may then be thought of as the rules by which the work shall be done.

The general principles of technical writing can well be followed in fixing the scope and purpose of the contract, as the chance for uncertainty or misunderstanding at this point would be fatal to the sales engineer. This is true not only from a legal and an engineering standpoint, but even more especially from a sales standpoint. These introductory statements must be worded so as to infer the quality of our mind, the measure of our ability, the responsibility and integrity of our employer, in order to win instant respect and open the door for a quick consummation of a profitable business transaction; for if a prospective customer is entirely satisfied with the outline of the scope and purpose of the contract, and the drawings, he will frequently pass over the body of the contract proposal, or the specifications, with but a hasty survey, and, if the price, terms and other general conditions are satisfactory, will accept the proposal with full confidence that he is quite safe in doing so. Needless to say, such confidence must *never* be violated, for the confidence of a purchaser is the one BIG asset of the sales engineer. The value of being able to execute a high class drawing, nicely lettered, as previously mentioned, is here emphasized in its true relation to sales engineering work.

Specifications.—We have shown that the work to be done should be described as a whole, and then in detail. That portion of an engineering contract that relates to and describes the work in detail is called the specifications.

The writing of specifications calls for the most careful application of the principles of technical writing, and every portion and detail of the work should be described in clear and simple language that can be understood by all. The descriptions should have reference to the ultimate end to be accomplished rather than to the means and methods to be employed, unless some particular method is preferable to all others. The clauses in the specifications should be made, so far as possible, mutually exclusive; that is to say, no part of the work should be specifically described in more than one place, as repetition weakens specifications and makes for ambiguity.

Before an attempt is made to prepare a specification, it is necessary to brief the work carefully and establish the proper major-headings, main-headings and sub-headings. This is necessary not only from the standpoint of English composition, technical writing and legality, but also from a sales standpoint. The suggestion has been made that if the first or "scope-and-purpose" section of the contract proposal be properly presented and the drawings well executed, it will materially assist the sales engineer to secure a quick acceptance of the contract proposal, other things being equal. While, in general, this is true, yet many buyers scrutinize the complete document most carefully; and if weaknesses are found in the specifications, even though the remainder of the contract proposal be well drafted, it tends to destroy confidence in the ability of the sales engineer to have the proposed work carried out in a satisfactory manner, and thus operates very much against him. Furthermore, specifications, correct in every detail, are essential to the construction corps, if difficulties are to be avoided while prosecuting the work. The importance of this correlation is usually either not well understood or carelessly disregarded by the sales engineer.

The most common errors committed by sales engineers when writing specifications are failure to brief the work properly and neglect to make the clauses mutually exclusive. Major-headings, main-headings and sub-headings are frequently jumbled so as to make the complete specification subject to many interpretations, even though the choice of words and their order of arrangement, the sequence of clauses composing sentences, and the arrangement of sentences in each paragraph, are above criticism.

General Clauses.—The general clauses in an engineering contract, which set forth the business relation of the parties to the contract, may relate to any or all of the following:

(1) The valuable consideration.
(2) Terms of payment.
(3) Time of commencement, rate of progress and time of completion.
(4) Provision for monthly and final estimates.
(5) Kind of workmen to be employed.
(6) Appliances to be used.
(7) Liquidated damages.
(8) Workmen's compensation insurance.
(9) Public liability insurance.
(10) Owners' liability insurance.
(11) Contractors' contingent liability insurance.
(12) Special contingent damage insurance.

(13) Landlords' and tenants' liability insurance.

(14) Fire and loss insurance.

(15) Surety bond.

(16) Protection against claims for use of patents.

(17) Provision for heat, light, water, drainage, elevator, telephone, drayage, storage, street traffic.

(18) Inspection of materials and work.

(19) Claims for damage due to unforseen difficulties, strikes, accidents, acts of the government, delays, suspension of the work, etc.

(20) Subsequent agreements.

(21) Assignment, release, cancellation and abandonment of contract.

(22) Protection of finished work.

(23) Discharge of unpaid claims of workmen and material men.

(24) Cleaning up after completion.

(25) Settlements of disputes and provisions for arbitration.

(26) Extra work and credits.

(27) Guarantee.

While this list is not intended to be complete, it will serve as a general guide, and other items may be added as desired or required.

Modified Forms.—Often an engineering contract is based on detailed plans and specifications of an architect or engineer. In such case the preparation of a contract proposal by the sales engineer is indeed hazardous, unless he makes a most careful study and correct interpretation of the complete plans and specifications so as to insure against errors of omission in estimating and to satisfy himself that no conditions or requirements are at variance with his employer's prescribed business policy. Once satisfied that all terms and conditions can be complied with, the contract proposal by the sales engineer should be very brief, simply setting forth the scope and purpose of the work to be done by specific reference to numbered and dated plans and specifications of the architect or engineer handling the commission, the commission number, the specific branch of the work involved, and close by stipulating the price or valuable consideration.

If certain terms or conditions can not be complied with, and it is the desire, nevertheless, to bid for the work, the objectionable terms and conditions should be carefully listed as exceptions; thus:

> The materials to be furnished and the work to be done under this proposal shall be in accordance with plans and specifications of Mr. Albert Q. Simmons, Architect and Engineer, Chicago, Illinois, his commission #7056, drawings #9852, sheets 1-5 inclusive, dated March 17, 1927, specifications #8540, pages 1-10 inclusive pertaining to General Conditions and pages 45-87 inclusive pertaining to Mechanical Equipment, with the following exceptions:

(1) Page #8, paragraph 3. A 1-year guarantee shall be extended instead of the 5-year guarantee specified.

(2) Page #9, paragraph 4. Bidder does not bind himself to receive payments only upon the certificate of the architect and engineer.

(3) Drawing #9852, sheet 3. Size of unit "B" is at variance with the specifications, page #48, paragraph 5; specifications are understood to take precedence.

PRICE: Nine Thousand ($9,000.00) Dollars.

Bidders are frequently provided with printed forms, especially for large projects and municipal, state and government work, that leave only the price to be inserted.

Many times an architect or engineer will prepare general plans and specifications, limit the bidders to a select class of reliable contractors and corporations with reputations to lose if inferior work is done, and allow them to fix the details within the limits of the general plans and specifications. In such case, the sales engineer should merely use the general plans and specifications as a guide in the preparation of his own drawings and his own complete contract proposal.

The sales engineer should always strive to make his contract proposal exclusive in itself, avoiding unnecessary entanglements, but this is not always possible or desirable when dealing with a reliable architect or engineer.

TOPICAL INDEX

A

B

C

D

E

J

K

L

M

N

O

P

Q

R

S

T

U

V

W

Y

Lightning Source UK Ltd.
Milton Keynes UK
UKHW010103150321
380354UK00001B/25

9 789354 010088